FIFTY
SOUTHERN
WRITERS
BEFORE
1900

FIFTY SOUTHERN WRITERS BEFORE 1900

A BIO-BIBLIOGRAPHICAL SOURCEBOOK

EDITED BY

ROBERT BAIN

AND

JOSEPH M. FLORA

GREENWOOD PRESS

NEW YORK • WESTPORT, CONNECTICUT • LONDON

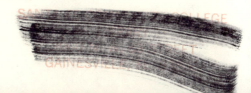

Library of Congress Cataloging-in-Publication Data

Fifty southern writers before 1900.

Includes index.
1. American literature—Southern States—History and
criticism.   2. American literature—Southern States—
Bio-bibliography.   3. American literature—19th century—
Bio-bibliography.   4. American literature—Colonial
period, ca. 1600–1775—Bio-bibliography.   5. Southern
States in literature.   6. Authors, American—Southern
States—Biography—Dictionaries.   7. Southern States—
Biography— Dictionaries.   I. Bain, Robert (Robert A.).
II. Flora, Joseph M.   III. Title: 50 southern writers
before 1900.
PS261.F543   1987   016.81′09′975   86-31832
ISBN 0-313-24518-5 (lib. bdg. : alk. paper)

Copyright © 1987 by Robert Bain and Joseph M. Flora

Library of Congress Catalog Card Number: 86-31832
ISBN: 0-313-24518-5

First published in 1987

Greenwood Press, Inc.
88 Post Road West, Westport, Connecticut 06881

Printed in the United States of America

The paper used in this book complies with the
Permanent Paper Standard issued by the National
Information Standards Organization (Z39.48-1984).

10   9   8   7   6   5   4   3   2   1

For my mother,
Gail Clark Bain Sexson,
whose Southern heritage has delighted,
amused, and sometimes shocked me.

—Robert Bain

Contents

PREFACE   xi

INTRODUCTION   1

George William Bagby ["Mozis Addums"] (1828–1883)   20
Harold Woodell

Joseph Glover Baldwin (1815–1864)   29
Merritt W. Moseley, Jr.

Robert Beverley (1673–1722)   38
Anne Margaret Daniel and *Jon Kukla*

William Wells Brown (ca. 1814–1884)   44
John Sekora

William Byrd of Westover (1674–1744)   55
Robert Bain

George Washington Cable (1844–1925)   75
Robert O. Stephens

William Alexander Caruthers (1802–1846)   86
Curtis Carroll Davis

Mary Boykin Chesnut (1823–1886)   96
Elisabeth S. Muhlenfeld

Charles Waddell Chesnutt (1858–1932)   107
William L. Andrews

Thomas Holley Chivers (1809–1858)   118
Charles M. Lombard

Kate Chopin (1851–1904)   132
Anne E. Rowe

Samuel Langhorne Clemens [Mark Twain] (1835–1910)   144
Everett Emerson

Ebenezer Cook(e) (ca. 1667–ca. 1732)   165
Robert D. Arner

John Esten Cooke (1830–1886)   174
Ritchie D. Watson, Jr.

Philip Pendleton Cooke (1816–1850)   184
Edward L. Tucker

Frederick Douglass (1818–1895)   190
Mary Kemp Davis

William Elliott (1788–1863)   205
Reed Sanderlin

Will N. Harben (1858–1919)   212
James K. Murphy

George Washington Harris (1814–1869)   220
M. Thomas Inge

Joel Chandler Harris (1848–1908)   227
Lucinda H. MacKethan

Paul Hamilton Hayne (1830–1886)   240
Rayburn S. Moore

Johnson Jones Hooper (1815–1862)   250
Robert L. Phillips

George Moses Horton (ca. 1797–ca. 1883)   257
William Carroll

Thomas Jefferson (1743–1826)   268
William Peden

Richard Malcolm Johnston (1822–1898)   277
L. Moody Simms, Jr.

John Pendleton Kennedy (1795–1870)   286
David O. Tomlinson

Grace King (1852–1932)   296
David Kirby

Sidney Lanier (1842–1881)   303
Jane S. Gabin

Augustus Baldwin Longstreet (1790–1870)   312
William E. Lenz

Robert Munford (ca. 1737–1783)   323
Jon C. Miller

Mary Noailles Murfree [Charles Egbert Craddock] (1850–1922)   336
Allison R. Ensor

Thomas Nelson Page (1853–1922)   348
Harriet R. Holman

Edward Coote Pinkney (1802–1828)   359
C. Michael Smith

Edgar Allan Poe (1809–1849)   365
Eric W. Carlson

Irwin Russell (1853–1879)   389
Marlene Youmans

William Gilmore Simms (1806–1870)   395
Mary Ann Wimsatt

Charles Henry Smith ["Bill Arp"] (1826–1903)   416
James C. Austin

Captain John Smith (1580–1631)   427
Jennifer R. Goodman

John Reuben Thompson (1823–1873)   435
Gerald M. Garmon

William Tappan Thompson (1812–1882)   440
Herbert Shippey

Thomas Bangs Thorpe (1815–1878)   452
Eugene Current-Garcia

Henry Timrod (1828–1867)   464
Jack De Bellis

George Tucker (1775–1861)   473
Donald R. Noble

Nathaniel Beverley Tucker (1784–1851)   483
J. V. Ridgely

St. George Tucker (1752–1827)   492
Carl R. Dolmetsch

Booker T. Washington (1856–1915)   502
Sondra O'Neale

Albery Allson Whitman (1851–1901)   514
Blyden Jackson

Richard Henry Wilde (1789–1847)   524
Elizabeth Dunn

Augusta Jane Evans Wilson (1835–1909)   530
Lynne P. Shackelford

William Wirt (1772–1834)   541
Richard E. Amacher

INDEX   557

CONTRIBUTORS   593

Preface

Fifty Southern Writers Before 1900, a companion volume to *Fifty Southern Writers After 1900*, takes as its province the work of half a hundred Southerners whose careers ended before 1900 or thereabouts, whose works often appear in anthologies of Southern and American writing, and whose books figure prominently in the history of Southern letters. The territory we have selected is huge, beginning with Captain John Smith and ending with Grace King and Charles W. Chesnutt, both of whom died in 1932. The historical events confronting Southern writers in the 293 years between 1607 and 1900 are staggering—the first settlements, the introduction of slavery, the Revolutionary War, the adoption of the Constitution, the Southern expansion across the mountains and into the Old Southwest, the growing controversy over slavery and secession, the devastating War Between the States and equally devastating Reconstruction, and the rocky road to reunion, just to mention a few. Although the format of this volume has dictated that we exclude many worthy authors, we have tried to include those writers who answer Shreve McCannon's question to Quentin Compson in William Faulkner's *Absalom, Absalom!*—*"Tell about the South."*

To tell about the South, *Fifty Southern Writers Before 1900* had to include essays about such major authors as Edgar Allan Poe, William Gilmore Simms, Frederick Douglass, Mark Twain, George Washington Cable, and Kate Chopin. To represent the seventeenth and eighteenth centuries, we chose Captain John Smith, Robert Beverley, William Byrd of Westover, Ebenezer Cook, Robert Munford, Thomas Jefferson, and St. George Tucker. This volume, however, focuses most upon those nineteenth-century authors whose works give a sense of the long background behind the Southern Renascence. In that background lie the works of very different writers—Mary Boykin Chesnut, Augusta Evans Wilson, George Moses Horton, William Wells Brown, Grace King, Charles W. Chesnutt, and the Southwest humorists, as well as William Alexander Caruthers,

Thomas Holley Chivers, Paul Hamilton Hayne, Henry Timrod, Sidney Lanier, John Pendleton Kennedy, and others. Although we are aware of omissions, we believe our fifty authors do a good job of telling about the South.

Fifty Southern Writers Before 1900 offers students and teachers an overview of the writers' lives and works. Each essay, written by a knowledgeable scholar, contains five parts: a biographical sketch, a discussion of the author's major themes, an assessment of the scholarship on each writer, a chronological list of the author's works, and a bibliography of selected criticism. Readers working their way through this volume and its companion will have, we hope, a valuable complement to *The History of Southern Literature* (1985), which emphasizes chronology and movements.

Fifty Southern Writers Before 1900, like its sequel, *Fifty Southern Writers After 1900*, owes its existence to many people. Foremost, we are indebted to the many scholars who have contributed to the making of this book. Their willingness to share their love for and knowledge of Southern letters constitutes an act of faith. To Fred Erisman and Richard W. Etulain, editors of *Fifty Western Writers* (1982), we owe the format of these volumes. We thank especially Louis D. Rubin, Jr., who has given us wise counsel about our work. We are grateful to Cynthia Harris and her associates at Greenwood Press for their patience and help in a complex job of editing. We also thank our colleagues at Chapel Hill and the Department of English for their support and advice.

Suzanne Booker proved an able sleuth at uncovering many of our errors. Cheryl Baxley, Toni Carter, Diana Dwyer, Jo Gibson, Kim Lassiter, Angela Miller, Sandi Moore, and Tobi Schwartzman helped us with typing and clerical duties. Nancy West aided us by compiling the index. Ramona Cook, Christine Flora, Maggie Boone Ford, and Charlotte McFall assisted us with numerous details. Erika Lindemann put her editor's eyes to work at improving sentences in our introductions. Frustrations there were, but these good people helped us to keep our sense of humor and our confidence in a good cause.

Introduction

After the tragedy of the Lost Colony at Roanoke and other early English failures to settle the Southern colonies, Captains Christopher Newport and John Smith tried again at Jamestown in 1607. George Percy, who accompanied the expedition, recorded his first impressions of Virginia with a mixture of disappointment, delight, and finally terror:

The six and twentieth of April [1607], about four o'clock in the morning, we described the land of Virginia. The same day we entered into the Bay of Chesupoic directly, without any let or hindrance. There we landed and discovered a little way, but we could find nothing worth speaking of, but fair meadows and goodly tall trees, with such fresh waters running through the woods as I was almost ravished at the first sight thereof.

The "nothing worth speaking of" probably betrays Percy's disappointment at not finding wealth; the ravishing sight of "fresh waters" and "fair meadows and goodly tall trees" later led Percy to call this new land a "paradise."

After dark on that first day, the terror came:

At night, when we were going abroad, there came the savages creeping upon all four from the hills like bears, with their bows in their mouths, charged us very desperately in the faces, hurt Captain Gabriel Archer in both his hands and a sailor in two places of the body very dangerous. After they had spent their arrows, and felt the sharpness of our shot, they retired into the woods with a great noise, and so left us.

By August 1607—after Captain Newport had returned to England in June, leaving "one hundred and four persons" to settle and explore the country—Percy cataloged a litany of dying. Between 6 August and 5 September, he recorded 21 deaths in his company: "Our men were destroyed with cruel diseases as swellings, fluxes, burning fevers, and by wars, and some departed suddenly, but for the most part they died of mere famine. There were never Englishmen left in a foreign country in such misery as we were in this new discovered Virginia." So began the first permanent British settlement in the South.

Like George Percy and Captain John Smith, the first "Southerners" were Englishmen who came to the New World looking for fame and fortune. Few of those who settled the South during the following decades were younger sons of the English nobility; many, like William Byrd I, were middling people on the make. Later, some were deported from England as undesirables, often for petty crimes like those of Daniel DeFoe's Moll Flanders; others arrived as indentured servants eager to escape the overcrowding and economic blight of their homeland. After 1619, thousands were involuntary colonists who came aboard the slaveships from Africa.

The earliest writers reported on the natural world and its native inhabitants, first in Virginia and later in Maryland, the Carolinas, and Georgia. Nearly all of these reports promoted the strange new world's possibilities for bringing wealth and empire to the "sceptered isle" and "demi-paradise" that Shakespeare's John of Gaunt called England in *Richard II*.

Foremost among these early Southern reporters and promoters was that doughty myth-maker John Smith (1580–1631), who wrote six books about his experiences in America and gave New England its name. A number of authors writing about North American exploration and colonization got out of the starting gate before Smith, among them Sir Walter Raleigh (in absentia), Arthur Barlow, Ralph Lane, John White (famous for his drawings), and Thomas Hariot, who published *A Brief and True Report of the New-Found Land of Virginia* in 1588. But John Smith had staying power as a writer. From *A True Relation* (1608) and *A Map of Virginia* (1612) to *The Generall Historie of Virginia, New England and the Summer Isles* (1624), and *Advertisements for the Unexperienced Planters* (1631), Captain John Smith championed the cause of American settlement, created himself as a hero equal to any task, defined the earliest version of the American Dream of Success, and recorded the Pocahontas story (in several versions) that would give great good glee to Mark Twain in *Pudd'nhead Wilson* (1894) and to John Barth in *The Sot-Weed Factor* (1960). The handsome new edition of Smith's works in three volumes (1986) should encourage a new generation of readers and scholars to look at his writing with fresh eyes.

Unlike the New Englanders who founded Harvard College in 1636 and printed books by 1640, Southerners were slower in acquiring the accoutrements of a literary culture. Virginia's Indian war of 1622 postponed the founding of the College of William and Mary until 1693, and printing came to the South much later. Book publishing usually accompanied the founding of the gazettes, and the *Maryland Gazette*, established by William Parks at Annapolis in 1726, was the first Southern newspaper. Parks moved to Williamsburg to publish the *Virginia Gazette* in 1732, and in Charleston Thomas Whitmarsh began the *South-Carolina Gazette* in the same year. North Carolina had its first newspaper in

1751 and Georgia in 1763. For the most part the early Southerners published their books in England and looked to London for their literary culture.

Though the South produced few books between 1631 and 1700, Southerners wrote and read. Most of their writing was in the form of letters, official reports, and state papers. The Burwell Papers, first printed in 1814, present a lively account of Nathaniel Bacon's Rebellion of 1676 and two poems upon Bacon's death. Like much of Southern writing of the early period, this manuscript probably circulated among readers at the time of its composition in the seventeenth century, but without printing presses, these authors seldom saw their work in print. Planters such as Robert "King" Carter and William Byrd I sent their sons to England to be educated in the classical schools and often in law. Most had libraries, often filled with books of law, medicine, and agriculture. None had a library the size of that of William Byrd II, who at his death in 1744 owned 3,600 volumes in his magnificent collection.

Among those early authors carrying their manuscripts to London for publication were Robert Beverley (1673–1722) and Ebenezer Cook (sometimes spelled Cooke) (ca. 1667–ca. 1732). Beverley's *The History and Present State of Virginia* (1705) is an account of his colony's history, natural products, Indians, and current conditions. Posing in his preface as an Indian not "exact in my Language," Beverley hopes the "Plainness of my Dress, will give him [the critic] the kinder impressions of my Honesty." Written partly to correct British misconceptions about Virginia, the *History*, which Beverley revised and published again in London in 1722, also wittily describes in its liveliest section Indian customs and culture. Cook's *The Sot-Weed Factor* (1708) recounts in Hudibrastic verse the rollicking adventures of an Englishman come to Maryland to make his fortune. After a picaresque journey through the countryside and encounters with settlers who fleece him, the poem's speaker returns to England cursing the colony: "May Wrath Divine then lay those Regions wast / Where no Man's Faithful, nor a Woman chast." As J. A. Leo Lemay has pointed out, the poem "satirizes not only America but also the popular English conceptions of America." Three centuries later, John Barth's novel would spin out Cook's story with the same wit and verve that the original author employed in his verses.

The most distinguished man of letters in the colonial South was William Byrd of Westover (1674–1744), author of *The History of the Dividing Line* (1841), *The Secret History of the Line* (1929), *A Progress to the Mines* (1841), *A Journey to the Land of Eden* (1841), numerous character sketches, three volumes of secret diaries (kept in a seventeenth-century shorthand and not published until the middle of this century), some occasional verses, a pamphlet on the plague, literary exercises and brief translations from the classics, a short and un-Puritan autobiography, and more than 200 surviving letters. A compulsive reader and writer, Byrd published little during his life but circulated his manuscripts among his Virginia friends and British correspondents. Publication of his work since 1841 has brought him literary fame denied him during his lifetime. Besides providing the single most comprehensive picture of plantation life during the Golden Age, Byrd has delighted readers with his portraits of the pork-eating poor whites of Lubberland and of himself as the Virginia Gentleman. He also created other Southern and American portraits, especially in *The Secret History* where he draws thumbnail sketches of his "pioneers," "foresters," and the noble Indian Ned Bearskin. Because he preoccupied himself with subjects and motifs central to his culture and because he explored these subjects with wit, grace, and insight, William Byrd stands foremost among Southern writers before Jefferson, Poe, and Simms.

With the coming of the gazettes and printing, Southerners began to publish books locally and to develop a literary character of their own. The typical gazette printed four pages weekly. Page 1 usually featured foreign news and occasionally a verse or an essay by a local writer. During the Stamp Tax disputes of the mid–1760s, news from other colonies might appear on page 2 along with the foreign news continued from page 1. A "Poet's Corner" on page 3 often gave Southern versifiers a chance to try their hands at an elegy, a love poem, some comic lines, or a poem for a special occasion. That page frequently printed local news and some advertising. The last page contained mostly advertising. The gazettes gave Southerners an outlet for original verse and essays, usually contributed anonymously or signed with such pseudonyms as "A Virginian," "A Cracker," or a host of classical names. The *South-Carolina Gazette* published in 1736 a series of original essays as "The Meddlers Club Papers," and in 1736–37 William Parks's *Virginia Gazette* printed some 22 original contributions under the title of "The Monitor Essays." Such books as William Dawson's *Poems on Several Occasions* (Williamsburg, 1736) and a new edition of Ebenezer Cook's *The Sot-Weed Factor* in *The Maryland Muse* (Annapolis, 1731) trickled from these presses. None of these authors was a professional writer; all were planters, doctors, lawyers, preachers, or merchants first—and writers second and third. Most imitated what their English cousins in London were writing; but the South was developing its own literary culture.

The "Revolutionary generation of the South," Richard Beale Davis has argued, produced the region's "finest literary expression before the twentieth century." Though Southerners in the years between 1765 and 1790 wrote few belletristic works that have endured, they wrote well and voluminously on the issues of their day. Their ranks are legion—Daniel Dulaney the Younger, Patrick Henry, William Eddis, Christopher Gadsden, Arthur Lee, Richard Henry Lee, James Iredell, Richard Bland, David Ramsey, Jonathan Boucher, John Joachim Zubly. Schooled in the art of rhetoric and the science of politics, these Southerners turned their pens—and often their swords—to the cause of Independence. Among these political writers, James Madison, contributor to *The Federalist* and author of the most complete account of the Constitutional Convention (not published until after his death), was the most original thinker and political scientist in the New World.

Because his work touches upon issues central to the Revolution and to the founding of the Republic, Thomas Jefferson (1743–1826) was the most important Southern writer of his generation. The author of the Declaration of Independence published only one book during his life, but his letters, state papers, speeches, essays, and posthumously published autobiography deal with everything from politics and planting to the metrics of classical and English verse and the list of books belonging in a gentleman's library. First published in France in 1785 and then in Jefferson's approved version in 1787, *Notes on Virginia* answers 23 queries from François de Marbois, secretary to the French legation in Philadelphia. Jefferson comments on Virginia's geography, natural resources, people, government, religion, and in William Peden's excellent edition (1954) lists an eighteen-page chronology of Virginia's history. In that book's most famous section, on "Manners," Jefferson analyzes the dehumanizing effects of slavery on both slaves and masters and hopes for "total emancipation," for the "Almighty has no attribute which can take sides with us [slaveholders] in such a contest." Lewis P. Simpson has described *Notes on Virginia* as being "more in the spirit of a poem than a scientific treatise"; he reads the book as Jefferson's attempt to create in prose "a modern secular state in the image of the rational, lettered, free mind." For Simpson, Jefferson defines clearly the dilemma for Southern writers before the Civil War; he writes, "In the inability of a modern man of letters like Jefferson to terminate his role as a slave master lies the chief key to the history of literature in the antebellum Southern states."

Of Jefferson's voluminous correspondence, his exchange of letters with John Adams toward the end of their lives tells much about differences between the South and New England. In one letter to Adams, Jefferson expresses his distrust of the "artificial aristocracy," based on "wealth and birth," and his faith in the "natural aristocracy," based on "virtue and talents," the "most precious gift of nature." To cultivate this natural aristocracy, the lifeblood of the new republic, Jefferson wrote his proposals for educating the youth of Virginia and founded his University at Charlottesville. Merrill D. Peterson has called these letters between two old comrades and adversaries "the finest fruit" of Jefferson's correspondence.

Two other Southerners of the Revolutionary Period—Robert Munford (ca. 1737–83) and St. George Tucker (1752–1827)—addressed many of the same problems Jefferson did, but chose different literary forms for their work. Munford's *The Candidates* and *The Patriots*, two comic dramas written in the 1770s but not published until 1798, are set in the newly settled Southside Virginia (near the North Carolina border) and parade before viewers the characters and conflicts of the new country. *The Candidates* farcically pits characters named Mr. Wou'dbe, Mr. Strutabout, Mr. Smallhopes, and Sir John Toddy against each other in an election campaign, complete with a political barbecue. *The Patriots*, a more ambitious work, explores the ambiguities of "patriotism" in the highly charged atmosphere of suspicion and intrigue during the Revolution. A major theme in this comedy is that "patriotism" is often the refuge of rascals.

Though much of St. George Tucker's work remains in manuscript, he contributed patriotic verses to newspapers and in letters to his family wrote realistic accounts of his soldiering in the Southern campaigns. A lawyer and judge, Tucker published after the war *Liberty, A Poem on the Independence of America* (1788), *A Dissertation on Slavery* (1796), and *Probationary Odes of Jonathan Pindar, Esq.* (1796). In *A Dissertation*, which he sent to members of the Virginia Assembly, he proposed the gradual abolition of slavery by allowing children born of slaves to be freed upon reaching adulthood. His *Probationary Odes* satirize the persons and policies of such Federalists as John Adams and Alexander Hamilton. In 1811 Tucker wrote some 27 or 28 "Old Batchellor" essays, Addisonian in style and subject; most of these works remain unpublished. Carl R. Dolmetsch argues in this volume that Tucker's literary stock will rise once his works become available. That work includes 210 poems, 29 Addisonian essays, 3 plays, and many letters.

A transitional writer between the Revolutionary generation and those young authors coming to the fore in the 1820s and 1830s, William Wirt (1772–1834) wrote between 1803 and 1817 three series of Addisonian essays and his most famous book, *Sketches of the Life and Character of Patrick Henry* (1817). *The Letters of the British Spy*, first published serially in Richmond's *Virginian Argus* in 1803, was so popular that it went through ten editions in Wirt's lifetime. But his biography of Patrick Henry is his most important contribution to Southern and American letters. Though Wirt had never met Henry, he gathered material from many sources to draw Henry's portrait as a new man from the western country—inspired backwoods orator, yeoman farmer, spokesman for the common man, and in some ways a precursor of Andrew Jackson, who would be president in 1829. Wirt's friend John Taylor of Caroline called the book a "splendid novel," and like Mason Locke Weems, whose biography of George Washington (1800) helped mythologize this national hero, Wirt created in his *Life* the Patrick Henry whose words every American schoolchild could recite once upon a time.

The next generation of writers, most coming to maturity in the 1820s and 1830s, responded to the pressures of growing sectionalism and began to give Southern writing a character distinct from that of the North. Southerners also established such literary magazines as the *Southern Literary Messenger* (1834–64) and the *Southern Quarterly Review* (1842–57), to which regional writers submitted their work. Richard Henry Wilde (1789–1847), Edward Coote Pinkney (1802–28), Thomas Holley Chivers (1809–58), and Philip Pendleton Cooke (1816–50) number among the poets of this period. They wrote love lyrics, nature poetry, some satirical verses, and lines about the South's past. Chivers, who published his first volume of verse in 1832, wrote of the death of a beautiful woman, a theme common to much antebellum verse. A friend to and biographer of Poe, Chivers ranks below Poe, Simms, and Henry Timrod as an antebellum poet and experimenter in verse.

Antebellum novelists, many of them Virginians writing historical romances, looked to their Southern past, to plantation life, to frontier adventures, and to sentimental love stories for their material. They had established, long before the Civil War, the "plantation novel" as a staple of Southern fiction. George Tucker's *The Valley of the Shenandoah* (1824) tells a "tale of the ruin of a once prosperous and respected family," the Graysons, complete with a perfidious Yankee villain named James Gildon. William Alexander Caruthers (1802–46), John Pendleton Kennedy (1795–1870), Nathaniel Beverley Tucker (1784–1851), and John Esten Cooke (1830–86) all wrote novels touching upon these Southern subjects. Nearly all of these novels are flawed by stereotyped characters, by inflated language (later called by some "Confederate Rhetoric"), by weak plotting, or by sentimentality, but they remain a rich source of telling how Southerners conceived of themselves and their world before the Civil War.

Kennedy's *Swallow Barn* (1832) set the image of plantation life that would prevail for 100 years. He followed *Swallow Barn* with his popular historical romances, *Horse-Shoe Robinson* (1835), set during the Revolution, and *Rob of the Bowl* (1838), set in colonial Maryland. Caruthers looked to Bacon's Rebellion for his subject in *The Virginia Cavaliers* (1834–35) and to Alexander Spotswood's expedition across the Blue Ridge in 1716 for *The Knights of the Golden Horse-Shoe* (1845). Nathaniel Beverley Tucker's *The Partisan Leader* (1836), a polemical novel set in 1849, predicts civil strife and Virginia's secession from the Union. Cooke's antebellum romances—among them *Leather Stocking and Silk* (1854), *The Virginia Comedians* (1854), and *Henry St. John, Gentleman* (1859)—tell tales of Virginia's Golden Age. In his postbellum novels, Cooke, who served valiantly with the Confederate Army, apotheosized Stonewall Jackson in *Surry of Eagle's Nest* (1866) and J.E.B. Stuart and Robert E. Lee in *Mohun* (1869). He portrays these leaders as the courageous noblemen of the doomed Lost Cause. Cooke's *The Heir of Gaymount* (1870) deals with the hero's struggles to maintain his estate during Reconstruction.

The most prolific and most representative antebellum Southern writer was William Gilmore Simms (1806–70) of Charleston, author of some 80 books of history, poetry, novels, drama, short stories and sketches, criticism, biography, and polemics. Simms's uncollected work, according to C. Hugh Holman and Mary Ann Wimsatt, would fill another twenty volumes.

Largely self-educated and widely traveled in the South, Southwest, and the North, where he met writers from Boston and New York, Simms took his Southern American past and present as the canvas for his work. An ardent advocate of a national and a Southern literature, Simms, who published his first book in 1824 when he was only nineteen, explored his region in almost everything he wrote, most notably in his biographies, histories, and especially in his historical romances. Mary Ann Wimsatt argues in this volume that four periods of Southern history preoccupied Simms throughout his career, early and late. Works of the first period of Southern history treat the French, Spanish, and English explorations to the founding of Jamestown. Among these books are a volume of poems, *The Vision of Cortes* (1829), and two romances, *The Damsel of Darien* (1839), a tale of Balboa's American adventures, and *Vasconselos* (1853), dealing with De Soto's explorations. The second period covers the era from the founding of Jamestown to the reign of George III and includes Simms's biography of Captain John Smith (1846) and *The Yemassee* (1835), about the Carolina Indian wars in 1715 and thought by some critics to be his finest work.

The seven Revolutionary War Romances and such biographies as those about Nathanael Greene (1849) and Francis Marion (1844) number among the books of the third historical period to interest Simms. Keen Butterworth believes that *The Forayers* (1855) and its sequel, *Eutaw* (1856), two of the Revolutionary War Romances, show Simms at "the height of his powers" as a novelist. The fourth historical period parallels Simms's own life; these works include such Border Romances as *Guy Rivers* (1834) and *Richard Hurdis* (1838).

Simms enjoyed great popularity among Northern and Southern reviewers of his day, but as the Civil War approached, his defense of slavery and the Southern cause cost him the favor of Northern critics. As editor of several magazines—among them *Magnolia* (1842–43), *Southern and Western* (1845), and the *Southern Quarterly Review* (1849–55)—Simms reviewed hundreds of books and set the literary taste of much of his region. In poor health and with his plantation burned by Sherman's troops, Simms continued to write after the war, contributing to magazines several serialized fictions about the Appalachian Mountains. When he died on 11 June 1870, he had unpublished manuscripts on hand. As Wimsatt notes in this volume, Simms's literary reputation after the war suffered the same decline as did his much-beloved South. But his works, now too often neglected, tell much about the South before and during the war.

Of the antebellum Southern writers, the enigmatic Edgar Allan Poe (1809–49) outstripped all of his contemporaries in the quality and quantity of his work, and in Eric W. Carlson's words, "helped to create the modern literary imagination." Though Poe was born in Boston and spent five years of his childhood in England, he identified himself as a Virginian. The most cosmopolitan of his contemporaries, Poe attended to art instead of politics, fighting his battles in critical reviews defending excellence in poetry and fiction rather than preoccupying himself with polemics justifying slavery and the Southern way of life. In these battles he referred to the Bostonians as "Frogpondians" for croaking their own praises, and he spoke slightingly of Longfellow's verses and of "the so called poetry of the so called transcendentalists." His other battles were with editors or publishers for whom he worked. As an assistant editor of the *Southern Literary Messenger*, Poe brought this periodical better writing and a wider readership, but throughout his life he battled with editors over his literary judgments, and he longed to finance and edit his ideal journal in which he could print worthy art. The *Broadway Journal*, which he briefly owned and edited and which was not his ideal periodical, failed.

Though he did not respond to Northern critics of the South as did Simms and others, Ellen Glasgow believed Poe "a distillation of the Southern." Many of Poe's themes link him with his successors: the fall of a house, his preoccupation with abnormal psychological states and with grotesques, his interest in incest, and his belief that art need not commit the "heresy of *The Didactic*," but should exist solely for its aesthetic beauties. The distance between "The Fall of the House of Usher" and the Fall of the House of Thomas Sutpen is not great, and Faulkner acknowledged his kinship to Poe with many allusions to his predecessor in *Absalom, Absalom!*

Poe's achievements, recognized by European critics before American, were in short fiction, poetry, criticism, and magazine editing. He gave the short story its form ("unity of effect") by his practice and his theory; he invented the modern detective story. His fine lyric and symbolic poems—"The City in the Sea," "Israfel," "To Helen," "The Raven," among others—anticipated the French Symbolists, who admired his work. Poe's poetic theory opposed the prevailing theories in New England and insisted on the poem's value for its own sake; his theory of the short story refined and intensified notions about the sketch he had inherited from Irving and the Knickerbocker school. His practical criticism recognized the genius of Nathaniel Hawthorne and others. He wrote hundreds of such reviews. Whenever he edited a magazine—and he edited several—the quality of that journal improved. Although he tried his hand at a novel and a drama, these were not his forms, but in the 22 years of his literary career, he wrote enough to fill seventeen volumes of *The Complete Works*, published in 1902. And ever since, scholars have been pointing out that *The Complete Works* was not complete.

Other antebellum Southern voices came from other rooms. George Moses Horton (ca. 1797–ca. 1883), Frederick Douglass (1817–95), and William Wells Brown (ca. 1815–84)—all born into slavery—wrote longingly of freedom, about the brutalizing effects of that "peculiar institution" upon the psyches of blacks, and about the injustices of chattel slavery. The earliest black Southern poet, Horton, who lived in Chatham and Orange counties in North Carolina, published his first volume, *The Hope of Liberty*, in 1829. He wrote love lyrics and religious verse, but in such poems as "Division of an Estate," he contrasts the fate of his master's heirs with that of his slaves, whose state is much like the master's livestock.

Born into slavery on a plantation on Maryland's Eastern Shore, Frederick Douglass wrote one of the most widely read books of the antebellum era, the *Narrative of the Life of Frederick Douglass, an American Slave* (1845). In this autobiography and two later versions of the work (1855, 1881), Douglass documented a black man's view of slavery's evils and championed the cause of liberty for all men. William Wells Brown, born on a farm near Lexington, Kentucky, wrote of his bondage and escape in the *Narrative of William W. Brown, a Fugitive Slave* (1847). Author of European travel books, of essays, and of histories, Brown is best known for *Clotel; or, The President's Daughter* (1853), the first novel by a black Southerner. In that work Brown recounts the plight of Clotel, daughter of an American President (Thomas Jefferson) and a slave mistress. Douglass, Brown, and later Horton all escaped to the North, a pattern that would hold true for many black writers until the middle of the twentieth century.

The most vital writing of the antebellum South and its chief contribution to the national literature, according to some historians and critics, was the work of the Southwest humorists. These writers often published their tales in the *Southern Literary Messenger*, in William T. Porter's New York sporting journal called *Spirit of the Times*, or in the newspapers of dozens of Southern towns. Other newspaper editors, looking for good copy, often reprinted these tales even before their authors collected them in book form. Their humorous stories and sketches, often earthy and filled with Southern characters speaking in dialect, sold well and circulated widely in the 1830s, 1840s, and 1850s. Few plantations appear in their tales about the common folk of the backcountry South.

Augustus Baldwin Longstreet's (1790–1870) *Georgia Scenes* (1835), the earliest book of Southwest stories to gain national prominence (eleven editions in the nineteenth century), featured two gentlemanly personae (''Hall'' and ''Baldwin'') reporting on backcountry customs and speech, often with amusement and sometimes with horror. Reviewing the book, Poe called the author ''a clever fellow, imbued with a spirit of the truest humor, and endowed, moreover, with an exquisitely discriminative and penetrating understanding of *character* in general, and of Southern character in particular.'' In such sketches as ''Georgia Theatrics'' and ''The Fight,'' Longstreet captured the ''raw idiom of frontier dialect'' and a sense of the new country's violence. In addition to being the first important book of Southwest humor, Longstreet's *Georgia Scenes* signaled, according to literary historians, the beginnings of both the realistic and local color movements.

In the three decades following publication of *Georgia Scenes*, many Southerners collected their humorous tales and sketches in book form. Though literary historians often group these humorists together, their works differ markedly, ranging from Thomas Bangs Thorpe's (1815–78) ''The Big Bear of Arkansas'' in *The Mysteries of the Backwoods* (1846), a hunting story that Faulkner praised and wrote his own version of, to George Washington Harris's (1814–69) *Sut Lovingood. Yarns Spun by a ''Nat'ral Born Durn'd Fool''* (1867). Using the frame story (as Longstreet and others had) as the device for allowing Sut to spin his comic yarns in highly vernacular prose, Harris created a character whom M. Thomas Inge has called ''a Tennessee backwoods individualist and crude philosopher who would play the roles of trickster and fool in working out a series of disastrous pranks and retributive schemes against the hypocritical society around him.'' A young reviewer of Harris's book, Mark Twain, allowed that the tales would be too bawdy for Eastern tastes. Mostly, they were.

Other humorists achieving national recognition included William Tappan Thompson (1812–82), Johnson Jones Hooper (1815–62), Joseph Glover Baldwin (1815–64), George William Bagby (1828–83), and Charles Henry Smith (1826–1903). Thompson's *Major Jones's Courtship* (1843) offered the adventures of

Major Joseph Jones of Pineville, Georgia, for readers' edification. Johnson Jones Hooper, creator of *Some Adventures of Captain Simon Suggs* (1845), has his hero declare that it was good to be shifty in a new country. *Flush Times of Alabama and Mississippi* (1853), by Joseph Glover Baldwin, recounted the boom-and-bust era of the Southwest frontier. George William Bagby, author of *Mozis Addums' New Letters* (1860) and *The Letters of Mozis Addums to Billy Ivvins* (1862), took the shenanigans of rural Virginia as his territory. In *Bill Arp, So Called* (1866) and its four sequels, Charles Henry Smith told tales of north Georgia from the Civil War to the end of the century. Mark Twain, William Faulkner, Flannery O'Connor, and Robert Penn Warren have all acknowledged the influence of these humorists upon their work.

The Civil War and Reconstruction devastated the South. During the war, writers turned their pens in one of several directions—patriotic verses, prose polemics, letters from the battlefronts, reportage, slave narratives, and diaries. After the war, people preoccupied with grubbing food and shelter and rebuilding a shattered society had little time for making stories, poems, and novels. J. Gordon Coogler's doggerel couplet has some truth to it; the self-proclaimed poet laureate of Columbia, South Carolina, lamented, "Alas for the South! Her books have grown fewer; / She was never much given to literature." But Southerners did write, and in the years following the war they found audiences in their own newspapers, where Joel Chandler Harris's Uncle Remus stories originally appeared. By the 1870s and 1880s Northern publishers and editors sought Southerners' work because they wanted someone to tell them about the South.

Two popular and oft-reprinted poems from the Civil War and Reconstruction era characterize the range of Southerners' feelings. Innes Randolph's "The Rebel," which he sang during the war at a meeting of the Mosaic Club in Richmond and which was apparently first printed in the Augusta, Georgia, *Constitutionalist* of 4 July 1867, seethes with anger, hurt, pride, and defiance. Randolph's vernacular speaker "followed old Mars Robert / For four year, near about" and "Got wounded in three places, / And starved at Pint Lookout." Randolph's speaker concludes:

> Three hundred thousand Yankees
>   Is stiff in Southern dust;
> We got three hundred thousand
>   Before they conquered us.
> They died of Southern fever
>   And Southern steel and shot;
> I wish it was three millions
>   Instead of what we got.
>
> I can't take up my musket
>   And fight 'em now no more,
> But I ain't agoin' to love 'em,
>   Now that is sartin sure.

> And I don't want no pardon
> For what I was and am;
> I won't be reconstructed,
> And I don't care a dam.

Randolph's speaker's sentiments lingered long in the South; in some places, they are not dead yet.

In "The Conquered Banner," Father Abram Joseph Ryan, known as the "Poet-Priest of the Confederacy," took a tack different from that in Randolph's "The Rebel." First published in Father Ryan's Augusta, Georgia, newspaper, the *Banner of the South*, on 21 March 1868, "The Conquered Banner" treats the Lost Cause in an elegiac tone. Ryan's last two stanzas counsel a putting away of the bloody conflict, but also exhort readers *never* to forget:

> Furl that Banner! True, 'tis gory,
> Yet 'tis wreathed around with glory,
> And 'twill live in song and story,
>   Though its folds are in the dust:
> For its form on brightest pages
> Penned by poets and by sages,
> Shall go sounding down the ages—
>   Furl its folds though now we must.
>
> Furl that Banner, softly, slowly!
> Treat it gently—it is holy—
>   For it droops above the dead.
> Touch it not—unfold it never,
> Let it droop there, furled forever,
>   For its people's hopes are dead!

In some ways, these two popular poems signal attitudes much Southern writing was to take after the war—Randolph's apotheosizing the Lost Cause and the Old South, and Ryan's resolution to furl but never to forget the conquered banner, symbol of a nation's death, and to get on with whatever was necessary to live.

The Southern author who achieved most following the Civil War was Mark Twain (1835–1910), whom Everett Emerson has called "America's favorite writer and a world favorite as well." Though he wrote many books having nothing to do with the South and though critics dispute whether he is a Southern or Western writer, Mark Twain's roots lie deeply embedded in the South, and his best works speak with a Southern accent. Born in Missouri, then a slave state, and briefly a Confederate volunteer during the war, Sam Clemens mined his richest imaginative vein in such Southern tales as "A True Story" (1874), "Old Times on the Mississippi" (1875), *The Adventures of Tom Sawyer* (1876), *Life on the Mississippi* (1883), *Pudd'nhead Wilson* (1894), "The Man That Corrupted Hadleyburg" (1899), and his masterpiece, *Adventures of Huckleberry Finn* (1885). In these books and stories, Mark Twain satirized his South's Bible-belt religiosity and hypocrisy, its penchant for Emmeline Grangerford's sentimentality, the pretensions of its "aristocratic" descendants of the First Families of Virginia, its redneck folks in the person of Pap Finn, its picaresque rogues from Southwest humor in the Duke and the King, the injustices of slavery, and its greed and grotesqueness. He transcended the white South's stereotyping of blacks by creating such characters as Jim and Aunt Rachel. With wit and humor, he punctured pomposity and pretentiousness wherever he saw it.

One of Mark Twain's principal achievements, one that may have prompted Ernest Hemingway's remark that American literature begins with *Huck Finn*, was harnessing vernacular language for something other than the humorous or the comic tale. Without falling into the trap of a completely eccentric spelling as George Washington Harris had in his *Sut Lovingood* (1867), Mark Twain captured on his pages the rhythms and sounds of folk-talk and put them to work. When Huck Finn muses on the loveliness and majesty of the River or when Jim scolds Huck for being trash and putting "dirt on de head er dey fren's en makes 'em ashamed," the vernacular voice becomes a vehicle for poetry and for serious fiction. More than any other writer in the nineteenth century, Mark Twain liberated the language of the common folk for those authors who came after him. Acknowledging his indebtedness, William Faulkner called Mark Twain "our grandfather."

The South's postbellum poets wrote few great works, but as Jack De Bellis remarks of Henry Timrod, these writers tell much about the "intellectual and emotional climate of the South before, during, and after the Civil War." Although Timrod (1828–67) and Paul Hamilton Hayne (1830–86) had published volumes before the war, they and Sidney Lanier did their most important work after 1860. Timrod's Civil War poems like "Ethnogenesis," "The Cotton Boll," "A Cry to Arms," and "Charleston"—all written in 1861–62—earned him the title of "Poet Laureate of the South," but also show his changing attitudes toward the war, beginning with a patriotic call to arms and ending with a recognition of the war's horrors. When Timrod died in 1867, his friend Hayne inherited the unofficial title of laureate of the South. In *Legends and Lyrics* (1872), *The Mountain of the Lovers* (1875), and *Poems* (1882), Hayne explored in verse his love for his homeland, his love of his family, his love of nature, and the theme of death. Always a derivative poet, Hayne nevertheless spoke in competent meters about common Southern concerns.

Attempting to escape the conventional rhythms he had inherited from his predecessors, Sidney Lanier (1842–81) experimented with sound and music in his *Poems* (1877) and his posthumously published *Poems of Sidney Lanier* (1884). A professional musician, a serious student of prosody, and author of *The Science of English Verse* (1880), Lanier struggled to find new and fresh forms for casting his poems. In such poems as "Corn" (1874), "The Symphony" (1877), and his oft-anthologized "The Marshes of Glynn" (1882), Lanier varied line lengths and sought new rhythms in an effort to make music and poetry one. Though his poems lack the bold originality of a Walt Whitman, who admired

Lanier's work, Lanier chose to follow "no school, no safe and established practices, no patterns except his own." In the process, argues Jane S. Gabin, he created dozens of poems memorable for their music. Of the postbellum poets, Lanier attempted more and achieved more than his contemporaries because he sought in his experimental verse to find a new voice for poetic expression. All anthologists of American writing recognize this achievement by including selections from his work.

Albery Allson Whitman and Irwin Russell present something of a paradox among the postbellum poets. Whitman (1851–1901), the black poet-preacher and author of the five thousand-line *Not a Man Yet a Man* (1877), wrote narrative poems imitating the rhythms and verse forms of his day. His *Twasinta's Seminoles, or The Rape of Florida* (1884, 1885), for example, is in Spenserian stanzas. Called the "mockingbird" poet by early critics, Whitman has received from recent commentators a more sympathetic estimate of his achievement. The short, unhappy life of the white poet Irwin Russell (1853–79) took another direction: he experimented with black dialects and hoped to write a "Negro novel." Although he published no collection during his lifetime, the dialect verse that he first published in magazines and that was collected posthumously in *Christmas Night in the Quarters* (1913, 1917) earned him the praises of Joel Chandler Harris and Thomas Nelson Page.

The "Queen Regnant of Southern Literature," according to one contemporary reviewer, and perhaps the most read Southern author just after the war was Augusta Jane Evans Wilson (1835–1909), who wrote nine sentimental novels between 1855 and 1902. Although Wilson had published two novels before the war (*Inez: A Tale of the Alamo*, 1855; *Beulah*, 1859), she came into her own with a popular Civil War novel, *Macaria; or Altars of Sacrifice*, published in Richmond in 1863 and smuggled to New York for a Northern edition in 1864. An ardent secessionist, Wilson in *Macaria* answered Harriet Beecher Stowe's criticism of the South in *Uncle Tom's Cabin*. But Wilson hit the jackpot with *St. Elmo* in 1866. Within four months of its publication, *St. Elmo*'s heroine, Edna Earl, had titillated and tearified over one million readers. St. Elmo Murray, Wilson's Byronic hero, sins until he falls under Edna's spell, recants, becomes a preacher, and marries the heroine. So successful was *St. Elmo* that Wilson received $15,000 from her publisher for the copyright to her next novel, *Vashti; or, Until Death Do Us Part* (1869). Mrs. E.D.E.N. Southworth (1819–99), also a popular author and Wilson's Southern soul sister, wrote more than 60 sentimental and melodramatic novels, but Southworth never achieved the vogue of *St. Elmo*.

Working in a literary form different from the sentimental novel, Mary Boykin Chesnut (1823–86) crafted the best "inside narrative" of the war years in *Mary Chesnut's Civil War*, recently edited and introduced by C. Vann Woodward (1981). Originally published in flawed texts as *A Diary from Dixie* in 1905 and again in 1949, *Mary Chesnut's Civil War* won for Woodward (and for Chesnut) the Pulitzer Prize in history and offered readers for the first time a reliable text.

Woodward and Elisabeth S. Muhlenfeld followed this work with *The Private Mary Chesnut: The Unpublished Civil War Diaries* (1984). Scholars and critics now have sound texts for reassessing Chesnut's achievement. Her achievement is large.

With her husband, James Chesnut, Jr., who held high military and civil offices in the Confederate government and who was a personal aide to Jefferson Davis, Mary Chesnut traveled throughout the South witnessing the great events and people of her time. Aware that she was watching history, Chesnut kept religiously her diary of the war years, writing her first entry in February 1861 and her last in July 1865. After the fall of the Confederacy, she put away her diaries and in the mid–1870s tried her hand at three novels, all unpublished. In *The Captain and the Colonel*, she drew upon her Civil War experiences for her fiction; in *Two Years; or The Way We Lived Then*, she used memories of her childhood in Charleston and on the Mississippi frontier for her work. Her third attempt, *Manassas*, survives as a fragment. Elisabeth Muhlenfeld calls these efforts "thoroughly unsuccessful," but believes Chesnut learned valuable fictional techniques that would help her shape her diary into a work of conscious artistry. After a partial revision of the diaries in the mid–1870s, Chesnut returned to them in 1881 for a wholesale reworking, which she completed in December 1884, two years before her death. This reshaped work, according to Muhlenfeld, presents "a panoramic view of the Confederacy teeming with life at its most intensely comic, most tragic, and most thoroughly grand." With a distance of twenty years on her experience, Chesnut rewrote her *Civil War* artfully, avoiding the sentimental, romanticized versions of the war that plagued so much Southern writing after 1865.

In the 1870s, 1880s, and 1890s, dozens of Southern writers gained regional and national recognition in what literary historians have labeled the "local color" movement in American letters. Encouraged by such Northern editors as Edward King, Richard Watson Gilder, and Robert Underwood Johnson, Southerners published stories and novels about the goings on in their localities. Northern readers eager to know more about the defeated nation devoured tales about the picturesqueness and quaintness of the several Souths: the mountaineers of Tennessee, the crackers of Georgia, the Cajuns and Creoles of Louisiana, the struggles of black Americans during Reconstruction, the plantation life of the Tidewater, and almost anything about the South "befo de wah." Paul Buck in *The Road to Reunion* (1937) credits the local color movement with helping to heal the wounds created by the war. But these "local colorists" did not paint their portraits with the same oils, the same brush strokes, or the same perspectives. Thomas Nelson Page's South differs mightily from the one in Charles W. Chesnutt's stories and novels.

Local color writing at its best inclines toward realism; at its worst, it is pathetic. At its best, local color writing shows ordinary characters struggling to deal with their lives, presents an accurate and sympathetic understanding of the region's manners and customs, renders setting with fidelity, eschews the sentimentalizing of characters and events, employs in dialogue the language of the place, refuses the author an attitude of superiority in point of view, and suggests the universal in the local. At its worst, local color writing suffers incurable ills: overdoses of sentimentality, stereotyped characters, weak plotting, superficial understanding of the region's manners and customs, overblown rendering of setting, improbable love matches with melodramatic resolutions, the author's looking down upon characters rather than viewing them from eye level, and exploitation of the region's quaintness, not its connection with the human family. Southerners wrote all kinds of local color—good and bad.

Thus, although "local color" is a useful term for describing much postbellum Southern writing, it also causes trouble. Lumping together such different writers as Page, Chesnutt, Grace King, Kate Chopin, Mary Noailles Murfree, Richard Malcolm Johnston, and George Washington Cable encourages readers to see similarities in their works when differences are more telling. The term also encourages habits of mind that may blind readers to a writer's virtues, but old literary terms, unlike old soldiers, seldom fade away. In *The History of Southern Literature* Merrill Maguire Skaggs argues that modern readers have difficulty evaluating these writers because "local color does not conform to the norms of modernism. Simply put, local color is primarily story-telling, not prophecy; narrative, not symbolism; character sketch, not psychological analysis." But Skaggs also recognizes "varieties of local color" and counsels readers to make distinctions. So do the authors of essays in this volume.

Taking Old Virginia and the plantation as his territory, Thomas Nelson Page (1853–1922) created a powerful and palatable (to white readers) mythology about the South. His first and most popular story, "Marse Chan," published in *Century* in 1884, features a former slave named Sam narrating in dialect the charming life and awful death of "Marse Channin' " in the Civil War. Using a frame story, Page has his black narrator recall nostalgically life before the war and the terrible impact the war had upon the South. His earliest books—*Marse Chan: A Tale of Old Virginia* (1885) and *In Ole Virginia: Marse Chan and Other Stories* (1887)—earned Page the reputation as a major interpreter of the South. His novel *Red Rock: A Chronicle of Reconstruction* (1898) was a best-seller. The author of histories, biographies, children's stories, and such sociological works as *The Negro: The Southerner's Problem* (1904), Page collected his work in eighteen volumes for The Plantation Edition in 1908–12. Though critics have charged him with representing a sentimental view of Southern plantation life and especially of "happy darkies," his work captured the imaginations of readers North and South. Harriet R. Holman suggests in this volume that *Gone with the Wind* owes much to Page.

Although Joel Chandler Harris (1848–1908) sets his Uncle Remus stories on the plantation, his black narrator's dialect tales about animals are really the center of his work. A journalist, Harris began writing Uncle Remus sketches for the Atlanta *Constitution* in 1877, gradually developing his characters and setting. *Uncle Remus: His Songs and His Sayings* (1880), Harris's first collection, sold

10,000 copies in its first four months. More followed. Between 1881 and 1900, Harris wrote twenty books, including such conventional tales as those in *Free Joe and Other Georgian Sketches* (1887). But his fame rests most securely on the Uncle Remus tales. Unlike the black narrators in Page's stories, Uncle Remus was a canny tale-teller, spinning yarns about the weak and powerless Brer Rabbit outwitting the stronger bears, wolves, and foxes. In these tales Harris portrays realistically slave strategies for gaining power and dignity in a society that denied them those qualities. Always attentive to folklore as well as dialect, Harris drew upon the Afro-American trickster figure for his Brer Rabbit. Uncle Remus and his alter ego Brer Rabbit endure as contributions to Southern and American letters.

George Washington Cable (1844–1925), wounded while serving with the Confederate cavalry, after the war openly championed Negro rights and became one of the South's harshest critics. Writing New Orleans tales and sketches in the 1870s, Cable found his fictional milieu in the conflicts between and within the polyglot culture (Creole, black, and Anglo) of his native city. Employing Creole dialects in his work, Cable collected six stories—among them "'Sieur George," "Posson Jone'," "Jean-ah Poquelin," and "Belles Demoiselles Plantation"—in his first book, *Old Creole Days* (1879). His novel and best work, *The Grandissimes*, appeared in 1880, followed by the short novel *Madame Delphine* (1881). Central to all these works is Cable's concern for private morality and public justice. In his early research into New Orleans's past, he discovered the *Code Noir*, which dictated treatment of slaves; his outrage at its injustice appears in *The Grandissimes* as "The Story of Bras-Coupé." Disenchanted with responses to his pleas for Negro rights, Cable moved in 1885 to Connecticut and later to Northampton, Massachusetts. But he continued to write about the South in such works as *The Silent South* (1885), *The Negro Question* (1890), and *John March, Southerner* (1894). Set in Georgia, *John March, Southerner* tests its hero's mettle as he struggles against corrupt politicians and greedy businessmen to lead and to rebuild his region. By 1898 Cable turned to writing popular romances; his best work was behind him.

Richard Malcolm Johnston (1822–98), Mary Noailles Murfree (1850–1922), and Grace King (1850–1932) all wrote in the so-called local color tradition. With Middle Georgia as his locale, Johnston published under the pseudonym of Philemon Perch *Georgia Sketches* (1864). But he is best remembered for his *Dukesborough Tales* (1871, 1874, 1883, 1892), which deal with white middle-class characters in a town much like Powelton, Georgia, near where Johnston grew up. Murfree, who used the pen name Charles Egbert Craddock, published her first story about Tennessee mountaineers in the *Atlantic Monthly* in 1878 and wrote 25 books. She gained national recognition for *In the Tennessee Mountains* (1884), a collection of stories, and *The Prophet of the Great Smoky Mountains* (1885). Her story "The 'Harnt' That Walks Chilhowee" often appears in anthologies. Grace King charged Cable with misrepresenting New Orleans Creoles and set to work correcting that impression in "Monsieur Motte," her first story, published in January 1886 in the *New Princeton Review*. There followed such works as *Tales of a Time and Place* (1892), *Balcony Stories* (1893), and her *Memories of a Southern Woman of Letters* (1932). Though she never married, King treated that subject much, presenting a "unique angle of vision into the psychology of American women."

Though Charles W. Chesnutt (1858–1932) was born in the North and never was a slave, he spent the years just after the war in Fayetteville, North Carolina, and focused much of his work on the lives of black Americans in the postbellum South. An early story, "The Goophered Grapevine," appeared in the *Atlantic Monthly* of August 1887, and Chesnutt collected his tales of Uncle Julius McAdoo in *The Conjure Woman* (1899). An ex-slave very different from Page's black narrators, Uncle Julius remembers the old days "not from nostalgia or a desire to entertain, but rather from self-interested schemes to secure his own economic advantage through artful manipulation of his white listening audience." The novels in Chesnutt's trilogy—*The House Behind the Cedars* (1900), *The Marrow of Tradition* (1901), and *The Colonel's Dream* (1905)—deal with black characters who pass for white, with the 1898 race riots in Wilmington, North Carolina, and with a white, ex-Confederate officer who tries to bring economic recovery and racial enlightenment to his hometown after the war. Chesnutt's stories and novels often treat "life along the color line."

Another black author, the controversial Booker T. Washington (1856–1915), spent much of his energy founding and nurturing Tuskegee Institute and writing prolifically about the education of Negroes, Negro history and social issues, and a biography of Frederick Douglass (1907). Washington earned national recognition with *Up From Slavery* (1901), first serialized in *Outlook* and then published in book form to critical acclaim. One of several of his autobiographical books, *Up From Slavery* became a best-seller immediately. Though Washington counseled accommodation to the segregationist movement in his famous 1895 Atlanta Exposition Speech and earned the scorn of other black leaders, he projected in his work images of hope for black Americans through education and industry. Scholars still debate Washington's significance as a writer, but his voice was an important one in the South's letters.

Kate Chopin (1851–1904), a Southern "local colorist" recently rescued from this epithet by feminist critics and by her biographer Per Seyersted, was one of the boldest and most talented writers of her day. The author of some 100 tales and *The Awakening* (1899), condemned by critics as immoral and obscene, Chopin questioned and finally shattered stereotypes of the Southern Lady by creating real women with minds and passions of their own. In "The Story of an Hour," Chopin portrays a wife exulting in the news of her husband's death by thinking "free, free, free!" In "The Storm," not published during Chopin's life, the heroine Calixta makes love with a former suitor, then welcomes home her husband and son without guilt and with laughter.

But Chopin's major achievement is her careful, artful psychological portrait of Edna Pontellier in *The Awakening*. Safe and secure in a good marriage to a decent and conventional man, Edna longs to fly her cage. Chopin develops in detail two foil characters—Madame Ratignolle, a devoted wife and mother, and Mademoiselle Riesz, an unmarried artist. Into this scene enter two men, Robert Lebrun and Alcée Arobin. What keeps Chopin's novel from descending into melodrama is her restraint as a writer and her sympathetic exploration of Edna's psyche. Though critics have called *The Awakening* a "minor classic," Chopin so controls her language and her art that "minor" simply will not do.

By the end of the first decade of the twentieth century, a new generation of writers had begun to make themselves heard, and the rumblings of the Renascence were under way. By 1910 Ellen Glasgow had written nine books, including *The Voice of the People* (1900), the first of her novels comprising her social history of Virginia. James Branch Cabell had published six books by 1910 and would shortly shock the reading public with his *Jurgen* (1919). In the second decade, H. L. Mencken roundly condemned the South for its lack of culture in his famous essay "The Sahara of the Bozart" (1917). His *Prejudices* began appearing in book form in 1919. Writers of this new generation—all with knowledge of and some distance on the Civil War and the literary heritage recorded in *Fifty Southern Writers Before 1900*—were tapping a rich past to create enduring works of art. Their works are the subject of *Fifty Southern Writers After 1900*, the sequel to this volume.

HAROLD WOODELL

George William Bagby ["Mozis Addums"] (1828–1883)

Called by Jay B. Hubbell "the best of the Virginia humorists," Dr. George William Bagby (essayist, journalist, editor) is a Southern writer who sums up much of the cultural history of the Old South from its rise at mid-century to its fall during Reconstruction. Although known today primarily as a humorist like Augustus Baldwin Longstreet, Joseph Glover Baldwin, and Charles Henry Smith, Bagby finally comes closer to resembling the clown who laughs though his heart is breaking. If a form of laughter comes from the depths of human suffering—from ill health, blighted dreams, and false starts—then Bagby has more in common with a Mark Twain than he does with those humorists with whom he is normally grouped.

BIOGRAPHY

George William Bagby was born on 13 August 1828 in Buckingham County, Virginia. George Bagby, his father, claimed that the date of birth was 25 August, and since no formal certificate was recorded, the day remains in doubt. His ancestors were among the First Families of Virginia. His mother, Virginia Young Evans, descended from pioneers who settled Buckingham County before the American Revolution, and the Bagby lineage could be traced to the founders of Jamestown. The Bagby clan was well-known and respected as pious, hard-working Baptists who farmed the land and entered the business professions. Mr. Bagby was a merchant, but only a marginally successful one who seems to have been more interested in the ministry. In letters to his son, he repeatedly asked the boy to read the Bible and to say his prayers, and he often encouraged him to become a clergyman, a desire that accounts for his son's excellent education.

Mr. Bagby married Virginia Evans with the full knowledge that she would soon die from tuberculosis. After the birth of their two children, George and his sister Ellen, the desperately ill mother moved to the mountain village of Covington for treatment, and the children moved in with an aunt. Mrs. Bagby died two years later when George was eight years old. Later, he wrote fondly of the mother he hardly knew and always described his childhood and early youth in Virginia in happy terms; yet by all accounts these years were filled with separation and grief. His beloved Aunt Betsy, Mrs. Elisabeth Hobson, for instance, is praised highly for her generosity, cooking skills, and understanding in an essay entitled "Good Eating" that appeared in the *Southern Literary Messenger* in May 1863.

Bagby's education was an outstanding one, even though it separated him from his father. He attended "Old Field" schools in Virginia until, at the age of ten, he entered Edgehill School in Princeton, New Jersey. At Edgehill, highly respected as one of the finest schools in the country and known for its strict discipline and rigorous curriculum, he fell in love with reading, especially the works of Charles Dickens, Charles Lamb, and Washington Irving, three authors who clearly exerted strong influences on his style. From 1843 until 1846, Bagby attended Delaware College and from there entered the University of Pennsylvania where he earned an M.D. in 1841 at age twenty-one. He then moved to Lynchburg to practice medicine. The reasons for Bagby's abortive pursuit of a medical career are not known (he never had more than six or seven patients at a time), but it is clear that his no-nonsense schooling and early career choice played a significant part in causing a major health problem, the digestive condition known as dyspepsia, that would follow him for the rest of his life.

Bagby's initial direction in a professional career proved a dead end not only because he failed to encourage the development of a good practice but also because he began to allow his interests to develop along a very different route—writing essays for local newspapers. So enthusiastic was he in this new effort that in 1853, at age twenty-five, Bagby and a nineteen-year-old friend, G. Woodville Latham, purchased the Lynchburg *Express*, a local paper they ran haphazardly until it folded in 1856. In an unpublished tribute to Latham entitled "Woody," Bagby implies that this publication, no copies of which survive, was more of a youthful frolic than a serious venture. Nevertheless, with the demise of the *Express*, Bagby suffered the first of a lifelong series of collapses from dyspepsia. Finding himself in a chronic condition, he moved to his uncle John Evans's plantation, Mountain View, in Prince Edward County, where he spent over a year recuperating. Afterwards, his uncle and the old plantation figured prominently in some of Bagby's most characteristic essays about the Old South—"The Old Virginia Gentleman," "Fishing in the Appomattox," and "My Uncle Flatback's Plantation."

During his rest at Mountain View, Bagby continued to write essays, when his health would permit, such as "The Sacred Furniture Warehouse" that appeared in the Lynchburg *Virginian* in 1856. More important, two additional developments in his writing career occurred while he was staying with his uncle. For the first time, he began to publish humorous essays, the first being "The

Local Takes a Turn on the Ice,'' an anecdote about a newspaper editor who gets his comeuppance while showing off his supposedly great skating talents. Second, Bagby began to achieve national recognition for his essays appearing in Northern periodicals. The first piece to earn him national fame was published in the December 1856 issue of *Harper's Magazine*. Entitled ''The Virginia Editor,'' the article satirizes arrogant, boastful Southern journalists who believe that the power of the pen should be augmented by the whiskey bottle and the pistol. Readers both North and South were amused by the attack, but one Southern editor took it as a personal affront and challenged Bagby to a duel that was stopped only at the last moment by the intervention of a mutual friend.

Encouraged by improving health and by his growing reputation as an essayist, Bagby moved to Washington, D.C., in December 1857 to pursue his writing career more vigorously. Here he became a regular political correspondent for two Southern papers, the New Orleans *Crescent* and the Memphis *Eagle and Enquirer*. In addition to two letters a week to the *Crescent* and three to the *Eagle and Enquirer*, Bagby also published occasionally in the Richmond *Daily Whig* and in a second New Orleans paper, the *Sunday Delta*. Unfortunately, even though his career was developing well, Bagby underwent at this time a severe state of depression, compounded by another dyspepsia attack. In a letter to a friend on 6 January 1859, he wrote that he could not ''reasonably expect to live long'' and that he hoped his ''hard'' life would allow him to perform ''at least one worthy and lasting deed'' (King, *Dr. George William Bagby*, p. 56).

Nevertheless, it was during this period so filled with brooding hopelessness that Bagby produced his most famous literary creation—the comic ''Mozis Addums'' character. Under the guise of an untutored native Virginian, Bagby began a series of eight letters that ran in the *Southern Literary Messenger* from February to December 1858. Cast in the comic vernacular similar to that of the humorists of the Old Southwest, ''The Letters of Mozis Addums to Billy Ivvins,'' as they came to be called, were immediately popular with readers all over the country. With his backwoods diction and homespun comparisons, the simple character of Mozis Addums was a welcome addition for the readers of the *Messenger*, who applauded him extravagantly. These ''Mozis Addums'' sketches and similar ones that followed were the finest and most original work in Bagby's career, but because of his religious and cultural heritage, he was never comfortable with their success. In the introduction to the 1878 edition of the letters, he states, ''I literally 'woke up and found myself famous,' much to my annoyance, for I was then ambitious to succeed in quite other and more elevated fields of literature. But the public would have its way. From that day to this I have gone by the name of 'Mozis,' and I am sure that, directly and indirectly, these letters have paid me better than all my other writings put together'' (*Original Letters of Mozis Addums to Billy Ivvins*, p. 3). Later in this revealing statement, Bagby laments, ''My best exertions have still left me plain 'Mozis Addums,' a name that for many years made me a little sick whenever I heard it'' (p. 4).

In spring 1859, Bagby left Washington discouraged by his health and disheartened by the country's political problems that were reaching a crisis. After a brief stay at Buckingham County, he moved in the winter to Richmond, where he would spend most of his remaining life. In Richmond, which was quickly replacing Charleston as the literary center of the South, Bagby became an editorialist for a number of the dozen newspapers and journals published there as well as the librarian for the Mechanics Institute, the Richmond Library Association, and the Virginia Historical Society. Like all Southern authors at this time, Bagby received little pay for his efforts and as a result began to supplement his small income by delivering essays on the lecture circuit. His first performance, entitled "An Apology for Fools," was well received by the Richmond Lyceum, the Fredericksburg Literary Association, the Danville Lyceum, and the Petersburg Library Association.

By 1859 Bagby was one of the best-known writers in Virginia, and when the editorship of the *Southern Literary Messenger* came open in June, he was appointed to the post, a position he held until exhaustion and failing health led him to resign in January 1864. As editor of this literary journal, Bagby enthusiastically championed the cause of Southern literature by encouraging new writing that would "smack of the soil," as he said in his first editorial (*SLM*, June, 1860, p. 466). He always insisted on an indigenous Southern literature and called for an end to the moonlight and magnolia school of sentimental poetry and fiction. He deplored the rosy literary portraits painted of Virginia and noted that "many weak and trashy productions receive undue praise at the hands of Southern critics, merely because they are written and published South of the Potomac" (*SLM*, Sept., 1860, p. 238). Southern writers, he concluded, should "kick Tennyson and all other models into the middle of next week, or elsewhere" (*SLM*, Jan., 1861, p. 53).

At the same time, Bagby began to express strong partisan views on the direction of the South's political future. He applauded South Carolina's withdrawal from the Union and chided Virginia for not doing the same: "What ails her? is she stricken with the palsy of fear? . . . For shame!" (*SLM*, Dec., 1860, p. 474). His tirades grew in intensity until they became almost uncontrollable rantings as in his blast at the supporters of William H. Seward, who wanted Virginia to remain in the Union: "The sons of patriots lick the coarse hand of an ill-bred, foulmouthed fanatical tyrant" (*SLM*, Jan., 1861, p. 152).

With Virginia's secession in April 1861 came Bagby's inevitable enlistment in the Confederate army. He was thirty-three years old, half-dead with his stomach problem, and totally unfit for cold water baths, hard tack meals, and early morning drills. Although he joined the Lynchburg Rifle Grays as a private, he was charitably appointed to General Beauregard's staff and was present at the Battle of Bull Run, which he observed from a distance, an experience he documents in "An Unrenowned Warrior: The Record of a Man Who Shivered Through the Manassas Campaign." In August he was discharged because of "infirm health," and he returned to Richmond where he continued to manage the *Southern Literary Messenger* as well as serve as correspondent for the Richmond papers, *Dispatch*, *Evening News*, *Enquirer*, and *Examiner*, plus the New Orleans *Crescent*, the Charleston *Mercury*, and the Mobile *Register*.

In the midst of an increasingly dismal war, Bagby, in typical fashion, wrote some of his better essays ("A Horrible Scrape," "Good Eating," "Getting Married," and "The Politician") and secured one enduring portion of happiness in his life by marrying Lucy Parke Chamberlayne on 16 February 1863. The daughter of a prominent Richmond physician, his new wife was a devoted woman who stood by her husband during poverty, despair, and bad health. They had six children and, after his death, she was the dedicated editor of two volumes of her husband's writings.

The end of the Civil War found Bagby, like the South, in a depressed, dispirited condition, and in desperation he traveled to New York to break into the writing market there, but to no avail. This time a flare-up of his old health problem was compounded by a disease that so inflamed his eyes that he was nearly blinded. He returned to Richmond with his nerves wrecked to find his wife desperately ill with the birth of their second child. With debts continuing to pile up, the family was forced to move into a two-room apartment. This was the low point of his life, but it was, in fact, also similar to that of other Southern writers just after the war. For sheer misery and frustration, these years are unparalleled in the history of the Southern man of letters, as the lives of William Gilmore Simms, Henry Timrod, and Paul Hamilton Hayne also reveal.

Bagby again returned to the lecture circuit on 4 January 1866 with an essay called "Bacon and Greens." It was a lifesaver, for it turned into a solid success and was delivered in towns and villages throughout Virginia as well as in Baltimore and New York. With his career rejuvenated, he was offered a partnership in an Orange County, Virginia, newspaper, the *Orange Expositor*. He became the editor and changed the name to the *Native Virginian*. The stated goal of this "First Class Literary and Humorous Paper," as it was subtitled, was to provide a decent livelihood for Southern writers, and, above all, to affirm the glorious past of the South, in fact, to view the South through rose-colored glasses—the very ones Bagby as editor of the *Southern Literary Messenger* had spoken against so adamantly.

Bagby's main productions during this concluding part of his career were such reminiscent essays as "John M. Daniel's Latch-Key," "The Old Virginia Gentleman," and "The Virginia Negro," all tributes to people and manners of an idealized Virginia "befo' de wah." And, while he continued to place essays in such national publications as the New York *Evening Post* and *Lippincott's Magazine*, he finally had a piece of good luck in March 1870 when he was appointed custodian of the State Library of the Commonwealth of Virginia. He held this post until 1878 when he was turned out of office through a cutback in state spending. Bagby spent the remainder of his life writing letters to newspapers, delivering lectures, and collecting his essays for publication in book and pamphlet form.

On 12 December 1882 in Trenton, New Jersey, Bagby gave his last public lecture. Entitled "Yorktown and Appomattox," it called for reconciliation between the North and the South. He returned to his home in Richmond a sick man. There he developed a disease of the tongue that prevented him from eating properly and aggravated his dyspepsia. His already poor health declined seriously, and he died on 29 November 1883.

MAJOR THEMES

It is tempting to conclude through a variation of an old remark that Bagby explored only three themes in his writing—Virginia, Virginia, and Virginia. It is certainly evident that the Commonwealth looms large as the most abiding subject matter of his professional career as a writer. The love he felt for his native state resembles that associated with two other Virginians, Thomas Jefferson and Robert E. Lee.

As a Virginian, Bagby came to his profession dedicated to the value of excellent writing. The ideal of the gentleman demanded a graceful prose style and pride in authorship. And, for the greater part of his career, Bagby lived up to the high standards his culture set for authors by composing essays that served a serious political purpose by asserting the rights of the state or essays that applauded a genteel way of life and manners that would be no more.

Politically, Bagby was a staunch conservative who forever supported Virginia and the Southern way of life. As editor of the *Southern Literary Messenger* before the Civil War, he called for Virginia to secede from the Union months before she did. His outspokenness agitated Northern readers and a few Southerners so much that the journal's subscription list suffered a dramatic decline. For example, in January 1861 he exclaimed in an editorial:

Let us tear from the national flag the fifteen stars which the despots of the North have attempted to sully with the imputation of barbarism. Let us give these stars a double brilliance by forming them into a cross—the Southern Cross—emblem of that pure and holy religion which has been reviled, trampled and spit upon in the interest of Abolitionism. (*SLM*, Jan., 1861, p. 71)

And for years after the war, he maintained a strong sense of righteous indignation over the plight of the South. As late as 1880 he privately issued a pamphlet entitled *John Brown and Wm. Mahone: An Historical Parallel Foreshadowing Civil Trouble, 1860–1880.* This 23-page work is a nightmarish dream about a possible new civil war based on the author's wrongheaded assumptions about present distressful political conditions. As editor of Southern newspapers and journals, as letter writer and lecturer, Bagby always asserted the primacy of the Southern life-style.

During the Civil War, Bagby discovered a new way to praise Southern life in a gentle manner through the personal essay of reminiscence. Published in periodicals and read on the lecture circuit, these essays secured his fame in

Virginia during his lifetime, but because of their topical matter and aristocratic tone, they were forgotten soon after his death. These first essays, however, are realistic in their depiction of local color material, "Cornfield Peas," for instance, and often contain passages of tender power, as in "Canal Reminiscences." Unfortunately, the more he depended on this mode after the war, the more the essays become sentimental and discursive.

The essays that display Bagby's congenial conversational style at its best are "John M. Daniel's Latch-Key," a superb character sketch of a Virginia journalist; "Bacon and Greens," a charming and entertaining account of eating habits of Virginians; and "The Old Virginia Gentleman," his single most famous essay. The latter is a sincere tribute not just to the gentleman but also to the "gentle" lady of Virginia and to the agrarian way of life. With his colloquial style in command, Bagby's writing here is sharp, bumptious, and informative: "But who shall tell of harvest-time, when the field fairly swarmed with cutters, the binders, the shockers, the gleaners, all agog with excitement and joy?"

Although Bagby always believed that his essays recalling the past and extolling the Southern cause were his most enduring work, he is better remembered today for his comic writings. And, contrary to his own estimation, his best talents lay in the field of humor. Hubbell's remark that Bagby is "the best of the Virginia humorists" notwithstanding, the truth is that the land of Washington, Jefferson, and Lee has never been a rich ground for comedians. By the time of the first great outpouring of native American wit from the humorists of the Old Southwest, Virginia had a 200-year history and one in which its inhabitants took a distinct pride. Had Bagby been a resident of Georgia or Mississippi, perhaps he would not have been so ambivalent about "Mozis Addums."

Bagby's comic creation "Mozis Addums" compares favorably with other characters from Southern humor: "Simon Suggs," "Major Jones," and "Sut Lovingood." In letters to the *Southern Literary Messenger* in 1858, Bagby sets his rural philosopher from Buckingham County on the road to fame and fortune in the nation's capital, which at the time was embroiled in passionate and occasionally uproarious debates over the slave status of Kansas and Nebraska. Into this cauldron steps the simple rustic Mozis Addums, who gets involved in ridiculous situations, who makes bumbling and provincial mistakes, but whose sharp eye for detail enables him to depict realistically the passing scene and to observe the absurdities in the national government.

Never having learned to spell, Mozis writes letters to his friend "Billy Ivvins" in dialect filled with comic misspellings. He tells Billy that he visited the "Supreme Kote" and found the behavior of the justices disgusting. He is similarly discouraged by his observation of "Kongris" who "uv all peepil on the fais uv erth to talk and talk and talk, and do nuthin, they is the beet."

In one of the funniest sequences in the letters, Mozis explains his visit to "the Ballay" where a ballerina, named "Seen-yo-reen-er Rollar," performs a solo:

Well, ser, she went a skippin and a hoppin and a pirootin aroun on the platform uv the stage, like a hummin berd, and pretty soon she cum rite in frunt uv me cleen to the edge of the stage, facing uv the congregashun and shot her foot rite smak up to the seelin. The owdashus, onmanered thing! in compny too!

Mozis Addums continued to observe the passing parade after the war in such pieces as "Uv Wimmin" and "History uv the Waw, by Mozis Addums," but the homely comparisons and flashes of wit become fewer. In "Meekins's Twinses," for example, the original unsophisticated Mozis Addums has faded from view, and Bagby simply speaks through the dialect of his character. Finally, in "What I Did with My Fifty Millions," with Mozis Addums the supposed author, Bagby drops the pose of the rustic speaker altogether.

SURVEY OF CRITICISM

Bagby is not an author who has been scrutinized by critics and scholars, nor is he one who cries out for rediscovery. By no means, though, should this lack of attention represent the final verdict on a body of work that contains a substantial number of essays and sketches worthy of close attention. Since no Southern author has ever been more of a product of his region, his essays that proved enormously popular in his day increase our understanding of a significant segment of Southern culture. Above all, Bagby's humorous writings would benefit from a fresh approach by students expert in the field of American humor.

Most of the standard reference works (*DAB, LHUS, Southern Writers*) include a paragraph or two on Bagby's life and writings. The venerable multi-volume work known as *The Library of Southern Literature*, edited by Joel Chandler Harris and others, contains a biographical sketch by Churchill Gibson Chamberlayne and selections from four of the essays. Biographical essays and general appraisals also appear in the three posthumous collections of his essays.

Finally, Wade Hall's *The Smiling Phoenix* (1965) and James C. Hall's *American Humor in France* (1978) discuss Bagby's work briefly, and Rayburn S. Moore's dissertation, "Southern Writers and Northern Literary Magazines, 1865–1890," examines Bagby's contributions to *Lippincott's Magazine*. The best treatments of Bagby are Hubbell's in *The South in American Literature* (1954) and Joseph L. King's *Dr. George William Bagby* (1927). King's biography, originally a dissertation at Columbia University, is the only book-length study of Bagby. Generally solid and informative, it places a great deal of emphasis on Virginia history and, following Bagby's lead, calls the comic essays "unfortunate" and condemns them as an "inferior" type of literature. A scholarly edition of Bagby's essays spanning the whole of his career would correct this judgment.

BIBLIOGRAPHY

Works by George William Bagby

Mozis Addums' New Letters: Letter Wun. Richmond: Macfarland & Ferdusson, 1860.
The Letters of Mozis Addums to Billy Ivvins. Richmond: West & Johnston, 1862.

John M. Daniel's Latch-key: A Memoir of the Late Editor of the Richmond Examiner. Lynchburg, Va.: J. P. Bell, 1868.

What I Did with My Fifty Millions. Philadelphia: J. B. Lippincott, 1874.

Meekins's Twinses: A Perduckshun uv Mozis Addums. Richmun: Westun, Johnsum & Kumpny, 1877.

Original Letters of Mozis Addums to Billy Ivvins. Richmond: Clemmitt & Jones, 1878.

Canal Reminiscences: Recollections of Travel in the Old Days on the James River and Kanawha Canal. Richmond: West & Johnston, 1879.

A Week in Hepsidam: Being the First and Only True Account of the Mountains, Men, Manners and Morals Thereof. Richmond: G. W. Gray, 1879.

John Brown and Wm. Mahone: An Historical Parallel, Foreshadowing Civil Trouble, 1860–1880. Richmond: C. F. Johnston, 1880.

Selections from the Miscellaneous Writings of Dr. George W. Bagby. 2 vols. Ed. Lucy C. Bagby, Edward S. Gregory, and James McDonald. Richmond: Whittet & Shepperson, 1884–85.

The Old Virginia Gentleman and Other Sketches. Ed. Thomas Nelson Page. New York: Charles Scribner's Sons, 1910.

The Old Virginia Gentleman and Other Sketches. Ed. Ellen M. Bagby. Richmond: Dietz Press, 1938 (5th ed. 1948).

Studies of George William Bagby

Freeman, Douglas Southall. "Introduction: George W. Bagby, Patriot." *The Old Virginia Gentleman and Other Sketches.* Ed. Ellen M. Bagby. Richmond: Dietz Press, 1938, pp. xvii–xxvii.

Gregory, Edward S. "George William Bagby." *Selections from the Miscellaneous Writings of Dr. George W. Bagby.* Ed. Lucy C. Bagby, Edward S. Gregory, and James McDonald. Richmond: Whittet & Shepperson, 1884. 1: xiii–xxxvii.

Hall, Wade. *The Smiling Phoenix: Southern Humor from 1865 to 1914.* Gainesville: University of Florida Press, 1965.

Hubbell, Jay B. "George William Bagby." *The South in American Literature, 1607–1900.* Durham, N.C.: Duke University Press, 1954, pp. 680–83.

King, Joseph L., Jr. *Dr. George William Bagby: A Study of Virginia Literature, 1850–1880.* New York: Columbia University Press, 1927.

Moore, Rayburn S. "Southern Writers and Northern Literary Magazines, 1865–1890." Ph.D. diss., Duke University, 1956.

Page, Thomas Nelson. "A Virginia Realist." *The Old Virginia Gentleman and Other Sketches.* Ed. Thomas Nelson Page. New York: Charles Scribner's Sons, 1910, pp. v–xiii.

Pickett, La Salle C. " 'Bacon and Greens,' Dr. George William Bagby." *Literary Hearthstones of Dixie.* Philadelphia: J. B. Lippincott, 1912, pp. 225–50.

Watson, Ritchie D., Jr. "George William Bagby." *Southern Writers: A Biographical Dictionary.* Ed. Robert Bain, Joseph M. Flora, and Louis D. Rubin, Jr. Baton Rouge: Louisiana State University Press, 1979, pp. 10–12.

Joseph Glover Baldwin
(1815–1864)

Joseph Glover Baldwin is best known as a Southwestern humorist, author of the popular *Flush Times of Alabama and Mississippi* (1853). He was also a distinguished attorney and judge (eventually associate justice of the Supreme Court of California), the chronicler of two frontiers—Alabama and Mississippi in the 1830s and California in the 1850s—and a political historian of some gifts. Baldwin believed, like many American humorists, that humor had something second-rate about it. He expected to make his reputation by his "serious" work. In his letters he expresses relief and satisfaction that reviewers have noticed his "gentlemanly scholarship and elevated taste and vigorous thought." Yet during his lifetime, the acclaim he gathered for his writing was for his comic frontier sketches, which sold some 20,000 copies in the first year of publication and were among Abraham Lincoln's favorite reading. He is now remembered solely as the author of *The Flush Times*. Though his other writings are by no means negligible, in this selective memory posterity is just.

BIOGRAPHY

Joseph Glover Baldwin was born on 21 January 1815 in Friendly Grove Factory, Virginia, where his father operated cotton and woollen mills. When Jo (as he was called in the family) was a year old, the Baldwins moved to Winchester, Virginia, where, for the next eight years, he was taught by his mother; in 1824, with the next move to Staunton, Virginia, the Baldwin boys began their formal education, first at Staunton English School and then at Staunton Academy. Though he had been considered a sluggish student, Jo began at this time to demonstrate his skill in writing, even composing papers for his classmates, and to excel in a traditional curriculum of English and Latin composition. He also read widely. His formal education ended when he was fourteen, but he was already well advanced, as readers of his essays can tell from his urbane allusiveness.

For the next few years, Baldwin's apprenticeship followed time-honored paths. Just out of school, he worked, like Dickens, as a law clerk. Unlike Dickens, he was attracted to the profession, and he read law, qualifying as an attorney when he reached his majority. While waiting for that time, he worked as a journalist; he began by helping his brother Cornelius on the *Lexington Union*, and also wrote for papers in Richmond and Buchanan, Virginia, where he coedited and published a newspaper, which failed in six months. Perhaps disillusioned by that experience, and by an unhappy love affair, Baldwin set out for the Southwest. He settled in DeKalb, Mississippi, in April 1836. Here, on the raw frontier of Alabama and Mississippi, during the "flush times" that accompanied the opening up of new lands, Baldwin lived for seventeen years, succeeded as a lawyer and politician, and began his career as a writer. The most important accomplishment of these years was, of course, his acquisition of the experiences and the characters who were to figure in *Flush Times*.

After one year in DeKalb, where he began to make a reputation as a criminal lawyer, Baldwin moved to Gainesville, Alabama. There he practiced thirteen years; there he married and began a family that eventually included six children; there he began a political career that included election to the Alabama House of Representatives and an unsuccessful campaign for the U.S. House. In 1850 Baldwin moved to Livingston, Alabama, where he resided until moving to California. At the same time as his move he began to write sketches of life during the flush times. These were published in the *Southern Literary Messenger* between July 1852 and September 1853. Unlike other Southwestern humorists, Baldwin was uninterested in publishing his sketches in newspapers, or, apparently, in such standard humor outlets as *Spirit of the Times* or the *Carpet-Bag*. Publication in a literary magazine, especially in Virginia, satisfied Baldwin's desire for respectability for his writing. Several of these sketches are clearly written with a specifically Virginian audience in mind. In December 1853, the New York firm of Appleton & Co. published *The Flush Times of Alabama and Mississippi*, which collected seventeen of the *Southern Literary Messenger* sketches and nine others previously unpublished. It was an immediate success.

Baldwin followed up with two very different sequels; one, called "California Flush Times," was an imaginative account of life in California—where he had never been. It is an exuberant collection of tall tales about the economy, society, and geology of California. He also began on a work of history, written between January and July 1854, and published in that year as *Party Leaders; Sketches of Thomas Jefferson, Alex'r Hamilton, Andrew Jackson, Henry Clay, John Randolph of Virginia. . . .* When it appeared he was already on his way to California.

From this point on Joseph Glover Baldwin's biography is interesting but essentially nonliterary. In California he again established a successful legal practice; again ran unsuccessfully for national office, this time for the U.S. Senate; and served with great distinction on the California Supreme Court, to which he was elected in 1858. His later years were troubled by deaths of children and by the Civil War, which caused a family rift (Baldwin was sympathetic to the Confederacy). Some time in the 1860s he began writing "The Flush Times of California," a sober and ambitious history of the Anglo-Saxon settlement in California and the riotous times he had experienced. Never completed, this work was left in manuscript until published in 1966. In September 1864 Baldwin, following a minor operation, complained his jaws felt stiff. This was the onset of tetanus, and he died, aged forty-nine, on 30 September 1864.

MAJOR THEMES

Baldwin wrote to his wife in 1854 that he hoped to make "a reputation which 'men will not willingly let die.' I think I can put myself on the roll of American authors somewhat above the names which are counted distinguished." When he wrote these words, of course, he had no idea that his last book was behind him, and that the "serious" writing for which he expected fame was to be forever unwritten or, if written, largely unread. Two books, *The Flush Times of Alabama and Mississippi* and *Party Leaders*, represent him to the world. In addition, his 1853 sketch, "California Flush Times," is extant, now combined in one volume with the longer California work, left in manuscript at his death, which Baldwin confusingly titled "The Flush Times of California." Of these works *The Flush Times of Alabama and Mississippi* is clearly the best and most important.

The *Flush Times* is identified on the title page as "A Series of Sketches." Though "sketches" was a conventional literary term, sometimes used for stories as well (by Irving, for instance), the term suggests that these productions are to be more static than "stories" or "tales"; and that suggestion is entirely borne out by the contents of the volume. It is partly for this reason that some commentators have censured Baldwin for his lack of narrative power, his tendency to abstract, to tell rather than show, to neglect verbatim rendering of colorful American vernacular. His works lack the racy vigor that characterizes some of the best Southwestern humorists. But Baldwin is genuinely writing sketches, and the broad canvas to which they are subordinate is a chronicle of the times. He is really a social historian rather than an embryonic novelist or romancer. If we sometimes miss the engaging particulars of Southwestern life in the *Flush Times*, this is because Baldwin writes with a fairly pronounced neoclassical bias toward depicting universals and "human nature" rather than vividly characterizing individuals, though there are some good individual sketches.

The book contains three basic kinds of "sketches." One of these is the character sketch, ranging from short and negligible pictures of rascals to careful and thoughtful full-length portraits of admired jurists. Another is the short humorous anecdote. The final category is the historical account, usually combined with generous amounts of ironic or savage commentary on the social, financial, and moral arrangements that characterize life on a frontier during flush times.

The most popular Baldwin sketch, judging by the frequency with which modern literary historians reprint, quote, or cite it as illustrative of his writing, is his "Ovid Bolus, Esq., Attorney at Law and Solicitor in Chancery: A Fragment." An accomplished liar, Bolus is particularly identified as a phenomenon of the boom days in the Southwest, "that golden era, when shin-plasters were the sole currency; when bank-bills were 'as thick as Autumn leaves in Vallambrosa,' and credit was a franchise." Yet, despite his many ironic encomia on Bolus's abilities, Baldwin never seems to descend to particulars. There is almost no quotation of Bolus's lies, and though some of them are paraphrased, these are brief and casual, almost offhanded. The main source of interest in the sketch is in the author's resourcefulness in *describing* Bolus as a liar: "There was nothing narrow, sectarian, or sectional, on Bolus's lying. . . . He did not confine himself to mere lingual lying: one tongue was not enough for all the business he had on hand . . . Ovid had early possessed the faculty of ubiquity. He had been born in more places than Homer. . . . Gossip and personal anecdote were the especial subjects of Ovid's elocution." These quotations capture the generalizing quality of the Ovid Bolus sketch and the elegance of Baldwin's style.

Baldwin's characteristic technique is also evident in the restrained, delicately ironic approach to Bolus—after all, a terribly immoral fellow who has bankrupted many of his friends. The author's judgment is implied in the choice of pseudonym for Bolus and the mock-heroic treatment by which Bolus is compared to Homer, Charles II, and Themistocles. The sketch is also distinctive (and, in this, perfectly representative of Baldwin's method) for its highly "literary" texture, full of classical tags, Latin phrases drawn from legal terminology, and frequent allusions. This passage captures the flavor well:

He never squandered his lies profusely: thinking, with the poet, that "bounteous, not prodigal, is kind Nature's hand," he kept the golden mean between penuriousness and prodigality; never stingy of his lies, he was not wasteful of them, but was rather forehanded than pushed, or embarrassed, having, usually, fictitious stock to be freshly put on 'change, when he wished to "make a raise." In most of his fables he inculcated but a single leading idea; but contrived to make the several parts of the narrative fall in very gracefully with the principal scheme.

The other character sketches in *Flush Times* include colorful accounts of "Cave Burton, Esq., of Kentucky" and "Uncle John Olive"—humorous and eccentric personalities; sometimes these sketches, though mostly expository, have an anecdote at the center. In addition, there are two long and lovingly developed sketches on the Honorables S. S. Prentiss and Francis Strother, attorneys and public gentlemen whom Baldwin reveres and treats without levity. In these articles Baldwin turns entirely from Southwestern humor devices and suggests the sober, judicious portraits of his later *Party Leaders*.

The humorous anecdote, the second type of sketch appearing in *Flush Times*, is usually short, casual, and more straightforwardly funny. Often set in a court and having to do with lawyers and their clients, these stories contain traditional

comic motifs, particularly practical jokes, tables-turning, comic assaults on outsiders, ignorance and malapropism, and witty repartee. "Squire A. and the
Fritters" is a good story based on a practical joke; "An Equitable Set-Off" is
a story of horse-trading, in which the injured party neatly turns the tables on his
deceiver; "Samuel Hele, Esq.: A Yankee Schoolmistress and an Alabama Lawyer" represents a comic reproof to an outsider whose interfering opinions (and
ugly visage) affront the community; the transcript created in "Examining a
Candidate for License" derives its humor from the ignorance and linguistic
befuddlement of the ne'er-do-well who wishes to practice law; and "A Cool
Rejoinder" is a bare, paragraph-long "sketch" in which a judge makes a snappy
comeback to a bibulous lawyer.

In these anecdotes, we can clearly see the connection between Baldwin and
the traditions of Southwestern humor, which is most obvious in his sketch
"Simon Suggs, Jr., Esq.: A Legal Biography," where he makes obvious homage
to and use of the famous character of Johnson J. Hooper. Baldwin focuses on
the son of the famous Captain Suggs, making him a lawyer, and, for once,
making extended use of the vernacular language of an ignorant man. Even more
noticeable, in his book as a whole, than the regional humor is Baldwin's use of
traditional English comic mannerisms. The "feel" of Baldwin's anecdotes is
often more English than Alabaman, with the frequent use of Courts of Chancery,
wigs and gowns, landowners referred to as "Squire," and comic Irishmen as
staple properties.

The final category of sketch is the furthest from comic anecdote; this is the
sociocultural, or sociomoral, picture of the times, focusing on the turmoil, the
disorder, the vitality, and the moral laxity of the flush times. The three sketches
called "The Bench and the Bar," "How the Times Served the Virginians," and
"The Bar of the Southwest" contain most of this chronicle (as well as some
autobiographical material on Baldwin's accommodation, as a Virginian, to the
rough conditions he found there). Here, though the author still writes to amuse,
there is an iron vein of moral diagnosis that produces some brilliant writing and
the most serious evaluation of the flush times. Baldwin makes clear that, exciting
as they may have been, wonderful opportunities for the hardworking or inventive
settler, the times were also morally shoddy. The collapse following the boom
was necessary, a predictable and well-deserved corrective to a paroxysm of
nonsense and fraud. He refers to the boom times as the "Rag Empire," and
characterizes them as "the reign of humbug, and wholesale insanity, just overthrown in time to save the whole country from ruin." Baldwin's moral anatomy
of the times is vigorous and suave:

Credit was a thing of course. To refuse it—if the thing was ever done—were an insult
for which a bowie-knife were not a too summary or exemplary a means of redress. . . .
In short, the country had got to be a full ante-type of California, in all except the gold.
Society was wholly unorganized: there was no restraining public opinion: the law was
well-nigh powerless—and religion scarcely was heard of except as furnishing the oaths

and *technics* of profanity. . . . Larceny grew not only respectable, but genteel, and ruffled it in all the pomp of purple and fine linen. . . . The man of straw, not worth the buttons on his shirt, with a sublime audacity, bought lands and negroes, and provided times and terms of payment which a Wall-street capitalist would have to re-cast his arrangements to meet. . . . The condition of society may be imagined:—vulgarity—ignorance—fussy and arrogant pretension—unmitigated rowdyism—bullying insolence, if they did not rule the hour, *seemed* to wield unchecked dominion.

Baldwin's tone here, and the more jocular treatment, in other sketches, of the excesses of the flush times, are like "California Flush Times" (1853), his other fully successful exercise in humorous writing. Baldwin wrote this sketch without any firsthand knowledge of California, though he apparently was already planning to emigrate. It abounds in the humorous exaggeration alternating with cool understatement that is sometimes found in *Flush Times* and flavor better-known contemporary sketches such as Thomas Bangs Thorpe's "The Big Bear of Arkansas." Baldwin explains the extravagance of what he has to report by the unreality of life in booming California: "Things here are turned upside down, wrong side out. What is the truth elsewhere is a lie here—a lie here is the truth everywhere." He comments in an amusing way on the marvels of Nature, but devotes most of his attention to the marvels of human affairs. For instance, he claims that clients pay him retainers up to $10,000 a month; that interest on loans is two percent a day; that flour costs $100 a barrel, and so on. He points out striking success stories: governors from the East have emigrated and struck it rich as headwaiters, bartenders, and hod-carriers. His laundress, he maintains, is a former university professor.

Baldwin also comments on the violence of the frontier, mentioning certain attempts to assassinate him, frequent lynchings, and the activities of the Vigilantes. The tone is one of ironic understatement, as when he explains the aftermath of his attempt to defend a client before a committee of vigilance, which threatened him as well as his client:

I abruptly left the court in precipitate indignation. Hearing a shout as I got about 300 yards off, I turned my head, and caught a glimpse of a man I took to be my client, apparently running up a rope, his hands tied behind him, to the third story of a warehouse, and, who, getting up some fifty feet, seemed vigorously kicking at the crowd below, much to their divertisement. I resolutely refused to practise any more before that court.

And he touches, here as in *The Flush Times of Alabama and Mississippi*, on social disorder—"Society is kept together on a principle of universal distrust. Nobody has confidence in any body else." Despite his moral concerns, this first California sketch is primarily comic, and equal to Baldwin's best work on Alabama and Mississippi.

The same cannot be said for the later, uncompleted history of California, now printed and titled by modern editors "Ebb Tide." It is a work without humor, without much order, and essentially without much interest. Its flashes of the old vitality do not really make it worth reading. It is surprisingly leaden, poorly organized and, despite being incomplete, repetitious.

Baldwin's second book, and other major work, is *Party Leaders*. Clearly a more worthwhile undertaking for him, it is by no means inconsiderable, despite its hasty composition. Modern readers will appreciate the judgments rendered there on the Revolution and the founders by one who saw them at close range and without the veneration that is now conventional. The most interesting parts of the books are on Jefferson and Hamilton. Baldwin admires Hamilton with little reservation; and, despite manful attempts at impartiality, shows marked distaste for Jefferson. His preference is partly due to his approach; he indeed considers Jefferson as a party leader—as a practicing politician—rather than as the author of the Declaration of Independence or the Enlightenment thinker.

The modern reader can easily find more reliable and scholarly histories of the early years of the Republic; and Baldwin's judgments of politicians are of no transcendent interest now; but the book is still highly readable. Its strengths are a lively and clear style, a judicious moral stance, and a nice mixture of admiration for his subjects and awareness of their deficiencies. At times it is epigrammatic: "Like all reformers, Jefferson was an enthusiast. Enthusiasm necessarily heightens the colors of the objects upon which it glows." At times it is fervent, as when the author offers this comment on Hamilton and Burr's dueling: "The defense of this moral cowardice by both is simply drivelling. It deceives no one. It had been more candid in both to have said: We fought from cowardice—from the fear of the scoffers." And at times, as in the explanation of how John Randolph (another hero of the book) spoke when "in the mere carte and tierce of digladiation," it is unintentionally funny through euphuism. Throughout it runs Baldwin's essential conservatism, his mistrust, evident in the *Flush Times*, too, of popular sovereignty.

Here, as in the other works, the reader is aware that the author's true literary tradition is neoclassical. His frequent allusions are to Burke, Dr. Johnson, Lord Byron. Elsewhere he refers often to Shakespeare, Dickens, Bulwer, Scott, and Sterne. The only American author to whom he alludes in this way is Washington Irving, who was himself something of an honorary Englishman. His style, likewise, more befits the age of Johnson than mid-century, frontier America: balanced, grave, decorous, allusive, generalizing, judicious, sometimes sententious. His evaluations of men and manners assume a stable morality that is unchanging and apparent to men of intelligence. He has more in common with his fellow Virginian, William Byrd, or with another favorite mentor, Charles Lamb, than with his American contemporaries of the Southwestern humor school.

His conservatism may help to explain the frequency of certain critical strictures against Baldwin. Walter Blair criticizes him for being primarily an essayist and making "little use of direct discourse"; Blair further complains that Baldwin is little influenced by oral anecdotes. Likewise, Jennette Tandy censures his lack of technique, as evidenced by his subordination of narration and colorful regionalisms to pictures of the age; Norris Yates objects to his "too-frequent striving for literary gentility and . . . the scantiness of his output." And he has been criticized for his genteel tone and neglect of dialect. By all these standards, Baldwin certainly falls short of the achievement of his contemporaries Thomas Bangs Thorpe, Johnson Jones Hooper, Augustus Baldwin Longstreet, and others. Many of these writers use the dignified, gentlemanly way of writing, but they combine it with the racy language of ignorant backwoodsmen. Hooper writes as elegantly as Baldwin, but his elegance constitutes a frame for the illiterate rascality and colorful vernacular of Simon Suggs. Baldwin seldom allows his characters (many of whom are laywers and judges, rather than eye-gougers and thieves, anyway) to flourish their own style. He makes a poor showing against Longstreet and Hooper; but perhaps they are not his real context.

SURVEY OF CRITICISM

There is little published criticism on Baldwin. Most treatments of American humor devote between one and three pages to him. Kenneth S. Lynn's *Mark Twain and Southwestern Humor* gives more extensive consideration to Baldwin, but it sees Baldwin as an example of a Southern defender of the Whig status quo and overemphasizes Baldwin's despondency. The best criticism of Baldwin is in Eugene Current-Garcia's "Joseph Glover Baldwin: Humorist or Moral-ist?"—which emphasizes Baldwin the moralist sensibly but somewhat superfi-cially—and in the introduction and afterword of the Richard E. Amacher and George W. Polhemus volume *The Flush Times of California*. There is room for further intelligent criticism of Baldwin, which should begin without preconcep-tions of what *all* Southwestern humor should be, preconceptions by means of which he will inevitably, but unjustly, be found inadequate.

BIBLIOGRAPHY

Works by Joseph Glover Baldwin

The Flush Times of Alabama and Mississippi. New York: D. Appleton, 1853.
Party Leaders; Sketches of Thomas Jefferson, Alex'r Hamilton, Andrew Jackson, Henry Clay, John Randolph, of Roanoke Including Notices of Many Other Distinguished American Statesmen. New York: D. Appleton, 1855.
The Flush Times of California. Ed. Richard E. Amacher and George W. Polhemus. Athens: University of Georgia Press, 1966.

Studies of Joseph Glover Baldwin

Amacher, Richard E. and George W. Polhemus, ed. Introduction to *The Flush Times of California*. Athens: University of Georgia Press, 1966, pp. 1–10.
Blair, Walter. *Native American Humor, 1800–1900*. New York: American Book, 1937. San Francisco: Chandler, 1960, pp. 78–79.

Blair, Walter and Hamlin Hill. *America's Humor: From Poor Richard to Doonesbury*. New York: Oxford University Press, 1978, pp. 195–96.

Cox, James M. "Humor of the Old Southwest." *The Comic Imagination in American Humor*. Ed. Louis D. Rubin, Jr. New Brunswick, N.J.: Rutgers University Press, 1973, pp. 104–8.

Current-Garcia, Eugene. "Joseph Glover Baldwin: Humorist or Moralist?" *Alabama Review* 5 (April 1952): 122–41.

Dillingham, William B. "Days of the Tall Tale." *Southern Review* 4 (1968): 569–77. Review of *The Flush Times of California*.

Farish, Hunter Dickinson. "An Overlooked Personality in Southern Life." *North Carolina Historical Review* 12 (1935): 341–53.

Hubbell, Jay B. *The South in American Literature, 1607–1900*. Durham, N.C.: Duke University Press, 1954, pp. 675–78.

Lynn, Kenneth S. *Mark Twain and Southwestern Humor*. Boston: Little, Brown, 1959, pp. 115–24.

McMillan, Malcolm C., ed. "Joseph Glover Baldwin Reports on the Whig National Convention of 1848." *Journal of Southern History* 25 (1959): 366–82.

Owens, William A. Introduction. *The Flush Times of Alabama and Mississippi*. By Joseph Glover Baldwin. New York: Hill and Wang, 1957, pp. v-ix.

Polhemus, George W. "Biographical Sketch of Joseph Glover Baldwin." *The Flush Times of California*. Athens: University of Georgia Press, 1966, pp. 65–78.

Rubin, Louis D., Jr. "Introduction: The Great American Joke." *The Comic Imagination in America*. Ed. Louis D. Rubin, Jr. New Brunswick, N.J.: Rutgers University Press, 1973, pp. 9–15.

Stewart, Samuel Boyd. "Joseph Glover Baldwin." Ph.D. diss., Vanderbilt University, 1941.

Tandy, Jennette. *Crackerbox Philosophers in American Humor and Satire*. New York: Columbia University Press, 1925. Port Washington, N.Y.: Kennikat Press, 1964, pp. 80–82.

— ANNE MARGARET DANIEL AND JON KUKLA —

Robert Beverley
(1673–1722)

Written in haste from various manuscript and printed sources, Robert Beverley, Jr.'s *The History and Present State of Virginia* nevertheless exhibits a contemporary sophistication of style and content that belies its author's pose as an unlettered rustic provincial.

BIOGRAPHY

Robert Beverley, Jr., was born in 1673 (the date of his birth is uncertain) at his father's plantation in Middlesex County, Virginia. He was the son of Major Robert Beverley, Sr., who had migrated to Virginia about 1663 and who was a leading planter and politician in the colony.

When fourteen-year-old Robert Beverley, Jr.'s father and namesake died in 1687, the frontier of English settlement already lay north and west of tidewater Middlesex County. During a busy and often controversial career at Jamestown, Robert Beverley, Sr., had himself shaped that settlement, claiming vast tracts of land north across the York River in Gloucester County and up the Rappahannock River into Middlesex. Land was both a commodity to be acquired and exploited and a natural landscape to be enjoyed and celebrated.

Throughout the last decade of the seventeenth century, the future historian found ready employment in the offices of the colonial capital. Sent to England for schooling, possibly at Beverly Grammar School in his father's native Yorkshire, Robert Beverley had returned to Virginia by April 1688. His career in government began at age twenty, when he petitioned the House of Burgesses (to which his brother Peter was clerk from 1691 to 1697) for a place. On 8 March 1693 he was named clerk of the committee for public claims. During 1693 he acted as temporary clerk to the General Court in his brother's absence and also began a five-year stint assisting Ralph Wormeley, who was secretary of the colony. During 1696 and 1697 Beverley acted as "clerk extraordinary" to the governor's Council while James Sherlock was seriously ill, and in the latter year he served briefly as register (or clerk) of the Virginia Court of Admiralty, an office that he occupied again from 1700 to 1704. Quite naturally, when fire destroyed the colony's third statehouse on 21 October 1698, Governor Edmund Andros and the Council employed Robert and Peter Beverley to rearrange and catalog the "Records and papers of this Countrey both those belong[ing] to the Assembly [and] those belonginig to the Generall Court and Secretaryes office"—archives that had been saved from destruction but "altogether disordered and mixed one with the other." Among these records Beverley first encountered the manuscripts by the late naturalist John Banister that he copied and later used extensively in his history.

In 1697 Beverley married Ursula Byrd, William Byrd II's sister, but she died the next year while giving birth to their only child, William. Beverley never remarried. The years immediately following his wife's death seem to have been unsettled. He had spent much of his time at Jamestown during the 1690s, had represented the borough in the assemblies of 1699, 1700–2, and 1705–6, and was appointed to the bench of Elizabeth City County (modern Hampton) on 27 December 1700. From 1699 to 1704 he was also clerk of King and Queen County and a justice of the peace there when his history was published in 1705, but in December an angry Governor Francis Nicholson and the Council removed him from the King and Queen bench, ostensibly because he was no longer a county resident.

On 19 March 1703, while his brother served as Speaker, Beverley was appointed clerk of the House of Burgesses, but that July he sought leave to sail for England to appeal a land dispute before the Privy Council. The Virginia councillors expelled him from office but let him sail. In England, Beverley lobbied for Governor Nicholson's recall, lost his suit, and wrote his book.

The History and Present State of Virginia appeared in London in 1705. When Beverley returned to Virginia, he seems to have lived a life of retirement. He revised his *History* for a second edition in 1722, and that same year published *An Abridgement of the Publick Laws of Virginia*. He died at his plantation, Beverley Park, on 21 April 1722.

MAJOR THEMES

Early in Beverley's eighteen-month stay in England, London bookseller Richard Parker invited him to read and correct the manuscript of John Oldmixon's *The British Empire in America* (London, 1708). Finding Oldmixon's treatment of Virginia "too imperfect to be mended"—as indeed it is—Beverley wrote a fresh account. He had some notes with him and memories from a decade's work in the provincial records, but literary piracy was common enough in his day, and Beverley readily found resources in London that enabled him to complete the manuscript quickly and return to Virginia in 1704. Richard Parker published

The History and Present State of Virginia in 1705. Although Louis B. Wright conjectures that Beverley wrote *An Essay upon the Government of the English Plantations on the Continent of America . . . By an American* (published by Parker in 1701), others attribute it to Ralph Wormeley or Benjamin Harrison.

Scholars have identified various of Beverley's sources from internal evidence, but there is textual detective work to be done. Beverley relied heavily on Captain John Smith and other published reports for historical narrative. He lifted passages about natural history and Virginia's Indians from John Banister's manuscripts, sometimes copying pages and paragraphs verbatim. The apparent lack of logical sequence in Book 3 may derive from Beverley's ''reliance on John White's drawings for illustrations and, possibly, as a guide to what subjects should be included,'' and many of his comments about Indians have parallels in Baron de Lahontian's *New Voyages to North-America* (London, 1703). For Book 4, Beverley borrowed extensively from Henry Hartwell, James Blair, and Edward Chilton's manuscript report to the Board of Trade (published in 1727 as *The Present State of Virginia and the College*). Finally, Richard Beale Davis argues that Beverley probably borrowed from his brother-in-law William Byrd II's lost manuscript history of Virginia.

Although literary appraisal of Beverley's style or meaning remains a treacherous enterprise until a critical edition of the *History* precisely documents whose hand wrote what, only a plodding reader turns the final page of *The History and Present State of Virginia* convinced that Beverley was a mere plagiarist or (as his preface claimed) ''an Indian'' incapable of being ''exact in his language.'' The Beverley who asked his readers ''not to Criticize too unmercifully upon my Stile'' was a talented, well-read man forced to write in haste and inclined, therefore, to cover his tracks with a stylish version of early-American rustic chic. Even Beverley's hastily written passages—choppy and repetitive and leaping backward and forward in time—fixed Beverley's Virginia of 1703–4 in the context of its Anglo-American past. Comfortably familiar with London literary fashion, Beverley had a knowledge of the American landscape and people that gave him confident dominion over Grub Street hacks who ''pester the Publick'' with books ''stuff'd with Poetic Stories.'' Beverley borrowed well from other writers, tested their observations against his direct experience, and made them his own with a disarming ''Plainness . . . , for Truth desires only to be understood.'' ''Like Beauty,'' Beverley proclaimed, it ''is rather conceal'd, than set off, by Ornament''—just as genius hides unseen beneath his well-crafted simile. With a single interjected phrase, Beverley could transform a passage stolen from Banister and make it reflect Lockean epistemology. And throughout *The History and Present State of Virginia*, amid passages already old when he copied them, one hears in Beverley echoes of John Dryden and Thomas Shadwell; John Wilmot, Earl of Rochester; John Sheffield, Earl of Mulgrave; and Jonathan Swift.

Beverley's *History* was popular in its day. Four editions of a French translation appeared between 1707 and 1718, and by 20 June 1720 Beverley had revised (and toned down) the *History* for a second edition issued in two London printings in 1722. The same booksellers issued Beverley's other published work, *An Abridgement of the Publick Laws of Virginia, In Force and Use, June 10. 1720*, in 1722 as well, and a second edition was printed six years later. Following Beverley's return from England and the publication of *The History and Present State of Virginia*, he nearly disappears from the extant records, virtually retiring from public affairs. John Fontaine's journal records impressions of a visit to Beverley Park in 1715, and the next year Beverley was a host and participant in Governor Alexander Spotswood's Knights of the Golden Horseshoe expedition to the Blue Ridge. The historian died at Beverley Park on 21 April 1722 and was buried on its grounds. By then his son, William, had built his own plantation house at Blandfield. In time Beverley Park was gradually broken into smaller tracts and the exact site of Robert Beverley's home was lost to memory.

SURVEY OF CRITICISM

Although Beverley's themes may include pastoralism in Southern letters, regional sloth, and ecological awareness, critics who advance these interpretations underestimate Beverley's individuality, conforming him to predefined categories seldom taking into account the sources of his *History*. The better recent scholarship has been historical, and the pressing need is for a critical edition of the *History* without which critics will remain unable to distinguish Beverley's artistry from that of his printed and manuscript sources.

BIBLIOGRAPHY

Works by Robert Beverley

The History and Present State of Virginia, In Four Parts. London: R[ichard] Parker, 1705. Trans. into French as *Histoire de la Virginie*. Orleans: Pierre Ribou, 1707; Amsterdam: Thomas Lombrial, 1707; Amsterdam: Claude Jordan, 1712; Amsterdam: J. F. Bernard, 1718.
An Abridgement of the Publick Laws of Virginia, In Force and Use, June 10. 1720. London: F. Fayram, J. Clarke, and T. Bickerton, 1722. 2d ed. London: F. Fayram, J. Clarke, and T. Saunders, 1728.
The History of Virginia, in Four Parts . . . The Second Edition, revis'd and enlarg'd by the Author. London: F. Fayram, J. Clarke, and T. Bickerton, 1722. Also London: B. and S. Tooke, F. Fayram, J. Clarke, and T. Bickerton, 1722.
"The Account of Lamhatty." Ed. David I. Bushnell, Jr. *American Anthropologist* n.s., 10 (1908): 568–74.
Title Book, 1652–1700. Mss. 5:9 B 4676: 1. Virginia Historical Society, Richmond.
The History of Virginia, in Four Parts. Ed. Charles Campbell. Richmond: J. W. Randolph, 1855. Text of 1722 edition.
The History and Present State of Virginia. Ed. Louis B. Wright. Chapel Hill: University of North Carolina Press, 1947. Text of 1705 edition.

The History and Present State of Virginia. Ed. and introd. David F. Hawke. Indianapolis and New York: Bobbs-Merrill, 1971. Text of 1705 edition.

Studies of Robert Beverley

Arner, Robert. "The Quest for Freedom: Style and Meaning in Robert Beverley's *History and Present State of Virginia.*" *Southern Literary Journal* 8 (Spring 1976): 79–98.

Bain, Robert A. "The Composition and Publication of *The Present State of Virginia, and the College.*" *Early American Literature* 6 (Spring 1971): 31–54.

Bertelson, David. *The Lazy South.* New York: Oxford University Press, 1967, pp. 63–84.

Daniel, Anne Margaret. "Robert Beverley's Writing as Tradition and Transition in Virginia." B.A. thesis, Harvard University, 1985.

Davis, Richard Beale. *Intellectual Life in the Colonial South, 1585–1763.* Knoxville: University of Tennessee Press, 1978. 1: 84–91.

Dunn, Richard S. "Seventeenth-Century English Historians of America." *Seventeenth-Century America: Essays in Colonial History.* Ed. James Morton Smith. Chapel Hill: University of North Carolina Press, 1959, pp. 195–225.

Ewan, Joseph and Nesta Ewan. *John Banister and His Natural History of Virginia, 1678–1692.* Urbana: University of Illinois Press, 1970.

Fitz, Virginia White. "Ralph Wormeley: Anonymous Essayist." *William and Mary Quarterly* 3d ser., 26 (October 1969): 586–95.

Harrison, Fairfax. "Robert Beverley, The Historian of Virginia." *Virginia Magazine of History and Biography* 36 (October 1928): 333–44.

Hubbell, Jay B. *The South in American Literature, 1607–1900.* Durham, N.C.: Duke University Press, 1954, pp. 26–30.

Jacobs, Wilbur. "Robert Beverley: Colonial Ecologist and Indian Lover." *Essays in Early Virginia Literature Honoring Richard Beale Davis.* Ed. J. A. Leo Lemay. New York: Burt Franklin, 1977, pp. 91–99.

Kukla, Jon. "Robert Beverley Assailed: Appellate Jurisdiction and the Problem of Bicameralism in Seventeenth-Century Virginia." *Virginia Magazine of History and Biography* 88 (October 1980): 415–29.

———. *Speakers and Clerks of the Virginia House of Burgesses, 1643–1776.* Richmond: Virginia State Library, 1981, pp. 103–5, 144–46.

Marx, Leo. *The Machine in the Garden: Technology and the Pastoral Ideal in America.* New York: Oxford University Press, 1964.

Rutman, Darrett B. and Anita H. Rutman. *A Place in Time: Middlesex County, Virginia, 1650–1750.* New York: W. W. Norton, 1984.

Seelye, John. *Prophetic Waters: The River in Early American Life and Literature.* New York: Oxford University Press, 1977, pp. 343–62.

Shammas, Carole. "Benjamin Harrison III and the Authorship of *An Essay upon the Government of the English Plantations of the Continent of America.*" *Virginia Magazine of History and Biography* 84 (April 1976): 166–73.

Simpson, Lewis P. *The Dispossessed Garden: Pastoral and History in Southern Literature.* Athens: University of Georgia Press, 1975, pp. 15–17.

Small, Judy Jo. "Robert Beverley and the New World Garden." *American Literature* 55 (December 1983): 525–40.

Wright, Louis B. "Beverley's *History . . . of Virginia (1705)*, A Neglected Classic." *William and Mary Quarterly* 3d ser., 1 (January 1944): 49–64.
———. *The First Gentlemen of Virginia: Intellectual Qualities of the Early Colonial Ruling Class*. San Marino, Calif.: Huntington Library, 1940, pp. 286–311.
———, ed. *An Essay upon the Government of the English Plantations on the Continent of America*. San Marino, Calif.: Huntington Library, 1945.

JOHN SEKORA

William Wells Brown
(ca.1814–1884)

A pioneer in Afro-American writing—especially fiction, drama, history, biography, and travel literature—William Wells Brown was the first black American man of letters. Without a day's schooling, he was one of the most widely read authors of the mid-nineteenth century; his work of the 1840s far outsold anything by Thoreau, Hawthorne, or Melville. He said he wrote "for the moment," addressing urgent issues of the day, yet he was more than representative of his time; he was its very ticking.

BIOGRAPHY

Looking back over a full and varied career, William Wells Brown simplified it into five stages: slave, laborer, lecturer, author, and physician. It was the condition of slavery that he was least likely to forget. He was born on a farm outside Lexington, Kentucky, most likely in 1814. He was the youngest, or one of the youngest, of seven children born to a field slave named Elizabeth, each of whom had a different father. His owner was John Young, a physician and farmer; his father, whom he did not know, was probably Young's half-brother.

Without the certainty of documents, the future historian gained instead a series of lessons into the workings of the "peculiar institution." One of his earliest recollections was of the cracks of a cowhide whip followed by his mother's cries. In his small world he saw two groups of people. The larger group, to which he and his mother belonged, had complexions ranging from ivory to ebony. Its members did all the work of the farm, but had little food or clothing, and lived in small, crowded, floorless, windowless cabins. Mostly but not entirely light-skinned, the smaller group did little or no work yet expected the best of everything and always wanted more than they could use. When the Youngs brought a nephew to live with them, Brown discovered how very little he could call his own. The boy's name was also William, confounding the Youngs, who now had in their household two nephews of the same name, one enslaved, the other not. Their confusion was increased when all noticed that the slave resembled his owner more than did the free child. The Youngs removed their embarrassment by changing the name of William the slave to Sandford, a designation he endured like a stigma until his escape.

In 1827 he and his family were moved to a farm four miles north of St. Louis. Because he was uncommonly alert, he was not sent to the fields but hired out to work in the city. During his final six years in slavery he was owned or hired out to ten different men—a circumstance that gave him a broad knowledge of the mechanics of slavery. He noted two brief periods of comparative happiness. For six months he was a printer's helper for Elijah P. Lovejoy, whose Saint Louis *Times* spurred his taste for learning. For another few months he served as assistant to Dr. Young, preparing medicines, treating slaves, running errands, and beginning a lifelong interest in medicine and physical detail. Yet these quieter moments were overwhelmed by more fearsome confrontations with bondage.

Between 1827 and 1833 Brown underwent a crisis of spirit that was also a rite of passage into freedom. All members of his family were sold off and dispersed, though his mother remained nearby in St. Louis. He himself spent much of the time as an understeward or general factotum on steamboats traveling up and down the Mississippi from the city. In most of his jobs he was but a pained observer of the slave trade; in early 1832, when he was seventeen or eighteen, he was hired out (at four times the current rate) directly to a slave trader, James Walker, whose business would appall him. His task was to tend large groups of slaves and ready them for sale in Natchez or New Orleans. On one occasion he saw Walker give away a month-old baby because the mother could not quiet its crying. On another Walker sold a small blind boy from his mother's grasp after the boy had stumbled in the slave coffle. From his year with Walker, Brown took several permanent scars over his body, including one over his right eye, and many more no one could see.

In spring 1833, threatened with sale by Young, he convinced his mother to try to escape. They walked 150 miles into central Illinois over eleven days of travel by night before being found by commercial slave catchers. He was punished by his uncle-owner, then sold; Elizabeth was sold south, never to be seen again, but not before obtaining a promise from her son that he would not allow himself to die a slave. Sold a final time later that fall to Enoch Price, he was already planning to fulfill the promise.

On New Year's Day 1834 Brown walked away from Price's steamer in an adventurous trek from Cincinnati to Cleveland. One episode epitomized his rebirth as a free man. After seven or eight days, ill with fever, frostbite, and hunger, he was taken in and nursed back to health by a kindly Quaker. Before resuming his journey, he asked the new friend to join him in a belated ceremony. A new birth requires a new baptism, and a free man requires a free name. Now about twenty years old and determined to restore the name Elizabeth had given him, he still lacked a proper surname. When his Quaker benefactor offered his own, we have the precise moment he became William Wells Brown. To his namesake he dedicated the first edition of the *Narrative*.

Between 1834 and 1842 Brown relished the chance to keep his own earnings and to start his own family. During the season he continued to work the lake steamers. Later in 1834 he married Elizabeth Schooner, in a largely unhappy marriage lasting, with several long separations, until her death in 1851. Three daughters were born to the Browns, two of whom, Clarissa and Josephine, lived into adulthood. Josephine became her father's biographer and close associate in anti-slavery work. He was also, he said, "a laborer in the vineyards of freedom," by 1836 declaring himself actively an Abolitionist, opening his home to the Underground Railroad, and ferrying fugitives across Lake Erie to Canada.

The year 1843 is another watershed in Brown's life, marking the transformation of the private man into the public figure. Inspired by a rousing address by Frederick Douglass, he began lecturing in churches and was soon embraced by the Garrisonian wing of the Abolitionist Movement. In the early 1840s followers of William Lloyd Garrison pressed for the immediate but peaceful end to slavery. They urged moral suasion toward a national reformation on the issue and eschewed conventional partisan politics. Brown's association with the American Anti-Slavery Society and major Abolitionist papers—which published reports of his activities as well as letters and essays by him—continued through Emancipation.

Defining the inner meaning of slavery to a tepid and often ignorant white audience was the initial task of the anti-slavery agent and lecturer. Brown carried his message through New England, New York City, Pennsylvania, the new farmlands from upstate New York across Ohio and Illinois, and into Canada. As Douglass became the impassioned preacher of the movement, so Brown developed into its accomplished storyteller. By turns plain, witty, ironic, erudite, and broadly humorous, he held audiences from a dozen persons to several thousand with his gift of narrative; it was apt training for a writer. Exhilarated by rapport with his listeners, he discovered how to lift flagging spirits with a song, turn heckling to his own advantage, and defend himself against pro-slavery mobs. In a normal week he would lecture in two or three different towns, depending upon their proximity; it was a schedule he maintained, except for periods of writing or ill health, for 40 years.

His first book in 1847 was an inevitable extension of his lecturing. The *Narrative of William W. Brown, a Fugitive Slave* soon became one of the best-selling and most influential works of anti-slavery literature, selling 10,000 copies in four editions within two years and many more in later British editions. While retaining those stories with greatest appeal, Brown could also achieve several ends not possible in lectures. He could render dialogue and dramatic scenes, provide detail and precision, integrate argument and narrative, and reach thousands who would never hear him speak. Soon one of his speeches was printed in its entirety, and he published an anti-slavery songbook and the earliest account of the flight of William and Ellen Craft, the most famous and most ingenious escape from American slavery on record.

By 1849 Brown was in demand abroad as well as at home. Elected to the World Peace Congress, presided over by Victor Hugo in Paris, he intended a stay of no more than a year, mostly in the British Isles. But the politics of slavery once more altered his plans. The Fugitive Slave Act was enacted in 1850, ensuring that upon returning he, as a famous fugitive, would certainly be arrested and remanded into slavery. (He glimpsed such difficulty when he applied for a passport. "Persons of color," he discovered, could obtain documents only if they traveled as slaves or servants of a white person.) His visit lengthened into five years. He reported traveling 25,000 miles and giving more than 1,000 lectures, an average of over one every two days, to audiences of up to 5,000 persons and including Dickens, Macaulay, and Tennyson. He spoke in every sizable town in England, Scotland, and Wales and found time to visit France, Italy, and Germany. Indefatigable as ever, he discovered yet new energy among the British: "For the first time in my life, I can say, 'I am truly free.' " Released from the daily racial tensions of the United States, he was eager to write and found in London editors and publishers equally eager to accommodate him. In the course of things he was able to earn his living by his pen—the first black American to do so.

In a season of innovations he produced *Three Years in Europe*, an important travel book, in 1852, and a year later the earliest black American novel, *Clotel; or, The President's Daughter*. Appearing just a year after *Uncle Tom's Cabin*, Brown's novel was as sensational in content as in effect. The spring of its plot is the rumor, already hoary when he first heard it, that Thomas Jefferson, the most enlightened statesman in the nation, had had a slave mistress and children and had callously sold them. With nearly as many subplots as Dickens, he traces the consequences of that sale into three generations. The main narrative follows the title character, Jefferson's gifted and beautiful older daughter. Sold as mistress to a weak but wealthy Virginian, she selflessly bears his child. When he is compelled to marry a white woman, the vengeful wife sells Clotel and enslaves her daughter. Desperate over separation from her daughter, Clotel flees but is seized and taken to the slave pens of Washington. Escaping again, she is finally trapped by slave catchers on the Long Bridge across the Potomac. There within sight of the Capitol, the president's daughter refuses capture and leaps to her death. While this harrowing plot tantalizes the imagination, what grips it is the frame of undeniable factuality with which Brown envelopes it: excerpts from pro-slavery laws, sermons, and editorials; descriptions of slave auctions, hunts, and lynchings; and glimpses of slave life and lore. Pathos and history so qualify one another that the result is a tale of mythic proportions.

For Brown writing was often rewriting, and he did not publish his novel in this form again when, his freedom bought by British friends, he returned to the United States in 1854 to continue his anti-slavery work, residing in Buffalo, New York. He instead revised it three times, each time with a different title.

Miralda; or, The Beautiful Quadroon. A Romance of American Slavery, Founded on Fact appeared in sixteen front-page installments of the New York *Weekly Anglo-African*, 1 December 1860 through 16 March 1861. It has never been reprinted in book form. Here the narrative is streamlined, most names are changed, and Clotel's daughter is the central figure. The next version, in 1864, is *Clotelle: A Tale of the Southern States*, which retains the structure and characters of *Miralda* but shortens the tale by 100 pages to fit the format of a series of reprints of briefer narratives. The final version of 1867, *Clotelle; or The Colored Heroine*, reproduces the 1864 edition and brings it through the end of the Civil War with the addition of four new chapters. In all of the American versions, Brown reduced or eliminated the connection with Jefferson.

His other books of the period include his first strictly historical work, *St. Domingo: Its Revolutions and Its Patriots* (1854); an enlargement of his travel book, *The American Fugitive in Europe* (1855); the first published black American play, *The Escape; or, A Leap for Freedom* (1858); and a further *Memoir* (1859). More in demand as a lecturer than ever as war approached, Brown found renewed personal hope in 1860 as he entered into a happy marriage with Annie Elizabeth Gray. In 1861 he began a nineteen-year career practicing medicine. An extended series of essays on "Celebrated Colored Americans" culminated in *The Black Man, His Antecedants, His Genius, and His Achievements* (1863), a long account of the historical importance of black civilizations and their contemporary position that gave him new prominence as a historian. His spirits needed lifting, for he was growing more and more pessimistic over the black plight after the war. While speaking for equal citizenship and full franchise, he predicted that in their absence wage slavery and peonage would replace legal slavery. At the opening of the conflict he had acted as a recruiting agent for a black regiment; now he was chagrined at the treatment of black soldiers, noting that they had been "cheated, robbed, deceived, and outraged everywhere."

Many of his worst fears were realized within a few years of the war's end. Yet Brown remained fixed on the reformer's path. His lectures emphasized black achievements and advocated equal suffrage and national temperance. His writing chronicled black accomplishments too soon forgotten. *The Negro in the American Rebellion: His Heroism and His Fidelity* (1867) is at once the first account of the black role in the Civil War and the first to join together black service in the American Revolution, the War of 1812, and the Civil War. His longest book and fourth history is *The Rising Son* (1873), which unites the story of previous black societies and blacks in the United States to brief lives of illustrious black Americans. *My Southern Home* (1880), his last book and one of his best, joins a history of slavery in the South to a report of a trip south he took in 1879–80.

Brown died at home in Chelsea, Massachusetts, of a tumor of the bladder 6 November 1884. He was buried at the Cambridge Cemetery in an unmarked gravesite.

MAJOR THEMES

In fall 1871, Brown, then fifty-seven and celebrated on two continents as author and lecturer, accepted an invitation to deliver a series of addresses in his native Kentucky. He was eager to make the trip, partly because he had not been in the state since he was a child, and partly because he fancied receiving a "home-boy makes good" welcome. En route to a meeting near Pleasureville one evening he was surrounded, captured, and threatened by a group of the Ku Klux Klan. Taken to a cabin to await a public, early morning lynching, he escaped only after his guards fell asleep—one with whiskey, the other with the help of Brown's hypodermic.

This episode reveals an irony bordering on the tragic for America as a nation. More than most writers of his time, however, Brown understood the abiding contradictions of American life and used the incident to assert his faith in the power of words. He reported that he was able to regain control over his spirits only by *writing* of the threat to his life—diffidently, humorously. Writing and lecturing had taught him that one could anticipate and control encounters with danger. They taught that one could be victimized without being degraded into a victim. They taught that it was one's duty to tell one's own story, not entrusting the task to others. Most important, they taught him to concentrate his formidable energies upon those problems human beings create for each other. Others could write about the mysteries of being and essence. He would expose the ways in which people were thoughtlessly, heartlessly, and pointlessly cruel to one another.

It was the role of the writer, he recorded in *The American Fugitive in Europe*, to add to the stock of national ideas, to bring novel and even painful ideas within the national ken, and thereby to serve as educator to the country at large, as effective in reform "as many of its legislators." Although quite painful at the time, his principles now seem commonplace, largely because they have been absorbed into present-day thinking. Belief in the indivisibility of the human family generated his lifelong struggle with the effects of slavery. He regularly asked his audiences, "Whom do you see standing before you?" When the reply was "A man," he responded, "Why do you not see a slave or a black man?" His own answer, for he was light-skinned, was that those were inventions, names designed to divide, to exclude, and to exploit. His arguments gained immediacy from his sympathy for, and analogies drawn from, other dependent, dispossessed, and disfranchised Americans: women, laborers, recent immigrants, American Indians, and poor whites in the South. Books and lectures he saw as opportunities to disclose and underscore that kinship, to move an audience to see resemblance where they had earlier seen only otherness.

It could be said that he was most adept as a translator, a carrier of experience from one group to another. An uninformed white audience, he found, was likely to dismiss the everyday workings of slavery and of black life generally as unfamiliar, if not incredible. To overcome such resistance, he in effect created a language that turned the cold and distant into the vivid, immediate, and mean-ingful. The form he chose was the life story, the style a native realism qualified by English restraint. From the *Narrative* of 1847 to *My Southern Home* more than 30 years later, his writing is one long excursion into personal history: of himself in the autobiographical narratives, of public figures in the histories, and of thinly fictional characters in the plays and novels. Whether describing himself, Clotel, Frederick Douglass, or Toussaint L'Ouverture, he is documenting the significance and influence of the single individual life; some of his most poignant songs and stories concern slave children, haunting examples of human potential destroyed. His search for a realistic, compelling form likewise led him to a reliance on factuality and a questioning of the usual boundaries between fact and fiction. He regularly pointed to factual sources of his plays and novels. ''The main features in the Drama are true,'' he wrote in the preface to *The Escape*. In 1848 he had read of a young woman with a child in her arms fleeing from slavery in Kentucky by crossing the Ohio River in midwinter—leaping from one ice floe to another. The scene so intrigued Brown that while in London he hired an English painter to reproduce it. A year later Harriet Beecher Stowe immor-talized the scene with Eliza in *Uncle Tom's Cabin*. Stowe had also been inspired by Brown's *Narrative*, and Brown acknowledged the influence of her novel upon *Clotel*. *Clotel* in its turn is the summary into one family of dozens of factual situations he had seen or read. Thus his writing is a continued interweaving of fact and imagination.

It is this penchant for hidden and neglected facts that distinguishes Brown's work as a travel writer, historian, and social critic. The travel books are re-markable where they observe people and places afresh, without the preconcep-tions of reputation and guidebook, from the naturally ambivalent view of a fugitive from slavery. Although drawn mostly from secondary sources, the four histories were indispensable in their time because most other historians refused to give black men and women their rightful place in the national story. Brown not only did so, with his customary narrative skill, but also provided the essential background of African civilization.

The need for social and historical understanding is the refrain of most of his later work. ''Slavery and Its Effect upon the American Character'' was one of his perennial lecture topics, through which he argued that white Americans who defend bondage or are indifferent to it begin in historical ignorance and end in moral blindness. The indictment of *Clotel* is less against the man Jefferson than against a country of many men who declare themselves free and innocent. When the ease and profit of the few are allowed to become customary, then custom hardens into institutions, and these are propped up by fear, greed, and ignorance. Soon the propagation of these evils grows into a national industry. For ordinary Americans, seeking innocence yet embracing ignorance, hardening of the heart becomes a certain virtue, while slavery yields a mode of self-justification and, by negation, of self-definition. Ordinary white Americans, especially in the

South, might not be able to say precisely what made them good or normal or patriotic citizens, yet they could at least testify that they were not slaves.

The terms of the American dilemma are stated as early as the title page of *Clotel*, where the enslavement of the president's daughter is juxtaposed with the egalitarian opening of the Declaration of Independence. Thereafter they are repeated in the form of hypocritical legislators, pious slaveholders, ranting preachers, bloody slave hunters, and ignorant mobs. A looming presence over the whole, Jefferson is brought forward during auction scenes, when his statements against the traffic in human beings serve as foreground music over the sale of his children. Brown ends such a chapter with, "But, sad to say, Jefferson is not the only American statesman who has spoken high-sounding words in favour of freedom, and then left his own children to die slaves." With but two exceptions, the slaves of the novel are victimized precisely because they are so friendly, open-hearted, nonviolent, and religiously inclined toward brotherhood. Indeed, they can be bought, abused, and sold precisely because they are genuinely good. The world Brown presents is a world of moral inversions, a world Kafka and Orwell would recognize, a world in which the truly evil are called Great and the truly good, Slaves.

Because Brown was an artist, his books are not mere chronicles of human woe. Slavery could be an abomination, but the human lives touched by it—and therefore their narratives—could transcend its squalor. Through rhetorical control, he indicated how injustice could be effectively overcome. In his lectures, after recounting an especially painful beating he received as a slave, he would break the tension in the hall with a comic aside revealing how ineffectual the slaveholder actually was. In the autobiographical narratives, he tells of the time he was forced to move from the passenger section of a Northern train to the baggage car; when the conductor came back demanding payment for a first-class ticket, Brown gave him a quarter of the amount—the rate for freight. He also describes the working of slave auctions, in one of which a beautiful young quadroon who had borne her owner's children was being sold, the bidding starting at $500. The auctioneer displayed a certificate attesting to the slave's "good moral character," and the bidding went to $700. He added that she was very intelligent, and the bids climbed to $800. When he said that she was "a devoted Christian," the bidding rose rapidly until she was sold for $1,000. Brown's ironic commentary serves equally to control his fury and to place the transaction in a greater perspective: "This was a southern auction, at which the bones, muscles, sinews, blood, and nerves of a young lady of twenty-eight years of age sold for five hundred dollars; her moral character for two hundred dollars; her improved intellect for another hundred, and her Christianity—the person of Christ in his follower—for two hundred more."

Rhetorical control is for Brown as much a lesson as a technique. Humor, irony, understatement, and other devices all release tension, subverting the threat and the power of the atrocities he describes. Injustice can thus be cut down to size, rendered manageable, and brought within the reformer's grasp. His first play, *Experience, or How to Give a Northern Man a Backbone*, is an extended series of reversals for a pro-slavery Boston preacher, who is sympathetically tolerant of slavery until, through comic mischance, he is himself enslaved. The most arresting instances of control appear in the narratives, when he explains how he not only survived bondage but also prospered over it. At the end of the *Narrative* of 1847 Brown remarks:

In the autumn, 1843, impressed with the importance of spreading anti-slavery truth, as a means to bring about the abolition of slavery, I commenced lecturing as an agent of the western New York Anti-Slavery Society, and have ever since devoted my time to the cause of my enslaved countrymen.

For the conclusion of a tale of survival, resistance, and escape, one might expect explosive effusion. Here humility and restraint are poised, and the passage gains a measured dignity by using the understated language Brown admired in eighteenth-century English writers. Readers can acknowledge the effort, the discipline of his control. Slavery is far worse than anything he can say about it. The tension created between the cruelties he recounts and his manner of presenting them— this tension he will use communally, not to win applause, but to go on working. The surplus of energy will be spent in the future: "devoted . . . to the cause of my enslaved countrymen." Throughout his career, Brown's tension would be active and creative, always renewing and always being renewed.

SURVEY OF CRITICISM

Brown's work has not yet been properly assessed. Virtually all abolitionist writers were in eclipse between 1870 and 1900; between 1900 and 1945 Brown's memory was kept alive by only a few, mostly black, scholars. The turning point was the mid–1960s, when his work became known to a broad spectrum of critics; since then studies have averaged about ten per year. Ten of his books were reprinted 1969–75. The high point came in 1969 with the appearance of the definitive biography by William Edward Farrison, who had spent a lifetime recovering Brown's significance for our day. All subsequent scholarship has depended upon Farrison's work.

Curtis W. Ellison and E. W. Metcalf, Jr., have compiled a valuable checklist of criticism. Farrison, Arthur Davis, and Jean Fagan Yellin have written introductions to *Clotel*, and J. Noel Heermance published a full-length study of the background of *Clotelle*. Important shorter studies have been done by William L. Andrews, Lucinda H. MacKethan, Robert Stepto, and Yellin. Five of the essays in *The Art of Slave Narrative* discuss the 1847 *Narrative*. Yet a substantial amount of work remains to be done. By 1980 all of Brown's books were once more out of print; new annotated editions are required. The connections among his work as lecturer, autobiographer, playwright, historian, novelist, and journalist have not yet been traced, far less examined. A bibliography of his newspaper articles is acutely needed, as are studies of particular periods of his life. Because Brown was so many-sided as a writer, he demands much of his critics.

BIBLIOGRAPHY

Works by William Wells Brown

Narrative of William W. Brown, a Fugitive Slave, Written by Himself. Boston: Anti-Slavery Office, 1847.

The Anti-Slavery Harp. Boston: B. Marsh, 1848.

A Description of William Wells Brown's Original Panoramic Views of the Scenes in the Life of an American Slave. London: Charles Gilpin, 1849.

Three Years in Europe. London and Edinburgh: C. Gilpin, 1852.

Clotel; or, The President's Daughter. London: Partridge & Oakey, 1853.

The American Fugitive in Europe. Boston: J. P. Jewett and New York: Sheldon, Lamport & Blakeman, 1855.

St. Domingo: Its Revolutions and Its Patriots. Boston: Bela Marsh, 1855.

The Escape; or, A Leap for Freedom: A Drama in Five Acts. Boston: R. F. Walcutt, 1858.

Memoir of William Wells Brown, an American Bondman. Boston: Anti-Slavery Office, 1859.

Miralda; or, The Beautiful Quadroon. Weekly Anglo-African, 1 December 1860–16 March 1861.

The Black Man, His Antecedents, His Genius, and His Achievements. Boston: R. F. Walcutt, 1863.

Clotelle: A Tale of the Southern States. Boston: J. Redpath, 1864.

Clotelle; or, The Colored Heroine. Boston: Lee & Shepard, 1867.

The Negro in the American Rebellion: His Heroism and His Fidelity. Boston: Lee & Shepard, 1867.

The Rising Son; or, The Antecedents and Advancement of the Colored Race. Boston: A. G. Brown, 1873.

My Southern Home. Boston: A. G. Brown, 1880.

Studies of William Wells Brown

Andrews, William L. *To Tell a Free Story: The First Century of Afro-American Autobiography, 1760–1825.* Urbana: University of Illinois Press, 1985.

Bell, Bernard W. "Literary Sources of the Early Afro-American Novel." *CLA Journal* 18 (1974): 29–43.

Butterfield, Stephen. *Black Autobiography in America.* Amherst: University of Massachusetts Press, 1974.

Ellison, Curtis W. and E. W. Metcalf, Jr. *William Wells Brown and Martin R. Delany: A Reference Guide.* Boston: G. K. Hall, 1978.

Farrison, William Edward. "Clotel, Thomas Jefferson, and Sally Hemings." *CLA Journal* 17 (1973): 147–74.

————. *"The Kidnapped Clergyman* and Brown's *Experience." CLA Journal* 18 (1975): 507–15.

————. *William Wells Brown: Author and Reformer.* Chicago: University of Chicago Press, 1969.

Gloster, Hugh M. *Negro Voices in American Fiction.* Chapel Hill: University of North Carolina Press, 1948.

Heermance, J. Noel. *William Wells Brown and Clotelle: A Portrait of the Artist in the First Negro Novel.* Hamden, Conn.: Shoe String Press, 1969.

Jackson, Blyden. "A Golden Mean for the Negro Novel." *CLA Journal* 2 (1959): 81–87.

————. "The Negro's Negro in Negro Literature." *Michigan Quarterly Review* 4 (1965): 290–95.

MacKethan, Lucinda H. "Huck Finn and the Slave Narratives: Lighting Out as Design." *Southern Review* 20 (1984): 247–64.

Redding, J. Saunders. *To Make a Poet Black.* Chapel Hill: University of North Carolina Press, 1939.

Sekora, John and Darwin T. Turner, eds. *The Art of Slave Narrative: Original Essays in Criticism and Theory.* Macomb: Western Illinois University, 1982.

Starling, Marion Wilson. *The Slave Narrative: Its Place in American History.* Boston: G. K. Hall, 1981.

Stepto, Robert B. *From Behind the Veil: A Study of Afro-American Narrative.* Urbana: University of Illinois Press, 1979.

Takaki, Ronald. *Violence in the Black Imagination.* New York: G. P. Putnam's Sons, 1962.

Thorp, Earl E. *Black Historians.* New York: Morrow, 1971.

Yellin, Jean Fagan. *The Intricate Knot: Black Figures in American Literature, 1776–1863.* New York: New York University Press, 1972.

ROBERT BAIN

William Byrd of Westover (1674–1744)

If posterity judged William Byrd of Westover by what he published during his lifetime, his work would merit little more than a footnote in the literary history of the South. Publication of three prose narratives in 1841 elevated Byrd's stature as a writer, but with the twentieth-century publication of another prose narrative, of three volumes of secret diaries and literary exercises, of his collected letters, and of other fugitive pieces, Byrd has earned the reputation as the major Southern colonial writer before Thomas Jefferson. Critics and historians admire his work for its wit, for the range of his literary achievements, and for his invaluable portraits of Virginia plantation life during the so-called Golden Age. Today, Byrd is not only the major Southern writer of the period but also a major colonial American author.

BIOGRAPHY

Born on 28 March 1674 at his father's frontier plantation near the falls of the James River, William Byrd II was the son of Mary Horsmanden Filmer Byrd (1653–99) and William Byrd I (1652–1704). His father, who was born in London and had migrated to Virginia in 1670, inherited from his kinsman Thomas Stegge some 3,000 acres and a lucrative Indian trade. In 1673 William Byrd I married Mary Filmer, the eighteen-year-old widow of Samuel Filmer and daughter of Warham Horsmanden, who had fled England during the civil war because he sympathized with the Cavaliers. Besides William, the Byrds had three daughters and another son, who died in infancy. When William Byrd I died on 4 December 1704, he left his son some 25,000 acres of land, a profitable Indian trade, and a legacy of public service to and political power in the Old Dominion.

From 1681 until 1696, William Byrd II lived in England where his grandfather Horsmanden saw to the boy's education. Under the supervision of Christopher

Glasscock, master of Felsted Grammar School in Essex, Byrd learned his Latin and Greek, a lifelong passion with him. In 1690 he studied business in Holland, then visited the court of France before returning to England to work in the mercantile house of Perry and Lane. Admitted to the Middle Temple in 1692 to study law, Byrd was licensed to practice in 1695. Through the influence of his friend and patron, Sir Robert Southwell, he was elected to the Royal Society on 29 April 1696. He was twenty-two years old.

Byrd returned briefly in 1696–97 to Virginia where he was elected to the House of Burgesses from Henrico County, but by October 1697 he was again in London representing his father and Governor Edmund Andros in a dispute before the Board of Trade. His first published work—"An Account of a Negro Boy That Is Dappled in Several Places on his Body with White Spots"—appeared in the Royal Society's *Philosophical Transactions* in 1698. This two-page account is a scientific curiosity.

Deciding when Byrd began to "scribble, scribble, scribble" is sheer guesswork. He probably became a compulsive reader and writer during his grammar school years. Though his earliest extant letters date from as late as 1697, evidence suggests that he had formed the habit of scribbling long before any of his surviving manuscripts indicate. His letters to Sir Robert Southwell in 1701, during Byrd's tour of England with John Perceval, Sir Robert's nephew, refer to a journal Byrd was keeping during this trip. He wrote to Sir Robert, "We are not negligent in our observations, but lay about for matter to put in our journall," and "I foresee that our journals are like to swell to a volume" (*Letters*, I, 211–12, 213). In his letters to "Facetia" (Lady Elizabeth Cromwell) in 1703, he refers to "characters of 2 of your freinds [*sic*]" that he is sending to her and talks of being venturesome "enough to send you a 3rd" (*Letters*, I, 222). The character sketches and prose narratives in his personal letters illustrate Byrd's pleasure at drawing a portrait or telling a story, a habit that stayed with him. And though no one knows exactly when he learned the shorthand in which he kept his secret diaries, he had mastered the skill by 1709, the date of his first surviving diary, and probably long before that. All evidence, circumstantial though it is, points to Byrd's being a lifelong scribbler, and one wonders how much of his work has been lost.

Byrd's second residence in England continued from 1697 until 1705, when he returned to Virginia after his father's death. During this time, he wrote ten witty letters to Lady Cromwell, then in Ireland, giving her the London gossip and proclaiming his love. Beginning with his third letter, Byrd created two characters for her—"Veramour," a wretched creature suffering love melancholy for the beautiful, pitiless "Facetia," who will not return his passion. Veramour and Facetia are alter egos for Byrd and Lady Elizabeth. Byrd writes, "Poor distressed Veramour leads a wretched life, and sees hardly any mortal but me, with whom he comes to sigh away some melancholy hours. He's the reverse of a ghost . . ." (*Letters*, I, 222). As a wit of the town, Byrd reports on poor

Veramour's misery, so in a sense, he has his wit and his wretchedness at the same time.

Though it is almost impossible to date Byrd's characters, he probably wrote those of Dr. Samuel Garth ("Dr. Glysterio") and Sir Robert Southwell ("Cavaliero Sapiente"), among others, during this period. His literary exercises include "A Poem Upon Some Ladies at Tunbridge 1700." Of "Mrs. E . . . k" he wrote: "Drusilla warms us with her fire, / Which her too Icy breast denies; / At every. smile, some swains expire, / At every frown some Hero dies." And he may have written during this time a history of Virginia, now lost, which Sir John Oldmixon used to write his *The British Empire in America* (1708, 1741).

From 1705 to 1715, Byrd lived in Virginia at Westover, a plantation located twenty miles east on the James River from his birthplace and purchased by his father in 1688 to be nearer the seats of government and commerce. Shortly after his return, he met Lucy Parke, daughter of Colonel Daniel Parke, and trotted out his old character of Veramour (and some lines he had used on Lady Cromwell) to court Lucy ("Fidelia") with love letters. They were married on 4 May 1706 and had four children, two of whom survived infancy—Evelyn and Wilhelmina. Byrd also found his business affairs in chaos and spent the next few years ordering them. In 1709 he won appointment to the Governor's Council and became much involved in the colony's politics.

From this period, too, comes Byrd's first *Secret Diary*, covering the years 1709 through 1712 and first published in 1941. Critics have called Byrd's diary entries formulaic, banal, dull, repetitive, monotonous. Although the entries may have little literary merit, they tell much about the man and about plantation life in Virginia. He kept his diaries in a seventeenth-century shorthand, not intending them for others' eyes. But he did from time to time reread them to refresh his memory about events and people.

Two entries below illustrate the form and content of Byrd's *Secret Diary*. Nearly all recount the time he arose, his morning reading, his plantation or government business, his diet, his health, his visitors, his concern with his people (servants and slaves), and his sexual activity. Most entries end with the phrase "thanks be to God Almighty" or "thank God Almighty." He uses a few code phrases. When he "dances his dance," he refers to a physical exercise he performed daily for most of his adult life. He uses the noun *flourish* and the verb *roger* to refer to sexual intercourse. The first entry is from 30 July 1710:

I rose at 5 o'clock and wrote a letter to Major Burwell about his boat which Captain Broadwater's people had brought round and sent Tom with it. I read two chapters in Hebrew and some Greek in Thucydides. I said my prayers and ate boiled milk for breakfast. I danced my dance. I read a sermon in Dr. Tillotson and then took a little [nap]. I ate fish for dinner. In the afternoon my wife and I had a little quarrel and reconciled with a flourish. Then she read a sermon in Dr. Tillotson to me. It is to be observed that the flourish was performed on the billiard table. I read a little Latin. In the evening we took a walk about the plantation. I neglected to say my prayers but had good health, good thoughts, and good humor, thanks be to God. This month there were many people sick of fever and pain in their heads; perhaps this might be caused by the cold weather which we had this month, which was indeed the coldest that ever was known in July in this country. Several of my people have been sick, but none died, thank God. (pp. 210–11)

The second, from 4 May 1711, almost a year later, has essentially the same form and content as all other entries:

I rose about 6 o'clock and read two chapters in Hebrew and some Greek in Lucian. I said my prayers and ate boiled milk for breakfast. I danced my dance. The weather was cold. I sent G-r-l with a letter to Colonel Hill which came from Mr. Perry concerning his ship. Nurse sent for her things which were delivered. I settled some accounts. My sick people were better, thank God Almighty. My sister Duke and Colonel Eppes came and stayed to dinner. I ate pork and peas for dinner. In the afternoon my sister went home and the Colonel went away and then I went and read some law till evening. Then I took a walk about the plantation to see how everything was but my wife stayed at home and was melancholy. At night I read more law. I said my prayers and had good health, good thoughts, and good humor, thank God Almighty. I gave my wife a flourish. (p. 339)

But as this litany of repetition with slight variation accrues, Byrd's portrait emerges. He frets over his accounts and his business losses; as amateur physician, he doctors his "people" as best he can and prays for them; though he seldom comments on his reading, he reads daily; he is a gracious host, worrying at times that he cannot afford to treat his guests as well as he does; he records more than 50 experiences with dreams and occult signs, often troublesome ones; occasionally he weeps when Lucy is not well. He worries that the governor will not pay him sufficient respect and is delighted when he receives proper acknowledgment. He prays daily, attends church regularly, and tries to practice an enlightened religion. As a farmer, he reads the rainfall and weather that affect his crops. He laments on his thirty-sixth birthday that he has done so little with his life. He recounts, sometimes with disarming candor, his passions and lusts. On 2 November 1709, three years after his marriage, he describes an evening at Dr. Barret's,

where my wife came this afternoon. Here I found Mrs. Chiswell, my sister Custis, and other ladies. We sat and talked till about 11 o'clock and then retired to our chambers. I played at [r-m] with Mrs. Chiswell and kissed her on the bed till she was angry and my wife also was uneasy about it, and cried as soon as the company was gone. I neglected to say my prayers, which I should not have done, because I ought to beg pardon for the lust I had for another man's wife. However I had good health, good thoughts, and good humor, thanks be to God Almighty. (p. 101)

A dispute with Governor Spotswood and business debts sent Byrd back to England in 1715, and except for a brief visit to Virginia in 1720–21, he lived in England from 1715 until 1726. Lucy, who joined him there in 1716, died of smallpox on 21 November 1716. Byrd wrote to his brother-in-law John Custis, "No stranger ever met with more respect in a strange country than she had done here, for many persons of distinction, who all pronounced her an honor of Virginia. Alas! how proud was I of her, and how severely am I punished for it. But I can dwell no longer on so afflicting a subject, much less can I think of anything else . . . " (*Letters*, I, 296). But Byrd spent the next few years looking for a second wife, and after courting unsuccessfully several heiresses, he married Maria Taylor, a wealthy young woman of 25, in May 1724. They had four children—Anne (1725–57), Maria (1727–45), William III (1728–77), and Jane (b. 1729).

Byrd's literary productions during these London years include his verses to ladies in *Tunbrigalia: or, Tunbridge Miscellanies, for the Year 1719* (1719) and *A Discourse Concerning the Plague* (1721). The verses, signed "Mr. Burrard," resemble his earlier efforts for the ladies of Tunbridge Wells, and critics cannot decide whether the *Discourse* is a satire or a serious scientific treatise, largely because Byrd recommends tobacco as a cure for the plague. Letters to various ladies date from this period, as do some of his characters. More important are *The London Diary* (1958), dealing with the years 1717 through 1721, and his self-portrait, "Inamorato L'Oiseaux" (The Enamored Bird), sent to an unidentified lady ("Minionet") in a letter dated 21 February 1723, though perhaps composed much earlier.

The London Diary, whose entries resemble those of *The Secret Diary*, recounts Byrd's attempts to buy the governorship of Virginia, his courtships of various ladies, his hobnobbing with London society and members of the Court, and his dallyings with whores, whom he sometimes "rogered" three times a night. Byrd was in his mid-forties. "Inamorato L'Oiseaux," which historians and biographers regard as a perceptive and psychologically sound self-portrait, has yet to receive sufficient critical attention. Although Byrd's purpose is to convince some lady of his worthiness and although his tone is that of a witty, worldly man, he builds his sketch from beginning to end on a series of conflicting opposites. In fact, the controlling metaphor of the first part is that of an embattled psyche. Byrd writes, "The struggle between the senate and the Plebians in the Roman Commonwealth, or betweext [*sic*] the King and the Parliament in England, was never half so violent as the Civil war between this Hero's Principles and his Inclinations" (*Another Secret Diary*, p. 276). In addition to the "Civil war" between "Principles" and "Inclinations," Byrd defines his psychological conflicts as struggles between Passion and Reason, Good and Evil, Laziness and Diligence, Resolution and wavering, fire and phlegm, "obscure merit" and "corrupt Greatness," retirement and society, and humility and "a cast of pride." He confesses that these conflicts have kept him from achieving "a great fortune" (p. 277). And though he claims he "never interlop't with anothers wife or mistress" (he may have forgotten Mrs. Chiswell), he admits candidly that "He cou'd return from one of the Convents of Drury Lane [a whorehouse] with as much innocence, as any of the saints from a meeting" (p. 280). Byrd's autobiographical portrait shows that he had more insight into the paradoxes of his character than many critics have granted him.

In 1726 Byrd sailed for Virginia with his new wife and growing family, never to return to England. He reentered politics immediately, acquired more land, struggled to pay his debts, and wrote his best work. He took his seat on Virginia's council on 28 April 1726 and was appointed in 1727 as one of three Virginia Commissioners to settle a long-standing boundary dispute with North Carolina. In spring and fall 1728, the Virginia and North Carolina Commissioners surveyed the boundary line from Currituck Inlet for 241 miles to the Appalachian foothills. On this journey, Byrd kept a journal, which he later rewrote as *The Secret History of the Line* (1929) and as *The History of the Dividing Line* (1841); for £200 he also claimed 20,000 acres in western North Carolina.

Byrd built in 1730–31 at Westover the house that still stands today and in 1733 laid out plans for Richmond and Petersburg. The two journals that he kept of his journey to Governor Spotswood's plantation at Germanna in 1732 and of his visit to his western lands in 1733 became the short prose narrative entitled *A Progress to the Mines* and *A Journey to the Land of Eden*. Land poor and beleaguered by debts, he considered selling Westover in 1735–36, and throughout the 1730s and 1740s tried to sell his western lands to Swiss immigrants. A Swiss agent named Samuel Jenner published in 1737 at Berne a volume entitled *Neugefundenes Eden*, a volume once attributed to Byrd, but really a compilation of information from John Lawson's *New Voyage to Carolina* (1709) and other sources. During these years Byrd kept up a lively correspondence with friends in England, and *Another Secret Diary* (1942), covering the years 1739–41 and less interesting than the earlier ones, survives from this period. He became president of the Council in 1743.

Though dating the composition of the four major narratives is impossible, the best guess is that Byrd began work on the histories as early as 1732 and finished them between 1738 and 1740. He undoubtedly kept journals—in the same shorthand as his secret diaries—of his running of the line, of his trip to Governor Spotswood's plantation, and of his journey to the Land of Eden. These journals are probably lost. In three letters to British correspondent Peter Collinson, Byrd mentions works in progress, though it is not always clear what works he refers to. On 18 July 1736, Byrd mentions "my history of the line" and "an Indian scribble," the latter probably a reference to *A Journey*. He told Collinson, who had asked to see the "history," that he never ventured "any thing unfinisht out of my hands," that what he had so far written was "only the skeleton and ground-work of what I intend," and that he wanted only the "leizure" to complete his work (*Letters*, II, 493–94). On 5 July 1737, Byrd hoped that Collinson had sent "by some of the latter ships . . . your critique upon my journal," which was "compos'd in the rough woods, and partakes of the place that gave it birth" (*Letters*, II, 523). And on 10 July 1739, Byrd told Collinson, "As to the generation of the opossum I will beg leave to answer your questions by a transcript from my journal of the line" (*Letters*, II, 533). From these references and from internal evidence, historians guess that Byrd first worked on *The Secret History* and then on *The History*. By 1736 he was also at work on one of the shorter narratives. These manuscripts circulated among British and American friends, but none saw publication until 1841.

Byrd's extensive revisions of and additions to *The Secret History* to produce *The History* make one point clear: *The Secret History* was a Southern American book for a Virginia audience; *The History*, nearly twice as long as its predecessor, was a Southern American book for a British audience. To the "skeleton and groundwork" of *The Secret History*, Byrd revised and enlarged *The History* with a conscious eye upon his audience. He (1) deleted the code names (Steddy, Firebrand, etc.) and many characters, all perhaps puzzling to British readers, (2) generalized his satire, directing it toward North Carolinians rather than individual characters, (3) wrote the comic introduction about Virginia's history to place his narrative in an understandable context, (4) defined unfamiliar words (a *tomahawk* as a "hatchet"), (5) added much natural history to interest his British audience, (6) advocated swift settlement of western lands to extend and protect the British Empire's frontier borders in the New World, (7) described Virginia and North Carolina scenes by comparing them with locations familiar to British readers, and (8) sprinkled his new history with classical allusions to clarify ideas and feelings.

When William Byrd died on 26 August 1744, he left the manuscripts that have since brought him fame as a writer. He had also paid off his debts and owned 179,440 acres of land. He was buried at Westover.

MAJOR THEMES

To talk of preoccupations or recurring motifs in Byrd's writing may be more precise than to talk of major themes. Because he practiced and often mingled a variety of literary forms (diaries, letters, characters, journals, light verse, tracts, histories, promotional writing), genre and formalist critics have some difficulty characterizing his work. For example, his letters sometimes include characters or brief tales; his two histories of the line take the form of journals; *The History* smacks of promotional writing, especially near the end. But several recurring motifs appear in nearly all of his works. In a way, Byrd's preoccupations in the secret diaries and letters spill over into his four prose narratives.

Byrd's preoccupations were many—his rage for order and fear of discord, his compulsiveness about reading and writing, his playing the role of comedian and wit, his fascination with observing and creating characters, his ambition for political power and preferment, his lust for wealth and empire, his interest in science, his insistent practice of his religion, his obsessions with women and sex, his portrayal of plantation life as pastoral, and his observations on slavery and Indians.

The comic conflict between order and discord stands at the center of *The Secret History* and *The History*. In the large cast of code-named characters in *The Secret History*, William Byrd is "Steddy," defender of industry and order, and his principal opponents are "Firebrand" (Richard Fitzwilliam of Virginia), the prince of discord, and the North Carolina rabble ("Jumble," "Shoebrush," "Plausible," and "Puzzlecause"), all names reflecting low birth or hoggish intelligence. The lazy North Carolinians and their "porcivorous countrymen" eat so much swine that they "seem to grunt rather than speak in their ordinary conversation" (pp. 60–61). But it is "Firebrand" who criticizes Byrd's journal as being "too poetical" (p. 85), who is a "disorderly fellow" (p. 73), who is responsible for "our perpetual discord" (p. 88), and who causes the stalwart "Steddy" to halt "as bad as old Jacob, without having wrestled with anything like an angel" (p. 59). When "Firebrand" and the Carolina Commissioners leave the party after "Steddy" stops an impending brawl between "Meanwell" (William Dandridge of Virginia) and "Firebrand," Byrd sighs deeply: "A general joy discovered itself through all the camp when these gentlemen turned their backs upon us . . . " (pp. 112–13). Then Byrd and the rest of his Virginians can complete in good order their mission in His Majesty's service.

In *The History*, Byrd represents the conflict between order and chaos by contrasting, often implicitly, the law-abiding, Christian society of Virginia with the Lubberland of North Carolina. He satirizes the pork-eating poor whites of North Carolina's backcountry as pagans (p. 195) and infidels (p. 221) living godlessly without ministers (p. 195) and sheltering fugitives, runaway slaves, criminals, and debtors (p. 186). Eating mostly pork, these people are "full of gross humors" (p. 185), and the men are "slothful in everything but the getting of children" (p. 192). "Surely," says Byrd, "there is no place in the world where the inhabitants live with less labor than in North Carolina. It approaches nearer to the description of Lubberland than any other, by the great felicity of the climate, the easiness of raising provisions, and the slothfulness of the people." The men make their wives do all the work while "they lie and snore till the sun has risen one-third of his course," and they "loiter away their lives, like Solomon's sluggard, with their arms across, and at the winding up of the year scarcely have bread to eat" (p. 204). But what threatens good order even more is that they treat their governors and other officials "with all the excesses of freedom and familiarity" (p. 207), that they "pay no tribute either to God or to Caesar" (p. 212), and that "everyone does what seems best in his own eyes" (p. 196). For Byrd, returning to Virginia is returning to "Christendom" (p. 222), for there most things seem to be in their place and good order prevails. Bryd's preoccupation with the struggle between order and chaos appears everywhere in his work.

Reading and writing were like breathing for Byrd. He begins most days reading in one of the many languages he knew—Latin, Greek, Hebrew, Dutch, and probably French—but seldom records his responses. He knew works by British writers (he talks of reading in English), but again seldom mentions authors or titles. His unpublished Commonplace Book contains some judgments about authors and books, but Byrd put his reading to work functionally in his own prose through the use of allusion. The secret diaries and letters refer to his writing (his history, verses, lampoons, etc.), but again he says little of those works. In a letter of 2 February 1727 to John Boyle, a British correspondent, Byrd congratulates Boyle for the vividness of his "historical epistle," saying "Every thing is described with so much life and propriety that I fanceyed [*sic*] the objects themselves present before my eyes" (*Letters*, I, 359–60). That seems to be Byrd's intention in *The Secret History* and *The History*—to put the reader in the scene in a delightful, informative way. He also knew that writing was an avenue to power, for his political and public correspondence shows an able rhetorician at work.

As a child of his literary age, Byrd worked hard to project an image of himself as a wit, as a master of the comic and satiric. His letters, characters, and prose narratives abound with comedy, humor, and satire. He says of "Shoebrush" and "Puzzlecause" in *The Secret History*, "We found Shoebrush a merry, good-humored man and had learnt a very decent behavior from Governor Hyde, to whom he had been *valet de chambre*, of which he still carried the marks by having his coat, waistcoat, and breeches of different parishes. Puzzlecause had degenerated from a New England preacher, for which his godly parents designed him, to a very wicked but awkward rake" (p. 57). At the camp, "Meanwell entertained the Carolina commissioners with several romantic passages of his life with relation to his amours, which is a subject he is as fond of as a hero to talk of battles he never fought" (p. 68). Of Dr. Humdrum, the clergyman who took a liking to bear meat, Byrd wrote, "Here we promoted our chaplain from the deanery of Pip to the bishopric of Beardom" (p. 133). Byrd's "The Female Creed," a satire on women's foibles, and "Upon a Fart," a parody of Anne Finch's poem "Upon a Sigh," illustrate his penchant for the bawdy. And the final stanza of "A Song," a poem about Mary Smith's rejecting his marriage proposal, vents Byrd's spleen: "Let Age with double speed oretake her; / Let Love the room of Pride supply; / And when the fellows all foresake her, / Let her gnaw the sheets & dy" (*Another Secret Diary*, p. 203).

Drawing characters preoccupied Byrd, but he has not received proper recognition for the originality of those in his histories. Critics disagree about whether his early characters are based on individuals or Theophrastan types, but often these exhibit moral and psychological insight. "Dr. Glysterio" depicts in about 500 words the portrait of "an amusing posturer whose dilettantism is dangerous" (Bain, p. 51), and "Cavaliero Sapiente" draws the likeness of the good man. His female characters range from portraits of ideal women to such satires as "The Female Creed."

But Byrd's most original characters, often drawn in miniature, are the later ones in *The History* and *The Secret History*. The generalized portrait of the pork-eating poor whites in *The History* is perhaps his most famous, but he also draws in *The Secret History*, in addition to the code-named portraits, some American characters who are precursors to those of James Fenimore Cooper and William Gilmore Simms. Old Captain Hix, a precursor of Natty Bumppo, joins the expedition for just a few days; Byrd writes, "I sent several of the men out a-hunting, and they brought us four wild turkeys. Old Captain Hix killed two of them, who turned his hand to everything notwithstanding his great age, disdaining to be thought the worse for threescore-and-ten. Beauty never appeared better in old age, with a ruddy complexion and hair as white as snow'' (p. 97). Later Captain Hix "entertained us with one of his trading songs, which he quavered out most melodiously, and put us all into a good humor'' (p. 99).

Byrd's thumbnail sketch of Epaphroditus Bainton has the ring of a less noble Daniel Boone. Bainton is "young enough at sixty years of age to keep a concubine and to walk twenty-five miles a day. He has foresworn ever getting on a horse's back, being once in danger of breaking his neck by a fall. He spends most of his time in hunting and ranging the woods, killing generally more than one hundred deer a year'' (p. 100). The portrait of Ned Bearskin, the company's Saponi Indian guide, anticipates Cooper's Chingachgook. In both versions of the history, Byrd talks of Bearskin's religion, but in *The Secret History* a fuller portrait emerges because Byrd deals with Bearskin's various superstitions. Byrd's "Orion," a mathematics professor at the College of William and Mary, is the tenderfoot who cannot adapt to the frontier, and young Robin Hix becomes the "independent yeoman who refuses to carry Orion's 'greatcoat' in the march through the Dismal Swamp. Admiring Robin, Byrd sees the justice of his refusal'' (Bain, p. 55). Some commentators find Byrd's personae in the two histories the most interesting of his characters—the Virginia Cavalier and Gentleman equal to any situation.

Byrd's ambition for political power and preferment appears most blatantly in his diaries and letters. For years he sought the governorship of Virginia and at one time offered a bribe for that post (*London Diary*, p. 259). In a wish-fulfilling dream that did not come true, he dreamed that the king had made him secretary of state (*London Diary*, p. 494). By implication in *The Secret History*, Byrd suggests that a good governor would bring a "Steddy" hand to colonial affairs.

In his quest for wealth and empire, Byrd did well enough, but he always had visions of more. He owned several plantations, built the fine house at Westover and furnished it handsomely, enjoyed one of the best libraries in America, owned more than 100,000 acres in the Land of Eden, and had many servants, slaves, and creature comforts. After claiming western lands, he tried unsuccessfully to sell the tracts to Swiss settlers. Describing a delightful landscape in the mountain foothills, he daydreams about another wish that went unfulfilled: "This [scene] had a most agreeable effect upon the eye and wanted nothing but cattle grazing in the meadow and sheep and goats feeding on the hill to make it complete rural landscape'' (*History*, p. 306). And, of course, cash-paying settlers. He wrote in *A Journey* of laying "the foundation of two large cities" to be called Richmond and Petersburg; "Thus,'' he says, "we did not build castles only, but also cities in the air'' (p. 388). One reason Byrd's air-built castles and cities never materialized immediately was, as he complained in a letter of June 1731, that the "merchants of England take care that none of us grow very rich'' (*Letters*, II, 444).

An amateur scientist, Byrd maintained a lifelong interest in nature and medicine. He corresponded with Sir Hans Sloane, Mark Catesby, Peter Collinson, and others about medicinal virtues of such plants as snakeroot and ginseng. He notes in letters and the diaries the cures he prescribes for friends, slaves, and servants, and he laments to Sloane in 1706 that Virginia has no skilled naturalists (*Letters*, I, 259). *The Secret History* and especially *The History* reflect these concerns.

Unlike the New England Saints, whom he frequently satirized, Byrd practiced his Anglican religion with "good health, good thoughts, and good humor, thank God Almighty." He kept the Sabbath faithfully and said his prayers regularly; he judged the effectiveness of Commissary James Blair's sermons; he read sermons, mentioning those of Archbishop John Tillotson most often. When the Dividing Line company argued for breaking the Sabbath in order to head home, Byrd wittily agreed on the condition that Dr. Humdrum "would take that sin upon himself" (*Secret History*, p. 135). He said of himself in "Inamorato L'Oiseaux": "His religion is more in substance than in form, and he is more forward to practice vertue [*sic*] than to profess it. . . . Of all cheats in the world he has least charity for the Holy Cheat, that makes Religion bawd for his Interest and serves the Devil in the Livery of Godliness" (*Another Secret Diary*, p. 280). Though Byrd sometimes fractured the Seventh and Tenth Commandments, he usually asked God's pardon and took both the form and substance of his religion seriously.

To account satisfactorily for Byrd's obsessions with women and sex would require a skilled psychiatrist. That he sought the company of women and generally admired them is evident from his letters. In "Inamorato L'Oiseaux," he wrote: "There is something in female conversation, that softens the roughness, tames the wildness, & refines the indecency too common amongst men. He laid it down as a maxime [*sic*] that without Ladys, a schollar is a Pedant, a Philosopher a Cynick, all morality is morose, & all behavior either too Formal or too licentious" (*Another Secret Diary*, p. 281). In both histories, much humor arises from his treatment of the battles of the sexes. His secret diaries, especially *The London Diary*, recount his trafficking with ladies and with whores, his keeping boxscores of his lovemaking, his performing "manual uncleanness" (probably masturbation), and his playing the fool, when he was in his sixties, with this-or-that woman. After a bout with gonorrhea, his "cousin Horsmanden" walked him home "lest I should pick up a whore," and months later he slept "but indifferently because I dreamed I was clapped" (*London Diary*, pp. 206, 356). As he notes in "Inamorato L'Oiseaux," he often played the fool when he was in love or lust, and he was often in love or lust.

Erotic visions filled even his dream life. One night he dreamed that "the King's daughter was in love with me," and on the following night, that he "made love to a young sister and made her in love with me while I intended to get the older" (*London Diary*, p. 444). While he was running the line, Byrd dreamed "the three Graces appeared to me in all their naked charms; I singled out charity from the rest, with whom I had an intrigue'' (*Secret History*, p. 120). How a psychiatrist might interpret these obsessions would make interesting reading, but as Byrd himself admitted, his passions often triumphed over his principles.

When William Byrd created his version of the Southern American pastoral, he built it around Westover's cultivated fields and a busy, seemingly benevolent patriarchy, not around any Forest of Arden or even Virginia's frontier. In letters to British correspondents from 1726 on, he compared his life at Westover to ''Canaan'' and ''Paradise,'' though he had trouble forgetting ''the onions, and flesh-pots of Egypt'' (that is, London). He wrote to Charles Boyle in 1726, ''Like one of my patriarchs, I have my flocks and my herds, my bond-men, and bond-women, and every soart [*sic*] of trade amongst my own servants, so that I live in a kind of independance [*sic*] on every one, but Providence.'' In this pastoral landscape, there were no ''housebreakers, highway-men, or beggers'' [*sic*] and all could ''rest securely in our beds with all our doors and windows open'' (*Letters*, I, 355–56). Although he praised the hardy ''pioneers'' and ''foresters'' who surveyed the line with him and although he admired the frontier's natural beauty, Byrd peopled his ideal ''rural landscape'' with good husbandmen and plenty of livestock.

But, as Byrd knew, all was not well in his Virginia Paradise: Indians threatened the frontiers from without and Negro slavery threatened from within. For friendly Indians, he had some sympathy: he approved intermarriage between the English and Indians as a way of civilizing them (*History*, p. 160), and he treated sympathetically Ned Bearskin's account of his religion in both histories. In *The History* especially he showed some understanding of Indian culture and warfare, but he recalled the Catawba uprising of 1713 (p. 317) and recommended using the mountains as a natural fortification against the French and the hostile tribes to the north and west (pp. 271–72). He advocated continued trade with the Cherokees and further exploration beyond the mountains.

Though Byrd viewed Negroes more ambivalently than he did Indians, he expressed for his time clear insights about slavery in the South. In 1718 he owned 220 slaves, ''many of them being tradesmen,'' whom he valued at £7000 (*Letters*, I, 312–14), and he wrote to Charles Boyle in 1727 that ''our poor Negroes are free-men in comparison of the slaves who till your ungenerous soil'' (*Letters*, I, 358). By 1736, when he was considering selling slaves to pay off his debts, Byrd seems to have changed his mind. Writing to John Perceval on 12 July 1736, Byrd listed the evils of ''this unchristian traffick of makeing [*sic*] merchandize of our fellow creatures.'' He laid part of the blame to the ''saints of New England,'' who ''import so many Negroes hither, that I fear this colony will some time or other be confirmed by the name of New Guinea.'' The ''bad consequences of multiplying these Ethiopians amongst us'' were numerous: the presence of Negro slaves blew ''up the pride'' and ruined ''the industry of our white people,'' who ''detest work for fear it shoud [*sic*] make them look like slaves''; the presence of so many slaves also made ''them insolent'' and rebellious in their servitude, and though Virginians practiced "nothing like the inhumanity" of masters "in the islands," they were often "severe"; and finally the threat of slave uprisings by "10,000 men" ready to make "sevile [civil] war" would "tinge our rivers as wide as they are with blood" (*Letters*, II, 487–88). Byrd's insights did not make him an Abolitionist, but they produced the clearest and most succinct analysis of slavery's woes by a white Southerner before Jefferson's *Notes on Virginia* (1785).

For his preoccupation with subjects and motifs central to the study of Southern culture and for his achievements as a writer of wit and insight, William Byrd stands foremost among those authors before Jefferson.

SURVEY OF CRITICISM

Several helpful bibliographies for the study of Byrd are available. Jay B. Hubbell's *The South in American Literature, 1607–1900* (1954), though dated, is still useful, as is Richard Beale Davis's *American Literature through Bryant, 1585–1830* (1969). Louis B. Wright's entry in *A Bibliographical Guide to Southern Literature* (1969) lists both biographical and critical studies. Two annotated studies are Rose Marie Cutting's *John and William Bartram, William Byrd II, and St. John de Crevecoeur: A Reference Guide* (1976) and Donald Yanella and John H. Roch, *American Prose to 1820: A Guide to Information Sources* (1976). Neither of these volumes is comprehensive, however. Pierre Marambaud's study (cited below) contains the best bibliography of Byrd's work, a catalogue of his letters, and a listing of secondary books and essays.

Byrd's works exist in a number of forms, most of them with informative introductions and often with indispensable annotations. Louis B. Wright has edited and written a long introduction to *The Prose Works of William Byrd of Westover* (1966). Included in this volume are *The Secret History, The History, A Progress to the Mines*, and *A Journey to the Land of Eden*. Wright's edition is the definitive text of the four prose narratives. In *William Byrd's Histories of the Dividing Line Betwixt Virginia and North Carolina* (1929), which prints the texts of *The History* and *The Secret History* on facing pages, William K. Boyd identifies the code names of the characters in *The Secret History* and provides an informed introduction. Percy G. Adams wrote a new introduction to Boyd's edition for Dover Publications (1967), adding manuscript pages missing from Boyd's edition and retaining the format of producing the two texts on facing pages.

Standard editions of the diaries, all with fine introductions and indispensable annotations, are *The Secret Diary of William Byrd of Westover, 1709–1712* (1941), edited by Louis B. Wright and Marion Tinling, *Another Secret Diary of William Byrd of Westover, 1739–1741, with Letters and Literary Exercises, 1696–1726* (1942), edited by Maude H. Woodfin and Marion Tinling, and *The London Diary (1717–1721) and Other Writings* (1958), edited by Wright and Tinling. An abridged edition of the earliest diary appeared as *The Great American*

Gentleman: William Byrd of Westover of Virginia, His Secret Diary for the Years 1709–1712 (1963), also edited by Wright and Tinling. This volume, evidently prepared as a classroom text, omits much. Marion Tinling has edited and annotated Byrd's letters in *The Correspondence of the Three William Byrds of Westover, Virginia, 1684–1776* (1977). Tinling supplies an excellent introduction and notes for her two volumes. Byrd's letters occupy the last half of volume one and the first part of volume two.

The earliest work on Byrd was editorial and biographical. Edmund Ruffin, that firebrand Confederate, first edited *The Westover MSS: Containing the History of the Dividing Line Betwixt Virginia and North Carolina; A Journey to the Land of Eden, A.D. 1733; and A Progress to the Mines* in 1841. Ruffin's introduction was quite brief, and he did not know about *The Secret History*. In 1866 T. H. Wynne edited *History of the Dividing Line and Other Tracts* in two volumes. In addition to the three prose narratives that Ruffin edited, Wynne added an essay on tobacco and other miscellaneous papers. In 1901 John S. Bassett edited *The Writings of "Colonel William Byrd of Westover in Virginia, Esquire."* Bassett's edition, really the first modern one, prints in addition to the prose narratives some letters and a catalogue of Byrd's library. His biography is the most comprehensive of the early ones, and his introduction sets forth clearly the context of Byrd's work.

Richmond Croom Beatty, who did not have access to the secret diaries but had read letters and other accounts, wrote the first book-length study, *William Byrd of Westover* (1932). Beatty portrays his subject romantically and at times fictionally, but treats with clarity and grace Byrd's economic woes. Beatty documents how the tobacco trade in the first half of the eighteenth century indentured Byrd and his contemporaries to British merchants and capitalists. Other accounts that introduce Byrd deftly are Louis B. Wright's "William Byrd II" in *The First Gentlemen of Virginia* (1940) and Wright's essay on Byrd in *Anglo-American Cultural Relations in the Seventeenth and Eighteenth Centuries* (1960). Alden Hatch in *The Byrds of Virginia: An American Dynasty, 1670 to the Present* (1969), recounts briskly Byrd's political life and quotes liberally from the letters and the works.

It was not until 1971 that the next book-length biography appeared, Pierre Marambaud's *William Byrd of Westover, 1674–1744*; it is now the standard biography. Marambaud has sorted carefully through the biographical accounts and presents the most solid narrative of Byrd's life. His chapters on Byrd as a man of letters, though sometimes repetitive, are judicious. His commentary on Byrd's character sketches and on the letters is particularly informed.

The best article on Byrd—and the place to begin one's critical reading—is Richard Beale Davis's "William Byrd: Taste and Tolerance" in *Major Writers of Early America* (1972), edited by Everett Emerson. Davis devotes sections of his essay to "Miscellaneous Minor Writings," to the "Diaries and Letters," and to "The Public Prose." Though Davis believes that the diaries as "literary pieces" have "little merit," they "are rich in historical value, indicating, when taken chronologically, the development of the colony from frontier fears to sophisticated political arguments in an established society, a nation in embryo'' (pp. 160–61). Of the four prose narratives, especially *The History* and *The Secret History*, Davis says: "Taken together, or as a unit, this is the first classic work by a native southern American" (p. 167). Davis traces the evolution of these works carefully and presents a balanced, informed view of the "Public Writings." Robert Bain surveys the life and work in *The History of Southern Literature* (1985).

Other essays or chapters in books that shed light on Byrd as a writer include Lewis P. Simpson's discussion in *The Dispossessed Garden: Pastoral and History in Southern Literature* (1975). Examining the impact of Negro slavery in the South, Simpson notes that "in the context of the adaptation of the pastoral convention in America, William Byrd of Westover is the full-fledged embodiment of a singular figure in America and, you might say, in Western literature: the patriarch-philosophe—the slave master and man of letters—of the Southern plantation world. He forecasts a greater and more intricate embodiment of this figure in Thomas Jefferson of Monticello" (p. 24). Simpson believes that Byrd and Jefferson illustrate a peculiarly Southern association of the life of the mind with chattel slavery, a fact that would increasingly alienate the Southern writers in the antebellum period. This alienation, caused by the need to defend slavery, would ultimately fail, but it would, Simpson believes, account for a resurgence of literary activity following the Civil War.

In his chapters on Byrd in *Prophetic Waters: The River in Early American Life and Literature* (1977), John Seelye views the Dividing Line histories as a "literary epitome of the Cavalier spirit" that characterizes the "mixture of gaiety and greed" typical of the "Virginian enterprise from the beginning" (p. 364). Seelye argues that the two histories

as an organic whole give literary shape to the essential dichotomy of the Virginian adventure, accommodating paradisiac myth as well as the picaresque reality. Imposing an imperial—indeed, literal—line upon the land, Byrd's twin testaments provide a heroic and a satiric complement to [Robert] Beverley's *History*, an aesthetic kinship carrying colonial enterprise beyond the falls. As the disjunctive dimension of Beverley's book is the difference between the wise and foolish Virginians, so Byrd's narrative twins project that dichotomy into a further range, drawing a line not only between Virginia and North Carolina, but between two ways of life. (p. 365)

The two ways of life, says Seelye, involve the issue of "law and order versus misrule" (p. 366), and Byrd in the character of Steddy in *The Secret History* stands for order, enterprise, and for faithfully fulfillng his commission in " 'His Majesty's Service' " (p. 367). Unlike the picaresque journey of *The Secret History*, *The History* is for Seelye a book that "promotes an epical elevation and size"(p. 374). The epic of *The History* is that of empire building.

Another useful chapter is that by Kenneth S. Lynn in *Mark Twain and South-*

western Humor (1959, repr. 1972). In "The Style of a Gentleman," Lynn contrasts the style of *The Secret History*—which he calls a "blunt jerky style, with a tough, unfooled directness that seems unmistakably American" (p. 16)— with the gentlemanly style of *The History*. Lynn argues, "From William Byrd to the Civil War, the humorists of the Southwestern tradition by and large remained loyal to the Southern myth, and to the image of themselves as gentlemen. Style was the principal means by which they defined that image, fleshed out their myth, gave the ring of authenticity to fantasy" (p. 18). Lynn finds *The Secret History*—with its cruelty, violence, and absence of "gentlemanly circumlocutions" (p. 16)—much more akin to Southwestern humor of the post– Civil War period than *The History*, whose style held sway among those humorists before the War.

Background studies that illuminate Byrd's literary training include Carl L. Cannon's "William Byrd II of Westover" (1938), a discussion of Byrd's reading and library. In *The American Colonial Mind and the Classical Tradition* (1963) and in "Byrd and Sewall: Two Colonial Classicists" (1975), Richard M. Gummere discusses Byrd's formidable classical learning, speculating that he was perhaps the best classicist in early America. And in "William Byrd II: Comic Dramatist?" (1971), Carl R. Dolmetsch proposes that Byrd collaborated with Colley Cibber on *The Careless Husband*. Though Dolmetsch admits that his evidence is inconclusive, he documents Byrd's lifelong interest in the drama.

Studies focusing on Byrd as writer include Edd Winfield Parks's "William Byrd as Man of Letters" (1960), which, though brief, stresses his careful preparation of his manuscripts. In "William Byrd: Satirist" (1947), Willie T. Weathers discusses the early verses and "The Female Creed," along with the later writings, to show how Byrd matured as a satirist because he worked from a conscious literary theory and was a conscious artist. Percy G. Adams's introduction, cited above, notes that the two histories, though different in language and tone, really "are complementary." He writes, "Where one gains in spontaneity, the other gains in detail. Where one may be impetuous in certain judgments or unfair in its attempt at sarcasm, the other may be the result of greater deliberation and a desire for more thoroughness. Taken together they reveal many sides of their author as well as many attitudes to life on the old frontier of Southern America" (pp. xiv-xv). Adams also links some of Byrd's outrageous anecdotes in *The History* with the tradition of the tall tale.

More recent criticism, tending to question or qualify observations by Marambaud and Richard Beale Davis, has looked at the artfulness of Byrd's work and has examined the psychological complexities of Byrd as author. In "Westover and the Wilderness: William Byrd's Images of Virginia" (1975), Robert D. Arner examines the imagery of the two histories and concludes, "Guided by Virgil, Horace, and the Bible, he has created an image of Westover which performs the vital psychological function of reconciling him to his misfortunes, chief among which at this point in his career is his financially enforced exile in the 'silent Country' of Virginia" (p. 108). Arner argues that Byrd's artistic achievement is to "fuse inextricably" literary forms he had inherited from his time (p. 116). For Arner, Byrd is the first Southern writer "to bring the pastoral, the epic, and the romance forcefully to bear upon the Old Dominion in an effort to establish its positive ties with the civilized and cultivated world of England, and to give Virginians the welcome shelter of a family tree in the Old World" (p. 123). Like some earlier commentators, Kenneth A. Requa—in *The Westering Experience in American Literature* (1977)—sees the central tension in the two histories coming from Byrd's fear of wildness and his rage for order. Believing Byrd's "conscious world" to be "England" (p. 62), Requa notes, "Fundamental in both accounts is his conviction that the West was a disordered wilderness, an uncultivated land that challenged the cultured Virginian to maintain at least his own order and perhaps like God himself to create order in so chaotic a landscape" (p. 59).

Two recent articles perhaps indicate the direction Byrd scholarship may take in the next few years. In "William Byrd's *Histories of the Line*: The Fashioning of a Hero" (1976), Donald T. Siebert, Jr., plumbs the psychological complexities of Byrd to speculate on his need to create a self in the prose. Comparing Byrd's career with that of Sir William Temple, Siebert discovers in Byrd's character not the self-assured gentleman and artist, but a man "with passions not always under control" and bedeviled "with fears and self-doubts, a man *struggling* to fashion himself in his own ideal image" (p. 536, Siebert's italics). Though Siebert admires Byrd's artful histories, he argues that "Byrd is not entirely successful in reaching this state of grace, grace by the fiat of *sprezzatura*. Wit is piled too high; it is everywhere; it begins to sound more like the expression of desperation than of confidence" (p. 541). Siebert believes that the William Byrd of "Inamorato L'Oiseaux" was trying to become the "Steddy" of *The Secret History* and the even more decorous narrator of *The History*, but the last two characters are simply assumed identities, not the real William Byrd (pp. 549–50). Finally, both the man and the works of art are flawed, but worthy, creations.

Ross Pudaloff, in " 'A Certain Amount of Excellent English': The Secret Diaries of William Byrd" (1982), argues that the diaries "are both the genesis and the product of his transformation of a conflict-ridden world to one determined and defined by the authority of the word" (p. 102). Instead of seeing the diaries as presenting a history of plantation Virginia or as routine and banal, Pudaloff believes that for Byrd,

the primary vocation of the American was to be a writer. In the order inherent in the idea of grammar, Byrd found a structuring principle for the self and the world. As the composer of "a certain amount of excellent English," he found in writing, as a writer and as an American, a way to impose a grammar of relationships and value upon worlds which might otherwise prove rebellious and chaotic. Writing is the origin and equivalent of civilizing the natural world; ultimately the perception (i.e., creation) of the American West and the American future is the issue here. (p. 110)

For Pudaloff, the diaries gave Byrd a way to control self and world.

Whatever direction future criticism takes, Byrd's works will continue to delight readers, casual and critical.

BIBLIOGRAPHY

Works by William Byrd of Westover

"An Account of a Negro Boy That Is Dappled in Several Places on His Body with White Spots." *Philosophical Transactions* 19 (London 1698): 781–82.

Verses by "Mr. Burrard." *Tunbrigalia: or, Tunbridge Miscellanies, for the Year 1719.* London, 1719. Repr. *Another Secret Diary*, pp. 403–9.

A Discourse Concerning the Plague, with Some Preservatives Against It. By a Lover of Mankind. London, 1721. Repr. *Another Secret Diary*, pp. 417–43.

Neu-gefundenes Eden, by "Wilhelm Vogel." Berne, Switzerland, 1737. Trans. Richard Croom Beatty and W. J. Malloy as *William Byrd's Natural History of Virginia* (1940), but mainly a collection of observations from John Lawson's *A New Voyage to Carolina* (1709) and other sources.

The Westover MSS: Containing the History of the Dividing Line Betwixt Virginia and North Carolina; A Journey to the Land of Eden, A.D. 1733; and A Progress to the Mines. Written from 1728 to 1736 and Now First Published. Ed. Edmund Ruffin. Petersburg, Va., 1841.

History of the Dividing Line and Other Tracts, from the Papers of William Byrd of Westover in Virginia. 2 vols. Ed. Thomas H. Wynne. Richmond: [Albany, N.Y.: J. Mumsell, 1866].

The Writings of "Colonel William Byrd of Westover in Virginia, Esquire." Ed. John S. Bassett. New York: Doubleday, 1901. Repr. New York: Burt Franklin, 1970.

William Byrd, Esq., Accounts as Solicitor General of the Colonies and Receiver of Tobacco Tax 1688–1704 . . . Letters Writ to Facetia by Veramour. Ed. Thomas F. Ryan. Baltimore: Privately Printed, 1913.

Description of the Dismal Swamp and a Proposal to Drain the Swamp, by William Byrd of Westover. Ed. Earl G. Swem. Metuchen, N.J.: Printed for C. F. Heartman, 1922.

A Journey to the Land of Eden, and Other Papers by William Byrd. Ed. Mark Van Doren. New York: Macy-Masius, 1928. Includes *The History* and *A Progress*.

William Byrd's Histories of the Dividing Line Betwixt Virginia and North Carolina. Ed. William K. Boyd. Raleigh: North Carolina Historical Commission, 1929. Repr. with new introduction by Percy G. Adams. New York: Dover, 1967.

The Secret Diary of William Byrd of Westover, 1709–1712. Ed. Louis B. Wright and Marion Tinling. Richmond: Dietz Press, 1941, abr. New York: Capricorn Books, 1963, as *The Great American Gentleman: William Byrd of Westover in Virginia, His Secret Diary for the Years 1709–1712.*

Another Secret Diary of William Byrd of Westover, 1739–1741, with Letters and Literary Exercises, 1696–1726. Ed. Maude H. Woodfin and Marion Tinling. Richmond, Dietz Press, 1942.

The London Diary (1717–1721) and Other Writings. Ed. Louis B. Wright and Marion Tinling. New York: Oxford University Press, 1958.

The Prose Works of William Byrd of Westover. Ed. Louis B. Wright. Cambridge: Harvard University Press, 1966.

The Correspondence of the Three William Byrds of Westover, Virginia, 1684–1766. 2 vols. Ed. Marion Tinling. Charlottesville: University Press of Virginia, 1977.

Studies of William Byrd of Westover

Adams, Percy G. "The Real Author of William Byrd's *Natural History of Virginia.*" *American Literature* 28 (1956): 211–20.

Arner, Robert D. "Westover and the Wilderness: William Byrd's Images of Virginia." *Southern Literary Journal* 7 (1975): 105–23.

Bain, Robert. "William Byrd of Westover." *The History of Southern Literature*. Ed. Louis D. Rubin, Jr., et al. Baton Rouge: Louisiana State University Press, 1985, pp. 48–56.

Beatty, Richmond Croom. *William Byrd of Westover*. Boston: Houghton Mifflin, 1932.

Cannon, Carl L. "William Byrd II of Westover." *Colophon* n.s. 3 (1938): 219–302.

Cutting, Rose Marie. *John and William Bartram, William Byrd II, and St. John de Crevecoeur: A Reference Guide*. Boston: G. K. Hall, 1976, pp. 73–105.

Davis, Richard Beale. *American Literature through Bryant, 1585–1830*. New York: Appleton-Century-Crofts, 1969, pp. 24–25.

———. "William Byrd: Taste and Tolerance."*Major Writers of Early America*. Ed. Everett Emerson. Madison: University of Wisconsin Press, 1972, pp. 151–77.

Dolmetsch, Carl B. "William Byrd II: Comic Dramatist?" *Early American Literature* 6 (1971): 18–30.

Gummere, Richard M. "Byrd and Sewall: Two Colonial Classicists." *Transactions of the Colonial Society of Massachusetts* 42 (1975): 156–73.

———. *The American Colonial Mind and the Classical Tradition*. Cambridge: Harvard University Press, 1963.

Hatch, Alden. *The Byrds of Virginia: An American Dynasty, 1670 to the Present*. New York: Holt, Rinehart and Winston, 1969, pp. 55–175.

Hubbell, Jay B. *The South in American Literature, 1607–1900*. Durham, N.C.: Duke University Press, 1954, pp. 40–51, 919–21.

Lynn, Kenneth S. "The Style of a Gentleman." *Mark Twain and Southwestern Humor*. Boston: Little, Brown, 1959, pp. 3–22. Repr. Westport, Conn.: Greenwood Press, 1972.

Marambaud, Pierre. *William Byrd of Westover, 1674–1744*. Charlottesville: University Press of Virginia, 1971.

Parks, Edd Winfield. "William Byrd as Man of Letters." *Georgia Review* 14 (1960): 172–76.

Pudaloff, Ross. " 'A Certain Amount of Excellent English': The Secret Diaries of William Byrd." *Southern Literary Journal* 15 (1982): 101–19.

Requa, Kenneth A. " ' As Far as the South Seas': The Dividing Line and the West in William Byrd's Histories." *The Westering Experience in American Literature*. Ed. Merrill Lewis and L. L. Lee. Bellingham: Western Washington University, 1977, pp. 59–68.

Seelye, John. *Prophetic Waters: The River in Early American Life and Literature*. New York: Oxford University Press, 1977, pp. 363–81.

Siebert, Donald T., Jr. "William Byrd's *Histories of the Line*: The Fashioning of a Hero." *American Literature* 47 (1976): 535–51.

Simpson, Lewis P. *The Dispossessed Garden: Pastoral and History in Southern Literature*. Athens: University of Georgia Press, 1975, pp. 14–33.

Weathers, Willie T. "William Byrd: Satirist." *William and Mary Quarterly* 3d ser. 4 (1947): 27–41.

Wright, Louis B. "William Byrd: Citizen of the Enlightenment." *Anglo-American Cultural Relations in the Seventeenth and Eighteenth Centuries*. Ed. Leon Howard and Louis B. Wright. Los Angeles: William Andrews Clark Memorial Library, 1960, pp. 26–40.

———. "William Byrd II." *The First Gentlemen of Virginia: Intellectual Qualities of the Early Colonial Ruling Class*. San Marino, Calif.: Huntington Library, 1940, pp. 312–47. Repr. Charlottesville: University Press of Virginia, 1964.

Yanella, Donald and John H. Roch. *American Prose to 1820: A Guide to Information Sources*. Detroit: Gale, 1979, pp. 223–28.

————— ROBERT O. STEPHENS —————

George Washington Cable
(1844–1925)

George Washington Cable's critical reputation is that of a New Orleans local colorist who early in his career expanded his vision to write stories and novels challenging the fundamental assumptions of the post–Civil War South, who expended his mid-career energies on the Negro Question and other reforms, and who late in his career wrote popular romances concerned more with individual morality than with public justice.

BIOGRAPHY

Born in New Orleans on 12 October 1844, Cable was the fifth of six children of George Washington and Rebecca Boardman Cable, who had moved to New Orleans from Indiana in 1837. His parentage reflected the divided loyalties later to be revealed in him. His father embodied a Virginia heritage dating from before the Revolutionary War and his mother a New England Puritan heritage from the seventeenth century.

Educated in New Orleans public schools and trained in his mother's Puritan ethic, Cable was nevertheless an enthusiastic observer of Creole life in the Southern city. His education was interrupted at fourteen when his father died after several business reverses, leaving young George as the chief support of his mother and sisters. After observing the fall and occupation of New Orleans, the Cables refused the loyalty oath and were banished from the city as registered enemies. Once in Mississippi, Cable joined the Confederate cavalry, fought in a number of skirmishes, was wounded, and after recovering, served on the headquarters staffs of Generals Wirt Adams and Nathan Bedford Forrest. In later years when his loyalties as a Southerner were questioned, he often pointed to his refusal to take the oath and to his military service as certificates of his right to criticize Southern culture from the inside.

Back home on parole, he worked briefly as a surveyor's apprentice, then served as accountant for a cotton factor and eventually as secretary of the New Orleans Cotton Exchange. In December 1869 he married Louisa Bartlett of New Orleans and, in addition to his business duties, began writing occasional pieces and later the "Drop Shot" column for the *Picayune*. By 1871 he was working full-time as reporter for the paper, but he later returned to work with the cotton factors and followed his literary interests when he agreed to write a series of historical sketches for the *Picayune* on "The Churches and Charities of New Orleans." While searching historical records, he saw the possibilities of fictional treatment of the old materials, began to write stories in the local color manner, and was discovered in 1873 by Edward King of Scribner's when King was traveling through the region in search of materials for his series on "The Great South."

Through King's encouragement and his recommendations to the Scribner editorial offices, Cable began his career-long, though not exclusive, association with Scribner's. During the next four years he published in *Scribner's Monthly* six of the seven stories later collected in *Old Creole Days* (1879) and profited by the suggestions of such Scribner editors as Richard Watson Gilder and Robert Underwood Johnson and later Roswell Smith. To these editors Cable owed much of the discipline he learned in managing his stories of picturesquely charming Creole characters and customs, told in a droll French-English dialect. To them he owed also much of the sentimentality that marks his stories written for popular, family-centered magazines. He also received important early encouragement and literary tutelage through a long correspondence with another Scribner author, H. H. Boyesen, then professor of Germanics at Cornell.

Cable followed his modest success in *Old Creole Days* with *The Grandissimes* (1880), his best work by most accounts and his best claim to continuing literary notice. *The Grandissimes* portrays the changes in an aristocratic Creole family, largely through the eyes of Joseph Frowenfeld, a recent Yankee immigrant, in 1803–4, a time when old Creole ways were being challenged by the flood of *Américains*. Besides such vivid Creoles as Agricola Fusilier, Raoul Innerarity, and Aurora Nancanou, the novel depicts such strong quadroons as Palmyre la Philosophe, the voodoo, and the colossal black rebel Bras-Coupé, whose resistance to slavery and whose destruction by the *Code Noir* becomes a paradigm for the treatment of blacks in the Old South. Cable said later that the novel had all the political implications one could find.

With the success of *The Grandissimes*, Cable committed himself to earning his living by his writing and when writing was not enough, through lectures and public readings. Part of the result of his Northern success, however, was a feeling by many Creoles that he had ridiculed them in his characterizations and dialect. Smoldering at first, this resentment later flared against Cable as he became an open champion of Negro rights. In 1881 he published *Madame Delphine*, a short novel later incorporated into the revised edition of *Old Creole Days* (1883). *Madame Delphine* tells of a quadroon mother who falsifies the parentage of her daughter so the young woman can marry a Creole husband, contrary to the laws against interracial marriage. Père Jerome, who absolves the dying mother in the confessional, clearly does not absolve a society that makes such laws.

His informal history *The Creoles of Louisiana* (1884) was written, at least partly, to show that his fictional treatment of Creoles was based on historical record. But the Creoles, as he had noted earlier, never forgave "a public mention."

To supplement his income from writing, Cable agreed with Mark Twain to tour American and Canadian cities from November 1884 to February 1885, during which time they read from their most popular pieces. Cable sang Creole songs, and both joked with their audiences to increasing acclaim. By the mid–1880s Cable, a small man (never more than five foot five) with courtly manners, enjoyed a literary and public reputation comparable to that of Mark Twain, Howells, and James.

But while his stature as a public spokesman for reform increased, his literary productivity and acclaim diminished. Out of his work for prison and asylum reform he produced his next novel, *Dr. Sevier* (1884). It is the story of John and Mary Richling, who experience the poverty of pre–Civil War New Orleans and the friendship of honest but caustic Dr. Sevier, who knows too well the city's failure to reform its parish prisons or to protect itself against yellow fever. Because picturesque Creoles figured only incidentally in the novel, it failed to attract Cable's usual audience. His zeal for including reformist ideas in *Dr. Sevier*, and later *John March, Southerner*, led to temporary alienations from his editors at Scribner's. The climax of Cable's advocacy to Negro rights came in 1884 with his address to the American Social Science Association and his publication in *Century Magazine* (1885) of "The Freedman's Case in Equity," an appeal to the South and the nation to provide full rights of citizenship to Negroes. The essay prompted a storm of protest from most Southern editors and politicians, made him persona non grata among many former friends, and confirmed his decision in summer 1885 to move from New Orleans to Simsbury, Connecticut, and later to Northampton, Massachusetts, his home for the remainder of his life. That same year he published *The Silent South*, his call to Southerners to rescue their literature, education, and politics from provincialism and the limitations of pre–Civil War thought.

Bonaventure (1888), a lyrical but sentimentalized depiction of Acadians, and *Strange True Stories of Louisiana* (1889), a retelling of stories Cable found during his later visits to the state, were minor efforts while he labored over *John March, Southerner* (1894), his last novel to confront seriously the problems of the New South. Set in the state of Dixie (Georgia was his model), the novel depicts the struggle of young John March to conquer his inner weaknesses as well as to survive the external dangers of rapacious businessmen and corrupt politicians before he can become a true leader for the reviving South.

But with the enactment of segregation and other Jim Crow laws in most Southern states by 1890, Cable knew that the freedman's cause was lost, at least in his time, and he began to turn his energies to other reforms. Reflecting his own shift from doctrinaire religion to ethical humanitarian efforts, he helped organize the Home Culture Clubs in 1886. Begun as Bible study groups, these clubs developed first into home study, and then group study, units dedicated to reform through education. The literary outcome for Cable was his compilation of *The Busy Man's Bible* (1891), a slim volume on how to study and teach the Bible. In a more practical way, his work with the Home Culture Clubs prompted his acquaintance with the philanthropist Andrew Carnegie and resulted in Carnegie's gifts of libraries or library funds to Northampton and several other cities.

Although his literary popularity had waned, Scribner produced the five-volume Tarryawhile Edition of Cable's fiction in 1898. The renewed relationship, after estrangement during Cable's work on *John March, Southerner*, coincided with his turn to popular romances centered on the inner moral struggles of characters in exotic or historical situations—the primary characteristics of his late work. In 1899 Scribner published his *Strong Hearts*, a collection of stories with heroes struggling for goodness in the morally ambiguous world of New Orleans. Central to several of those late works was his presiding narrator Richard Thorndyke Smith, a character much like Cable himself. In *The Cavalier* (1901), a best-selling work, Smith is a Confederate cavalryman involved in the romance of Confederate double agent Charlotte Oliver and heroic cavalry scout Ned Ferry. In *Kincaid's Battery* (1908), Smith is a peripheral figure in the struggles of Confederate artillerist Hilary Kincaid to fight an honorable war, with battle accounts of Shiloh, New Orleans, Vicksburg, and Mobile rendered through the reconciling haze of more than 40 years. *Gideon's Band* (1914) returns to the pre–Civil War period to chronicle the voyage of the Mississippi River steamboat *Votaress*, complicated by a cholera outbreak on board and a Romeo-Juliet love affair of Ramsay Hale and Hugh Courtney separated by their feuding families of steamboat owners. *Bylow Hill* (1902), however, was a grim and somewhat sentimentalized account of a New England minister's moral disintegration prompted by sexual jealousy.

Cable's wife Louise died after an operation in 1904, and with his family grown and scattered, he married Eva C. Stevenson of Kentucky. During their marriage (1906–23) they traveled frequently, including trips to New Orleans, where Cable found he had not only been forgiven by the Creoles but was welcomed as a local hero. His literary work during the period, however, was painfully slow and showed a fatigued creativity. *The Flower of the Chapdelaines* and *Lovers of Louisiana* (both 1918) were set in New Orleans and reused old materials in stories of runaway slaves and temperamental differences between Creole and Anglo families.

After Eva died and Cable married a third time, he passed into old age, inactivity, and sickness and died in St. Petersburg, Florida, on 31 January 1925—a man and author who had survived to a time strange to his genteel values.

MAJOR THEMES

Cable's principal place in literary memory is that of chronicler of New Orleans places and people and as recorder of the Creole-English patois of his settings. To many late nineteenth-century readers, his version of New Orleans was the only one, and travelers came to the city with his stories in hand as enriched guides to the French Quarter. When Mark Twain and Joel Chandler Harris visited New Orleans, they, like other distinguished visitors, depended on Cable to show them the city through his eyes.

Yet what made his stories more than tales of quaint manners was his concern for private morality and public justice. Both were involved in his career-long exploration of black slavery and its repercussions on freedmen and their former masters.

Cable's concern with private morality came directly from the New Testament ethic he learned as a youth. Despite his doctrine-dominated Presbyterianism, he took quite literally the biblical injunctions to strive for personal goodness and considered such teachings personal imperatives. Throughout much of his adult life he taught Bible classes, whether in New Orleans or Northampton, and commonly used biblical allusions in his fiction and his polemical writings. His integration of personal conduct and feeling with biblical imperatives appeared in his address to a meeting of New Orleans teachers on implications of the Negro Question: "Now, I did not myself feel a brother love for the South's Samaritan, but I believed it my duty not to wait for that belated feeling, but to act as if I had it" ("My Politics," *The Negro Question*. Ed. Turner, p. 16). And when he observed the expedient morality of Southern leaders after the Civil War, he insisted that "no course of action could be practical unless it was founded in morality and justice" (*The Negro Question*, p. xii).

That concern for practical, individual morality marked his fiction from the first. The stories of *Old Creole Days* show characters in his newly exotic setting of New Orleans coming at last to a moral stance, often in contrast to their earlier shortcomings and crimes. In "Jean-ah Poquelin," old Jean redeems his past as smuggler and slave runner by looking after his younger brother Jacques, a leper, after their last slave voyage. Considered a warlock and the embodiment of evil by the local citizenry, Jean protects his brother until his own death, and as Jacques and their mute African slave carry his body into the wilderness and go on to leperland, his worth is stated by Little White to the watching group of self-righteous neighbors: "Hats off, gentlemen, . . . here come the last remains of Jean Marie Poquelin, a better man, I'm afraid, with all his sins,—yes a better—a kinder man to his blood—a man of more self-forgetful goodness—than all of you put together will ever dare to be." That same concern for personal morality runs throughout *Dr. Sevier* as the New Orleans physician, through the sufferings of John and Mary Richling, learns that individual goodness must be realized by helping the poor and reforming the asylums and prisons into which they too often fall. And in *Madame Delphine* Cable is careful to note that the secret to good Père Jerome's preaching was that "he took more thought as to how he should feel, than as to what he should say."

But it was even more the connection between private conduct and public justice that concerned Cable, and that concern was focused on the Negro Question. As he recounted it in "My Politics," his discovery of the full impact of the issue came while he was researching the colonial history of Louisiana in the city archives and came across the old *Code Noir* for the treatment of slaves. From that point on, he became aware of the implications of slavery upon the morality of the slaveholders, both those who held them before the war and those whose mentality had been shaped by that experience. That outrage at the *Code Noir* prompted him to write "Bibi" (1871), the story of a rebellious New Orleans slave destroyed by the code. That episode, retold as "The Story of Bras-Coupé," became the moral paradigm at the center of *The Grandissimes* (1879–80). The similar story of Phyllis in his late novel *Gideon's Band* (1914) indicated his continued interest in the relationship between individual morality and public justice. Just as the story of Bras-Coupé causes Honoré Grandissime to reconsider his Creole convictions and serves as the cause of enmity between the Grandissimes and Nancanous, the story of Phyllis prompts the aristocratic Creole Madame Hayle to become an abolitionist and explains the differences between the feuding Hayles and Courtneys, owners of rival steamboat fleets.

Although treatment of the Negro might be a matter of personal ethics on the one hand and of political morality on the other, in Cable's fiction it was typically presented as a question of manners. In "My Politics," despite his assertion that literature meant to him "belles-lettres, not essays whether political or other," he presented the argument that informed most of his fictional treatment of manners:

What our fathers called their "peculiar institution" tended, when it was in force, to promote in us a certain spirit of command—of dictation—that made our wills seem to us nearly or quite as authoritative as the laws, and sometimes more so. We were a race of masters. We were dictators. The main thing to be kept in sight was the discipline of the plantation. Hence a most lamentable laxness of parental discipline; a similar laxness of that defensive discipline by which society lays down its conditions of membership; and springing distinctly from these deficiencies, a group of outrageous vices: shameless hard drinking, the carrying of murderous weapons, murder, too, and lynching at its heels, the turning of state and county prisons into slavepens, the falsification of the ballot, night riding and whipping, and all the milder forms of political intolerance. (*The Negro Question*, p. 22)

His depictions of proud Southerners, Creole and Anglo—from Colonel De Charleu in "Belles Demoiselles Plantation" to Agricola Fusilier and his fellow Grandissimes, Brahmins, and Mandarins to the Hayle twins in *Gideon's Band*— all illustrate that thematic code of manners.

In *Madam Delphine* (1881), written in light of the Compromise of 1877, Cable developed another part of the theme—the complicity of the entire nation in acquiescing to the abandonment of the Negro. The story poses an indictment of society for its failure to ''fix dat law'' prohibiting interracial marriage. When Madame Delphine dies in the confessional after admitting her perjury, Père Jerome's prayer that the Lord lay not that sin to her account clearly indicates that it should be laid to society's account, and he charges his parishioners with Saul's sin of standing by and consenting to the denial of the freedman's rights and humanity. That became Cable's explicit theme in his controversial essay ''The Freedman's Case in Equity'' (1884).

As he extended his advocacy of the freedman's cause in the 1880s, Cable began to express his doubts about the New South movement. Not only did he see the New South advocates as deficient in their doctrine of racial inequality but also in their reckless drive to develop industry and exploit the region's natural resources. In *John March, Southerner* (1894) he attempted to present in fictional form what he had said in polemical writings during the decade before. Through the experience of John March, he confronted the pieties and deceptions of New South leaders who professed loyalty to the public good and to progress while making self-serving deals for their own private fortunes. In March's encounters with Reverend Garnett, ex-Confederate major, war hero, and president of Rosemont College, he showed a symptomatic New South leader who professed religion while making dubious deals for use of public monies, abusing his family, and betraying his friends. And in Jeff-Jack Ravenel he saw a typical Southern editor who, though personally honest, acquiesced in praising activities he knew to be corrupt.

In his address to the graduating class at the University of Mississippi (1882) and later in his essay ''Literature in the Southern States,'' Cable began to call for a renaissance of Southern culture on the principles of equality found in the Declaration of Independence—pointedly, not the Constitution. Saying ''You know how large a part of the governing of a people consists in the directing of its thought,'' he called on Southerners to rejoin the mainstream of American and modern thought and, in effect, to be Americans rather than Southerners: ''When we have done so we shall know it by this—there will be no more South. . . . [The New South] is a term only fit to indicate a transitory condition. What we want—what we ought to have in view—is the No South!'' (*The Negro Question*, p. 47).

With the failure of the freedman's cause by the early 1890s and the confirmation of the region's commitment to the New South program, Cable gave up controversial public issues and developed less debatable interests such as the Home Culture Clubs and his amateur gardening campaign. In his fiction he wrote historical romances, such as *The Cavalier* and *Kincaid's Battery*, whose heroes struggled with the fine points of honor and rectitude as they participated in events of the Civil War. Typical of the thought in these romances is Richard Thorndyke Smith's observation in *The Cavalier* as he talks with Lieutenant Ned Ferry and Charlotte Oliver about the conflict between their love and duty in time of war:

" . . . no two persons, and above all no one man and one woman, can ever be sure of their duty, or even of their happiness, till they consider at least one third person. . . . " Notable also in his late fiction was a recurring theme of sexual jealousy, particularly in "The Entomologist" (*Strong Hearts*) and *Bylow Hill*. But for all his late probing of psychological states and delicate social situations, Cable failed to demonstrate the self-knowledge of Jamesian characters or the power of analysis exhibited in his earlier work. As Louis D. Rubin, Jr., has provocatively surmised, for Cable the energy and astuteness involved in addressing external injustices may have been a way of avoiding looking within himself (Rubin, p. 150).

SURVEY OF CRITICISM

By any reckoning, Arlin Turner was the dominant figure in Cable studies from the late 1940s until his death in 1980. His thoroughly documented and readable *George W. Cable: A Biography* (1956) is the definitive biographical study. Later critical biographers such as Philip Butcher (1962) and Louis D. Rubin, Jr., (1969) have largely followed Turner's factual data while providing critical interpretations of the works based on biographical readings. In addition to the biography, Turner wrote his account of the Boyesen-Cable correspondence in "A Novelist Discovers a Novelist" (1951), still useful for critical insights; *Mark Twain and George W. Cable: The Record of a Literary Friendship* (1960), based on Cable's letters to his wife and Twain's letters to J. B. Pond, their manager during their celebrated lecture tour; *George W. Cable* (1969), a summary of biography and criticism; and edited *Critical Essays on George W. Cable* (1980) with an introduction tracing the development of scholarship on Cable.

The two best critical biographies are Philip Butcher, *George W. Cable* (1962), a Twayne U.S. Authors study, and Louis D. Rubin, Jr., *George W. Cable: The Life and Times of a Southern Heretic* (1969). Both take a more critical view of Cable's mind and character than Turner does. Butcher's view is that Cable's public persona was often at variance with his deeper instincts, sometimes insidious, and the discrepancy led him into flawed performances. Rubin sees Cable captured by his public roles and finally unable to achieve the true self-knowledge necessary for a novelist in the company of Henry James. Both provide insightful readings of the major works in light of Cable's biography. Earlier and uncritical memoirs are those by his daughters Lucy Leffingwell Cable Biklé, *George W. Cable: His Life and Letters* (1928), which includes material later reused by Turner, and Mary Cable Dennis, *The Tail of the Comet* (1937), a tribute to her father and her husband. Griffith Thompson Pugh's *George Washington Cable* (1947) provides an early, pre-Turner view of Cable's life and work.

Kjell Ekström's *George Washington Cable: A Study of His Early Life and Work* (1950), though limited to Cable's treatment of the Creoles and their reactions to his work, is based on manuscript materials and provides useful reprintings of those sources. Philip Butcher's *George W. Cable: The Northampton*

Years (1959) also provides access to new source materials, some biased by informants involved in controversies of Cable's later career. Guy A. Cardwell's *Twins of Genius* (1953) is a specialized study of the Cable and Twain relationship from 1881 to 1906.

Turner's biography in 1956 was the occasion for Edmund Wilson to reread Cable's works and to write his reassessment, "The Ordeal of George Washington Cable," for the *New Yorker* (1957). Wilson pointed out the unexpected richness and complexity of Cable's work even as he found him shaped by his editors to fit genteel tastes. Wilson's reappraisal, Turner's biography, and the availability of Cable's works in reprint helped stimulate new interest in Cable by the late 1950s, and the following two decades saw a resurgence in critical notice of Cable's works, especially *The Grandissimes*. That development was the background for *Southern Quarterly*'s special issue on *The Grandissimes* in summer 1980, marking the centennial of its publication. Thomas J. Richardson, ed., *The Grandissimes: Centennial Essays* (1981) reprinted the essays of the special issue and provided an annotated bibliography of criticism on the novel—now a marking point for those who propose further studies of the work.

William H. Roberson's *George Washington Cable: An Annotated Bibliography* (1982) is likely to be a sine qua non for further serious study of Cable. Its notation of printing editions and bibliographical variations as well as its coverage of criticism should provide tools for a new generation of post-Turner researchers.

Most needed now to maintain interest in Cable studies are inexpensive reprints of his works for use as texts. The correlation between their availability and critical interpretation of them has been a notable phenomenon over the last two decades.

BIBLIOGRAPHY

Works by George Washington Cable

Old Creole Days. New York: Scribner, 1879; 1883 edition and since enlarged by the addition of "Madame Delphine."
The Grandissimes: A Story of Creole Life. New York: Scribner, 1880; revised 1884.
Madame Delphine. New York: Scribner, 1881.
The Creoles of Louisiana. New York: Scribner, 1884.
Dr. Sevier. Boston: J. R. Osgood, 1884. New York: Scribner, thereafter.
The Silent South. New York: Scribner, 1885.
Bonaventure: A Prose Pastoral of Acadian Louisiana. New York: Scribner, 1888.
Strange True Stories of Louisiana. New York: Scribner, 1889.
The Negro Question. New York: Scribner, 1890.
The Busy Man's Bible. Meadville, Pa.: Chautauqua-Century Press, 1891.
A Memory of Roswell Smith. New York: DeVinne Press, 1892.
John March, Southerner. New York: Scribner, 1894.
Strong Hearts. New York: Scribner, 1899.
The Cavalier. New York: Scribner, 1901.

Bylow Hill. New York: Scribner, 1902.
Kincaid's Battery. New York: Scribner, 1908.
Posson Jone' and Père Raphaël. New York: Scribner, 1909.
The Amateur Garden. New York: Scribner, 1914.
Gideon's Band: A Tale of the Mississippi. New York: Scribner, 1914.
The Flower of the Chapdelaines. New York: Scribner, 1918.
Lovers of Louisiana. New York: Scribner, 1918.

Cable also published a vast number of newspaper and magazine items, pamphlets, and occasional pieces, for which see Arlin Turner, *George W. Cable: A Biography*, or William H. Roberson, *George Washington Cable: An Annotated Bibliography*.

Collections

The Negro Question: A Selection of Writings on Civil Rights in The South by George W. Cable. Ed. Arlin Turner. Garden City, N.Y.: Doubleday, 1958. Includes "My Politics," not published during Cable's lifetime.
Creoles and Cajuns; Stories of Old Louisiana. Ed. Arlin Turner. New York: Doubleday, 1959.
The Silent South. Ed. Arlin Turner. Montclair, N.J.: Patterson Smith, 1969.
Collected Works. Ed. with introd. and notes by Arlin Turner. 6 vols. American Author Series. New York: Garrett Press, 1970.

Studies of George Washington Cable

Biklé, Lucy Leffingwell (Cable). *George W. Cable: His Life and Letters*. New York: Scribner, 1928. Repr. New York: Russell and Russell, 1967.
Butcher, Philip. *George W. Cable*. New York: Twayne, 1962. Repr. New Haven: College and University Press, 1964.
―――. *George W. Cable: The Northampton Years*. New York: Columbia University Press, 1959.
Cardwell, Guy A. *Twins of Genius*. East Lansing: Michigan State University Press, 1953.
Dennis, Mary Cable. *The Tail of the Comet*. New York: E. P. Dutton, 1937.
Ekström, Kjell. *George Washington Cable: A Study of His Early Life and Work*. Cambridge: Harvard University Press, 1950.
Pugh, Griffith Thompson. *George Washington Cable: A Biographical and Critical Study*. Nashville: Joint Universities Library, 1947.
Richardson, Thomas J., ed. *The Grandissimes: Centennial Essays*. Jackson: University Press of Mississippi, 1981.
Roberson, William H. *George Washington Cable: An Annotated Bibliography*. Metuchen, N.J.: Scarecrow Press, 1982.
Rubin, Louis D., Jr. *George W. Cable: The Life and Times of a Southern Heretic*. New York: Pegasus, 1969.
Turner, Arlin. *George W. Cable*. Austin, Texas: Steck-Vaughan, 1969 (paper).
―――. *George W. Cable: A Biography*. Durham, N.C.: Duke University Press, 1956. Repr. Baton Rouge: Louisiana State University Press, 1966 (paper).
―――. *Mark Twain and George W. Cable: The Record of a Literary Friendship*. East Lansing: Michigan State University Press, 1960.

————. ''A Novelist Discovers a Novelist: The Correspondence of H. H. Boyesen and George W. Cable.'' *Western Humanities Review* 5 (Autumn 1951): 343–72.

————, ed. *Critical Essays on George W. Cable*. Boston: G. K. Hall, 1980.

Wilson, Edmund. ''The Ordeal of George Washington Cable.'' *New Yorker* 33 (9 November 1957); 180–228 passim. Repr. in *Patriotic Gore: Studies in the Literature of the American Civil War*. New York: Oxford University Press, 1962.

William Alexander Caruthers
(1802–1846)

William Alexander Caruthers was the first important novelist from Virginia and with William Gilmore Simms and John Pendleton Kennedy, one of the first important novelists of the South. He styled himself a "humble literatuer." In *American Literature, As an Expression of the National Mind* (1931), Russell Blankenship declared: "Dr. William A. Caruthers is probably today the most unjustly neglected novelist in our whole literary history. The South . . . has totally forgotten one of its most deserving sons."

BIOGRAPHY

William Alexander Caruthers was born in the village of Lexington, in western Virginia, on 23 December 1802, the second son and fourth child of a prosperous Rockbridge County merchant, William Caruthers and his wife Phebe Alexander. He attended local Washington College (now Washington and Lee University) during 1817–20 without graduating, and then took a degree in 1823 from one of the country's leading medical schools, the University of Pennsylvania. That same summer he married a Georgia girl he had met there, Louisa Catherine Gibson, daughter of an affluent Whitemarsh Island planter, the late Robert S. Gibson. The young couple settled in the groom's hometown and in due course produced three sons and two daughters.

At Lexington, Caruthers became a representative citizen. He belonged to both of the college's literary and debating societies and to the village Franklin Library Company as well. He practiced medicine (developing a "secret method of curing stammerers") and became a Master Mason. He dabbled in agriculture, purchased a pew in the Presbyterian church, and became active in the nascent Whig Party. He owned two properties, the larger just outside Lexington as his residence. His library grew to 150 volumes. He was named one of the dozen trustees of the town. Alas, all of these accomplishments were conducted without due attention to solvency. Although Louisa had inherited a handsome estate from her father, and William himself was benefiting from his share of the senior Caruthers's will, by late 1829 the Doctor was broke. Everything went under the auctioneer's hammer. In November that year he took his family north and settled in New York City.

Caruthers's five-and-a-half year residence there transformed a small-town squire into a professionally oriented man of affairs. For one thing, his sojourn embraced the terrible plague year of 1832 which, though it gave him matter to incorporate into his first novel, *The Kentuckian in New-York*, left him economically stricken. As his uncle by marriage, the Presbyterian minister Benjamin H. Rice, put it: "The cholera thro' which he labored faithfully, at the hourly risk of his life attending the poor and miserable not only brought him no profits, but so scattered those who employed him before that he gets less practice than formerly. I wish I could do more for him, but I cannot." The Doctor survived, however. Among other activities he was instrumental in selecting a new president for Washington College: the New York University mathematician Henry Vethake. He acted as middleman for sales of pig iron between the Manhattan firm of Byrnes, Trimble & Co. and the Lexington merchants Jordan & Irvine. He placed an article with the popular monthly *Knickerbocker Magazine* on the vogue of Italian music (he did not like it). He became friends with one of the country's better known authors, James Kirke Paulding, Navy Agent for the port of New York. As Caruthers some years later described their relationship, "Though we were politically opposed to each other, we had been personal & literary friends for years, used to meet together at the coteries of the Harpers—published books together &c—. . . . '' (A scanning of Paulding's work suggests as the likeliest single product of dual authorship his *Westward Ho!* [1832], the story of a Virginia planter and his family who pioneer into Kentucky.) And within the space of seven months the prestigious house of Harper released two two-volume novels by Caruthers that were, between them, so widely reviewed they caused his name, in the words of an unfavorable Boston critic, to be "liberally plastered by every McGrawler, from Maine to Mexico." These books were *The Kentuckian in New-York* (1834) and *The Cavaliers of Virginia* (1834–35).

Presumably, because of his straitened circumstances Caruthers left New York in spring 1835 and returned to Lexington with his family. There they probably remained—their whereabouts is unknown—until spring 1837. By that date they lived in a handsome residence in the bustling little port city of Savannah, Louisa's hometown. In this dwelling, at what is now the northwest corner of Hull and Whitaker streets, the Doctor lived the remaining nine years of his life.

In Georgia, Caruthers resumed a diversified career. He practiced medicine, joined the Georgia Medical Society, and served on the city's Board of Health. He lectured to the Temperance Society on the evils of alcohol and on "the art of living." He became a charter member of the Georgia Historical Society and lectured to it on "The History and Progress of Civilization with Regard to This

Country.'' He became active in Whig politics, took a seat on the Board of Aldermen, and involved himself with real estate. He sent off an article to the *Knickerbocker* about the first ascent of the Natural Bridge of Virginia; the essay winged away on a career of its own that saw manifestations until at least the year 1959. (For example, it is cited, without ascription, in Mitford M. Mathews's *A Dictionary of Americanisms on Historical Principles*, 1951.) During January-October 1841 he saw his last known romance, "The Knights of the Golden Horse-Shoe,'' through the press of a local monthly, the *Magnolia*, and then its publication in book form in Alabama in 1845. He served on the Board of Arbiters in a duel between two Savannah newspapermen. He converted from Presbyterianism to the Episcopal Church. He caught tuberculosis, died from it at a health resort in the mountains of Georgia on 26 August 1846, and is buried in an undiscovered grave at Marietta. He left no known likeness. Since he left an estate in the red, Louisa had to take in boarders.

MAJOR THEMES

William A. Caruthers was a novelist wholly committed to the Sentimental School. Before discussing his themes, let us take note of his literary practice. It was comprised of four main elements: employment of the Sentimental mode, incidental employment of its gothic aspect, a largely unvarying dramatis personae, and what might be termed "matrimonial" endings.

Caruthers's view of Romanticism is in the mainstream of English aesthetic tradition as enunciated by Wordsworth in the preface to the second edition of *Lyrical Ballads*. His view proclaims a sort of sublime common sense, the origins of which are a gift from God. It is a pietistic view that includes a psychological element: the "escapist" desire of the writer to create that archetypal Arcadia that once existed on earth as the Garden of Eden. Hence it is, affirmed Caruthers in "Excerpts from the Portfolio of an Old Novelist," that "a great writer of Romance is communicating in spirit with a whole world of ideal personages, and rousing up, like an enchanter, the dead heroes of a thousand Romances in real life." As the ablest examplar of such evocation his choice was Sir Walter Scott.

Concerning the gothic element, Caruthers deemed it no better than "a bastard romantic vein." He employed it in all of his novels but, as the mode for an entire book, condemned it out of hand. "Cervantes has, fortunately for common sense, gibbeted the whole class to the everlasting gaze and derisions of posterity." In his last two works, *The Cavaliers* and *The Knights*, Caruthers introduces a variation on the mode: "Indian Gothic." Although there is a good deal of gore, he did not belong to the Indian-hating, "yaller vermint" coterie. His perception of the animosity between white and red saw it as a grand, impressive drama but also a bitter, tragic drama for the losers. Though aware of the potential for viciousness in the aboriginals, he was also aware of their bravery and their endurance under suffering. In *The Cavaliers* the speech that Caruthers assigns to the Indian girl Wyanokee, in which she excoriates the white man's concept of justice, is the best prose Caruthers ever wrote.

In his cast of characters Caruthers's heroines—all of them—are petite, blonde, and blue-eyed. They and their successors in Southern fiction developed into that stereotype of the belle so nostalgically described by Thomas Nelson Page in his essay "Social Life in Virginia before the War" (1892). Each heroine has a girl chum with whom she is contrasted physically and temperamentally. Caruthers's heroes are—all of them—paragons, and hence inaccessible to analysis. As has been observed by Alexander Cowie of William Gilmore Simms's protagonists, these figures are simply "animated ideals." Each has a male friend who is even less individualized. Caruthers's two villains—strictly speaking, there is no villain in *The Kentuckian*—are about as black as his heroes are white. There is also a "westerner," a backwoods comic type, in both *The Cavaliers* and *The Knights*.

Caruthers's slave characters are likewise stratified. There are the butler, or house servant, and the handyman, or field laborer. They are preceded notably in American fiction only by those in James Fenimore Cooper's *The Spy* (1821), George Tucker's *The Valley of Shenandoah* (1824), and John Pendleton Kennedy's *Swallow Barn* (1832). Although Caruthers was one of the earliest American authors to perceive the literary value of Negro speech, his attempts at dialect—for the handyman; the butler speaks a language worthy of college sophomores—are not persuasive. Their names, however, reflect a firsthand acquaintance. At Lexington, he owned at least six slaves, whereas his wife, Louisa, had inherited no fewer than 79 from her father. Accordingly, Caruthers's names for his fictional blacks reflect both a Virginian and a sea-island background: Cato, Essex, Tombo, Congo. There was a slave named Bullutah belonging to Louisa whose name is probably a Mahometan derivative, and Caruthers's fascination with the African origin of the Negroes is manifest in both *The Kentuckian* and *The Knights*. In the former the slave Charno is credited with knowing the opening chapter of the Koran, which the novelist inserts in the original Arabic— a possibly unique instance in American fiction up to that time.

Perhaps because his own union with Louisa may be presumed to have been a happy one, Caruthers terminates all three of his romances with multiple marriages. Double weddings are the minimum, and triple weddings are preferred. With the so-called domestic novelists of the 1850s and 1860s, the nuptial scene would blossom into a treasured sine qua non.

His first known romance—one must bear in mind his claim that he had "published books together" with Paulding—*The Kentuckian in New-York*, stands as the earliest "intersectional" novel of any significance. Its South Carolina hero and his comrade take horse up to the big city; and their correspondence, along with that of their future fiancées, describes for stay-at-homes the many and diverse sights they encounter in the America of 1832. These include an almost guidebook-like account of Manhattan's landmarks, the falls of the Passaic River in New Jersey, the High Hills of Santee in South Carolina, and, in North Carolina, a poor-white area and the Moravian settlement in what is now Winston-Salem.

Along the way Caruthers instructs his reader in how to step to the Virginia reel, notes the "juba" dance of the Negroes, distinguishes between Tucks and Cohees (cited in William A. Craigie's *A Dictionary of American English on Historical Principles*, 1936), and confers the immortality of print upon Jesse Scott, that "coloured gentleman of Charlottesville, Virginia," who is supposed to have inherited Thomas Jefferson's violin.

Here, in sum, was a pleasant little story of four young people flirting with one another against a passing parade of local color. All Caruthers hoped to accomplish was to get his name known to the reading public, despite the fact that "there is evidently a current in American literature, the fountain-head of which lies north of the Potomac, and in which a southern is compelled to navigate upstream if he jumps in too far south."

He succeeded, but just barely—in 1834. Not until a century later did *The Kentuckian* bathe its author in an unanticipated critical praise. This was because he had elected to introduce a bit of social commentary into its text. Of the 452 pages in the two little volumes, just fifteen are concerned with sociopolitical issues in general and with the slavery question in particular. As a western Virginian of Scots Presbyterian background, Caruthers was opposed to the slave system for its dehumanizing attrition upon master and servant alike (especially the employment of "drivers"). He preferred colonization for the Negroes. He hoped that the increasing number of white farmers migrating to the lower South and West could "be induced to stay in the land of their sires" and that a reinvigorated yeomanry would learn to till their depleted soil more wisely. *The Kentuckian in New-York* is the first prominent expression of agrarianism in the history of Southern literature, taking its place well in advance of similar utterances stretching from John Esten Cooke's novel *The Heir of Gaymount* (1870) up to the authors of the symposium *I'll Take My Stand* in 1930.

Modern critics often describe the tone of Caruthers's novels as "genial." Nowhere is it more so than in the presentation of his titular character, Montgomery Damon, a Kentucky drover paying his first visit to Gotham. Making gentle fun of the man, Caruthers utilizes him for his earliest attempt at dialect, and Damon's resultant epistle has been called, by Vernon Louis Parrington, "a little masterpiece in the vein of the free frontier humor that was competing with the cavalier romantic for popular approval." A quarter century later the apogee of this type of humor in the South would produce the Mozis Addums letters by the Virginia journalist George W. Bagby.

There is little doubt that Caruthers's drover is a mildly satirizing appraisal of that celebrated backwoodsman from east Tennessee, David Crockett. Caruthers had witnessed the first literary emergence of the Crockett legend some time in 1831 or 1832 at the Park Theater, New York, where he saw a burlesque entitled *The Lion of the West* . . . by his "old personal friend," James K. Paulding. Some months later he may also have attended an adaptation thereof, W. B. Bernard's play *The Kentuckian; or, a Trip to New York*. Moreover, Caruthers's uncle by marriage, Henry McClung of Lexington, was a Crockett acquaintance.

For his "second" novel Caruthers turned to the historical romance, choosing as his mise-en-scène the rebellion in Virginia by the young planter Nathaniel Bacon in 1676. In that episode Caruthers saw "sown the first germ of the American revolution," and "the *army of the people*" flocking to Bacon's standard represented to him a justified uprising of an oppressed minority against a privileged few. Far and away the most widely reviewed of Caruthers's works, *The Cavaliers* put a seal on the incipient mystique of the Cavalier—and by extension that of the First Families of Virginia—as the hallmark of a regional uniqueness, and lent basic support to the future concepts of both the "Virginia novel" and the "plantation novel." Over the years the term *Cavalier* has become so nationalized that one finds it doing duty not merely as the sobriquet for the state university but as a tag for everything from a railroad train to a brand of cigarette. Southern intellectuals began to ponder the term: see, for example, William Archer Cocke in *De Bow's Review* for September 1861 or Hugh Blair Grigsby's Phi Beta Kappa oration as noted in the *Richmond Whig*, 6 June 1856.

James K. Paulding went on record with his admiration for *The Cavaliers*. A Philadelphia critic did not "hesitate to say that the author gives promise of becoming one of our most popular American writers," and in Richmond a reviewer took note of "the fact that several of the London critics are praising [Caruthers's] work to the skies." In sum, if the fixing of the "cavalier" tradition in American mores can be attributed to any single phenomenon, it is to the anonymous appearance of this romance about an uprising in Tidewater Virginia from the pen of a Western Virginian who probably composed much of it in New York City while practicing medicine.

The secondary lead in *The Cavaliers*, that mystery-shrouded "recluse of Jamestown," turns out to be none other than Major General Edward Whalley, one of the three Puritan regicides of Charles I who had fled to New England about 1660. A small library of lore has accumulated around the trio, usually centering on the figure of John Goffe—Paulding and Nathaniel Hawthorne, among others, have treated the subject—but it would seem to be Caruthers's tiny distinction to become the first writer to focus on Whalley and to transplant the regicide from his Northern hideaway to the soil of the Old Dominion.

Despite the fact that it is a textbook example of its author's besetting sins—periphrasis, awkward dialogue, and verbosity—*The Cavaliers of Virginia* tells a rather complicated story with adequate plotting, a dashing cast of characters, and an outspokenly nationalistic thesis. It stands at the head of a lengthy caravan of novels treating the subject. The authors of at least three of these may well have done more than just turn its pages, since each has several plot elements in common with Caruthers's work: Daniel P. Thompson's *The Green Mountain Boys* (1839), Emerson Bennett's *The Fair Rebel* (1853), and St. George Tucker's *Hansford* (1857).

" . . . I wish you," Caruthers assured Sarah Griffin, a Georgia magazine editor, "and all other *southern* enterprises of the kind, all possible success. There is no lack of literary labourers in this region—it is the 'ways & means' that our people generally fail to furnish." Probably for reasons of sectional pride the ex-Harper's author elected to have his last novel, *The Knights of the Golden Horse-Shoe*, published by an obscure Alabama printer (of Virginia background). Set in the Old Dominion a generation after that of *The Cavaliers*, the plot centers on the expedition led by Lieutenant Governor Alexander Spotswood in 1716 across the Blue Ridge and down into the Shenandoah Valley in an effort to scout the possibilities of utilizing what would come to be called "the western waters." The work is the earliest extended treatment of this episode and the first book-length tribute in any genre to Spotswood's career.

As with *The Cavaliers*, Caruthers's sources cajoled him into a variety of factual errors. But his plot—a very gymkhana of jouncing episodes—and an appreciably improved style combined to make "the Tramontane Expedition" easily the best wrought of Caruthers's romances. By at least 1869 the subject was being called a "legend," and the tiny golden horseshoes that the governor bestowed upon his fellow venturers have spurred fruitless quests for them from that day to this. Their elusiveness may, indeed, be said to constitute the most glamorous conundrum in Virginia history. The overall subject of the expedition has, across the years, prompted historical commentary and interpretations in song and story up to at least 1968. It seems fair to say that in transforming the Spotswood riders into Horse-Shoe Knights pursuing a Manifest Destiny, Caruthers created in our literature one of the more glowing examples of the American romantic ideal.

SURVEY OF CRITICISM

The course of Caruthers's literary reputation is a record of almost complete neglect for a quarter century following his death. Interest began in the early 1870s and continued at a low level until 1910; and then, commencing in 1920, there was an increasing flow of commentary—rarely extensive—every decade through 1950; and since then there has been a slender continuance of academic attention. His place in his home-state annals was formally assigned to him (it has not been gainsaid) in 1884 when John Esten Cooke affirmed, in his *Virginia: A History of the People*, that "Virginia literature may be said to begin" with *The Cavaliers* and *The Knights*.

Upon publication, *The Kentuckian* earned a bare majority of critical approval, which saw the novel as a harmless tale in traditionally acceptable format of young people pirouetting across a local color landscape. Today's criticism dismisses all this as an irrelevant politicoeconomic element in his story. In 1927 Parrington emphasized that novel in the five and a half pages he gave to Caruthers in *The Romantic Revolution in America*. A variety of like-minded commentators have followed suit.

The Cavaliers of Virginia has undergone a similar volte-face. Initially, it was far and away Caruthers's most remarked-upon piece of fiction. Of eighteen known early notices eleven were cordial, two were casual, and only five were unfavorable. The critics' interest focused on the fact that here was an early, seriously projected *American historical* romance. But commentators nowadays are much less enthusiastic. Its author is derogated for the use of overly melodramatic episodes and an unduly rhetorical style. As to his nationalist theme, scholars now argue whether Nathaniel Bacon was an authentic paladin and whether his "rebellion" was anything more than an internecine power squabble over what to do about the Indian menace.

The Knights of the Golden Horse-Shoe is in every respect Caruthers's best-written piece of fiction. Because of its obscure original publication, however, formal criticism has all but passed it by. Since 1900 only fourteen commentators have deigned to take note of it; the intelligentsia have ignored it; and the saga of gallant horsemen penetrating unknowable frontiers has remained in the folk mind. In 1859 in Clarke County, Virginia, a jousting attracted a competitor who tagged himself as "The Knight of the Golden Horse-Shoe." And consider such phenomena from the 1920s and 1930s that have claimed the same titles: a float in a Fredericksburg municipal parade; a segment of Robert L. Ripley's cartoon series, *Believe It or Not*; a tourist camp near the Blue Ridge and a tavern for blacks in Chesterfield County; a fancy-dress ball at Washington and Lee University and a similar affair for society in Richmond; a national patriotic group in Virginia Beach; and the logo of a bank in Orange County. A title—no author. Caruthers and his brainchild have, over the decades, glided silently into the slipstream of anonymous Virginiana. Not until 1970 would a full-fledged renascence occur.

It seems clear that, for a part-time scribbler, Caruthers's shade may take pride in the multihued coloration his two historical romances have added to the spectrum of Southern life and lore. An uncomplicated storyteller with good stories to tell, he stayed in the realm in which he wanted to wander. What he set out to do he did. And time, that unwearying winnower of the incompetent—in literature, if not in life—has decreed that what he did shall stand.

BIBLIOGRAPHY

Works by William Alexander Caruthers

The Kentuckian in New-York, or the Adventures of Three Southerns. By a Virginian. 2 vols. New York: Harper, 1834.

The Cavaliers of Virginia, or the Recluse of Jamestown. An Historical Romance of the Old Dominion. 2 vols. New York: Harper, 1834–35.

"Daniel Boone." *National Portrait Gallery of Distinguished Americans.* 4 vols. Ed. James Herring and James B. Longacre. New York: Monson Bancroft, 1834–39.

"A Musical Soiree." *Knickerbocker Magazine* 5 (April 1835): 337–39.

"Climbing the Natural Bridge. By the Only Surviving Witness of That Extraordinary Feat." *Knickerbocker Magazine* 12 (July 1838): 32–35.

The Drunkard; from the Cradle to the Grave. A Lecture, delivered before the Savannah Temperance Society.... Savannah: W. T. Williams, 1840.

"A Lecture on the Art of Living. Delivered at the Request of the Savannah Temperance Society. . . . " *Southern Ladies' Book* 2 (December 1840): 306–14.

"Excerpts from the Portfolio of a Physician. Blushing." *Magnolia: or, Southern Monthly* 3 (January 1841): 24–26.

"The Ruins of Jamestown." *Magnolia: or, Southern Monthly* 3 (January 1841): 14–15.

"Mesmerism." *Magnolia* 4 (March 1842): 178–82.

"Excerpts from the Portfolio of an Old Novelist." *Family Companion and Ladies' Mirror* 2 (April-June 1842): 56–57, 79–80, 173.

"The Bardolphian Nose." *Orion: A Monthly Magazine of Literature, Science, and Art* 1 (June 1842): 176–79.

"Excerpts from the Portfolio of an Old Novelist. Love and Consumption." *Magnolia* n.s. 1 (July-September 1842): 35–38, 103–8, 177–82.

A Lecture, Delivered before the Georgia Historical Society. . . . Savannah: Locke & Davis, 1843.

The Knights of the Horse-Shoe: A Traditionary Tale of the Cocked Hat Gentry in Old Dominion. Wetumpka, Ala.: Charles Yancey, 1845.

The Knights of the Golden Horse-Shoe. . . . Ed. Curtis Cararoll Davis. Southern Literary Classics Series. Chapel Hill: University of North Carolina Press, 1970.

"Dr. Caruthers Aids a Lady." *Georgia Historical Quarterly* 56 (Winter 1972): 583–87. Letters to Mrs. Sarah Lawrence Griffin.

Studies of William Alexander Caruthers

Blankenship, Russell. *American Literature as an Expression of the National Mind.* New York: Holt, 1931.

Cowie, Alexander. *The Rise of the American Novel.* New York: American Book, 1948.

Davis, Curtis Carroll. *Chronicler of the Cavaliers: A Life of the Virginia Novelist, Dr. William A. Caruthers.* Richmond: Dietz Press, 1953, with bibliographies and digests of Caruthers's novels.

———. "That Daring Young Man." *Virginia Cavalcade* 9 (Summer 1959): 11–15. Reverberations of the Natural Bridge ascent.

———. "Dr. Caruthers Confronts the Bureaucrats." *Georgia Historical Quarterly* 56 (Spring 1972): 101–11.

———. "William Alexander Caruthers." *A Bibliographical 128de to the Study of Southern Literature.* Ed. Louis D. Rubin, Jr. Baton Rouge: Louisiana State University Press, 1969, pp. 169–70.

———. "William Alexander Caruthers." *AnteBellum Writers in New York and the South.* Ed. Joel Myerson. Vol. 3 of *Dictionary of Literary Biography.* Detroit: Gale Research, 1979.

Davis, Richard Beale. *Intellectual Life in Jefferson's Virginia, 1790–1830.* Chapel Hill: University of North Carolina Press, 1964.

———. *Literature and Society in Early Virginia, 1608–1840.* Baton Rouge: Louisiana State University Press, 1973.

Holliday, Carl. *A History of Southern Literature.* New York and Washington: Neale, 1906.

Hubbell, Jay B. *South and Southwest: Literary Essays and Reminiscences.* Durham, N.C.: Duke University Press, 1965.

————. *The South in American Literature, 1607–1900*. Durham, N.C.: Duke University Press, 1954.

Parrington, Vernon L. *Main Currents in American Thought*. Vol. 2. New York: Harcourt, Brace, 1927.

Taylor, William R. *Cavalier and Yankee: The Old South and the American National Character*. New York: George Braziller, 1961.

ELISABETH S. MUHLENFELD

Mary Boykin Chesnut
(1823–1886)

Although Mary Boykin Chesnut may be the most widely quoted Southern woman of the Civil War era, some readers may find it surprising to find her included in this gathering of Southern writers, for Chesnut is generally—if inaccurately— known simply as a diarist. Nevertheless, the single incomparable work for which we remember her is not, as its early title announced, a diary, but rather a thoroughly conscious literary work that employs the diary form to evoke the chaotic immediacy of Confederate life. *Mary Chesnut's Civil War* (ed. C. Vann Woodward, 1981) was first published some twenty years after the author's death, in truncated form, as *A Diary from Dixie*, a title Chesnut had no part in devising. Meticulously based on private diaries kept during the war, fewer than half of which have survived (*The Private Mary Chesnut: The Unpublished Civil War Diaries*, ed. Woodward and Elisabeth Muhlenfeld, 1984), Chesnut's book expands and transforms her diary material to achieve a panoramic view of the Confederacy teeming with life at its most intensely comic, most tragic, and most thoroughly grand. By using the diary form, Chesnut was able in the 1880s to write with perspective of the central event of nineteenth-century America without succumbing to the softening and romanticizing that hindsight visited upon other writers of her day. Inasmuch as scholars have only recently made us aware of the true nature of *Mary Chesnut's Civil War*, Chesnut has a special place in this volume, as not only one of our finest nineteenth-century Southern writers but also in a sense our newest.

BIOGRAPHY

Mary Boykin Miller was born in South Carolina on 31 March 1823 in Statesburg (now Stateburg), a town near the center of a state traditionally highly patriotic and highly political. The eldest child of Mary Boykin and Stephen

Decatur Miller, a lawyer and former U.S. Congressman then serving as a senator in the South Carolina legislature, Mary lived even her earliest years in a world permeated by politics. Her father, a strong proponent of Nullification, was elected governor of the state when Mary was five, and two years later won a seat in the U.S. Senate. Mary's daily life was perhaps more strongly shaped by a vast network of kin headed by her maternal grandmother, Mary Whitaker Boykin, who instructed her namesake almost from infancy in the arts and duties of running a large plantation.

Mary's early education began at home, where reading and writing were natural and inevitable parts of every day, before she began formal schooling in Camden, seven miles to the north. Stephen Decatur Miller sold his property in Statesburg in 1835 and determined to move his family to frontier Mississippi, where he owned cotton plantations. Mary, now twelve, was sent to Charleston to a French boarding school for girls run by Madame Ann Marson Talvande. Madame Talvande's school offered its well-heeled pupils an excellent education. There Mary learned to speak French fluently enough that she was occasionally taken for a native speaker, and received sound instruction in German, English literature, history, rhetoric and the natural sciences. More important, the school exposed Mary to Charleston and all it had to offer—the arts, high society, the beauty of a Southern port city rich in history. Mary Miller blossomed under Madame Talvande's tutelage, quickly earning her teacher's approbation as a natural leader and a witty, reliably proper yet independent-minded conversationalist.

After little more than a year, however, Mary's father put an abrupt end to her burgeoning independence. Disturbed by rumors that his thirteen-year-old daughter had been seen walking in the moonlight with a young man, Miller removed Mary from gossip and took her with him to join the rest of the family in Mississippi, a land then so primitive that wolves sometimes gathered under the house at night to howl. Mary survived the ordeal by reading everything she could get her hands on, and by thinking of the young man of the moonlight walks—James Chesnut, Jr., a recent graduate of Princeton and son of one of the wealthiest planters in the state. After several months in Mississippi she returned in 1837 to Charleston and Madame Talvande's (this time with her mother and younger sisters in attendance) for another year or so of formal schooling.

Schooling ended in 1838 with word of her father's death. After a brief visit to Mississippi to settle the estate, the family returned to Camden, and Mary became formally engaged to Chesnut. On 23 April 1840, less than a month after her seventeenth birthday, the couple were married and went to live at Mulberry, the Chesnut plantation south of Camden.

From the first, the life of the new Mrs. Chesnut was anomalous. Expecting the happily-ever-after of the novels she so loved, Mary Chesnut found instead that few aspects of her life were fulfilling. Her husband, heir to an immense fortune, was nevertheless dominated by his parents, James Chesnut, Sr., and Mary Chesnut, both in their sixties, who had no intentions of abdicating any responsibility. Mary, intelligent, outgoing, frankly passionate and headstrong by nature, found herself a perpetual guest in a house run impeccably by her mother-in-law and two unmarried sisters-in-law considerably older than herself. Her quiet and dignified young husband, deeply involved in his law practice and increasing responsibilities in the state legislature, could do little to stem her frustration. Most difficult was her failure to have any children on whom she might have lavished her love and creativity, children who also would have given her status within the Chesnut household.

Vaguely dissatisfied and discontented, Mary Chesnut spent the next twenty years of life alternately engaging her antagonists in pitched battles of wit and emotion and retreating in shame or fury to calm herself by reading. Mulberry had a superb library of classics and contemporary works, and the young Chesnuts developed a fine collection of their own, amassing the latest in French, German, and English literature and history. The years were broken for Mary by occasional trips to the famous vacation spots of the day; occasional "borrowings" of relatives' children for extended visits; Mary's unspecified illnesses, probably in part psychosomatic; and constant, intense interest in (and ambition for) her husband's political career.

When James Chesnut, Jr., was elected to the U.S. Senate in 1858, Mary moved finally into her element. Washington was a medium reminiscent of the Charleston of her youth—full of social events, important personages, literary and political talk. Mary Chesnut, armed with the political acumen that was her birthright, quickly established a reputation as an astute hostess and desirable guest, and came to know most of the Southern politicians who were to become the elite of the Confederacy. As tensions mounted in the fall of 1860 following Lincoln's election, Mary was more reluctant than her husband to leave Washington. When James resigned his Senate seat and returned to South Carolina to help draft an Ordinance of Secession, his wife's comment was telling: "I am not at all resigned." Nevertheless, Mary Chesnut's first allegiance was to her husband and to South Carolina, and she soon embraced the Confederate cause and became an ardent supporter of Jefferson Davis, whose wife Varina had been a friend when both husbands served in the U.S. Senate. Sorry that she had not done so earlier, she began to keep a diary in February 1861.

Mary Chesnut seems to have been conscious from the beginning of the immense import of the events she was witnessing, and of the remarkable vantage point she would have as recorder. Steeped in history, she apparently early determined to examine her world with as much perspective as possible while at the same time involving herself wholeheartedly. And her vantage point was indeed remarkable. She accompanied James to Montgomery and watched as the fledgling Confederate States of America formed itself and inaugurated its president. While James served in the Provisional Congress, Mary entertained the leaders of the new government and their wives, renewed her friendship with Varina Davis, and jotted down the details of every day in her diary.

From Montgomery, the Chesnuts went to Charleston, where James, now an aide to Beauregard, carried on negotiations over Fort Sumter and Mary sat on the rooftop of the Planters Hotel and watched the firing on the fort. Most of the next several months were spent in Richmond, where she renewed family connections with Mrs. Robert E. Lee, went with Mrs. Joseph E. Johnston to review the troops, waited anxiously with Mrs. Davis for news of a battle at Manassas, nursed the first sick and wounded of the war at Sally Tompkins's hospital, and grew accustomed, though never indifferent, to the dreaded "dead march," accompaniment to funerals of the war dead.

In the midst of all the excitement, confusion, elation and fear, and despite the constant discomfort and crowding of hotel life, Mary Chesnut found time almost daily for the next four years to record the events she witnessed, the people she saw, snatches of conversation, private opinions, quiet musings, unspoken fears. On days when, by her own account, she had hardly a moment alone, she who had never before kept a diary wrote almost religiously, carrying the mounting number of volumes with her from town to town even when, late in the war, she apparently could take little else. Certainly the diary served as an important outlet, for it is replete with explosions of frustration over what seemed to her the petty stupidities of the men in authority: in February 1861, "It is hard for me to believe these people are in earnest. They are not putting the young, active, earnest, efficient in place any where. When ever there is an election they hunt up some old fossil ages ago laid on the shelf. There never was such a resurrection of the dead and forgotten. This does not look like business"; in August of the same year, "Jeff Davis ill & shut up—& none but *noodles* have the world in charge"; and four years later, in February 1865, "We do not look among gentlemen for our rulers—but in the dust & ashes we rake them from Dunghills."

Much of Mary's frustration stemmed from the fact that as a woman, she could neither join the army nor hold office, and thus her involvement depended on her husband's position. But James, cool and reserved, refused to curry favor or even to press his case; through much of 1861, he vacillated between the army and a bid for a Senate seat. His wife, unwilling to return to the cotton batting of Mulberry, hoped he would be appointed ambassador to France, and wrote revealingly in her diary, "I wish Mr. Davis would send *me* to Paris." The appointment did not come, and the Chesnuts returned to Camden. When Chesnut lost his bid for the Confederate Senate, he assumed the chairmanship of a wartime Executive Council of Five empowered to oversee the defense concerns of South Carolina. The new position was powerful, for the Executive Council virtually ran the state. The Chesnuts moved to Columbia, another favorite city, but Mary was ill throughout much of 1862 with what she called "hospital fever" contracted during her nursing stints the previous summer. Her recovery was slow and painful; not until late 1862 was she ready to join her husband, who had accepted a commission as colonel and personal aide to Jefferson Davis in Richmond.

The Chesnuts spent most of the next sixteen months in Richmond. Renting quarters close to the White House of the Confederacy, they saw the Davises almost daily. For most of the period, Mary had as guests Sarah (called Sally or "Buck") and Mary Preston, the beautiful daughters of close Columbia friends.

She oversaw the flirtations of the two lovely girls and watched and counseled as both fell in love: Buck with General John Bell Hood and Mary with John Darby, a surgeon in Hood's division. Mrs. Chesnut's skill as a hostess meant that here, as everywhere, her home served as a salon in which genteel guests congregated to gossip, to dine, to play, to plot, to mourn. As the war advanced, mourning became a constant emotion. Nevertheless, the Chesnut home remained a place for support, where for an evening, one could relax and remember for a few hours the luxuries of good food, good humor, good conversation. Thus, the contrasts of pleasure and pain, amusement and terror, high glee and grim death filled Mary Chesnut to fever pitch, leaving her exhilarated one moment, exhausted the next.

The contrasts, the chaos, the political quarrels all took their toll on James, who welcomed reassignment to South Carolina in April 1864 as a brigadier general. The Chesnuts' last visit in Richmond was with the President and his wife, whose five-year-old son Joe had fallen to his death from a balcony of the Davis home. Once Mary was settled in Columbia, Varina Davis sent her sister Maggie Howell for an extended visit to get the young woman away from the atmosphere of tension and mourning in the capital. And in October, Jeff Davis himself came for a day, grateful for Mary's hospitality, grateful as well to spend a few moments with old friends whose support had been unequivocal. Once more, as always, the Chesnuts' rented quarters were filled with visitors, now defeated generals and ragged troops—and two nieces, daughters of her sister Kate. Mary's days began at 5:00 A.M. with a visit to the hospital and ended late at night as the last guest left.

Sherman's capture of Atlanta announced in clarion tones Columbia's vulnerability, and so in January 1865 James counseled his wife to flee. Among the last to leave the city by rail, Mary found herself in Lincolnton, North Carolina, waiting anxiously for news and dreading to hear the awful truth: Columbia was burned. Soon, James found three rooms in Chester, South Carolina, and the grand Mrs. Chesnut, now sporting threadbare dresses that she exchanged for food, took up her last wartime residence. After Appomattox, even the cramped quarters in Chester served as Mary's salon, and there came generals, senators, governors, friends and relatives—all passing through, spinning out the last act of ruin. One of the final visitors was Varina Davis with her four small children, fleeing arrest.

The Chesnuts' return to Camden was ignominious; they lacked even the small change required to pay for the ferry ride across the Wateree River. Mulberry had been badly damaged and pillaged by Yankee troops following Sherman, and the Chesnut fortunes had become worthless Confederate bonds. Mary's mother-in-law had died in 1864; the old Colonel, her husband's father, died in 1866, stipulating in his will that no land could be sold until the Chesnut holdings were free of debt. Thus James's long-awaited inheritance was a bitter one, and Mary, now in her early forties, spent the next several months gathering strength for the task ahead. The diary entries tapered off until, in July 1865, they ceased.

Money was a constant worry, and Mary expanded a small butter-and-egg business run during the war by her maid, set about to manage the cottage industries that supplied the plantations with clothing and other necessities, shared the produce from Mulberry's gardens with those less fortunate, and provided a haven for destitute family members. Finally, she had children under her care for longer than a mere visit; Miller Williams, then his younger brother David, sons of her beloved sister Kate, came to live with her.

During the next several years, true to his class and his convictions, James tried with little success to mitigate the indignities of Reconstruction while the day-to-day details of the household fell to Mary. Long troubled by a heart condition, she found life eased by the construction in the early 1870s of a new home in Camden: Sarsfield, built from bricks of dismantled outbuildings at Mulberry. In a spacious ground-floor library of the new house, Mary Chesnut began, like so many Southern women of her day, to experiment with literary projects. Writing was a potential source of funds, but at least as important was the intellectual outlet it provided for a lonely woman accustomed to the excitement of national capitals and the stimulation of intelligent, well-informed debate.

Her diaries of the war years were apparently never far from her mind, but because they were so candid, filled with acerbic comments on many of her husband's associates and relatives, her first serious attempts to deal with her material were in fiction. In the mid–1870s she apparently set about to teach herself to write, drafting one novel of the war, *The Captain and the Colonel*; a second entitled *Two Years; or, The Way We Lived Then*, based on her childhood experiences in Charleston and Mississippi; and a third, of which only a fragment survives, entitled *Manassas*. The novels, although thoroughly unsuccessful (their author seems to have lost interest in them), nevertheless taught Mary Chesnut much about creating character, establishing tone, and writing lively dialogue, and revealed to her a narrative voice that she would ultimately sustain throughout *Mary Chesnut's Civil War*. Even more important, the attempts at fiction suggested structures and thematic concerns that would appear fully realized in her work of the 1880s.

At one point, perhaps ten years after the war, Chesnut tried a full-scale readying of her diaries for publication by recopying, smoothing out, expanding phrases into sentences, and the like, but abandoned the effort nearly three-quarters of the way through the project. Her ongoing experiments at fiction suggested to her that even in polished form the diaries could not do justice to the events they recorded and, in particular, to the people they mentioned. As she had written them day by day, they told *her* story—not the story of a doomed world. Accordingly, in 1881 she bought a sheaf of copybooks and began a major revision and expansion, using the literary techniques with which she had experimented in her fiction. Although she had discovered neither an appropriate beginning nor a satisfactory ending, she had substantially completed the work by December 1884, when her husband fell seriously ill. James Chesnut died in February 1885, only a few days before the death of her mother. Exhausted by two months of nursing the two people she most loved, Mary Chesnut was badly shaken, and before she could recover, she found herself entangled in the settlement of James's estate. Despite twenty years of hard work after the war, Mary was left almost nothing; even her dower lands were seized against debts. Retaining only Sarsfield and several cattle that produced the milk for her little dairy business, Chesnut spent the last year of her life attempting to extricate herself from financial difficulties and to get her husband's papers in order. Before she could return to her own book, she died on 22 November 1886, victim at last of the old familiar heart trouble.

Shortly before her death, Mary Chesnut had asked a younger friend, Isabella Martin, to oversee the publication of her book. Accordingly, Martin took diaries and manuscript to Columbia and tried halfheartedly to interest a publisher, but finding no ready takers, put the assignment out of her mind. The manuscript rested under Martin's bedroom armoire for almost twenty years. Fortunately, in 1905 Martin mentioned the manuscript to a visiting editor for the New York firm of D. Appleton, and shortly afterwards *A Diary from Dixie* was published. Its editors made no mention of the fact that the book was not, strictly speaking, a diary or that its title had been supplied by the *Saturday Evening Post*, which published extensive excerpts prior to book publication. Nor did they note that their edition had cut more than 100,000 words from the manuscript and had heavily edited and rewritten the remainder. Novelist Ben Ames Williams edited a somewhat fuller edition in 1949, but again made no mention of the true nature of the work.

In fact, *Mary Chesnut's Civil War* is a wholesale revision, expansion, and shaping of the wartime diaries on which it is based. Scrupulously faithful to the diaries in many ways, it nevertheless omits much that its author deemed (almost always correctly) trivial or extremely personal and weaves into the texture of the diary passages skillfully designed to introduce personages the author knew perfectly well (and, in the original diaries, felt no need to introduce, much less describe), to underscore contrasts or similarities, to establish a sense of place, and to create living dialogue. Most important, the material of the original diaries was, in the revision process, shaped to heighten themes or images inherent in the experiences themselves.

MAJOR THEMES

Mary Chesnut's Civil War represents a kind of *Vanity Fair* of the Confederacy. Like Thackeray, an author Mary Chesnut particularly admired, she subtly ties the concepts of love, marriage, and divorce with partriotism, political conflict, and war. Lovers' quarrels are battles; civil war is a kind of cosmic marital discord. In the process of showing the noble in the quotidian and the petty in the grand, she emphasizes the cyclical nature of historical events, rooted as they must be in the simple lives and deaths of mere human beings.

The Civil War itself, of course, provides the structure of the book, which begins as the Provisional Congress convenes in Montgomery to establish a government and ends in the aftermath of Appomattox. A central thematic device, which she had first worked out in her unpublished novel *The Captain and the Colonel*, is the three generations of Chesnut men who appear throughout the work. James Chesnut's father, the old Colonel, holds a central place in the book; as he and his entourage are described, Mary Chesnut brings alive the antebellum world in all its glory—and all of its tyrannies, hypocrisies, and stagnation. In 1861 the old Colonel is monarch of all he surveys, charming when he chooses to be, unbending when he pleases, unaffected by political upheavals beyond his property lines. The patent to his lands dates back to King George II, and he and his wife represent American nobility, as symbolized by the Charles Stuart portraits of each of them and of George Washington hanging on the walls of Mulberry.

James Chesnut, Jr., son of the monarch, represents the war itself. Chesnut notes that he was the first senator to resign following Lincoln's election, was involved in the firing on Fort Sumter, the first engagement of the war, and participated in perhaps the last skirmish in South Carolina four years later. Throughout, he is a man troubled, at once enmeshed by the cause and yet not wholly invested in it. Essentially a rational man, James is reserved, and his nature draws back from the fiery spirit of the military engagement; yet he resolutely pursues the only possible course he can: to aid in the winning of the war and so to bring about peace once again. He is the public servant, the man of duty, and, as such, increasingly out of step with the time.

James's nephew Johnny Chesnut is the new generation, the hope. He rides with J.E.B. Stuart and other plumed cavalry heroes. Devoid of personal ambition, he fights simply to fight, because it is his duty to fight and because he loves the ride and the chase. At war's end, Mary's father-in-law, the old Colonel, is blind and lost—a figure immensely dignified and deeply moving. Her husband is cognizant of all that has passed, all that has been wasted, and of the superhuman energy that will be required to rebuild. Johnny, however, is not tied to the past. He, too, has lost everything, and yet by the book's end, he is busily engaged in flirtations, dances, and parties. His is a soul of tempered steel, ready to embrace whatever the future brings, but unwilling to dwell too deeply on the meaning of the events he has lived through. One testament to Mary Chesnut's fidelity to her chosen genre, the diary form, is that the book contains no hint of a dark future for Johnny, who in fact died intestate in 1868, fifteen years before the book was written.

Other important themes surface in *Mary Chesnut's Civil War* as well. Of particular interest is the emphasis Chesnut places on subtle distinctions of Southern caste and class, through all layers of which runs an elaborate code of manners, the concept of honor and the scourge of slavery. Herself the proud daughter of a patriarchal slave society, Chesnut embraced most of the elitist prejudices of her class; nevertheless, she was from at least her teen years both abolitionist and feminist. She was opposed to slavery in any form, and wrote of the similarity between literal slavery and the willing enslavement of women by men in marriage. Throughout *Mary Chesnut's Civil War*, the abridgement of freedom is signaled by an inability to communicate: white masters are unable to read the faces of their servants; husbands and wives (including the Chesnuts themselves) are unsure of one another's thoughts and motives; and even the capture of a town or territory in war is symbolized by the inability to send or receive news.

The reader of *Mary Chesnut's Civil War* takes from the book a sense of chaos—a riot of episodes, quips, tragic tag lines, all represented by the Greek chorus of characters who move into and out of Chesnut's drawing room, talking endlessly of the trivial and the profound, the petty and the crucial, the dressing of bonnets and the dressing of wounds. The Confederacy, a doomed cause, is a study in contrasts in this work, a world filled with ironies. But the contrasts and the ironies come directly from lived experience, giving the book a power and immediacy that few works portraying the Confederacy can match.

SURVEY OF CRITICISM

Mary Boykin Chesnut's work has been widely quoted from its first publication in 1905, but until very recently most of the attention it has received has focused on two things: the events and conversations related in the book and the personality of its author. Because the book's true nature was obscure until the publication of the Woodward edition of 1981 and the Muhlenfeld biography of the same year, *Mary Chesnut's Civil War* in its earlier dresses as *A Diary from Dixie* was treated as historical material rather than as a literary work.

As soon as literary critics began to produce extended studies of the American Civil War, however, Mary Chesnut received serious attention. Edmund Wilson, writing in 1962 in *Patriotic Gore: Studies in the Literature of the American Civil War*, believed the work to be a diary. Nevertheless, he assessed the book as a structured literary work. "This diary," he wrote, "is an extraordinary document—in its informal department, a masterpiece." Its author was able to take advantage of "the actual turn of events to develop" the people and relationships she described "and round them out as if she were molding a novel." A decade later, Daniel Aaron in *The Unwritten War: American Writers in the Civil War* (1973) agreed with Wilson that *A Diary from Dixie* was "more genuinely literary than most Civil War fiction," and dubbed Chesnut the "most likely candidate to write the unwritten Confederate novel."

By the time of Aaron's evaluation, scholars were beginning to turn their attention to Chesnut's papers. Bell Irvin Wiley wrote an extended essay on Chesnut in *Confederate Women* based in part on his own examinations of the "diary" manuscripts, and drawing attention to revisions between various versions of the work and to the complexity of textual material. Also in the mid–1970s, Eileen Gregory made initial transcriptions of two novel drafts in the Chesnut papers, reporting her findings in "The Formality of Memory," originally presented at a conference on South Carolina Women Writers in 1978. At the same conference, essays by George Hayhoe and Elisabeth Muhlenfeld explored the literary qualities of the diary manuscripts.

Woodward's introductory essays to *Mary Chesnut's Civil War* in 1981 and Muhlenfeld's *Mary Boykin Chesnut: A Biography*, marked the first extended discussions of Chesnut's book of the 1880s as a conscious literary work. The publication of the Woodward edition created renewed interest in Chesnut, winning for Woodward (and, it might be fair to say, for Chesnut as well) the Pulitzer Prize for history and prompting an array of thoughtful reviews. Woodward's 1984 "Mary Chesnut in Search of a Genre" discussed Chesnut's deliberate choice of the diary form, and Woodward and Muhlenfeld's introduction to *The Private Mary Chesnut: The Unpublished Civil War Diaries* (1984) explored the relationship of the wartime diaries to the book. To date, however, most discussions of Chesnut continue to respond to *Mary Chesnut's Civil War* as if it were a diary—certainly testimony to the author's success in applying fictional techniques to the diary form.

BIBLIOGRAPHY

Works by Mary Boykin Chesnut

Chesnut's only work intended for publication has appeared in three editions:

A Diary from Dixie, as written by Mary Boykin Chesnut, wife of James Chesnut, Jr., United States Senator from South Carolina, 1859–1861, and afterward an Aide to Jefferson Davis and a Brigadier-General in the Confederate Army. Ed. Isabella D. Martin and Myrta Lockett Avary. New York: D. Appleton, 1905.
A Diary from Dixie. Ed. Ben Ames Williams. Boston: Houghton, Mifflin, 1949.
Mary Chesnut's Civil War. Ed. C. Vann Woodward. New Haven: Yale University Press, 1981.
The Private Mary Chesnut: The Unpublished Civil War Diaries. Ed. C. Vann Woodward and Elisabeth Muhlenfeld. New York: Oxford University Press, 1984.

Manuscript drafts and draft fragments of several novels and related biographical material are in the South Caroliniana Library, University of South Carolina, Columbia. For edited versions of them, see Elisabeth S. Muhlenfeld, "Mary Boykin Chesnut: The Writer and Her Work" (Ph.D. diss., University of South Carolina, 1978). Many of Chesnut's letters are collected in Allie Patricia Wall, ed., "The Letters of Mary Boykin Chesnut" (M.A. thesis, University of South Carolina, 1977).

Studies of Mary Boykin Chesnut

Aaron, Daniel. *The Unwritten War: American Writers and the Civil War*. New York: Knopf, 1973.
Childs, Margaretta P. "Chesnut, Mary Boykin Miller." *Notable American Women: 1607–1950*. Ed. Edward T. Jones et al. Cambridge, Mass.: Belknap Press of Harvard University Press, 1971, pp. 327–30.
Gregory, Eileen. "The Formality of Memory: A Study of Literary Manuscripts of Mary

Boykin Chesnut." *South Carolina Women Writers*. Ed. James B. Meriwether. Columbia: Southern Studies Program, University of South Carolina, 1979, pp. 229–43.

Gwin, Minrose C. *Black and White Women of the Old South: The Peculiar Sisterhood in American Literature*. Knoxville: University of Tennessee Press, 1985, pp. 102–9.

Hayhoe, George F. "Mary Boykin Chesnut's Journal: Visions and Revisions." *South Carolina Women Writers*. Ed. James B. Meriwether. Columbia: Southern Studies Program, University of South Carolina, 1979, pp. 211–21.

Lynn, Kenneth S. "The Masterpiece That Became a Hoax." *The Air-line to Seattle: Studies in Literary and Historical Writing about America*. Chicago: University of Chicago Press, 1983. Revised from *New York Times Book Review*, 26 April 1981, pp. 9, 36.

Muhlenfeld, Elisabeth S. *Mary Boykin Chesnut: A Biography*. Baton Rouge: Louisiana State University Press, 1981.

———. "Of Paradigm and Paradox: The Case of Mary Boykin Chesnut." *Feminist Visions: Toward a Transformation of the Liberal Arts Curriculum*. Ed. Diana L. Fowlkes and Charlotte S. McClure. University, Ala.: University of Alabama Press, 1984.

Wiley, Bell Irvin. *Confederate Women*. Contributions in American History, No. 38. Westport, Conn.: Greenwood Press, 1975.

Wilson, Edmund. *Patriotic Gore: Studies in the Literature of the American Civil War*. New York: Oxford University Press, 1962.

Woodward, C. Vann. "Mary Chesnut in Search of Her Genre." *Yale Review* (Winter 1984): 199–209.

WILLIAM L. ANDREWS

Charles Waddell Chesnutt
(1858–1932)

Charles W. Chesnutt was the South's—and America's—first important black writer of fiction. The tale-teller of his first stories, Uncle Julius, owed something to Joel Chandler Harris's Uncle Remus, who was a major impetus to Harris's design of writing fiction that would lead to recognition of the rights of black Americans. Although Chesnutt had never been a slave, having been born in the North, he understood better than white authors who had portrayed it what plantation life had been for slaves. Himself light-skinned, Chesnutt also wrote powerfully of life along the color line, making it an important topic for fiction.

BIOGRAPHY

Charles W. Chesnutt was born on 20 June 1858 in Cleveland, Ohio, the son of Andrew Jackson Chesnutt and his wife, Ann Maria Sampson, both free Negro émigrés from Fayetteville, North Carolina. During the Civil War, Andrew Jackson Chesnutt served as a teamster in the Union Army, but after the fighting ended he returned to Fayetteville, where his father, Waddell Cade, helped him start a grocery business. Charles and his mother followed in 1866. While working part-time in the family store, Charles attended a school funded by the Freedman's Bureau. In 1872 financial necessity forced him to begin a teaching career in Charlotte, North Carolina. Five years later Chesnutt returned to Fayetteville to become an instructor of reading and writing in the new State Colored Normal School. Married in 1878 to Susan Perry, he was appointed principal of the normal school at age twenty-two.

Despite these successes, Chesnutt longed for broader opportunities than segregated Fayetteville could offer him or his family. His private studies of English and continental literature, along with the growing vogue of postwar Southern racial conditions as a subject in American writing, helped stir his latent ambition to make a name for himself in the North with his pen. Legal stenography became his ticket to a new life in the city of his birth. After settling his wife and three children in Cleveland in 1884, Chesnutt worked as a court reporter, passed the Ohio bar examination in 1887, and established a prosperous legal stenography firm that gave him a solid financial base on which to build his literary career.

Chesnutt's advent as an Afro-American man of letters was inauspicious. From 1885 to 1889 his name appeared under the titles of humorous sketches and mildly sentimental or didactic squibs for home journals, humor magazines, and the Sunday supplements used by the S. S. McClure newspaper syndicate. Through his friendship with George W. Cable, who introduced him to the Open-Letter Club, a private forum for the discussion of social issues in the South, Chesnutt wrote his first commentary on racial questions. From this literary apprenticeship his first memorable work of fiction emerged in August 1887, when the *Atlantic Monthly* published "The Goophered Grapevine," an unusual dialect story that displayed intimate knowledge of the black folk culture of the South. This short story was the first by an Afro-American to appear in such a prestigious literary magazine.

Two more stories narrated by Chesnutt's distinctive ex-slave persona, Uncle Julius McAdoo, found their way into the *Atlantic* before the magazine's publisher, Houghton Mifflin, decided in 1899 to bring out a collection of tales in this vein entitled *The Conjure Woman*. Meanwhile, Chesnutt had begun writing short stories about the origins, aspirations, and social and psychological dilemmas of light-skinned Afro-Americans like himself in the post-Civil War era. After the appearance of "The Wife of His Youth" in the *Atlantic* in 1898, Chesnutt's convincing depiction of the manners and mores of Cleveland's "blue-veined" mulatto bourgeoisie won him attention and praise as a new voice of racial realism in American fiction. Growing public curiosity about him, along with the approving response of reviewers to *The Conjure Woman* and the evidence of an untapped audience for nondialect fiction like "The Wife of His Youth," convinced Houghton Mifflin in 1899 to add another book of Chesnutt's short stories to its list. The nine stories of *The Wife of His Youth and Other Stories of the Color Line* ranged over a broader area of racial experience in the United States than had been previously delineated by any author, black or white, in American writing.

On 30 September 1899 Charles Chesnutt closed his court reporting business in order to pursue his lifelong dream, a career as a full-time author. He regarded his short story collections as only an entering wedge into the literary world. By the end of the year he had two novel manuscripts ready to show to Walter Hines Page, his editor at Houghton Mifflin. The autumn of 1900 saw the publication of his first novel, *The House Behind the Cedars*, a tragic story of two Negroes who pass for white in Reconstruction North Carolina. The possibility and consequences of racial intermixing between whites and upwardly mobile mulattoes had become a familiar theme in American literary as well as political discourse by the turn of the century. Against this background, Chesnutt's first novel achieved a modest sales record and spurred its author on to write a second race problem novel, which Houghton Mifflin published in time for the 1901 Christmas trade.

The Marrow of Tradition is a *roman à clef* based on the so-called race riot of 1898 in Wilmington, North Carolina. In this nationally reported incident, Wilmington's municipal government was overthrown by a cadre of white supremacists, who unleashed a pogrom in which more than a score of black people were killed. Hoping to write the *Uncle Tom's Cabin* of his generation, Chesnutt indited a plea for racial justice in the New South that William Dean Howells praised for its moral forcefulness even as he worried over its apparent bitterness. *The Marrow of Tradition* was widely reviewed but narrowly discussed, usually in terms of the accuracy of a mixed-blood doctor as the epitome of embattled progressivism in the New South.

When the sales of Chesnutt's second novel fell short of the author's expectations, he reopened his court reporting business and relegated his literary activities to the status of an avocation. Reports on Southern disfranchisement and peonage of blacks moved him to write trenchant essays on these developments, linking him with Booker T. Washington and W.E.B. Du Bois as black America's most compelling commentators on the race problem in the South. In June 1904 Chesnutt the belletrist resurfaced in the *Atlantic* with his best crafted short story, "Baxter's Procrustes," a satirical portrait of a fraternity of bibliophiles patterned after Cleveland's Rowfant Club, which had earlier refused Chesnutt membership because of his race. A year later, Doubleday, Page and Company published Chesnutt's third race problem novel, *The Colonel's Dream*, in which a former Confederate officer tries to revive his North Carolina hometown from an economic and spiritual depression. While Thomas Dixon's virulently racist novel, *The Clansman*, became a best-selling sensation in 1905, *The Colonel's Dream* was largely ignored by reviewers and readers.

After 1905 Chesnutt continued to tinker with the materials of his art in the hope of holding onto his dwindling literary audience. He wrote a four-act mystery that did not venture into the realm of race; he created a short historical romance about the free people of color in antebellum New Orleans. None of these works aroused an interest in the publishers to whom Chesnutt sent them. A handful of his short stories appeared sporadically in *The Crisis*, the official organ of the National Association for the Advancement of Colored People (NAACP), but these tales added nothing to his literary stature. Nevertheless, during the first three decades of the twentieth century, Chesnutt's fiction came to be regarded as literary standards by the black American reading public and by many whites sympathetic to the causes Chesnutt espoused. As a result, in 1928 the NAACP awarded the dean of Afro-American fiction writers its Spingarn Medal for his "pioneer work as a literary artist depicting the life and struggles of Americans of Negro descent, and for his long and useful career as scholar, worker, and freeman of one of America's greatest cities."

Between the close of his active literary career and his death on 15 November

1932, Chesnutt the business and family man prospered considerably more than Chesnutt the literary figure. A member of the Cleveland Chamber of Commerce as well as the city's Bar Association and several private clubs, Chesnutt parlayed his business success and his literary reputation into the social respectability of a self-made man. His influence was often courted by civic leaders and political aspirants, and he appeared in a number of local and national symposiums, where he promoted the welfare of black people and agitated for social justice. He sent all four of his children to college and lived to see them all established in their chosen professions. Through his correspondence he traded ideas with a wide range of writers, pundits, and power brokers on both sides of the color line. Although for many years after his death Chesnutt's writing remained underread and undervalued, in his native city he was memorialized by a street and a school named after him and by his induction into the Cleveland Hall of Fame.

MAJOR THEMES

Charles W. Chesnutt was the first Afro-American fiction writer to enlist the white-controlled mass media in the service of a serious social message. He was also the first black storyteller to touch a significant portion of the white American reading audience with his art. Despite, or perhaps because of, the fact that he lived during a period in American history that has been called the nadir of black America's sociopolitical fortunes, Chesnutt set his sights early on the ideal of success in the literary world, where, he hoped, merit, not race, was the desideratum for recognition. His personal literary ambition was fired by his growing sense of outrage over the racism and social injustice that he felt were undermining the foundations of American democracy. Consequently, he became a willing literary advocate, if not a spokesman, for the interests of Afro-Americans with whom he most identified, namely, middle-class mixed bloods like himself and working-class blacks of the small-town South whom he had known from his youth in eastern North Carolina. Although a Midwesterner by birth and lifetime adult residence, Chesnutt's literary heart and soul gravitated toward the South, the source, he believed, of America's complex racial fate and the site, as well, of its destined resolution.

From the beginning of his literary career, Chesnutt's subject matter and narrative perspective bore the earmarks of his Southern experience. Stemming from an oral tale that his father-in-law's gardener had told him in Fayetteville, "The Goophered Grapevine" revealed its author to be intimately acquainted with the black folkways of the Old South and the progressive spirit of the New. At first glance, Uncle Julius, the ex-slave raconteur of *The Conjure Woman* who spins wonderful tales about times "befo' de wah," seems cast in the mold of the aging black retainers who evoke the past for the plantation literary tradition. Julius's reminiscences stem not from nostalgia or a desire to entertain, but rather from self-interested schemes to secure his own economic advantage through the artful manipulation of his white listening audience. This motivation revealed a side of Afro-American character that readers of Southern local color and plantation fiction were not accustomed to seeing.

Chesnutt's conjure stories unveiled the most revisionistic assessment of the myth of the Old South yet attempted in post–Civil War fiction. Instead of celebrating the romantic and heroic exploits of idealized whites in the manner of Thomas Nelson Page's *In Ole Virginia* (1887), Chesnutt's conjure stories concentrate on the struggles of ordinary slaves to maintain their essential dignity and human identity in the face of white oppression. The Southern slaveholder in *The Conjure Woman* is no sweet-tempered, benevolent plantation aristocrat such as may be found in profusion in the work of Page, F. Hopkinson Smith, and Harry Stillwell Edwards. With notable realism, Chesnutt depicts the parsimonious Scots of down-east North Carolina cheating each other, indulging their gambling vices, hunting down their runaways, arguing with their wives, and perpetually scrambling for financial gain. The whites' preoccupation with profit inevitably clashes with their slaves' determination to preserve marriage ties, family solidarity, love relationships, and the general group welfare.

Through the magic of conjuration—i.e., black hoodoo spells, charms, and other forms of witchcraft—slaves in "Sis' Becky's Pickaninny," "Mars Jeems's Nightmare," and "Hot-Foot Hannibal" find ways to resist successfully the power wielded by their would-be exploiters. In *The Conjure Woman*'s more tragic stories, such as "The Conjurer's Revenge" and "The Gray Wolf's Ha'nt," hoodoo power is put to vengeful purposes in internecine conflicts between slaves and free blacks. Employing such universal folk motifs as the metamorphosis and the trickster figure (epitomized in Uncle Julius himself) as well as materials specific to Southern black folk culture, Chesnutt rivaled Joel Chandler Harris as an adapter of Southern folklore to literary art. Chesnutt's ironies are subtle and intricate, whether they stem from his explicitly revisionistic image of the Old South or his implicit debunking of the complacency and naïveté of the supposedly "progressive" New South. By pitting the narrator of *The Conjure Woman*, a literal-minded white Ohioan to whom Julius is merely a reciter of quaint "fairy tales," against his wife, who gradually realizes the moral significance of the ex-slave's reminiscences, Chesnutt quietly launched his campaign to challenge the social and aesthetic premises on which genteel post–Civil War Southern literature had been founded.

Life along the color line in the contemporary North as well as the South is the overarching subject of Chesnutt's second book. The fundamental social issue, as well as the unifying theme, in most of the stories of *The Wife of His Youth* is the causes and effects of miscegenation in the United States. The social aspirations and prejudices of the light-complexioned black bourgeoisie in "Groveland," Ohio, are analyzed with both irony and pathos in the title story of Chesnutt's book and in such tales as "A Matter of Principle" and, to a lesser extent, "Her Virginia Mammy." Many of the characters in these stories were

modeled on people whom Chesnutt knew from membership in the Cleveland
Social Circle, an exclusive society of upwardly mobile mulattoes who were
reputed to discriminate against anyone whose color was darker than theirs.

"The Wife of His Youth" describes how a leader of the Groveland "Blue
Veins" triumphs over his class, if not color, prejudices by acknowledging after
decades of separation his dark-skinned antebellum wife. The pretense and hypocrisy of another "blue-veined" middle-class mulatto are satirically deflated
in "A Matter of Principle." "Her Virginia Mammy" presents this class of Afro-
Americans in a more sympathetic light and depicts the betrothal of a Groveland
woman unaware of her black ancestry to a bona fide Boston Brahmin. This was
the first time Chesnutt broached the question of miscegenation directly in his
fiction; nothing in the story suggests that crossing the color line or racial intermixture through marriage is inherently perverse. On the other hand, "Her Virginia Mammy" does not present a brief for miscegenation or "social equality"
in the abstract. "Uncle Wellington's Wives" argues that blacks who think that
prestige and equality in the North can be achieved by marriage to a white woman
are foolishly deluded. Throughout his fiction and nonfiction, Chesnutt championed the cause of black assimilation into the mainstream of American life, but
he always predicated such upward mobility on black education, preparation, and
application of the traditional work ethic. Though he believed that the eventual
solution of the race problem lay in the intermixture of blacks and whites through
marriage, Chesnutt's fiction looked as seriously for answers to the black majority's immediate socioeconomic plight as it acquitted the cases of individual
mixed-bloods who cross the color line in search of opportunities commensurate
with their abilities.

When *The Wife of His Youth* turned to the Southern scene, such stories as
"The Sheriff's Children" and "The Web of Circumstance" confront racial
problems that cast grave doubt on Chesnutt's faith in the ameliorative power of
traditional American rugged individualism. The ex-slave hero of "The Web of
Circumstance" tries to pull himself up by his bootstraps via Booker T. Washington's self-help philosophy, but a combination of adverse circumstances, racism, and betrayal leaves him broken and degraded at the end of the story. "The
Sheriff's Children" originates in an incident of miscegenation in the antebellum
South and erupts into a near-violent confrontation between an aspiring mulatto
and a respected white aristocrat in the small-town New South. As in each of
Chesnutt's novels, the aristocrat, in this case the sheriff himself, is compelled
at the climax of the story to make a moral decision about the responsibility he
has to the Southern Negro and to social justice in his region. In "The Sheriff's
Children" Chesnutt combined the two predominant purposes of all his color-
line fiction: analysis and exposure of the caste system in the South together with
a sympathetic portrayal of the mulatto as the human product and victim of that
unjust system.

In these and other stories Chesnutt's pessimistic reaction to the rise of white
supremacy and the eclipse of black opportunity in the New South of the 1890s

was manifest. The urbane Clevelander could play the Horatian ironist when surveying isolated examples of color consciousness among mulattoes of his own social set. But when the North Carolina expatriate looked southward, he found it difficult to accommodate his sense of the enormity of the race problem to the constraints of conventional American literary realism. Hence, he experimented with a naturalistic perspective in "The Web of Circumstance," with deliberate sentimentality in "The Bouquet," and with a heightened melodrama of theme and form in "The Sheriff's Children." His goal was to find ways to dramatize the urgency of the contemporary racial crisis in the South and to compel his reader to view racial issues in the clarifying light of purely ethical consideration, unclouded by custom or prejudice.

During the ten years that Chesnutt spent writing and revising *The House Behind the Cedars*, he became convinced that "the distinctions on which the story is based" were his "métier as a story writer." "There is scarcely an incident in it," he wrote to Walter Hines Page, "that has not been paralleled in real life to my actual knowledge." The first half of the novel narrates the attempt of Rena Walden, product of an illicit union between an antebellum Southern gentleman and his light-skinned slave concubine, to assimilate into the white upper class of a South Carolina town. When unexpected circumstances betray her background to her prospective husband, he breaks off the match. In the second half of the story, Walden seeks fulfillment among her "own people" by becoming a country schoolteacher, but harassment from her former fiancé and from a black suitor combine with her own growing sense of desperation to bring about her tragic death.

The novel of "passing" and miscegenation was not a new thing when Chesnutt published *The House Behind the Cedars*, but his treatment of the causes and significance of passing for white was virtually unprecedented. He treated the controversial action of Rena Walden and her brother John, a successful sub-rosa assimilator into the white world, as morally and socially defensible given the bigotry and Jim Crow conditions that barred blacks from any other way of gaining social or economic opportunity. A woman like Rena Walden, who had only the most tenuous links to the Negro race, was not, as most American writers tended to believe, "tainted" or "cursed" by her black heritage. The tragedy of Rena Walden stemmed from the fact that she was, in her creator's words, "a fine character forced into a false position" by Southern society's obsession with whiteness as the sine qua non of respectability and advancement. Chesnutt traces the Southern reverence for whiteness through the blue-blooded aristocrats of South Carolina and into the "bright mulatto" class of "Patesville," North Carolina, from which the Waldens come. He is equally critical of this disease of the social imagination on both sides of the color line, but he urges that those most victimized by the sickness, namely, mixed-bloods, be given the most credit for refusing to accept meekly the artificial status appointed for them outside the privileged sphere. "To undertake what [the Waldens] tried to do required great courage," Chesnutt argues as narrator of *The House Behind the Cedars*.

As a novel of purpose, *The House Behind the Cedars* is remarkably subdued and nonpolemical; *The Marrow of Tradition* is more outspoken. It contains Chesnutt's most probing analysis of the sources and consequences of the turn-of-the-century South's racial and social situation. The novel incorporates the largest and most diverse cast of characters, the most complicated plot, and the most problematic themes that Chesnutt would ever ponder in one literary work. The main thread of action knits together the lives of two families in "Wellington" (Wilmington), North Carolina: the Carterets, who represent the New South aristocracy, and the Millers, a mixed-blood couple who embody their creator's idea of the progressive New Negro. Carteret's successful conspiracy with other white reactionaries to take over Wellington leads to a race riot in which Dr. Adam Miller's son is killed and the hospital he has built is destroyed. Miller's philosophy of prudent diplomacy in race relations and Christian fortitude in the face of personal wrongs is put to a severe test at the conclusion of the novel, but in choosing mercy instead of revenge as his guiding principle, the mulatto doctor transcends the evils inflicted on him and becomes the true healing agent for the Southern body politic.

Monitoring the social ills of the South left Chesnutt with this basic diagnosis: the patient suffered most profoundly from the corruptive grip of the past upon the present. Specifically, it was the tradition of white mastery and black servitude that held the New South in thrall to the Old. Despite the fact that the trend of the time was toward celebrating the legacy of the Old South in historical romances, Chesnutt determined that his magnum opus should "show the efforts of the people of a later generation to adjust themselves in this traditional atmosphere to the altered conditions of a new era." In the throes of a difficult transition, the people of the South, Chesnutt believed, had to "adjust themselves" to the fact that theirs was now a biracial society instead of trying to live in the past or revolutionize the present. The white supremacist leadership of Wellington tries to block the inevitable social evolution of the town and as a result leads it to the brink of chaos. This action allows Chesnutt to condemn the so-called redeemer Democrats of the New South whose false "progressivism" masked their plan to re-create the region in the image of its discredited past. The alternative to this element in the South is symbolized by Dr. Miller, whose moral ascendancy at the end of the novel allows Chesnutt to conclude *The Marrow of Tradition* on a hopeful note without spelling out exactly what kind of power such a man might be able to exert in white-controlled Wellington.

In his last novel of purpose, *The Colonel's Dream*, Chesnutt tried to enhance his white readers' identification with his protagonist by making him a white man, an enlightened ex-Confederate officer who has earned his fortune in Northern manufacturing without losing his aristocratic sense of noblesse oblige. Colonel French returns to North Carolina to find his hometown suffering under the pall of economic stagnation, political corruption, and racial oppression. Like many other heroes of the economic novels that flourished during the Progressive era, French sets about reforming the backward, often repressive and exploitative, systems of education and production in his region. Resistance steadily mounts from Bill Fetters, a prototype of Faulkner's Flem Snopes, whose political and economic power holds blacks and poor whites alike in virtual serfdom. In the end, the colonel renounces his dream in despair and, with the handful of other forward-looking Southerners in the novel, returns to the North.

The Colonel's Dream is the final volume of what might be called Chesnutt's New South trilogy. Each of his previous novels tests a particular means of alleviating the racial injustices that Chesnutt believed were endemic in the South. In *The House Behind the Cedars*, the individualistic, clandestine strategies of the Waldens are shown to be very risky, often self-defeating, ways of gaining rights and opportunities for a marginal group of Afro-Americans. In *The Marrow of Tradition*, both violent resistance and diplomatic accommodation are weighed as choices for aspiring Southern blacks, with neither proving itself potent enough to stop the rise of institutionalized racism. *The Colonel's Dream* asks whether white philanthropy, cooperative enterprise, and the pursuit of enlightened self-interest among whites and blacks could raise the socioeconomic prospects of both races and thus create a climate in which justice might thrive. In a number of public statements and in private correspondence, Chesnutt endorsed programs very similar to the ones that French espouses in *The Colonel's Dream*. Yet, for all his moderation and good intentions, Chesnutt's hero fails because he does not realize until the end of the novel that piecemeal reforms in education, economics, and civil rights cannot cure a society in which, as the narrator of the novel concludes, "the very standards of right and wrong had been confused by the race issue." Colonel French decides that somehow "a new body of thought must be built up" in the South, but he never discovers a way to do this. Neither did Chesnutt, except by writing such books as *The House Behind the Cedars, The Marrow of Tradition*, and *The Colonel's Dream*.

Chesnutt's last novel was the harshest, most lurid, and most thoroughgoing fictional exposé of the New South myth in its era. Perhaps sensing that this would be his last Southern book, he wrote into the culmination of *The Colonel's Dream* a grim finality that registered his increasing despair over the prospects of forward-looking blacks or whites in the Jim Crow South. Much of his analysis of the region's problems has been borne out by subsequent historians, qualifying Chesnutt for recognition as one of the precursors of twentieth-century Southern literary realism, of such writers as Ellen Glasgow and Stark Young. Even more important, with George W. Cable in *The Grandissimes* and Mark Twain in *Pudd'nhead Wilson*, Chesnutt anticipated Faulkner in focusing on miscegenation, even more than slavery, as the repressed myth of the American past and a powerful metaphor of Southern post–Civil War history. To the question of the origins and ramifications of miscegenation, he brought an intimate knowledge unprecedented in American literature, which instilled in his writing a deeper appreciation of the comic absurdities and tragic realities generated by the color line than any American writer had imagined before him.

SURVEY OF CRITICISM

Until the 1960s critical interest in the life and work of Charles Chesnutt was slight. The only substantial work that had been done on the first important black fiction writer was his daughter's eulogistic biography, *Charles Waddell Chesnutt: Pioneer of the Color Line* (1952). Helen M. Chesnutt's treatment of her father is understandably adulatory and does not offer a detailed estimate of his writing, but because it includes a generous selection from his journals and letters it is a useful sourcebook. The standard scholarly biography is Frances Richardson Keller's *An American Crusade: The Life of Charles Waddell Chesnutt* (1978). Here, too, the focus is on the making of a racial leader and opinion-maker, with a somewhat sketchy analysis and evaluation of Chesnutt's literary work.

After the reprinting of Chesnutt's fiction in the 1960s, scholarly articles and essays on his writing have proliferated. In the absence of a representative collection of these shorter studies of Chesnutt, readers interested in the status of Chesnutt criticism must begin by consulting the three books on the writer that are currently available. The first of these to be published was J. Noel Heermance's *Charles W. Chesnutt: America's First Great Black Novelist* (1974). Although Heermance demythologizes the man behind the writing, his criticism of Chesnutt's fiction is uneven, and his assessments are often laudatory to the point of special pleading. Sylvia Lyons Render's *Charles W. Chesnutt* (1980) provides a helpful introduction to the writer without exploring the more complex literary issues that have been raised about the man or his work. William L. Andrews's *The Literary Career of Charles W. Chesnutt* (1980) offers a unified, systematic, and extensive examination and evaluation of Chesnutt's entire literary corpus. Its primarily literary historical approach, however, is but one of a number of promising methods of investigating Chesnutt's literary experimentation and significance.

BIBLIOGRAPHY

Works by Charles W. Chesnutt

The Conjure Woman. Boston: Houghton Mifflin, 1899.

Frederick Douglass. Boston: Small Maynard, 1899.

The Wife of His Youth and Other Stories of the Color Line. Boston: Houghton Mifflin, 1899.

The House Behind the Cedars. Boston: Houghton Mifflin, 1900.

The Marrow of Tradition. Boston: Houghton Mifflin, 1901.

"Baxter's Procrustes." *Atlantic Monthly* 93 (June 1904): 823–30.

The Colonel's Dream. New York: Doubleday, Page, 1905.

The Short Fiction of Charles W. Chesnutt. Ed. Sylvia Lyons Render. Washington: Howard University Press, 1974.

Studies of Charles W. Chesnutt

Andrews, William L. *The Literary Career of Charles W. Chesnutt*. Baton Rouge: Louisiana State University Press, 1980.

Bone, Robert. *Down Home: A History of Afro-American Short Fiction from Its Beginnings to the End of the Harlem Renaissance*. New York: Putnam, 1975.

Chesnutt, Helen. *Charles Waddell Chesnutt: Pioneer of the Color Line*. Chapel Hill: University of North Carolina Press, 1952.

Ellison, Curtis and E. W. Metcalf, Jr. *Charles W. Chesnutt: A Reference Guide*. Boston: G. K. Hall, 1977.

Heermance, J. Noel. *Charles W. Chesnutt: America's First Great Black Novelist*. Hamden, Conn.: Shoe String Press, 1974.

Keller, Frances Richardson. *An American Crusade: The Life of Charles Waddell Chesnutt*. Provo, Utah: Brigham Young University Press, 1978.

Render, Sylvia Lyons. *Charles W. Chesnutt*. Boston: Twayne, 1980.

CHARLES M. LOMBARD

Thomas Holley Chivers
(1809–1858)

Among nineteenth-century Southern poets, Thomas Holley Chivers occupies a unique position. He became friends with Edgar Allan Poe and was influenced by him. In turn, Poe apparently also borrowed ideas from Chivers, who thought Poe borrowed even more. Chivers, however, wanted to be seen in his own right as an innovator in poetry.

BIOGRAPHY

Born in Washington, Georgia, on 18 October 1809, Thomas Holley Chivers grew up in a rough frontier community. His father's thriving mill and cotton farm assured Chivers a comfortable living. In those days Georgia was a violent territory threatened by outlaws and Indians. Methodist and Baptist preachers denounced crime and vice and engaged in theological debates. The promise of eternal reward comforted a society with a high death rate.

Readers searching for biographical details in Chivers's writings find reports of a carefree lad living close to nature. He always had great affection for the family homestead, spoke respectfully of his father, and made his mother the focus of reverence in his poetry. But there is also ample evidence that Chivers was aware of the social turbulence around him.

The oldest of three sons and four daughters, Chivers had a special attachment to one sister whose death had a lasting effect on him; she is the Adaline honored in his poems. His first marriage in 1827 was an equally sorrowful experience. Frances, his bride and a first cousin, left Chivers after a few months, even though already pregnant. He was never allowed to see his daughter. After extensive litigation, he finally obtained a divorce on grounds of desertion.

The quick-tempered and high-strung Chivers underwent painful readjustment. One of his in-laws, Franky Albert, spread rumors that Chivers was a wife beater.

Her gossip forced him to leave town, and he enrolled in medical school in 1828 at Transylvania University in Kentucky, where on 17 March 1830 he received his degree.

Chivers practiced medicine for a short time and then abandoned it to wander in the wilderness near Cincinnati and to visit the Cherokee Indians. A volume of poems, the *Path of Sorrow* (1832), is a record of his wanderings. Popular interest in the theatre led him to write a verse drama, *Conrad and Eudora*, based on the Beauchamp-Sharpe murder case of the 1820s; later it came to be known as the Kentucky Tragedy.

After returning to Georgia in 1835, Chivers devoted himself to writing. *Nacoochee* (1837) was published at his own expense, as were subsequent works. Chivers was often in the North, where he met and married Harriet Hunt of Springfield, Massachusetts. The wedding took place on 21 November 1837 in New York. Eleven years of personal tragedy followed his second marriage. In addition to the death of his mother, Chivers faced the deaths of favorite daughter, Allegra Florence, and his three other children.

Chivers's residence in the East brought him into personal contact with Poe. They met by chance on a street in New York in early summer 1845 when Poe was accosting one of his most vitriolic critics, Lewis Gaylord Clark. Poe and Chivers had previously corresponded with each other. Their brief association has raised questions about their influence on each other's poetry in the matter of symbols and versification.

In the late 1840s alleged supernatural manifestations accomplished by mesmerists and spiritualists caused Chivers to compose *Search After Truth*, an apology for Swedenborg's teachings on immortality and a refutation of materialism. The Swedenborgianism in *Search After Truth* formed the basis for the aesthetic and poetic theory underlying *Eonchs of Ruby* in 1850. Rebuffed by critics, a disappointed Chivers nonetheless continued to write. Three works, *Virginalia*, *Atlanta*, and *Memoralia*, were published in 1853.

By 1855 the rising tide of abolitionism made Chivers feel uneasy in the North, so he terminated his residence there. Back home in Georgia, he expressed his views on the slavery question: loyalty to the Union was important for the moment to Chivers, but he foresaw the possibility of secession. A work written in 1856, *Birth-Day Song of Liberty*, was nevertheless optimistic in tone and made no mention of civil war. Afflicted with a sudden illness, Chivers wrote his will and died on 18 December 1858 in Decatur, Georgia.

MAJOR THEMES

The Native American had an important place in Chivers's plays and poetry. Like Poe and other Southern writers, Chivers was acquainted with Chateaubriand and his views of the American Indian. In *Atala* (1801) and *Les Natchez* (1826–31) the French writer glorified the Indian in a manner that appealed to Romantic tastes: noble, stoical warriors courted comely, sentimental maidens who were either Christians or about to be converted. Instead of a description of authentic Indian customs, readers were given a picture of Europeanized red men.

Although Chivers followed the prevailing trend in America to idealize Indians in his works, he also depicted them as warlike tribesmen. Although he was certain of his Indian names and his terms were reasonably accurate, his poetry about the Indian varied in quality; one of his best is "Atala's Prayer," which received special praise from Poe. In most of Chivers's Indian poems the theme concerns an Indian maid on an enchanted isle who is sought by both heroic and villainous warriors. Chivers's borrowing from themes and models from Chateaubriand was a practice among Longfellow, Poe, and other American Romantics. In Chivers this trend had one of its better expressions.

In *Search After Truth* (1848), written in the form of a dialogue between a seer and his pupil Politian, none other than Chivers and Poe under obvious pseudonyms, Chivers refuted materialism and proposed the theology of Swedenborg in its stead. Primarily an exposition of the Swedish mystic's thought, the work was also designed in all probability to convert Poe, with whom Chivers had had lively discussions on many topics during their brief acquaintance. The work is an important indicator of Chivers's thought.

Chivers was especially indebted to Swedenborg, whose teaching he knew as early as the 1830s. The religious thought of Swedenborg gave Chivers the ideas that formed the basis of his aesthetics and provided themes for his poetry. The Swedish mystic depicted humanity as only a step away from eternal life, since man had two bodies, one material, the other spiritual. Death separated man from his material body, but he continued to live in his spiritual body in the spiritual world. Through this theory Swedenborg explained his own alleged contact with the world of spirits.

Man's quest for truth, according to Swedenborg, led thim through the material world and ultimately into the world of spirits. After passing through various stages, man gradually became aware of the spiritual truths behind the material forms of the physical world. This theory of correspondences between natural and spiritual truths inspired Chivers's concept of aesthetics and explains his striving for novel and singular effects in rhythm and harmony; poetry had to reveal spiritual truths behind the material sounds and the moods evoked by harmonious rhyme. Chivers's interest in the notion of correspondence was undoubtedly first aroused by Emerson's *Nature* (1836). Besides his search for corresponding relationships in the world, Chivers sought to verify the reality of Swedenborg's spirit world when interpreting in poems his own dreamlike encounters with departed loved ones. For Chivers, there was a thin wall separating life on earth from eternity.

There was already some evidence of an interest in dream and visions in the *Path of Sorrow* (1832), his first volume of poems, but the work has little artistic value.

Chivers showed more promise in *Nacoochee* (1837), where in a preface he defined poetry in terms symbolic of the mysteries and infinity of the sea. The

society of angels, which departed souls joined, and divine emanation were proposed as Swedenborgian concepts that lent themselves aptly to poetry. True to
Romantic tradition, Chivers acclaimed the poet's role as priest and prophet, a
theme repeated in subsequent prefaces.

In *Nacoochee* Swedenborgian and Chateaubriandesque themes exist side by
side, indicating Chivers's search for some form of mystic exaltation. The Indian
maiden in *Atala* chooses death over carnality, and her counterpart in *Nacoochee*
escapes a lustful suitor by ascending to heaven. What Chivers had created was
a Swedenborgian Indian determined to control her sexual drives and achieve
perfection on a celestial plane.

Nacoochee, unlike the melancholy and frustrated Atala, anticipates eagerly
the joys of heaven. Seraphims behold her from above as she harmonizes her life
with heavenly precepts:

> There gushed upon her cheeks, beneath her eyes,
> A vigilant sublimity, that seemed
> To those, who gazed upon her with surprise,
> As if they had, despairingly, but dreamed
> Of some Utopian loveliness, they deemed
> Of some celestial sphere, which God had given
> To make Creation heaven! . . .
>
> *(Nacoochee, p. 18)*

"The Soaring Swan," written in blank verse, affords a better example of
Chivers's talent. He set the mood in the first line; the physical heights to which
the swan soars correspond to the poet's sensation of spiritual elevation:

> Thou art soaring away, beautiful bird!
> Upon thy pinions into distant lands
> Bathing thy downy bosom's loftiest flight
> In welkin zephyrs! Whither art thou borne
> From snowy home through heaven's empyrean depths?
>
> *(Nacoochee, p. 25)*

"The Soaring Swan" probably had some effect on Rossetti and marks a step
forward in Chivers's effort to stimulate the reader's imagination by softly suggesting color and sound.

The Lost Pleiad (1845) contains 68 pieces composed between 1836 and 1844.
Most of the poems deal with love and death and are rather short. Poe praised
The Lost Pleiad; and although he made no mention of plagiarism, other critics
accused Chivers of being an outrageous copycat in borrowing openly from the
language and meter of "The Raven," most notably, the use of the refrain
"Nevermore!" There were other critics, however, who joined Poe in praise of
The Lost Pleiad, among them William Gilmore Simms. After some initial success

the work declined in popularity, but not before Chivers enjoyed momentary recognition.

In the title poem of over 800 lines, "The Lost Pleiad," Chivers portrays the death of his daughter, Allegra Florence, using starkly realistic details of typhoid fever. The grimness is alleviated by the vision of her ascent to heaven in conformity with Swedenborg's teachings. The outer shell of the material body is cast aside, and Allegra emerges clothed in her spiritual body. Transfused with light, a visual phenomenon recorded by Swedenborg as occurring in his own trances, she is ready to enter into angelic society:

> So does the soul cast off its form
> Even as the chrysalis the worm
> And rise up from its mortal night,
> A spiritual body, clothed in light,
> As different from its body here,
> As Heaven is from this sinful sphere.
>
> (*Lost Pleiad*, p. 6)

One form which Chivers felt at home with was the ballad. "Awake from Thy Slumbers" has some of the gentle lilting movement associated with Stephen Foster. The poet's enthusiasm for the countryside imparts sprightliness to the lines

> Awake from thy slumber! the wild birds are tuning
> Their voices to greet thee so loud in the brake,
> While the roebucks are watching the swans that are pruning
> Their white silver wings on the glass of the lake.
>
> (*Lost Pleiad*, p. 23)

Chivers had the Romantic's love of nature expressed in terms of his own fondness of the Georgia landscape. In *The Lost Pleiad* he deftly handles symbols and versification. Stimulated by Swedenborg's emphasis on correspondence, he sought material images that reflect celestial truths and lines that demonstrate the interrelation of poetry and music.

Eonchs of Ruby (1851) aroused interest by its odd title. Eonch, explained Chivers, was simply a variation of *Concha* and was used for its euphony. In Swedenborg's language of correspondences, Ruby connoted Divine Love. The work at first was favorably received, but charges again arose about his plagiarizing Poe.

"The Vigil of Aiden," the first poem in the collection, was a homage to Poe. Skeptical critics, however, refused to concede that Chivers intentionally borrowed from Poe out of respect. The mood and rhythm of "The Raven," imitated creditably by Chivers, were scorned by his opponents. Its cadence and melody, nevertheless, recall in a measure Poe's lyrics:

> And the voice of that sweet Maiden,
> From the Jasper Groves of Aiden
> With her lily lips love-laden
> Answered, "Yes! forever more!"

                                                         (*Eonchs*, p. 14)

Like his other volumes of verse, *Eonchs*, although uneven in quality and inspiration, contains noteworthy stanzas. One such passage in "The Mighty Dead" pays an unaffected and moving tribute to Shelley:

> Like that sweet Bird of Night,
> Startling the Ebon silence from repose,
> Until the stars appear to burn more bright
> From its excessive gush of song, which flows
> Like some impetuous river to the sea—
> So thou didst flood the world with melody.

                                                         (*Eonchs*, p. 16)

In "The Lusiad" Chivers displays his ability to describe a Georgian rural scene with zest and vigor. The repetend, "Long time ago," reflects Chivers's interest in folk music and gives a whimsical cast to the lines. Chivers's regionalism, as witnessed here, is too often overlooked by critics when it is in reality one of the fresh and bright elements in his poetry:

> On the banks of Talapoosa,
> Long time ago.
> Where it mingles with the Coosa,
> Southward to flow—
> Dwelt the Maid I love, sweet Lucy!
> Lucy, long time ago.

                                                         (*Eonchs*, p. 57)

When Chivers resided in the East for long periods of time, he frequently attended plays and concerts. After hearing a famous soprano on one occasion, he jotted down his reactions in "To Ceclia":

> Like mellow moonlight in the month of June
> Waning serenely on some far-off sea,
> Died the soft pathos of that spiritual tune—
> Soft as the liquid hues of Heaven to me.

                                                         (*Eonchs*, p. 82)

Chivers defined "liquid hues" as "the harmony between a soft sound and a blue color" (*Eonchs*, p. 68).

Preoccupation with the unity of sensory perceptions is also in evidence in "Lord Uther's Lament for Ella." Chivers produces pleasant results in rhyme and refrain through the judicious use of descriptive terms in a series of evenly cadenced and smoothly paced lines:

> By her side Cherubic Aster
> With white limbs of Alabaster
> Circled through Heaven's azure pasture,
> Half the fields of night to mow,
> When her heart to mine was given—
> Then she sang to me at even
> Golden melodies of Heaven
> In the days of long ago.
>
> (*Eonchs*, p. 83)

Some poems in *Eonchs of Ruby* may provide grounds for accusing Chivers of plagiarizing Poe, but more often they indicate aims and techniques common to both. A more profitable subject of inquiry would be the way in which Poe and Chivers represented a special trend in American poetry, one apart from the main current.

Memoralia (1853) was nothing more than a reissue of *Eonchs of Ruby*, to which 26 pages were added. One poem in the new edition, "The Poet," sums up Chivers's role as a priest-prophet revealing heavenly secrets to mankind, a Romantic notion common to Novalis and Hugo, among others:

> The Poet, through all things on Earth, can see
> Glimpses of that Celestial state to be.
> The Voices of all Ages, from their dim
> Abodes, (his foregone echoes,) answer him.
> God's holy Messenger to ignorant men
> To lead them safely back to Heaven again.
>
> (*Memoralia*, p. 24)

The foregoing lines suggest that Chivers was probably convinced the soul could, as Swedenborg claimed, leave the body on occasion to visit the world of spirits. In his final years, Chivers dwelt on such mystical experiences.

Atlanta: or the True Blessed Isle of Poesy (1853) has the same general story line as *Nacoochee*. The narrative serves as the framework for an allegory on the quest for spiritual truth. The two lovers sublimate their sexual drives and rise to a celestial plane in keeping with Swedenborgian precepts. In its better passages *Atlanta* has lines that convey pleasant sensations of sound, color, and taste as Chivers makes skillful use of meter, refrain, and imagery.

Virginalia (1853) consists of short lyric poems. Generally ignored, except for a few favorable comments, *Virginalia* represented Chivers's continuing work to develop poetry as an instrument of sound. This resulted at times in poems that, when read aloud, produced a series of irregularly recurring impulses painful to hear. More often in *Virginalia* Chivers literally generated a sustained vibrational energy from felicitous word combinations that conveyed to the reader notions, impressions, and sensations that brought into play all the reader's faculties: mind, imagination and intuition are simultaneously stimulated.

In 1855 Chivers left the North never to return. His last poem, *Birth-Day Song of Liberty* (1856), was a lackluster summary of the deeds of leading figures in American history, ending with a florid eulogy of the Lord's selection of the United States to play a crucial part in the divine strategy to spread democracy throughout the world. *Birth-Day Song of Liberty*, reiterative and tedious, was a sorry swan for the author of *Eonchs of Ruby* and *Virginalia*.

But despite that poem, Chivers deserves praise for his poetic achievements. He often obtained singular effects in his poems through a variety of sounds, even to coining words when necessary. He imitated the lively patterns in black songs. He always took a keen interest in form and structure and experimented with stanzaic forms. In *The Lost Pleiad* Chivers attempted several variations of the sonnet with fair success, although on the whole he had little awareness of the intricacies of that form.

Never inclined to use a standard poetic form without altering it, Chivers discarded blank verse after trying it briefly in the 1830s. Even when using quatrains, one of his favorite forms, Chivers alternated trimeter, tetrameter, and pentameter lines. His stanzas often vary from three to eleven lines in length.

Experimentation for its own sake led Chivers astray. For example, his variation of the Spenserian stanza was seldom successful. In the *Path of Sorrow* blank verse was a problem, and his experiments with it were primitive. The refrain is not found in the *Path of Sorrow*, but by 1853 *Virginalia* scarcely has a poem without one. Since Chivers was determined to expand the function of rhythm and sound in poetry, the refrain was a logical choice. His fondness for folk ballads made him aware of the suggestive effects attained by the skillful use of repetends. Repetitive strains could convey to the reader the auditory and visual sensations of a woodland scene.

Oratory in the South was glorified as a manly expression of patriotism, a viewpoint that affected Chivers. He tried declamatory verse in *Conrad and Eudora* as well as in *Birth-Day Song of Liberty*.

The coining of new terms and phrases was closely related to Chivers's experiments with meters and refrains. *Smile-beams, zephyr-dimpled lake, island-clouds*, and *shell-tones* were among his early neologisms. Chiversian words could conjure up images of hues and colors.

Of secondary consideration to Chivers was the literal meaning of words since he was more concerned with the connotations of the terms he used. Apparently he was aware of the far-reaching implications of altering the literal meaning of words in poetry.

Color and sound became one in Chivers's mind since identical terms could be used to describe both sensory reactions. The word portrait in "The Angelus" illustrates this point:

> A wave-like, azure sound,
> Upon the pavement of new-fallen snow

Pure as an Angel's garment upon the ground—
Trembling the atmosphere with its soft flow—
Comes swiftly, with its Heaven-dialating swell,
From the Noon-ringing of yon far-off Hell.

(*Virginalia*, p. 108)

Absorbed in the study of color and its sonic connotations, Chivers examined the possibility of a stronger stress on onomatopoeia with a corresponding deemphasis on the literal meaning of words. He realized as well the need for alliteration and assonance. In seeking a form where beauty of sound was of primary importance, Chivers hoped to develop novel verbal magic. There are moments in Chivers's poems when an unanalytical reader might find himself in a bizarre world of unconventional word combinations that conjure up startling images of sound and color. One poem in particular, "Chinese Serenade," records the sounds of a Chinese fretted instrument in an attempt at a phonetic reproduction of the strange sounds of a different musical tradition:

Tien-Tsze
Tu Du
Skies Blue—
All Clear—
Fourth Year,
Third Moon.
High Noon.

("Chinese Serenade," p. 344)

Another poem, somewhat similar to "Chinese Serenade," is "Railroad Song," where a clever use of sound leads to a vivid picture of a train pulling out of a station. Here Chivers recognized that a proper choice of onomatopoeic words and end-rhymes could conjure up the image of a locomotive:

All aboard! Yes—Tingle, tingle
Goes the bell as we all mingle—
No one sitting solely single—
As the steam begins to fizzle—
With a kind of sighing sizzle
Ending in a piercing whistle.

("Railroad Song," p. 1)

Chivers displays his craftmanship in the juxtaposition of similar sounds. He always insisted that his contemporaries did not understand the function of sound in poetry and regretted what he considered their refusal to experiment. As early as the *Path of Sorrow* in "The Retrospect" he dealt with the thin line separating sleep from wakefulness where dream and reality seemingly become one. The clarity of his depiction of the oneiric state demonstrates unusual insight:

My chamber has become an alcove
For the watchers of the sky! and in my
Bed, at midnight of my sleep, I people
Worlds, and dream unnumbered things, till silence
Wakes for lethargy, and shocks my burning
Brain.

(Path of Sorrow, p. 116)

Chivers recognized the evocative quality of words but did not always put his knowledge to the best possible use. For him the poet's function was to give to readers through poetry some inkling of heavenly truths; his role was, as he saw it, essentially sacerdotal in performing what amounted to a religious ritual.

Although he opposed cruel treatment of blacks, Chivers, as a slaveholder, defended slavery as an economic and social institution essential to the South. He always appreciated and admired the various rhythms of slave singing and felt that white writers could profit by studying them. With his frequent stress on the pristine quality of writers in the early period of man's history, it is not surprising he would draw upon sources in his own surroundings that reflected the spontaneity of the poetic and musical traditions of a simpler society. For this reason the folk heritage of the blacks he knew would naturally attract him.

Most slaves of the time expressed their misery in song. Outwardly mirthful and lighthearted, their music voiced the inner despair caused by their bondage. The lyrics usually concerned the singer himself, fellow slaves, or some physical point of reference, whether a river or an animal. Rhyme and rhythm were convenient memory devices and helped singers recall the lines of a song. A captivating sound pattern was more important than communicating a precise message. Final consonants were usually dropped at the end of a line. Short lines were coordinated with long ones, and long words were scanned in the same way as shorter ones. Such a flexible prosody allowed a composer to produce unusual effects when two syllables could be counted as one. Pronouns and conjunctions were deleted, and considerable latitude was permitted in the pronunciation of words. Thus a composer could invent subtle harmonies with few strained rhymes or dissonant sounds.

Chivers sneered at the Northern writer's ignorance of black music and language and cited Harriet Beecher Stowe, Stephen Foster, and G. P. Morris as notorious offenders in this regard. Blacks themselves, insisted Chivers, resented Northern indifference to their folk customs. To remedy the situation, he suggested, a learned Southerner should make a serious study of black music. Chivers himself was well qualified to undertake such a research project. His own renditions of black songs capture the spirit of their forceful and almost hypnotic rhythm. The "Corn Shucking Song" (1855) demonstrated his sensitivity to their energy and vigor:

Jinny broke de hoecake, Sally make de cawphy,
Nancy bile de bakyon wid de bracky-ey pea;

Cuffy blow de Ram's Hawn, Juba beat de banjo—
Dinah ring de Tin Pan to cawl us awl to Tea.

("Corn Shucking Song," p. 2)

Chivers's love of black music with its rhythm and harmony resulted in sweeping statements, for example, his assertion that even Greek poetry lacked some of the harmony of black verse. Always outspoken in his regionalism, Chivers was convinced that black melodies, like all folk art, had lessons for more conventional art forms.

SURVEY OF CRITICISM

Every student of Chivers is indebted to S. Foster Damon, whose *Thomas Holley Chivers: Friend of Poe* (1930) is scholarly and comprehensive. The work contains a bibliography of the periodical publications, poems, and articles by Chivers as well as a bibliography of reviews and criticisms of his work. There is still need, however, for a definitive bibliography of Chivers's work.

In 1931 Landon C. Bell criticized Damon for his praise of Chivers. Joel Benton in his 1899 *In the Poe Circle* had viewed the Poe-Chivers controversy with much greater objectivity. In "Poe and Chivers" (1902), James A. Harrison also made valuable, if incomplete, comparisons.

Charles Henry Watts's *Thomas Holley Chivers, His Literary Career and Poetry* (1956) is, like Damon's work, indispensable. Charles M. Lombard's *Thomas Holley Chivers* (1979) is also a useful summary of the poet's career and work.

The most fascinating part of Chivers's criticism remains the Poe-Chivers controversy. Chivers first met Poe in New York in June 1845. They discussed the publication of *The Lost Pleiad*, later favorably reviewed by Poe. They had corresponded earlier, and when the Georgian returned home, they exchanged further letters. After the latter's death Chivers wrote a *Life of Poe*; it remained unpublished until 1952. In the biography Chivers denounced Poe's detractors, at the same time responding to charges that he plagiarized "The Raven"; he insisted that Poe was indebted to him personally for thematic and metrical techniques.

In the nineteenth century there was in actual practice an easygoing attitude to the contrary. Even before Poe's death the fact of their mutual borrowing was plainly in evidence. Damon has concluded that Chivers was justified in claiming that Poe took the format of "The Raven" from him and that there is a strong resemblance between Poe's "Ulalume" and Chivers's "Nacoochee."

Long before they met in 1845 the two poets were acquainted with each other's work. Chivers claimed that in 1831 he read a volume of Poe's poems. Sometime after that Poe came across some of Chivers's poetry sent to him when he was editor of the *Southern Literary Messenger* in the 1830s; Poe might also have been familiar with *Nacoochee*. Unquestionably, both poets must have recognized that they used similar methods and imagery.

Charges that *Eonchs of Ruby* contained passages taken directly from Poe infuriated Chivers. Unable to restrain himself, he proclaimed publicly that "The Raven" owed much to his "To Allegra Florence in Heaven"; moreover, Chivers insisted that Poe was indebted to him for poetic innovations and technique.

Much of the controversy revolved around similarity in the use of meter and refrains. To a certain extent Chivers's protests can be attributed to his resentment of public indifference to his work. Yet there is some evidence in his favor. The refrain "Nevermore" may be read in the "Lament on the Death of My Mother" (1829). Furthermore, in Chivers's manuscripts at Duke University Library a passage from an unpublished poem "No More" composed in 1829 is similar to "The Raven" (1845):

> A voice then answered faint and low,
> From yon far-distant shore;
> Whose name I sought at once to know—
> Said he to me—'No more!'
>
> (Duke University Chivers Manuscripts)

Conceivably "No More" might have been printed in one of the countless magazines or newspapers of the time, only to remain buried there. Perhaps "No More" was one of the poems sent to the *Southern Literary Messenger* when Poe was editor. Be that as it may, the poem's refrain is not comparable to "Nevermore," used by Poe within a poetic context of greater complexity and power. In the furor over his alleged theft of Poe's material, the excitable Chivers apparently forgot a poem in his files that might have supported his arguments. Many commentators today would claim any comparison between "No More" and "The Raven" is unconvincing and would attribute any resemblance to a generally shared literary style and translation of subject matter and theme. At the very least, "No More" provides evidence that Chivers was in a certain sense correct in claiming he first used the basic theme, pattern, and refrain of "The Raven" with its haunting imagery and echo.

On the subject of the origin of specific lines in "The Raven" there is reason to believe that a line from "Isadore" in the *Eonchs of Ruby*, "Back to Hell, thou ghostly Horror!", was written prior to the publication of "The Raven." In a letter to Poe, 21 February 1847, Chivers implies that "Isadore" was a poem familiar to Poe for several years.

Some of the confusion is caused by significant gaps in the Poe-Chivers correspondence, which covers a period of nine years. Many letters, referred to by both poets in their existing correspondence, ostensibly were lost. There are nineteen letters in manuscript collections, but at least seventeen letters remain undiscovered—two from Poe to Chivers and fifteen or more from Chivers to Poe. Some questions will remain unsolved unless additional letters are found, a fact that some critics are inclined to overlook; Chivers's claims, owing to Poe's stature, are too often lightly dismissed. If further letters are found, Chivers may yet have a fair hearing in which some of his arguments may be substantiated. Until that time the Poe-Chivers controversy cannot be fully resolved. The dispute over Poe notwithstanding, Chivers at the very least remains a significant figure in Southern letters by reason of his unique approach to poetry, the use of Swedenborgian and Chateaubriandesque themes, and pioneer efforts in reproducing black songs and verse.

BIBLIOGRAPHY

Works by Thomas Holley Chivers

The Path of Sorrow, or, The Lament of Youth: A Poem. Franklin, Tenn.: Western Weekly Review, 1832.

The Constitution of Man. Memphis, Tenn. 1833. Title from the *Western Monthly Magazine* 1 (July 1833): 321–25.

Conrad and Eudora; or, The Death of Alonzo. A Tragedy. In Five Acts. Founded on the Murder of Sharpe, by Beauchamp, in Kentucky. Philadelphia: n.p., 1834.

Nacoochee; or, The Beautiful Star, with Other Poems. New York: W. E. Dean, 1837.

The Lost Pleiad; and Other Poems. New York: Edward O. Jenkins, 1845.

Search After Truth; or, A New Revelation of the Psycho-Physiological Nature of Man. New York: Cobb & Yallalee, 1848.

Eonchs of Ruby, A Gift of Love. New York: Spalding and Shephard, 1851.

"The Railroad Song." *Georgia Citizen* (21 June 1851), p. 1.

"Chinese Serenade." *Dodge's Literary Museum* 5 (30 October 1852): 344.

Atlanta; or, The True Blessed Island of Poesy. A Paul epic. Macon: Georgia Citizen, 1853.

Memoralia; or, Phials of Amber Full of the Tears of Love. A Gift for the Beautiful. Philadelphia: Lippincott, 1853.

Virginalia; or, Songs of My Summer Nights. A Gift of Love for the Beautiful. Philadelphia: Lippincott, 1853.

"Corn Shucking Song." *Georgia Citizen* (12 June 1855), p. 2.

Birth-Day Song of Liberty. A Paean of Glory for the Heroes of Freedom. Atlanta: C. R. Hanleiter, 1856.

The Sons of Usna: A Tragi-Apotheosis, in Five Acts. Philadelphia: C. Sherman, 1858.

Chivers' Life of Poe. Ed. Richard Beale Davis. New York: Dutton, 1952.

The Correspondence of Thomas Holley Chivers. Ed. Emma Lester Chase and Lois Ferry Parks. Providence, R.I.: Brown University Press, 1957. This work was originally intended as the first volume of a complete set of Chivers's works.

Unpublished Plays. Ed. Charles M. Lombard. Delmar, N.Y.: Scholar's Facsimiles & Reprints, 1980.

Studies of Thomas Holley Chivers

Bell, Landon C. *Poe and Chivers*. Columbus: Trowbridge, 1931.

Benton, Joel. *In the Poe Circle*. New York: Mansfield and Wessels, 1899.

Damon, S. Foster. *Thomas Holley Chivers: Friend of Poe*. New York: Harpers, 1930.

Harrison, James A. "Poe and Chivers." *The Complete Works of Edgar Allan Poe*. New York: Crowell, 1902. 7: 266–88.

Hubbell, Jay B. *The South in American Literature, 1607–1900*. Durham, N.C.: Duke University Press, 1954, pp. 555–59.

Lombard, Charles M. *Thomas Holley Chivers*. Boston: Twayne, 1979.

Watts, Charles Henry. *Thomas Holley Chivers, His Literary Career and Poetry*. Athens: University of Georgia Press, 1956.

Kate Chopin
(1851–1904)

Considered today as an important innovator among nineteenth-century Southern writers, Kate Chopin was condemned by her contemporaries for writing an indecent novel. After her death, critics largely ignored her work until she was rediscovered in the mid-twentieth century.

BIOGRAPHY

Katherine O'Flaherty was born 8 February 1851 in St. Louis, Missouri. Her family background not only molded her personality but also provided her with a wealth of material for her fiction. On her mother's side, O'Flaherty's family traced its roots to French-Creole settlers who came to America in the early 1700s. Her great-grandmother, Victoria Verdon Charleville, told the young Katherine not only of their family but also of the early history of the Louisiana Territory. These tales of larger-than-life figures such as LaSalle were often embellished, becoming as much fiction as fact. Many of her tales were also quite frank in details, a quality later influencing Kate Chopin's realistic writing.

In contrast to her mother's Creole background, her father immigrated to America from Ireland, arriving in St. Louis in 1825. Thomas O'Flaherty became a successful merchant accepted into the upper classes of St. Louis. His first wife died in childbirth. His second marriage in 1844 to Eliza Farris resulted in three children, Thomas, Jr.; Kate; and another daughter who did not survive childhood. Kate was the only child who lived into middle age. Thomas drowned when he was twenty-five, and George, her half-brother, died of typhoid fever in 1862 after being captured and imprisoned by Union forces.

As a child, O'Flaherty enjoyed the luxury and security of life in a handsome home and gardens. Although these comforts continued throughout her childhood, the O'Flaherty household became much more subdued after the death of her father in a train wreck in 1855. Kate was only four years old.

Kate O'Flaherty's education was characteristic of a young girl of a prominent Catholic family. She entered the St. Louis Academy of the Sacred Heart in 1860, where she became an avid reader and a talented musician. At home the influence of her great-grandmother, Mme. Charleville, continued, especially because Kate was expected to speak French to her; thus Kate learned to read French literature in the original. The death of her great-grandmother and her half-brother when she was twelve brought about a period when she was somewhat a recluse, remaining away from school while she and her mother grieved. She sought an escape in literature, especially poetry and fiction, but eventually returned to school where she was a good student and kept a commonplace book in which she sometimes wrote her own essays and poems.

In her writing, Chopin would often portray conflicts felt by women in fulfilling the role expected by family and society, and even as a young girl she experienced these conflicts herself. After graduating from the Academy in 1868, she led the life of a belle, attending parties and dances and receiving visits from eligible young bachelors. Although she was exceptionally popular and apparently never neglected any of the entertainments of her social set, she confided to her commonplace book that much of this activity was a nuisance, for it took her away from what she loved best—her reading and writing.

Little of her writing from that time survives, and she apparently never wrote seriously until many years later, but there is documentation of her reading, including French and German authors in the original, as well as Dante, Coleridge, Longfellow, Jane Austen, and others. She read both standard writers and current literature being published in magazines, and one of her special interests was in reading books about writers, indicating that even this early in her life, her literary aspirations were serious.

An exciting diversion in spring 1869 was a three-week trip to New Orleans. In her commonplace book she wrote her impressions of the city, which she liked, and of her excitement at meeting a successful actress. In New Orleans she also began to smoke cigarettes, reflecting her willingness to deviate from the prescriptions of how a proper young lady should behave.

Although she had confided to her commonplace book that she was chafing in her role as a belle, O'Flaherty apparently hesitated little in entering into marriage and motherhood. Not long after the trip to New Orleans she met Oscar Chopin, a native of Louisiana who had come to St. Louis to work in a bank. They were married 9 June 1870 and embarked on an extended honeymoon in Europe, a journey abbreviated by the outbreak of the Franco-Prussian War.

Kate and Oscar Chopin were married twelve years and had six children. Although friends characterized her as moody, there is much evidence that, unlike the heroine of her novel *The Awakening*, she loved her husband devotedly and was always close to her children. As newlyweds the Chopins lived in New Orleans where she enthusiastically explored the city she had earlier enjoyed.

Oscar Chopin became a successful cotton factor, and they eventually established their home in the Garden district and played an active role in New Orleans society. As their family grew, Kate Chopin often spent summers with her children at Grand Isle, a Gulf Coast island resort she later depicted in *The Awakening*.

When Oscar Chopin suffered financial losses in 1879, the family moved to Cloutierville in Natchitoches in northern Louisiana, site of the Chopin family lands. Oscar Chopin managed his plantations in addition to running a general store in Cloutierville, described by Kate Chopin as a little French village. A land of cotton plantations now worked by sharecroppers and inhabited by a variety of people—white landowners, blacks, and Cajuns—Natchitoches offered a rich variety of material for Kate Chopin to incorporate into many of her short stories. This way of life ended abruptly when in 1883 Oscar Chopin died of swamp fever, leaving his wife a widow at the age of 30. Although she continued her husband's work in Cloutierville for a year or so, in 1884 she gave in to her mother's pleas to return to St. Louis, only to suffer another unexpected loss when her mother died suddenly the following year.

Kate Chopin's literary career began only after she had suffered these great personal losses. One of the greatest influences in her life at this time was Dr. Frederick Kolbenheyer, her family doctor, who visited her frequently, recommended reading to her, and suggested that she write fiction. In 1888 after a visit to Natchitoches she took his advice and began writing, first poetry and short stories. Her first published work was "If It Might Be," a poem appearing in *America*, 10 January 1889. She was at this time reading Maupassant, whose work she termed "life, not fiction," and she reportedly destroyed a 30,000 word manuscript as she began rethinking her own ideas about fiction. Two stories, "Wiser Than a God" and "A Point at Issue," both treating the problems of women's choices, also appeared in 1889.

Chopin's first novel, *At Fault*, published at her own expense in 1890, marked the first major point in her literary career. The story of a love affair between a young widow and a man who had divorced his wife because of her alcoholism was praised by critics for the skillful depiction of characters and setting. Some critics, however, were offended by the moral issues touched upon in the novel.

Much more popular were her short stories and sketches, 23 of which she collected in *Bayou Folk*, published in 1894. Her stories of life in Louisiana, especially Natchitoches, were well received by a reading audience that enjoyed the local color stories in vogue during the 1880s and 1890s. The exotic setting and complex relationships among characters of the various social orders were fascinating to Northern, often urban, readers. Although she was disappointed that most reviewers were unable to see beyond the surfaces of her fiction, Chopin must have enjoyed the fact that *Bayou Folk* brought her national recognition and enabled her to place easily many of her subsequent short stories.

Chopin continued to write prolifically, almost 40 stories between the publication of *Bayou Folk* and her next collection, *A Night in Acadie* (1897). Similar in setting to the earlier collection and containing some of the same characters,

A Night in Acadie received less enthusiastic reviews, chiefly because the increasing frankness with which Chopin treated her characters and their emotions offended some readers.

In January 1898 Chopin completed what would be her final novel, *The Awakening*, published by Herbert S. Stone in April 1899. Nothing had prepared Chopin for the overwhelming negative reaction to her novel of a young wife and mother who in a search to fulfill her growing desires for independence commits adultery and eventually takes her own life. The book was labeled "poison" by one St. Louis paper, and the consensus was that it was an indecent book. Although many of Chopin's friends wrote to praise the book and to encourage her, she was crushed by the reaction. In the July 1889 number of *Book News*, she defended *The Awakening*, saying that by the time she realized the heroine had made "such a mess of things," it was too late to exclude her from the novel.

Kate Chopin wrote little after *The Awakening*, and she found publishers were now less willing to accept her work. Her health began to fail as well, and on 20 August 1904 she suffered a brain hemorrhage from which she died on 22 August. She was buried in St. Louis.

MAJOR THEMES

During her lifetime Kate Chopin wrote about 100 short stories and sketches; she completed three novels (Chopin destroyed the manuscript of "Young Doctor Gosse," written after *At Fault*, and rejected by publishers), as well as poems, a one-act comedy, and a number of essays. Throughout her work the theme persists that it is important to make choices consistent with one's needs and desires, even if those choices fly in the face of society's expectations. Some critics have noted an ambiguity in Chopin's attitudes toward women (whose characters are predominantly, although not exclusively, her focus). They believe that while she sometimes argues that her characters must achieve their independence, in the form of a career or freedom from the domination of men, at all costs, at other times her female protagonists find that the price of such freedom is an even greater unhappiness. Although Chopin was sometimes ambivalent in her treatment of her fictional heroines, she was also not offering a single answer to the problems the women in her fiction face. There is not a "right" choice for everyone; rather, each one must struggle to find what is right for oneself.

An early tale, written before her marriage, contains the germs of the theme Chopin would develop throughout her work. "Emancipation: A Life Fable" is a brief, overwritten piece describing an animal that has lived in a cage from birth, with his needs provided for. One day the animal finds the door of his cage open and after several false starts musters up enough courage to leave. Chopin concludes: "So does he live, seeking, finding, joying and suffering. The door which accident had opened is open still, but the cage remains forever empty!" (p. 38).

Chopin's first two published stories, both appearing in 1889, show her willingness to explore the dilemmas of her protagonists while demonstrating a variety of responses to such situations. In "Wiser Than a God" the central character, Paula Von Stoltz, a talented but impoverished young pianist, must choose between her music and the rich young man who loves her. When he tells her that she can have marriage *and* her music, she responds, "What do you know of my life? . . . Is music anything more to you than the pleasing distraction of an idle moment? Can't you feel that with me, it courses with the blood through my veins?" (p. 46). For Paula marriage cannot be reconciled easily with one's art— a dilemma faced by many of Chopin's protagonists.

In contrast to the problems of this story is the situation of one written only a few months later. "A Point at Issue" opens with the announcement of the marriage of Eleanor Gail and Charles Faraday, a couple who have decided to have a "modern" marriage, "a form, that while fixing legally their relation to each other, was in no wise to touch the individuality of either" (p. 50). Chopin quickly destroys this premise as she shows how Eleanor and Charles find that they grow jealous of one another's freedoms. By the story's end, Chopin suggests that they will subscribe to a more conventional marriage.

Chopin returned to a similar theme in her first novel, *At Fault* (1890). The young, recently widowed Thérèse Lafirme agrees to allow David Hosmer to manage a sawmill on her Cane River plantation. They fall in love, but when Thérèse learns that David has divorced his wife because of alcoholism, she persuades him that it is his moral duty to return to his wife. David abides by Thérèse's wishes and brings his wife to live with him on the plantation. Having done the "right" thing does not guarantee happiness to the characters in this novel. Hosmer's wife continues to drink, and only after the wife is killed accidentally does Chopin manage to save the situation and allow Thérèse and David to marry.

At Fault is a flawed novel. The dialogue is often stilted; characters are not developed as well as they are in Chopin's later work; and the plot is noticeably contrived. But even in this early work Chopin raises the kind of moral questions that would become so well-defined in her later work, for Thérèse Lafirme takes what she (and society) judge is the "right" course of action when she refuses David Hosmer and persuades him to return to Fanny. But after he takes her advice and she sees the sad result, she begins to doubt the wisdom of her advice: "She had always thought this lesson of right and wrong a very plain one. So easy of interpretation that the simplest minded might solve it if they would. And here had come for the first time in her life a staggering doubt as to its nature" (p. 840). Chopin solves this question by removing David's wife; her later treatment of such questions would be much less simplistic.

Bayou Folk (1894) was the best received of Chopin's books during her lifetime. Most stories in this collection are typical of local color with great attention to Louisiana plantation and small-town life, and in many stories Chopin's main purpose seems to be simply to evoke the way of life she knew there. Some of her stories, however, go beyond mere surface portrayals, such as "Beyond the

Bayou,'' the story of a black woman, La Folle, who has never crossed the bayou since she was frightened there as a child: "Through the woods that spread back into unknown regions the woman had drawn an imaginary line, and past this circle she never stepped'' (p. 175). La Folle worships the young son of the plantation owner and only when he is wounded by a rifle does she overcome her fear and cross the bayou to take him to safety. The story has a happy ending because Chéri is saved, but, even more important, La Folle has become a whole person again as she watches "for the first time the sun rise upon the new, the beautiful world beyond the bayou" (p. 180).

Another story in this collection illustrates Chopin's exploration of male-female relationships and the importance of acting for oneself (or the consequences of not doing so). In "Désirée's Baby," Chopin treats the usually avoided topic of miscegenation and, in doing so, parallels the role of the slave and the wife in Southern society. Désirée, an adopted orphan, has married Armand Aubigny of the neighboring plantation. Armand worships his beautiful wife until after their baby is born and he realizes that it is of mixed blood. When Armand blames her and sends her away from him, Désirée walks with the baby into the bayou and disappears. But Chopin does not end her story here; Armand discovers from the scrap of an old letter that it was his own mother who was of mixed blood. Désirée accepted too readily her husband's condemnation of her, and Chopin paints a grim psychological portrait of a woman who has never dared to think independently.

Chopin's "The Story of an Hour," published in 1894 but not included in either of the short story collections, is a daring study of the response of a young wife to the news of her husband's death: "When she abandoned herself a little whispered word escaped her slightly parted lips. She said it over and over under her breath: 'free, free, free!' " (p. 353). Mrs. Mallard knew that she would mourn her husband: "But she saw beyond that bitter moment a long procession of years to come that would belong to her absolutely. And she opened and spread her arms out to them in welcome" (p. 353). When at the end of the story, Brently Mallard enters his home (the report of his death had been an error) and his wife falls dead of shock, Chopin concludes ironically, "When the doctors came they said she had died of heart disease—of joy that kills" (p. 354).

In the stories collected in *A Night in Acadie* (1897), Chopin was even more explicit in her psychological depiction of the inner turmoil felt by her female characters, and in some of the stories she also dealt frankly with their sensual feelings. "A Respectable Woman," for example, depicts a wife who is at first bored with her husband's guest at their plantation, but eventually her feelings change: "Her mind only vaguely grasped what he was saying. Her physical being was for the moment predominant. She was not thinking of his words, only drinking in the tones of his voice. . . . She wanted to draw close to him and whisper against his cheek—she did not care what—as she might have done if she had not been a respectable woman" (p. 335). She sees no more of her husband's friend in this visit, but not many months later she encourages her husband to invite his friend again. It seems that in this case her emotions have won a victory over her values as a "respectable woman," for Chopin concludes with this conversation between husband and wife: " 'Oh,' she told him, laughingly, after pressing a long, tender kiss upon his lips, 'I have overcome everything! you will see. This time I shall be very nice to him!' " (p. 336). Although Chopin refrains from making any authorial comment on the wife's decision, the implication is that she is happy with her choice.

Another story in *A Night in Acadie* contains one of Chopin's most fully developed characters. "Athénaïse" tells of the marriage of Cazeau, a widower for ten years, to the spirited Athénaïse. The young bride soon becomes disenchanted with married life and leaves for a visit with her family, only to be brought home again by her husband. Chopin writes: "Cazeau's chief offense seemed to be that he loved her, and Athénaïse was not the woman to be loved against her will. She called marriage a trap set for the feet of unwary and unsuspecting girls" (p. 434). Athénaïse complains, " 'It's jus' being married that I detes' an' despise. . . . I can't stan' to live with a man: to have him always there; his coats an' pantaloons hanging in my room; his ugly bare feet—washing them in my tub, befo' my very eyes, ugh!' " (p. 431).

Chopin skillfully depicts through her imagery the problem and its resolution. In one scene, when Cazeau has brought his wife back home from her parents, he passes an old live-oak tree that he has seen many times before, but this time he remembers that the oak had once served as a resting place for Black Gabe, a runaway slave whom his father, known to everyone as a kind master, was bringing home again. The parallel with Cazeau and Athénaïse is clear.

In contrast, however, is a scene at the end of the story. Aided by her brother, Athénaïse has "escaped" from Cazeau and taken a room in New Orleans. She enjoys her freedom from married life, but after a few weeks learns she is pregnant. Now when she thinks of Cazeau "the first purely sensuous tremor of her life swept over her" (p. 451). The story ends with Athénaïse's return home where Cazeau feels for the first time "the yielding of her whole body against him" (p. 454). Athénaïse hears the crying of a baby in the distance, and her sympathetic comments to this sound reflect her complete reconciliation with her own married life.

"Athénaïse," almost 30 pages in length, was much longer than most of Chopin's stories, and she soon completed an even more comprehensive treatment of marriage and a woman's place, *The Awakening* (1899), which has inspired more critical commentary than any of Chopin's other work. The novel has been frequently compared with *Madame Bovary*, and although similarities exist between these two portraits of women who are unsatisfied with their married lives, take lovers, and eventually commit suicide, Chopin's treatment of her heroine, Edna Pontellier, is much more sympathetic and avoids the moral commentary present in Flaubert's novel. A more evident influence on Chopin's style is Maupassant, whose works she admired and translated into English.

The Awakening opens on the Gulf Coast resort of Grand Isle where Edna

Pontellier and her two children are summering, visited on weekends by her husband Léonce, a successful New Orleans businessman. Edna, a Kentuckian by birth, has married into Creole society and is this summer's recipient of the attentions of Robert Lebrun, the resort owner's son who each summer "courts" one of the young matrons. Robert's actions are approved by Creole custom, for it is assumed that he has no intention of overstepping any moral boundaries. Robert's attention, however, awakens in Edna new feelings about herself. When she returns to New Orleans at the end of the summer, she refuses to keep up many of her prescribed duties, neglecting her Tuesdays at home to receive guests, and eventually, when her husband is away on business, moving out of her home into a smaller rented house, where she pursues her interest in painting. In the meantime Robert Lebrun has left for Mexico, and Edna succumbs to the advances of Alcée Arobin, a well-known man about town. When Robert returns and realizes that Edna loves him, he hopes that some way Edna might be released from her marriage and marry him. He cannot understand Edna's response, "I am no longer one of Mr. Pontellier's possessions to dispose of or not. I give myself where I choose" (p. 992). Robert's code of honor will not allow him to accept this statement, and when Edna learns that he has left her, she fears what the future will bring. For herself she envisions a series of Alcée Arobins, and she thinks of her children who "appeared before her like antagonists who had overcome her; who had overpowered and sought to drag her into the soul's slavery for the rest of her days. But she knew a way to elude them" (p. 999). Edna returns to Grand Isle where she had first learned to swim; she slips off her clothes and swims out to her death.

One way Chopin develops Edna's character is through the use of two women as foils, and her choice of types reflects and continues the dichotomies appearing in the earlier fiction. On the one hand, there is Adèle Ratignolle, a beautiful Creole devoted to her husband and children. Chopin describes her as a "mother woman" who spends her summer at Grand Isle making winter garments to protect her children from threatening drafts and who plays the piano well, but keeps up her music only for the entertainment of her family. Adèle has a pivotal role in the novel, for she calls Edna away from her final scene with Robert in order to be with her during childbirth, and she warns Edna that she must always think of her children.

In sharp contrast to Adèle is Mademoiselle Reisz, a physically unattractive and sharp-tongued spinster, but an artist whose piano playing touches Edna's soul. Mademoiselle Reisz, who also summered at Grand Isle before returning to her modest apartment in New Orleans, is sympathetic to Edna's longing for independence and her passion for Robert. She advises Edna that the true artist must be able to defy convention, and she feels Edna's shoulder blades to see if she has the wings to surmount life's obstacles. Significantly, when Edna swims out into the Gulf, a bird with a broken wing hovers overhead. Neither role—that of the conventional mother-woman or of the unconventional artist—is a satisfying one for Edna, and although her suicide may be a less than satisfactory solution, Edna at least attempts to come to terms with her own individuality, to think for herself, illustrating again Chopin's concern with her characters' ability to make difficult choices.

In *The Awakening* Chopin deals frankly with Edna's passion both as an artist and as a lover. A story she wrote after she had completed *The Awakening*, and before she was disheartened by the criticism of it, is even more explicit in its depiction of sensuality. "The Storm," written in July 1898 but unpublished during Chopin's lifetime, tells the story of an afternoon in which Calixta, whose husband and son are detained away from home by a storm, is visited by her former suitor, Alcée Laballière, who seeks shelter from the rain. It takes only one touch from Alcée to rekindle their passion, and this time it will be consummated: "If she was not an immaculate dove in those days, she was still inviolate; a passionate creature whose very defenselessness had made her defense, against which his honor had forbade him to prevail" (p. 594). Chopin vividly parallels the power of the storm outside with the love-making within Calixta's room. The storm ends, and Alcée rides away. Calixta prepares a meal for her returning family, and the three laugh and enjoy themselves. Once home Alcée writes a letter to his wife urging her to stay in Biloxi with their children if she wishes. Thus, Chopin concludes, "the storm passed and every one was happy" (p. 596).

In "The Storm" Chopin avoids authorial moralizing as she had in *The Awakening*. Chopin's major themes deal not with what choice each of her protagonists makes, but with the fact that they (and the reader) realize that each character is an individual who must weigh society's expectations in relation to personal needs, and forge, sometimes painfully, an answer that is uniquely her own. Nineteenth-century readers were not ready for this iconoclastic thinking, but Kate Chopin's works have today a contemporary quality that makes many readers feel her themes are speaking directly to them.

SURVEY OF CRITICISM

It has taken more than 50 years for Kate Chopin to receive the recognition she deserves. After her death in 1904 her work was generally ignored, although in the *Library of Southern Literature* (1907) Leonidas Rutledge Whipple commented on *The Awakening* and praised Chopin's short stories. The most important work during the early decades of the twentieth century was Father Daniel S. Rankin's *Kate Chopin and Her Creole Stories* (1932); Rankin viewed Chopin primarily as a short story writer and dismissed *The Awakening* as less important.

A Frenchman, Cyrille Arnavon, treated Chopin along with other realists in a 1946 essay, and in 1953 he translated *The Awakening* into French. In the 1950s several important articles appeared, including two in 1956 by Robert Cantwell and Kenneth Eble praising *The Awakening*.

Chopin criticism continued to increase in the 1960s. *The Awakening* was reprinted in 1964 with Eble's article introducing it. *The Ferment of Realism* (1965) by Warner Berthoff devoted a page to the novel, and Larzer Ziff treated the realism of Chopin's *The Awakening* in *The American 1890s* (1966). George Arms noted the importance of *The Awakening* among American novels and also included a discussion of Chopin's short stories in an article published in 1967. But the greatest debt of Chopin scholars is owed to Per Seyersted, who in 1969 published the definitive biography of Kate Chopin and a two-volume edition of her works. The abundance of criticism since then is the result, in part, of convenient, accessible editions of her writing. Seyersted's biography also provides invaluable information about Chopin's life and helps to establish the importance of her place in American literary history.

An even greater amount of Chopin criticism appeared in the 1970s. The 1975 MLA Bibliography, for example, lists more than twenty entries on Chopin. Much credit should be given to Emily Toth, who edited *The Kate Chopin Newsletter* during this period and who has also written a number of perceptive articles on Chopin, as well as coediting with Seyersted *A Kate Chopin Miscellany* in 1979. Several bibliographies of Chopin's work have also appeared, including Marlene Springer's *Edith Wharton and Kate Chopin: A Reference Guide* (1976; with an article supplementing the Kate Chopin material appearing in 1981). Another useful and perceptive bibliographical essay by Tonette Bond Inge is included in *American Women Writers: Bibliographical Essays* (1983).

Although the articles and studies appearing in the 1980s have decreased in number, what is important in current Chopin scholarship is the variety of treatment her work is receiving. Careful attention is being paid not only to her novels but to the short stories as well. No longer does it seem necessary to prove that her work deserves study; her fiction is being examined for her realistic themes but is also being given linguistic and stylistic analysis. It is fitting that a writer who was so misunderstood in her own time is now receiving the attention she richly deserves.

BIBLIOGRAPHY

Works by Kate Chopin

Page numbers given in the text refer to Per Seyersted, ed., *The Complete Works of Kate Chopin.*

At Fault. St. Louis: Nixon-Jones, 1890.
Bayou Folk. Boston: Houghton, Mifflin, 1894.
A Night in Acadie. Chicago: Way & Williams, 1897.
The Awakening. Chicago: Herbert S. Stone, 1899.
The Complete Works of Kate Chopin. 2 vols. Ed. Per Seyersted. Baton Rouge: Louisiana State University Press, 1969.

Studies of Kate Chopin

Arms, George. "Kate Chopin's *The Awakening* in the Perspective of Her Literary Career." *Essays on American Literature in Honor of Jay B. Hubbell.* Ed. Clarence Gohdes. Durham, N.C.: Duke University Press, 1967, pp. 215–28.

Arnavon, Cyrille. Introduction. *Edna*. Paris: Le Club Bibliophile de France, 1952.

Arner, Robert. "Kate Chopin." *Louisiana Studies* 14 (1975): 11–139 [Special issue; Lewis P. Simpson, Foreword, 5–10].

———. "Pride and Prejudice: Kate Chopin's 'Désirée's Baby.' " *Mississippi Quarterly* 25 (Spring 1972): 131–40.

Bonner, Thomas, Jr. "Kate Chopin: An Annotated Bibliography." *Bulletin of Bibliography* 32 (1975): 101–5.

Cantwell, Robert. "*The Awakening* by Kate Chopin." *Georgia Review* 10 (Winter 1956): 489–94.

Cather, Willa. Review of *The Awakening*. *Pittsburgh Leader* 8 July 1899, p. 6.

Dyer, Joyce. "Gouvernail, Kate Chopin's Sensitive Bachelor." *Southern Literary Journal* 14 (Fall 1981): 46–55.

Eble, Kenneth. "A Forgotten Novel: Kate Chopin's *The Awakening*." *Western Humanities Review* 10 (Summer 1956): 261–69.

Fletcher, Marie. "The Southern Woman in the Fiction of Kate Chopin." *Louisiana History* 7 (Spring 1966): 117–32.

Fluck, Winfried. "Tentative Transgressions: Kate Chopin's Fiction as a Mode of Symbolic Action." *Studies in American Fiction* 10 (Autumn 1982): 151–71.

Inge, Tonette Bond. "Kate Chopin." *American Women Writers: Bibliographical Essays*. Ed. Maurice Duke, Jackson R. Bryer, and M. Thomas Inge. Westport, Conn.: Greenwood Press, 1983, pp. 47–69.

Jones, Anne Goodwyn. *Tomorrow Is Another Day: The Woman Writer in the South, 1859–1936*. Baton Rouge: Louisiana State University Press, 1981.

Justus, James H. "The Unawakening of Edna Pontellier." *Southern Literary Journal* 10 (Spring 1978): 107–22.

Lattin, Patricia Hopkins. "Kate Chopin's Repeating Characters." *Mississippi Quarterly* 33 (Winter 1979–80): 19–37.

———. "The Search for Self in Kate Chopin's Fiction: Simple versus Complex Vision." *Southern Studies* 21 (Summer 1982): 222–35.

Leary, Lewis. "Kate Chopin's Other Novel." *Southern Literary Journal* 1 (Autumn 1968): 60–74.

May, John R. "Local Color in *The Awakening*." *Southern Review* 6 (Autumn 1970): 1031–40.

Miner, Madonne M. "Veiled Hints: An Affective Stylist's Reading of Kate Chopin's 'Story of an Hour.' " *Markham Review* 11 (Winter 1982): 29–32.

Rankin, Daniel S. *Kate Chopin and Her Creole Stories*. Philadelphia: University of Pennsylvania Press, 1932.

Ringe, Donald A. "Romantic Imagery in Kate Chopin's *The Awakening*." *American Literature* 43 (January 1972): 580–88.

Seyersted, Per. *Kate Chopin: A Critical Biography*. Baton Rouge: Louisiana State University Press, 1969.

Seyersted, Per, and Emily Toth, eds. *A Kate Chopin Miscellany*. Natchitoches, La.: Northwestern State University Press, 1979.

Simpson, Claude M., ed. *American Short Stories 1857–1900*. New York: Harper, 1960.

Skaggs, Merrill Maguire. *The Folk of Southern Fiction*. Athens: University of Georgia Press, 1972.

Skaggs, Peggy. *Kate Chopin*. Boston: Twayne, 1985.

Springer, Marlene. *Edith Wharton and Kate Chopin: A Reference Guide*. Boston: G. K. Hall, 1976.

———. "Kate Chopin: A Reference Guide Updated." *Resources for American Literary Study* 11 (Autumn 1981): 280–81. [Supp. to 1976 bibliography.]

Thornton, Laurence. "*The Awakening*: A Political Romance." *American Literature* 52 (1980): 50–66.

Toth, Emily. "Kate Chopin and Literary Convention: 'Désirée's Baby.' " *Southern Studies* 20 (Summer 1981): 201–8.

Whipple, Leonidas Rutledge. "Kate Chopin." *Library of Southern Literature*. Ed. Edwin Anderson Alderman and Joel Chandler Harris. Atlanta: Martin and Hoyt, 1907. 2: 863–67.

Wilson, Edmund. *Patriotic Gore: Studies in the Literature of the American Civil War*. New York: Oxford University Press, 1962, pp. 587–93.

Wolff, Cynthia G. "Kate Chopin and the Fiction of Limits: 'Désirée's Baby.' " *Southern Literary Journal* 10 (Spring 1978): 123–33.

———. "Thanatos and Eros: Kate Chopin's *The Awakening*." *American Quarterly* 25 (October 1973): 449–71.

Ziff, Larzer. *The American 1890s: Life and Times of a Lost Generation*. New York: Viking Press, 1966, pp. 296–305.

EVERETT EMERSON

Samuel Langhorne Clemens [Mark Twain] (1835–1910)

Mark Twain is America's favorite writer and a world favorite as well. A writer whose forte was humor, he was such a complicated person that it is fitting that he had two names.

BIOGRAPHY

Samuel Langhorne Clemens was born in Florida, Missouri, on 30 November 1835, the Clemens family having moved west from Tennessee earlier that year. In 1839 the family settled in Hannibal, a hundred miles north of St. Louis on the Mississippi River. Later this town was to be celebrated in Mark Twain's fiction as St. Petersburg. After the death of John Marshall Clemens, Samuel's father, in 1847, the family was in such financial need that Sam was soon out of school and at work as a printer's apprentice. His first writings were for a Hannibal newspaper where he was employed. A few years later as a journeyman printer he traveled to St. Louis, then to New York, Philadelphia, and Washington; in each city he wrote letters about what he saw for newspaper publication. Then he lived for a time in Keokuk, Iowa, and Cincinnati.

In 1857 Clemens left printing and journalism to become first an apprentice, then a pilot on the Mississippi River. Later he was to provide an account of his experiences in "Old Times on the Mississippi" (1875). During the four years he worked on the river, he wrote very little. The Civil War ended his piloting, and in 1861 he traveled westward with his older brother, who had been appointed secretary of the Nevada Territory. There for a time Clemens combined silver mining with writing for newspapers. In 1862 he became a full-time writer for the Virginia City *Territorial Enterprise*, and shortly thereafter adopted the pen name Mark Twain. Later he was to explain that he signed his Nevada newspaper letters "using the Mississippi leadsman's call, 'Mark Twain' (two fathoms =

twelve feet) for this purpose.'' In the 1860s he soon made the name famous in the West. In 1864 he moved to San Francisco, where he wrote sketches for magazines and continued to work as a newspaper reporter. His first piece to draw national attention was "Jim Smiley and his Jumping Frog," published in a New York weekly in 1865. On assignment in the Hawaiian Islands for a Sacramento paper, he wrote a series of letters that he later attempted to publish in book form. Again on assignment, he left the West in late 1865 for New York and a visit home to Missouri.

In New York he arranged for the publication of *The Celebrated Jumping Frog of Calaveras County and Other Sketches* (1867), but it was not profitable to the author. At age thirty-one he still had not found his métier. Fortunately, he had the opportunity to travel to Europe and the Holy Land as correspondent for the San Francisco *Alto California*; he was a member of the first American tour group, on board the *Quaker City*. The letters he wrote, like the earlier ones from Hawaii and New York, are a mixture of reporting and humor. They describe France, Italy, Damascus, Jerusalem, Egypt. At the end of the five-month trip Mark Twain was still a journalist, but soon an invitation to convert his letters into a book for a Hartford publisher permitted him to become an author. The result, *The Innocents Abroad* (1869), sold well, to the author's surprise, and thereafter he devoted most of his energies for several years to composing books.

Two other important events took place after his return from Europe. He undertook a lecture tour (he had given an occasional lecture earlier) and enjoyed such success that lecturing became a part of his life for twenty years, off and on. And he met the sister of a *Quaker City* shipmate; he courted and in 1870 married Olivia Langdon of Elmira, New York, whose genteel ways were in striking contrast to those Mark Twain had known in the West. The newlyweds lived for a time in Buffalo, where Clemens owned an interest in and wrote for a newspaper. Because of the success of *The Innocents Abroad*, his Hartford publisher sought another book, and he began an account, heavily fictionalized, of his Western years. *Roughing It* (1871) was completed at Quarry Farm, near Elmira, at the home of Olivia's sister; there Mark Twain was to do most of his writing during the next two decades, in the summertime. He made his residence now in Hartford, where he built a substantial house, which survives as one of the city's sights. His family grew as his wife gave birth to three daughters, Olivia Susan (called Susy) in 1872, Clara in 1874, and Jane (called Jean) in 1880.

In 1872 Clemens made the first of several visits to England, which he expected to make the subject of his next book; there was, however, to be no such book. His next completed book was *The Gilded Age* (1874), a novel written with Charles Dudley Warner, his Hartford neighbor, about the contemporary scene. More significant, Mark Twain wrote during the next two summers *The Adventures of Tom Sawyer* (1876), based on memories of his Hannibal boyhood. During winter 1874–75, he wrote for the *Atlantic Monthly* a series of sketches on "Life on the Mississippi."

But the author now fell into a fallow period. He tried his hand at the writing of comedies, none of which was successful. He began at least five books that he was unable to finish. Then in December 1877 he spoke at a Boston birthday party for the poet John Greenleaf Whittier, and though the story he told was entertaining, to William Dean Howells, Clemen's friend and editor of the *Atlantic*, and to some others, it was offensive. Fortunately, the Clemenses had already planned to go to Germany in order for the author to get his writing career back in order. In Heidelberg he began an account of his European adventures, such as they were, but the writing went badly. Travels through Switzerland and Italy did not help, and the book remained unfinished when the Clemenses returned to America after seventeen months abroad. He was now calling it a "hated book." *A Tramp Abroad* was finally published successfully in 1880.

More enjoyable to the author, though it was not a financial success, was his next book, an attempt at a decorous historical novel. *The Prince and the Pauper*, dedicated appropriately to the author's daughters, appeared in 1882. That year Clemens returned to the Mississippi River to obtain matter for another book. Despite the pleasure he took from the trip, writing the book proved difficult, even though it included the "Old Times" account published in the *Atlantic* earlier. *Life on the Mississippi* was published in 1883.

To one of the unfinished books from the 1870s he now returned, vivified by his Mississippi visit, and in 1883 he completed *Adventures of Huckleberry Finn*, his best book. Set in the pre–Civil War South, the work is ostensibly a sequel. It bears on the title page the description of its hero as "(Tom Sawyer's Comrade)." The author imagines Huck telling his own story, and one source of the book's greatness is the freshness of the telling. The book was moderately successful, though some newspapers were critical of its vulgarity and irreverence.

After *Huckleberry Finn*, Clemens found himself prosperous. He engaged in business activities. He created a publishing company, lucrative for a time as publisher of Ulysses S. Grant's *Memoirs*. He invested some $200,000 in a typesetting machine that failed to operate properly. He now thought of writing as "holiday amusement." He did produce another novel in the years 1886–89, *A Connecticut Yankee in King Arthur's Court*, intended as a social and political statement, for Mark Twain was beginning to think of himself as something of a philosopher. The response to the novel was distinctly mixed; it was called both offensive and delicious.

Early in 1891 Clemens realized that his financial needs required him to return to writing. His next work, a novel, was *The American Claimant* (1892). It reintroduces the exuberant inventor Colonel Sellers, one of Mark Twain's most memorable characters; he had appeared in *The Gilded Age*. Despite his appearance and Mark Twain's interest in his novel as a vehicle for political and social commentary, the book is badly botched, overcrowded with plot and satire.

Later in 1891 the Clemenses closed their Hartford house to visit Europe. They could live more cheaply there, and both Olivia and Samuel Clemens were in bad health, from which they sought relief. Mark Twain's literary health was also poor. The family traveled, chiefly in Germany; rheumatism interfered with the writer's productivity, except for some hackwork—travel letters. He attempted another sequel, little better than a fragment, *Tom Sawyer Abroad* (1894), with Huck as narrator. More ambitious was a work badly marred by complications of plot: it was finally cut into two and appeared as *The Tragedy of Pudd'nhead Wilson and The Comedy of Those Extraordinary Twins* (1894). The book deals with the switching of a light-skinned son of a slave and a look-alike of free parentage—and the consequences. The author's editing prevented the effective conveying of the ideas that had led to the writing of the book.

At this time Mark Twain was writing intensely. He produced short stories and essays, mostly of little value, in order to make money. His publication house was rapidly failing, requiring him to make several trips to America, though his family and his residence remained abroad. It was in Europe, chiefly in France, that he undertook his longest novel, *Personal Recollections of Joan of Arc* (1896), really a fictionalized biography based on French and English sources. Though not as bad as it is now usually thought to be (it was a favorite—perhaps *the* favorite of its creator), its combination of sentimentality and cynicism, plus its author's ignorance of the Middle Ages, make it a badly marred work. The book is usually considered an unfortunate aberration, and indeed the subject was unsuitable for the author's talents. The best and worst feature of the book is the portrayal of Joan, based in part on Susy Clemens, then in her early twenties. Joan is both heroic and sentimentalized. The defeat of the heroine made the story a suitable vehicle for the author's growing pessimism.

This pessimism, which had among its sources the author's reading in medieval history, was augmented when in late 1894 Clemens's financial adviser, Henry H. Rogers, forced him to recognize his desperate financial status. He was deeply in debt. He had planned a round-the-world lecture tour, and now he saw that it could produce needed income. The Clemenses returned to America in spring 1895. Jean and Susy remained there while Clara and Olivia went westward with Clemens, who did readings in Australia, New Zealand, India, and South Africa. The travelers then settled in England. The trip, which lasted a year, was not a great financial success; Clemens made only about $30,000. Now, however, he was able to write a book about his travels.

At this point word reached England that Susy Clemens was ill, and soon after she died of meningitis. This event gave focus to the author's pessimism. Nevertheless, he went to work and completed *Following the Equator* (1897, entitled *More Tramps Abroad* in England). Though less forced than *A Tramp Abroad*, the book is not engaging. But it served its purpose. His royalties, along with other income including that from his lecture tour, permitted Clemens to pay off his debts.

To express his pessimism, as he needed to do, Mark Twain began a novel based on his sense that his earlier life now seemed to him a dream. He could not finish the story, and from this point to the end of his life, he began a whole series of works that remained unfinished and until recent years unpublished. One of the best of these fragments is not pessimistic. "Tom Sawyer's Conspiracy" is perhaps the best sequel to *Huckleberry Finn*. More significant, Mark Twain was beginning to write his autobiography. In fall 1897, during the period when the Clemenses lived in Vienna, he wrote "Early Times," one of the best parts of the miscellany that goes by the name of Mark Twain's autobiography.

More systematic but less attractive is "What is Man?", drafted in 1897–98, elaborated and published anonymously in 1906. It is an explicit statement of the author's determinism. The publication was anonymous because Mark Twain was increasingly aware of how offensive his philosophy would seem to his readers, who continued to provide him with income. They thought of him as a genial humorist. The most attractive presentation of Mark Twain's deterministic philosophy is in the fragment entitled "The Chronicle of Young Satan," written over the years 1897–1900; it is a magical story of the education of a boy at the hands of the author's spokesman, who disguises himself as a boy but is actually the nephew of Satan.

The Clemens family returned to the United States in October 1900, after nearly a decade abroad. They settled in New York City. Mark Twain was now sought out by newspapers who asked for his opinion on world affairs. He had become strongly anti-imperialist as a result of his world tour and expressed his views in "To the Person Sitting in Darkness," published in 1901. Another effort to tell the story of his "dream" experience, "Which Was It?" occupied him for two summers, spent at Saranac Lake, New York, and York Harbor, Maine. It remains a 100,000 word fragment. It was in Maine that Olivia suffered a severe heart attack, and in October 1903 the Clemenses moved to Florence, Italy, where the author continued to write. He bagan "No. 44, The Mysterious Stranger," in which he used memories of his experience as a printer and offered his ideas about multiple personalities. There, too, he wrote the remarkable preface to his autobiography, "As From the Grave." But on 5 June 1904, Olivia Clemens died. Though her death was not the shock that Susy's had been, it did reaffirm Clemens's pessimism.

Returning to New York, Mark Twain resumed his anti-imperialism by publishing *King Leopold's Soliloquy*, a skillful attack on the Belgians' treatment of the Congo. Another piece of political criticism, "The War Prayer," was not published till 1923, after having been rejected by a women's magazine. During two summers at Dublin, New Hampshire, Mark Twain worked on novels he left unfinished.

In early 1906 Albert Bigelow Paine entered Mark Twain's life and soon became his authorized biographer. (Later he became his literary executor.) The writer provided Paine with materials by dictating his memoirs, in random fashion. These dictations were also intended for posthumous publication. During the years 1906–9 there were nearly 250 sessions. Twenty-five selections were published during the author's lifetime. In 1924 Paine published two volumes of selections, and Paine's successor as literary editor, Bernard De Voto, published a volume in 1940. Other portions remain unpublished, for the work is highly uneven. One result of this undertaking is that Mark Twain almost stopped writing. He did publish in 1907 a charming fragment begun in the 1870s, one that Olivia Clemens had not wanted published, *Extract from Captain Stormfield's Visit to Heaven* (1907).

In 1907 the remaining Clemenses moved to a house built for them and named for the recent book, Stormfield, at Redding, in western Connecticut. There Mark Twain wrote one more work of continuing interest, "Letters from the Earth," in which under the guise of reporting Satan's findings from his visit to our planet, he combined striking frankness with good humor. The author was now in failing health. The death of Jean Clemens, drowned in the bathtub during an epileptic fit at Christmas time 1909, led him to write a final piece for his autobiography, "The Death of Jean." At his Connecticut home, his heart gave out on 10 April 1910.

MAJOR THEMES

Mark Twain's complete writings consist of some 800 pieces. Thirty volumes from his pen appeared during his lifetime, and nearly that many have appeared since 1910, as well as ten volumes of his letters. His themes range from celebration of youthful innocence to angry expressions of pessimism, too many for all to be taken up here.

Mark Twain is probably most famous for his semiautobiographical portrayals of his youth. *Tom Sawyer* is described in the author's preface: "Most of the adventures recorded in this book really occurred; one or two were experiences of my own, the rest those of boys who were schoolmates of mine." To emphasize the appeals of the freedom known to youth, Mark Twain characterizes the adults who surround Tom as rigid and restrictive. Aunt Polly seeks to manipulate Tom not chiefly by discipline but by pity and guilt. Tom flees for a time to Jackson's Island, where he and his friends experience an idyllic life. In *Tom Sawyer* youth is a time for adventures, concocted ones or real ones, before one assumes the routine of adult life. Though Tom is highly imaginative, he is clearly destined to become a responsible adult, probably a leader. Another portrayal of youth, that of the cub pilot in "Old Times on the Mississippi," shows the boy becoming an adult. Mark Twain here distorts reality by making the cub pilot seem much younger than Clemens, whose story is ostensibly being told, was at that time. In "Old Times" youth is characterized as a time when romantic attitudes dominate, before experience teaches one to see, realistically, what is really there. Mark Twain makes good-humored fun of the cub's innocence, whereas Tom is presented sympathetically.

In his sequel to *Tom Sawyer* Mark Twain creates a different and much less attractive Tom, who is now an egotist and hypocrite, though—ironically—Huck, now the narrator, continues to worship Tom. In *Huckleberry Finn* Huck's own modesty, his lack of any sense of self-worth, contributes powerfully to his appeal. Like Tom, he is imaginative, but he uses his imagination to escape, time after time, from threatening situations. Huck's gradual recognition of the virtues of his companion, the escaped slave Jim, as they travel together on a raft, adds to Huck's appeal. His goodness, moreover, is in sharp contrast to the corruption of the society he meets when he goes ashore. When two semicomic but threatening representatives of that corruption, the Duke and the King, come aboard the raft, Huck becomes even more sympathetic. His goodness and naïveté are balanced by his shrewdness.

Mark Twain had no good idea of what the freedom-loving Huck was to do at the end of the book, when Tom reenters and makes a game of Huck's concern for Jim's freedom. In the sequels, such as the fragments "Huck Finn and Tom Sawyer Among the Indians" (1885) and "Tom Sawyer's Conspiracy" (1897), as well as in *Tom Sawyer Abroad* (1894), Tom is once again the central figure though Huck tells the story, each of which emphasizes boyhood adventurousness.

The Prince and the Pauper, written after *Tom Sawyer*, also deals with youthful innocence. The prince, who finds himself confused with his look-alike, a pauper, learns that the world is full of cruelty, much as Huck does. Like the cub pilot, he discovers, as does the pauper who is identified as the prince, that experiences correct youthful romantic attitudes towards life.

Although the narrator of *The Innocents Abroad* is not a boy, the book has as one of its central themes the contrast between the naive American's expectations and the reality he finds in his travels. This difference is greatest in the Holy Land, where Mark Twain uses contemporary guidebooks to emphasize the distance between the anticipated and the actual. His growing sense that his Western irreverence was likely to offend Easterners prevented him from being as outspoken as he might have been.

The theme of innocence occurs also in *Roughing It*, in which Mark Twain relates a whole series of adventures that had led to his own antiromantic attitude. He described his outlook on the verge of his departure in 1861 for the West. His brother Orion was going to travel:

I had never been away from home, and that word "travel" had a seductive charm for me. Pretty soon he would be hundreds of miles away on the great plains and deserts, and among the mountains of the Far West, and see buffaloes and Indians, and prairie dogs and antelopes, and have all kinds of adventures, and maybe get hanged or scalped, and have ever such a fine time, and write home about it, and be a hero. . . . What I suffered in contemplating his happiness, pen cannot describe.

The author was in fact 26 in 1861, but he is characterized as if he were fourteen. The book presents, then destroys, all of the romantic myths of the West. Mark Twain buys a "Genuine Mexican Plug," only to find, after many futile attempts to ride the animal, that he has been taken in. He is a humiliated victim of Western ways.

As early as 1864, when he was a San Francisco reporter, Mark Twain was a social critic. He brought attention to political corruption and the incompetence of public officials. Especially notable is his sketch "The Christmas Fireside for Good Little Boys and Girls. *By Grandfather Twain*," subtitled "The Story of the Bad Little Boy That Bore a Charmed Life." This thoroughly wicked child "grew up, and married, and raised a large family, and brained them all with an axe one night, and got wealthy by all manner of cheating and rascality, and now is the infernalist wickedest scoundrel in his native village, and is universally respected, and belongs to the Legislature." Here spoke the Mark Twain who would describe himself in 1868 as one who has "been through the world's 'mill,' " one who knows the world "through and through, and from back to back—its follies, its frauds, and its vanities—all by *personal* experience."

In the West Mark Twain satirized the pious, the moralizers, the pretentious. When he went to Europe in 1867, he found himself in the midst of the people he had made his enemy, and one of the themes of *The Innocents Abroad* is the hypocrisy of those he calls the "pilgrims," his fellow tourists. He satirizes the reverence, often badly misplaced, of the pilgrims as they explore the Holy Land. Mark Twain saw dirt, flies, and beggars. He was sure that Jesus would not come again to such a place.

To his discomfort, Clemens knew by the time he wrote the final version of *The Innocents Abroad* that his ambitions would soon take him into the very society he had satirized. He could be more comfortable with what was not so near at hand, and his presentation in *The Gilded Age*, subtitled *A Tale of Today*, of the Washington scene is memorable, with its mixture of speculators, lobbyists, and politicians. Later Mark Twain recognized that this "partnership novel" was a failure because the two authors' "ingredients refused to mix, & the book consisted of *two* novels—and remained so, incurably and vexatiously."

In *Tom Sawyer* Mark Twain makes gentle fun of Sunday schools and the rigidities of adult society, but such criticism is not the central focus of the novel. It is much more important in *Huckleberry Finn*. The whole of the trip down the river is an exposé of the brutality, hatred, hypocrisy, and violence of American society. Particularly effective is the episode in which Huck finds shelter and almost a home with the Grangerfords, whose parlor, a masterpiece of overelaborated Victorian decor, he admires, along with the poetry of Emmeline Grangerford. When he discovers the hypocrisy of the feuding Grangerfords and Shepherdsons, who take their weapons to church to hear a sermon on brotherly love, Huck is devastated.

The Prince and the Pauper is also a vehicle for Mark Twain's social criticism. Miles Herndon, the exiled son of a nobleman, befriends young Prince Edward and protects him from the harshness of the kingdom's laws. As a result of his exposure to man's inhumanity to man, Edward develops a sensitivity to immorality rather like the one Huck possesses. Social criticism can be found in *Life on the Mississippi*, but two chapters severely critical of the America of the past—its chauvinism, the vulgarity of its newspapers—were dropped when the book was published. They can be found in a 1944 edition of the book, published by the Limited Editions Club. The author's expectation that he could incorporate social criticism into *A Tramp Abroad* was largely disappointed: Mark Twain told his friend Howells that he would have liked to write sharp satires of European life but found he was not "in a good enough humor with ANYTHING to satirize it: no, I want to stand up before it and curse it, and foam at the mouth, or take a club and pound it to rags and pulp."

In the book most fully intended to permit an agenda of social and political criticism, *A Connecticut Yankee in King Arthur's Court*, Mark Twain's hero, Hank Morgan—the superintendent of a Connecticut arms factory—wakes up in the early Middle Ages. Soon he is given the opportunity to introduce modern technology into the rather primitive society. Writing under the inspiration of a work of English radical polemics, George Standring's *People's History of the English Aristocracy*, Mark Twain attacked British devotion to nobility and the concepts of primogeniture and entail. Another book that he admired, William E. H. Lecky's *History of European Morals*, had persuaded him that the villain behind the ills of medieval society was the church. As in *Huckleberry Finn* and *The Prince and the Pauper*, Mark Twain exposes man's inhumanity to man, but now he permits himself to comment, even to philosophize, as he had not in *Huckleberry Finn*. Here he tells his reader directly that "any Established Church is an established crime, and established slave-pen," and "when every man in a State has a vote, brutal laws are impossible."

An American Claimant, the author's least successful novel, is as full of social criticism as the *Yankee*, criticism that seems pointed because of the contemporary setting. The ambition of Americans to assume British titles is the starting point of the novel. When Colonel Sellers claims that he is the rightful heir to an earldom, the "American Claimant," he calls himself Rossmore and changes his daughter's name from Sally to Gwendolyn. In contrast, the rightful earl comes to America and is captivated by the American Dream that anyone can succeed by dint of hard work. He seeks a clerkship only to learn that he lacks the necessary political connections. After several defeats, he records in his diary, "It does look as if in a republic where all are free and equal, prosperity and position constitute rank." Thus the democratic spirit that conceived *A Connecticut Yankee* was followed by a much more critical attitude towards democracy in *An American Claimant*.

In *Pudd'nhead Wilson*, Mark Twain attacked American racial attitudes. The difference between the free child Tom Driscoll and the slave Valet de Chambres (Chambers) is that the latter has a teaspoon of black blood. The story centers upon the results of the actions of Roxy, Chambers's mother, who switches the two as babies. Unfortunately, the thesis that Mark Twain intended to offer, that "Training is everything; cauliflower is nothing but cabbage with a college education," is blurred by Roxy's telling her son, when he has become an adult, that his cowardice is the consequence of his black blood: "It's de nigger in you, dat's what it is." What Mark Twain intended to say was lost when he deleted an explanation. There Chambers is made to think:

In his brooding in the solitudes, he searched himself for the reasons of certain things, and in toil and pain he worked out the answers:
Why was he a coward? It was the "nigger" in him. The nigger *blood*? Yes, the nigger blood degraded from original courage to cowardice by decades and generations of insult and outrage inflicted in circumstances which forbade reprisals, and made mute and meek endurance the only refuge and defence.

Mark Twain was offering a kind of Mendelian explanation of inheritance.

After his trip around the world in the 1890s, Mark Twain offered much of his social and political criticism in nonfictional form. He was beginning to have clearer views of the sources of some of society's faults, and in "Corn Pone Opinions" he provided an almost Marxist interpretation of society. "You tell me where a man gets his corn-pone, en I'll tell you what his 'pinions are." For the mature writer, man's attitudes and behavior were determined by outside influences and his need for self-approval. This philosophy is set forth in "What is Man?", best read in the 1973 edition published by the University of California Press.

"The Chronicle of Young Satan," the most admired of the late philosophical and pessimistic fragments of fiction, forms the basis of the work concocted by A. B. Paine and Frederick A. Duneka and entitled *The Mysterious Stranger* (1916). In the "Chronicle" Mark Twain provides some of his most caustic criticisms of men's cruelty. His spokesman Philip Traum (Young Satan) objects to the term "brutal" by noting, "No brute ever does a cruel thing—that is the monopoly of the snob with the Moral Sense. When a brute inflicts pain he does it innocently; it is not wrong; for him there is no such thing as wrong. And he does not inflict pain for the pleasure of inflicting it—only man does that. Inspired by that mongrel Moral Sense of his!" Philip provides the narrator with a quick rehearsal of human history to demonstrate man's maliciousness.

Although Mark Twain had long been critical of the Christian church, which is attacked with particular vehemence in *A Connecticut Yankee*, it is only in his late work that he attacks God himself. In a dictation made in June 1906 and published only in 1963 as "Reflections on Religion," Mark Twain said,

In His destitution of one and of all of the qualities which could grace a God and invite respect for Him and reverence and worship, the real God, the genuine God, the Maker of the mighty universe is just like all the other gods in the list. He proves every day that he takes no interest in man, nor in the other animals, further than to torture them, slay them, and get out of this pastime such entertainment as it may afford—and do what he can not to get weary of the eternal and changeless monotony of it.

In *Letters from the Earth*, written in 1909, Mark Twain blames God for man's physical ills in an analysis that is both amusing and disturbing.

Readers who identify Mark Twain as primarily a humorist are often disturbed to learn that he became a pessimist in his later years. Usually the explanation given is that his personal disasters—his bankruptcy, the death of his daughter Susy and then his wife, as well as his own poor health—were responsible. But there is evidence of the direction his thoughts were taking him long before these calamities occurred, indeed while he was still affluent. In the 1880s he drafted a series of statements, published only in 1973 in *What is Man? and Other Philosophical Writings*, in which he asserts that no system of divine reward or punishment exists and that the Scriptures were "imagined and written by man" and that moral laws were created by experience. In 1896, before news had come to the Clemenses that Susy was dead, Mark Twain had begun "Man's Place in the Animal World." Here he argued that man descended from animals, not ascended from them. To man alone he ascribed revenge, indecency, vulgarity, obscenity, cruelty, slavery, patriotism, religion, and the Moral Sense. "Since the Moral Sense had but the one office, the one capacity—to enable man to do wrong—it is plainly without value to him. In fact it is manifestly a disease." The Moral Sense was to become a favorite theme in such later works as "The Chronicle of Young Satan."

Throughout his career, one of Mark Twain's favorite themes was the double. The idea appeared early in his work, when Mark Twain was fascinated by Chang and Eng, the Siamese twins, two separate individuals joined by a ligature. The earliest version of *Pudd'nhead Wilson* was about twins, Angelo and Luigi, who had one body, two heads, four arms, and two legs. Later he separated them into two, and that is how they appear in the published story. But in "Those Extraordinary Twins" the two are—as Mark Twain put it—"conglomerate." Luigi explains that he and his brother have "utter and indisputable command" of their joint body during alternate periods.

In both *The Prince and the Pauper* and in the Tom Driscoll-Chambers part of *Pudd'nhead Wilson*, it is the notion that training creates individual differences that interests Mark Twain. Later, after reading Robert Louis Stevenson's *Dr. Jekyll and Mr. Hyde* and learning about French experiments with hypnosis and the work of William James, he became interested in multiple personalities within one individual. He found that each person consisted of three selves: a waking self, a somnambulic self, and a dream self. This idea dominates the story Mark Twain wrote in the early years of the new century, "No. 44, The Mysterious Stranger," and here he found a way to return to his celebration of freedom by arguing that one aspect of man's self is immortal, and that when it is freed from the body, it experiences "forces, passions and emotions of a quite tremendous character." The story of the interaction of the various selves is both playful and serious. Here Mark Twain was exploring the conflicts of human needs, the desire to be "a person who wants the earth, and cannot be satisfied unless he can have the whole of it," and the desire to be liberated, to be free from the deterministic forces he had described in "What is Man?"

Although Mark Twain tried to play the role of sage and philospher in his last years, he remained inconsistent. The opening of one of his best short stories, "The Man That Corrupted Hadleyburg" (1898), is deterministic, but ultimately the story implies man's responsibility for his actions. The pieces he collected and published as *Christian Science* (1907) offer no consistent view of the subject, though Mark Twain had great fun examining Mary Baker Eddy's prose style. He was a democrat in principle but so attracted to royalty that he was obliged to present King Arthur as a superior person, and his Connecticut Yankee, Hank Morgan, is allowed to become virtually a dictator. Mark Twain's complexity is perhaps best shown in a story he wrote about himself, "The Facts Concerning the Carnival of Crime in Connecticut" (1876), a small masterpiece. Here Mark Twain explores his divided self by explaining how he was visited by his conscience, who has been so mistreated that he is "a shriveled, shabby dwarf . . . not much more than two feet high." In this story Mark Twain is a victim, not only of society but of himself. With great good humor he tells how after much provocation he rose up, tore apart, and killed his conscience, a death that freed him to undertake a criminal career. Mark Twain's humor, even at his own expense, was his greatest virtue.

SURVEY OF CRITICISM

Because Mark Twain's life and work were closely interwoven, most of the criticism about his work has a biographical orientation. Unfortunately, there is no satisfactory biography. The three-volume work written by Albert Bigelow Paine and published in 1912 provides a great deal of information not available elsewhere; Paine interviewed many people who had known Clemens, and Paine himself knew the author during his last years. Paine intended to present his subject in an attractive light, and he succeeded. Some indication of the limitations of his work can be obtained by comparing Paine's presentation of Clemens's last decade with that in Hamlin Hill's *Mark Twain: God's Fool* (1973), which provides a much less attractive picture. Many readers find that Hill overcompensated for Paine's bias.

In 1920 Van Wyck Brooks published *The Ordeal of Mark Twain*, in which he offered an interpretation of the life of the author, arguing that he had moved from the sterility of the frontier to the restrictiveness of Eastern respectability. Bernard De Voto in *Mark Twain's America* (1932) offered a rebuttal, in which he argued that the frontier had a salutary effect on the author. In 1933 Brooks published a revised version of his book; in it the argument is largely what it was. Neither Brooks nor De Voto had access to materials that would have made their books of continuing value, though Brooks's ideas continue to be stimulating. Neither writer attempted a biography.

Thirty years after Paine's volumes appeared, DeLancey Ferguson's *Mark Twain: Man and Legend* (1943) was published. It provides an overview of both life and works. Ferguson is more critical than Paine, and his book is still readable, but it now needs both correction and amplification. Dixon Wecter, who acted as literary editor of the Mark Twain Estate after Paine (and after Bernard De Voto) was engaged in a full-length biography when death interrupted his work, and only a good account of Clemens's first seventeen years was published, *Sam Clemens in Hannibal* (1952).

In 1966 Justin Kaplan published a highly readable, scholarly biography, but it covers only the years after Mark Twain left the West. *Mr. Clemens and Mark Twain* makes rather less of the author's duality than the title suggests, and it emphasizes the man much more than the writer. Kaplan's book would be more valuable had he chosen to explore his subject's formative years. Another interesting portrait of Samuel Clemens can be found in Edward Wagenknecht's *Mark Twain: The Man and His Work*, first published in 1935, then revised in 1961. (A third edition appeared in 1967; it simply adds a commentary on scholarship since 1960.) This is not a biography but a psychograph, a consideration of the writer under such headings as "The Man of Letters," "Charts of Salvation," and "The Damned Human Race." Everett Emerson's *The Authentic Mark Twain: A Literary Biography of Samuel L. Clemens* (1984) focuses on the writer and his work; only those aspects of the author's life that touched his work are explored. Emerson had access to information not available to Kaplan. Edgar M. Branch is preparing an account of the years from Hannibal to Hartford and has already located much new information, including previously unknown publications of the years when Clemens was a pilot. Thomas Tenney is preparing a documentary biography of Clemens.

Of the dozens of critical books on Mark Twain, two have become recognized as most helpful. Henry Nash Smith's *Mark Twain: The Development of a Writer* (1962) focuses on nine works, all of the most admired ones. A leading American studies specialist, Smith shows how Mark Twain's works reveal "a conflict between the dominant culture of his day and an emergent attitude associated with the vernacular language of the native American humorist," as Smith himself put it. He is especially good on Mark Twain's style. James M. Cox's *Mark Twain: The Fate of Humor* (1966) is a more brilliant book, but it rides its theses too hard. It is much the best study of the place of humor in Mark Twain's work.

The Mark Twain Papers, by far the largest collection of materials on the author, is in the Bancroft Library in the University of California, Berkeley. It is the headquarters for the valuable scholarship on Mark Twain being undertaken by the editors of two series being published by the University of California Press, the Mark Twain Papers, gathered from unpublished writings, and the Works of Mark Twain, chiefly editions of his familiar works. The texts and the scholarship in the volumes of *Early Tales and Sketches* and the forthcoming *Collected Letters* are highly valuable. Robert Hirst is now in charge of the Mark Twain Project. One of the editors of this vast undertaking, John S. Tuckey, published important work in 1963, *Mark Twain and Little Satan: The Making of "The Mysterious Stranger."* Tuckey determined the time of composition of the several related stories in which Mark Twain employed the figure of Little Satan and shows that the book published in 1916 as *The Mysterious Stranger* was an edited conglomeration of two separate manuscripts. In 1969 an edition of *The Mysterious Stranger Manuscripts* appeared, edited by William M. Gibson. Until the edition of *Pudd' nhead Wilson* being prepared by Hershel Parker appears, readers interested in that work should consult Daniel M. McKeithan's *The Morgan Manuscript of Mark Twain's "Pudd' nhead Wilson"* (1961), which includes excerpts from the manuscript before it was cut, disastrously. These passages help a reader make sense of the published novel.

It is doubtful that there will ever be a satisfactory edition of the autobiography, because Mark Twain worked into his dictations such a variety of materials and spoke in such a disorganized way that there is unlikely to be a readership for a complete edition. At present the reader should begin with the two volumes edited by Paine in 1924 as *Mark Twain's Autobiography*. (Paine might have published at least one additional volume if interest had seemed to demand one.) Bernard De Voto, who succeeded Paine as literary editor, published *Mark Twain in Eruption: Hitherto Unpublished Pages about Men and Events* (1940). Charles Neider tried to organize chronologically the materials Paine had published; he also included some previously unpublished material from dictations in *The Autobiography of Mark Twain* (1959). One of the most valuable autobiographical writings, not to be thought of as part of what the author called his autobiography, remains unpublished. It is called "A Family Sketch" (1906) and describes in amusing fashion the servants of the Clemens household.

Other significant problems of text should be mentioned. Some excellent passages were omitted from *Life on the Mississippi* at the suggestion of James R. Osgood, at the time Mark Twain's publisher. They appear in the 1944 version of the book edited by Willis Wager. Another publisher, Clemens's nephew Charles L. Webster, persuaded the author to omit the "Raft Passage" he had borrowed from the *Huckleberry Finn* manuscript and inserted into the text of *Life on the Mississippi*. Since without it there is a gap in the novel, it ought to be restored. Henry Nash Smith included it as an appendix to his edition of *Huckleberry Finn* (1958). The 1979 University of California Press edition of *A Connecticut Yankee in King Arthur's Court* includes many passages omitted from the novel. There was good reason for this pruning, but examination of the deleted passages is informative. Probably the work most damaged by editing is *Tom Sawyer Abroad*. The American publication suffered at the hands of Mabel Mapes Dodge, editor of *St. Nicholas Magazine*, where it first appeared. The restored text appears in the 1980 University of California Press edition, along with *Tom Sawyer*. *Following the Equator* was also heavily edited by both the American Publishing Company and Mark Twain's English publisher, Chatto and Windus. The manuscript survives at the New York Public Library.

There are valuable materials in the many volumes of the Mark Twain Papers being published by California. Those in *Mark Twain's Hannibal, Huck & Tom*, edited by Walter Blair (1969), are of particular interest. One of the masterpieces of American literary scholarship is the two-volume *Mark Twain–Howells Letters*, edited by Henry Nash Smith and William M. Gibson (1960). A minor masterpiece, "A Singular Episode" (1891–92), lies buried in *Mark Twain's Quarrel with Heaven*, edited by Ray B. Browne (1970), which also contains the fullest published text of "Captain Stormfield's Visit to Heaven." Good texts must precede sound criticism.

Two books that help explain Mark Twain's relationship with England are Howard G. Baezhold's *Mark Twain and John Bull: The British Connection* (1970), which traces the author's attitude towards England and its writers and thinkers, and Dennis Welland's *Mark Twain in England* (1978), which explores his connection with British publishers, especially Chatto and Windus. Mark Twain's connection with the American Publishing Company of Hartford is explored in Hamlin Hill's *Mark Twain and Elisha Bliss* (1964). Hill shows what an important impact subscription publishing had on the shape of Mark Twain's work. How Mark Twain shaped the public perception of himself is explained by Louis J. Budd in *Our Mark Twain: The Making of His Public Personality* (1983).

Of the many studies of Mark Twain's thought, two are most helpful: Roger B. Salomon's *Twain and the Image of History* (1961), an exploration of the conflicts between the author's conception of history and his concept of human nature, and Louis J. Budd's *Mark Twain: Social Philosopher* (1962), an analysis of Mark Twain's social and political positions. How Mark Twain thought about American blacks is intelligently examined in Arthur G. Pettit's highly readable *Mark Twain & the South* (1974). The Clemens family's Hartford milieu is explored in Kenneth R. Andrews's *Nook Farm: Mark Twain's Hartford Circle* (1950). Two studies of Mark Twain as a lecturer are Paul Fatout's *Mark Twain on the Lecture Circuit* (1964) and Fred W. Lorch's *The Trouble Begins at Eight: Mark Twain's Lecture Tours* (1968). The title of William G. Macnaughton's work explains what his subject is: *Mark Twain's Last Years as a Writer* (1979). More fundamental than any of the above is Alan Gribben's *Mark Twain's Library: A Reconstruction* (1980), which explores fully the influence of his reading. Not so much a book to be read as one to consult, the two volumes are arranged dictionary-fashion, with an entry for each work that Mark Twain is known to have owned or read.

Adventures of Huckleberry Finn is naturally Mark Twain's most discussed work. The fundamental study, perhaps the most learned book yet written on the author, is Walter Blair's *Mark Twain & Huck Finn* (1960), an attempt to explain how the book came to be written. It explores the man's life, his reading, thinking, and writing between 1874 and 1884. Blair deals perceptively with both *Tom Sawyer* and *Huckleberry Finn*. He answered the question "When Was *Huckleberry Finn* Written?" in a valuable essay published in 1958. The most admired critical essay on the novel is Henry Nash Smith's introduction to his 1958 edition. Based solidly on Blair's scholarship, this essay helps to explain the structure and the meaning of the book. The striking difference between the central figure of *Tom Sawyer* and Tom as he appears in *Huckleberry Finn* is explored by Judith Fetterley in "Disenchantment: Tom Sawyer in *Huckleberry Finn*," a 1972 essay. A quite different kind of criticism is supplied by John Seelye, who revised Mark Twain's novel to make it conform more fully to modern critical standards. The result, *The True Adventures of Huckleberry Finn* (1970), is an exciting critical statement, in unexpected ways. An up-to-date account of the critical reception of the novel is Victor Fischer's 1983 essay, "Huck Finn Reviewed." (Fischer is preparing the California edition of the novel.) See also *Mark Twain: The Critical Heritage* (1971), edited by Frederick Anderson, which contains a well-chosen compendium of criticism. There is a "critical edition" of *Huckleberry Finn* that includes relevant documents and a collection of critical essays edited by Sculley Bradley, Richmond Croom Beatty, E. Hudson Long, and Thomas Cooley (2d ed., 1977).

A Connecticut Yankee in King Arthur's Court has also been the subject of much discussion. Henry Nash Smith's lectures on the book are gathered as *Mark Twain's Fable of Progress: "A Connecticut Yankee in King Arthur's Court"* (1964); it analyzes the book in terms of the thought of the time on the subject of industrialism. Everett Carter's 1979 essay "The Meaning of *A Connecticut Yankee*" rehearses what others have said about the book and offers a persuasive reading.

The Mark Twain Journal is now edited by Thomas A. Tenney at the College of Charleston (South Carolina). Whereas for many years its publication record was highly uneven, under Tenney it should be a useful journal of Mark Twain scholarship and criticism. Tenney edited a valuable secondary bibliography, *Mark Twain: A Reference Guide* (1977), to which he provides annual supplements in the journal *American Literary Realism*. There is no complete bibliography of Mark Twain's writings. A useful census, which includes comments on unpublished materials, is Robert L. Gale's *Plots and Characters in the Works of Mark Twain* (1973).

BIBLIOGRAPHY

Works by Mark Twain

With one notable exception, only book publications are listed. Much early work has been gathered in such volumes as *Early Twain and Sketches*.

The Celebrated Jumping Frog of Calaveras County, and Other Sketches. New York: C. H. Webb, 1867.
The Innocents Abroad, or The New Pilgrims' Progress. Hartford: American, 1869.
Mark Twain's (Burlesque) Autobiography and First Romance. New York: Sheldon, 1871.
Roughing It. Hartford: American, 1872.
The Gilded Age, in collaboration with Charles Dudley Warner. Hartford: American, 1874.
Mark Twain's Sketches. Number One. New York: American News, 1874.
Sketches, New and Old. Hartford: American, 1875.
The Adventures of Tom Sawyer. Hartford: American, 1876.
A True Story and the Recent Carnival of Crime. Boston: James R. Osgood, 1877.
Punch, Brothers, Punch! and Other Sketches. New York: Slote, Woodman, 1878.
1601, or Conversation as It Was by the Fireside in the Time of the Tudors. Cleveland edition of 1880, n.p., n.d.

A Tramp Abroad. Hartford: American, 1880.

The Prince and the Pauper. Boston: James R. Osgood, 1882.

Life on the Mississippi. Boston: James R. Osgood, 1883.

The Stolen White Elephant. Boston: James R. Osgood, 1883.

Adventures of Huckleberry Finn. New York: Charles L. Webster, 1885.

A Connecticut Yankee in King Arthur's Court. New York: Charles L. Webster, 1889.

The American Claimant. New York: Charles L. Webster, 1892.

Merry Tales. New York: Charles L. Webster, 1892.

The $1,000,000 Bank-Note and Other New Stories. New York: Charles L. Webster, 1893.

Tom Sawyer Abroad. New York: Charles L. Webster, 1894.

The Tragedy of Pudd'nhead Wilson and The Comedy of Those Extraordinary Twins. Hartford: American, 1894.

Personal Recollections of Joan of Arc. New York: Harper, 1896.

Tom Sawyer Abroad, Tom Sawyer, Detective, and Other Stories. New York: Harper, 1896.

Following the Equator. Hartford: American, 1897.

How to Tell a Story and Other Essays. New York: Harper, 1897.

English as She Is Taught. Boston: Mutual Book, 1900.

How to Tell a Story and Other Essays. Hartford: American, 1900.

The Man That Corrupted Hadleyburg and Other Stories and Essays. New York: Harper, 1900.

Edmund Burke on Croker and Tammany. New York: Economist Press, 1901.

A Double Barrelled Detective Story. New York: Harper, 1902.

My Debut as a Literary Person with Other Essays and Stories. Hartford: American, 1903.

A Dog's Tale. New York: Harper, 1904.

Extracts from Adam's Diary. New York: Harper, 1904.

King Leopold's Soliloquy: A Defense of His Congo Rule. Boston: P. R. Warner, 1905.

Eve's Diary. New York: Harper, 1906.

The $30,000 Bequest and Other Stories. New York: Harper, 1906.

Christian Science. New York: Harper, 1907.

A Horse's Tale. New York: Harper, 1907.

Extract from Captain Stormfield's Visit to Heaven. New York: Harper, 1909.

Is Shakespeare Dead? New York: Harper, 1909.

Mark Twain's Speeches. New York: Harper, 1910.

The Mysterious Stranger. New York: Harper, 1916.

Mark Twain's Letters. Ed. Albert Bigelow Paine. New York: Harper, 1917.

What Is Man? and Other Essays. New York: Harper, 1917.

The Curious Republic of Gondour and Other Whimsical Sketches. New York: Boni and Liveright, 1919.

The Mysterious Stranger and Other Stories. New York: Harper, 1922.

Europe and Elsewhere. New York: Harper, 1923.

Mark Twain's Speeches. Ed. Albert Bigelow Paine. rev. ed. New York: Harper, 1923.

Mark Twain's Autobiography. 2 vols. Ed. Albert Bigelow Paine. New York: Harper, 1924.

Sketches of the Sixties by Bret Harte and Mark Twain. San Francisco: John Howell, 1926. rev., enl. ed., 1927.

The Adventures of Thomas Jefferson Snodgrass. Chicago: Pascal Covici, 1928.

Mark Twain's Notebook. Ed. Albert Bigelow Paine. New York: Harper, 1935.

Slovenly Peter (Der Struwwelpeter) translated by Mark Twain. New York: Harper, 1935.

Mark Twain in Eruption: Hitherto Unpublished Pages about Men and Events. Ed. Bernard De Voto. New York: Harper, 1940.

Mark Twain's Travels with Mr. Brown. Ed. Franklin Walker and Ezra C. Bane. New York: Alfred A. Knopf, 1940.

Mark Twain's Letters to Will Bowen. Ed. Theodore Hornberger. Austin: University of Texas, 1941.

Mark Twain's Letters in the Muscatine Journal. Ed. Edgar M. Branch. Chicago: Mark Twain Association of America, 1942.

Life on the Mississippi. Ed. Willis Wager. With an introduction by Edward Wagenknecht and a number of previously suppressed passages now printed for the first time. New York: Limited Editions Club, 1944.

The Love Letters of Mark Twain. Ed. Dixon Wecter. New York: Harper, 1949.

Mark Twain to Mrs. Fairbanks. Ed. Dixon Wecter. San Marino: Huntington Library, 1949.

Report from Paradise. Ed. Dixon Wecter. New York: Harper, 1952.

Mark Twain to Uncle Remus, 1881–1885. Ed. Thomas English. Atlanta: The Library, Emory University, 1953.

Mark Twain: San Francisco Correspondent. Ed. Henry Nash Smith and Frederick Anderson. San Francisco: Book Club of California, 1957.

Mark Twain of the "Enterprise": Newspaper Articles and Other Documents, 1862–1864. Ed. Henry Nash Smith and Frederick Anderson. Berkeley: University of California Press, 1957.

Traveling with the Innocents Abroad: Mark Twain's Original Reports from Europe and the Holy Land. Ed. Daniel Morley McKeithan. Norman: University of Oklahoma Press, 1958.

The Autobiography of Mark Twain. Ed. Charles Neider. New York: Harper, 1959.

Mark Twain–Howells Letters. Ed. Henry Nash Smith and William M. Gibson. Cambridge: Harvard University Press, 1960.

"Ah Sin," a Dramatic Work by Mark Twain and Bret Harte. Ed. Frederick Anderson. San Francisco: Book Club of California, 1961.

Letters to Mary. Ed. Lewis Leary. New York: Columbia University Press, 1961.

Life as I Find It: Sketches, Tales, and Other Material, the Majority of Which Is Now Published in Book Form for the First Time. Ed. Charles Neider. Garden City, N.Y.: Hanover House, 1961.

The Pattern for "Roughing It." Ed. Franklin R. Rogers. Berkeley: University of California Press, 1961.

Letters from the Earth. Ed. Bernard De Voto. New York: Harper, 1962.

"Reflections on Religion." Ed. Charles Neider. *Hudson Review* 16 (1963): 329–52.

Simon Wheeler, Detective. Ed. Franklin R. Rogers. New York: New York Public Library, 1963.

On the Poetry of Mark Twain. With Selections from His Verse. Ed. Arthur L. Scott. Urbana: University of Illinois Press, 1966.

Mark Twain's Letters to His Publishers. Ed. Hamlin Hill. Berkeley: University of California Press, 1967.

Mark Twain's Satires and Burlesques. Ed. Franklin R. Rogers. Berkeley: University of California Press, 1967.

Clemens of the "Call": Mark Twain in San Francisco. Ed. Edgar M. Branch. Berkeley: University of California Press, 1968.

Mark Twain's Which Was The Dream? and Other Symbolic Writings of the Later Years. Ed. John S. Tuckey. Berkeley: University of California Press, 1968.

Mark Twain's Correspondence with Henry Huddleston Rogers. Ed. Lewis Leary. Berkeley: University of California Press, 1969.

Mark Twain's Hannibal, Huck & Tom. Ed. Walter Blair. Berkeley: University of California Press, 1969.

The Mysterious Stranger Manuscripts. Ed. William M. Gibson. Berkeley: University of California Press, 1969.

"Colonel Sellers as a Scientist." *The Complete Plays of William Dean Howells*. Ed. Walter J. Meserve. New York: New York University Press, 1970.

Mark Twain's Quarrel with Heaven: "Captain Stormfield's Visit to Heaven" and Other Sketches. Ed. Ray B. Browne. New Haven: College & University Press, 1970.

Mark Twain's Fables of Man. Ed. John S. Tuckey. Berkeley: University of California Press, 1972.

A Pen Warmed Up in Hell: Mark Twain in Protest. Ed. Frederick Anderson. New York: Harper and Row, 1972.

Roughing It. Ed. Franklin R. Rogers and Paul Baender. Berkeley: University of California Press, 1972.

What is Man? and Other Philosophical Writings. Ed. Paul Baender. Berkeley: University of California Press, 1973.

Mark Twain's Notebooks & Journals, Volume 1 (1855–1873). Ed. Frederick Anderson, Michael B. Frank, and Kenneth M. Sanderson. Berkeley: University of California Press, 1975.

Mark Twain's Notebooks & Journals, Volume 2 (1877–1883). Ed. Frederick Anderson, Lin Salamo, and Bernard Stein. Berkeley: University of California Press, 1975.

The Mammoth Cod and Address to the Stomach Club. Ed. G. Legman. Milwaukee: Maledicta, 1976.

Mark Twain Speaking. Ed. Paul Fatout. Iowa City: University of Iowa Press, 1976.

Adventures of Huckleberry Finn. Ed. Sculley Bradley, Richmond Croom Beatty, E. Hudson Long, and Thomas Cooley. 2nd ed. New York: Norton, 1977. [A Norton Critical Edition.]

A Connecticut Yankee in King Arthur's Court. Ed. Bernard L. Stein. Berkeley: University of California Press, 1979.

Early Tales & Sketches, Volume 1, 1851–1864. Ed. Edgar M. Branch and Robert H. Hirst. Berkeley: University of California Press, 1979.

Mark Twain's Notebooks & Journals, Volume 3 (1883–1891). Ed. Robert Pack Browning, Michael B. Frank, and Lin Salamo. Berkeley: University of California Press, 1979.

Mark Twain Speaks for Himself. Ed. Paul Fatout. West Lafayette, Ind.: Purdue University Press, 1979.

The Prince and the Pauper. Ed. Victor Fischer and Lin Salamo. Berkeley: University of California Press, 1979.

The Adventures of Tom Sawyer, Tom Sawyer Abroad, Tom Sawyer Detective. Ed. John C. Gerber, Paul Baender, and Terry Firkins. Berkeley: University of California Press, 1980.

Early Tales & Sketches, Volume 2, 1864–1865. Ed. Edgar M. Branch and Robert H. Hirst. Berkeley: University of California Press, 1981.

Wapping Alice. Berkeley: Friends of the Bancroft Library, 1981.

Adventures of Huckleberry Finn. Ed. Walter Blair and Victor Fischer. Berkeley: University of California Press, 1985.

Studies of Mark Twain

Anderson, Frederick, ed. *Mark Twain: The Critical Heritage*. New York: Barnes and Noble, 1971.

Andrews, Kenneth R. *Nook Farm: Mark Twain's Hartford Circle*. Cambridge: Harvard University Press, 1950.

Baezhold, Howard G. *Mark Twain and John Bull: The British Connection*. Bloomington: Indiana University Press, 1970.

Blair, Walter. *Mark Twain & Huck Finn*. Berkeley and Los Angeles: University of California Press, 1960.

———. "When was *Huckleberry Finn* Written?" *American Literature* 30 (March 1958): 1–25.

Brooks, Van Wyck. *The Ordeal of Mark Twain*. New York: Dutton, 1920: rev. ed., 1933.

Budd, Louis J. *Mark Twain: Social Philosopher*. Bloomington: Indiana University Press, 1962.

———. *Our Mark Twain: The Making of His Public Personality*. Philadelphia: University of Pennsylvania Press, 1983.

Carter, Everett. "The Meaning of *A Connecticut Yankee*." *American Literature* 50 (November 1978): 418–40.

Cox, James M. *Mark Twain: The Fate of Humor*. Princeton: Princeton University Press, 1966.

De Voto, Bernard. *Mark Twain's America*. Boston: Little, Brown, 1932.

Emerson, Everett. *The Authentic Mark Twain: A Literary Biography of Samuel L. Clemens*. Philadelphia: University of Pennsylvania Press, 1984.

Fatout, Paul. *Mark Twain on the Lecture Circuit*. Bloomington: Indiana University Press, 1964.

Ferguson, DeLaney. *Mark Twain: Man and Legend*. Indianapolis: Bobbs-Merrill, 1943.

Fetterley, Judith. "Disenchantment: Tom Sawyer in *Huckleberry Finn*." *PMLA* 87 (1972): 69–74.

Fischer, Victor. "Huck Finn Reviewed: The Reception of *Huckleberry Finn* in the United States, 1885–1897." *American Literary Realism* 16 (1983): 1–57.

Gale, Robert L. *Plots and Characters in the Works of Mark Twain*. 2 vols. Hamden, Conn.: Archon Books, 1973.

Gribben, Alan. *Mark Twain's Library. A Reconstruction*. 2 vols. Boston: G. K. Hall, 1980.

Hill, Hamlin. *Mark Twain and Elisha Bliss*. Columbia: University of Missouri Press, 1964.

———. *Mark Twain: God's Fool*. New York: Harper and Row, 1973.

Kaplan, Justin. *Mr. Clemens and Mark Twain*. New York: Simon and Schuster, 1966.

Lorch, Fred W. *The Trouble Begins at Eight: Mark Twain's Lecture Tours*. Ames: Iowa State University Press, 1968.

McKeithan, Daniel M. *The Morgan Manuscript of Mark Twain's "Pudd'nhead Wilson."* Uppsala: American Institute, Uppsala University, 1961.

Macnaughton, William G. *Mark Twain's Last Years as a Writer*. Columbia: University of Missouri Press, 1979.

Paine, Albert Bigelow. *Mark Twain: A Biography*. 3 vols. New York: Harper, 1912.

Pettit, Arthur G. *Mark Twain & the South*. Lexington: University of Kentucky Press, 1974.

Salomon, Roger B. *Twain and the Image of History*. New Haven: Yale University Press, 1961.

Seelye, John. *The True Adventures of Huckleberry Finn*. Evanston, Ill.: Northwestern University Press, 1970.

Smith, Henry Nash. Introduction to *Adventures of Huckleberry Finn*. Boston: Houghton Mifflin, 1958.

————. *Mark Twain: The Development of a Writer*. Cambridge: Harvard University Press, 1962.

————. *Mark Twain's Fable of Progress: "A Connecticut Yankee in King Arthur's Court."* New Brunswick, N.J.: Rutgers University Press, 1964.

Tenney, Thomas A. *Mark Twain: A Reference Guide*. Boston: G. K. Hall, 1977.

Tuckey, John S. *Mark Twain and Little Satan: The Writing of "The Mysterious Stranger."* West Lafayette, Ind.: Purdue University Studies, 1963.

Wagenknecht, Edward. *Mark Twain: The Man and His Work*. 3d ed. Norman: University of Oklahoma Press, 1967.

Wecter, Dixon. *Sam Clemens of Hannibal*. Boston: Houghton Mifflin, 1952.

Welland, Dennis. *Mark Twain and England*. London: Chatto and Windus, 1978.

Ebenezer Cook(e)
(ca. 1667–ca. 1732)

Ebenezer Cook (sometimes spelled Cooke) is the author of the first wholly belletristic writing to be published in the colonial South, his *ELOGY on the Death of Thomas Bordley*, which issued as a broadside from William Parks's press in Annapolis in October 1726. In *The Sot-Weed Factor* (1708), Cook also shows himself to be the most accomplished colonial satirist before Benjamin Franklin. Styling himself the ''Poet Laureate'' of Maryland, a title he probably assumed in jest, Cook created in that poem and several others a gentleman narrator who mocks the ''planting Rabble'' and who is also revealed by their actions to be vain and foolish as well. Like many later Southern writers, Cook was unimpressed by man's pretense of rationality and found the flesh and the appetites to be the lowest comic denominators of human nature.

BIOGRAPHY

Not much is known for certain about Cook's life. Born in London sometime around 1667, he was the son of the Maryland merchant Andrew and his wife, Anne Bowyer Cook. Perhaps hoping to follow in his father's footsteps, he came to Maryland sometime before 1694, when he signed a remonstrance protesting the removal of the capital from St. Mary's City to Annapolis. This first written record of Cook's presence in Lord Baltimore's province finds an echo in *The Sot-Weed Factor* when Cook's narrator explains for the benefit of English readers unfamiliar with Maryland's history that ''St. *Mary's* once was in repute'' as the provincial capital and describes Annapolis as ''A City Situate on a Plain, / Where scarce a House will keep out Rain.'' Perhaps Cook's portrait of Annapolis as a raw frontier town populated by pettifogging lawyers, quack physicians, cozening Quakers, and dishonest judges reflects his disapproval of the decision to locate the new capital there instead of leaving it at St. Mary's.

Cook appears to have left Maryland and returned to London sometime late in 1700, where, in September of that year, he was appointed the "true and Lawfull Attorney" of one "Edwd Ebbitt Citizen." Whether this commission applied in London or in Maryland is not certain. Perhaps Cook remained in London until 1708, when *The Sot-Weed Factor* was published by "*B. Bragg*, at the *Raven* in *Pater-Noster Row*," and he may, indeed, have stayed long enough to probate his father's will on 2 January 1712. By the terms of that will, he inherited half-interest in an estate in Maryland, Malden, to which he had already referred obliquely in *The Sot-Weed Factor* ("And had my Doctress wanted skill, / Or Kitchin Physick at her will, / My Father's Son had lost his Lands") and which he sold to a cousin, Edward Cook, on 30 October 1717. He was, apparently, back in Maryland to stay.

During the 1720s, Cook was admitted to the bar of Prince Georges County and, from all appearances, sided with the Lower House of the Assembly against the Lord Proprietor and his Governors (Charles Calvert between 1720 and 1727 and then Benedict Leonard Calvert from 1727 to 1731) in the Statute Law controversy that led to the eventual composition and publication of Daniel Dulany's *Rights of the Inhabitants of MARYLAND, to the Benefit of the ENGLISH Laws* (1728). Dulany's position, which was also supported by Cook's friend and former attorney general of Maryland, Thomas Bordley (until the Proprietors dismissed him in 1725), was essentially that both Common Law, including the Habeas Corpus Act, and Statute Law, which in practice upheld Common Law, ought to be allowed full jurisdiction in Maryland; he attacked especially the Proprietors' contention that they could and should determine which articles of the Common Law were relevant to their province, which they initially argued was a conquered country rather than a colony of England. The Habeas Corpus Act, they said, although it was a general act, was never meant to extend to the plantation of Maryland.

Despite Cook's later authorship of an elegy "In Memory of the Honble Benedict Leonard Calvert Esqr. Lieutenant Governor in the Province of Maryland" (1732), his sympathies during this controversy may be reliably inferred from an ironic remark he made in the so-called Preface to the lost (or entirely fictitious) second edition of *The Sot-Weed Factor*. In that fragment, he noted that some readers had charged him with plagiarism in the original poem but that, even if the charge were true, he could not be prosecuted because "the Laws of Great Britain are not allow'd to extend to the wilds of America." His sympathetic portrait of Bordley's public service in the *ELOGY* of 1726, together with some sly references to "Party Discords" and other veiled political allusions in the poem, further help to establish Cook's position in this hotly debated contest, in which students of American history may detect foreshadowings of issues that ignited the Revolution some 50 years later.

However well the pettifogging lawyers of *The Sot-Weed Factor* may have fared financially, Cook's own legal practice, if indeed he practiced at all, could not sustain him. Throughout the 1720s, he seems to have survived chiefly on the proceeds of his services as a deputy of Henry Lowe II, receiver-general of the province in 1720, and as a land agent for Lowe, Lowe's brother Bennett, and John Gresham. After 1722, his name disappears entirely from public records, and his continued existence can be established only by the publication of a handful of poems written between 1726 and 1732, when he would have been in his middle sixties, impoverished, and probably in poor health. A poem by the Virginia historian Hugh Jones affectionately inscribed at the head of Cook's "History of Colonel Nathaniel Bacon's Rebellion in Virginia" in *The Maryland Muse* speaks of Cook as an "Old Poet," and within the "History" itself are several references to Cook's poverty, a theme that reappears in the elegy on Benedict Leonard Calvert. Given Cook's age and financial circumstances, it is not surprising that after 1732 nothing further is heard from or about the "Poet Laureate" of colonial Maryland.

No account of Cook's career could be complete without special reference to his association with the public printer William Parks. Parks had been induced to set up shop in Annapolis by Cook's friend and benefactor Thomas Bordley, who wanted Parks to print the *Debates and Proceedings of the Assembly* (first publication 1725) in order to make Maryland's laws public and expose the Proprietors during the Statute Law controversy. But Parks's presence also encouraged literary activity, first in Annapolis and later in Williamsburg, Virginia. Cook was, of course, part of this new interest in local literature. Though he may have been writing all the while, the fact is that no poems by his hand have come to light written between *The Sot-Weed Factor* in 1708 and the *ELOGY* on Bordley in 1726, just shortly after Parks's arrival in Annapolis. Then in quick succession appeared "An Elegy on the Death of the Honorable Nicholas Lowe" (*Maryland Gazette*, 24 December 1728), *Sotweed Redivivus* (1730), and the so-called third edition of "The Sot-Weed Factor" and "The History of Colonel Nathaniel Bacon's Rebellion in Virginia" for *The Maryland Muse* (1731)—all published by William Parks. The subject matter and topical nature of Cook's other two surviving poems, "An Elegy on the Death of the Honourable William Lock, Esqr." and the verses on Benedict Leonard Calvert (both 1732), suggest that these works, too, were destined in Cook's mind for publication by William Parks. The inference that Parks's arrival in Maryland awoke long dormant literary ambitions in Cook's heart (and in the hearts of Richard Lewis and other Marylanders as well) seems unavoidable.

MAJOR THEMES

Cook declares the major themes of his poetry on the title page of his first and best poem, *The Sot-Weed Factor*: "The Laws, Government, Courts and Constitutions" of Maryland, together with "the Buildings, Feasts, Frolicks, Entertainments, and Drunken Humours of the Inhabitants of that Part of America." He will spend his career, in other words, writing about the people in that remote, almost fantastic region of the world, at first for English audiences and then increasingly for local American ones. If *The Sot-Weed Factor* itself does not fulfill all the title page promises, such later poems as *Sotweed Redivivus* and "The History of Bacon's Rebellion" eventually make good on Cook's pledge. From first to last, Cook wrote as a Southerner, from a perspective at first ambivalently and then unequivocally American.

The subtitle of *The Sot-Weed Factor*, "a Voyage to Maryland," makes it clear that Cook was familiar with the promotional and, occasionally, antipromotional "voyage" literature about America, much of it written by people who had never seen the places they attempted to describe. In his poem, Cook was careful to cover the kind of material an audience acquainted with such "voyage" narratives would expect. Cook's narrator's encounter with the Indian "Tom," for instance, was almost obligatory in writing that purported to be about America, as were speculations (which Cook mocks) about the origins of the American natives. Cook's sources for this episode, accordingly, seem to be literary rather than personal. The allusion to the Indian as a "naked Pict," for example, points to Theodore de Bry's engravings of Picts and Indians, themselves inspired by John White's drawings of American Indians in Thomas Harriot's *A Briefe and True Report of the New Found-Land of Virginia* (1588), as a primary source. The same is true of the many references to Spanish exploration of the New World, which seem to originate in Spanish reports rather than in Cook's own experiences. Cook saw America through a literary glass, darkly, and with the shades and shadows of the European imagination clearly visible in the final product.

Nevertheless, despite Cook's dependence upon literary resources to fashion his images of America—Samuel Butler's *Hudibras* is, of course, a ubiquitous influence—there is about his verses the authentic quality of a true resident in the New World. Probably Cook's crossings and recrossings of the Atlantic Ocean, for example, contributed to the complexly ironic point of view, part English and part American, and to the instability evident in his best poem, *The Sot-Weed Factor*. As an Englishman, Cook's narrator condemns rustic Maryland for failing to achieve civilized standards of morals and manners; Maryland's courts are but provincial parodies of courts, her justice a mere travesty of the real article. Yet the narrator as Englishman is also pompous and egotistical, assured of his innate superiority to the poor white trash of Maryland, and so he, too, becomes a legitimate object of satire. He represents, in fact, the logical literary culmination of a familiar type in writing about America, the disgruntled merchant adventurer, and his misadventures lead to disastrous economic consequences largely as a result of his own naïveté. This arrogant British visitor would, of course, remain a fixture in American humor for many generations to come.

In many ways, Cook's narrator's depiction of America as a land where aspiration has degenerated into appetite and most of the humans, like all of the animals, are predatory merely represents an extension of the economic society that had been developing in England since the late Middle Ages. Maryland, that is, stands as a uniquely capitalistic kind of Underworld, the cursed "Land of

Nod'' that results when brother turns against brother in economic competition. In this view, the twin curses from which the sotweed factor suffers, the curse of an "empty Purse" and of "Friends unkind," are one and the same, and England no less than Maryland is a lost Eden. Fraud, usury, and double-dealing abound in both places. Cook's narrator's quest for economic status is a quest for identity in the strictest sense, for a way to measure and assert the value of the self in a world where economic considerations alone have importance. In the allusion to the Ship of Fools (*das Narrenschiff*) early in the poem, Cook deftly brings together a familiar image of the old moral order—the ship without a destination and the Fool as alien from God—and an image of the modern mercantile world—the ship as symbol of commerce and the immigrant as the new alien, economically dispossessed. The double irony of the poem is, of course, that the speaker voyages to recoup his fortunes toward a land made in the very image of imperialism and colonialism, with no prior traditions of brotherhood to disguise or in any way ameliorate the rule of economic aggression. Further, the identity the speaker has assumed, that of a merchant, though he will ultimately prove unworthy of it, marks him as yet another aspirant to membership in the class of oppressors—in the language of the poem, a "Vagrant *Cain*" indeed.

A mythic pattern underlies Cook's economic themes in *The Sot-Weed Factor*. One important myth, as comments may already have indicated, is the myth of Cain and Abel, the betrayal of brother by brother—a post-Edenic fable, to be sure. Another frequently encountered mythic image of America, and of the South in particular, in early promotional literature is the myth of America as a new Arcadia, an actual Garden of Eden located within the confines of time, geography, and history. This myth, of course, portrays man in harmony with nature, other men, and God. But in *The Sot-Weed Factor* Cook offers us, instead of the myth of the Garden, the story of Jason and the Argonauts as an archetype of colonial exploration and exploitation. Jason's quest for the Golden Fleece, it will be recalled, involves greed, lust, murder, betrayal, and revenge, all for the sake of personal fame and—above all else—fortune. In Cook's poem, historical types of the mythic Jason include (besides the sotweed factor himself, a parodic Jason if ever there was one) the ancient Phoenicians, who Cook's narrator hypothesizes may have been the ancestors of the Indians, and especially the conquistador Pizarro—"a Man" (in Cook's own words) "of most bloody Disposition, base, treacherous, covetous, and revengeful." Pizarro, in short, is just the sort of man to succeed where the petty sotweed factor has failed, though the factor, too, dreams of America as a "Golden Shoar" and imagines the act of discovery as virtually synonymous and simultaneous with vast profits. There have long been two conflicting and contradictory dreams of America, the dream of Edenic innocence and the dream of economic advancement. In *The Sot-Weed Factor*, Cook becomes the first American writer to bring the two dreams so forcefully and ironically into collision.

One need not transform Cook into an incipient Marxist in order to understand

The Sot-Weed Factor as, in part, a satire on capitalism. Cook envisions no revolution, after all, and his myth of a communal society rests upon a simple Edenic model, not upon notions of a developing conflict between classes. But it is clear from his next major poem, *Sotweed Redivivus* (1730), that he remained interested in economic issues. This poem on the title page declares itself a satire but is really a poem of counsel and advice in the Horatian mode and manner. Cook here employs the Augustan metaphor so common in eighteenth-century English poetry, drawing upon both Horace and Aesop for sententiae, exempla, and moral fables to illustrate his remedies for Maryland's economic woes. Those woes include a scarcity of currency and coin in the province (a common problem in colonial America), economic dependence on the single crop of tobacco, the power of English merchants to regulate the price of tobacco and to influence taxes on all imports, absentee landlords, and the increasing Southern dependence on African slaves for labor. The speaker of this poem claims to be the same fellow who narrated his misadventures as the sotweed factor, but, possibly like Cook himself, he has mellowed considerably after long residence in the province. There are tavern scenes in the poem and drunken, long-winded orations, but on balance the work possesses greater interest for historians than for students of Southern humor.

Cook's next major work, "The History of Colonel Nathaniel Bacon's Rebellion in Virginia," continues Cook's poetical examination of the Southern frontier, this time through the historical metaphor of a famous rebellion in the neighboring colony of Virginia. Until recently, American historians have treated Bacon's Rebellion as a precursor of the American Revolution, a struggle of the frontier against Tidewater aristocrats who did the bidding of the King. In Cook's poem, however, the British governor, Sir William Berkeley, clearly comes off better than Bacon, who is viewed as a rabble-rouser comparable to "Straw, or Kett, or Wyatt rude"—leaders of peasants' revolts in medieval England. This time Cook's appropriation of Butler's Hudibrastic meter serves as a persistent reminder of another social upheaval, the Puritan revolution of the 1640s, but Cook so unambiguously mocks the pretensions of Colonel Bacon (the poet never promotes him, though to appease the people Berkeley did) that the American uprising seems but a poor parody of the Puritan action—itself (in Butler's view anyway) but a parody of true military activity. There are some memorable comic portraits in the poem, notably the portrait of Hubert Farrell, one of Berkeley's leaders, and the Southern frontier develops as a symbol of some complexity. Cook's loyalties, however, never waver, and he applauds the death of Colonel Bacon—"So Vermin slew this public evil, / That fear'd not God nor man nor Devil"—and the eventual restoration of order. A would-be gentleman himself and a Southern loyalist, he had no wish to further the image of the Southerner as an instigator of insurrection.

Printed with the "History" is a revised version of *The Sot-Weed Factor* that purports to be the third edition of the poem. In general, Cook touched up the satire a bit, adding or changing a couplet here, a verse there, but he made no substantial changes until the final dozen lines or so. The original *Sot-Weed Factor*, aesthetically and psychologically superior to the later version, concludes with a "dreadfull Curse" upon all who live in Maryland, invoking divine wrath in the form of a slave insurrection and cannibalism (the cannibalistic metaphor is, of course, the logical extension of Cook's treatment of the evils of Maryland's commercial, capitalistic society). The revised version of the poem, however, edits out the ferocity, concluding instead with a "Wish" that all residents of the province and all traders will deal fairly with each other. This new ending testifies to Cook's altered allegiances to the South, though not to the shrewdness of his editorial eye.

Cook's minor poems, the four elegies already mentioned in other contexts, mostly extol the civic virtues of some early leaders of Maryland, often employing veiled political allusions or personal references. With the exception of the verses on Nicholas Lowe, which may have been inspired by Cook's acquaintance with Henry Lowe II and his brother, Bennett, but which seem mocking and satiric in their tone, Cook's elegies praise Southern aristocrats and genteel professionals for contributions and leadership that are typically misunderstood by Maryland's rude mechanics. A strong antidemocratic element, in other words, links these poems to Cook's major work and indicates the essentially conservative cast of his imagination. In this, too, as in so many other attitudes and opinions that seem to underlie his writings, Cook reveals the distinctly Southern aspects of his mind and art.

There is, perhaps, additional biographical evidence about Cook lurking in some dusty archives somewhere, and there may even be a poem or two surviving as yet undiscovered. But at this late date, it seems unlikely that new information will significantly alter Cook's position in American literary history or illuminate very much the obscurity in which, for the most part, he lived and moved and had his being. It is in the nature of humor, moreover, to seem less significant than tragedy, romance, or even melodrama, and surely that is one reason Cook's status is not yet secure, and perhaps never will be. His work appears in and disappears from the standard anthologies of American literature for no apparent or sound critical reasons. But the ironies of *The Sot-Weed Factor* at least, and of occasional passages in the "History of Bacon's Rebellion" as well, seem more tragic than comic in their implications, offering us the Southern frontier as a habitat that challenges all moral sureties upon which human identity, as a construction of civilized thought, has come to depend. It is a sobering experience to encounter such dark statements about human nature being made so forcefully and so early in the American enterprise.

SURVEY OF CRITICISM

Most scholarly effort devoted to Cook and his work has been concerned with the question of his identity and with the lost "second edition" of *The Sot-Weed Factor*. Lawrence C. Wroth's introduction to *The Maryland Muse* still holds the clearest explanations of both these problems, although the chapter on Cook in J. A. Leo Lemay's *Men of Letters in Colonial Maryland* (1972) is also necessary reading. Lemay is the first of Cook's critics to discuss the differences between Cook himself and Cook's persona, the sotweed factor, and to understand the importance of this distinction for a reading of Cook's best poem. In "Ebenezer Cooke's *The Sot-Weed Factor*: The Structure of Satire" (1971), Robert D. Arner anticipated some of Lemay's conclusions, and in several other pieces Arner has attempted to apply techniques of close reading, combined with relevant historical information, as a way of explaining and estimating Cook's accomplishments as a writer of satire. Despite the publication of Edward H. Cohen's *Ebenezer Cooke: The Sot-weed Canon* in 1975, the best full-length overview of Cook's work will be found in Donald V. Coers's unpublished dissertation, "A Review of the Scholarship on Ebenezer Cook and a Critical Assessment of His Works" (1974). Cook is also discussed briefly in Jay B. Hubbell's *The South in American Literature, 1607–1900* (1954), Richard Beale Davis's *Intellectual life in the Colonial South, 1585–1763* (1978), and Louis D. Rubin, Jr., et al., eds., *The History of Southern Literature* (1985), among other standard works of reference.

BIBLIOGRAPHY

Works by Ebenezer Cook

The Sot-Weed Factor, Or, a Voyage to Maryland. . . . London: Printed and sold by B. Bragg, 1708.
An ELOGY on the Death of Thomas Bordley, Esq. . . . [Annapolis: William Parks], 1726.
"An Elegy on the Death of the Honorable Nicholas Lowe." *Maryland Gazette*, 24 December 1728.
Sotweed Redivivus: Or the Planters Looking-Glass. . . . Annapolis: Printed by William Parks, 1730.
The Maryland Muse. Containing I. The History of Colonel Nathaniel Bacon's Rebellion in Virginia. Done in Hudibrastic Verse, from an Old Ms. II. The Sotweed Factor, or Voiage to Maryland. The Third Edition, Corrected and Amended. Annapolis: Printed by William Parks, 1731.

Unpublished Works

"An Elegy on the Death of the Honourable William Lock, Esqr. . . . " Maryland Historical Society, Baltimore, Maryland.
"In Memory of the Honble Benedict Leonard Calvert Esqr. Lieutenant Governor in the Province of Maryland. . . . " U.S. Naval Academy, Annapolis, Maryland.

Studies of Ebenezer Cook

Arner, Robert D. "The Blackness of Darkness: Satire, Romance, and Ebenezer Cooke's *The Sot-Weed Factor.*" *Tennessee Studies in Literature* 21 (1976): 1–10.
———. " 'Clio's *Rhimes*': History and Satire in Ebenezer Cooke's 'History of Bacon's Rebellion.' " *Southern Literary Journal* 6 (Spring 1974): 91–106.

————. "Ebenezer Cooke: Satire in the Colonial South." *Southern Literary Journal* 8 (Fall 1975): 153–64.

————. "Ebenezer Cooke's *Sotweed Redivivus*: Satire in the Horatian Mode." *Mississippi Quarterly* 28 (Fall 1975): 489–96.

————. "Ebenezer Cooke's *The Sot-Weed Factor*: The Structure of Satire." *Southern Literary Journal* 4 (Fall 1971): 33–47.

————. "Literature in the Eighteenth-Century Colonial South." *The History of Southern Literature*. Ed. Louis D. Rubin, Jr., et al. Baton Rouge: Louisiana State University Press, 1985, pp. 34–47.

Coers, Donald V. "New Light on the Composition of Ebenezer Cook's *Sot-Weed Factor*." *American Literature* 49 (1978): 604–5.

————. "A Review of the Scholarship on Ebenezer Cook and a Critical Assessment of His Works." Ph.D. diss., Texas A & M University, 1974.

Cohen, Edward H. *Ebenezer Cooke: The Sot-weed Canon*. Athens: University of Georgia Press, 1975 [reproduces much material from Cohen's two articles on the "second edition" of *The Sot-Weed Factor* and Cook's elegies].

Lemay, J. A. Leo. *Men of Letters in Colonial Maryland*. Knoxville: University of Tennessee Press, 1972, pp. 77–110.

Poole, James Talbot. "Ebenezer Cooke and the Maryland Muse." *American Literature* 3 (1931): 296–302.

Steiner, Bernard C. *Early Maryland Poetry*. Baltimore: John Murphy, 1900.

Wroth, Lawrence C. "The Maryland Muse." *American Antiquarian Society Proceedings* n.s. 44 (1934): 267–335.

John Esten Cooke
(1830–1886)

John Esten Cooke's literary influence far surpassed his distinctly limited fictional achievement. Though his historical romances today seem clichéd and mediocre, they popularized more effectively than any other novels of the antebellum period a romantic, rose-colored view of Virginia's past, and they fixed the figure of the Southern aristocrat or Cavalier firmly in the minds of both Southern and Northern readers.

BIOGRAPHY

This popularizer of the plantation romance was born on 3 November 1830 in Winchester, Virginia. The Cookes were relative newcomers to the region, having established themselves in the state shortly after the conclusion of the Revolutionary War; however, John Esten's mother, Maria Pendleton, bore one of the Old Dominion's most distinguished names and supplied the family with a solid social pedigree.

Though Cooke's earliest years were spent in the Shenandoah Valley of northern Virginia, the part of the state he would always consider home, his father's law practice drew the family to Richmond in 1840. Here John attended school and, during his adolescent years, was an active member of a literary-debating club called the Franklin Debating Society. Such activities were widely assumed to help prepare young men for the practice of law, and Cooke's father apparently planned for John to follow him in the profession. But the son's professional ambitions were hampered by his father's inability to finance further education at the University of Virginia.

Ironically, Cooke's frustrated educational hopes seem to have hastened his development as a writer; for by the time he began the practice of law in 1851 he was fully immersed in the cultural and literary life of Richmond, having contributed poems, stories, and essays to publications such as the *Southern Literary Messenger*. Cooke seemed destined to emulate the literary career of his older brother, Philip Pendleton Cooke, a well-known antebellum poet. By the time his first novels appeared in 1854 he had effectively abandoned the legal profession.

Leather Stocking and Silk (1854) gave an early indication of Cooke's subject matter and of the literary influences that would help to shape that subject matter. Drawing on James Fenimore Cooper's figure of the backwoods hunter as well as on the familiar essay style of Washington Irving and John Pendleton Kennedy, Cooke skillfully concocted a frontier romance that, for extra flavor, included the aristocratic characters of Lord Fairfax and George Washington. *Leather Stocking and Silk* was quickly followed by *The Virginia Comedians* (1854), a novel of colonial Virginia that received flattering reviews in Northern newspapers and magazines and that remains Cooke's most substantial work.

Curiously, Cooke turned away from the historical romance with *Ellie* (1855), a Dickensian social novel set in contemporary Richmond that contrasts dire poverty with the superficial social life of the city. Cooke believed that *Ellie* would "create a great talk" (Beaty, *John Esten Cooke*, p. 55), but readers simply ignored it. They wanted more colorful descriptions of colonial Virginia, not appeals to social conscience. After this brief bow to the problem novel, Cooke returned to his true métier in *Henry St. John, Gentleman* (1859). This work followed the action of *The Virginia Comedians* and constituted with the earlier novel the author's most successful romantic evocation of the Old Dominion's pre-Revolutionary Golden Age.

By 1860 John Esten Cooke was, in the words of George Cary Eggleston, "chief among the literary men of Richmond" (Beaty, *John Esten Cooke*, p. 63). Eggleston paints a picture of a proud young man so punctilious in his sense of honor that he chose to discharge slowly through "toilsome literary activity" (p. 63) the debts his father had left behind him at his death, even though he was not legally responsible for them. The numerous titles that helped to cancel those debts included stories, verse, essays, and a number of articles on Virginia for Appleton's *New American Cyclopoedia*.

Early in his career Cooke's varied publications had secured him an established reputation beyond the boundaries of the Old Dominion. He numbered among his acquaintances New York literati such as E. C. Stedman and the Duyckinck brothers, George and Evert. Yet he turned his back on this hard-earned Northern audience with apparent ease. He considered the election of Abraham Lincoln a catastrophe for the South, and he believed that secession was Virginia's only honorable course. The coming of the Civil War ushered his career into a new phase.

After Virginia's secession Cooke promptly joined the Confederate army as a sergeant, commanding a gun emplacement at the Battle of First Manassas and quickly rising to the rank of first lieutenant. He eventually was promoted to captain, saw service with J.E.B. Stuart as a member of his staff, and acquired the reputation of a soldier who remained steadfast and calm in the midst of fire. Amazingly, though he served throughout the war and was present with Lee at Appomattox, he escaped serious injury. Even more amazing was the appearance of the *Life of Stonewall Jackson* (1863), which he managed to write in camp between military engagements along with numerous poems and dispatches for the Richmond newspapers.

After the war the penniless soldier-writer returned to his boyhood home in northern Virginia and began to write furiously, drawing on his considerable store of Civil War experiences. He published an expanded biography of Jackson in 1866 and a biography of Lee in 1871. His Civil War novels, *Surry of Eagle's Nest* (1866), dealing with Jackson's campaigns, and *Mohun* (1869), focusing on Lee's generalship, presented a fictional treatment of the material of the biographies and were nearly as popular with readers from all sections of the country as *The Virginia Comedians* had been a decade earlier. In addition to these books, Cooke collected and reworked his Civil War dispatches, expanding this material into full-length war histories, *Wearing of the Gray* (1867) and *Hammer and Rapier* (1870).

In 1867 Cooke married Mary Frances Page, member of a northern Virginia branch of the distinguished Page family. Eggleston quipped that with this ceremony John Esten "had married into all the good families he didn't belong to himself" (Beaty, *John Esten Cooke*, p. 112). Cooke later revealed that his marriage had kept him in the Old Dominion. Rather than pursuing his career in the North he did his writing, first at his father-in-law's house, and later at his own northern Virginia farm, The Briars. Here he combined his literary endeavors with supervising the raising of his three children as well as the activities in his fields and gardens. The substantial profits from his books supported the enthusiasms of an amateur farmer and the prodigality of a house that entertained frequent visitors.

Cooke's years at "The Briars" produced a large number of works, including novels set variously from seventeenth-century England, *Her Majesty the Queen* (1873), to contemporary America, *Pretty Mrs. Gaston* (1874). None of his later fiction, however, equaled the popularity of his earlier colonial Virginia romances and his Civil War novels. Of the works composed during these years, probably the most interesting is *The Heir of Gaymount* (1870), a novel of Reconstruction Virginia in which the hero struggles to maintain his ancestral estate by accommodating himself to the realities of the present. *Gaymount* bears an interesting resemblance to Thomas Nelson Page's better known *Red Rock* (1898).

The sudden death of Cooke's wife in 1878 ended a period of frequent entertaining. Hereafter the novelist-farmer spent his time quietly and routinely, writing in the morning and supervising his farm and visiting neighbors in the afternoon. Of his last works, *Virginia: A History of the People* (1883) was by far his most influential. Though today it seems hardly historical in its grandiose picture of the state's aristocratic heritage, E. C. Stedman, reflecting a widespread contemporary critical acceptance, described it as a "graceful and scholarly" work

(Beaty, *John Esten Cooke*, p. 150). For many years it remained the most popular history of Virginia.

Quiet farm life, interrupted by occasional trips to New York, ended abruptly for Cooke on 27 September 1886 when he died from typhoid fever. The writer's demise occasioned less commentary than it might have twenty years earlier, when his popular romances were widely read. He was buried next to his wife in his beloved Shenandoah Valley, not far from the place of his birth. This burial seems a fitting one for a writer who never chose to leave his native state and who remained physically, mentally, and spiritually faithful to his vision of her sacred heritage.

MAJOR THEMES

John Esten Cooke's romances of the Old Dominion reflect a historical perspective that accepts as essentially true Virginia's cherished notions of its aristocratic past. This subjective approach to his state's heritage is clearly present in *Virginia: A History of the People* (1883). Although a product of Cooke's later years, this work reflects the three fundamental convictions about Virginia's history underlying his fiction from his earliest novels to his later books.

Cooke's first conviction was that Virginia's culture had been profoundly influenced by large numbers of immigrants of Cavalier ancestry. "One of the highest authorities in American history," he observed, "has described the Cavalier element in Virginia as only 'perceptible.' It was really so strong as to control all things,—the forms of society, of religion, and the direction of public affairs. The fact was so plain that he who ran might read it" (*Virginia*, p. 230).

Cooke's second conviction was that the years from 1700 to 1774 had constituted Virginia's Golden Age. The years before this period had been years of formation; those that followed would be years of transition, and even of chaos. But during the Golden Age, he believed, the colony's society had remained a stationary "democratic aristocracy." In this period slaves and white servants had been contented, and the class of middling yeoman farmers had willingly deferred to the directives of the dominant planter class. "The planter in his manorhouse, surrounded by his family and retainers," he concluded, "was a feudal patriarch mildly ruling everybody . . . and everybody, high and low, seemed to be happy" (*Virginia*, pp. 370–371).

This sympathetic view of eighteenth-century Virginia led to Cooke's third conviction. This notion, though not directly expressed, is implicit in the final pages of his history, which deal with post–Revolutionary War Virginia. In these pages the reader clearly perceives that for Cooke the "Republican Ascendency" and the declining influence of the ancient aristocratic families had produced a new society, which, if more egalitarian, was duller, less picturesque, and less distinguished than the society that had preceded it. "Democratic equality had become the watchword and controlled society," he observed in a passage redolent with a wistful and nostalgic tone that is the special province of the Virginia romance writer. With democracy, he lamented, had come a "brusque address," which had rudely supplanted "the old ceremonious courtesy . . . " (*Virginia*, p. 478).

It is essentially this romantic and nostalgic view of Virginia's Golden Age that permeates Cooke's most popular antebellum novel, *The Virginia Comedians*. Cooke himself believed that his novel was a critique of the Virginia aristocracy; and there is, in fact, evidence to suggest that he set out to free his fiction from the clichés of plantation fiction. *The Virginia Comedians* sets up an interesting contrast between the haughty and aristocratic Champ Effingham and plebeian Charlie Waters, one of the radical political leaders who will shortly propel the Old Dominion toward revolution. Between the bewigged Champ and the close-cropped Charlie, Cooke places Beatrice Hallam, one of the Virginia Company of Actors, who provides the love interest and furnishes the conflict between the two men.

Cooke underlines and deepens the aristocrat-yeoman conflict by contrasting the extremely conservative social views of Virginia's planter aristocracy with the Jeffersonian democratic creed of Waters. "Men are not by nature destitute of truth and love, nobility and purity," Charlie proclaims (*Virginia Comedians*, I: 13). The masses, with the help of improved education, can learn to rule themselves wisely. In the character of Charlie Waters, Cooke presents and initially seems to support the most sanguine hopes of democratic idealism.

If Cooke had consistently developed the contrast between Champ and Charlie, if he had emphasized the weaknesses within the aristocratic framework that had brought its destruction in the Revolutionary War, he would probably still be read today. But he was above all else a Virginian; and democratic sentiments to the contrary, he was hopelessly entangled in the romance of the myth, in the very charm and grace of those people that he said he did not like. Because of these warring sentiments, it is not completely surprising to discover that toward the end of *The Virginia Comedians* Cooke has abandoned the Champ-Charlie conflict.

After gravely wounding Charlie in an abortive attempt to abduct the unwilling Beatrice Hallam, Champ catches an outward-bound ship for Europe. Charlie recovers from his wounds and withdraws with Beatrice, who has all along favored him, to live in the mountains of western Virginia. There she dies of consumption. Charlie reappears only in the novel's last scene, inflaming the Williamsburg mob to revolution. Onto the stage vacated by Charlie and Beatrice returns Champ, chastened by experience, a wiser and stronger man.

In the concluding half of the novel Champ Effingham improves in character until, by its conclusion, it is clear that Cooke intends him to be the major object of the reader's sympathy. Those admirable qualities he possesses in the first part of the novel—courage and a strong sense of honor—are augmented by a humility born of a sense of past iniquity. Above all, Champ's triumph of character is suggested by his noble and pure passion for a plantation belle he had earlier scorned in order to pursue Beatrice Hallam. He commits himself to love this lady and to cherish her memory "always, as that of the tenderest soul, the warmest, purest heart that ever was in human bosom" (*Virginia Comedians*, II: 177). The pure and refined sentiment, the religious and devotional tone of praise, represent the most refined aspects of the Cavalier love code.

One cannot read *The Virginia Comedians* without feeling that Cooke is essentially confused in his attitude toward his characters. He claims to be giving his aristocrats the worst of things, but in the final portion of the novel he allows his aristocratic characters to dominate the action. Charlie and Beatrice are forgotten as one views with increasing sympathy the exquisitely high-minded sentiments of Champ Effingham and his fellow First Families of Virginia. This confusion is not lessened by the return of Charlie at the end of the book. The storm of revolution contrasts strangely with the happy conclusion of an aristocratic love affair, and Cooke seems oblivious to the irony his narrative has created.

Cooke's sensibility, like that of John Pendleton Kennedy, seems to have been truly divided. One part of him was strongly attracted to the romantic vision of Virginia's splendidly colorful past. Another part responded to the democratic ideal of the equality of all men, an ideal propounded by Charlie Waters. In *The Virginia Comedians* the aristocratic vision prevailed in the end.

Whatever objectivity Cooke strove to achieve in his fiction regarding his native state vanished entirely in the aftermath of the Civil War. In *Surry of Eagle's Nest*, published immediately after the War in 1866, and in *Mohun*, a sequel published in 1869, Cooke used the historical novel to embellish the reputations of Virginia's greatest military commanders—Lee, Jackson, and Stuart. The novels are linked by a common protagonist, "Surry of Eagle's Nest," a Virginia gentleman of unblemished aristocratic credentials. Surry's ancestral Rappahannock River plantation is the legacy of the first Surry, a "gay gallant" who had served with valor under Prince Rupert and who had repaired to the Old Dominion after his defeat. Both *Surry of Eagle's Nest* and *Mohun* juxtapose realistic and factual descriptions of Civil War battles against the labyrinthine and highly melodramatic action of Cooke's fictional plot.

The protagonist of *Surry* serves under General Stonewall Jackson. Although turning this plain and pious Presbyterian soldier into a Cavalier figure presented Cooke with difficulties, he did the best he could with the material at hand. For example, before his death on the eve of the battle at Chancellorsville Jackson utters sentiments that identify his personal honor with that of his native state in a way that strongly suggests the nobility of the more aristocratic Lee: "It was duty no less than pleasure to fight for the land I loved. . . . There is not a foot of Virginia soil that is not dear to me—not a river, a stream, or a mountain that is not sacred . . . " (*Surry*, p. 458).

Cooke found more promising material available in the person of General Turner Ashby, "the Knight of the Valley," a valiant cavalryman who served under Jackson in the early Shenandoah Valley campaigns. When Ashby encounters Northern ladies stranded in the town of Winchester, they claim they have no contraband and that he is welcome to search them. Ashby's reply is typical of a knightly Confederate hero: "I am a Virginia gentleman; we do not search the trunks or persons of ladies here, madame" (p. 217). A sample of the diction lavished on Ashby within the space of a single page after his death in battle gives a good indication of the assiduousness with which Cooke maintained the Cavalier stereotype in his Civil War novels. Ashby, the narrator opines, was "heroic," a "dauntless cavalier," a "noble gentleman," and a "splendid chevalier."

In *Mohun* Cooke's focus shifts from Stonewall Jackson to Jeb Stuart, whose staff Surry joins after the death of Jackson. Cooke's sequel is characterized, like *Surry of Eagle's Nest*, by a blatantly apotheosizing tone. The objects associated with these legendary military heroes become objects of veneration. "The great tree of the grassy knoll" of a northern Virginia plantation "under which Stuart erected his own tent," is known ever after as "Stuart's Oak." "To this day," the narrator observes, "no ax will ever harm it, I hope; gold could not purchase it; for tender hearts cherish the gnarled trunk and huge boughs, as a souvenir of the great soldier whom it sheltered . . . " (*Mohun*, p. 107). The death of Stuart at Yellow Tavern combines with the death of Jackson in the Wilderness to prefigure the ultimate destruction of the Old South, a land comparable in its perfection to Arthur's Camelot. "These two kings of battle," the narrator ruminates, "had gone down in the storm, and, like the knights of Arthur, I looked around me with vacant and inquiring eyes. . . . Jackson! Stuart!—who could replace them?" (p. 216). No one can, of course; and the action of *Mohun* proceeds, despite the heroic struggles of Lee, inexorably to its conclusion at Appomattox.

Amidst the bitterness of defeat and Reconstruction, John Esten Cooke created some of the most romantic images of the glorious though doomed South. As much as any postbellum Southern writer, he gave fictional validity to the myth of the Lost Cause. His Civil War novels showed that the South's surrender was to be only a partial one. Though the region was defeated, Cooke's postbellum romances celebrated the noble ideals for which Dixie's chivalric, gray-clad knights had bravely fought.

SURVEY OF CRITICISM

John Esten Cooke's historical romances, virtually lost in the wake of modern realism, have attracted relatively little critical notice in this century. One of the earliest significant surveys of his life and literary career is John O. Beaty's *John Esten Cooke, Virginian* (1922), which remains the only published biography. Beaty's book gives the essential biographical details; but, with the exception of some interesting personal observations of George Cary Eggleston, there is little evidence in the book to suggest the complexities of the inner man. Critically it overestimates Cooke's fictional achievement and ignores the obvious ways that his books romantically distort Virginia's past. Jay B. Hubbell's *The South in*

American Literature, 1607–1900 (1954) provides a brief but interesting biography as well as a more balanced critical assessment of the Cooke canon.

Cooke's novels have attracted brief notice from three critics in their surveys of American fiction. Arthur Hobson Quinn's *American Fiction: An Historical Survey* (1936) contends that the writer does not "deserve the comparative neglect which has befallen him." It is an examination that is interesting today chiefly for its comment on Cooke's use of middle-class and mountain characters in *Leather Stocking and Silk*. Carl Van Doren's *The American Novel* (1940) contains a brief commentary astutely linking *The Virginia Comedians* to the antebellum South's rejection of the present and to its yearning for a legendary past. In *The Rise of the American Novel* (1948) Alexander Cowie presents a reasonably thorough survey of Cooke's works and compares his fiction favorably with that of William Gilmore Simms. He also bestows special attention on an otherwise little-known novel, *Fairfax: or, The Master of Greenway Court*.

Probably the most interesting general evaluations of Cooke's writing have been made by Francis Pendleton Gaines and Edmund Wilson. In *The Southern Plantation* (1924) Gaines observes that Cooke "crystallized in a few novels all the sentiment entertained by highly bred Southerners . . . concerning the magnificence of the plantation" and "supplied a scale of operation and some structural material to innumerable writers who have since entered the field." Wilson includes a brief but penetrating discussion of Cooke's Civil War fiction in a review (1958) of Sherman's *Memoirs* that detects a discrepancy between the author's firsthand experience of war and the "dreamlike" romantic quality of his fictional treatment of it.

There have been a few more scholarly treatments of Cooke's work. Carvel Collins's "John Esten Cooke and Local Color" (1944) considers Cooke a pioneer in fiction dealing with the Southern mountains and a precursor of postbellum local color writing. Though its thesis is forced, this essay contains analyses of otherwise unknown Cooke short stories. In "John Esten Cooke, Civil War Correspondent" (1953) Richard Barksdale Harwell argues that the eighteen articles Cooke wrote for the *Southern Illustrated News* are, unlike the romanticized novels drawn from the same war experience, a "vivid record" that established the writer as a war correspondent "without rival." Marshall Fishwick's "Civil War II," in his *Virginia: A New Look at the Old Dominion* (1959), contains brief mention of *Surry of Eagle's Nest* and *Mohun* in an interesting discussion of the ways in which the South's postbellum writers achieved the literary vindication denied the Confederacy on the battle field.

Two more recent analyses of Cooke's writing deserve mention. In "John Esten Cooke and His 'Confederate Lies' " (1981), Mary Jo Bratten draws on unpublished journals and letters to buttress her thesis that defeat and Reconstruction moved Cooke away from the more critical treatment of the Cavalier ideal of his antebellum novels and caused him to abandon altogether his yeoman characters, resorting to "Confederate lies" to embellish the myth of the Lost Cause. Ritchie D. Watson, Jr.'s *The Cavalier in Virginia Fiction* (1985) contains an extended discussion of *The Virginia Comedians* and *Henry St. John, Gentleman* that focuses on Cooke's unsuccessful resolution of the tensions inherent in his juxtaposition of Cavalier with yeoman characters. Watson links Cooke's failure to reconcile the Southern aristocratic myth with the larger democratic ideals of the nation with that of other antebellum Virginia writers.

BIBLIOGRAPHY

Works by John Esten Cooke

Page numbers given in the text for *Virginia: A History of the People* are from the 1894 edition. Page numbers given in the text for *The Virginia Comedians* are from the 1968 edition. Page numbers given for *Surry of Eagle's Nest* and *Mohun* are from the 1894 and 1896 editions respectively.

Leather Stocking and Silk. New York: Harper, 1854.
The Virginia Comedians. 2 vols. New York: D. Appleton, 1854; Ridgewood, N.J.: Gregg Press, 1968. Vol. 1 reissued as *Beatrice Hallam* (1892); Vol. 2 as *Captain Ralph* (1892).
The Youth of Jefferson. New York: Redfield, 1854.
Ellie. Richmond: A. Morris, 1855.
The Last of the Foresters. New York: H. W. Derby and Jackson, 1856.
Henry St. John, Gentleman. New York: Harper, 1859. Reissued as *Bonnybel Vane* (1883) and as *Miss Bonnybell* (1892).
The Life of Stonewall Jackson. New York: C. B. Richardson, 1863.
Stonewall Jackson: A Military Biography. New York: D. Appleton, 1866.
Surry of Eagle's Nest. New York: Bunce and Huntington, 1866; New York: G. W. Dillingham, 1894.
Wearing of the Gray. New York: E. B. Treat, 1867.
Fairfax. New York: Carleton, 1868.
Mohun. New York: Huntington, 1868; New York: G. W. Dillingham, 1896.
Hilt to Hilt. New York: Carleton, 1869.
Hammer and Rapier. New York: Carleton, 1870.
The Heir of Gaymount. New York: Van Evrie, Horton, 1870.
A Life of General Robert E. Lee. New York: D. Appleton, 1871.
Out of the Foam. New York: Carleton, 1871.
Doctor Vandyke. New York: D. Appleton, 1872.
Her Majesty the Queen. New York: G. W. Dillingham, 1873.
Justin Harley. Philadelphia: To-day Painting and Publishing, 1874.
Pretty Miss Gaston and Other Stories. New York: Orange Judd, 1874.
Canolles. Detroit: E. B. Smith, 1877.
Professor Pressensee. New York: Harper, 1878.
Mr. Grantley's Idea. New York: Harper, 1879.
Stories of the Old Dominion. New York: Harper, 1879.
The Virginia Bohemians. New York: Harper, 1880.
Franchett. Boston: J. R. Osgood, 1883.
Virginia: A History of the People. New York: Houghton, Mifflin, 1883; Boston: Houghton, Mifflin, 1894.

The Maurice Mystery. New York: D. Appleton, 1885. Reissued as *Colonel Ross of Piedmont* (1892).

My Lady Pocahontas. New York: Houghton, Mifflin, 1885.

Poe as a Literary Critic. Baltimore: Johns Hopkins University Press, 1946.

Stonewall Jackson and the Old Stonewall Brigade. Charlottesville: University Press of Virginia, 1954.

Outlines from the Outpost. Chicago: Lakeside Press, 1961.

Studies of John Esten Cooke

Beaty, John O. *John Esten Cooke, Virginian.* New York: Columbia University Press, 1922.

Bratten, Mary Jo. "John Esten Cooke and His 'Confederate Lies.' " *Southern Literary Journal* 13 (Spring 1981): 72–91.

Collins, Carvel. "John Esten Cooke and Local Color." *Southern Literary Messenger* 6 (January-February 1944): 82–84.

Cowie, Alexander. *The Rise of the American Novel.* New York: American Book, 1948.

Fishwick, Marshall. "Civil War II." *Virginia: A New Look at the Old Dominion.* New York: Harper, 1959.

Gaines, Francis Pendleton. *The Southern Plantation: A Study in the Development and the Accuracy of a Tradition.* New York: Columbia University Press, 1924.

Gross, Theodore L. "John Esten Cooke." *A Bibliographical Guide to the Study of Southern Literature.* Ed. Louis D. Rubin, Jr. Baton Rouge: Louisiana State University Press, 1969.

Harwell, Richard Barksdale. "John Esten Cooke, Civil War Correspondent." *Journal of Southern History* 19 (November 1953): 501–16.

Holliday, Carl. "John Esten Cooke as a Novelist." *Sewanee Review* 13 (1905): 216–20.

Hubbell, Jay B. *The South in American Literature, 1607–1900.* Durham, N.C.: Duke University Press, 1954.

———. "The War Diary of John Esten Cooke." *Journal of Southern History* 7 (1941): 526–40.

Quinn, Arthur Hobson. *American Fiction: An Historical Survey.* New York: D. Appleton Century, 1936.

Van Doren, Carl. *The American Novel, 1789–1939.* New York: Macmillan, 1940.

Watson, Ritchie D., Jr. *The Cavalier in Virginia Fiction.* Baton Rouge: Louisiana State University Press, 1985.

Wilson, Edmund. "Books: Uncle Billy." *New Yorker* 34 (June 7, 1958): 114, 116–24, 127–44.

EDWARD L. TUCKER

Philip Pendleton Cooke
(1816–1850)

Philip Pendleton Cooke, of a distinguished Southern family that also produced John Pendleton Kennedy and John Esten Cooke, is known today primarily for one poem, "Florence Vane." But he wrote some 38 poems as well as short prose fiction and some of the best literary criticism of the period.

BIOGRAPHY

Philip Pendleton Cooke was born in Martinsburg, Berkeley County, Virginia (now West Virginia), on 26 October 1816, the son of Maria Pendleton and John Rogers Cooke. The Pendletons and the Cookes, who had come originally from England, boasted of lawyers, physicians, and statesmen in their genealogy. Many of the best Tidewater families, after the Revolution, had settled in the Shenandoah Valley. John Rogers Cooke, a lawyer, was one of the framers of the Virginia Constitution of 1830.

Philip was the oldest of thirteen children, only four of whom survived their father. A younger son was John Esten Cooke, born in 1830, who became a well-known novelist. A cousin was John Pendleton Kennedy of Baltimore, who wrote *Swallow Barn*. Another cousin was David H. Strother, who, under the pen name "Porte Crayon," became famous for his illustrations in Union periodicals during the Civil War.

After attending local schools, Philip in 1831, at age fifteen, entered Princeton College. His life there was uneventful, and he was not a particularly good student. Although he was suspended one month before he was to receive his degree because he and a fellow student were guilty of a personal assault upon each other, he was admitted to his examinations and received his degree in 1834.

Then, feeling that he must have an occupation, he settled on law. By age twenty-one he had read enough in Blackstone to pass the required examination.

He hoped to have a life of leisure and contentment, but one big problem stood in his way: lack of money. There were numerous creditors, and at one time he planned bankruptcy proceedings. He had to depend, to his embarrassment, on the generosity of his father. But sometimes John R. Cooke was not able to help his son financially. The Panic of 1837 had plunged the father into financial troubles; these were heightened by the burning in 1839 of Glengary, the family home near Winchester.

Fortunately, Philip Pendleton Cooke made a good marriage. On 1 May 1837 he married Willie Anne Corbin Tayloe Burwell, whom he called "Willie," of an excellent family. She lived nearby at "Saratoga" with her uncle Nathaniel Burwell, who had adopted her after her father's death. Although Burwell was wealthy, he did not allow his niece much money. He did build a home for her and Cooke and their children in 1845, a beautiful place named the Vineyard, two miles from Millwood, Virginia. The two-story brick structure had a view of the Blue Ridge Mountains, the Valley of Virginia, and the Alleghenies. The actual management of the estate, however, remained in the hands of Mr. Burwell until his death in November 1849. With his death, Willie Annie received a handsome inheritance, and Cooke's financial worries were at last over. Unfortunately, he died the next year. His wife lived until 1899, though she was blind for the last 30 years of her life.

Cooke had a few poems accepted for publication in the *Knickerbocker Magazine* while he was at Princeton. His chief work, though, was for the *Southern Literary Messenger*. In 1835 its editor, Thomas W. White, wrote to John Rogers Cooke asking for a literary contribution. Since the father did not have enough time for writing, he gave the request to his son, who began to send prose and verse. Cooke, therefore, had a close acquaintance with the magazine from its beginning; in all, he contributed to 44 issues.

Cooke knew some important literary figures: John Pendleton Kennedy, his cousin, often encouraged him; John R. Thompson, editor of the *Southern Literary Messenger* from 1847 to 1860, carried on an extensive correspondence with him; and Rufus W. Griswold, the well-known anthologist, wanted to include him in his *Poets and Poetry of America*.

But the most important figure Cooke corresponded with was Edgar Allan Poe. Poe, in his various editorial positions, sought contributions from Cooke for the *Southern Literary Messenger*, the *Gentleman's Magazine*, and *Graham's*. At least three long and important letters from Poe to Cooke—dated 21 September 1839, 16 April 1846, and 9 August 1846—exist. Poe believed that the publication of Cooke's one volume of poems, *Froissart Ballads, and Other Poems*, would make the poet famous. Through the efforts of Rufus Griswold, Carey and Hart of Philadelphia brought out 750 copies of the book in 1847; but the work, dedicated to Kennedy, received little attention.

In spite of his lack of fame as an author and his lack of any great success as a lawyer, Cooke led an enviable life. He often spoke of his contentment. He had a pleasant existence with his wife and five children, though he had to depend rather heavily on the generosity of his wife's uncle. Burwell managed to separate the wife and husband briefly, but gradually he was reconciled to the marriage.

Cooke loved his region of the country and especially hunting. It was ironical that he died on 20 January 1850 in the way he did. During a hunting trip, he waded into the icy Shenandoah River to retrieve a wounded duck. Cold developed from the exposure, and pneumonia swiftly followed. He died and was buried in the churchyard cemetery of Old Chapel, near Millwood, Virginia.

MAJOR THEMES

Cooke's writings fall into three groups: essays, poetry, and short fiction. The essays are on a number of authors, such as Edgar Allan Poe, Alexandre Dumas, Alexander Pope, Edward Bulwer, Sir Walter Scott, James Fenimore Cooper, and Dante. He published at least 38 poems, often under the name of "Larry Lyle," or, because of confused handwriting, "Zarry Zyle," or the initials "L. L." and "E. D." He was the author of five short novels, as well as several shorter works of prose fiction.

In the poems, Cooke, like other Southern poets of the time, places woman—even though she is sometimes a child—on a pedestal. Often she is dead, and the poet is grieving because he adored her. Rosalie Lee has "gone to her early rest" (p. 6). Florence Vane, who "wast lovelier than the roses / In their prime," is now "glorious clay" lying under the "green sod"; elements of nature—the "lilies of the valley," the "pansies"—as well as the poet weep for her (p. 11). Generally, the women in the medieval works are noble and virtuous, though at times they can be treacherous.

A second theme is the love of nature. Cooke was fond of the outdoors and became known as one of the best hunters in the Shenandoah Valley. The prose selection "The Turkey-hunter in the Closet" contains a discussion of hunting, followed by a description of Cooke's first turkey hunt. In the poem "Life in the Autumn Woods," set in October, the poet says that he loves "the woods / In this best season of the liberal year," and "What passionate / And wild delight is in the proud swift chase." If someone has "griefs," that person can surely find a "cure in the forest" (pp. 12–13). The same feeling is in "The Mountains" with its praise of the maple, the ash, the pines, the dogwood, the oak, the hickories. When we have "cares" and "despairs," we learn that "nature is a foe severe / To pallid brow, and shadowy fear / And lifts the fallen to valiant cheer" (pp. 18–21).

A third theme is the presentation of problems facing aristocratic society of the Shenandoah region. Three novelettes—*The Gregories of Hackwood*, *The Two Country Houses*, and *The Crime of Andrew Blair*—fit this mold. They present life in western Virginia during the 1830s and 1840s. The central male characters are men of breeding; for instance, Andrew Blair is "a man of wealth, talent, political training, and a fair degree of distinction" (p. 200). They live in old homes: Miles Gregory lives at Hackwood and is the "owner of many thousand acres of the land about it'' (p. 162). Their family members are attractive, but these central male figures have problems of various kinds: for example, Miles Gregory is a miser; and Andrew Blair, in a fit of rage, has killed a neighbor and has thrown his body into a well (in this second case, the lower classes give opposition—a poor white has seen the deed and is blackmailing Blair). Sentimental trappings abound: a blind son; a daughter-in-law dying of a cough; lingering, tearful deaths.

Several works present frontier life in colonial times—a fourth theme, illustrated well by poems entitled ''The Song of the Sioux Lovers'' and ''The Last Indian.'' In ''The Murder of Cornstalk,'' based on an actual historical event, the Shawnee chief Cornstalk, head of the great northern confederacy of tribes, is murdered by whites at Point Pleasant in 1777. The novelette *John Carper, the Hunter of Lost River*, written under the influence of James Fenimore Cooper, is set in the frontier region during the time of the Revolution. The central figure, John Carper, loves a Quaker, Nelly Blake, who, unfortunately, is captured by Indians. But Carper, a ''noble specimen of the best class of frontiersmen'' (p. 130), follows the Indians and manages to rescue Nelly.

A fifth theme—perhaps his most distinctive—is his fascination with the past. His unfinished short novel *The Chevalier Merlin* is about a Norwegian, Merlin Brand, who, after entering the services of Charles XII of Sweden, encounters a number of important figures, including Czar Peter. Possibly Cooke's most interesting works are based on the *Chronicles* of the Frenchman Jean Froissart (ca. 1337–ca. 1410). The title character in ''Emily,'' the proem to the work, with her ''temples fair'' and ''gliding limbs,'' loves ''ancient lays,'' not Arthurian stories but those from the continent (p. 21). In one ballad, ''The Master of Bolton,'' the sport of falconry is praised; the work presents jousting scenes, including a knight fighting desperately for the hand of his lady. In another, ''Geoffrey Tetenoire,'' the title character has wronged Lady Jane; in anger, she tells an admirer, Count Gaston, that she will marry him if he brings her the head of Geoffrey Tetenoire. But the count is killed instead, and the evil Tetenoire sends her the head of her lover in a casket.

SURVEY OF CRITICISM

The name that is most prominent in Cooke studies is John D. Allen. His dissertation at Vanderbilt was condensed into a shorter work and published as *Philip Pendleton Cooke* in 1942. Of considerable value is a collection that Allen made in 1969 entitled *Philip Pendleton Cooke: Poet, Critic, Novelist*. This publication brings together in one volume the best of Cooke's works: all the seventeen poems that originally appeared in *Froissart Ballads, and Other Poems*, though not in the order in which they appear in that work; three other poems; three short novels—*John Carper, the Hunter of Lost River, The Gregories of Hackwood*, and *The Crime of Andrew Blair*—as well as two other short prose works; generous selections from *English Poetry* and *Living Novelists*; and a few letters. The bibliography of the 1942 biography is repeated.

Outside the work of John D. Allen, little scholarly attention has been given to Cooke. David K. Jackson wrote an article on Cooke in *American Studies in Honor of William Kenneth Boyd*. Edd Winfield Parks discusses Cooke as a literary critic in his *Ante-Bellum Southern Literary Critics*. Edward L. Tucker reproduces photographs of Cooke and his home in an article in *Virginia Cavalcade* and, in an article in the *Mississippi Quarterly*, publishes for the first time eight letters by Cooke, mainly to editors of the *Southern Literary Messenger* (Benjamin Blake Minor, John R. Thompson), dealing with the problems of publication.

Charles H. Bohner in *John Pendleton Kennedy* gives a few references to Cooke. Although most biographies of Poe, such as Arthur Hobson Quinn's *Edgar Allan Poe*, mention Cooke, one that is highly revealing is *Poe: Journalist and Critic*, in which the author, Robert D. Jacobs, who evaluates Cooke as "the best of the *Messenger* poets except for Poe," compares the two men—Cooke and Poe—as to background, themes and interests, and eventual success.

BIBLIOGRAPHY

Works by Philip Pendleton Cooke

Page numbers given in the text refer to John D. Allen, *Philip Pendleton Cooke: Poet, Critic, Novelist*.

English Poetry. *Southern Literary Messenger* 1 (April, June 1835): 397–401, 557–65; 2
         (January 1836): 101–6.
Living Novelists. *Southern Literary Messenger* 13 (June, September 1847): 367–73, 529,
         745–52.
Froissart Ballads, and Other Poems. Philadelphia: Carey and Hart, 1847.
John Carper, the Hunter of Lost River. *Southern Literary Messenger* 14 (February, March,
         April 1848): 90–94, 167–75, 222–28.
The Two Country Houses. *Southern Literary Messenger* 14 (May, June, July 1848): 307–
         18, 349–56, 436–50.
The Gregories of Hackwood. *Southern Literary Messenger* 14 (September, October 1848):
         537–43, 612–22.
The Crime of Andrew Blair. *Southern Literary Messenger* 15 (January, February, March
         1849): 46–54, 101–8, 148–54.
The Chevalier Merlin. *Southern Literary Messenger* 15 (June, July, August, September,
         November, December 1849): 326–35, 417–26, 473–81, 641–50, 727–34; 16 (Jan-
         uary 1850): 42–50 (not completed).
Philip Pendelton Cooke: Poet, Critic, Novelist. Ed. John D. Allen. Johnson City: East
         Tennessee State University Research Advisory Council, 1969.
"Philip Pendelton Cooke and *The Southern Literary Messenger*: Selected Letters." Ed.
         Edward L. Tucker. *Mississippi Quarterly* 27 (Winter 1973–74): 79–99.

Studies of Philip Pendleton Cooke

Allen, John D. "Philip Pendleton Cooke: A Critical and Biographical Study." Ph.D. diss., Vanderbilt, 1939.

———. *Philip Pendleton Cooke*. Chapel Hill: University of North Carolina Press, 1942.

———. "Philip Pendleton Cooke." *A Bibliographical Guide to the Study of Southern Literature*. Ed. Louis D. Rubin, Jr. Baton Rouge: Louisiana State University Press, 1969, pp. 181–82.

Bohner, Charles H. *John Pendleton Kennedy, Gentleman from Baltimore*. Baltimore: Johns Hopkins University Press, 1961.

Cooke, John Esten. "Recollections of Philip Pendleton Cooke." *Southern Literary Messenger* 26 (June 1858): 419–32.

Hubbell, Jay B. "Philip Pendleton Cooke." *The South in American Literature, 1607–1900*. Durham, N.C.: Duke University Press, 1954, pp. 502–11.

Jackson, David K. "Philip Pendleton Cooke: Virginia Gentleman, Lawyer, Hunter, and Poet." *American Studies in Honor of William Kenneth Boyd*. Durham: Duke University Press, 1940, pp. 282–326.

———. *Poe and "The Southern Literary Messenger."* Richmond: Dietz Press, 1934.

———. "The Writings of Philip Pendleton Cooke." *Southern Literary Journal* 2 (Spring 1970): 156–58. A review of Allen's 1969 volume.

Jacobs, Robert D. "Campaign for a Southern Literature: *The Southern Literary Messenger.*" *Southern Literary Journal* 2 (Fall 1969): 66–98.

———. *Poe: Journalist & Critic*. Baton Rouge: Louisiana State University Press, 1969.

Ostrom, John. *The Letters of Edgar Allan Poe*. 2 vols. Cambridge: Harvard University Press, 1948.

Parks, Edd Winfield. *Ante-Bellum Southern Literary Critics*. Athens: University of Georgia Press, 1962.

Pemberton, James M. " 'An Inward and Spiritual Grace': The Southern Gentleman of the Antebellum Novel." Ph.D. diss., University of Tennessee, 1973.

Quinn, Arthur Hobson. *Edgar Allan Poe: A Critical Biography*. New York: Appleton-Century-Crofts, 1941.

Thompson, May Alcott. "Philip Pendleton Cooke." M.A. thesis, Columbia, 1923.

Tucker, Edward L. "Philip Pendleton Cooke." *Virginia Cavalcade* 19 (Winter 1970): 42–47.

Frederick Douglass
(1818–1895)

Frederick Douglass's life as a freeman is flanked by two enduring autobiographies. When he was twenty-seven years old and just seven years "up from slavery," he wrote the *Narrative of the Life of Frederick Douglass, an American Slave*, an undisputed classic in the slave narrative genre. In the twilight of his life 47 years later, he enlarged his third autobiography, the *Life and Times of Frederick Douglass*. This book is reminiscent of the classic "rags to riches" story except that it is more profound. For Douglass did not rise merely from poverty or even from obscurity; rather, he transcended his subhuman chattel status to become a man walking among and, in many respects, towering above, men. At least two other works within this broad span are of interest to students of literature. But had he written nothing else, Douglass's place in American literature would have been assured.

BIOGRAPHY

In *My Bondage and My Freedom* (1855), Frederick Douglass stated crisply and bitterly, "Genealogical trees do not flourish among slaves." His inability to determine his exact birth date and his father's name troubled him until his death. From his mother he inferred that he may have been born on Valentine's Day. Other calculations convinced him that he must have been born in 1817. As for his paternity, slave gossip had it that his father was his master, but no evidence confirms either his paternity or his exact birth date. His birthplace was a plantation on Maryland's Eastern Shore.

Recent researchers have discovered that Frederick Augustus Washington Bailey was born one year later than he assumed, in February 1818. Although Douglass thought that his resounding name was rather "pretentious," his mother had linked him symbolically to one of his ancestors when she named him "Augustus.'' For generations, family names had been recycled in the Bailey clan. Not surprisingly, then, she chose to honor her brother who had died two years earlier.

On his mother's side, Douglass's roots extended to at least just before the middle of the eighteenth century when the Bailey clan belonged to the Richard Skinner family of Talbot County, Maryland. His mother, Harriet Bailey (born 28 February 1792), was the granddaughter of a slave named Jenny born in 1745. Jenny, in turn, may have been the daughter of a male slave named Baly (by 1781 spelled ''Bailey'') who was born in 1701 and lived to be over eighty years old. The Bailey clan remained in the Skinner-Rice family until around 1797 when Ann Skinner, the granddaughter of Richard Skinner, married Aaron Anthony, Douglass's master. Aaron Anthony soon moved the Skinner slaves to a farm on the Tuckahoe Creek fifteen miles away.

Among these uprooted slaves was Douglass's maternal grandmother, Bett or Betsey. She would eventually bear eight additional children, but in 1797 the then twenty-three-year-old Betsey had only two young daughters, Milley and Harriet. At some point either before or after 1797, Betsey married a free black sawyer named Isaac Bailey. In fact, Aaron Anthony explicitly acknowledged the marriage in one of his ledgers. Little is known about Isaac Bailey except that he sometimes worked for Colonel Edward Lloyd, Aaron Anthony's employer, and that he was industrious enough to hire a slave from Aaron Anthony on two separate occasions (in 1797 and 1812). Aaron Anthony allowed the couple to live together in a small cabin on his property. He also permitted Betsey to work as a fisherwoman and a paid midwife to his slave women.

In the late 1700s, Douglass's owner, Aaron Anthony, had been a captain on schooners belonging to Colonels Edward Lloyd IV and V. Near the turn of the century, he became chief overseer at Colonel Edward Lloyd V's magnificent estate on the Wye River. Since he lived on the Lloyd estate, Anthony rented his two farms and most of his slaves to others. Such a fate befell Douglass's mother, an attractive and literate slave who was hired out repeatedly between 1809 and 1816.

Douglass had one older brother, two older sisters, and two younger sisters. Until he was six, he lived in his grandmother's cabin with five cousins and his younger uncle, Harry. Although Douglass implied in his first autobiography that his mother lived twelve miles away, his mother actually lived at the nearby Holme Hill farm between 1817 and 1821 when Perry Ward Steward rented the farm from Aaron Anthony. Thus, Harriet's reputed lack of contact with the young Douglass remains a mystery. In any event, Douglass's relatively happy life with his grandmother came to an abrupt end in summer 1824 when his grandmother carried him to Aaron Anthony's house twelve miles away.

At this time, Colonel Edward Lloyd V owned thirteen farms, nearly 10,000 acres of land, and more than 500 slaves. Some 181 slaves lived on the central farm alone. Historically, the estate looked like one of those fabled Southern plantations supposedly endemic to the region; however, slave life was far from idyllic. Under the iron sway of Anthony's head cook (Douglass's cousin, "Aunt" Katy), Douglass experienced some of the harsher realities of slave life. He also saw firsthand the glaring contrast between the ostentatious life-style of the wealthy Lloyds and the bleak, sometimes brutal, life-style of the Lloyd and Anthony slaves.

Out of about 80 slave children living on the central farm, Douglass was selected to be the companion of Daniel Lloyd, Colonel Lloyd's twelve-year-old son. In addition, he became the pet of Aaron Anthony's daughter, Lucretia Anthony Auld. Even though Lucretia's solicitude eased the pain in his life, it was not until Douglass moved to Baltimore in March 1826 that a white mistress's affection had a pivotal influence on his development.

Douglass was sent to Baltimore because Hugh Auld, the brother of Aaron Anthony's son-in-law, wanted a black boy to be a servant and companion to his young son Thomas (born in January 1824). Not long after he arrived, Sophia Keithley Auld began teaching him to read, and she continued to give him rudimentary instruction until her husband forbade her to do so. Such instruction was not illegal in Maryland, but Hugh Auld believed that education would make Douglass unfit to be a slave. This opposition forced Douglass to pursue his self-education surreptitiously.

On 14 November 1826, Aaron Anthony died, leaving 29 slaves to be divided among his heirs. Douglass returned to Tuckahoe in October 1827 to be valued with the rest of Anthony's chattels and to be assigned to a new owner. Because Lucretia Anthony Auld had also died in summer 1827, Douglass fell to Thomas Auld, who promptly sent him back to Baltimore to live with his brother Hugh. Douglass's mother was already dead by this time, having died late in 1825 or early in 1826. The remaining 28 slaves were divided among Anthony's two sons, Andrew and Richard, and Thomas Auld.

For the next five years (1827–32), Douglass stayed in Baltimore. Living there allowed him to continue to educate himself, to hear and read abolitionist propaganda, and to meet and mingle with free blacks. It also spared him from seeing his family slowly disintegrate. Although it is true that Aaron Anthony had sold three of Douglass's close relatives before he died in 1826, his wastrel son Andrew sold double that number before he died in 1833. These developments were unparalleled in Douglass's family history. In the eighteenth century, none of his family was sold out of the Eastern Shore region. Yet by 1832 his younger sister Sarah, two of his aunts, numerous relatives, and dozens of his acquaintances had been sold south. Had his aunt Jenny and her husband Noah not fled north earlier in 1825, they, too, might have been in this group.

Douglass was probably unaware of these family disruptions that occurred while he lived in Baltimore; however, he himself was uprooted in March 1833. After a dispute with Hugh Auld, Thomas Auld ordered him to send Douglass to St. Michaels to live with him and his new wife, Rowena Hambleton Auld. Douglass was so unhappy about the move that not even his reunion with his older sister Eliza and his aunt Priscilla could reconcile him to his new life. At the Thomas

Aulds, life was harsh; they were a stingy couple, and Rowena Auld particularly disliked him. Soon Douglass's untoward disposition caused Thomas Auld to hire him out to Edward Covey, a twenty-eight-year-old overseer turned farmer with a reputation for subduing rebellious slaves.

Douglass left for Covey's rented farm on 1 January 1834 and remained there for the rest of the year. During the first few months, he was initiated into the rigorous life of a field hand and reduced for a time to the level of a brute. Then in August 1833 he fought valiantly and wrested his manhood from Covey's vise. This famous battle was the turning point in Douglass's life as a slave. Henceforth, though his master still owned his body, he no longer enslaved his spirit.

In January 1835 Douglass was hired out to William Freeland, a cousin of Thomas Auld's wife, whose farm was two or three miles northwest of St. Michaels. Freeland was a mild master, but Douglass could not forget that he was still a slave. Eventually, he organized a secret school for younger blacks (some of whom later escaped to the North), and he began working on an escape plan. Had they not been betrayed earlier that day, Douglass and five other blacks would have tried to escape on the Saturday night before Easter, 2 April 1836. Instead, five of the six were jailed in Easton. Slave traders could not persuade Thomas Auld to sell his troublesome property. Rather, in mid-April 1836 Auld sent Douglass back to Baltimore to live with the Hugh Aulds.

During this next period in Baltimore (1836–38), Douglass worked as an apprentice calker, reestablished his connections with free blacks, and joined a secret debating club where he polished his verbal skills. In spring 1838, he convinced Hugh Auld to let him hire himself out for a set fee. After allowing him to live independently until August, Auld ordered Douglass to move back home after Douglass failed to turn over his wages to him at the stipulated time. Douglass remained there until he escaped on Monday, 3 September 1838.

Douglass's method of escape was conditioned by the special circumstances in which he found himself. Since he lived and worked in a seaport community, he knew how to impersonate a sailor. One sailor named Stanley lent him his uniform and his "protection papers." Furthermore, since the railroad line heading north had only recently opened (1837), security was not as strict as it would be in ensuing years. Thus, this bold "sailor" simply boarded an overland train and rode north to freedom.

He arrived in New York City, not particularly hospitable to fugitives, the next day. There, he was befriended by still another black sailor and by David Ruggles, a black man who was secretary of a local organization assisting fugitives. A few days later, on 15 September 1838, Douglass married Anna Murray, a free black woman from Baltimore who had helped to finance his escape.

On 17 September 1838 Douglass and his new wife moved to New Bedford, Massachusetts, where they were befriended by the Nathan Johnson family. When Douglass decided to adopt still another last name to avoid detection, Johnson suggested that Douglass change his last name to Douglass, a name Johnson borrowed from the character named Douglas in Sir Walter Scott's *The Lady of the Lake*. White hostility prevented Douglass from working as a calker in New Bedford; therefore, he held all sorts of odd jobs to support his growing family. Meanwhile, he aligned himself closely with the black community, particularly black abolitionists, and became a local leader and a preacher.

In early 1839 Douglass read a copy of William Lloyd Garrison's abolitionist newspaper, the *Liberator*. This newspaper had a searing impact on him. It was not until two years later, on 9 August 1841, that he heard Garrison speak for the first time. The next day, Douglass accompanied Garrison and 40 others to a convention in Nantucket where, on 12 August 1841, a New Bedford abolitionist named William Bedford convinced him to speak of his life as a slave. Douglass was timid at first, but soon he relaxed and spoke so movingly that the audience shouted with Garrison that they had heard a *man* speak, not a *thing*. He spoke again that evening and the next morning to much approbation.

Douglass's meteoric rise from self-educated slave to renowned anti-slavery orator dates from this Nantucket meeting. Enlisted thereafter as a "traveling agent" for the Massachusetts Anti-Slavery Society, Douglass was a stunning success. He traveled some 3,500 miles before he accepted the position permanently in January 1842. Ironically, by 1844, he had developed so rapidly that many people in his audience doubted that he had ever been a slave. Therefore, in 1845, he published the *Narrative of Frederick Douglass, an American Slave, Written by Himself* to prove that he was not an imposter and to buttress the anti-slavery cause. This book was a best-seller, selling tens of thousands of copies in America, Great Britain, France, and Germany.

Douglass's autobiography dispelled doubts about his true identity, but it also endangered his freedom. Consequently, in August 1845 he fled to Great Britain, where he remained for eighteen months. There he delivered hundreds of lectures on slavery, temperance, universal suffrage, and pacifism.

He returned to America in spring 1847 a free man. His English friends had raised about $710 to purchase his freedom from Hugh Auld, who had previously bought him from his brother, Thomas, for $100. Before the year was out, he had begun publishing his own newspaper, the *North Star*, which was renamed *Frederick Douglass' Paper* in June 1851. In this paper he first published his only known work of short fiction, "The Heroic Slave," which was based on the *Creole* slave mutiny of 1841. Two years later, in 1855, he published a more detailed, updated version of his life entitled *My Bondage and My Freedom*, which sold 18,000 copies in two years and, like the *Narrative*, was translated into German.

Succeeding years saw Douglass crusade against slavery in his *Paper* and in *Douglass' Monthly*. The latter, begun in 1858, was originally meant for British consumption. His most important platform, though, was the lecture circuit. He vociferously denounced discrimination, segregation, and colonization; and he championed the rights of women (including women's suffrage), land reform, temperance, the abolition of capital punishment, and universal peace. During the Civil War, he fought for the abolition of slavery and the enlistment and just treatment of blacks in the Union Army; after the war, he waged a battle for the full citizenship of the newly emancipated slaves and for all black Americans.

A staunch but not uncritical Republican, Douglass received several political appointments. He was appointed assistant secretary of a commission sent to the Dominican Republic in 1871; president of the tottering Freedman's Bank in 1874; U.S. Marshal of the District of Columbia in 1877; Recorder of Deeds for the District of Columbia in 1881; Minister-Resident and Consul-General to the Republic of Haiti in 1889; and Haitian Commissioner at the World's Columbian Exposition in Chicago in 1893.

In 1881 Douglass published still another version of his life entitled *Life and Times of Frederick Douglass*. This edition and the enlarged and revised edition of 1892 sold fewer than a thousand copies in America. Nevertheless, after his sudden death at his Washington home on 20 February 1895, he received numerous tributes befitting his stature. The legislature of North Carolina adjourned for the day; four other legislatures adopted resolutions of regret. Survived by Helen Pitts, his wife of eleven years, and four children from his first marriage, Douglass was buried on 26 February 1895 in Rochester, New York, the state that had given him his first brief asylum in 1838 and had been his home from 1847 to 1872.

MAJOR THEMES

In the 1892 edition of *Life and Times of Frederick Douglass*, Douglass clarifies his primary reason for writing his autobiographies: "I write freely of myself, not from choice, but because I have, by my cause, been morally forced into thus writing. Time and events have summoned me to stand forth both as a witness and an advocate for a people long dumb, not allowed to speak for themselves, yet much misunderstood and deeply wronged." Although this is the underlying motive of all four autobiographies, it is especially true of the *Narrative of the Life of Frederick Douglass, an American Slave, Written by Himself* (1845) and of *My Bondage and My Freedom* (1855), which were written during the height of the anti-slavery movement. In these, Douglass devoted his pen to the crusade he considered "the noblest and best part" of his life. He endeavored to expose "the direful nature of the slave system, by telling [of his] own experiences while a slave, and to do what [he] could thereby to make slavery odious and thus hasten the day of emancipation" (1892).

In the *Narrative*, Douglass exposes the inhumanity and brutality of slavery and traces his own developing awareness of and resistance to the system. The work opens with a stark image of slavery's assault on the slave's identity and on the slave family. Douglass knows neither his birth date nor his father's name because such information is superfluous for human chattel. Even if he knew his white father's name, the knowledge would arraign his master or some other white man, but it would not mitigate his slave status. Slave children follow the condition of their mothers, not their fathers. This insidious law insures that the sexual exploitation of slave women will not result in free offspring. Slavery also weakens or even severs family ties. Young Douglass is separated from his mother, his grandparents, his siblings, and his relatives whenever his master decides to plant him elsewhere.

Douglass slowly learns that the slave is subject to the arbitrary will of his master. If the master so chooses, he can overwork him, half-starve him, or scantily clothe him; he can whip, torture, or murder him with impugnity. The slave must passively endure his hardships or risk incurring his master's wrath. Physical resistance is foolhardy, if not suicidal; and verbal resistance, construed as impudence or insubordination, is risky. The slave must ever play the role of an insensitive, unaspiring, unquestioning mute.

Douglass also perceives that slave masters jealously guard the Tree of Life. On Colonel Lloyd's flourishing plantation, a garden abounds in all types of fruit, but the Colonel forbids the slaves to pluck it. Masters like Hugh Auld also deny them access to the Tree of Knowledge lest their enlightenment make them discontent. Their resulting ignorance augments their degradation, and their degradation provides an easy rationale for their continued enslavement.

Once Douglass comprehends the nature and mechanisms of slavery, he is in a much better position to resist it. Essentially, he learns that his interests are antagonistic to his master's interests. What his master forbids, he desires, whether this be education, self-respect, manhood, or physical freedom. The slave-breaker Covey tries to crush him under his iron heel, but he cannot destroy Douglass's natural yearning for freedom. His divine spirit recoils and springs back on his oppressor.

Once Douglass's psychic liberation is complete, he is already half-free. He need only bide his time and search for that weak link in his chains. Given his determination and his acuteness, his eventual escape comes as no surprise. And given his deep, abiding hatred of slavery, we are even less astonished when he becomes slavery's "witness" and the slaves' "advocate" at the end of the *Narrative*.

Douglass's anti-slavery crusade continues in the short story "The Heroic Slave" (1853). In this treatment of the *Creole* mutiny (1841), Douglass modifies a number of the historical details and develops themes that appear repeatedly in his autobiographies and other writings. Naturally, he denounces America for continuing the domestic slave trade and praises Britain for freeing the mutineers. Thus, the story's plot embodies the triumph of a just order over an unjust one. Second, in his portrait of Madison Washington, historically the most prominent of at least four leaders of the mutiny, Douglass creates the quintessential American hero. Madison bears the names of two of America's most illustrious leaders during the American Revolution, for example. Similarly, in their violent defense of their natural right to liberty, the slaves imitate the actions of the insurgent colonists. In this case, however, the slaves' enemies are the erstwhile victims of British tyranny, and their allies are the former tyrants.

This analogy between the slave mutiny and the American Revolution is intertwined with a third theme, America's moral decline in the post-Revolutionary era. Virginia, parent of statesmen, has kept one of its noblest sons in bondage. Douglass chastizes both Virginia and America for their apostasy to ideals they once held sacred.

A final theme is the efficacy of moral suasion and, paradoxically, of slave violence. Mr. Listwell, a Northerner, becomes an active abolitionist when he learns the truth about slavery. Also, although Tom Grant, the first mate of the *Creole*, denies that he has become an abolitionist, he vows that he will never sail another slaver or risk his life in an immoral cause. On the other hand, the slaves' violence wins them their nominal freedom, whereas Britain's moral enlightenment makes it permanent. Thus, Douglass implies that both moral suasion and a stout arm are potent weapons and that the former reinforces the efficacy of the latter.

With emancipation, Douglass's crusade against slavery ended, but he realized that he could not abandon his role as witness and advocate, either in his life or in his autobiographies. Thus, the earlier motive is just as apparent in the two versions of *Life and Times* (1881 and 1892) as it was in the earlier auto-biographies.

One of the most distressing features of *Life and Times* is that Douglass retains, with some modifications, the description and critique of his life in slavery. This feature of the work is practically unbearable to readers who have patiently read the *Narrative* and the more detailed *My Bondage and My Freedom*. The key here, though, is that Douglass feels that his former slave status not only heightens the singularity of his life but also furnishes a point of reference from which he, and his reader, can evaluate his life as a freeman.

The *Narrative* ends with Douglass's first speech before a white audience. Later, in *My Bondage and My Freedom*, he mentions the Garrisonians' misguided attempt to fetter his speech whenever he delivers anti-slavery lectures. He is supposed to present the facts or the narration, and they are to furnish the critique and the philosophy. Moreover, he is to retain "a *little* of the plantation manner of speech" so that his auditors will not doubt that he has ever been a slave. Douglass feels, however, that his narrow orbit is too confining. As he later explains in *Life and Times* (1892), "These misguided friends were actuated by the best of motives and were not altogether wrong in their advice, and still I must speak just that word that seemed to *me* the word to be spoken by *me*." Since he had been a slave, it did not take Douglass long to realize that he was, in effect, behaving slavishly. Both *My Bondage* and *Life and Times* chronicle his growing independence.

In *Life and Times* (1892), Douglass especially analogizes his battle against color caste and color prejudice to his resistance to slavery. Here, Douglass makes it clear that he wants to be accepted both into the human family and the American family. Previously, slave masters had tried to keep blacks "beyond the circle of brotherhood." Similarly, in 1866 when Douglass is a delegate to the National Loyalist Convention in Philadelphia, the white delegates shun him as if he is an outsider. He comments, "I was the ugly and deformed child of the family, and to be kept out of sight as much as possible while there was company in the house" (1892). Douglass fights vigorously for his rightful place in society, and he rejoices whenever he and other blacks set precedents. Each "first" testifies to blacks' potential and paves the way to still other accomplishments.

The burden of color is wearisome at times, the battle against racial proscription seemingly unending. Hence, when Douglass takes a trip to Europe, the Middle East, and Africa in 1886–87, he feels invigorated. He is thankful that "there was left to [him] a space in life when [he] could and did walk the world unquestioned, a man among men." His is not the voice of despair, however. On the contrary, at the end of the 1892 edition, he observes, "Servitude, persecution, false friends, desertion, and depreciation have not robbed my life of happiness or made it a burden." This essential optimism is vintage Douglass. Since he believes that human rights, when trampled, will yet "revive, survive, and flourish again," optimism runs like a golden thread through *Life and Times*. In fact, it might be said that this attitude informs all of his writings. Even when he rails like an Old Testament prophet, Douglass evinces a firm belief in human progress. This belief made him a crusader in the beginning and kept him one until the end.

SURVEY OF CRITICISM

Interest in Frederick Douglass's *Narrative* (1845) intensified in the 1970s and 1980s and, at present, shows no sign of waning. By contrast, neither *My Bondage and My Freedom* (1855) nor the two versions of *Life and Times* (1881 and 1892) have received as much attention as they warrant. Until recently, almost no attention had been focused on Douglass's only known short story, "The Heroic Slave" (1853). Fortunately, this oversight is slowly being corrected.

As for the autobiographies, researchers have been interested primarily in genre, narrative mode, structure, thematic and imagistic patterns, language, and point of view. Douglass's influence on later black writers and his relationship to contemporary white authors have received less attention. Generally, critics have compared two or more autobiographies with one of two purposes in mind: to trace Douglass's artistic growth or deterioration or to provide a psychological portrait of him. Many critics have mentioned the constraints placed on Douglass and other slave narrators, but one critic in particular has focused an entire essay on this issue.

Critics have been almost unanimous in classifying Douglass's *Narrative* as both a slave narrative and "true" autobiography, but there is one provocative voice of dissent. Whereas Albert E. Stone ("Identity and Art," 1973) and James Olney (" 'I Was Born,' " 1985) consider Douglass a "true" autobiographer because he consciously shapes the events of his life and creates a metaphorical image of himself, John Sekora ("Comprehending Slavery," 1985) argues that the *Narrative* is not "true" autobiography at all. Borrowing an older term, he calls it "the first comprehensive personal history of slavery." Sekora notes that slave narrators did not, in fact, shape their own narratives; the narratives were shaped by white abolitionists, editors, and printers, a point he developed more comprehensively in "The Dilemma of Frederick Douglass" (1983). Basically, Douglass shows that he has mastered the preexistent "language of abolition" in the *Narrative*; he would not write "true" autobiography for another ten years. Robert B. Stepto ("I Rose and Found My Voice," 1979) concedes that not all slave narratives are autobiographies; however, "Douglass inaugurates the autobiographical mode in Afro-American letters." In an essay describing the four modes of narration in slave narratives, he concludes that Douglass's *Narrative* belongs to a subclass of the "Generic Narrative" because its "authenticating documents" are "*totally* subsumed by the tale," evidence of Douglass's authorial control.

In his *Long Black Song* (1973), Houston A. Baker, Jr., calls the *Narrative* "a *Bildungsroman*, which records the growth to manhood of a small slave boy," and "a spiritual autobiography akin to the writings of such noted authors as Cotton Mather, Benjamin Franklin, and Henry Adams." Yet he primarily discusses the work's themes, style, and folk motifs. A concrete and elaborate discussion of the *Narrative*'s links to spiritual autobiography appears in G. Thomas Couser's *American Autobiography* (1979). Couser believes that the "analogy between the process of conversion and that of liberation" is the central structural pattern of the work. This analogy is common in slave narratives, as Francis Smith Foster's *Witnessing Slavery* (1979) makes clear. But Douglass handles the motif more artistically, Couser argues.

Charles T. Davis and Lucinda H. MacKethan have also discussed the architectonics of the *Narrative*. Both find that interlinked metaphorical patterns determine the shape of the *Narrative*. In "The Slave Narrative" (1982), Davis unwinds three threads: Douglass's "growth in . . . intellectual competence, the increase in his yearning for freedom, and the search for a community in which he could achieve an amount of self-realization." Similarly, in "Metaphors of Mastery" (1982) MacKethan describes a "network of metaphors," specifically, "the metaphor of the trick," "the metaphor of the word and of language," and "the metaphor of narrative order" or "design." In contrast to these authors, Henry Louis Gates, Jr., limits his discussion to chapter 1 of the *Narrative*. In "Binary Oppositions" (1979), he explains that Douglass uses antitheses to undermine the "arbitrary," culturally mandated "symbolic code" that created specious similarities between slaves and other animate chattel.

Thematic and imagistic patterns in Douglass have received a great deal of attention. Literacy, which has manifold ramifications for Douglass, is a favorite topic. In the works noted above, Stone, Couser, Davis, MacKethan, Olney, and Sekora treat this theme in varying degrees; however, Baker in *The Journey Back* (1980) and Annette Niemtzow in "The Problematic Self" (1982) devote their entire essays to this topic. Both authors recognize the positive benefits of the quest for literacy, particularly the existential and political dimensions. They argue, though, that Douglass's uncritical acceptance of the dominant language is problematical since he also accepts a white perspective.

Other critics have explored Douglass's extensive use of animal and nautical images in the *Narrative*. In his article discussed above, Stone considers nautical imagery to be far more important to the narrative design of the *Narrative* than its animal imagery. In fact, it constitutes Douglass's "metaphor of self." Conversely, in "Animal Farm Unbound" (1977), H. Bruce Franklin argues cogently for the centrality of animal imagery, echoing an observation Baker had made earlier in *Long Black Song* (1973).

Still other critics have analyzed the *Narrative*'s biblical imagery. Lisa Margaret Zeitz's "Biblical Allusion and Imagery" (1981) is a useful guide to Douglass's allusions to the Old and New Testaments. G. Thomas Couser (*American Autobiography*, 1979) links the Edenic overtones of the *Narrative* to the conversion pattern, but Baker's treatment is more complex. In *Blues, Ideology, and Afro-American Literature* (1984), Baker applies the Edenic paradigm to the garden, Douglass's trip to Baltimore, Hugh Auld's prohibition of Douglass's instruction, Edward Covey's appropriation of the "fruits" of the slave Caroline's womb, and, of course, to the slaveholder's appropriation of the "fruits" of the slaves' labor. When Douglass "steals away" from slavery, he "steals the fruits of his own labor," thereby exploiting the "economic imperatives of the system."

In the article noted above, Stepto ("I Rose") treats briefly four major types of writing in the *Narrative*. Stephen Butterfield, by contrast, isolates nine characteristic features of Douglass's polemical rhetoric. His chapter in *Black Autobiography* (1974) is by far the most expansive analysis of Douglass's style. Robert G. O'Meally takes a different approach to language in his article "Frederick Douglass' 1845 *Narrative*." His thesis is his subtitle: "The Text Was Meant to Be Preached" (1979). He describes the content, voice, tone, biblical allusions and oratorical techniques of Douglass's "black sermon."

Several additional studies exhibit sundry approaches. Nancy T. Clasby in "Frederick Douglass's *Narrative*" (1971) asserts that slavery was designed to kill the slave's spirit or destroy his personality. Figuratively, Douglass "died" to be "reborn of violence." In another article, Paul D. Johnson (" 'Goodbye to Sambo,' " 1972) notes the polemical ramifications of Douglass's presentation of himself as an "intelligent and militant reformer" in the *Narrative*. He also mentions Douglass's influence on Harriet Beecher Stowe's *Uncle Tom's Cabin* (1852). Similarly, Richard O. Lewis ("Romanticism in the Fiction of Charles W. Chesnutt," 1982) discusses the influence of the train incident in *My Bondage* on Chesnutt's *The Marrow of Tradition* (1901). William W. Nichols's "Individualism and Autobiographical Art" (1972) compares certain themes and techniques in *My Bondage* with those in Henry David Thoreau's *Walden* published a year earlier. In an article comparing Douglass's *Narrative* with James W. C. Pennington's, Lillie Butler Jugurtha ("Point of View in the Afro-American Slave Narrative," 1982) discusses the ways in which the participant-narrators manipulate the distance between the reader and the story "to maximize meaning."

A final group of studies compares two or more versions of the autobiographies. Two critics from the 1930s, Vernon Loggins (*The Negro Author*, 1931) and J. Saunders Redding (*To Make a Poet Black*, 1939), disagree about the relative merits of the autobiographies. Of the four versions, Loggins feels that *My Bondage* is superior, whereas Redding calls the 1881 version the "most American of American life stories" and Douglass's "best book." In a pioneering study of the slave narrative, Marion Wilson Starling (*The Slave Narrative*, 1981) describes all four versions and assigns the *Narrative* to "the position of top-ranking slave narrative."

More recent comparative studies are those by Henry Dan Piper, James Matlack, and Thomas De Pietro. In "The Place of Frederick Douglass's *Narrative* . . . in the Development of a Native Prose Style" (1977), Piper argues that the *Narrative* is superior because it belongs to the tradition of "an indigenous prose style." Matlack ("The Autobiographies," 1979) also gives the *Narrative* the highest rating because of its plain style. De Pietro ("Vision and Revision in the Autobiographies," 1983) takes a different stance, arguing that *My Bondage* "suffers unduly" from critical neglect. Whereas these writers focus on the literary merits of the autobiographies, Peter F. Walker and Waldo E. Martin, Jr., probe Douglass's psychology. In three extremely detailed chapters in *Moral Choices* (1978), Walker argues that Douglass became an abolitionist because he had a "hopeless secret desire to be white." Eventually, he learned "the absurdity of selecting abolition as the instrument to blot out his blackness." Consequently, in his sequence of autobiographies, he identifies more and more with "his black heritage," especially his mother. Martin (*The Mind of Frederick Douglass*, 1984) asserts that Douglass "carefully delineated his self-image" in his autobiographies. "It betrayed a conscious and unconscious elaboration of his idealized self—a self-conscious hero complex," he observes.

Douglass's short story "The Heroic Slave" (1853) has only recently begun to attract critical attention. In 1972 Ronald T. Takaki republished and discussed the work in *Violence in the Black Imagination*. He argues that even though Douglass projected the rebellious part of himself onto Madison Washington, the rebel leader, he was actually quite ambivalent toward violent resistance. He uses a biographical approach to account for this ambivalence. A brief treatment of the story appears in William L. Van Deburg's *Slavery and Race in American Popular Culture* (1984). This work is useful not so much for its limited discussion of the story as for its larger context: the contemporary ideological battle over the presumed nature of blacks. Finally, Stepto's "Storytelling in Early Afro-American Fiction" (1984) is a subtle and insightful analysis of the story's narrative design. Stepto discusses the specific occasion for the work, the impact of personal and contemporaneous factors on the work, and, most important, the story's complex relationship to the slave narrative tradition. He especially emphasizes the work's craft or its combination of "artfulness" and "usefulness."

For further criticism, readers might consult the sections on Douglass and on the slave narrative in volume 1 of *Black American Writers: Bibliographical*

Essays, ed. M. Thomas Inge, Maurice Duke, and Jackson Bryer (1978), and the checklist of criticism on slave narratives in the appendix of *The Art of the Slave Narrative* (1982), ed. John Sekora and Darwin T. Turner.

BIBLIOGRAPHY

Works by Frederick Douglass

Narrative of the Life of Frederick Douglass, an American Slave, Written by Himself. Boston: Anti-Slavery Office, 1845. Repr., ed. Benjamin Quarles; Cambridge, Mass.: Harvard University Press, 1960. Repr., ed. Houston A. Baker, Jr.; New York: Penguin Books, 1982.

My Bondage and My Freedom. New York: Miller, Orton and Mulligan, 1855. Repr. New York: Arno Press, 1968. Repr. with Intro. by Philip S. Foner; New York: Dover, 1969.

Life and Times of Frederick Douglass. Hartford, Conn.: Park, 1881 and 1882. rev. and enl., Boston: De Wolfe, Fiske, 1892, 1893, 1895. Repr. of 1892 ed. with Intro. by Rayford B. Logan; New York: Macmillan, 1962.

The Life and Writings of Frederick Douglass. Ed. Philip S. Foner. 5 vols. New York: International Publishers, 1950–75. Biography, letters, addresses, essays, editorials, reviews; "The Heroic Slave," in 5: 473–505.

The Frederick Douglass Papers, Series One: Speeches, Debates and Interviews. 2 vols. Ed. John W. Blassingame et al. New Haven: Yale University Pess, 1979–82. Covers 1841–46 and 1847–54; third volume covering 1855–63 forthcoming.

Frederick Douglass: The Narrative and Selected Writings. Ed. Michael Meyer. New York: Random House, 1984.

Studies of Frederick Douglass

Baker, Houston A., Jr. *Blues, Ideology, and Afro-American Literature: A Vernacular Theory.* Chicago: University of Chicago Press, 1984, pp. 39–50.

————. *The Journey Back: Issues in Black Literature.* Chicago: University of Chicago Press, 1980, pp. 27–46.

————. "Revolution and Reform: Walker, Douglass, and the Road to Freedom." *Long Black Song: Essays in Black American Literature and Culture.* Charlottesville: University Press of Virginia, 1973, pp. 71–83.

Butterfield, Stephen. "Frederick Douglass: Language as Weapon." *Black Autobiography in America.* Amherst: University of Massachusetts Press, 1974, pp. 65–89.

Clasby, Nancy T. "Frederick Douglass's *Narrative*." *CLA Journal* 14 (March 1971): 242–50.

Couser, G. Thomas. "Frederick Douglass: Abolitionism and Prophecy." *American Autobiography: The Prophetic Mode.* Amherst: University of Massachusetts Press, 1979, pp. 51–61.

Davis, Charles T. "The Slave Narrative: First Major Art Form in an Emerging Black Tradition." *Black Is the Color of the Cosmos: Essays on Afro-American Literature and Culture, 1942–1981.* Ed. Henry Louis Gates, Jr. New York: Garland, 1982, pp. 89–93, 107–15.

Davis, Mary Kemp. "The Historical Slave Revolt and the Literary Imagination." Ph.D. diss., University of North Carolina at Chapel Hill, 1984.

De Pietro, Thomas. "Vision and Revision in the Autobiographies of Frederick Douglass." *CLA Journal* 26 (June 1983): 384–96.

Foster, Francis Smith. *Witnessing Slavery: The Development of Antebellum Slave Narratives*. Westport, Conn.: Greenwood Press, 1979.

Franklin, H. Bruce. "Animal Farm Unbound Or, What the *Narrative of the Life of Frederick Douglass, an American Slave* Reveals about American Literature." *New Letters* 43 (Spring 1977): 25–46.

Gates, Henry Louis, Jr. "Binary Oppositions in Chapter One of *Narrative of the Life of Frederick Douglass, an American Slave, Written by Himself*." *Afro-American Literature: The Reconstruction of Instruction*. Ed. Dexter Fisher and Robert B. Stepto. New York: Modern Language Association, 1979, pp. 212–32.

Inge, M. Thomas, Maurice Duke, and Jackson R. Bryer, eds. *Black American Writers: Bibliographical Essays*. Vol. 1. New York: St. Martin's, 1978.

Johnson, Paul D. " 'Goodbye to Sambo': The Contribution of Black Slave Narratives to the Abolitionist Movement." *Negro American Literature Forum* 6 (Fall 1972): 79–84.

Jugurtha, Lillie Butler. "Point of View in the Afro-American Slave Narratives: A Study of Narratives by Douglass and Pennington." *The Art of Slave Narrative: Original Essays in Criticism and Theory*. Ed. John Sekora and Darwin T. Turner. Macomb: Western Illinois University Press, 1982, pp. 110–19.

Lewis, Richard O. "Romanticism in the Fiction of Charles W. Chesnutt: The Influence of Dickens, Scott, Tourgee, and Douglass." *CLA Journal* 26 (December 1982): 145–71.

Loggins, Vernon. *The Negro Author and His Development in America to 1900*. New York: Columbia University Press, 1931; repr. Port Washington, N.Y.: Kennikat Press, 1964, pp. 134–56.

MacKethan, Lucinda H. "Metaphors of Mastery in the Slave Narratives." *The Art of the Slave Narrative*. Ed. John Sekora and Darwin T. Turner. Macomb: Western Illinois University Press, 1982, pp. 55–69.

Martin, Waldo E., Jr. *The Mind of Frederick Douglass*. Chapel Hill: University of North Carolina Press, 1984.

Matlack, James. "The Autobiographies of Frederick Douglass." *Phylon* 40 (March 1979): 15–27.

Nichols, William W. "Individualism and Autobiographical Art: Frederick Douglass and Henry Thoreau." *CLA Journal* 16 (December 1972): 145–58.

Niemtzow, Annette. "The Problematic Self in Autobiography: The Example of the Slave Narrative." *The Art of the Slave Narrative*. Ed. John Sekora and Darwin T. Turner. Macomb: Western Illinois University Press, 1982, pp. 96–109.

Olney, James. " 'I Was Born': Slave Narratives, Their Status as Autobiography and as Literature." *The Slave's Narrative*. Ed. Charles T. Davis and Henry Louis Gates, Jr. New York: Oxford University Press, 1985, pp. 148–75.

O'Meally, Robert G. "Frederick Douglass' 1845 *Narrative*: The Text Was Meant to Be Preached." *Afro-American Literature: The Reconstruction of Instruction*. Ed. Dexter Fisher and Robert B. Stepto. New York: Modern Language Association, 1979, pp. 192–211.

Piper, Henry Dan. "The Place of Frederick Douglass's *Narrative of the Life of [Frederick*

Douglass] an American Slave in the Development of a Native American Prose Style." *Journal of Afro-American Issues* 5 (Spring 1977): 183–91.

Preston, Dickson J. *Young Frederick Douglass: The Maryland Years.* Baltimore: Johns Hopkins University Press, 1980.

Quarles, Benjamin. *Frederick Douglass.* Washington, D.C.: Associated Publishers, 1948; repr. New York: Atheneum, 1968.

Redding, J. Saunders. *To Make a Poet Black.* Chapel Hill: University of North Carolina Press, 1939, pp. 30–38.

Sekora, John. "Comprehending Slavery: Language and Personal History in Douglass' *Narrative* of 1845." *CLA Journal* 29 (December 1985): 157–70.

———. "The Dilemma of Frederick Douglass: The Slave Narrative as Literary Institution." *Essays in Literature* 10 (Fall 1983): 219–26.

Sekora, John and Darwin T. Turner, ed. *The Art of the Slave Narrative: Original Essays in Criticism and Theory.* Macomb, Ill.: Western Illinois University Press, 1982.

Starling, Marion Wilson. "The Most Important Narrative." *The Slave Narrative: Its Place in American History.* Boston: G. K. Hall, 1981, pp. 249–93.

Stepto, Robert B. "I Rose and Found My Voice: Narration, Authentication, and Authorial Control in Four Slave Narratives." *From Behind the Veil: A Study of Afro-American Narrative.* Urbana: University of Illinois Press, 1979, pp. 3–31.

———. "Storytelling in Early Afro-American Fiction: Frederick Douglass's 'The Heroic Slave.' " *Black Literature and Literary Theory.* Ed. Henry-Louis Gates, Jr. New York: Methuen, 1984, pp. 175–86.

Stone, Albert E. "Identity and Art in Frederick Douglass's *Narrative.*" *CLA Journal* 17 (December 1973): 192–213.

Takaki, Ronald T. "Not Afraid to Die: Frederick Douglass and Violence." *Violence in the Black Imagination: Essays and Documents.* New York: G. P. Putnam, 1972, pp. 17–35.

Van Deburg, William L. *Slavery and Race in American Popular Culture.* Madison: University of Wisconsin Press, 1984, pp. 51, 60–61.

Walker, Peter F. "Frederick Douglass: Orphan Slave." *Moral Choices: Memory, Desire, and Imagination in Nineteenth Century American Abolition.* Baton Rouge: Louisiana State University Press, 1978, pp. 209–61.

Zeitz, Lisa Margaret. "Biblical Allusion and Imagery in Frederick Douglass' *Narrative.*" *CLA Journal* 25 (September 1981): 56–64.

William Elliott
(1788–1863)

William Elliott, a member of the planter class in the coastal region of Beaufort, South Carolina, in many ways typified what came to be the stereotypical image of Southern aristocracy in post–Civil War romances. A gentleman farmer and politician who also produced literary works, he was described by Jay B. Hubbell as ''one of the most gifted of the type.'' In several respects Elliott illustrates how the talents and energies of a particular class in the Old South were invested in a variety of interests—agricultural, political, literary, social, and recreational. His fame now derives mostly from a collection he wrote about hunting and fishing adventures near Hilton Head and Beaufort.

BIOGRAPHY

Born on 27 April 1788 at Beaufort, South Carolina, William Elliott was from a line of Elliotts who had come to that section of the state as early as 1685 from Barbados. His grandfather, William Elliott, had moved to Beaufort from Charleston and married a granddaughter of John Barnwell, one of the original recipients of a large land grant from the King of England. William Elliott II (1761–1808), the author's father, had a distinguished public career in both houses of the state legislature and was the first to raise long-stapled cotton successfully in the region. In 1787 Elliott II married Phebe Waight of Beaufort, and the next year William was born.

As a youngster Elliott enjoyed hunting and fishing and developed for these sports an enthusiasm that continued until his death. His early education took place at home, and he attended Beaufort College for a year. In 1806 he took entrance examinations to Harvard and enrolled there as a sophomore that fall, already proficient in French when he arrived. He distinguished himself academically at Harvard and apparently formed close friendships, but by the end of his junior year he had developed a bronchial infection that forced him to return home without completing his degree. In 1810 he was granted an honorary B.A. from Harvard and an M.A. in 1815.

His father had died in 1808, so when Elliott returned home he began to help his mother manage several plantations owned by the family. (His mother, who lived until 1855, resided at Myrtle Bank, a plantation of approximately one thousand acres located on Hilton Head near the present-day Port Royal.) In 1814 Elliott was elected to the state legislature from the St. Helena Parish, occupying the seat his father had held earlier.

On 23 May 1817 he married Ann Hutchinson Smith, the daughter of Thomas Rhett Smith, Sr., of Charleston, another family that could trace its family line back to one of the original land grants. The marriage increased the plantation holdings, for Ann brought to the marriage three rice and two cotton plantations. With the addition of these plantations, the Elliott family owned at least thirteen plantations, with summer houses at two of the plantations (Adams Run and Bay Point), a winter home at Oak Lawn near Osborn, South Carolina, a permanent residence on Bay Street in Beaufort, and a mountain home in Flat Rock, North Carolina. At one time Elliott also owned over 300 slaves.

In the late 1820s Elliott became interested in improving agricultural practices. His research had shown the wisdom of diversifying crops and not relying solely upon cotton. He repeatedly called for the establishment of agricultural schools, crop diversification, reductions of cotton production, the establishment of an experimental farm, and eventual establishment of manufacturing plants in the upland parts of the state. In addition to contributing articles on farming to the *Southern Agriculturalist* over a period of years, he spoke several times at meetings of various agricultural societies, with some of these addresses being reprinted as pamphlets.

He remained active in one or other of the state houses until 1832, when he resigned his position over the issue of Nullification. Declining cotton prices, competition from other cotton-growing areas, and other factors had plagued the South for several years. In addition, Congress had passed in 1828 a protective tariff designed to help Northern manufacturing. John Calhoun had proposed that, in the name of states rights, South Carolina should nullify the tariff since it was hurting the sale of cotton to England and forcing up the prices of manufactured goods needed by the South. Elliott did not believe the tariff was entirely just, but he foresaw that pursuing Nullification would lead to dire consequences. When his constituents insisted that St. Helena's representatives to the state legislature support calling a state convention to vote for nullification of a bill that extended the tariff, Elliott resigned his office. Later he wrote *Address to the People of St. Helena Parish*, in which he tried to calm his fellow planters and appeal to "the nobler convictions of your reason" (p. 1). In 1838 he once more entered a local race for the state legislature, but he was defeated, possibly because of his negative remarks on lawyers and his previous Nullification position. At any rate, he never again ran for a legislative office.

Around 1829 Elliott began to submit a series of hunting and fishing stories to

John Skinner of Baltimore, who published the *American Turf Register and Sporting Magazine*. By 1843 he had also contributed similar pieces to the *Southern Literary Journal* and various Charleston newspapers, signing them with the pen names "Piscator" and "Venator." In 1846 he collected seven of these sketches and stories, along with six new ones, in a volume entitled *Carolina Sports by Land and Water*. This work was republished in 1850 with a new preface by Elliott. Another edition was printed in New York by Derby and Jackson in 1859, this one containing illustrations, a completely new chapter, and a revision of two others. The same volume was reprinted in London in 1867, and a third edition appeared in 1918 at Columbia, South Carolina, edited by Ambrose Elliott Gonzales, Elliott's grandson.

In 1850 Elliott tried his hand at writing a historical drama called *Fiesco: A Tragedy*. Printed privately in New York and distributed as gifts to some close friends, the five-act play, written in blank verse, tells the story of the unsuccessful effort of Giovanni Luigi Fiesco to usurp the throne of his uncle in Genoa. Elliott himself recognized the inadequacies of the play and acknowledged in a letter to his wife that it "does not become me!" (Jones, p. 381).

Elliott spent the rest of his life traveling, planting, lecturing, writing, and helping develop agricultural societies. By the early 1850s the issue of secession from the Union was again heating up, and he debated Robert Barnwell Rhett, a neighbor and opponent, in a series of public letters in the Charleston *Southern Standard*. These were eventually collected and published in 1852 as *The Letters of Agricola*.

Elliott traveled in 1853 and again in 1855 in Europe to learn about foreign cotton production, new agricultural techniques, and possible markets for Southern cotton. During the 1855 trip he represented South Carolina at the Universal Exhibition sponsored by Napoleon III in Paris, delivering an address about cotton to the Imperial Agricultural Society of France on 4 July. In 1857 he made a trip to Cuba to visit a daughter who had married Ambrosio Gonzales, a leader in the freedom movement. He reported his observations in a series of seven accounts published in *Russell's Magazine* during the latter part of 1857 and early 1858.

Though he opposed secession until late 1861, once the South declared war he took sides with the Confederacy, and his three sons volunteered. Despite his earlier opposition, it was natural for him to side with family and friends and with his native region. When federal troops took the coastal area around Beaufort in 1861, the plantations were confiscated and a federal direct tax was levied on all seized property. When the taxes went unpaid, for whatever reasons, the lands were either sold off to bidders, some white and some black, or held by the government itself. Elliott sent his wife and daughters to Flat Rock, North Carolina, and returned himself to Oak Lawn from where he tried to save as much property as he could. His home in Beaufort was ransacked in 1862, the Myrtle Bank plantation home and Oak Lawn homes were eventually burned, and most of the other land was confiscated. He died on 3 February 1863 on a trip to Charleston. He is buried at Magnolia Cemetery in Charleston.

In 1872 Congress passed special legislation permitting land owners to reclaim any land still under government possession by paying the old wartime tax plus interest. Elliott's widow tried to regain what had not been sold off in 1874, but much had already been disposed of by court order to pay cash bequests. Two of his daughters rebought Myrtle Bank at a sheriff's sale in 1884 for $1,000.

MAJOR THEMES

Elliott's public career divides itself into essentially agricultural, legislative, and literary interests.

Throughout his life he supported major reforms in agricultural policies and production and even chided his fellow planters for their shortsightedness. He suggested that greater crop diversity was absolutely essential for survival. He also urged the development of manufacturing as a way of broadening the economic structure of the state. At the same time, he was a spokesman for the planter class. Generally speaking, the emergence of new professional and business elites in Charleston and elsewhere was undermining the political and economic clout of the planters. In his exchange with Edmund Rhett in 1841 he argued that agriculture is the true basis of wealth.

Though he opposed Nullification and secession, he was also very orthodox in his views on slavery, believing in the gradual ameliorative effects of slavery upon the blacks and justifying the institution by the moral agruments commonly cited in that day.

In the *Address to the People of St. Helena Parish* Elliott sought to show that the effects of the tariff were not as bad as had been portrayed; it would be impossible to maintain free ports in South Carolina; Nullification would be a violation of the Constitution; and the federal government would have to intervene with force. Though a couple of commentators detect a tone of bitterness in the address, it is amazingly controlled and indicates Elliott's firm grasp of rhetorical principles. Besides marshaling factual evidence and structuring his points logically, he repeatedly tries to establish what Kenneth Burke has called "identification." He knows the concerns of his audience and addresses them skillfully, though the enthusiasm of the planters was so high for Nullification he could not dissuade them. Able to maintain a consistency of tone and perspective, he in some respects does his best writing in these kinds of essays.

The hunting and fishing stories collected in *Carolina Sports by Land and Water* are a mixture of chapters on fishing and hunting adventures enjoyed by the author and his friends, a hunting piece that is almost a short story, and a concluding essay on hunting rights. The longest is the devilfish chapter, which contains several accounts of fishing for the devilfish in the Port Royal River and around the islands near Beaufort. The large, winged fish, with a spread of as much as twenty feet, could be harpooned from a small boat. Swiftly accelerating, the fish would tow the boat around the harbor until it pulled free from the harpoon or beached itself, exhausted, upon the shore. Capturing such fish was mostly a sport for the planters, though the liver contained an oil that could be recovered and the fish could be used as fertilizer. The hunting section contains four small chapters on deer hunting at one of his plantations on a spot called Chee-ha, and these, along with "The Fire Hunter" story, are probably overall the best written.

One of the best assessments of Elliott's strengths and weaknesses as a writer is that by Louis D. Rubin, Jr., in his essay "William Elliott Shoots a Bear." Unfortunately, Elliott was not able to move beyond his unquestionably rhetorical sophistication and mild, genial irony or satire to let the narrative incidents resonate with some larger significance. Rubin attributes Elliott's limitations to either an unwillingness or an inability to confront the tensions, class frictions, and moral dilemmas inherent in a slaveholding, planter-class society. Elliott had a good eye for detail, a sound sense of narrative pacing, and the ability, though not fully developed, to handle narrative incident. In some of the narrative pieces perhaps the most awkward feature is Elliott's tendency to shift back and forth from direct to indirect personal address. Rubin's point is that whereas Faulkner could tell a bear-hunting story and let characters and plot function as a moving and insightful unveiling, Elliott's stories remain largely polished surface, satisfied with light humor and interesting incident.

SURVEY OF CRITICISM

For a relatively minor literary figure Elliott has had a surprising amount of investigative work devoted to him. Perhaps much of the more recent attention derives from his belonging to the planter aristocracy of South Carolina during a period of much interest to historians, though certainly his *Carolina Sports* is worthy of some consideration in its own right.

He had already gained attention in 1856, as his inclusion in the *Cyclopaedia of American Literature* indicates. A two-page entry by George Wauchope appeared in Edwin A. Alderman and Joel Chandler Harris's *The Library of Southern Literature*. Entries for Elliott also were included in the *Bibliographical Guide to the Study of Southern Literature* and *Southern Writers: A Biographical Dictionary*.

The first extensive examination was done by Lewis Pickney Jones, in a still quite useful article in the *Journal of Southern History* (1951) and then in a dissertation on the Elliott and Gonzales families (1952). Two years later Jay B. Hubbell devoted some four pages to a discussion of Elliott's biography and his major literary productions in *The South in American Literature* (1954).

B. N. Skardon, who also wrote the *Southern Writers* entry, completed an M.A. thesis on Elliott in 1964. A well-written summary of the contents of *Carolina Sports* appears in Charles A. Anderson's article on Thoreau's reactions to the book. James E. Kibler, Jr., wrote a full and helpful biographical entry for the *Dictionary of Literary Biography*, though in his eagerness to defend Elliott's literary abilities he takes perhaps unnecessary offense at Louis D. Rubin, Jr.'s "William Elliott Shoots a Bear," still the best single piece on Elliott.

The most extensive recent work on Elliott is by Beverly Scafidel, who wrote a dissertation on Elliott's letters (1978) and has published two articles since then. A book not exclusively about Elliott but one that contains information about the Elliott family and the settlement of Beaufort and Hilton Head is Virginia C. Holmgren's *Hilton Head: A Sea Island Chronicle* (Hilton Head, 1959).

BIBLIOGRAPHY

Works by William Elliott

"Reflections on the State of Our Agriculture in South Carolina." *Southern Agriculturist* 1 (1828): 61–66.
"On the Cultivation of Male Cotton." *Southern Agriculturist* 2 (1829): 354.
Address to the People of St. Helena Parish. Charleston: W. Estill, 1832.
"An Address Delivered Before the Beaufort (S.C.) Agricultural Society." *Southern Agriculturist* 11 (July 1838): 346–60.
Examination of Mr. Edmund Rhett's Agricultural Address. Charleston: A. E. Miller, 1841.
The Planter Vindicated: His Claims Examined—To be Considered a Producer: And Chief Tax-Payer of South Carolina. Charleston: Burges & James, 1842.
Carolina Sports by Land and Water. Charleston: Burges & James, 1846.
Anniversary Address of the State Agricultural Society of South Carolina, Delivered in . . . House of Representatives, 30 November 1848. Charleston, 1849.
Address Delivered by Special Request Before the St. Paul's Agricultural Society, May, 1850. Charleston: Agricultural Society, 1850.
Fiesco: A Tragedy. New York: Trehern & Williamson, 1850.
Letters of Agricola. Greenville, S.C.: Office of the Southern Patriot, 1852.
"Report of William Elliott, Commissioner of the State of South Carolina, to Gov. J. H. Adams." Charleston *Courier,* 29 January 1856.
Speech of Mr. Elliott before the Commercial Convention at Knoxville, Aug. 10, 1857. Columbia: Carolina Times, 1857.
"A Trip to Cuba." *Russell's Magazine* 2 (1857): 59–63, 116–23, 235–39, 322–27, 439–45, 536–43; 3 (1858): 60–69.

Studies of William Elliott

Albrecht, Frank. "William Elliott (1788–1863)." *A Bibliographical Guide to the Study of Southern Literature.* Ed. Louis D. Rubin, Jr. Baton Rouge: Louisiana State University Press, 1969, pp. 190–91.
Anderson, Charles. "Thoreau Takes a Pot Shot at *Carolina Sports.*" *Georgia Review* 22 (Fall 1968): 289–99.
Hubbell, Jay B. "William Elliott." *The South in American Literature, 1607–1900.* Durham, N.C.: Duke University Press, 1954, pp. 564–68.
Jones, Lewis Pickney. "Carolinians and Cubans: The Elliotts and Gonzales, Their Work and Their Writings." Ph.D. diss., University of North Carolina at Chapel Hill, 1952.
————. "William Elliott, South Carolina Nonconformist." *Journal of Southern History* 17 (August 1951): 361–81.

Kibler, James E., Jr. "William Elliott." *Antebellum Writers in New York and the South*. Ed. Joel Myerson. Vol. 3 of *Dictionary of Literary Biography*. Detroit: Gale Research, 1979, pp. 111–18.

Rubin, Louis D., Jr. "William Elliott Shoots a Bear." *William Elliott Shoots a Bear: Essays on the Southern Literary Imagination*. Baton Rouge: Louisiana State University Press, 1975, pp. 1–27.

Scafidel, Beverly. "The Author-Planter William Elliott (1788–1863)." *Proceedings of the South Carolina Historical Association, 1981*. Aiken, S.C.: South Carolina Historical Association, 1981.

———. "The Letters of William Elliott." Ph.D. diss., University of South Carolina, 1978.

———. "William Elliott, Planter and Politician: New Evidence from the Charleston Newspapers, 1831–1856." *South Carolina Journals and Journalists*. Ed. James B. Meriwether. Spartanburg, S.C.: Southern Studies Program of the University of South Carolina, 1975, pp. 109–19.

[Simms, William Gilmore]. "Carolina Sports." *Southern Quarterly Review* 12 (July 1847): 67–90.

Skardon, B. N. "William Elliott: Planter-Writer of Antebellum South Carolina." M.A. thesis, University of Georgia, 1964.

———. "William Elliott (1788–1863)." *Southern Writers: A Biographical Dictionary*. Ed. Robert Bain, Joseph M. Flora, and Louis D. Rubin, Jr. Baton Rouge: Louisiana State University Press, 1979, pp. 144–45.

Wauchope, George. "William Elliott." *The Library of Southern Literature*. Ed. Edwin A. Alderman and Joel Chandler Harris. Atlanta: Martin & Hoyt, 1907–1923. 4: 1569–70.

"William Elliott." *Cyclopaedia of American Literature*. Ed. Evert A. and George L. Duyckinck. Vol. 2. New York: Charles Scribner, 1856, pp. 100–103.

Will N. Harben
(1858–1919)

Will N. Harben was one of the most popular writers of fiction in America during the 1890s and the first two decades of the twentieth century. His popularity and prestige have declined drastically, but at his best he was a master interpreter of the mountaineers of north Georgia. He knew his native land intimately and wrote effectively and colorfully about it, its backwoods inhabitants and their customs, in numerous novels and short stories.

BIOGRAPHY

William Nathaniel Harben was born on 5 July 1858 near the Cohutta Mountains in Dalton, Georgia, which became the "Darley" of most of his novels. The Harbens were prominent citizens of Dalton, and Will was reared in a refined environment. An indifferent student in the local public schools, he claimed that he learned to write by studying the romantic tales of James Fenimore Cooper and then composing his own rousing stories for school assignments. His first attempt, "Old Buckskin, the Silent Hunter of the Great West," was written when he was twelve and made him a hero among his classmates.

At the age of twenty, Harben opened a general store, Harben's Emporium, where he met and became thoroughly acquainted with the mountain people he later vividly portrayed. The country store became an important fixture in practically every novel Harben wrote about his mountain friends. After seven years of merchandising, he sold the store in Dalton and moved to Denison, Texas, and then to Knoxville, Tennessee, where he opened novelty shops. The advertisements that he wrote for his shops attracted such attention that he began to channel his creativity toward the writing of short stories, several of which he sold to the Atlanta *Constitution*. The criticism and encouragement of Henry Grady, the newspaper's editor, and Joel Chandler Harris, its famed columnist, inspired Harben to submit his stories to national magazines. He later stated that Harris's encouragement in particular had helped him to decide on a literary career, "the most delightful profession known to workers." In 1888, at age thirty, Harben abandoned his business career to write full-time.

After a long trip to Europe in 1888 with his close friend, poet Robert Loveman of Dalton, Harben moved to New York City, which became his home base except for summer sojourns to Dalton to visit relatives and to gather new material for his works. One of his stories, "White Jane," had been published in the magazine *Youth's Companion* (where Harben later became an editor for several years), and his first novel, *White Marie*, was an expansion of this story. Based on an account of a slave of Harben's mother's family, the book concerns a white girl who is brought up as a black slave. Harben overwrote descriptive passages, created caricatures instead of characterizations, and gave ultracorrect, artificial dialogue to his aristocratic characters, but he showed strength by realistically reproducing mountaineer and black dialects and by authentically depicting rural customs of Georgia. Although *White Marie* is a curiosity today, it sold well when it was published in 1889, and it generated several heated arguments in national magazines and newspapers: Was it pro-slavery or anti-slavery? Quaintly typical or disgracefully atypical of the South? Harsh reality or glossy romance?

During the 1890s Harben experimented with several different types of novels: religious, romantic, science fiction, and detective. In 1891 the first of his works advocating a social gospel appeared. *Almost Persuaded* is generally effective, despite some unrealistic plot situations. Harben's theme is the contrast between theological dogma and personal character; he implies that non-Christians seem to do more for their fellow man than professing Christians. The novel was an international success; Queen Victoria requested an autographed copy, a request Harben eagerly granted.

When *A Mute Confessor* was published in 1892, critics praised it for its pleasant realism, and they pointed to Harben as the possible future author of the Great American Novel. But *A Mute Confessor* is one of the most hackneyed novels of Harben's career. The stale plot about a vain novelist from Massachusetts who is softened by the pristine love of a young belle from a small Georgia town is filled with forced, often unintentionally comic situations and contains more overdone, artificial dialogue of the learned characters.

The next two years were occupied with his editorship at *Youth's Companion* magazine, a long trip to England, the composition and sale of many short stories, and the completion of his fourth novel, *The Land of the Changing Sun*, his only work of science fiction. Published in 1894, this utopian novel, concerning two aeronauts who discover an underground civilization lighted by an electric sun, is so well constructed and entertaining that even today it is cited as one of the best early science fiction works; it was reprinted in 1975.

During summer 1896, when he was almost thirty-eight years old, Harben made one of his frequent visits to Dalton and married seventeen-year-old Maybelle Chandler, daughter of one of his former classmates. Their honeymoon trip was a tour of Europe, accompanied by Robert Loveman, and they made their permanent home in New York City.

Sherlock Holmes was at the height of popularity at this time, and Harben's remaining three novels of the decade were detective stories similar to Arthur Conan Doyle's tales. In each novel, Minard Hendricks is the scholarly, sophisticated sleuth; Dr. Lampkin, a hypnosis expert, is the Dr. Watson figure; and the dense police officers, simple clues, and logical solutions are all used. Harben's detective novels—*From Clue to Climax* (published in *Lippincott's Monthly Magazine*) in 1896, *The Caruthers Affair* in 1898, and *The North Walk Mystery* in 1899—are verbose but generally entertaining. They mirror one segment of public taste during the unsettling 1890s, as did all of Harben's novels during his experimental period.

Before the publication of his first novel in 1889, Harben was occupied with writing short stories. He continued to be especially prolific in this genre during the 1890s and was a popular contributor to leading periodicals of the day. Most of these short stories were local color sketches about his north Georgia region; with only a few exceptions, he wisely avoided stories of aristocrats. In 1900 Harben collected ten of his best stories in *Northern Georgia Sketches*, still considered one of the best collections of local color tales. Dedicated to Joel Chandler Harris, this modest book (reprinted in 1970) brought Harben instant recognition as a regional writer, and it marked a turning point in his career. William Dean Howells was so impressed with Harben's realistic storytelling ability that he became Harben's mentor and was responsible for Harben's long association with Harper and Brothers, Howells's own publisher. Howells's chief advice was to urge Harben to write about Georgia, the place he knew best, and the majority of Harben's remaining 23 novels of the twentieth century were, in fact, set in Georgia.

The Harbens settled into a comfortable life in New York, socializing with many of the leading literary figures of the day. Part of Harben's early life in the city is told in *The Woman Who Trusted* (1901), an entertaining and informative novel about an inexperienced Georgia writer struggling in New York. Harben's first novel to be published by Harper appeared in the same year. *Westerfelt* is full of vivid mountain characters and customs, and it has an intriguing plot. In it Harben had found his best subject: the plain, simple folk of Darley. With his first Harper novel, he put his knowledge of these people to work.

Abner Daniel (1902) became Harben's most popular book, and the title character was his most delightful creation; Harben used Abner, the Southern counterpart to David Harum, in several of his subsequent novels. Full of homespun Southern wisdom, Abner produces such lines as "The wust things I ever seed was sometimes at the root o' the best. Manure is a bad thing, but a cake of it will produce a daisy bigger 'n any in the field" (p. 81). Pole Baker, Abner's desperado friend, is equally memorable; when asked how he would like to die, Pole says, "Well, boys, ef I had to go, I'd like to be melted up into puore corn whiskey an' poured through my throat tell thar wasn't a drap left of me" (p. 299).

Harben used neither of these backwoods heroes in *The Substitute* (1903), a novel about the effects of guilt on a Darley man, but in *The Georgians* (1904) he put Uncle Abner through relentless detective work to save a friend from a murder conviction. Pole Baker returned in 1905 as the title character in *Pole Baker*, but he played a minor role in the surprisingly disappointing novel about lovers' mishaps in Darley.

Ann Boyd (1906) is perhaps Harben's most powerful book, offering a comprehensively gritty portrayal of a middle-aged heroine who was persecuted for twenty years after having been unjustly accused of adultery. Ann is the most fully drawn of Harben's mountaineers; she is a proud, bitter, and practical mountain woman. Lucille LaVerne dramatized the novel and played the leading role in a short-lived Broadway production in 1911.

In 1907 Harben took a stand on racial issues in *Mam' Linda*. Despite the unfortunate title, the novel clearly demonstrates Harben's message of equality of the races, especially through his liberal hero, a young lawyer of Darley, and through a forceful, outspoken minor character, a hill matron who defies and calms a mob through forthright, powerful logic. Impressed with Harben's views, President Theodore Roosevelt invited him to the White House to discuss the country's racial problems.

In *Gilbert Neal* (1908) Harben emphasized the ambition and sense of honor among poor mountaineers. It is a capable novel, unlike the one published the following year, *The Redemption of Kenneth Galt*, which is hackneyed nonsense. With *Kenneth Galt*, Harben began to alternate between realistic novels of merit and romantic trivialities. *Dixie Hart* (1910) is his most charming story. The plot is slight, but the title character, a young, feminine version of Abner Daniel, completely ingratiates herself with the reader. It was a splendid climax to Harben's most distinguished decade.

In 1910 and 1911 Harben used the pseudonym of Virginia Demarest for two sophomoric, sentimental potboilers, *The Fruit of Desire* and *Nobody's*, but he succeeded in 1911 with *Jane Dawson* because of his realistic picture of the cynical heroine-adulteress. Written under Harben's own name, this book, as *Almost Persuaded* was twenty years before, is a social gospel novel that depicts the spiritual unrest and religious concerns of the Georgia mountain people. *Paul Rundel* (1912) is an excessively somber, weak novel, and *The Desired Woman* (1913) contains maudlin situations written in a plodding style. Harben needed another success, so he brought back Abner Daniel and Pole Baker in his 1914 novel, *The New Clarion*; his strategy worked. These two pillars of the hills make this novel about Abner's ownership of the Darley newpaper a pleasant exception to Harben's growing list of failures. The first three sections of *The Inner Law* (1915) are effective, but the unabashed sentimentality of the last part of the novel weakens the work and turns it into bathos. *Second Choice* (1916) is a mediocre novel with some good character sketches overshadowed by a contrived plot line.

The novel that might have made Harben's literary reputation secure was *The

Triumph (1917), a historical novel set in pre–Civil War days, during the war, and in Reconstruction. The chief characters are the families of two brothers who are on opposing sides during the war. As it is, *The Triumph* is a believable, moving novel, one of Harben's best. If Harben had brought this work to a more finished artistic completion, it might have been a powerful, lasting narrative since it has all the epic ingredients. Although his next novel, *The Hills of Refuge* (1918), became a motion picture melodrama, it is a third-rate romance with no redeeming qualities. It was especially disappointing since it followed *The Triumph*.

Harben remained a popular celebrity in New York during his last years. As he grew older, his white hair and mustache, piercing brown eyes, and tall, slim build made him an even more striking figure than he had been as a young man. He was a member of the Authors Club and the National Institute of Arts and Letters, but he began to prefer mingling with the common people he met on the streets and in the parks of New York. After a sudden, brief illness, he died at his home in New York on 7 August 1919, at age sixty-one. He was buried in West Hill Cemetery in Dalton and was survived by his wife, Maybelle, and two children. His obituary in the *New York Times* accurately noted that "in his writings he remained faithful to the surroundings of his youth."

Harben's first posthumous novel was published in 1919, shortly after his death. *The Cottage of Delight* also became a motion picture, but this story of religious bigotry, although one of Hayden's personal favorites, is rather listless and outworn. *The Divine Event* (1920), an inferior work, begins as a story about mystical experiences and ends as a routine detective tale. The last decade of Harben's life had produced some of his worst novels, one of his finest, and several respectable ones.

MAJOR THEMES

From the beginning of his career to the end, Harben's writings were curious mixtures of romanticism and realism. As a novelist who desired popular success, he satisfied readers' cravings for conventional, romantic stories with stereotyped heroes and heroines. Such sentimentality is common to most local colorists who attempt to capture quaint and charming worlds, but Harben's local color assumed a truer tone when he wrote of his hill people, for he revealed their normal, unglamorous lives. He treated them seriously, seeing in them a self-reliance and perseverance that would lead to better lives for their descendants. Most of them were based on actual people whom Harben knew, so his Georgians are not merely colorful hillbillies in romantic vignettes; they are accurate depictions of enterprising, honest, and proud Americans ambitious to improve their lot in life.

One source of pride for these mountain people was their fundamentalist religion, and most of them held fast to the accepted orthodoxy of their community. Some, however, rebelled against such strict beliefs and searched for a less dogmatic faith. Stanley Clayton (*Almost Persuaded*), Abner Daniel, George

Dawson (*Jane Dawson*), and John Trott (*The Cottage of Delight*) represent society's (and Harben's) conflict with religious issues; they are individuals who will not embrace a faith they cannot believe in. Often, the extreme individualism or rebellion of such characters leads to isolation from the community. These isolated characters are sometimes lonely, but they are always proud, and their isolation does not result from religious differences alone. Ann Boyd and Jane Dawson are outsiders because of youthful sexual indiscretions, yet they maintain dignity in their isolation. Carson Dwight (*Mam' Linda*) and Andrew Merlin (*The Triumph*) are shunned for political views; both are champions of rights for blacks. This isolation, whether caused by religious, social, or political beliefs, is common in many of Harben's characters.

Harben's attitude toward blacks was ambiguous early in his career. He knew that the Southern mistreatment of freed blacks was wrong, yet he frequently depicted his black characters as old-fashioned "darkies," endowing them with shuffles, eye-rollings, and servile gestures. But in 1907, with the publication of *Mam' Linda*, Harben committed himself to the side of equal rights and never strayed from this position, even though some Southerners considered him a traitor. Thus Harben was able to look beyond strictly regional concerns.

The author of 30 novels and numerous short stories, Harben wrote too much. There is merit in most of his work, but because of the excessive sentimentality in some dialogue, plots, and characters, he could never be considered a major writer. Nevertheless, his honesty and sincerity in depicting the people and customs of his own north Georgia region enabled him to make a distinct contribution, however minor, to American literature.

SURVEY OF CRITICISM

Since Harben's writing is generally neglected, little recent criticism has been written about his work. In his own day, his books were reviewed regularly by major newspapers and magazines, and several articles and interviews concerning Harben appeared sporadically, including an appreciative but honest analysis of his works by William Dean Howells in 1910 in *North American Review*. In his 1917 book, *Literature in the Making by Some of Its Makers*, Joyce Kilmer devoted a chapter to Harben, chiefly in Harben's own words, about the writing of novels and their current state in America.

Because Harben left no personal papers, biographical information is scarce, but there exist several unpublished works about him, including two handwritten volumes of his sister's memoirs containing insights into his early life.

Robert Bush began the Harben "revival" in 1967 in an article in *Mississippi Quarterly*; this essay is the most perceptive discussion of Harben's work to date. It led to renewed interest in Harben in a 1972 article about *Land of the Changing Sun* by Kenneth M. Roemer and to two articles by James K. Murphy in 1975, one dealing with Harben's mountain characters, and one about Harben's "Virginia Demarest" novels. Murphy also wrote for the Twayne series the only book on Harben (1979); this overview of Harben's works also has a bibliography that includes some of the minor sources dealing with Harben.

BIBLIOGRAPHY

Works by Will N. Harben

White Marie: A Story of Georgia Plantation Life. New York: Cassell, 1889.
Almost Persuaded. New York: Minerva, 1891.
A Mute Confessor: The Romance of a Southern Town. Boston: Arena, 1892.
The Land of the Changing Sun. New York: Merriam, 1894; Boston: Gregg Press, 1975; New York: AMS Press, 1975.
"From Clue to Climax." *Lippincott's Monthly Magazine* 57 (June 4, 1896): 737–816.
The Caruthers Affair. London and New York: F. Tennyson Neely, 1898.
The North Walk Mystery. New York: Street and Smith, 1899.
Northern Georgia Sketches. Chicago: A. C. McClurg, 1900; Freeport, N.Y.: Books for Libraries Press, 1970.
Westerfelt: A Novel. New York and London: Harper, 1901.
The Woman Who Trusted: A Story of Literary Life in New York. Philadelphia: H. Altemus, 1901.
Abner Daniel. New York and London: Harper, 1902.
The Substitute. New York and London: Harper, 1903.
The Georgians: A Novel. New York and London: Harper, 1904.
Pole Baker: A Novel. New York and London: Harper, 1905.
Ann Boyd. New York and London: Harper, 1906.
Mam' Linda. New York and London: Harper, 1907.
Gilbert Neal: A Novel. New York and London: Harper, 1908.
The Redemption of Kenneth Galt. New York and London: Harper, 1909.
Dixie Hart. New York and London: Harper, 1910.
The Fruit of Desire. Published under the name "Virginia Demarest." New York and London: Harper, 1910.
Jane Dawson: A Novel. New York and London: Harper, 1911.
Nobody's. Published under the name "Virginia Demarest." New York and London: Harper, 1911.
Paul Rundel: A Novel. New York and London: Harper, 1912.
The Desired Woman. New York and London: Harper, 1913.
The New Clarion: A Novel. New York and London: Harper, 1914.
The Inner Law. New York and London: Harper, 1915.
Second Choice: A Romance. New York and London: Harper, 1916.
The Triumph: A Novel. New York and London: Harper, 1917.
The Hills of Refuge. New York and London: Harper, 1918.
The Cottage of Delight. New York and London: Harper, 1919.
The Divine Event. New York and London: Harper, 1920.

Studies of Will N. Harben

Bush, Robert. "Will N. Harben's Northern Georgia Fiction." *Mississippi Quarterly* 20 (Spring 1967): 103–17.

Howells, William Dean. "Mr. Harben's Georgia Fiction." *North American Review* 191
    (March 1910): 356–63.
Kilmer, Joyce, ed. *Literature in the Making by Some of Its Makers*. New York: Harper,
    1917.
Murphy, James K. "The Backwoods Characters of Will N. Harben." *Southern Folklore
    Quarterly* 39 (September 1975): 291–96.
———. *Will N. Harben*. Boston: Twayne, 1979.
———. "Will N. Harben's 'Virginia Demarest' Novels: An Addendum." *Mississippi
    Quarterly* 29 (Winter 1975–76): 105–8.
Roemer, Kenneth M. "1984 in 1894: Harben's *Land of the Changing Sun*." *Mississippi
    Quarterly* 26 (Winter 1972–73): 28–42.

George Washington Harris
(1814–1869)

Even though his name has by no means become widely known among general readers, George Washington Harris of Tennessee has always had his following. During the late 1850s when he was doing his best writing for Southern newspapers and New York journals, an editor friend who had brought a good deal of his work into print could write that Harris's tales "have obtained a circulation and popularity, throughout the country, which no similar productions in modern times have enjoyed. . . . His stories are sought with avidity wherever genuine wit and humor are appreciated." When Harris's one book appeared in 1867, an admiring young reviewer named Mark Twain predicted that it would be too bawdy for Eastern tastes, which proved to be true, but the book enjoyed an underground reputation for a hundred years as dog-eared copies passed from father to son and countless reprints were quietly sold in brown paper wrappers. Copies found their way into the hands of prominent writers—William Faulkner, Flannery O'Connor, Robert Penn Warren, and Stark Young were among those to read and pay tribute to the artistry of Harris. In the past twenty years numerous critics have set out to elucidate the complex qualities of his comic genius, but we have only begun to understand the exact nature of his accomplishment in narrative strategy and his control of the American vernacular as a source of action, imagery, and symbolism.

BIOGRAPHY

George Washington Harris was born 20 March 1814 in Allegheny City, Pennsylvania, near Pittsburgh, but at a very early age he was brought by his half-brother to Knoxville, a center for trade and industrialization on the Tennessee River. After seeing the first steamboat to reach Knoxville in 1826, the twelve-year-old Harris reproduced it in a mechanical model that sailed in a local pond to the amazement of the townspeople. His exposure to school and formal education was brief before he was apprenticed to learn metalworking and developed skills in making jewelry and silverware, repairing timepieces and weapons, and building machinery.

His fascination with steamboats led him, after finishing his apprenticeship at age nineteen, to become captain of the steamboat *Knoxville*, which suggests considerable earlier experience on the river. As Mark Twain would point out, this was an exalted position for a young man, and it indicates an early aspiration to achieve professional and social respectability. He married the daughter of the inspector for the Port of Knoxville and owner of a racetrack, where he acquired experience with horses and racing, and continued on the river until 1838. He would always be known thereafter as Captain Harris.

As the family expanded (six children would eventually be born), Harris tried the life of the gentleman farmer in 1839 by purchasing 375 acres of land in the foothills of the Great Smoky Mountains. With three slaves, fine furniture, and a library of 75 books, Harris must have pursued more leisure than labor, since the note on the loan to buy the farm was foreclosed and by February 1843 he was back in Knoxville operating a metalworking shop, a trade for which there was always a market. Although the shop lasted for seven years, Harris was never thereafter to experience much stability or continuity in his life as he moved through a series of jobs and unsuccessful ventures.

The details are sketchy, but we know that he was superintendent of the Holston Glass Works in 1849, captain of the steamboat *Alida* in 1854, owner of a sawmill that failed, and surveyor for the newly explored copper mines at Ducktown, Tennessee, where he first met Sut Miller, the model for his fictional creation Sut Lovingood. During the political ferment of 1856 in Tennessee, he joined the Democratic party, was alderman from the Fourth Ward of Knoxville, and was a delegate to the Southern Commercial Convention in Savannah. He was appointed postmaster of Knoxville for only six months in 1857 and in 1859 was sent to Nashville to attend the state Democratic convention, where he was elected to the state Central Committee. Harris stayed on in Nashville to work for the Nashville and Chattanooga Railroad until the city was occupied by the Union troops in 1862.

During the Civil War he moved with his family to several Southern cities in Tennessee, Alabama, and Georgia. The postwar period was a bitter time for a man of Harris's ardent sentiments, but he went to work on one final business venture and bought the right-of-way for the Wills Valley Railroad then under construction. His first wife died in 1867, and he remarried an attractive widow just two months before his own death on 10 December 1869. Harris died under mysterious circumstances while returning by train from a business trip to Lynchburg, Virginia.

MAJOR THEMES

If the exterior facts of George Washington Harris's life are sketchy and incomplete, the interior life of his imagination was richly and thoroughly preserved in his writings. Except for the books he owned, there was little in his background or experience to encourage him to become a writer. References in his work suggest that he read, besides the Bible, William Shakespeare, Charles Dickens, Alexander Pope, William Congreve, Lord Byron, Robert Burns, Elizabeth Barrett Browning, and Henry Wadsworth Longfellow. Literary affinities suggest that he must have known Miguel Cervantes, François Rabelais, and Jonathan Swift. Whatever inspired Harris, his becoming a writer seems to have been a matter of incidental opportunity. He never pursued it as a profession.

It was politics that first moved Harris to write several political sketches for the Knoxville Democratic organ *Argus and Commercial Herald* in the 1840s while he was farming (no one has succeeded in identifying which contributions were his). Then he turned to that other major masculine preoccupation of the time, sports, and wrote a series of letters for the New York *Spirit of the Times* sporting journal about quarter horse racing, hunting, drinking, and partying in East Tennessee. The local color and lively style of these early efforts, otherwise undistinguished, soon earned for Harris some reputation as a writer and further invitations to publish.

Seeking a suitable content and form for his talent, he next turned to full sketches and tales about life and incidents in the Tennessee backwoods. This turning was first prompted in 1845 by a *Spirit of the Times* correspondent from Mississippi who accused East Tennesseans of having no amusements outside politics and religion. Harris responded with ''The Knob Dance—A Tennessee Frolic,'' in which he created a fictional character to describe an extravagant neighborhood party from his own point of view and in his own native dialect, crucial devices for the later fiction. In this and the sketches to follow, Harris was opening up new literary territory by his imaginative handling of the rich texture of folk speech to describe backwoods America in joyful pursuit of food, dancing, women, and fighting for the pure fun of it. These pieces appeared in the *Spirit of the Times* as well as in papers in Nashville and Knoxville.

Harris hit his stride and achieved literary distinction when he published in the *Spirit of the Times* for 4 November 1854 ''Sut Lovingood's Daddy, Acting Horse.'' Sut Lovingood stepped onto the stage of American literature full-blown, a Tennessee backwoods individualist and crude philosopher who would play the roles of trickster and fool in working out a series of disastrous pranks and retributive schemes against the hypocritical society around him. The technique of allowing Sut to speak for himself in his own dialect had been used earlier by Harris, but this time he created a continuing personality for Sut consistent from tale to tale in accordance with the integrity of his own independence of thought and action. In other words, Harris discovered on his own the aesthetic values of the first person point of view in fiction and the remarkable flexibility of American language and dialect as a tool in literary narrative. Mark Twain would learn these lessons well from Harris and put them to effective use in his *Adventures of Huckleberry Finn*.

During the remaining fifteen years of his life, Harris would publish primarily stories about Sut, either as straight humorous tales or as symbolic political satires, mostly in Nashville, Knoxville, Chattanooga, and New York papers. A collection entitled *Sut Lovingood. Yarns Spun by a "Nat'ral Born Durn'd Fool"* was published by Dick & Fitzgerald of New York in 1867. Just before his death, Harris had completed a second manuscript to be called "High Times and Hard Times," but it was lost and has never been recovered. In addition to the 24 stories collected in *Sut Lovingood. Yarns*, the known canon of Harris's work includes at least another 48 separately published pieces. His claim to the attention of posterity resides in this slim body of writing, and especially his creation of Sut Lovingood.

What makes the character of Sut both attractive and repellent is the combination in his nature of such human failings as vulgarity, cowardice, bigotry, and brutality along with the admirable trait of steadfast opposition to dishonesty, hypocrisy, and abuse of authority. Sut appeals to readers who enjoy seeing hypocritic sinners revealed and those who abuse the innocent and the impotent appropriately if brutally punished. He has been seen by some critics to represent a spirit of rough justice or homespun retribution, although there is no conscious aim on his part to rectify the wrongs of the world. His aim is to cause trouble and have fun.

Although most readers would be against the same things that Sut opposes, what he stands for can be disturbing, depending on one's point of view. Sut represents a total rejection of all restraints on personal and social freedom. From the very first yarn, in which he takes delight in seeing his naked father nearly killed by a nest of hornets, Sut struggles against and overcomes not only parental authority but nearly every other type of authority essential to civilization—civil, social, natural, and religious. The irony is that in his personal life, George Washington Harris was politically reactionary and religiously conservative. Through his writings, he attacked reformers, abolitionists, transcendentalists, New England Yankees, Radical Republicans, industrialism, education, and progress. Yet he invested Sut with the kind of freedom that borders on anarchy and sometimes moves beyond the limitations of morality and good sense.

Despite his seemingly superior point of view that places him above normal restraints, Sut never sees himself as a superior person. Quite the opposite is the case. He engages in the most extreme forms of self-deprecation: "Did yu ever see sich a sampil of a human afore?" he asks. "I feel like I'd be glad *tu be* dead, only I'se feard ove the dyin. I don't keer fur herearter, fur hits onpossibil fur me to hev ara soul. Who ever seed a soul in jis' sich a rack heap ove bones an' rags es this? I's nuffin but sum newfangil'd sort ove beas', a sorter cross atween a crazy ole monkey an' a durn'd wore-out hominy-mill." Rather than dwell upon his inadequacies and those of the absurd world around him, Sut pursues with ardor what pleasures life has to offer: "Man wer made a-purpus jis' to eat, drink, and fur stayin awake in the yearly part ove the nites, an' wimen were made to cook the vittils, mix the sperits, an help the men du the stayin awake." Good food, strong liquor, and plenty of sex are Sut's main concerns as he moves through the boisterous, violent society of nineteenth-century Tennessee. Like his literary descendant Huckleberry Finn, Sut celebrates life by remaining high-spirited and free in a world where corruption and gullibility all too often prevail.

SURVEY OF CRITICISM

In the process of establishing the foundations for modern scholarship in American literary humor in the 1930s, Franklin J. Meine, Constance Rourke, and Walter Blair all pointed out the importance of Harris's work, as did F. O. Matthiessen, whose few pages devoted to Harris in *American Renaissance* (1941) constitute the first effort to define his artistry. The first extensive biographical and critical work on Harris was completed in 1942 by Donald Day for his doctoral dissertation at the University of Chicago, from which he drew three definitive essays on the humor, satire, and life of Harris.

Norris W. Yates's standard study of the *Spirit of the Times*, where much of Harris's work appeared, and Kenneth S. Lynn's contested exploration of Mark Twain's backgrounds in the humor of the Old Southwest added valuable information during the 1950s. The liveliest debate, however, was instigated by Brom Weber's 1954 edition of the Sut stories translated into modern English to escape the impediments of the original dialect. So stirred was Edmund Wilson that he attacked both the editor for what he saw as a desecration of the text and Harris for the cruel and sadistic elements in his fiction. While Wilson found the style and language admirable, he felt Sut to be squalid and the yarns to be morally questionable.

The 1960s were particularly good years for Harris scholarship. Milton Rickels expanded on his excellent essay of 1959 on imagery in the Sut Lovingood yarns to produce the only single-volume and still the best critical study of Harris in print. Ben Harris McClary edited four annual issues of *The Lovingood Papers* between 1962 and 1965, reprinting some of the uncollected yarns with scholarly introductions; the volumes contain valuable critical essays. After publication of his essay on parallels between the fiction of Harris and William Faulkner, M. Thomas Inge edited *Sut Lovingood's Yarns* (1966) and *High Times and Hard Times* (1967). Edited according to traditional patterns rather than the new principles of textual scholarship then under development, the texts have not been found satisfactory by everyone. Although undiscovered tales undoubtedly exist in nineteenth-century newspapers (there are evidences of a few), nothing of any significance has been added to the Harris canon since the Inge editions were published.

Critical debate about the meaning and morality of Sut Lovingood intensified during the 1970s. Elmo Howell found Sut to be "inspired by right reason in human conduct" (p. 319), and Eugene Current-Garcia concluded that the ribald and repellent qualities of Sut and his world symbolized "the old South's vigor and fertility" (p. 129). In their study of American humor, Walter Blair and Hamlin Hill applied such epithets to the vision of Harris as "amoral" and "even fatalistic and anarchical'' (pp. 213–14). Lewis Leary contributed a playfully suggestive essay on Sut's literary relations; Ormonde Plater wrote two interesting studies of folklore in the early works and the sexual imagery in the Sut yarns, and Stephen M. Ross probed with intriguing results more deeply into parallels between Faulkner and the Harris school of humor. Noel Polk, however, came down on all fours against nearly everything that had previously been done or said about Harris, both the editing and the criticism. Rickels, Inge, and all the rest were either simplistic, wrongheaded, or both. Polk saw no redemption in Harris's vision; man appears hell-bent on self-destruction; and the *Yarns* is a pessimistic book, ''among the darkest in nineteenth century American literature'' (p. 49). On the positive side, Polk wants to make out a case for it as ''a major work of American fiction'' (p. 49), to which he might have more profitably devoted his attention.

The 1980s have brought new and interesting reassessments of Harris and his formidable creation, Sut Lovingood, among them Robert Micklus's appreciation of the use of creative repetition as a comic technique in the yarns and Milton Rickels's careful analysis of the differences between what Harris published in newspapers and what he prepared for book publication, particularly in the comparative use of the grotesque. Rickels and Robert Bain each also contributed useful essays on Harris's life and work to separate volumes of the *Dictionary of Literary Biography*. Despite the growing body of commentary (and additional materials can be found in the bibliographies and footnotes in all of the above), the final meaning of the yarns, the nature of Sut's character, and the qualities of Harris's fictional artistry are only beginning to come to light. The sometimes sharp diversity of opinion may be taken as a tribute to the actual complexity of his achievement.

BIBLIOGRAPHY

Works by George Washington Harris

Sut Lovingood. Yarns Spun by a "Nat'ral Born Durn'd Fool." New York: Dick & Fitzgerald, 1867.

Sut Lovingood: Travels with Old Abe Lincoln. Ed. Edd Winfield Parks. Chicago: Black Cat Press, 1937.

Sut Lovingood. Ed. Brom Weber. New York: Grove Press, 1954.

Sut Lovingood's Yarns. Ed. M. Thomas Inge. New Haven, Conn.: College & University Press, 1966.

High Times and Hard Times. Ed. M. Thomas Inge. Nashville: Vanderbilt University Press, 1967.

Studies of George Washington Harris

Bain, Robert. "George Washington Harris." *Antebellum Writers in New York and the South.* Ed. Joel Myerson. Vol. 3 of *Dictionary of Literary Biography*. Detroit: Gale Research, 1979, pp. 138–43.

Blair, Walter. *Native American Humor, 1800–1900*. New York: American Book, 1937, pp. 96–101.

Blair, Walter and Hamlin Hill. *America's Humor: From Poor Richard to Doonesbury*. New York: Oxford University Press, 1978, pp. 213–21.

Current-Garcia, Eugene. "Sut Lovingood's Rare Ripe Southern Garden." *Studies in Short Fiction* 9 (Spring 1972): 117–29.

Day, Donald. "The Humorous Works of George Washington Harris." *American Literature* 14 (January 1943): 391–406.

———. "The Life of George Washington Harris." *Tennessee Historical Quarterly* 6 (March 1947): 3–38.

———. "The Political Satires of George Washington Harris." *Tennessee Historical Quarterly* 4 (December 1945): 320–38.

Howell, Elmo. "Timon in Tennessee: The Moral Fervor of George Washington Harris." *Georgia Review* 24 (Fall 1970): 311–19.

Inge, M. Thomas. "William Faulkner and George Washington Harris: In the Tradition of Southwestern Humor." *Tennessee Studies in Literature* 7 (1962): 47–59.

Leary, Lewis. *Southern Excursions: Essays on Mark Twain and Others*. Baton Rouge: Louisiana State University Press, 1971, pp. 111–30.

Lynn, Kenneth S. *Mark Twain and Southwestern Humor*. Boston: Little, Brown, 1959.

McClary, Ben Harris, ed. *The Lovingood Papers*. 4 vols. Knoxville: University of Tennessee Press, 1962–65.

Matthiessen, F. O. *American Renaissance*. New York: Oxford University Press, 1941, pp. 641–45.

Meine, Franklin J., ed. *Tall Tales of the Southwest*. New York: Alfred A. Knopf, 1930.

Micklus, Robert. "Sut's Travels with Dad." *Studies in American Humor* n.s. 1 (October 1982): 89–101.

Plater, Ormonde. "Before Sut: Folklore in the Early Works of George Washington Harris." *Southern Folklore Quarterly* 34 (June 1970): 104–15.

———. "The Lovingood Patriarchy." *Appalachian Journal* 1 (Spring 1973): 82–93.

Polk, Noel. "The Blind Bull, Human Nature: Sut Lovingood and the Damned Human Race." *Gyascutus: Studies in Antebellum Southern Humorous and Sporting Writing*. Ed. James L. W. West III. Atlantic Highlands, N.J.: Humanities Press, 1978, pp. 13–49.

Rickels, Milton. *George Washington Harris*. New York: Twayne, 1965.

———. "George Washington Harris." *American Humorists, 1800–1950*. Ed. Stanley Trachtenberg. Vol. 11 of *Dictionary of Literary Biography*. Detroit: Gale Research, 1982. Part 1, pp. 180–89.

———. "George Washington Harris's Newspaper Grotesques." *University of Mississippi Studies in English* n.s. 2 (1981): 15–24.

———. "The Imagery of George Washington Harris." *American Literature* 31 (May 1959): 173–87.

Ross, Stephen M. "Jason Compson and Sut Lovingood: Southwestern Humor as Stream of Consciousness." *Studies in the Novel* 8 (Fall 1976): 278–90.

Rourke, Constance. *American Humor*. New York: Harcourt, Brace, 1931.

Wilson, Edmund. "Poisoned!" *New Yorker* 31 (7 May 1955): 150–49. Repr. in *Patriotic Gore: Studies in the Literature of the American Civil War*. New York: Oxford University Press, 1962.

Yates, Norris W. *William T. Porter and the "Spirit of the Times": A Study of the Big Bear School of Humor*. Baton Rouge: Louisiana State University Press, 1957.

LUCINDA H. MACKETHAN

Joel Chandler Harris (1848–1908)

Joel Chandler Harris's reputation rests on his creation of Uncle Remus and his character's unique manner of rendering the Afro-American trickster figure, Brer Rabbit. Far more than simply a transcriber of tales, Harris was particularly careful in matters of both setting and dialect and designed his work to respond to the world of the postbellum South that he helped to shape.

BIOGRAPHY

Joel Chandler Harris was born on 9 December 1848 in the small, middle Georgia town of Eatonton. This area had already produced a number of southwestern humorists (Augustus Baldwin Longstreet, William Tappan Thompson, Charles Henry Smith, and Richard Malcolm Johnston) whose work Harris would assimilate. Harris was illegitimate and never knew his father, an Irish laborer who deserted shortly after he was born. His mother, Mary Harris, gained the respect of the people of Eatonton through her work as a seamstress. Harris often led his peers in good-natured pranks that made him a town favorite, yet then, as afterward, his outgoing behavior contrasted with other qualities—problems with stuttering, embarrassment over his short stature and his bright red hair, a horror of strangers, and feelings of self-consciousness, if not rejection, because of his background. He had a close relationship throughout his life with his mother, who introduced him to the stories of a rich, oral Southern tradition as well as to formal literature, reading to him from *The Vicar of Wakefield* and other classics. Her economic dependence on him meant that after a few years in local schools, his tuition paid in part by a charitable townsman, Harris had to go to work. The job that he found at age fourteen as a printer's devil on a country newspaper was one that he turned into a lifelong vocation.

Harris went to work at Turnwold plantation for Joseph Addison Turner, an energetic, intellectual planter who, in addition to publishing a weekly paper, the *Countryman*, made hats for the Confederate army and managed his extensive lands with the labor of 25 slaves. As an editor he displayed a fierce sectional pride and a commitment to the world of letters. The four years 1862–66, which brought violence and destruction to the South, were among the most tranquil, yet stimulating, that Harris would ever know. He learned every aspect of the printer's trade, he was encouraged to read in Turner's extensive library, and he witnessed firsthand plantation life. By the time that the Yankees marched by Turnwold, late in the war, Harris knew how to set type, how to write book reviews and poems (mostly bad), and most important in the long run, how to befriend Turner's slaves and listen to their stories. Both Turner and some of the old black uncles on the plantation doubtless acted as father figures and mentors. In his ambivalent position between master and slaves, Harris developed toward the antebellum South attitudes that provide persistent tension in his writing. He saw the lost plantation world as a benevolent, paternal society yet also saw slaves as people who did not conform to the image of helplessness and inferiority ascribed to them, and he knew himself to be an outsider who fit nowhere in the arrangement of social hierarchies in the Old South.

When the war's outcome forced Turner to suspend his operations, Harris was ready for the world. For the next ten years he worked as typesetter, then printer, then editor on newspapers throughout the South, first in Macon, then in New Orleans, then in Forsyth, Georgia, and in Savannah, where in 1873 he married a vivacious Catholic girl, Esther La Rose, the daughter of a French-Canadian couple. During these years the humorous paragraphs that he penned for his papers began to receive admiring coverage throughout the state, so that when he took his young family to Atlanta to escape a yellow fever epidemic, he was offered a position on one of the South's most prestigious papers, the Atlanta *Constitution*.

By 1876, when Harris moved to Atlanta, both he and the city that was to be his permanent home were in positions of great potential. Harris, at the apex of a journalistic career, had assembled all the ingredients that he would soon need in an even more publicly rewarding profession. Atlanta had made a remarkable recovery from its destruction in 1864; it was the fastest-growing city in the Southeast, full of opportunities, opportunities the *Constitution* promoted in its New South philosophy. Harris's coeditor, Henry Grady, was the apostle of a gospel of progress and spoke eloquently for the merits of industry and nationalism. Harris in this atmosphere found another set of oppositions in his life; as his shyness competed with his craving for attention and his pleasant plantation memories competed with what he knew of the wrongs of slavery, so now his exposure to the improvements that industry could bring to the South warred with his loyalty to the agrarian scenes of his boyhood. Harris reconciled himself to life in the city in part by posturing as a country fellow, "a cornfield journalist," who would call his home the "Wren's Nest" or "Snap Bean Farm" and who would wear old-timey broad-brimmed hats in his office.

Harris never took up the economic cause of the New South in Grady's manner. He did, however, write about the need for a new kind of Southern literature and took the step that would make him a practitioner of it when, during his first year on the *Constitution* staff, he filled in for a regular humor columnist with some sketches of a black uncle who spoke in the dialect Harris had heard in Putnam County. One of the earliest of these sketches, "Jeems Robinson," appeared on 26 October 1876 and is of special note because it contains the prototype of the Uncle Remus who would soon take over Harris's imagination. At first this old man was conceived as an Atlanta "darky," a refugee from the country not unlike Harris himself, who could be heard pontificating comically on political problems or social habits of the city. The plantation Uncle Remus appeared full-blown in October 1877 in a story called "Uncle Remus as a Rebel."

By 1878 Harris was regularly contributing sketches using the Atlanta "darky" Remus, but he was also trying out another literary form with a novel of Georgia crackers entitled *The Romance of Rockville*, which was serialized in the *Weekly Constitution* for several months. His editorials of the period offered significant commentary on two subjects in particular, Southern race relations and the potential for a regional literature that would be national in its appeal. His research in both of these areas might have been what led him to read a December 1878 *Lippincott's* article by William Owens entitled "Folklore of the Southern Negroes," which included a version of the Tar Baby story. Through this avenue he was led back to his plantation Uncle Remus, who told his first animal fable, "The Story of Mr. Rabbit and Mr. Fox," in the *Constitution* on 20 July 1879. The framework elements of this sketch became the staple for all of the later ones: an old "faithful retainer" storyteller, a little boy listener, the backdrop of a cabin near the Big House, and the aura of slave songs and happy, family-style relations between master and slaves. The folklore elements immediately attracted the attention of scholars, so Harris began to take care to authenticate the fables and the dialect of their tellers. So popular were these sketches that in 1880 Harris was able to collect them, with new materials, into his first book, *Uncle Remus: His Songs and His Sayings*. Although the book bears the date 1881, it actually appeared in November 1880 in order to capitalize on the Christmas trade. Attracting a market proved no problem, for the book sold ten thousand copies in its first four months.

Harris had found the formula for success by combining the tales with frames dominated by an old man who could be both simple and wily, both shuffling and wise, like the rabbit who was his hero. Calling himself only a "compiler," Harris avowed (in a letter to Mark Twain) that it was "the matter and not the manner" that attracted attention to his work. Yet fitting an appropriate narrator to subtle folk materials constituted Harris's greatest gift, and despite his disclaimers, he was deeply concerned to create the right effect. His introduction to the first collection emphasized that he hoped "to give vivid hints of the really poetic imagination of the Negro" and to suggest his "curious exaltation of mind and temperament." Uncle Remus developed from the minstrel buffoon of the earliest *Constitution* sketches into a powerful propaganda weapon, Harris's own answer, as he said in his introduction, to Harriet Beecher Stowe. He was eager to bring out a second collection, which appeared prefaced by an essay on folklore in 1883 as *Nights with Uncle Remus*. Harris had no choice but to join the ranks of the famous and soon found them, in the persons of Mark Twain, Eugene Field, and Rudyard Kipling, paying their respects to his genius.

Though he called himself "An Accidental Author" in a biographical essay published by *Lippincott's* in April 1886, this image is belied by his almost nonstop production of works between 1881 and 1900. Twenty different books appeared in that twenty-year period while Harris continued to work full-time on the *Constitution* staff. In addition to the first two Uncle Remus collections, he brought out two more, *Daddy Jake the Runaway* (1889) and *Uncle Remus and His Friends* (1892). Collections of non-Remus stories using black characters and folk materials appeared with *Mingo and Other Sketches* (1884), *Free Joe and Other Georgian Sketches* (1887), *Balaam and His Master* (1891), and *The Chronicles of Aunt Minervy Ann* (1899). The stories in these books give us a gallery of black characters who range from childlike clowns to tragic mulattoes to devoted, doglike slaves, to shrewd, enterprising freedmen and freedwomen.

In Harris's other major topical category, he put together stories of the white yeoman folk, beginning with his autobiographically based novel, *Sister Jane*, in 1896. This poorly organized effort was followed by other collections of middle Georgia scenes, *Tales of the Home Folks in Peace and War* (1898) and *On the Wing of Occasions* (1900), which used for the first time the "cracker" persona, Billy Sanders. The latter collection contained a popular story, "The Kidnapping of President Lincoln," first published in the *Saturday Evening Post*. Harris's love of children and childhood manifested itself in a series of five adventure books that he wrote during these years. Another book for young readers, the idealized narrative of his time at Turnwold, *On the Plantation*, was published in 1892. During the 1890s he attempted a tale of an African prince loyal to the colonies during the American Revolution, but he seems to have found that he could not master materials from the distant past, and *Qua: A Romance of the Revolution*, remained unfinished. And still he found time to create a juvenile history reader (*Stories of Georgia*, 1896), to edit in 1890 a biography commemorating the untimely death of Henry Grady, and to help his wife with a translation of French folktales (*Evening Tales*, 1893).

During the last two decades of the nineteenth century, Harris was able to capitalize on a particular development in literary taste that secured a profitable Northern market for writers mining Southern locales and habits. Like Thomas Nelson Page, George Washington Cable, and a host of lesser known authors, Harris tapped into the phenomenon of local color. He intoned in an early editorial ("Literature of the South," 1879) that "The very spice and essence of all literature is localism," and while for him this did not mean enshrining "Miss Sweetie Wildwood's" productions simply because they were Southern, localism did mean that his ear for Southern speech, his eye for middle Georgia customs, and his reverential but never shrill celebration of the Old South would serve him well in attracting Northern magazines and publishing houses that were the arbiters of public taste.

When Harris retired from the *Constitution* in 1900, he did not slow down but continued to work in the vein of local color even while a new group of writers—Stephen Crane, Frank Norris, Theodore Dreiser, and others—were experimenting with far less sentimental, more violent, and more realistic materials. He turned once more to the novel form to publish *Gabriel Tolliver* (1902), a work that, despite the serious flaws in construction, still stands out among similar works by Page, Cable, and Thomas Dixon because it uses a more balanced, less dogmatic tone as it looks at the Reconstruction period. Also in 1902 he collected a series of stories that had appeared in magazine format (*The Making of a Statesman*). In magazines Harris serialized two Civil War novels, *A Little Union Scout* (published in book form in 1904) and *The Shadow Between His Shoulder-Blades* (published posthumously in 1909). Although he had indicated with the publication of *Uncle Remus and His Friends* that he was retiring his most famous character, Harris turned again to the best of his mediums with the major collection, *Told by Uncle Remus* (1905), and two smaller ones, *The Tar Baby and Other Rhymes* (1904) and *Uncle Remus and Brer Rabbit* (1907). In three articles for the *Saturday Evening Post* published in 1904, he found a national forum for his moderate, though nonreformist and paternalistic, program for handling deteriorating race relations. A year before his death he decided to go into the magazine business himself, calling his venture *Uncle Remus's Magazine*. It became a showcase for much of his own material—articles, reviews, and stories—including one set narrated by his alter ego, Billy Sanders, and collected in book form posthumously as *The Bishop and the Boogerman* (1909).

Harris had almost named his magazine "The Optimist," and that title is a rather ironic reflection both of Harris and the world in which he found himself in 1908. By the early 1900s muckraking was the preferred trend in journalism, and race-baiting and negrophobia of the kind represented in Thomas Dixon's novels were taking hold in the South. Yet Harris clung obsessively to the values of simplicity, goodwill, and good humor. When President Theodore Roosevelt visited him in Atlanta in 1905 to offer a testimonial, he indicated that these were the values that the world most appreciated in Harris. Yet as his own private emotions show, in letters written in any period of his career, his optimism was a posture disguising chronic feelings of depression and self-doubt. Much of his fiction also carries undertones of disruption, isolation, and violence that he held in check through comedy. Thus the writer publicly associated with a humorous, hopeful, cheerful view of race and region seems to have viewed himself, as well as his world, with more ambiguous feelings. While his home and family meant everything to him, he was driven to work by much more than financial necessity, and he succumbed to periodic bouts of heavy drinking. Illness, both physical and mental, slowed him even during his most productive periods, and when his own voice came through the later Uncle Remus volumes, it spoke in no uncertain terms of the diminishments he associated with modern times. Harris died of acute nephritis, complicated by cirrhosis of the liver, on 3 July 1908. Shortly before his death, in one last act of faith, he was baptized a Catholic.

MAJOR THEMES

Harris's first collection of Remus's narratives established the view of the antebellum South that dominated all of his work, no matter how diverse the medium. In the introduction to *Uncle Remus: His Songs and His Sayings*, he stresses the point that it is not difficult to see why slaves would tell stories in which "the weakest and most harmless of all animals" is able to be "victorious in contests with the bear, the wolf, and the fox." This comment is not just an astute analysis, for its time, of power strategies as slaves invoked them, but it is also an indication of Harris's consistent concern for individuals who were deprived of power in a society that granted status to those who could manipulate others. His characters are frequently outsiders, potential victims, who struggle to gain control of their lives. The caste and class structure of the antebellum South made this matter an understandable preoccupation for a writer with Harris's past, or lack of it. Beginning with Uncle Remus and Brer Rabbit, Harris's works ask how men can come to terms with each other, evaluate each other, appreciate each other justly, without the imposition of artificial social standards or controls. In this respect Harris was a kind of Jeffersonian democrat; the term *democracy* is one he frequently used to describe middle Georgia, a region he associated with a kind of "natural aristocracy," which slavery did not, for Harris as for Jefferson, complicate.

The rabbit tales of Uncle Remus clearly divide into stories of getting free, stories of outdoing, and stories of exploiting. Brer Rabbit gets a lion to let himself be tied; he gets the fox to throw him into what, for him, is an hospitable briar patch; he steals butter and arranges for another animal to be punished for the deed; he tricks Mr. Fox into carrying him to one of Miss Meadows's galas. In other tales a crawfish causes the deluge to get revenge on an elephant, and Mr. Terrapin beats a bear in a game of tug-of-war. Uncle Remus never moralizes about the sometimes inexplicable acts of trickery or actual malevolence that the rabbit inflicts upon the physically superior animals. All is fair in a world that gives some an arbitrary, illogical advantage, a principle that the slaves enacted in their tales and one to which Harris seems to have been especially sensitive. About blatantly unjust outcomes of events, Uncle Remus will say only, "Looks like hit's mighty onwrong, but hits des dat away."

In the world that Uncle Remus displays with such relish, all of the moral standards as well as social classifications have been expunged, and there is instead a primitive balance of power that keeps any one creature from being able to exploit any other for very long. In the frame sketches, Remus insists upon his right to respect through a subtle contest of wills with those around him. While in Harris's day Remus was seen as a conservative spokesman for the benignity of master-slave relations before the war, Harris endows Remus with trickster qualities in his own right; he teases and poses in order to captivate and win favors from his audience. The inviolability of his stories, like the indestructibility of the rabbit, affords Remus a control as narrator that Harris himself found only through authorship. Further, in his Remus frames Harris was managing, as Louis D. Rubin, Jr., has pointed out in "Southern Local Color and the Black Man," to make an instinctive identification with his black narrator that was fostered by his "powerful sympathy for the underprivileged, the discriminated against."

In Harris's non-Remus local color fiction, where the magic of Brer Rabbit could not produce victories for the underdog, his attempt to bring human relations into just alignments took two different paths. In the collections of the 1880s and 1890s, most of Harris's stories used black characters, while the later works increasingly portrayed the plain white folk of the rural interior of Georgia. In some collections there are stories of both kinds, but in those dealing with slaves or freedmen, Harris's supremacist sympathies complicated his attempts to endow his characters with realistic responses to the situations in which he places them. In his stories of whites inhabiting agrarian havens, Harris used rustic yeomen to rebuke the ethic of the modern capitalist who had replaced the master as the inhumane power broker of the postwar South.

In portraits of slaves of antebellum times, blacks are sometimes victims, like the characters in "Free Joe," a story of a pathetic freed slave and his slave wife who are kept apart by a vicious master, or like the mother in "Mom Bi," whose child was sold away from her. Sometimes the victim rises up to protest or even to wreak revenge. The title characters in "Daddy Jake the Runaway" and "Blue Dave" run away to escape unjust treatment. "Where's Duncan?", one of Harris's most somber tales, gives us a slave woman as she plots and carries out the murder of the master who sold their mulatto son. In the stories of plantation times, Harris's emphasis on the devotion even of ill-used slaves in not surprising though it does undercut his sometimes sensitive insights into his characters' feelings. What is surprising is his willingness to indict many of his master figures for their lack of humanity. His black characters very often are his most stable, energetic, and sympathetic ones, but for modern audiences, their unwavering loyalty to white interests cannot be squared with the reality of their denial of their own dignity.

In stories with postwar settings, the freedmen and freedwomen are usually shown as far more adaptable and productive than their former owners, but freedom does not make them fully men and women for Harris. Usually he shows them as childlike pawns of craftier whites or as self-deprecating proclaimers of the virtues of the old times. Mingo, Aunt Minervy Ann, and Ananias, title character of a story in *Balaam and His Master*, are all former slaves who survive the war with their humanity and energy strengthened, unlike the whites around them, who are bitter, demoralized, often incapacitated. Aunt Minervy Ann, in the collection of her "Chronicles" of life during Reconstruction, comes closest to Uncle Remus in being a person in her own right; however, like him, she herself is a composite who can be at one moment comical and shuffling and at another shrewd and aggressively proud. Harris never vocally supported the full equality of blacks and preferred to show them as most worthy of respect when they were being most helpful to the causes of those who had enslaved them. It can only be said that his commitment to tolerance of human nature and his own experiences of exclusion caused him to grant individual strengths to his black characters in moments when he allowed himself to see them apart from the societal norms he felt compelled to uphold as a white leader of his place and time.

Harris's efforts to debunk the New South's "cult of Progress," as Wayne Mixon has called it, is much in evidence in the stories of whites inhabiting settings based on his own Putnam County. Such characters are independent; they live in isolated mountain or rural communities in which, in theory at least, neighborliness balances self-sufficiency. Sometimes, as in "Mingo," Harris is more effective in dramatizing class bitterness among whites than he is at portraying the nurturing value of agrarian societies. Yet the voice of Billy Sanders, who takes center stage in Harris's later works (*On the Wing of Occasions, The Shadow Between His Shoulder-Blades, The Bishop and the Boogerman*), speaks in an earthy, direct way for the values of a yeoman South opposed both to the aristocrats of the plantation and the bureaucratic businessmen of the city. Many of Harris's stories dramatize the threat of progress to the plain man's South, employing plots turning more on social dislocations than on idyllic continuities. In "At Teague Poteet's," a story in the *Mingo* collection, a group of sturdy mountaineers resists all attempts to force them into conformity with the outside world's standards. In "Aunt Fountain's Prisoner" from the *Free Joe* collection, a wounded Union officer nursed to health on a plantation stays after the war to save his new home through a prosperous dairy farm. In *Gabriel Tolliver* the hero battles the greed not only of conquering Yankees but of local politicians who betray the pastoral ethic of the village.

In the works outside the Uncle Remus canon, assertion of the values of equality, simplicity, and brotherhood are set within plots where disturbing threats are contrived away; improbable happy endings reconcile enemies, unite storm-tossed lovers, reveal hidden truths that explain away old wrongs, and allow everyone to receive a just valuation of his or her true worth. The Uncle Remus books represent Harris's interests in this area most effectively because his favorite black storyteller freed Harris's imagination from the restraints of the political and the literary climate that marred his other efforts. In particular Uncle Remus was able to give voice to Harris's concern for the past, especially in the plaintive tones of the later collections.

Remus's wistful remembrance of a bygone era sometimes operates, as it did in Thomas Nelson Page's work, as an exercise in nostalgia. Harris and Page have consistently been coupled as writers who glorified the antebellum South for a Northern public at last ready to be conquered by images of the innocent simplicity of the life that Northern armies had destroyed; however, the later

Uncle Remus volumes exhibit a more personally grounded form of pastoralism than Page's romanticized apologies provide. Uncle Remus's plea, "You may think dat dez times is de bes; well, den, you kin have um if you'll des gi' me de ol' times . . . ," is indistinguishable in its simple candor from Harris's own remark to James Whitcomb Riley that someone who did not like his commitment to "old times, and the old timey people," could "just go ahead speculating in futures, and I'll speculate on the past." There is little indication that Harris was promoting a view of Remus as one who longed for the actuality of the world that enslaved him; likewise, Harris can hardly be conceived of as preferring his precarious status as a boy in Eatonton to his position as revered editor and author in Atlanta. Harris has Remus call up memories of the past, as he himself increasingly did, as a kind of weapon against the confusion of the present. The little boy who stands in a sense for Harris's general audience changes, "progresses," from book to book, becoming more acquisitive and narrow-minded, less open to the magic of Remus's arguments that somewhere there is a world in which the weak gain equal footing with the powerful. Uncle Remus's response to this new little boy shows how Harris needed the past as an image of a stable world, a place in which he could re-create himself as one who belonged as well as a place that would stand as a rebuke to a new era of materialism that depersonalized and devalued the individual.

SURVEY OF CRITICISM

Criticism of Harris during his lifetime was shaped by the impact of his first book, an achievement of genius that automatically qualified him for fame. Uncle Remus became at birth "One of the immortal 'real folks' of literature," as Stella Brewer Brookes puts it. Yet *Uncle Remus: His Songs and His Sayings* used more than Uncle Remus to establish Harris's stature. His superior handling of dialect was acknowledged by both of his serious competitors in that area, Mark Twain and Thomas Nelson Page. In addition, he brought together the first collection of Afro-American folklore, exhibiting an attention to detail that is still praised. One entire category of research on Harris has been, since the first book, concerned with his contributions as a folklorist.

Contemporary reviews of non-Remus fiction were mixed. As a short story writer Harris frequently geared his work to magazine publication, and he often wrote to fit editors' explicit specifications. Still, he was hailed in the 1880s as one of the South's best local color writers. In his own time his studies of black character, coupled with his editorials on race relations, made him for many the highest authority on the Negro Question. Today, his belief in black inferiority and his segregationist stance shows quite obviously in his stories and have been one cause of a diminishment of his reputation as a realistic delineator of black experience; another cause is the sentimentality and superficiality that he, like all local color writers, was obliged to deliver. Harris's novels were never very well received. He excused himself from the task of imposing coherent form on his plots, which ramble and twist their way to implausibly tidy conclusions. Contemporary reviews did not overlook these flaws. In our time only *Sister Jane* and *On the Plantation* are given much attention, and in both cases it is because of the psychological insights that they provide because they are so closely autobiographical.

Full-length critical work on Harris began after his death with two biographies (1918) that stressed the events of his life but included helpful data on circumstances surrounding his writings. Robert Lemuel Wiggins's admiring *The Life of Joel Chandler Harris: From Obscurity in Boyhood to Fame in Early Manhood* carries Harris in Horatio Alger style up through his early years as an Atlanta writer and editor. More useful is the biography, still considered standard, by Harris's daughter-in-law, Julia Collier Harris; her *Life and Letters of Joel Chandler Harris* gives some psychological insights but also includes valuable letters and reminiscences. In 1931 she published a second book, *Joel Chandler Harris: Editor and Essayist*, which compiled some of Harris's more important newspaper and magazine essays. This side of Harris's career, spanning over 40 years of full-time work, has been neglected. Three studies emphasizing technical aspects of the Uncle Remus tales are Sumner Ives's *The Phonology of the Uncle Remus Tales* (1954); Stella Brookes's valuable classification by genre of the folk tales, *Joel Chandler Harris—Folklorist* (1950); and Florence E. Baer's monograph, *Sources and Analogues of the Uncle Remus Tales* (1980).

The first full-scale treatment of Harris as a man of letters was Paul M. Cousins's *Joel Chandler Harris: A Biography* (1968), which emphasized the formative early years and tended to praise more than to evaluate Harris's productions. Yet students of Harris are now in a position to move ahead on many fronts of research thanks to the recent efforts of R. Bruce Bickley, Jr. His 1978 *Joel Chandler Harris: A Reference Guide* provides annotated listings of 1,400 pieces dating from 1862 through 1976. He contributed to one of two essays listing Harris's magazine publications (*American Literary Realism*, Summer 1976 and Spring 1978). Bickley's Twayne biography (1978) is a sensible and sensitive as well as a meticulously researched reading of the interplay between Harris's mental state, his background, and his voluminous output as a writer. Finally, he has collected essays and reviews for a volume, *Critical Essays on Joel Chandler Harris* (1981), which contains materials from Harris's time and also some original pieces. The collection provides a clear overview of the range of intelligent response that Harris has aroused since his first work proved to be the start and in some ways also the high point of his literary career.

While editions of the Uncle Remus tales have remained popular, selling well for over a century now, his other works have long been out of print, except for a recent republication of *On the Plantation* (University of Georgia, 1980, with a foreword by Erskine Caldwell) and the reprinting of twenty stories in *Free Joe: Stories of Joel Chandler Harris* (Beehive Press, 1975). There are no full-length works of literary analysis except for Bickley's indispensable collection of essays, but Harris has been well represented in books covering Southern history during the post-Reconstruction era, American humor, Afro-American studies, and the literature of the "poor white" or "plain folk" tradition. The 1970s saw a resurgence of interest in Harris's treatment of black character because of that decade's attempt to reassess the Old South as a slave culture and to evaluate Afro-American literature, which in some ways begins with Brer Rabbit.

Certainly interest in Harris's connections to Afro-American culture will remain strong, for few of the questions of his relationships there have been fully answered, although many have been perceptively explored. Yet emphasis on his positions on race problems has deflected interest in questions of how he fits in other ways into several narrative traditions attracting American writers, from the slave narrators to the naturalists to such novelists as William Faulkner, Ernest Gaines, and Ralph Ellison. A collection of his letters that will soon be brought out by Joseph Griska will open Harris materials to new psychoanalytic scrutiny. Finally, in Southern studies, Harris's influence on the literature of that region needs renewed emphasis, not just because of the debt of Mark Twain, Faulkner, and the Agrarians but because a new generation of Southern fiction writers is turning to the comic, sometimes grotesque world of rural folk that Harris defined with insight as well as humor.

BIBLIOGRAPHY

Works by Joel Chandler Harris

Uncle Remus: His Songs and His Sayings. New York: D. Appleton, 1881 [1880].
Nights with Uncle Remus: Myths and Legends of the Old Plantation. Boston: James R. Osgood, 1883.
Mingo and Other Sketches in Black and White. Boston: James R. Osgood, 1884.
Free Joe and Other Georgian Sketches. New York: Charles Scribner's Sons, 1887.
Daddy Jake the Runaway and Short Stories Told After Dark. New York: Century, 1889.
Joel Chandler Harris' Life of Henry W. Grady. New York: Cassell, 1890.
Balaam and His Master and Other Sketches and Stories. Boston and New York: Houghton, Mifflin, 1891.
On the Plantation: A Story of a Georgia Boy's Adventures During the War. New York: D. Appleton, 1892.
Uncle Remus and His Friends: Old Plantation Stories, Songs, and Ballads with Sketches of Negro Character. Boston and New York: Houghton, Mifflin, 1892.
Evening Tales Done into English from the French of Frédéric Ortoli. New York: Charles Scribner's Sons, 1893.
Little Mr. Thimblefinger and His Queer Country: What the Children Saw and Heard There. Boston and New York: Houghton, Mifflin, 1894.
Mr. Rabbit at Home: A Sequel to Little Mr. Thimblefinger and His Queer Country. Boston and New York: Houghton, Mifflin, 1895.
Sister Jane: Her Friends and Acquaintances. Boston and New York: Houghton, Mifflin, 1896.
Stories of Georgia. New York, Cincinnati, Chicago: American Book, 1896.
Aaron in the Wildwoods. Boston and New York: Houghton, Mifflin, 1897.

Tales of the Home Folks in Peace and War. Boston and New York: Houghton, Mifflin, 1898.
The Chronicles of Aunt Minervy Ann. New York: Charles Scribner's Sons, 1899.
Plantation Pageants. Boston and New York: Houghton, Mifflin, 1899.
On the Wing of Occasions. New York: Doubleday, Page, 1900.
Gabriel Tolliver: A Story of Reconstruction. New York: McClure, Phillips, 1902.
The Making of a Statesman and Other Stories. New York: McClure, Phillips, 1902.
Wally Wanderoon and His Story-Telling Machine. New York: McClure, Phillips, 1903.
A Little Union Scout. New York: McClure, Phillips, 1904.
The Tar-Baby and Other Rhymes of Uncle Remus. New York: D. Appleton, 1904.
Told by Uncle Remus: New Stories of the Old Plantation. New York: McClure, Phillips, 1905.
Uncle Remus and Brer Rabbit. New York: Frederick A. Stokes, 1907.
The Bishop and the Boogerman. New York: Doubleday, Page, 1909.
The Shadow Between His Shoulder-Blades. Boston: Small, Maynard, 1909.
Uncle Remus and the Little Boy. Boston: Small, Maynard, 1910.
Uncle Remus Returns. Boston and New York: Houghton Mifflin, 1918.
The Witch Wolf: An Uncle Remus Story. Cambridge, Mass.: Bacon & Brown, 1921.
Joel Chandler Harris: Editor and Essayist. Ed. Julia Collier Harris. Chapel Hill: University of North Carolina Press, 1931.
Qua: A Romance of the Revolution. Ed. Thomas H. English. Sources and Reprints, Series 3, no. 2. Atlanta: Emory University, 1946.
Seven Tales of Uncle Remus. Ed. Thomas H. English. Sources and Reprints, Series 5, no. 2, Atlanta: Emory University, 1948.
The Complete Tales of Uncle Remus. Ed. Richard Chase. Boston: Houghton Mifflin, 1955.

Studies of Joel Chandler Harris

Baer, Florence E. *Sources and Analogues of the Uncle Remus Tales.* Helsinki: Academia Scientiarum Fennica, 1980.
Bickley, R. Bruce, Jr. *Joel Chandler Harris.* Boston: Twayne, 1978.
———. *Joel Chandler Harris: A Reference Guide.* Boston: G. K. Hall, 1978.
———, ed. *Critical Essays on Joel Chandler Harris.* Boston: G. K. Hall, 1981.
Brookes, Stella Brewer. *Joel Chandler Harris—Folklorist.* Athens: University of Georgia Press, 1950.
Buck, Paul. *The Road to Reunion: 1865–1900.* Boston: Little, Brown, 1937.
Cook, Sylvia Jenkins. *From Tobacco Road to Route 66: The Southern Poor White in Fiction.* Chapel Hill: University of North Carolina Press, 1976.
Cousins, Paul M. *Joel Chandler Harris: A Biography.* Baton Rouge: Louisiana State University Press. 1968.
English, Thomas H., ed. *Mark Twain to Uncle Remus: 1881–1885.* Sources and Reprints, Series 7, no. 3. Atlanta: Emory University, 1953.
Hall, Wade. *The Smiling Phoenix: Southern Humor from 1865 to 1914.* Gainesville: University of Florida Press, 1965.
Harris, Julia Collier. *The Life and Letters of Joel Chandler Harris.* Boston and New York: Houghton Mifflin, 1918.

Hedin, Raymond. "Uncle Remus: Puttin On Ole Massa's Son." *Southern Literary Journal* 15 (Fall 1982): 83–90.

Ives, Sumner. *The Phonology of the Uncle Remus Tales*. Publication of the American Dialect Society, no. 22. Gainesville: University of Florida Press, 1954.

McIlwaine, Shields. *The Southern Poor White from Lubberland to Tobacco Road*. Norman: University of Oklahoma Press, 1939.

MacKethan, Lucinda. *The Dream of Arcady: Place and Time in Southern Literature*. Baton Rouge: Louisiana State University Press, 1980.

Mixon, Wayne. *Southern Writers and the New South Movement, 1865–1913*. Chapel Hill: University of North Carolina Press, 1980.

Rubin, Louis D., Jr. "Southern Local Color and the Black Man." *Southern Review* n.s. 6 (October 1970): 1014–22.

Stafford, John. "Patterns of Meaning in *Nights With Uncle Remus*." *American Literature* 18 (May 1946): 89–108.

Wade, John Donald. "Profits and Losses in the Life of Joel Chandler Harris." *American Review* 1 (April 1933): 17–35.

Wiggins, Robert Lemuel. *The Life of Joel Chandler Harris: From Obscurity in Boyhood to Fame in Early Manhood*. Nashville: Methodist Episcopal Church, South, 1918.

RAYBURN S. MOORE

Paul Hamilton Hayne
(1830–1886)

Of the many Southern writers of the nineteenth century, Paul Hayne is surely one of the most representative. If William Gilmore Simms was the preeminent Southern author of the antebellum period and Henry Timrod the laureate of the Confederacy, Hayne was certainly the poet laureate of the South and spokesman for Southern literary ideas in the postwar period.

BIOGRAPHY

Paul Hamilton Hayne was born on 1 January 1830 in Charleston, South Carolina. His father, the senior Paul Hamilton Hayne, was a member of one of South Carolina's most prominent families (two of his brothers were U.S. senators, and one of them, Robert Young Hayne, was the leading advocate of states' rights in the Senate debate on Nullification in 1830–31) and his mother, Emily McElhenney Hayne, was the daughter of a Carolina Presbyterian minister with important connections in Virginia. Hayne grew up and was educated in Charleston, and because his father, a naval officer, died of yellow fever before Hayne was two, he was reared by his mother and uncle, Robert Y. Hayne. He attended Christopher Cotes's school and sat near Henry Timrod. At age nine he began writing verse, and at fifteen he published his first poem in the Charleston *Courier* on 11 September 1845. Two years later he matriculated at the College of Charleston and graduated in 1850 with honors in English composition and elocution. Then, at his mother's urging, he began to study law in the office of James Louis Petigru, one of the state's most distinguished lawyers. Meanwhile, he had begun in the late 1840s to contribute verse to the *Southern Literary Messenger*, the *Southern Literary Gazette*, and, shortly thereafter, to *Graham's Magazine* and the *Home Journal*. In May 1852 he married Mary Middleton Michel, the daughter of a French émigré physician in Charleston, and became associate editor of the

Gazette. He assumed the editorship in the following December and gave up law in order to concentrate his energies on his weekly. From this date until he died in July 1886, Hayne, with the encouragement and support of his wife, devoted himself to literary matters. In 1856 his only son, William Hamilton, was born, and Hayne, at the urging of Simms and Timrod, became editor of the projected *Russell's Magazine*. He served in that capacity, with the exception of two or three brief periods of illness or vacation, from 1857 to 1860. *Russell's* was the last important Southern literary magazine founded before the Civil War, and Hayne was largely responsible for its quality and for its three-year effort to balance sectional politics with literary standards not restricted by geography.

At the same time he managed to bring out at his own expense (usually with his mother's help) three collections of verse. *Poems* (1855) appeared in November 1854; it contains mainly juvenilia, but also an ambitious long poem entitled "The Temptation of Venus" and a few promising sonnets and short pieces. The second book, *Sonnets, and Other Poems* (1857), reflects Hayne's continuing interest in and increasing mastery of the sonnet form, although its publication in Charleston occasioned less critical attention than *Poems*, published by Ticknor and Fields in Boston, had received. *Avolio; A Legend of the Island of Cos* (1860), Hayne's third volume, accordingly, was published in Boston in November 1859. This edition of his verse contains as title piece another long narrative and his best lyrics and dramatic pieces of the antebellum period.

The approach of the war, however, not only temporarily halted the development of Hayne's national reputation, but also brought about the demise of *Russell's*; Hayne turned to military service and to support of the Confederacy with his pen. Because his health had been delicate for much of his life, he was able to serve actively for only four months (as Governor Francis Picken's aide-de-camp in 1861–62), but he regularly lectured on the war and contributed verse to periodicals in Virginia, South Carolina, and elsewhere. By 1864 he had undertaken a serious study of English poetry from Chaucer to Tennyson; it resulted in "The Wife of Brittany," a long, ambitious narrative based upon Chaucer's "Franklin's Tale." But the war forced Hayne into uncongenial themes (a fervent supporter of his state and of the Confederacy as well, he was not so consistently successful a writer of patriotic verse as was Timrod, nor was he uncritical of various political and military means of promoting the Cause). The disruptions of war also limited his growth as a poet. "When one is knocked about as I was," he wrote a friend in 1866, "deprived of all tranquility, how *can* one compose properly, or artistically?" Finally, the war destroyed his home, reduced him to poverty, and generally ruined him in "fortune and prospects."

In July 1865 Hayne went to Augusta, Georgia, as news editor of the *Constitutionalist*. But his frail health could not endure the ten-hour work day, and he resigned in October to become a free-lance writer and editor. The following April he moved his family—wife, son, and mother—to a cottage near Grovetown, sixteen miles from Augusta, his home for the last twenty years of his life. At Copse Hill, as he called it, he devoted himself to writing—poems, essays, criticism mostly—and made a precarious and eventually a modest living from contributions to newspapers and magazines, among them *Scott's Monthly, Southern Opinion, Southern Society*, the *South-Atlantic, Home and Farm* and the *Southern Bivouac*. In the North the *Round Table*, the *Old Guard*, the *Galaxy, Appleton's Journal, Lippincott's, Scribner's Monthly* (later the *Century*), the *Independent*, the *Christian Union, Harper's Bazaar, Harper's New Monthly*, and the *Atlantic Monthly* published his writing. He also served in various editorial and critical capacities on numerous periodicals in the Southeast, including several of the magazines already mentioned, and on newspapers in Georgia, the Carolinas, and Kentucky.

Hayne's criticism has been only partially appraised. Edd Winfield Parks's *Ante-Bellum Southern Literary Critics* (1962) bespeaks its boundaries in its title, but Parks's conclusion that Hayne is an eclecticist and traditionalist characterizes fairly his total output. Rayburn S. Moore has indicated something of Hayne's critical views in *Paul Hamilton Hayne* (1972), *A Man of Letters in the Nineteenth-Century South: Selected Letters of Paul Hamilton Hayne* (1982), and in articles on Hayne's response to Shakespeare, Poe, Whitman, and Howells. Hayne asserted that Shakespeare, Milton, and Chaucer were the great English poets of the past, and Wordsworth, Keats, and Tennyson the chief bards of the nineteenth century. Among the novelists, he enjoyed Scott and Dickens and admired Thackeray, Bulwer, George Eliot, Charles Reade, and Charlotte Brontë. As for American poets, he considered Longfellow, Lowell, Bryant, Whittier, and Poe (despite his moral limitations) to be the most important. Whitman he despised. He respected Holmes as much for his fiction and essays as for his poems. Among the fiction writers he praised Hawthorne, Poe, Cooper, and Simms (although he acknowledged Simms's weaknesses), and he caustically denominated George W. Cable as a traitor to the South, and James and Howells as practitioners of fiction without a "story."

In his own time, Hayne was known primarily as a poet. The three volumes he published after the Civil War—*Legends and Lyrics* (1872), *The Mountain of the Lovers* (1875), and *Poems*, Complete Edition (1882)—brought him a reputation as the "poet laureate of the South," an honor earned not just by his poetry but also by his standing as a literary spokesman on a wide range of social, political, and intellectual matters. His older contemporaries, Longfellow and Whittier, respected him, and he was praised by such important Northern critics as E. C. Stedman and E. P. Whipple. In the South he was widely lauded, especially by Simms, Timrod, John Esten Cooke, John R. Thompson, Margaret Junkin Preston, and Sidney Lanier. His work now seems largely derivative and conventionally romantic. It is sentimental, personal, and too often lacks intellectual substance. Yet, these limitations relate directly to some of the strengths in Hayne's verse. His work does derive sustenance from his sources in Chaucer, Spenser, Wordsworth, Keats, Poe, and Tennyson; it also reflects a versatility in the range of forms, metrical schemes, and techniques. In this versatility and in the scope of his work, Hayne appears to be the most substantial Southern poet of the century (with the possible exception of Simms), though he is not the equal of Poe or Timrod or even of Simms or Lanier, nor has his best work lasted as well as theirs.

Hayne is chiefly remembered as a writer whose dedication to literature was as sincere and persistent as that of Poe or Simms; his letters are among his main contributions to nineteenth-century Southern writing. His correspondence with his British and American contemporaries reveals the depth and scope of his achievement even as it measures his standing among his peers. He wrote Tennyson, Swinburne, and Charles Reade (even Browning and Arnold on rare occasions) and, more regularly, William Black, Wilkie Collins, Jean Ingelow, R. D. Blackmore, and Philip Bourke Marston. He also corresponded with such American authors as Longfellow, Whittier, Holmes, Lowell, Howells, Whipple, Stedman, Bayard Taylor, Constance Fenimore Woolson, John Esten Cooke, John R. Thompson, and Lanier. His exchanges with Simms, Margaret Junkin Preston, Andrew Adgate Lipscomb, and Charles Gayarré fully express the range of his social, philosophical, literary, and personal views; and his communications with such minor contemporaries as Edgar Fawcett, Maurice Thompson, and Francis Saltus help complete the picture of man and artist in his correspondence. The emerging persona demonstrates consistently for 30 years a commitment to literature rare in nineteenth-century American literary history, and although Hayne's reach surely exceeded his grasp, he never stinted the effort.

Hayne's health, always frail, declined further in fall 1884 as he suffered from a "nervous asthma," which kept him "gasping off & on for hours." Following a stroke in June 1886, Hayne died on 6 July 1886 and was buried in Magnolia Cemetery in Augusta, Georgia.

MAJOR THEMES

Hayne found certain topics congenial to his spirit and these appear in his poetry throughout much of his career. Among these are home (including his state, region, and the Confederacy), friends, other writers, and such traditional themes as love, nature, religion, philosophy, and death.

His early poems celebrate his city and its environs and the brave men of South Carolina who fell in the Mexican War; indeed, his first published poem, "The Ashley at the Battery" (1845), praises the natural world where "beauty, taste, and fashion meet." Less than four years later, a martial elegy entitled "Lines—On the Death of Colonel Pierce M. Butler" (1849) honors the memory of the fallen leader of the Palmetto Regiment. Such themes of approbation for place and sacrifice continue in Hayne's Civil War poems, including "My Mother-Land" (1862) and "Charleston" (1862), both paeans to his native land and its cause. Even in his last years he still harped on similar notes in two long, commissioned pieces: the "Sesqui-Centennial Ode" (1883), which memorializes the 150th anniversary of the founding of Georgia and the so-called "Charleston Centennial Poem" (1883), which celebrates the "constancy and martyr-like courage" of his hometown. Summoning all the nostalgia accrued from almost twenty years of "exile," he bids farewell to the "City of my youth" and hears Saint Michael's bells pealing in his dreams.

Such public poems paralleled Hayne's lyrics on the members of his own immediate family—his father, mother, uncle, wife, and son. Because Lieutenant Paul Hamilton Hayne, U.S.N., died before his son was two, Hayne's "My Father" (1851) expresses the yearning for a parent he had never really known. His poems on his mother are more direct and declare his love and gratitude for her support of his literary ambitions, especially in the dedicatory piece of *Sonnets* (1857) and in the end piece to *Legends and Lyrics* (1872). In the same volume he confesses his joy in the prospect of his new son's possible future as a poet; a few years later, in "My Mother-Land" (1862), he honors his uncle Robert, now long dead, as the "gallant knight" who led the Senate debate on Nullification against Daniel Webster. His main contributions in this vein, however, are pieces celebrating his love for his wife. From the dedicatory lyric to *Poems* (1855) to "The Bonny Brown Hand" (1869), "Love's Autumn" (1880), and "A Little While I Fain Would Linger Yet" (1882), Hayne acknowledges his debt to "the hand which points the path to heaven, yet makes a heaven of earth."

In his poems, Hayne expresses his feelings toward friends and fellow writers almost as fervently as those toward his family and country. In a sonnet he invites Simms to visit Copse Hill (1866) and later memorializes his old friend and mentor in "Monody" (1877). He remembered Timrod in "Under the Pine" (1868) and "By the Grave of Henry Timrod" (1874), both elegiac considerations of his close friend and fellow artist. Thanking Margaret Junkin Preston for "deathless sympathy" in the dedication to *The Mountain of the Lovers* (1875), he similarly acknowledges Longfellow, Whittier, Holmes, Lanier, and R. D. Blackmore. Tributes to Lipscomb (1885) and to Gayarré (1886; indeed this sonnet to the venerable historian of Louisiana was one of Hayne's last poems) are among the most successful of his compliments to friends.

The theme of love manifests itself in his poetry as an expression of the dearest relationship between human beings and as a spiritual relationship between God and man. Love is not only the central theme of such long poems as "The Temptation of Venus" (1854), "The Wife of Brittany" (1870), and "The Mountain of the Lovers" (1875), but it is also basic to most of the poems addressed to Mary Middleton Michel Hayne—including "From the Woods" (1868), "The Bonny Brown Hand," "An Anniversary" (1871), "Love's Autumn," and "A Little While I Fain Would Linger Yet." Hayne touches on the spiritual side of love in "The Temptation of Venus" and "Avolio" (1859), but it is in such briefer lyrics of a later period as "Closing In" (1882), "Easter" (post 1882), and "Face to Face" (1886) that Hayne finds the true "glory of love."

Nature is another theme that appears throughout the canon. Present in a general romantic sense in "The Temptation of Venus," and in "Nature the Consoler. An Ode" (1858), and "Avolio," it appears with a local habitation and a name in the Copse Hill poems of the 1870s: "Aspects of the Pines" (1872), "The Voice of the Pines" (1873), and "The Woodland" (1874). It emerges again in the 1880s in the poems written for a rural audience: "In the Wheat Field" (1882), "Harvest Time" (1882), and "Midsummer. (On the Farm.)" (1884). The theme of nature finds its loveliest manifestation in such brief lyrics as "The Spirea" (1876), "Hints of Spring" (1877), "The Pine's Mystery" (1880), "To a Bee" (1880), and "On a Jar of Honey" (post–1882); and it achieves general philosophical expression in "Muscadines" (1876), a paean to the South's "magic" grape that Moses Coit Tyler always characterized as the "immortal 'Muscadines,' " "Unveiled" (1878), to Hayne himself the "highest water mark" of his accomplishment. In "The Snow Messengers" (1880) the philosophical view of nature is subordinated to the tributes to Longfellow and Whittier ("pen portraits" Hayne called them), as it is in "The Return of Peace" (1881) in which the natural resources of a devastated region risen from the ashes provide magnanimous and peaceful ties with the rest of the world.

Religious and philosophical themes also receive serious consideration as early as "Nature the Consoler," where nature offers a "sphere" from whence a mortal may "put on immortality." In "Unveiled" the natural world hints at "remoter meanings" as of the "far tone / Of ante-natal music faintly blown / From out of the misted realms of memory. . . . " "The True Heaven" (1879), on the other hand, suggests a marriage of action and quietude, a "marvellous state" leading to "true 'rest' or 'peace.' " A much more Christian poem, "Easter," stresses the importance of Christ and celebrates the meaning of Calvary and the risen Lord in the midst of "April's *palingenesis.*" Hayne, indeed, was convinced that through poetry one could catch "Brief glimpses of life divine" and that "through poetic thought spiritualized," one could " . . . pass from earth to heaven." He is not, it will readily be seen, essentially a cerebral poet. With generally conventional and derivative ideas, he is chiefly a poet of feeling and "outer weather."

Nevertheless, one of Hayne's great themes is death. As one who contemplated ill health throughout much of his life and who consequently dealt with death in one form or another from an early age, Hayne in "Nature the Consoler" asserts rather than arrives at immortality. In his war poems he exhorts Confederates to stand firm and to give all for glory ("Charleston!" [1862] and "Beyond the Potomac" [1862] are good examples). "Cambyses and the Macrobian Bow" (1873), conversely, portrays death as meaningless. Nonetheless, in two of his best late poems—"In Harbor" (1882) and "Face to Face" (1886)—Hayne serenely confronts death and discovers that it not only relates to life but also leads to union with the spirit of God and thus should not be feared. "In Harbor" is valedictory in purpose and function and seeks to provide "suffering Humanity" with a view of the goal: "Those lights in the harbor at last, / The heavenly harbor at last!" Hayne lived for four more years, but his second valedictory, published only six weeks before his death, proved indeed to be his farewell. In "Face to Face" the poet faces death and tranquilly accepts the outcome:

But beyond the stars and the sun
  I can follow him still on his way,

Till the pearl-white gates are won
   In the calm of the central day.
Far voices of fond acclaim
   Thrill down from the place of Souls,
As Death, with a touch like flame,
   Uncloses the goal of goals;
And from heaven of heavens above
   God speaketh with bateless breath—
My angel of perfect love
   Is the angel men call Death!

In general, we find little that is unusual in the nature or application of Hayne's themes. Assuredly a poet of his time, and a Southern poet at that, he accepts and embraces the past and is proud of the poetic and intellectual tradition that is his inheritance. His gift to the future is to add to this literary heritage whatever he can in an appropriate language, style, and form and to pass it along to the next generation. This he does in such a competent and unobtrusive way that the seriousness of his effort and the significance of its result have often been overlooked. Hayne's due is neither that of a neglected genius nor that of a poet to whom proper rank has been denied. Rather he is a poet of minor stature whose overall importance is as a man of letters and spokesman for the literary and intellectual values he held dear for over 35 years.

SURVEY OF CRITICISM

In his own day many considered Hayne the chief Southern poet and literary spokesman, as well as an American poet of consequence. Longfellow, Whittier, and Holmes praised him publicly and privately; and Stedman, Whipple, Howells, and Maurice Thompson reviewed him favorably. In 1882 Thompson characterized him, along with Longfellow, Whittier, and Lowell, as one of the four "best known" living poets of America. Even those critics in the North who did not regard him so highly viewed him as an honorable minor poet. At the same time Hayne's high reputation in the South remained secure; and although for a brief period in the late 1870s and early 1880s, Lanier's star was bright, it was not steadfast, and Hayne remained the laureate of the South.

After his death in 1886, Hayne's own star began to fade. No new edition of his poems appeared, and negotiations for such a volume between Mrs. Hayne, Will Hayne, and Lothrop in Boston, and the Scribner's and Holt firms in New York all eventually failed. The public was accordingly left with a "cabinet" edition of the poems that was too complete on the one hand and yet that did not include, on the other, any work from the last four years of his life. Moreover, Thompson, who had praised Hayne profusely during his lifetime, began to change his mind after Hayne's death; and in three essays written in 1887, 1888, and 1901, he sharply revised his opinion of Hayne's achievement, concluding in

1901 that the body of his work "is full of the quality *temporis acti* . . . and out of date."

Meanwhile, Hayne's reputation fluctuated among more academic critics. He received full recognition in Samuel A. Link's *Literary Pioneers of the South* (1899–1900), in F.V.N. Painter's *Poets of the South* (1903), in Carl Holliday's *History of Southern Literature* (1906), in *The Library of Southern Literature* (1908–23), and in Montrose J. Moses's *The Literature of the South* (1910). Yet in studies of American literature such as William B. Cairns's *History* (1912) he attracted far less attention, although Cairns compares him favorably with Timrod. Fred Lewis Pattee offered similar treatment in his *History of American Literature Since 1870* (1915), but decided that Hayne is less "sensitively imaginative" than Timrod.

Subsequent critical considerations follow the changing tastes and standards of the 1920s and 1930s, and as Tennyson's reputation receded and Whitman, Emily Dickinson, and gradually T. S. Eliot and Ezra Pound began to loom large, Hayne's status declined. He was adequately discussed and represented in Edd Winfield Parks's *Southern Poets* (1936) and in Jay B. Hubbell's *American Life in Literature* (1936); and he was also included proportionately in the various editions of Pattee's *Century Readings in American Literature* (1919–32). A few articles appeared in magazines before World War II, but the most important considerations of the period appeared in the early 1940s—Charles R. Anderson's long essay on Hayne and Charles Gayarré in 1940, Jay B. Hubbell's discussion of Hayne and Timrod in *The Last Years of Henry Timrod* (1941), Victor H. Hardendorff's "Paul Hamilton Hayne and the North" (M.A. thesis, Duke University, 1942), and, most significant, Daniel M. McKeithan's *Collection of Hayne Letters* (1944). Nevertheless, Hayne's reputation had declined substantially in two generations and, despite the acquisition of his papers and books by the Duke University Library in the late 1920s, work based upon this archive would not bear much fruit until well after the end of World War II.

The aftermath of that war, as was true in so many areas of study, brought about a gradual resurgence of interest in Hayne. The Centennial Edition of Lanier in 1945, for example, published Lanier's letters to Hayne and excerpts from Hayne's to Lanier. More important, the *Literary History of the United States* (1946, 1947) discussed Hayne briefly and provided a helpful bibliography. During this period, Charles Duffy edited Hayne's letters to Bayard Taylor (1945) and to Mrs. Julia C. R. Dorr (1951–52), and McKeithan published his edition of John G. James's letters to the Haynes (1946). But the chief work of this time was Hubbell's *The South in American Literature, 1607–1900* (1954), which includes a long chapter on Hayne's writing in its Southern context. A few years later, after providing several articles, Parks published *Ante-Bellum Southern Literary Critics* (1962), a careful survey and analysis of Hayne's criticism.

The chief effort, subsequently, to appraise Hayne's life and work has come from Rayburn S. Moore. Since 1968 Moore has written twelve articles on Hayne as poet and man of letters; that work has now reached book length and is still in progress. In the interim his *Paul Hamilton Hayne* (1972), a critical study of the life and poetry, and *A Man of Letters in the Nineteenth-Century South: Selected Letters of Paul Hamilton Hayne* (1982) have been published.

"Tho' much is taken," Ulysses says, "much abides." Hayne's reputation is now relatively fixed. His main importance stems from his insistent espousal of a literary standard whose nature and aesthetic had been changed drastically by the Civil War and Reconstruction. His poetry needs final appraisal, but such an estimate is unlikely until an adequate selected edition of his verse is available. A full-scale biography is also much to be desired. Nevertheless, for a minor poet, Hayne has been treated well.

BIBLIOGRAPHY

Works by Paul Hamilton Hayne

Poems. Boston: Ticknor and Fields, 1855. copr. 1854.

Sonnets, and Other Poems. Charleston: Harper & Calvo, 1857.

Avolio; A Legend of the Island of Cos. With Poems, Lyrical, Miscellaneous, and Dramatic. Boston: Ticknor and Fields, 1860. copr. 1859.

Legends and Lyrics. Philadelphia: J. B. Lippincott, 1872. copr. 1871.

Ed. *The Poems of Henry Timrod*. New York: E. J. Hale & Son, 1873.

The Mountain of the Lovers; With Poems of Nature and Tradition. New York: E. J. Hale & Son, 1875.

Lives of Robert Young Hayne and Hugh Swinton Legare. Charleston: Walker, Evans & Cogswell, 1878.

Poems. Complete Edition. Boston: D. Lothrop, 1882.

"Seven Unpublished Letters of Paul Hamilton Hayne." Ed. William Stanley Hoole. *Georgia Historical Quarterly* 22 (September 1938): 273–85.

"A Correspondence Journal of Paul Hamilton Hayne." Ed. Daniel M. McKeithan. *Georgia Historical Quarterly* 26 (September-December 1942): 249–72.

A Collection of Hayne Letters. Ed. Daniel M. McKeithan. Austin: University of Texas Press, 1944.

The Correspondence of Bayard Taylor and Paul Hamilton Hayne. Ed. Charles Duffy. Baton Rouge: Louisiana State University Press, 1945.

Selected Letters: John Garland James to Paul Hamilton Hayne and Mary Middleton Michel Hayne. Ed. Daniel M. McKeithan. Austin: University of Texas Press, 1946.

"Paul Hamilton Hayne to Dr. Francis Peyre Porcher." Ed. Richard B. Davis. *Studies in Philology* 44 (July 1947): 529–48.

"A Southern Genteelist: Letters of Paul Hamilton Hayne to Julia C. R. Dorr." Ed. Charles Duffy. *South Carolina Historical and Genealogical Magazine* 52 (April 1951): 65–73, to 53 (January 1952): 19–30.

A Man of Letters in the Nineteenth-Century South: Selected Letters of Paul Hamilton Hayne. Ed. Rayburn S. Moore. Baton Rouge: Louisiana State University Press, 1982.

Studies of Paul Hamilton Hayne

Anderson, Charles R. "Charles Gayarré and Paul Hayne: The Last Literary Cavaliers." *American Studies in Honor of William Kenneth Boyd*. Ed. David K. Jackson. Durham, N.C.: Duke University Press, 1940, pp. 221–81.

———. "Poet of the Pine Barrens." *Georgia Review* 1 (Fall 1947): 280–93.

Griffin, Max L. "Whittier and Hayne: A Record of Friendship." *American Literature* 19 (March 1947): 41–58.

Hardendorff, Victor H. "Paul Hamilton Hayne and the North." M.A. thesis, Duke University, 1942.

Harwell, Richard B. "A Confederate View of the Southern Poets." *American Literature* 24 (March 1952): 51–61.

Hayne, William Hamilton. "Paul H. Hayne's Methods of Composition." *Lippincott's Magazine* 50 (December 1892): 793–96.

Hubbell, Jay B. "Paul Hamilton Hayne." *The South in American Literature, 1607–1900*. Durham, N.C.: Duke University Press, 1954, pp. 743–57.

Lang, Cecil. "Swinburne and American Literature." *American Literature* 19 (January 1948): 336–50.

McKeithan, Daniel M. "Paul Hamilton Hayne and the *Southern Bivouac*." *University of Texas Studies in English* 17 (1937): 112–23.

Moore, Rayburn S. " 'The Absurdest of Critics': Hayne on Howells." *Southern Literary Journal* 12 (Fall 1979): 70–78.

———. " 'A Great Poet and Original Genius': Hayne Champions Poe." *Southern Literary Journal* 16 (Fall 1983): 105–12.

———. "Hayne the Poet: A New Look." *South Carolina Review* 2 (November 1969): 4–13.

———. "The Land of His Fathers: Paul Hamilton Hayne and South Carolina." *South Carolina Review* 11 (April 1979): 58–68.

———. " 'The Literary World Gone Mad': Hayne on Whitman." *Southern Literary Journal* 10 (Fall 1977): 75–83.

———. "The Old South and the New: Paul Hamilton Hayne and Maurice Thompson." *Southern Literary Journal* 5 (Fall 1972): 108–22.

———. *Paul Hamilton Hayne*. New York: Twayne, 1972.

———. "Paul Hamilton Hayne and Andrew Adgate Lipscomb: 'Sweet Converse' Between Poet and Preacher." *Georgia Historical Quarterly* 66 (Spring 1982): 53–68.

———. "Paul Hamilton Hayne and Northern Magazines, 1866–1886." *Essays Mostly on Periodical Publishing in America: A Collection in Honor of Clarence Gohdes*. Ed. James Woodress et al. Durham: Duke University Press, 1973, pp. 132–47.

———. "Paul Hamilton Hayne as Editor, 1852–1860." *South Carolina Journals and Journalists*. Ed. James B. Meriwether. Columbia: Southern Studies Program, University of South Carolina, 1975, pp. 91–108.

Parks, Edd Winfield. *Ante-Bellum Southern Literary Critics*. Athens: University of Georgia Press, 1962.

Preston, Margaret J. "Paul Hamilton Hayne." *Southern Bivouac* n.s. 2 (September 1886): 222–29.

Young, Thomas Daniel. "How Time Has Served Two Southern Poets: Paul Hamilton Hayne and Sidney Lanier." *Southern Literary Journal* 6 (Fall 1973): 101–10.

ROBERT L. PHILLIPS

Johnson Jones Hooper
(1815–1862)

On 8 December 1856 the temporary chairman of the Southern Commercial Convention, Savannah mayor J. P. Scriven, heard a motion that while the convention awaited the opening day report of its rules committee that it hear Mr. Simon Suggs of Alabama give an "account" of his activities for the past two years. Johnson Jones Hooper, editor of the Montgomery *Mail*, ardent supporter of Southern interests, creator of Captain Simon Suggs and an appointed delegate to the convention, did not stir from his seat when Scriven invited him to the platform. Hooper's Simon Suggs had become one of the most acclaimed figures in Southern humorous writing, but Hooper by 1856 had come to feel that identification of his own interests with the unscrupulous characters of his creation ill-served his serious political and commercial purposes.

BIOGRAPHY

Johnson Jones Hooper, born 9 June 1915 in Wilmington, North Carolina, was the youngest of three sons of Archibald and Charlotte De Berniere Hooper. Archibald Hooper, a lawyer and plantation owner, had inherited a modestly large estate, but by the time "Jonce" was seven the family had fallen on hard times and had come to depend on Archibald's editorship of the *Cape Fear Recorder* for its livelihood. In 1835 Johnson left Wilmington to read law in his brother's office in LaFayette, Alabama, and eight years later, on 9 September 1843, his first sketch appeared in the most prominent sporting journal in the nation, the *Spirit of the Times*, edited in New York City by William Trotter Porter.

Those eight years had been busy ones for Hooper. He had practiced law periodically with his brother George in LaFayette and briefly with Edward Stone in Dadeville, Alabama. He had traveled to Louisiana, Texas, and South Carolina observing the life of the developing Old Southwest, and in 1842 he had married

Mary Brantley and become editor of the *East Alabamian* in LaFayette. Of his experiences during these years, perhaps the most significant for his literary career was his service in 1840 as a census taker, or "Chicken man," as the census takers were sometimes called that year because they were required to report the number of chickens that families raised. This experience provided Hooper the material for the sketch Porter published—" 'Taking the Census in Alabama' by a 'Chicken Man' of 1840."

Hooper's rapid rise to national prominence as one of the leading humorists of the South was capped in 1845 with the publication of his first collection of sketches, *Some Adventures of Captain Simon Suggs, Late of the Tallapoosa Volunteers; Together with "Taking the Census," and Other Alabama Sketches, By a Country Editor*. These sketches featuring Suggs, a rustic confidence man and trickster, had begun to appear in the *East Alabamian* in 1843 and were republished by Porter in the *Spirit of the Times* soon after. Porter published and encouraged a number of Southern humorists, but Hooper was always one of his favorites. It was at Porter's urging that Carey and Hart, the Philadelphia publishers, brought out Hooper's book and gave it national circulation.

In 1846 Hooper moved to Montgomery, following a brief appointment as editor of the Wetumpka, Alabama, *Whig*. In Montgomery he was first a junior editor of the *Alabama Journal*, but soon joined owners John Bates and E. Sanford Sayer as a full partner. By 1849 he was back in LaFayette and Chambers County where for a four-year term he served as solicitor for the North District, known locally as the "Bloody North." He continued to contribute to the *Alabama Journal*, sending notices of "Chambers Gossip" to his friends in Montgomery. He also briefly edited the Chambers County *Tribune*, but more significantly he continued to write and publish sketches, some of which were collected in book form by M. D. J. Slade in Tuscaloosa, Alabama, under the title *A Ride with Old Kit Knucker, and Other Sketches, and Scenes of Alabama*. This book received very limited circulation, but an enlarged edition published in Philadelphia by Hart in 1851, entitled *The Widow Rugby's Husband, A Night at the Ugly Man's, and Other Tales of Alabama*, was distributed much more widely.

Of all of Hooper's interests the most consuming was politics. When the Whig Party, which he had ardently supported, foundered, he turned first to the Know-Nothings and then to the secessionists led in Alabama by William L. Yancey. He came to believe that his reputation as a humorist interfered with his being taken seriously as a politician and even as a serious commentator and editorialist. Consequently, during the decade of the 1850s he turned away from his humorous sketches and contributed articles about hunting and racing to the *Spirit*. From July 1853 to April 1860, under the pseudonym "Number Eight," he contributed fourteen such pieces to the *Spirit of the Times*, and in 1856 he published with a New York firm, C. M. Saxton & Company, a book, *Dog and Gun: A Few Loose Chapters on Shooting, Among Which Will Be Found Some Anecdotes and Incidents*.

The Whig Party was in the minority of the Alabama legislature in 1853, which meant an end to Hooper's career as solicitor for the "Bloody North"; however, the lure of politics and the advantages of being associated again with a newspaper in the state capital were too great for him to resist. In 1854 he became editor of the Montgomery *Mail*, a position he held until he sold his interest in the paper in order to devote his full time to his duties as secretary of the Provisional Congress of the Confederate States of America. Most of what Hooper published after 1853 that was not about the hunt or the turf was about politics. His 1855 booklet of sixteen pages, *Read and Circulate: Proceedings of the Democratic and Anti–Know-Nothing Party in Caucus*, criticized in a humorously critical tone the caucus method the Democratic majority in the legislature used to exclude the Know-Nothings. In 1857 he wrote "Thirteen Sages of Antiquity Carica-tured," a humorous sketch about Masonic ritual that remained unpublished until 1886 when it appeared in *Magnum Opos. The Great Book of the University of Comus*. . . . He also wrote an introduction for the republication in book form of a series of letters that Thomas S. Woodward, one of the original settlers in northeast Alabama, had contributed to the *Mail*. Hooper's major concerns were increasingly with a defense of Southern institutions, and finally with promoting the cause of secession.

When representatives of the Southern states met in Montgomery on 4 February 1861, Hooper was acclaimed secretary of the Southern Convention, his nomi-nation having been made by W. P. Chilton of Alabama and seconded by Robert Toombs of Georgia. In May he moved to Richmond, where he continued to serve as secretary and librarian of the Confederate Congress until the Congress was reorganized early in 1862, and he was defeated in an effort to become secretary of the new Senate. The weeks before his death on 7 June 1862 in Richmond he spent preparing the records of the Provisional Congress for pres-ervation and publication.

MAJOR THEMES

Hooper's Simon Suggs is the hero of a book shaped from the sketches Hooper had printed in the *East Alabamian* and the *Spirit of the Times* during the early 1840s; the book presents itself as a campaign biography, *Some Adventures of Captain Simon Suggs, Late of the Tallapoosa Volunteers* . . . (1845). Suggs has not actually declared for office, but his biographer assumes that "Suggs thinks it 'more than probable' he shall 'come before the people of Tallapoosa.' " In fact, at the conclusion the narrator announces that he "seeks the Sheriffalty." Like the campaign biographies of Jackson, Van Buren, Clay, and Polk, Suggs's biography purports to present "the prominent events of his life with accuracy and impartiality." The invention of the campaign biography gives the sketches a form, however, which, except for a few collections like W. T. Thompson's letters of Major Joseph Jones, is unusual for antebellum Southern humor.

The Suggs sketches resemble many that had appeared in the pages of the *Spirit of the Times* both in the character of the protagonist and the framework in which he is presented. Suggs is characteristically a dissembler and trickster who often gets the better of his opponents—first his father, an evangelist who does not know about his son's accomplishments at card tricks, then the others, an office seeker who believes that Suggs is a member of the state legislature; the young blade who thinks Suggs is his rich uncle; the sheriff and judge who are convinced Suggs's dogs are deathly ill; the people of his district who believe that he can lead them in battle against the Indians and vote him their captain; and the minister at the camp meeting who thinks Suggs is "saved." In each case the captain follows his cardinal principle—"It is good to be shifty in a new country"—and usually his rewards are financial in a way that makes appropriate the metaphor by which he describes himself—"Let who will run, gentlemen, Simon Suggs will allers be found sticking thar like a tick onder a cow's belly—." Suggs inhabits a world of vicious, ruthless economic competition in which piety and ethics, however forcefully stated, are ironic and superfluous. After he has capitalized on the weaknesses of others—weaknesses that derive from pride of family, evangelical enthusiasm, greed, and self-righteousness—Suggs often declares that he sees the hand of providence in his success. Life for Suggs is a game; the reward is not so much the money or material goods he might win as it is the pleasure he gets from outwitting his companions.

Hooper is remembered primarily for *Some Adventures of Captain Simon Suggs*. His other sketches, most of them collected in *The Widow Rugby's Husband, A Night at the Ugly Man's, and Other Tales of Alabama* (1851), are of a kind with other sketches in the humor of the South and Old Southwest, though Hooper's superior artistry is usually apparent. The practical joke played on the unsuspecting is a favorite; usually the victim is a man of some pretension—a lawyer who wears a wig, a judge who has no sense of humor. Suggs himself appears in some of these. Several sketches feature characters who are vulnerable to victimization by others or even of nature itself because of their love for money or alcohol or because of laziness. There is the man, for example, who is so lazy that he can only raise his head when the water of the Tallapoosa rises over the bank where he is lying on his back.

Irishmen caught Hooper's interest. They told tales of old Ireland (elephants came from Ireland, of course), and they spoke an Irish brogue that made them different. Jimmy Owen, the doorkeeper of the Alabama House of Representatives, was Irish and figured in two of Hooper's sketches as he did in many of those of Hooper's colleague John G. Barr (*Rowdy Tales from Early Alabama*, ed. G. Ward Hubbs).

SURVEY OF CRITICISM

Hooper's tales were popular with readers and editors of Southern humor. Almost every significant collection, from those edited by William Trotter Porter to the most recent edited by Henig Cohen and William P. Dillingham, contains selections from Hooper. The introduction and headnotes to these place Hooper solidly among the realistic humorists of the Old South. These were writers who not only sought to enjoy the oddities of dialect or bumptiousness, but who also sought to record the manners of antebellum Southerners, usually poor whites. As W. Stanley Hoole has pointed out, Suggs may have resembled a little too clearly Hooper's acquaintance, Bird H. Young.

The influence of Hooper on Mark Twain and later Southern writers has been studied by Bernard De Voto (*Mark Twain's America*), Kenneth S. Lynn (*Mark Twain and Southwestern Humor*), Willard Thorp ("Suggs and Sut in Modern Dress: The Latest Chapter in Southern Humor"), and others. Lynn is also convinced that the narrative structure of the Simon Suggs stories, together with that found in a large number of antebellum Southern stories, was designed to serve the political and social interests of the Whigs. The Southern yeoman speaks, Lynn observes, but usually within a framework controlled by an educated, sophisticated, Whig gentleman.

Alias Simon Suggs: The Life and Times of Johnson Jones Hooper, the biography of Hooper by W. Stanley Hoole, is a relatively full account of what is known about Hooper's life and can be supplemented by Norris W. Yates's *William T. Porter and the "Spirit of the Times"* and Edgar E. Thompson's M.A. thesis, "The Literary Career of Johnson Jones Hooper: A Bibliographical Study of Primary and Secondary Material (With a Collection of Hooper's Letters)," remains the best primary bibliography and is still useful for a summary of secondary resources. Howard Winston Smith's Vanderbilt University dissertation, "An Annotated Edition of Hooper's *Some Adventures of Captain Simon Suggs*," is useful, and his *Johnson Jones Hooper: A Critical Study*, published on microcard, needs to be made available in a more usable form.

BIBLIOGRAPHY

Works by Johnson Jones Hooper

Some Adventures of Captain Simon Suggs, Late of the Tallapoosa Volunteers; Together with "Taking the Census," and Other Alabama Sketches. Philadelphia: Carey and Hart, 1845.

A Ride with Old Kit Knucker, and Other Sketches and Scenes of Alabama. Tuscaloosa: M. D. J. Slade, 1849.

The Widow Rugby's Husband, a Night at the Ugly Man's, and Other Tales of Alabama. Philadelphia: A. Hart, 1851.

Read and Circulate: Proceedings of the Democratic and Anti–Know-Nothing Party in Caucus; or the Guillotine at Work. . . . Montgomery: Barret and Wimbish, 1855.

Dog and Gun: A Few Loose Chapters on Shooting. New York: C. M. Saxton & Company, 1856.

Simon Suggs' Adventures and Travels, Comprising All of the Scenes, Incidents, and Adventures of His Travels . . . With Widow Rugby's Husband, and Twenty-Six Other Humorous Tales of Alabama. . . . Philadelphia: T. B. Peterson, 1856.

"An Annotated Edition of Hooper's *Some Adventures of Captain Simon Suggs*." Ed. Howard Winston Smith. Ph.D. diss., Vanderbilt University, 1965.

"The Porter-Hooper Correspondence." Ed. Edgar E. Thompson. *Gyascutus: Studies in Antebellum Southern Humorous and Sporting Writing*. Ed. James L. W. West III. Atlantic Highlands, N.J.: Humanities Press, 1978, pp. 219–34.

Studies of Johnson Jones Hooper

Anderson, John Q. "For the Ugliest Man: An Example of Folk Humor." *Southern Folklore Quarterly* 28 (1964): 199–209.

Bettersworth, John K. "The Humor of the Old Southwest: Yesterday and Today." *Mississippi Quarterly* 17 (1964): 87–94.

Blair, Walter. "Burlesques in Nineteenth-Century American Humor." *American Literature* 2 (1930): 236–47.

———. "Traditions in Southern Humor." *American Quarterly* 5 (1953): 132–42.

Budd, Louis J. "Gentlemanly Humor in the Old South." *Southern Folklore Quarterly* 17 (1953): 232–40.

Current-Garcia, Eugene. "Alabama Writers in the *Spirit*." *Alabama Review* 10 (1957): 243–69.

———. "Newspaper Humor in the Old South, 1835–1855." *Alabama Review* 2 (1949): 102–21.

De Voto, Bernard. *Mark Twain's America*. Boston: Little, Brown, 1932.

Ellison, Rhoda C. *Early Alabama Publications: A Study in Literary Interests*. University: University of Alabama Press, 1947.

Hoole, W. Stanley. *Alias Simon Suggs: The Life and Times of Johnson Jones Hooper*. University: University of Alabama Press, 1952.

Hopkins, Robert. "Simon Suggs: A Burlesque Campaign Biography." *American Quarterly* 15 (1963): 459–63.

Lynn, Kenneth S. "The Confidence Man." *Mark Twain and Southwestern Humor*. Boston: Little, Brown, 1959.

———. "Johnson Jones Hooper." *The Comic Tradition in America*. Garden City, N.Y.: Doubleday, 1958, pp. 94–97.

Parks, Edd Winfield. "The Intent of Antebellum Southern Humorists." *Mississippi Quarterly* 13 (1960): 163–68.

———. "The Three Streams of Southern Humor." *Georgia Review* 9 (1955): 147–59.

Smith, Howard Winston. *Johnson Jones Hooper: A Critical Study*. Nashville: South Atlantic Modern Language Association, 1962 (Microcard edition).

Thompson, Edgar E. "The Literary Career of Johnson Jones Hooper: A Bibliographical Study of Primary and Secondary Material (with a Collection of Hooper's Letters)." M.A. thesis, Mississippi State University, 1971.

Thorp, Willard. "Suggs and Sut in Modern Dress: The Latest Chapter in Southern Humor." *Mississippi Quarterly* 13 (1960): 169–75.

Turner, Arlin. "Realism and Fantasy in Southern Humor." *Georgia Review* 12 (1958): 451–57.

———. "Seeds of Literary Revolt in the Humor of the Old Southwest." *Louisiana Historical Quarterly* 39 (1956): 143–51.

Watterson, Henry. "The South in Light and Shade." *The Compromises of Life and Other Lectures and Addresses*. New York: Fox, Duffield, 1903.

Wellman, Manly W. Introduction. *Adventures of Captain Simon Suggs*. Chapel Hill: University of North Carolina Press, 1969.

West, H. C. "Simon Suggs and His Similes." *North Carolina Folklore* 16 (1968): 43–57.

Yates, Norris W. "Johnson Jones Hooper." *A Bibliographical Guide to the Study of Southern Literature*. Ed. Louis D. Rubin, Jr. Baton Rouge: Louisiana State University Press, 1969, pp. 223–24.

———. *William T. Porter and the "Spirit of the Times": A Study of the Big Bear School of Humor*. Baton Rouge: Louisiana State University Press, 1969.

George Moses Horton
(ca.1797–ca.1883)

Though his birth and death dates are unverified and even the place where he died is not known, George Moses Horton, the self-styled Sable Bard of North Carolina, achieved a number of impressive ''firsts'' during his remarkably long life. He has been called the first black professional poet in America and one of the first professional writers in the South. Horton was the first black poet in the South to publish a volume of poetry, and he must have been one of the few poets anywhere to have had a book of his poems published before he had even learned to write down his own ideas for himself.

BIOGRAPHY

George Moses Horton was born a slave on the farm of one William Horton in Northampton County, North Carolina. The year of his birth is generally believed to have been 1797 or 1798, but since the birth of a slave child was almost never entered in the courthouse records and only rarely entered in the master's family Bible, the date of his birth probably will never be known.

In 1800, when George was a toddler, William Horton moved his household into the rolling hills of Chatham County. The Hortons' new farmstead was situated less than ten miles from the towns of Chapel Hill and Pittsborough (now Pittsboro), to the north and south respectively. It was here that George's earliest lasting impressions of the world were formed, according to his recollections in the autobiographical introduction to his second volume of poems in 1845.

Horton does not say much about his father except that he was his mother's second husband and that Mother Horton had ''left her husband behind'' when George was very young, evidently when she was forced to move to Chatham County. Horton's father may have been the slave of another family (he is never mentioned as a slave of William Horton), or he may have been a free Negro who was not able to accompany his family to their new home. The poet himself was to have a somewhat similar experience in his adult life, with his own wife and children being the legal property of his master's neighbor and carrying the surname of their master rather than that of their husband and father. Such was life in some slave families. The poet later commented in several poems on the forced separation of slave families.

On the new farm in Chatham, George was assigned the task of tending cows. During the ten years or so which he spent as a "cow-boy" he evidently had time during some of his workdays to work toward a twofold goal that occupied an ever increasing portion of his efforts: the mastery of reading and writing. His efforts to learn to read included gleaning bits of information from white school-children, acquiring scraps of paper and pieces of discarded schoolbooks, and poring over his mother's old worn Bible and Wesley hymnal, struggling to match familiar passages to the words he was learning to recognize.

George's younger brother (whose name does not appear in any of George's poetry or prose) learned to read along with the future poet. In fact, the younger Horton learned to write much sooner than George did. The two brothers spent much of their "free" time on Sabbath days working at their studies until the younger brother grew tired of scholarly pursuits and joined the other children in more orthodox leisure activities. But George had discovered the special allure of a particular kind of writing called poetry. He preferred this material to any other kind of writing and wondered if he would ever be able to compose in this manner.

The only person who knew about Horton's early compositions was his younger brother, but the budding poet's audience was destined to be broadened dramatically before 1820. In 1814, when William Horton divided part of his assets with his children, Old Master's son James became George's new master. Shortly thereafter, George began carrying produce to Chapel Hill on weekends for sale to the students and other buyers around the state university. The students had a custom of requiring prospective salesmen to entertain them before they would consider purchasing the proffered produce.

When he was told to entertain the students, Horton launched into streams of oratory and poetry. The students were impressed, but skeptical. Horton demonstrated the extent to which he had mastered the verse-maker's craft by composing original pieces on the spot. Soon students were offering Horton 25 cents or more to compose poems and love letters for them to send to their sweethearts. The legend of Poet Horton had begun!

One part of the legend says that one of the first students to befriend Poet Horton was James Polk, destined to be elected eleventh president of the United States in 1844. This story is highly improbable in view of the fact that when Horton wrote his autobiography in 1845 Polk was already president, and Polk was not named among the seventeen students that Horton recalled as having aided him. With Horton's tendency to play to the grandstand and attempt to exploit his connections with famous and quasi-famous people, he would certainly have mentioned that the president was his friend; he would also have written several poems about him. The Polk story is fairly typical of various legends that arose around the Black Bard of Chapel Hill.

As Horton continued to make his weekly trips to Chapel Hill, delivering the poems that had been commissioned the previous week, he continued to receive money as well as clothes, books, liquor, and literary assistance from interested students and faculty.

The most notable of Horton's literary helpers at Chapel Hill was Mrs. Caroline Lee Hentz. A native of Massachusetts, she was the wife of Professor Nicholas Hentz, who taught at the university from 1826 to 1830. Mrs. Hentz was herself a published author of poetry, fiction, and drama. In 1826 Caroline Hentz took Horton as her personal protégé. Not only did she assist him with his writing techniques; she also helped him to get his work into print in the North as well as in North Carolina.

In 1828 and 1829 two attempts to purchase Horton's freedom were made. These campaigns brought together diverse and widely separated people and agencies. Actively interested persons included Caroline Hentz; Dr. James Henderson, a Chapel Hill physician; English-born newspaper editor, Joseph Gales, and his Carolina-born son, Weston Raleigh Gales; the native Carolinian polemicist, David Walker, then residing in Boston; and a certain anonymous "philanthropic gentleman." Organizations and publications involved in these efforts included the North Carolina Colonization Society, the North Carolina Manumission Society, *Freedom's Journal* of New York (the first American newspaper edited by blacks), and the *Raleigh Register*, edited by the Gales family.

The first of the two campaigns was reported in *Freedom's Journal* between August and October 1828. The newspaper and the "philanthropic gentleman" established contact with James Horton regarding the possible purchase of his plowboy poet. The *Journal* reported in October that Mr. David Walker, a free man and a native of Horton's home state, had become a subscriber to the Free-Horton Fund and was serving as coordinator of the effort in Massachusetts. The plan was to raise enough money to offer James Horton $100 more than any reasonable person would say George was worth. James refused to accept the offer.

James Horton's refusal to respond favorably evidently did not convince George and his well-wishers in North Carolina that obtaining the poet's freedom by legal means was impossible. In 1829 the North Carolina Colonization Society joined forces with the Hentz and Gales families and other interested Carolinians in a new effort to bring about Horton's manumission. The new project involved the publication and sale of a book of Horton's poems. Horton's supporters hoped that the money derived from the sale of the book and from sympathetic contributors would make possible an offer Master Horton could not refuse—especially since the Colonization Society stood ready to guarantee the newly freed bard's speedy departure for Liberia on the earliest available vessel.

The book, entitled *The Hope of Liberty* (1829), did not gain its author his liberty; however, it did accomplish some important "firsts," the complex ironies of which can hardly be overemphasized. A slave had written a book. The slave's book was published in a slaveholding state, and although teaching a Negro to read and write was not yet a crime in North Carolina (it was declared illegal in 1830), it certainly was not a common practice. People of means residing in this slaveholding state were expected to give their money to help get this gifted African-American out of the "peculiar institution" that the state laws declared to be his rightful place. But in order for the slave poet to claim his freedom, he would have to leave behind the land of his birth, and people, black and white, whom he had esteemed for nearly a third of a century. Peculiar institution, indeed!

Regardless of the ironies involved in its publication, Horton's *Hope of Liberty* was the first book of poetry by a black American in half a century. It was the first book of any kind by a black person in the South and, evidently, the first poetic protest of his status by any slave. It was a slim volume containing 21 poems. The subject matter was largely confined to love, death, religion, and slavery. The collection provided a good sampling of Horton's talents, although the publishers explained that they had excluded a number of the slave poet's offerings to keep down costs.

During the decade following publication of Horton's first book, several events occurred that affected his life profoundly, not all for the better. One event was the departure of Professor Hentz from Chapel Hill, along with his wife, George's mentor and champion. Another of Horton's champions, David Walker, made a contribution to the conditions of the black poet's life that same year, but hardly the kind of contribution either Walker or Horton would have wished. In 1830 Walker published his *Appeal*, in which he cited history and Scripture in his condemnation of American slavery as doomed to feel the wrath of a just and vengeful God. Slaveholders and proslavery sympathizers offered a reward for Walker's capture—in addition to placing more stringent restrictions on their own slaves. That same year, the North Carolina legislature enacted a law requiring any slave upon being freed to leave the state and never return, and another law making it a crime to teach Negroes to read and write.

During the 1830s George and his master reached an agreement whereby the poet would "hire his time," an arrangement that would allow George to live in Chapel Hill in exchange for paying 25 cents a day to James Horton (later 50 cents a day to James's brother, Hall Horton).

Also in the 1830s, Dr. Joseph Caldwell, who as president of the university had befriended Horton, died and was replaced by former Governor David Swain. Horton, expecting Swain to be as helpful as his predecessor, entrusted the new president with his plans to obtain his freedom, including letters to such diverse persons as Master Horton, Horace Greeley, William Lloyd Garrison, and President Swain himself. Swain filed all the letters in what would be compiled as the Swain Papers. Horton probably did not know what became of his letters, but not receiving replies must have frustrated him.

In his curiously truncated autobiography, Horton never mentions any attempts (or even any strong desire) to obtain his freedom. His accounts of his life break off abruptly with the departure of the Hentzes from Chapel Hill in 1830, without mentioning *The Hope of Liberty*, which had been published the previous year. This autobiography served as a preface to Horton's second volume of poems, *The Poetical Works of George M. Horton*, published in 1845. Another ingredient significantly absent from Horton's *Works* was any outward sign of protest; the words *free, freedom, slave, slavery*, and *liberty* never appear in the titles of any of the poems in *Works*, although they appear frequently in the titles of poems in Horton's other volumes.

Only two of the poems in *Works*, "Farewell to Frances" and "Division of an Estate," contain any anti-slavery protest. The protest in "Farewell" is so generalized that a reader might not associate the poem's loneliness with the particular agonies brought on by the forced separation of a slave family.

The issue is presented much more forcefully in "Division of an Estate," which may be Horton's best protest poem. Though its title does not have any of those tell-tale key words that usually signal the Horton protest poem, "Division" is an emotion-charged description of an estate whose old master is dead or dying. The masterless estate is first depicted as a body without a head, its various members struggling for ascendancy and control. The stark contrast between the upward aspirations of the family heirs, looking toward the heavens to read their fate in the stars, and the abjectly apprehensive prospects of the slaves, whose fate is bound up with that of the family livestock, faced with the strong possibility of being split up and sold to various bidders, makes a powerful argument.

Despite having "potentially objectionable" material omitted from it, and despite its inclusion of a list of nearly a hundred supporters (many of them prominent Carolina citizens), *Poetical Works* did not sell well. Horton was not able to use it to convince his master or President Swain or anyone else of his ability to earn substantial amounts of money.

Of course, students were still buying poems from Horton, but the novelty of the Sable Bard had worn off. He was around all day every day, not just on weekends. When Hall Horton raised the "rent" on the quasi-freedom of his verse-making vassal from 25 to 50 cents per day, George was unable (or unwilling) to keep up the payments, so he then lived only sporadically in Chapel Hill, sometimes doing odd jobs and becoming increasingly familiar with the Demon Rum.

One event in Horton's life that is never mentioned in his extant writings is his marriage to a slave of Franklin Snipes, a Chatham County farmer. The union produced two children; the children and their mother carried the surname Snipes rather than Horton. The son died as a young adult; the daughter married and lived in Raleigh. Horton's writings make no mention of his children or his wife (unless some of the poems Horton wrote later in his life deriding and ridiculing women could be seen as expressing dissatisfaction with his own marriage).

Although the happiness or unhappiness of Horton's married life may be a matter for conjecture, his experiences at the university were unquestionably fraught with mixed emotions. His special status on campus had lost the element of novelty; the president, rather than promoting the slave poet's cause, was dragging his feet, or perhaps pulling in the opposite direction. Horton was no longer a young man: he had had three masters; he had seen generations of students come and go. Yet his position as "slave poet in part-time residence" had not lost all of its attractiveness. In the 1840s and 1850s campus literary publications carried several of Horton's poems. That is not remarkable in itself. What is remarkable is the number of "Hortonesque" poems that were attributed to authors other than Horton, suggesting that he may have been the founder of a literary "school."

As the years went by, Horton continued to write. As 1860 approached, there were stories of slave revolts and murmurs of impending war. Life in central North Carolina became increasingly uncertain. With the start of the Civil War, students left school to fight. Apprehension quickened late in the war when reports circulated that Sherman's forces had marched through Georgia and were headed through the Carolinas.

When Horton heard that Union forces were in Raleigh, he set out for the capital city (and long-sought freedom) with his precious manuscripts in hand. He soon found a new champion in Captain Will Banks of the 9th Michigan Cavalry.

In late summer 1865 Captain Banks and his new protégé rushed into print with a volume called *Naked Genius*. The new book, with well over one hundred poems, exceeded the combined contents of the two books that had been published while Horton was still legally a slave. Unfortunately, the haste with which the book evidently was published resulted in numerous printing errors and factual mistakes.

Despite its flaws, *Naked Genius* did show some facets of George Horton's varied interests and poetic techniques that had not been seen in his two earlier volumes or in the pieces that had been published in periodicals. Especially notable were the antimarriage poems that could be called collectively the "Contrathalamia." It is particularly curious that these poems were written by a man who, in his earlier years, had literally made his living from the existence of love and prospective marriages; in his declining years, he was lambasting love and mocking marriage.

Naked Genius fared no better financially than its predecessors, despite Captain Banks's invitation to enterprising persons to send money in exchange for a copy of a second edition of *Naked Genius* and a full prospectus outlining the soon-to-be-released *The Black Poet*, which was to be larger and more comprehensive than *Genius*. There is no evidence that either *The Black Poet* or the second edition of *Naked Genius* was ever published. Will Banks returned to Michigan, and George Moses Horton went to Philadelphia. In 1866 Philadelphia's Banneker Institute, an organization of progressive black intellectuals, reported rejecting the publication of a book of poems by a Mr. George Horton of North Carolina because the project was too expensive.

Horton's life from 1866 onward is shrouded in mystery. It was reported that he turned to writing prose fiction based on cleverly updated plots of Bible stories. It was also suggested that Horton sold the same stories to several publications simultaneously, thus becoming a syndicated author, but no such stories can be found.

Exhaustive searches have failed to detect any record of George Moses Horton's death in either North Carolina or Pennsylvania. The body of this proud black man who longed for fame and fortune lies somewhere unknown and unnoted. His writing deserves a better fate.

MAJOR THEMES

In 1974 M. A. Richmond wrote a book entitled *Bid the Vassal Soar* about the lives and writings of both Phillis Wheatley and George Moses Horton. Its title comes from a line that appears in several of Horton's poems; this concept of soaring is a predominant theme in much of his poetry. It should not be surprising that poetry protesting against slavery would make use of images of rising, flying, floating free, in a word, soaring; but the soaring concept is fundamental to many of Horton's poems on religion, love, and other subjects as well as those that are obvious antislavery protests.

According to Horton's own accounts, the first poems he ever made up were religious. These were the earliest lines of verse he could recall composing (many years before he had learned to write):

> Rise up, my soul, and let us go
>   Up to the gospel feast;
> Gird on the garment white as snow,
>   To join and be a guest.
> Dost thou not hear the trumpet call
>   For thee, my soul, for thee?
> Not only thee, my soul, but all
>   May rise and enter free.

The idea of "rising" and entering "free" reinforces the idea of rising up, with which the piece began. At the same time, it anticipates the notion of fleeing by flying, which undergirds much of Horton's poetry. His 1829 poem "Heavenly Love," from *Hope of Liberty*, is filled with references to rising, floating, and soaring.

The religious poems in Horton's last published volume, *Naked Genius* (1865), include two particularly noteworthy pieces. They are noteworthy because of their verse form and rhyme scheme and also because of the way Horton was able to incorporate the ideal of religious virtue in the person of a woman in each poem.

One of these poems, "Rachael or Virtue," is based on the Old Testament story of Jacob and Rachel, wherein Jacob loved Rachel above all other women, but had to labor long and hard (and even marry her sister) before he could have her for a wife. Horton's poem, showing preference for Rachel (identified with virtue) over mere mortal women, devotes short, choppy lines to Kate, Annie, Molly, Fanny, and other mortal women in studied contrast to the longer, flowing lines devoted to Rachel.

"Rosabella—Purity of Heart," like "Rachael or Virtue," personifies a religious virtue in the guise of a woman. "Rosabella" concludes with this stanza:

> When other pleasures tire,
>   And mortal glories fade to glow no more,
> She with the wing of truth augments her fire,
>   And still prevails to soar;
> All else must die, the good and wise,
> But Rosabella never dies.

Thus, virtue (Rosabella) herself is portrayed as undying and as prevailing "to soar" on the "wing of truth" in the poem's final image. Horton's techniques had changed over the years, but the image of soaring was as important as ever.

Although Rosabella and Rachael were not real women, the subjects of many Horton poems were very human and evidently very female. These were the women of Horton's love poems, most of them composed for quick sale and therefore usually not infused with serious poetic concerns. Yet even in these commercial compositions, Horton's ideas of floating and flying can be seen frequently. Sometimes the speaker in a Horton love poem speaks of wafting or floating on the very wings of love; at other times he talks of fleeing or flying *away* from love's influence, perhaps seeing it as a kind of imprisonment or enslavement.

Love as enslavement, something to be avoided or escaped, is the dominant theme in that special group of Horton poems first published in 1865, the Contrathalamia poems. As one might expect, these poems are loaded with direct and indirect references to flying, fleeing, escaping, and just plain avoiding. A good example of such avoidance: "Woman, thou bloom of every danger, / From whom all my sorrows rise, / To thee I'd live and die a stranger; / He who shuns thee must be wise." The tone of these pieces may be angry, sarcastic, bitter, humorous, playful, or some combination thereof. Whatever the tone, the message seems to be that women and marriage should be avoided by single men and fled by those already married.

Of a far less speculative nature is the motivation behind the flight imagery in Horton's anti-slavery protests. His poems depicted slavery as unjust and unnatural, a wrong bound to be righted by a just God. Images such as wings, pinions, angels, birds, and even songs, as well as such qualities as strength, endurance, and patience are seen lifting the vassals out of their misery, enabling them to soar away to a better existence.

"Division of an Estate" uses images of the heavens and earth to show the contrast between the situation of the heirs to an "estate" that is being "divided" at the death of the Old Master and that of the slaves who are part of the estate—to be "divided" just as the other assets are. The heirs are described as arriving like evening stars appearing in the sky at the disappearance of the sun, "the donor of their lamps" (Old Master). The heirs look up in anticipation of their good fortune. The fate of "poor vassals" is not, however, written in the celestial sphere; it is on the earthly plane with the livestock (other items of property to be divided). If the slaves look up, they see only the "spire of chance" or the "trembling pinnacle" (symbols of the auction block) on which they "soon must stand." This poem shows the anguish and hopelessness that prevail when people are earthbound and all hope of soaring is denied.

Horton wrote poems on many other subjects: the seasons, history, current events, famous and not-so-famous people, poetry itself, and Horton himself. The soaring motif is the dominant theme of most of his work.

Another theme that figures prominently in Horton's poetry is the concept of home, or more accurately, homegoing. Perhaps this theme would be expected in religious poetry, but it operates in many of Horton's other poems as well. The two related themes of flying and homegoing are frequently combined, as one flies not only from something but to something as well: "Fly away home."

The interrelated concepts of soaring on wings of inspiration, fleeing from bondage and trouble, floating on clouds of fame, and flying home to God were particularly appropriate for a farm-bound poet who longed for opportunities to soar while circumstances and powers were conspiring to force his Pegasus to pull a plow.

SURVEY OF CRITICISM

George Moses Horton's work has not received much attention. Most of it has never been seen by the people who might have an interest in it. Pre–twentieth-century writings about Horton were mainly expressions of wonder and admiration that an unschooled slave could write any kind of poetry at all. They tended to add to the Horton legend, but usually contributed little to an assessment of his work.

The 1920s and 1930s saw a new interest in Afro-American literature. Such scholars as Benjamin G. Brawley, Hugh Gloster, Vernon Loggins, and Jay Saunders Redding attempted to shed more light on the "forerunners" of the Harlem Renaissance. Horton was treated as one of them.

With the coming of the Black Power and Black Is Beautiful movements of the 1960s and 1970s, more attention came to George Horton. The many black anthologies that were printed or reprinted always contained a few Horton poems. Unfortunately, the poems anthologized were almost all from Horton's 1829 *Hope of Liberty* and Garrison's *Liberator*, since the poems of Horton's 1845 and 1865 volumes were practically inaccessible; thus, the anthologizers generally copied each other's offerings.

Richard Walser's *The Black Poet* (1966) and Merle A. Richmond's *Bid the Vassal Soar* (1973) were book-length studies that provide valuable information. Among the most valuable shorter studies are William Edward Farrison's "George Moses Horton: Poet for Freedom" (1971), which examines Horton's protest poetry, and John L. Cobbs's "George Moses Horton's Hope of Liberty: Thematic Unity in Early American Black Poetry" (1981), which discusses soaring imagery as the unifying principle in Horton's first volume.

Although the University of North Carolina Press has issued a facsimile edition of *Naked Genius*, much still needs to be done toward making Horton's poetry more accessible. Critical editions with careful annotations are needed. Attempts might be made to identify and collect more of Horton's "fugitive" pieces, since it is possible that the best of his love poems may be those that he sold, and they may now be falling apart in somebody's great-grandmother's old hope chest. Although neither *The Black Poet* nor the second edition of *Naked Genius* was ever published, there is evidence that both volumes existed in manuscript form. Their discovery and publication could add greatly to our knowledge of Horton, as could the discovery of some of the writings of his Philadelphia period. Much of the mystery of the legendary Sable Bard lives on; we need to keep working on solving the mystery.

BIBLIOGRAPHY

Works by George Moses Horton

The Hope of Liberty. Raleigh, N.C.: J. Gales & Son, 1829.
"The Slave." *Liberator* 4 (29 March 1834): 52.
"Poems." *Southern Literary Messenger* 19 (April 1843): 33–36.
The Poetical Works of George Moses Horton, the Colored Bard of North Carolina. Hillsborough, N.C.: Dennis Heartt, 1845.
"Poems." *North Carolina University Magazine*. Published by the Dialectic and Philosophical Societies. Various Issues, 1852–60.
Naked Genius. Raleigh, N.C.: Wm. B. Smith, 1865.
"Address to Students of UNC." Manuscript Copy. North Carolina Collection, University of North Carolina at Chapel Hill.
"Letters" to Garrison, Greeley, and Swain. Unpublished Manuscripts. The David L. Swain Papers. Southern Historical Collection, University of North Carolina at Chapel Hill.
"Poems." Pettigrew Papers. Southern Historical Collection.

Studies of George Moses Horton

Battle, Kemp Plummer. "George Horton, The Slave Poet." *North Carolina University Magazine* n.s. 7 (May 1888): 229–32.

Brawley, Benjamin G. *Early Negro American Writers*. Chapel Hill: University of North Carolina Press, 1935. repr. New York: Books for Libraries Press, 1968.

————. *The Negro Genius: A New Appraisal of the Achievement of the American Negro in Literature and the Fine Arts*. New York: Dodd, Mead, 1937.

————. "Three Negro Poets: Horton, Mrs. Harper, and Whitman." *Journal of Negro History* 2 (October 1917): 384–92.

Carroll, William. "Naked Genius: The Poetry of George Moses Horton, Slave Bard of North Carolina, 1797?–1883." Ph.D. diss., University of North Carolina at Chapel Hill, 1978.

Cobb, Collier. "An American Man of Letters." *The University Magazine* (North Carolina) n.s. 27 (October 1909): 25–32.

Cobbs, John L. "George Moses Horton's *Hope of Liberty*: Thematic Unity in Early American Black Poetry." *CLA Journal* 24 (June 1981): 441–50.

Farrison, William Edward. "George Moses Horton: Poet for Freedom." *CLA Journal* 14 (March 1971): 227–41.

Garrett, Thomas Miles. *Diary*. Unpublished Typescript. North Carolina Collection.

Jackson, Blyden and Louis D. Rubin, Jr. *Black Poetry in America: Two Essays in Historical Interpretation*. Baton Rouge: Louisiana State University Press, 1974.

Lakin, Mattie T. "George Moses Horton." M.A. thesis, North Carolina Central University (then North Carolina College), 1951.

Loggins, Vernon. *The Negro Author: His Development in America to 1900*. New York: Columbia University Press, 1931; repr. Port Washington, N.Y.: Kennikat Press, 1964.

Redding, Jay Saunders. *To Make a Poet Black*. Chapel Hill: University of North Carolina Press, 1939; repr. College Park, Md.: McGrath, 1968.

Richmond, Merle A. *Bid the Vassal Soar: Interpretive Essays on the Life and Poetry of Phillis Wheatley and George Moses Horton*. Washington, D.C.: Howard University Press, 1974.

Rush, Theresa G. et al. *Black American Writers Past and Present: A Biographical and Bibliographical Dictionary*. 2 vols. Metuchen, N.J.: Scarecrow Press, 1975.

Turner, Darwin T. *Afro-American Writers*. New York: Appleton-Century-Crofts, 1970. (A Goldentree Bibliography.)

Walser, Richard. *The Black Poet: The Story of George Moses Horton, A North Carolina Slave*. New York: Philosophical Library, 1966.

Thomas Jefferson
(1743–1826)

Governor of Virginia (1779–81), minister to France (1784–89), secretary of state under George Washington (1789–93), vice-president under John Adams (1797–1801), president of the United States (1801–9)—Thomas Jefferson was all of these. For his epitaph, he chose other items: "Here was buried / Thomas Jefferson / Author of the Declaration of American Independence / of the Statute of Virginia for religious freedom / And Father of the University of Virginia." Giving primacy to his achievement as author, Jefferson highlighted his role as maker, and he was a master with words. His *Notes on the State of Virginia* (1785) is the most important scientific and political book by an American to that time. Following his death, publication of his journals, letters, and other materials has confirmed his literary importance.

BIOGRAPHY

Thomas Jefferson was born on 13 April (2 April Old Style) 1743, at Shadwell, Virginia, one of several tobacco plantations owned by his father, Peter Jefferson, in what was then the Virginia "up country," a few miles from Charlottesville. His mother, Jane Randolph, was from one of the most distinguished Tidewater families in the Commonwealth. An intelligent man, though formally uneducated, Peter Jefferson became a prosperous landowner and member of the Virginia legislature. Thomas, the oldest of their several children, was educated by private tutors, in a nearby school, and at the College of William and Mary in the colonial capital of Virginia, Williamsburg.

Following his graduation in 1762, Jefferson studied law with the celebrated jurist George Wythe; became a member of the Virginia House of Burgesses; married a much-courted young widow, Martha Wayles Skelton; and returned to Albemarle County and his still incomplete mansion at Monticello.

Jefferson's first action as a public servant had been an unsuccessful attempt to allow owners to free their slaves. Subsequently, he became a major actor on a much larger stage. As indignation against the British grew throughout the colonies, Jefferson was appointed delegate to the Second Continental Congress where, in 1776, he chaired a committee that included Benjamin Franklin and John Adams to prepare a declaration of independence; he alone wrote the final version, the culmination of his early career.

The next decade was a tumultuous one. As a member of the Virginia House of Delegates, Jefferson made a thorough revision of the laws of Virginia, a revision highlighted by what eventually became his Act for Establishing Religious Freedom, 1779; was elected Governor of Virginia; began what was to be his only full-length book, the *Notes on the State of Virginia*; was a delegate to the Confederation Congress in 1783; and the following year, two years after the death of his wife, was appointed Minister Plenipotentiary of the United States to the Court of France.

The next five years were perhaps the richest of Jefferson's entire life. Apart from his many duties on the "vaunted scene of Europe," Jefferson was for the first time really able to indulge what he called his "canine appetite" for reading, and to satisfy his insatiable curiosity about the natural world and the achievements of "Old Europe's" scientists, scholars, philosophers, and artists. A tireless tourist, Jefferson reveled in the Continent's museums, galleries, and remnants of the past; with equal curiosity and delight, he traveled through the French and Italian countryside noting and recording the characteristics of the people, their farms and vineyards, their ways of life. Most important, perhaps, was his friendship—if it can be called that—with Maria Cosway, the vivacious, intelligent, and beautiful wife of an idiosyncratic English painter; no other woman was to engender the emotions Jefferson expressed so eloquently—and, perhaps, naively—in the controversial "My Head and My Heart" dialogue written in Paris, 12 October 1786.

Jefferson returned to the United States in 1789. The next two decades were the most important of his public career, highlighted by his serving as secretary of state during the presidency of George Washington, as vice president under John Adams, and as president from 1801 to 1809. At the same time, he continued his scientific and literary pursuits, which included gathering an invaluable collection of early Indian dialects; maintaining an astonishing correspondence among scholars, intellectuals, and political figures of all persuasions; aiding in establishing a national library and compiling the catalogue of the books that would be its basis; and, in the midst of pressing domestic and foreign crises, collecting a magnificent personal library of some 6,500 volumes, which he later sold to the government to replace the original national library, destroyed by the British in 1814.

In 1809 Jefferson retired to his beloved Monticello. His so-called retirement years were highlighted by his fulfillment of a long-cherished dream, the founding of the University of Virginia (his supervision ranged from designing the buildings and grounds to preparing the curriculum, sending an emissary to Europe to select a faculty, and supervising the purchase of books for the university library, the catalog of which he himself, of course, had prepared). He died at Monticello on the 50th anniversary of the day that had changed the world—4 July 1776. Ancient John Adams's often-quoted words, as he too lay dying on 4 July 1826, are as meaningful today as they were then: "Thomas Jefferson still lives."

MAJOR THEMES

Jefferson wrote only one full-length book, the *Notes on the State of Virginia*. The genesis of the *Notes* was a series of questions prepared in 1780 by François Marbois, then secretary of the French Legation at Philadelphia, a kind of semi-official questionnaire concerning the American states at a time when the outcome of the Revolution was "extremely hazardous." One set of these questions was sent to a member of the Virginia delegation who in turn forwarded it to Jefferson, then governor of a beleaguered Virginia. Following his resignation as governor, and while at his "country retreat" at Poplar Forest, recovering from a fall from a horse, Jefferson undertook the task of answering the Marbois queries. From his youth, he had been a tireless collector of any kind of material concerning Virginia. An assiduous taker of notes, amateur scientist, and student of everything from astronomy to zoology, Jefferson revised, organized, and expanded these masses of material about his native state and, late in 1781, completed the man-uscript that became the *Notes on the State of Virginia*.

After subsequent revisions and enlargements, the *Notes* was published—anon-ymously and at Jefferson's expense—in Paris, 10 May 1785, in an edition of 200 copies intended "solely for private distribution." Revised and enlarged, the "definitive" Stockdale edition was published in London in summer 1787.

The *Notes* consists of 23 "Queries" concerning such subjects as "Rivers," "Climate," "Laws," and "Manners"; it includes Jefferson's map of Virginia, and appendices highlighted by "An Act for Establishing Religious Freedom." Years later, Jefferson added a long commentary "Relative to the Murder of Logan's [an Indian chief] Family." Begun as a matter-of-fact and often prosaic compilation and survey of the resources and history of a specific state, the *Notes on Virginia* grew until the commentary involved a whole continent. Although *Notes* was in concept essentially factual, Jefferson proceeded from an "exact description of the boundaries of Virginia" to a discussion of the relationships between the individual and society, and from there his soaring mind inevitably led him to comment and speculate upon most of the major social, intellectual, and scientific developments of the eighteenth century. He attacks the tyranny of the church; questions the dogmas of the schoolmen, the injustice of slavery, and the usurpation and misuse of power by the few; and ultimately contemplates the supreme paradoxes and enigmas of man's being. It is this speculation that makes the *Notes on Virginia*—this "measure of a shadow," Jefferson once called it—

a vital and living work, a book aptly labeled by one major Jefferson scholar as "one of the finest masterpieces of American literature."

In what is generally regarded as the golden age of letter-writing, Jefferson has to acknowledge few if any peers and no superiors. From his youth almost—literally—until the day of his death, he was an indefatigable letter-writer, despite the encroachments of age upon a hand previously crippled when he was in France during the 1780s (presumably, it has been said, incurred while vaulting over a stile to impress Maria Cosway). The actual number of Jefferson's letters has been estimated to be between 50,000 and 75,000, and they are in themselves, one specialist has concluded, sufficient to enshrine their author as a national treasure. Nowhere is Jefferson's search for knowledge, his curiosity, or the depth of his mind and the largeness of his vision more amply displayed than in his letters. More important, perhaps, they display the *humanness* of the man sometimes labeled an austere intellectual: in them we see the Jefferson who stood "gazing whole hours at the Maison Quarré like a lover at a mistress," or who said he was "in love with a Diana . . . a delicious morsel of a sculpture"; the same Jefferson who had said of the Natural Bridge of Virginia that "it is impossible for the emotions arising from the sublime to be felt beyond what they are here; so beautiful an arch, so elevated, so light, and springing as it were up to heaven!"

Here, too, are portraits of many of the major people of Jefferson's day: politicians, scholars, statesmen, lawyers, Indian chiefs, ordinary citizens—a teeming cross-section of eighteenth- and early nineteenth-century society. Above all else, the letters illustrate Jefferson's never-failing belief in the ideas and ideals of his country; and his eloquence, vigor, optimism, and clarity of thought, all suggested in his last extant letter, written just a few days before his death:

All eyes are opened, or opening, to the rights of man. The general spread of the light of science [by which Jefferson meant knowledge in general] has already laid open to every view the palpable truth, that the mass of mankind has not been born with saddles on their backs, nor a favored few booted and spurred ready to ride them legitimately, by the grace of God. These are grounds of hope for others. For ourselves, let the annual return of this day [4 July] forever refresh our recollections of these rights, and an undiminished devotion to them.

In his interest in philology, as in so many other areas of learning, Jefferson again was a man ahead of his time. In an age in which the study of Anglo-Saxon was largely neglected, he included it in the curriculum of the University of Virginia, and wrote a small book on it, *An Essay Toward Facilitating Instruction in the Anglo-Saxon and Modern Dialects of the English Language for the Use of the University of Virginia.* Jefferson's early interest in the subject had been largely utilitarian: "I was led to . . . the study of . . . Anglo Saxon," he wrote to an English philologist in 1798, "while I was a student of the law by being obliged to recur to that source for explanation of a multitude of law terms.'' Subsequently revised and expanded, the complete work was not published until 1851. Today of only contemporary historical interest, the *Essay* is one more example of the breadth of Jefferson's interests in general, and his insistence on the importance of the study of languages in particular.

"At the age of 77, I begin to make some memoranda, and state some recollections of dates and facts concerning myself, for my own more ready reference, and for the information of my family.'' Dated 6 January 1821, so begins Jefferson's *Autobiography*. Compiled from notes, reminiscences, letters, and the like, the *Autobiography* is a matter-of-fact record of a remarkable life, often prosaic but always candid. Though of relatively little literary significance, it is an invaluable documentary and commentary on the epoch-making years in which Jefferson played a major role.

The *Anas*, or *Notes*, are in effect a continuation of the *Autobiography*, from 1791, Jefferson's second year as secretary of state, until his retirement from the presidency in 1809. Jefferson at one time thought the *Anas* hardly worth preserving, but it remains valuable for its commentary on the conflicts between Federalists and Republicans, and for Jefferson's portrayal of the major participants in this struggle for power.

Jefferson's travel journals deserve to be much better known. While minister to the court of Louis XI, Jefferson had time and leisure to travel: to England where he was presented to the king and, among other sight-seeing tours, visited Shakespeare's grave; to Southern France and Northern Italy in spring 1787; and to Amsterdam and Strasburg, from February to April 1788. A habitual note taker, Jefferson provides observations and commentaries that are among the most pleasant and readable of any of his writings: "I observe women and children carrying heavy burdens, and laboring with the hoe . . . an unequivocal indication of extreme poverty'' (Champagne, 3 March 1787); "I see few beggars. Probably this is the effect of the police'' (Milan, 22–23 April 1787); "About five years ago [in Milan] there was such a hail as to kill cats'' [Milan, 29 April 1787]; "I heard a nightingale to-day at Chanteloup'' (8 June 1787); "Courts. To be seen as you would see the tower of London or Menagerie at Versailles with their lions, tigers, hyenas and other beasts of prey'' (3 June 1788).

During his later years, Jefferson frequently answered letters of inquiry from historians and biographers concerning the major participants in the founding years of the nation. Characteristic are some of his comments on George Washington, written in response to one such query: "His mind was great and powerful, without being of the very first order . . . [but] no judgment was ever sounder than his. . . . It was slow in operation, being little aided by invention or imagination, but sure in conclusion. . . . His integrity was most pure, his justice the most inflexible I have ever known.''

Like any major public figure, Thomas Jefferson has meant many things to many people. It is difficult to recall that this spokesman for freedom and equal rights under law was censured and threatened with impeachment because of his conduct as governor of Virginia during the Revolution, or that in 1800 the president of Yale College warned a Federalist audience that should Jefferson defeat John Adams in the upcoming presidential election Bibles would be destroyed, children compelled to chant *Ca ira*, and women forced into legal prostitution. Few American statesmen have been more criticized than he, or become the target for the savage persecution reserved only for the truly great. Thomas Babington Macaulay, for example, who feared and detested democracy, labeled Jefferson a man he could not "reckon among the benefactors of mankind"; and Henry Adams described him as a confused, inaccurate visionary, "superficial in his knowledge, and a martyr to the disease of omniscience." Only relatively recently has Jefferson been admitted to the "hierarchy of our great men" and have such diverse statesmen as Woodrow Wilson, Herbert Hoover, and Franklin D. Roosevelt rejected Macaulay's estimate to agree with Henry Steele Commager's appraisal that "Jefferson is the central figure in American history and—if freedom and democracy survive in our generation—he may yet prove to be the central figure in modern history."

SURVEY OF CRITICISM

The writings about Jefferson are so voluminous and so varied that only a few of the most important or the most representative can be mentioned here. Henry S. Randall's *The Life of Thomas Jefferson*, three massive volumes published in 1858, though partisan and sympathetic, is extremely valuable as the major Jefferson biography based upon actual knowledge of the subject. So, too, is Sarah N. Randolph's *Domestic Life of Thomas Jefferson*, 1871. The major biography is Dumas Malone's six-volume *Jefferson and His Time*, 1949–81; others include those by Claude G. Bowers, John Dos Passos, Marie Kimball, and Nathan Schachner. Individual book-length studies are as varied as their subject's interests and achievements; a sampling is included in the secondary bibliography.

More recently, Fawn M. Brodie's *Thomas Jefferson: An Intimate History* (1974) revived the long-standing controversy over Jefferson's alleged liaison with Sally Hemings, a quadroon slave, a subject carried to almost ludicrous extremes in Barbara Chase-Riboud's *Sally Hemings* (1979) (*Clotel, or the President's Daughter*, the first fictionalized treatment of the subject, had been published in England in 1853 by William Wells Brown). Other fictionalized portraits of Jefferson range from the rather conventional and sedate portrayal in Elizabeth Page's *The Tree of Liberty* (1939) to Robert Penn Warren's superb *Brother to Dragons* (1953, revised 1979). Gore Vidal's *Burr: A Novel* (1973) contains an often brilliant but frequently infuriating portrayal of Jefferson, climaxed by the author's belief that "around 1807 Jefferson was mad."

BIBLIOGRAPHY

Works by Thomas Jefferson

Multivolume Editions

The Writings of Thomas Jefferson. 10 vols. Ed. Paul L. Ford. New York: G. P. Putnam's, 1892–99.

The Writings of Thomas Jefferson. 20 vols. Ed. Andrew A. Lipscomb and Albert Ellery
    Bergh. Washington, D.C.: Thomas Jefferson Memorial Association, 1903–4.
The Papers of Thomas Jefferson. Ed. Julian P. Boyd, Lyman H. Butterfield, and Mina
    R. Bryan. Vols. 1–18 of a projected 50-plus vols. Princeton, N.J.: Princeton
    University Press, 1950–   .
*The Adams-Jefferson Letters; the Complete Correspondence between Thomas Jefferson
    and Abigail and John Adams.* Ed. Lester Cappon. Chapel Hill: University of North
    Carolina Press, 1959.
The Family Letters of Thomas Jefferson. Ed. Edwin M. Betts and James A. Bear.
    Columbia: University of Missouri Press, 1966.

One-Volume Editions

The Commonplace Book of Thomas Jefferson. Ed. Gilbert Chinard. Baltimore: Johns
    Hopkins University Press, 1926.
*The Literary Bible of Thomas Jefferson, His Commonplace Book of Philosophers and
    Poets.* Ed. Gilbert Chinard. Baltimore: Johns Hopkins University Press, 1928.
The Complete Jefferson as Revealed in His Letters. Ed. Saul K. Padover. New York:
    Tudor, 1943.
The Life and Selected Writings of Thomas Jefferson. Ed. Adrienne Koch and William
    Peden. New York: Random House, Modern Library, 1944.
Notes on the State of Virginia. Ed. William Peden. Chapel Hill: University of North
    Carolina Press, 1955; New York: Norton, Books That Live, 1972.
The Portable Thomas Jefferson. Ed. Merrill D. Peterson. New York: Viking Press, 1975.
Jefferson. The Library of America. New York: Viking Penguin, 1984.

Studies of Thomas Jefferson

Adams, Randolph G. *Three Americanists* (chapter 3, "Thomas Jefferson, Librarian").
    Philadelphia: University of Pennsylvania Press, 1939.
Adams, William Howard, ed. *The Eye of Thomas Jefferson.* Washington, D.C.: National
    Gallery of Art, 1976.
————. *Jefferson and the Arts: An Extended View.* Washington, D.C.: National Gallery
    of Art, 1976.
————. *Jefferson's Monticello.* New York: Abbeville Press, 1983.
Bear, James A., ed. *Jefferson at Monticello.* Charlottesville: University Press of Virginia,
    1967.
Berman, Eleanor Davidson. *Thomas Jefferson Among the Arts.* New York: Philosophical
    Library, 1947.
Boorstin, Daniel J. *The Lost World of Thomas Jefferson.* New York: Holt, 1948.
Bowers, Claude G. *Jefferson and Hamilton; the Struggle for Democracy in America.*
    Boston: Houghton Mifflin, 1925.
————. *Jefferson in Power; the Death Struggle of the Federalists.* Boston: Houghton
    Mifflin, 1936.
————. *The Young Jefferson, 1743–1789.* Boston: Houghton Mifflin, 1945.
Brodie, Fawn M. *Thomas Jefferson: An Intimate History.* New York: Norton, 1974.
Bullock, Helen D. *My Head and My Heart, a Little History of Thomas Jefferson and
    Maria Cosway.* New York: G. P. Putnam's, 1945.

Chinard, Gilbert. *Thomas Jefferson, Apostle of Americanism*. Baltimore: Johns Hopkins University Press, 1929.

Cunningham, Noble. *The Image of Thomas Jefferson in the Public Eye*. Charlottesville: University Press of Virginia, 1981.

Davis, Richard Beale. *Francis Walker Gilmer: Life and Learning in Jefferson's Virginia*. Richmond: Dietz Press, 1939.

Dos Passos, John. *The Head and Heart of Thomas Jefferson*. Garden City, N.Y.: Doubleday, 1954.

————. *The Shackles of Power: Three Jeffersonian Decades*. Garden City, N.Y.: Doubleday, 1966.

Dumbauld, Edward. *Thomas Jefferson, American Tourist*. Norman: University of Oklahoma Press, 1946.

Foote, Henry W. *Thomas Jefferson: Champion of Religious Freedom, Advocate of Christian Morals*. Boston: Beacon Press, 1947.

Huddleston, Eugene. *Thomas Jefferson, a Reference Guide*. Boston: G. K. Hall, 1982.

Jones, Howard Mumford. *Jeffersonianism and the American Novel*. New York: Teachers College, Columbia University Press, 1966.

Kimball, Fiske. *Thomas Jefferson, Architect*. Cambridge: Riverside Press, 1916.

Kimball, Marie. *Jefferson: The Road to Glory, 1743–1776*. New York: Coward-McCann, 1943.

————. *Jefferson: War and Peace, 1776–1784*. New York: Coward-McCann, 1947.

————. *Jefferson: The Scene of Europe, 1784–1789*. New York: Coward-McCann, 1950.

Koch, Adrienne. *The Philosophy of Thomas Jefferson*. New York: Columbia University Press, 1943.

Lehmann, Karl. *Thomas Jefferson: American Humanist*. New York: Macmillan, 1947.

Malone, Dumas. *Thomas Jefferson and His Times*. 6 vols.: *Jefferson the Virginian* (Boston: Little, Brown, 1948); *Jefferson and the Rights of Man* (Boston: Little, Brown, 1951); *Jefferson and the Ordeal of Liberty* (Boston: Little, Brown, 1962); *Jefferson the President. First Term, 1801–1805* (Boston: Little, Brown, 1970); *Jefferson the President. Second Term, 1805–1809* (Boston: Little, Brown, 1974); *Jefferson in Retirement, 1809–1825* (Boston: Little, Brown, 1981).

Mayo, Bernard. *Jefferson Himself: The Personal Narrative of a Many-Sided American*. Boston: Houghton Mifflin, 1942.

Mott, Frank Luther. *Jefferson and the Press*. Baton Rouge: Louisiana State University Press, 1943.

Peden, William. "Thomas Jefferson: Book Collector, Bibliophile, and Critic." Ph.D. diss., University of Virginia, 1942.

Peterson, Merrill D. *The Jefferson Image in the American Mind*. New York: Oxford University Press, 1960.

————. *Thomas Jefferson and the New Nation: A Biography*. New York: Oxford University Press, 1970.

Randall, Henry S. *The Life of Thomas Jefferson*. 3 vols. New York: Derby & Jackson, 1858.

Randolph, Sarah N. *The Domestic Life of Thomas Jefferson*. New York: Harper's, 1871.

Russell, Phillip. *Jefferson, Champion of the Free Mind*. New York: Dodd, Mead, 1957.

Schachner, Nathan. *Thomas Jefferson: A Biography*. 2 vols. New York: Appleton-Century-Crofts, 1951.

Smith, Page. *Jefferson: A Revealing Biography*. New York: American Heritage, 1976.

Sowerby, E. Millicent. *Catalogue of the Library of Thomas Jefferson.* 5 vols. Washington,
    D.C.: Library of Congress, 1952–59.
Wiltse, Charles M. *The Jeffersonian Tradition in American Democracy.* New York: Hill
    and Wang, 1960.
Wright, Louis B. *The First Gentlemen of Virginia. Intellectual Qualities of the Early
    Colonial Ruling Class.* San Marino, Calif.: Huntington Library, 1940.

———————— L. MOODY SIMMS, JR. ————————

Richard Malcolm Johnston
(1822–1898)

Richard Malcolm Johnston will be remembered primarily for his *Dukesborough Tales*, a title that made four separate appearances (1871, 1874, 1883, 1892), though no two of the collections are exactly the same. Focusing national attention on Johnston, this work—specifically the 1883 edition—profited from the contemporary widespread interest in local color fiction. His tales about the right place appeared at the right time. The *Dukesborough Tales* reveal Johnston as a link between humorists of the Old Southwest and later Southern local colorists.

BIOGRAPHY

The son of a planter who was also a Baptist minister, Richard Malcolm Johnston was born on 8 March 1822 near Powelton, Georgia, to Malcolm and Catherine Johnston. Having begun classes at a rural old-field school when he was five, he completed his formal preparatory education in 1837 at Powelton Academy. In 1841 he graduated from a manual-labor institute that later became Mercer University. The twenty years between his graduation and the outbreak of the Civil War were divided between teaching and the law.

In 1841 Johnston began teaching school in Mt. Zion, Georgia. After a short period of study, he was admitted to the bar in Augusta, Georgia, in 1843. The same year he began law practice as a partner of Eli Baxter in Sparta, Georgia. In 1844 he married Mary Frances Mansfield, whose father, a Connecticut native, kept a tailor's shop. After serving for a time as headmaster of Mt. Zion Academy, he practiced law in Sparta as a partner of James Thomas. Johnston became schoolmaster at Sparta Academy in 1849. During the early 1850s he entered a law partnership with Linton Stephens, a half-brother of Alexander Stephens, whose biography Johnston and William Hand Browne were to publish in 1878. Having refused a circuit judgeship and the presidency of Mercer University,

Johnston accepted the professorship of belles lettres and oratory at the University of Georgia in 1857.

It was the vogue of Augustus Baldwin Longstreet's *Georgia Scenes* (1835) that led Johnston to write his first humorous sketches. He published "Five Chapters of a History" (later retitled "The Goosepond School") in 1857 in William T. Porter's *Spirit of the Times*. While at the University of Georgia, Johnston became one of the ablest pioneers in the study of English literature. In 1860 he published *The English Classics: A Historical Sketch* (revised with William Hand Browne and republished in 1872 as *English Literature: A Historical Sketch*). In later life, he often lectured on English literature and published two volumes of literary and historical essays (1891, 1892) that reflect his wide reading but are otherwise of little importance.

When the Civil War began, Johnston, who was no secessionist, resigned his university post and opened a school for boys near Sparta. In 1864 an Augusta firm brought out his first book, *Georgia Sketches*, under the pseudonym of "Philemon Perch." Johnston's stories of Middle Georgia life as it was before the coming of railroads show clearly the influence of both Longstreet and William Tappan Thompson. Dissatisfied with conditions in Reconstruction Georgia and pessimistic about the future of his state, Johnston moved to Baltimore in 1867 and established the Pen Lucy School.

Johnston's best-known work, *Dukesborough Tales*, appeared in 1871 (a second enlarged edition was published in 1874). The sketches in this book preserve Johnston's memories of Powelton and, like much of his later work, deal with ordinary people in situations that are awkward, humorous, and sometimes pathetic. In 1879 Johnston's first paid story, "Mr. Neelus Peeler's Conditions," was published in *Scribner's Monthly Magazine*. Although at first successful, the Pen Lucy school gradually declined after Johnston joined the Roman Catholic Church in 1875. The school closed in 1883, and Johnston began his efforts to become a professional man of letters. Also in 1883, Harper and Brothers brought out an enlarged edition of *Dukesborough Tales*, and for the first time Johnston prefixed his own name to the sketches and received payment for them. He found himself a national literary figure at age sixty-one.

The remaining fifteen years of Johnston's life, 1883 to 1898, were prolific and active ones almost to the very end. The *Life of Alexander H. Stephens* by Johnston and Browne was issued in a new and revised edition after Stephens's death in 1883. A travel book called *Two Gray Tourists* appeared in 1885. Johnston, for the most part, spent the decade after 1883 creating stories about Middle Georgia. Having written to such established literary figures as Charles Dudley Warner and Frank Stockton, he followed their advice, first publishing his stories in magazines and then collecting them in books.

Collections of stories appeared in 1888 (*Mr. Absalom Billingslea and Other Georgia Folk*); 1891 (*The Primes and Their Neighbors*); two in 1892 (*Mr. Billy Downs and His Likes* and *Mr. Fortner's Marital Claims and Other Stories*); 1894 (*Little Ike Templin and Other Stories*); and 1897 (*Old Times in Middle*

Georgia); these in addition to yet another but abbreviated and reworked *Dukes-borough Tales* in 1892. Johnston also published four novels, two of which had previously appeared in magazines: *Old Mark Langston* (1884), *Ogeechee Cross-Firings* (1889), *Widow Guthrie* (1890), and *Pearce Amerson's Will* (1898). The raw material for all of these works was the same. As he noted in his autobiography (1900), he intended these writings to illustrate scenes and characters among the rural folk of Middle Georgia during the period of his childhood.

Appropriately enough, Johnston is remembered for this local color fiction. Yet the writing and marketing of this work made up only part of the literary activity he engaged in during the 1880s and early 1890s. The financial precariousness that had shadowed much of his life was still far from being over. He gave public lectures on literature at an accelerated pace. In 1897 some of his later presentations were published as part of the Catholic Summer and Winter School Library as *Lectures on Literature: English, French and Spanish*. Long having had a reputation in Georgia as a fascinating storyteller, Johnston in the early 1880s added readings from original sources to his scholarly lecture series. He lectured with several contemporary humorists—once, in 1889, with Mark Twain, who was the guest of the Johnstons in Baltimore and, so the story goes, gave Johnston his share of the proceeds.

Johnston's narrowness of range has been noted by critics of his work. Even while being honored for his writings, he knew that it was time to stop mining a vein that perhaps had been mined too long. In 1894 he asked his friend E. C. Stedman to help him secure a position in Washington, D.C., with the federal government (income from his writings was getting smaller). Johnston ceased to be a professional storyteller in March 1895 when Stedman and others secured him a position in the U.S. Department of Labor. He eventually moved to the Bureau of Education and worked as a secretary to the commissioner for an annual salary of $1,200. One of his assignments led to what is probably the most complete record of the picturesque old-field schools of his boyhood in Georgia ("Early Educational Life in Middle Georgia," 1896, 1897).

Johnston's health and spirits declined after his wife's death in February 1897. Becoming ill in May 1898, he was soon confined to his room under the care of his daughters. He died in a Baltimore hospital on 23 September 1898. Though Richard Malcolm Johnston never became the poet and playwright he wished to be, he must have gained much satisfaction from the recognition he received as a writer of stories during the latter part of his life. And yet this fame he belatedly achieved on the crest of the wave of local color fiction surely exceeded the dreams and expectations of a young lawyer and teacher in Georgia during the 1850s.

MAJOR THEMES

Generally seen as the best of Johnston's works, the tales and sketches published in *Dukesborough Tales* are regarded as typical of much of his fiction. They are typical in subject—middle-class white people of Middle Georgia in the 1820s, 1830s, and 1840s—and type—shorter prose sketches and tales. "Also," observes Bert Hitchcock, in his *Richard Malcolm Johnston* (1978), "because several [sketches and tales] undergo successive, rather extensive revision for their several appearances, they evidence a typicality of treatment or style which is at once both personal and historical" (p. 44). As his style evolved, Johnston sacrificed vitality for formula and polish, genuineness for more sentiment and sophistication. Gaining in narrative tightness, he lost in originality of characterization, which was his real strength.

In *The Small Town in American Literature* (1939), Ima Honaker Herron maintains that Johnston "deserves recognition as a recorder of . . . the ante-bellum rural community and small town of Middle Georgia" (p. 328). Johnston, through his single-minded use of Dukesborough as a setting, made the town (essentially the real-life Powelton of his early days) come alive for many American readers in the 1880s and 1890s. "The story of a country town" according to Johnston— with its common setting, some common characters, and a sense of loving, nostalgic proprietorship—was quite different from the desolation and despair of Edgar Watson Howe's novel of this title (1883).

In *Dukesborough Tales*, plots are weak and incident is dependent upon personality. Practically every major social institution of the day is depicted in detail. The physical setting is sketched with care, even to locating the various houses in Dukesborough. Nevertheless, people are what is extremely important. Events and setting are given meaning by Johnston's characters.

According to Johnston, his old-time lawyer friends probably recalled more fondly and more often than anything else their days in the old-field schools, despite the primitive principles that prevailed and the sometimes cruel schoolmasters. Of his fictional Middle Georgia characters, 91 are either teachers or students. Johnston's own long-lived and reform-minded interest in pedagogy reveals his deep concern with education. Some critics believe that his major achievement was his faithful record of early educational life in his native region.

As one who recognized the humorous potential in a variety of situations, Johnston did not overlook the district military organization. Its rather ludicrous activities had led to the awarding of numerous military titles and to pomposity in many of their possessors. Public drunkenness and affairs of honor stemmed from the periodic militia musters. Among other familiar motifs found in the various pieces in *Dukesborough Tales* are the Yankee trickster, courtship rivalries, and the marital and domestic ups-and-downs of many of the characters.

From the beginning to the end of Johnston's work, Dukesborough is the hub of Middle Georgia, his fictional world. Sixty-six of the 67 stories and sketches that followed in time the 16 *Dukesborough Tales* echo them in form and subject. (These stories are collected in *Mr. Absalom Billingslea and Other Georgia Folk* [1888]; *The Primes and Their Neighbors* [1891]; *Mr. Fortner's Marital Claims and Other Stories* [1892]; *Mr. Billy Downs and His Likes* [1892]; *Little Ike Templin and Other Stories* [1894]; and *Old Times in Middle Georgia* [1897].)

In language and plot, they reflect the growing professionalism of a local color writer of limited range. Nevertheless, they deal further with the subjects and themes delineated in *Dukesborough Tales*: schools, religion, lawyers and courts, blacks and slavery, courtship and marriage, muster days, athletic contests, practical jokes and swindles, and physical discomfiture.

Four of Johnston's works—*Old Mark Langston: A Tale of Duke's Creek* (1884), *Ogeechee Cross-Firings* (1889), *Widow Guthrie* (1890), and *Pearce Amerson's Will* (1898)—have usually been called novels. They are like his short fictions in their local color and Middle Georgia setting; they differ in their more serious intentions and generally darker outlooks. Johnston's novels reinforce the judgment that characterization was his prime literary skill.

Hardly unexpectedly, the guilty are punished and the good and long-suffering are rewarded in *Old Mark Langston*. *Ogeechee Cross-Firings* is a tale of the triumph of true love and true manhood, whereas *Widow Guthrie* is an oedipal tale, one of psychopathic evil, selfish near-adultery, and homicide. The most melodramatic of all of Johnston's longer fictions, *Pearce Amerson's Will* deals with deceit and troubled marriages. Especially important in any consideration of Johnston's novels are the nostalgic and autobiographical elements of his fiction.

In many ways, Johnston is a fine generic example of the local colorists. A reading of his fiction reveals clearly his ties with the other local color writers of his day: the nostalgic idealization of the past; the careful, detailed delineation of a limited geographical area; the concentration on the peculiarities of a region and its people; the concern for the common folk; the avoidance of the unpleasant; the use of sentiment; and the frequent happy endings.

SURVEY OF CRITICISM

Four works provide essential biographical information about Richard Malcolm Johnston. Though not exclusively biographical, Jimmy Ponder Voyles's University of Georgia dissertation, "Richard Malcolm Johnston: A Biographical and Critical Study" (1971), is to date the single most valuable and trustworthy source of information on Johnston's life. More accessible though intentionally limited in scope are Edd Winfield Parks's "Professor Richard Malcolm Johnston" (1941), a detailed account of Johnston's association with the University of Georgia, and Francis Taylor Long's three-part treatment of Johnston's Baltimore years (1939, 1940, 1941). In the biographical first chapter of *Richard Malcolm Johnston* (1978), Bert Hitchcock provides an objective depiction of Johnston's life based heavily on primary and near-primary materials, including letters of Johnston and his family, contemporary newspaper clippings, and various manuscripts. Other secondary sources provide valuable specific biographical information, but they lack either the reliability or depth of the above-mentioned works.

Despite an overgenerous critical assessment and some errors of fact, Edmund

Clarence Stedman and Stephen B. Weeks's "Literary Estimate and Bibliography of Richard Malcolm Johnston" (1898) remains an essential beginning-point document for a study of Johnston. Other early studies and assessments of Johnston include: Charles W. Coleman, Jr.'s "The Recent Movement in Southern Literature" (1887), which examines Johnston's place in the great surge of interest in Southern writing during the 1880s; Sophia Bledsoe Herrick's "Richard Malcolm Johnston" (1888), which is informative if overly appreciative of Johnston and his work; and Regina Armstrong's "Richard Malcolm Johnston, Gentleman and Man-of-Letters" (1898), which focuses on Johnston's concept of a gentleman. Two of the earliest attempts at scholarly evaluation of Johnston appear in William A. Webb's "Richard Malcolm Johnston" (1903) and Carl Holliday's *A History of Southern Literature* (1906). Holliday's final assessment is too glowing; Webb presents a sympathetic but well-balanced account of the author and his works.

Later treatments of Johnston's work begin with Walter Blair's *Native American Humor* (1937), which associates Johnston with Mark Twain as an important transitional figure, and chapter 12 of Edd Winfield Parks's *Segments of Southern Thought* (1938), which has been described by Bert Hitchcock as "the finest twenty-one consecutive pages on Johnston in existence" (p. 156). Ima Honaker Herron's *The Small Town in American Literature* (1939) praises Johnston's work—especially *Dukesborough Tales*—in the context of an important theme in American literature. In *The South in American Literature, 1607–1900* (1954), Jay B. Hubbell views Johnston, even in his later years, primarily as "a writer of humorous sketches rather than a creator of artistically constructed short stories" (p. 781).

In "Richard Malcolm Johnston's Marriage Group" (1964), Robert Bush examines the persistent theme of courtship and marriage in an effort to establish the social value of Johnston's fiction. Wade Hall's *The Smiling Phoenix: Southern Humor from 1865 to 1914* (1965) finds the changing humor of the Civil War period illustrated best in the work of Johnston; Hall associates Johnston with the post–Civil War literary penchant for examining life through children's eyes. Clement Eaton, in his *The Waning of the Old South Civilization, 1860–1880s* (1968), labels Johnston as the most important local color humorist during the post–Civil War period for a study of Southern folk mores.

Robert L. Phillips, Jr.'s "The Novel and the Romance in Middle Georgia Humor and Local Color" (1971) reveals that, despite their claims, Johnston and other Middle Georgia writers did not examine the area and its people with realistic honesty. In his above-mentioned dissertation (1971) and his "Richard Malcolm Johnston's Literary Career: An Estimate" (1974), Jimmy Ponder Voyles argues that Johnston's literary accomplishments warrant him recognition as an author of historical significance. He finds Johnston's fiction and humorous local color sketches interesting culturally—as stories of Middle Georgia life and character—but not particularly distinguished artistically. Voyles suggests that Johnston's greatest contributions to American letters (both written in collaboration with

William Hand Browne) may be his biography of Alexander Stephens and his history of English literature, one of the first literary histories by an American. Clara Ruth Coleman Wood's "The Fiction of Richard Malcolm Johnston" (1973) is to date the most thorough survey of Johnston's work; it includes a categorization and critical discussion of all of Johnston's fiction. Bert Hitchcock's volume on Johnston (1978) in the Twayne's United States Authors Series is an informative introduction as well as a useful and authoritative reference about Johnston and his work. Both Wood and Hitchcock see Johnston not as a great but as an important Southern writer.

BIBLIOGRAPHY

Works by Richard Malcolm Johnston

"Religious Intoleration." *De Bow's Review* 22 (February 1857): 166–80.

The English Classics: A Historical Sketch of the Literature of England from the Earliest Times to the Accession of King George III. Philadelphia: J. B. Lippincott, 1860.

Georgia Sketches (under the pseudonym Philemon Perch). Augusta, Georgia: Stockton, 1864.

Dukesborough Tales (under the pseudonym Philemon Perch). Baltimore: Turnbull Brothers, 1871; 2d enl. ed., Baltimore: Turnbull Brothers, 1874.

English Literature: A Historical Sketch of English Literature from the Earliest Times, with William Hand Browne. New York: University Publishing, 1872.

Life of Alexander H. Stephens, with William Hand Browne. Philadelphia: J. B. Lippincott, 1878.

Dukesborough Tales. New York: Harper, 1883.

Old Mark Langston: A Tale of Duke's Creek. New York: Harper, 1884.

Two Gray Tourists: From the Papers of Mr. Philemon Perch. Baltimore: Baltimore Publishing, 1885.

Mr. Absalom Billingslea and Other Georgia Folk. New York: Harper, 1888.

Ogeechee Cross-Firings: A Novel. New York: Harper, 1889.

Widow Guthrie: A Novel. New York: D. Appleton, 1890.

The Primes and Their Neighbors: Ten Tales of Middle Georgia. New York: D. Appleton, 1891.

"Reading Bores." *Lippincott's* 47 (March 1891): 401–3.

Studies, Literary and Social. First Series. Indianapolis: Bowen-Merrill, 1891; Second Series. Indianapolis: Bowen-Merrill, 1892.

Dukesborough Tales: The Chronicles of Mr. Bill Williams. New York: D. Appleton, 1892.

"Middle Georgia Rural Life." *Century* 43 (March 1892): 737–42.

Mr. Fortner's Marital Claims and Other Stories. New York: D. Appleton, 1892.

Little Ike Templin and Other Stories. Boston: Lothrop, 1894.

"My Schools." *Lippincott's* 54 (November 1894): 703–8.

"Early Educational Life in Middle Georgia." *Report of the* [United States] *Commissioner of Education for the Year 1894–95.* Washington, D.C.: Government Printing Office, 1896. 2, 1699–1733.

"Early Educational Life in Middle Georgia." *Report of the* [United States] *Commissioner*

of Education for the Year 1895–96. Washington, D.C.: Government Printing
   Office, 1897. 1, 839–86.
Lectures on Literature: English, French and Spanish. Akron, Ohio: D. H. McBride,
   1897.
Old Times in Middle Georgia. New York: Macmillan, 1897.
"The Planter in the Old South." Southern History Association *Publications* 1 (January
   1897): 35–44.
"Dogs and Railroad Conductors." *Lippincott's* 61 (June 1898): 862–64.
Pearce Amerson's Will. Chicago: Way and Williams, 1898.
Autobiography of Colonel Richard Malcolm Johnston. Washington, D.C.: Neale, 1900.

Studies of Richard Malcolm Johnston

Armstrong, Regina. "Richard Malcolm Johnston, Gentleman and Man-of-Letters." *Cath-
   olic World* 68 (November 1898): 261–70.
Blair, Walter. *Native American Humor, 1800–1900*. New York: American Book, 1937;
   repr. San Francisco: Chandler, 1960.
Bush, Robert. "Richard Malcolm Johnston's Marriage Group." *Georgia Review* 18
   (Winter 1964): 429–36.
Coleman, Charles W., Jr. "The Recent Movement in Southern Literature." *Harper's
   New Monthly Magazine* 74 (May 1887): 837–55.
Eaton, Clement. *The Waning of the Old South Civilization, 1860–1880's*. Athens: Uni-
   versity of Georgia Press, 1968.
Edwards, Corliss Hines, Jr. "Richard Malcolm Johnston's View of the Old Field School."
   Georgia Historical Quarterly 50 (December 1966): 382–90.
Hall, Wade. *The Smiling Phoenix: Southern Humor from 1865 to 1914*. Gainesville:
   University of Florida Press, 1965.
Herrick, Sophia Bledsoe. "Richard Malcolm Johnston." *Century Illustrated Monthly
   Magazine* 36 (June 1888): 276–80.
Herron, Ima Honaker. *The Small Town in American Literature*. Durham, N.C.: Duke
   University Press, 1939.
Hitchcock, Bert. *Richard Malcolm Johnston*. Boston: Twayne, 1978.
Holliday, Carl. *A History of Southern Literature*. New York: Neale, 1906.
Hubbell, Jay B. *The South in American Literature, 1607–1900*. Durham, N.C.: Duke
   University Press, 1954.
Long, Francis Taylor. "The Life of Richard Malcolm Johnston in Maryland, 1867–1898:
   Country Gentleman, Teacher, and Writer, 1867–1881." *Maryland Historical
   Magazine* 34 (December 1939): 305–24.
———. "The Life of Richard Malcolm Johnston in Maryland, 1867–1898: Some Literary
   Friendships—The Lecture Platform, 1882–1889." *Maryland Historical Magazine*
   35 (September 1940): 270–86.
———. "The Life of Richard Malcolm Johnston in Maryland, 1867–1898: The Closing
   Years, 1889–1898." *Maryland Historical Magazine* 36 (March 1941): 54–69.
Parks, Edd Winfield. "Professor Richard Malcolm Johnston." *Georgia Historical Quar-
   terly* 25 (March 1941): 1–15.
———. *Segments of Southern Thought*. Athens: University of Georgia Press, 1938.
Phillips, Robert L., Jr. "The Novel and the Romance in Middle Georgia Humor and
   Local Color: A Study of Narrative Method in the Works of Augustus Baldwin

Longstreet, William Tappan Thompson, Richard Malcolm Johnston, and Joel Chandler Harris.'' Ph.D. diss., University of North Carolina at Chapel Hill, 1971.

Skaggs, Merrill Maguire. *The Folk of Southern Fiction*. Athens: University of Georgia Press, 1972.

Stedman, Edmund Clarence and Stephen B. Weeks. ''Literary Estimate and Bibliography of Richard Malcolm Johnston.'' Southern History Association *Publications* 2 (October 1898): 315–27.

Voyles, Jimmy Ponder. ''Richard Malcolm Johnston's Literary Career: An Estimate.'' *Markham Review* 4 (February 1974): 29–34.

———. ''Richard Malcolm Johnston: A Biographical and Critical Study.'' Ph.D. diss., University of Georgia, 1971.

Webb, William A. ''Richard Malcolm Johnston.'' *Southern Writers: Biographical and Critical Studies*, Vol. 2. Nashville and Dallas: Publishing House of the M.E. Church, South, 1903; repr. New York: Gordian Press, 1970.

Wood, Clara Ruth Coleman. ''The Fiction of Richard Malcolm Johnston.'' Ph.D. diss., University of North Carolina at Chapel Hill, 1973.

DAVID O. TOMLINSON

John Pendleton Kennedy
(1795–1870)

A lawyer and politician and only secondarily a man of letters, John Pendleton Kennedy is best-known today for *Swallow Barn* (1832), the novel credited, and sometimes condemned, for setting the fictional image of the plantation for a century. Although Kennedy supported the cause of the Union, his true fictional subject matter was the South. His *Horse-Shoe Robinson* (1835) is a romance about the Revolutionary War in the lower South. *Rob of the Bowl* (1838) is set in colonial Maryland.

BIOGRAPHY

Born on 25 October 1795, John Pendleton Kennedy was the eldest son of a prosperous Baltimore merchant. He enjoyed the town's best society and education of the most exclusive of its private academies until his father's business, faltering since the imposition of the embargo in 1807, failed entirely. In 1809 John, ready to enter college, had to forgo attending Princeton, the perennial favorite of his Virginia kin. Instead he entered the less costly and less prestigious Baltimore College, finishing in November 1812 as one of three members of its first graduating class.

Kennedy did not immediately pursue a career as a writer. Indeed, he never settled on a single profession, preferring to work in law, politics, corporate administration, the university, and letters more or less simultaneously during much of his life. This breadth of activity has caused some to term him a dabbler; but his substantial successes in each field call for fairer treatment. His interest in writing spans the whole of his adult life, but the fiction on which his reputation as the most talented Southern novelist before the Civil War rests was written between 1829 and 1840.

Kennedy began legal training, reading under Edmund Pendleton; and when

Pendleton left Baltimore, he continued his work under Judge Walter Dorsey. By 1816 he was admitted to the bar. An affable young man, Kennedy soon gained the friendship of two rival giants in the Baltimore legal community— William Pinckney and William Wirt. Both had been attorney general of the United States: Pinckney, under Madison; and Wirt, under Monroe and Adams. Wirt had also gained a literary reputation principally for his *Letters of a British Spy*. The young Kennedy envied and admired Wirt's dual rights to public acclaim and sought to model himself on Wirt.

Kennedy had begun to write for the local newspapers in 1812, blanketing them with patriotic fare. His first literary essays, five linked pieces called "The Swiss Traveler," appeared in 1816 in *The Portico*.

Joining with another young lawyer of puckish bent, Peter Hoffman Cruse, Kennedy wrote the wickedly satirical *Red Book* between 1819 and 1821. The two authors never revealed their identities either to public or publisher during the magazine's run, a technique that left them free to observe the foibles of Baltimore's upper crust and freed them from suffering reprisals for the barbs they flung.

Publication of the *Red Book* ceased after Kennedy began a political career in the Maryland House of Delegates (1820–23) and no longer had time to work on the periodical. Though he virtually abandoned writing until 1829, his effort on the *Red Book* completed his literary apprenticeship. When he began to write again, it was with a new maturity and vision.

Marriage in 1824 to Mary Tenant ended with her death later the same year and was followed by their infant son's shortly afterward. Kennedy withdrew from society, reentering the swirl again in 1827. He met and fell in love with Elizabeth Gray, the daughter of a wealthy textile manufacturer. Their marriage in 1829 seemed to allow him to write once again. The earliest parts of his magnum opus, the unpublished journal, date from this period.

Soon his political critiques were appearing in newspapers. His "Confessions of an Officeholder," first printed in the Baltimore *Republican* in October 1829, were copied by at least 42 other papers across the country.

While he worked on *Swallow Barn*, a book of lively fictional sketches about plantation life, Kennedy also entered the heated national debate over the tariff laws. His *A Review of Mr. Cambreleng's Report* (1830), written under the pseudonym Mephistopheles, provoked outcries from the antitariff press and strong support from important public figures. The pseudonym was soon penetrated; and because of his expertise as a writer, Kennedy became the darling of the Friends of Domestic Industry.

If Kennedy was receiving recognition as a political writer, he was, at nearly the same time, gaining recognition as a master of imaginative prose. *Swallow Barn*, published under the pseudonym Mark Littleton, was even attributed to Washington Irving by some reviewers; but the mystery of authorship was soon solved. The book—a composite of Kennedy's experiences in Virginia, the plantation life he observed there, the gentle attitudes and foibles of his Pendleton kin, and portraits of such acquaintances as his professor William Sinclair—was powerful enough that Henry Carey, Kennedy's publisher, urged him to continue penning fiction:

I most earnestly hope that the success of this book will be as such as to warrant you in abjuring the law & giving yourself up to amusing yourself & delighting your readers with your excellent descriptions of the scenery & manners of our country—I will be sadly in want of authors—Irving will write little—Cooper says he will write no more—& I fear we shall slowly see all our lights extinguished, unless you take and keep the field.

Carey's concern was for American letters and for his own financial health. He was the publisher of both Irving and Cooper and was, no doubt, wondering where future successes might be found.

Three years before Carey's letter of encouragement, Kennedy had begun collecting materials for a novel. In February 1830 he confided to his journal that he was inviting Warren R. Davis, a member of Congress from South Carolina, to dinner "to get the story of Horse Shoe Robinson from him. . . . " On a journey through the Pendleton district of South Carolina in 1818, Kennedy had met both Davis and the rough Revolutionary War veteran he knew as Robinson (the name was actually Robertson).

By the time he became involved in writing, however, Kennedy had two stories to tell: the tale of Robinson and that of Mildred Lindsay, a young woman torn between her loyalist father and her patriot betrothed. He hesitated over which story should control the book, even striking through the title "Horse Shoe Robinson" on one manuscript and substituting "Mildred Lindsay." Some critics have argued that *Horse-Shoe Robinson* (1835) is flawed because Kennedy never resolved the issue in any place but the title. Flawed or not, the book is one of the best early fictional views of the Revolution.

A second foray into historical fiction came in 1838 with *Rob of the Bowl*. The story, set in seventeenth-century Maryland, used the proprietary government of the Calverts under Puritan siege as a backdrop for dealings with supposed wizards, actual pirates, and the love between young people of disparate backgrounds. Kennedy used the handwritten journals of the Maryland Provincial Council from 1677 until 1686 to provide him with an accurate historical setting.

In the campaign for the House of Representatives in 1837, Kennedy, a Whig candidate, found that the fact that he wrote fiction was used against him. In addition, though the books sold well, they did not bring a return he felt equal to the effort of producing them. Though he lost that election, the death of a Congressman in 1838 left a vacancy to which he was named.

In 1840 Kennedy published *Quodlibet*, a satire on Jacksonian democracy, causing quite a stir. The book, published under the pseudonym Solomon Secondthoughts, soon was attributed to Kennedy; and the perception of him as a writer of political cunning may have helped him regain a seat in the U.S. House of Representatives in 1841, a seat he held for two terms, during that time championing an appropriation to test Morse's telegraph and entertaining Charles Dickens, who was seeking congressional support for an international copyright law.

In 1846 Kennedy was drafted by the Whigs to run for the Maryland House of Delegates. Democratic Baltimore elected him, and members of the House made him speaker. By 1847 an unsuccessful attempt to regain his seat in the U.S. House of Representatives caused him to give up seeking elective office ever again.

His writing during the 1840s was largely political. *Defense of the Whigs* (1844), a long pamphlet, tried to connect American Whigs to early strains in American and British political life; and *Memoirs of the Life of William Wirt* (1849) portrayed at length the life of his mentor, a man who was an attorney, writer, and politician. John Quincy Adams had been asked to compose the biography. When he felt he would never complete it, he suggested to Wirt's family that Kennedy be given the task. Like *Quodlibet*, it has not endured; but at the time it sold more copies than had any of Kennedy's other works.

In 1850 Kennedy became provost of the University of Maryland, a largely ceremonial post, which he held until his death. When William Graham resigned from President Fillmore's cabinet to run on the Whig ticket as vice president, Kennedy served as secretary of the navy for eight months.

During the mid–1850s, Kennedy worked with financier George Peabody and others to found and organize the Peabody Institute in Baltimore. The Institute, whose board Kennedy headed during the last decade of his life, later was frequented by literary luminaries from Sidney Lanier to John Dos Passos, who found the library facilities and the quiet work space it furnished conducive to literary work.

Though he was convinced that his political writing was ephemeral, Kennedy wished to keep his fiction in print. Accordingly, he contracted with George P. Putnam to issue a new edition of *Swallow Barn* in 1851. Kennedy did some textual revision, eliminating the long essay on Captain Smith; and he employed David Hunter Strother (Porte Crayon) to illustrate the text. Putnam also issued *Horse-Shoe Robinson* in 1852 and *Rob of the Bowl* two years later. Lippincott reissued these three works, *Quodlibet*, and the biography of Wirt in 1860.

In 1860 Kennedy began to oppose secession publicly. In "The Border States," he urged those states between the North and the South to mediate the disputes pulling those two regions further and further apart. His suggestion was not, unfortunately, accepted. When secession and then war ensued, Kennedy reflected on the situation in a group of articles printed in the *National Intelligencer* under the pseudonym Paul Ambrose. Collected in 1865, they were printed in book form as *Mr. Ambrose's Letters on the Rebellion*.

During the last decade of his life, Kennedy was elected a fellow of the Academy of Arts and Sciences, given an honorary doctor of laws by Harvard, and made U.S. Commissioner to the Paris exhibition.

He died on 18 August 1870 at Newport, Rhode Island, and was buried at

Greenmount Cemetery in Baltimore. His will left money for republication of previously published works and for his literary executors to comb his papers for other publishable materials. They carried out his wishes, publishing ten volumes in 1872, including Henry T. Tuckerman's *Life of Kennedy*.

MAJOR THEMES

Politically John Pendleton Kennedy was a nationalist, fearful that regionalism might pull the Union apart. Artistically, he drew heavily on one region, the South, for setting and dialogue in all his fiction but *Quodlibet*. Kennedy's relationship to the South was not unruffled, however. Like Faulkner's Quentin Compson in *Absalom, Absalom!*, he was of two minds about the region and its customs. This love-hate relationship is especially apparent in *Swallow Barn* (1832).

Begun in 1829 as a satire on Southern manners, the narrative finally became a book filled with love for the characters it created and with horrified disbelief at some of the society's ways, a disarming combination. Nowhere is this love-hate more evident than in the Tracy-Meriwether millpond feud. Meriwether and his opponent, Tracy, have been fighting for 40 years, for "principle" in the way that only Southerners can. What the courts award Meriwether, Tracy will not give. Seeing that Tracy will never give in, Meriwether decides to show his magnanimous side. He rigs the proceedings—in favor of his opponent—without letting the opponent know, of course. The feud is ended. The battle is, after all, a dispute over manners; and Meriwether's victory is the victory of gentlemanly behavior.

Kennedy was married in 1829, just before he began writing *Swallow Barn*. He could hardly leave a love story out. That love between a hero, slightly tainted, and the most attractive girl in the book is presented in *Swallow Barn* and repeated in *Horse-Shoe Robinson* and *Rob of the Bowl* with some slight variations. That story is the most conventional and, in some senses, the least satisfying part of each book. Nick Hazard is not quite Tom Jones; but he has the same propensity for getting into scrapes and for winning hearts while the lovely Bel Tracy stereotypically stands for all that is virtuous. Mildred Lindsay in *Horse-Shoe Robinson*, while she fits the stereotype generally, has a somewhat stronger role. She must act, traveling through three states on horseback to save the life of Major Arthur Butler. Butler is tainted, at least in the eyes of Mildred's father, by being in the Revolutionary Army. But by the end of the novel he gains acceptance from Mr. Lindsay as well as his daughter. Blanche Warden, both as pure and as colorless as her name implies, finds herself in love with Albert Verhayden, tainted by lack of a family and therefore presumed illegitimate. He proves a hero, finds a father, and the situation is resolved predictably.

Of more interest in *Horse-Shoe Robinson* is the role of the title character, a frontier man whose ingenuity and generosity mark him as the spirit for the new republic. To bring Robinson's exploits to the fore, Kennedy has to jail Major

Butler, Robinson's military superior, for all but 20 of the 58 chapters; but Horse-Shoe's daring exploits in the South Carolina countryside are worth having even if the author has to take such liberties.

Horse-Shoe Robinson does not, like *Swallow Barn*, take place on the plantation. Rather it focuses, at least in those chapters dominated by Robinson, upon the common man. Kennedy depicts life on what was the American frontier of the 1770s, revealing its joys and its privations.

The novel is historical fiction, concluding with the Battle of King's Mountain, a battle championed by some historians as the turning point of the Revolution in the South; and historical personages including Francis Marion, the Swamp Fox, weave in and out of the story.

Rob of the Bowl is also historical fiction. Like *Swallow Barn* and, to a lesser degree, *Horse-Shoe Robinson*, the book contrasts the life of the aristocrat and that of the common man; but it does so without rancor. It is more depiction than social commentary.

Quodlibet (1840) breaks that mold. It is pointed social commentary. The satire, supposedly an account of the growth of the town Quodlibet, is an attempt to defeat Martin Van Buren, Jackson's man, in the election of 1840. Jackson's war on the United States Bank, the factionalization of a party, and the voting of ignorant masses all are subjected to Kennedy's wit.

SURVEY OF CRITICISM

In 1840 John Pendleton Kennedy stopped writing fiction. By January 1842 the *New York Review* was publishing the first retrospective of the four volumes, promulgating judgments that have been for the most part reaffirmed in the following century and a half. John H. B. Latrobe, ostensibly the author of the unsigned review, said the supreme achievement of authorship came in "creating and describing an imaginary character, that ever after remains in the memories of men ranked among the real existences of the past." *Horse-Shoe Robinson*, he felt, created a title character of that stature. *Swallow Barn*, in spite of the masterful development of characters, would be chiefly remembered for its "pure Americanism." The book appeared to second the effort of Irving and Cooper to declare a literary declaration of independence. Followed, as it was, by works of Hawthorne, Simms, and Melville, it seems now an early and powerful document in the new cultural wave.

Latrobe found the two other fictions—*Rob of the Bowl* and *Quodlibet*—less powerful: *Rob*, because of the confusion generated by its large cast of characters; and *Quodlibet*, because of its attachment to the minute details of the campaign of 1840, details that two years later were already being forgotten.

Not until Vernon Louis Parrington's chapter on Kennedy in *The Romantic Revolution in America, 1800–1860* (1927) was such a sweeping evaluation of Kennedy's work made again. Surprisingly, he championed *Rob of the Bowl* as the best book of fiction, complimented *Quodlibet* for its satirical strength and played down *Horse-Shoe Robinson* as a book offering nothing unique to letters.

Other general estimates of the fiction worth reading are William S. Osborne's dissertation "John Pendleton Kennedy: A Study of His Literary Career" (1960), Charles H. Bohner's biography *John Pendleton Kennedy: Gentleman from Baltimore* (1961), and J. V. Ridgely's *John Pendleton Kennedy* (1966). Ridgely, devoted to *Swallow Barn*, gives his best in discussing it, though sections on *Horse-Shoe Robinson* and *Rob of the Bowl* are incisive.

It is the historical dimension of Kennedy's work that has most consistently captured the attention of critics. A. B. Meek sparked the interest when he discovered the original of Kennedy's Horse-Shoe Robinson living near Tuscaloosa, Alabama. His interview published in *The Flag of the Union* in January 1838 might have prompted Kennedy to reveal the historical seed of the story in his introduction to the 1852 edition of the novel. Lyman C. Draper discovered that Mary Musgrove also had an original in life and reported his finding in *King's Mountain and Its Heroes* (Cincinnati: 1881 rpt. Baltimore: Genealogical, 1971).

In spite of the evidence for historical connections, John Robert Moore maintained that the book was romantic fiction of the type created by Irving, Cooper, and Simms and was therefore not intended to convey matters of fact ("Horse-Shoe Robinson: Fact or Fiction?" 1932). Rhoda Coleman Ellison redirected scholars, reminding them in two articles of Meek's meeting with Robinson: "Early Alabama Interest in Southern Writers," (1948), and "An Interview with Horse-Shoe Robinson" (1959).

William S. Osborne, in addition to confirming the historicity of Robinson and Mary Musgrove, established that of Wat Adair, Hugh Habershaw, and Mrs. Markham. Remembering that Kennedy was a historian, Osborne looked for sources the academic might have used in describing the battle at King's Mountain and found David Ramsay's *History of South Carolina* (Charleston: n.p., 1809). Osborne's conclusion about the relationship of history and fiction in the novel is expressed in the title of his articles: "John Pendleton Kennedy's *Horse-Shoe Robinson*: A Novel with 'Utmost Historical Accuracy' " (1964).

That *Horse-Shoe Robinson* had historical sources was by the mid–1960s unmistakable. Nevertheless, the book was fiction, not history. The sources needed to be put in proper perspective. J. V. Ridgely did just that in *John Pendleton Kennedy* (1966), quoting from Kennedy's preface to prove the book "*both* factual and legendary, both instructive and entertaining." Kennedy used sources; but when he was writing fiction, he used them as a novelist, not a historian. He allowed his story to fit in around the facts; but the center of the work was *his* story lived out by *his* characters, whatever their origins or names.

Charles H. Bohner had previously uncovered a similar use of historical material in *Rob of the Bowl*, making the notation public in " 'As Much History as . . . Invention'; John P. Kennedy's *Rob of the Bowl*" (1960) and making the information available to a wider audience in *John Pendleton Kennedy: Gentleman from Baltimore* a year later.

The view that Kennedy gave historically accurate descriptions of two buildings in *Rob* has been championed by Henry Chandlee Forman. "The Rose Croft in Old St. Mary's" not only finds Kennedy's description of Blanche Warden's home accurate but also discusses three different houses built successively on the same site. In "The St. Mary's City 'Castle,' Predecessor of the Williamsburg Palace," Forman recounts Kennedy's accurate description of a building destroyed long ago.

Charles H. Bohner in "J. P. Kennedy's *Quodlibet*: Whig Counterattack" gives the best available commentary on the book, carefully spelling out the historical-political conditions of 1840 that pushed Kennedy to write and publish. Much, though not all, of the information in the article finds its way into Bohner's biography of Kennedy.

The most perplexing judgments about any of the works have involved *Swallow Barn* and its place in literary history. By 1924, Francis Pendleton Gaines was claiming in *The Southern Plantation* that *Swallow Barn* was the first important book in the plantation tradition. Sterling Brown, willing to grant that *Swallow Barn* was first, condemns it as first in a corrupt fictional tradition. In *The Negro in American Fiction* (1937), Brown judges the book largely by its attitude toward slavery. Not only did it implicitly support slavery, but it was not even original in doing so. Kennedy relied on the stereotypes created by others rather than on his own observation in depicting Negroes, Brown charges. Jay Hubbell, in his introduction to *Swallow Barn* (New York: Harcourt, Brace, 1929), found the novel at the end of an idealistic tradition, the Jeffersonian liberalism that guided the Virginia legislature in its effort to emancipate slaves in 1831–32. The effort and the tradition were dashed by the Nat Turner rebellion. What Hubbell calls "the Virginia tradition in fiction," a more conservative vision claiming slavery as its cornerstone, began after *Swallow Barn* with Caruthers's *The Cavaliers of Virginia*.

Richard Beale Davis has spoken twice about *Swallow Barn*'s place in American literary history. In "Literary Tastes in Virginia Before Poe" (*William and Mary Quarterly*, January 1939), he finds the book devoid of imitation of Scott and showing an attitude unique to Virginia. In "The 'Virginia Novel' before *Swallow Barn*" (*Virginia Magazine of History and Biography*, July 1963), he recognizes that unique Virginia attitude in novels produced from 1805 through 1828. This fiction preceded Kennedy but contained virtually every major feature of the work he, Caruthers, Cooke, and Page would produce.

An exhaustive bibliographic essay containing reaction to the nonfiction as well as the fiction is David O. Tomlinson's "John Pendleton Kennedy: An Essay in Bibliography" (1979).

BIBLIOGRAPHY

Works by John Pendleton Kennedy

The Red Book, with Peter Hoffman Cruse. Baltimore: J. Robinson, 1819–21.
Swallow Barn. Philadelphia: Carey & Lea, 1832. New York: George P. Putnam, 1851.

Philadelphia: J. B. Lippincott, 1860. New York: G. P. Putnam, 1872. New York: Harcourt, Brace, 1929, with intro. by Jay B. Hubbell. New York: Hafner, 1962. Baton Rouge: Louisiana State University Press, 1986, intro. by Lucinda H. MacKethan.

Horse-Shoe Robinson. Philadelphia: Carey, Lea & Blanchard, 1835. London: Richard Bentley, 1835. Philadelphia: Carey, Lea & Blanchard, 1836. London: J. Pratt, 1845. New York: George P. Putnam, 1852. Philadelphia: J. B. Lippincott, 1860. New York: G. P. Putnam, 1872. New York: American Book, 1937. New York: Hafner, 1962. Philadelphia: R. West, 1977.

Rob of the Bowl. Philadelphia: Lea & Blanchard, 1838. London: Richard Bentley, 1838. New York: G. P. Putnam, 1854. Philadelphia: J. B. Lippincott, 1861. New York: G. P. Putnam, 1872. New Haven: College and University Press, 1965.

Quodlibet. Philadelphia: Lea & Blanchard, 1840. Philadelphia: J. B. Lippincott, 1860. New York: G. P. Putnam, 1872. Upper Saddle River, N.J.: Literature House/ Gregg, n.d. New York: Irvington, n.d.

Defence of the Whigs. New York: Harper, 1844.

Memoirs of the Life of William Wirt. Philadelphia: Lea & Blanchard, 1849. Philadelphia: Lea & Blanchard, 1850. Philadelphia: J. B. Lippincott, 1860. New York: G. P. Putnam, 1872.

"The Border States, Their Power and Duty in the Present Disordered Condition of the Country." n.p., 1860. Philadelphia: J. B. Lippincott, 1861.

Mr. Ambrose's Letters on the Rebellion. New York: Hurd and Houghton, and Baltimore: James S. Waters, 1865. Printed with *Occasional Addresses*. . . . New York: G. P. Putnam, 1872.

At Home and Abroad. New York: G. P. Putnam, 1872.

Occasional Addresses. . . . New York: G. P. Putnam, 1872.

Political and Official Papers. New York: G. P. Putnam, 1872.

Studies of John Pendleton Kennedy

Bohner, Charles H. " 'As Much History as . . . Invention': John P. Kennedy's *Rob of the Bowl*." *William and Mary Quarterly* 17 (July 1960): 329–40.

———. *John Pendleton Kennedy: Gentleman from Baltimore*. Baltimore: Johns Hopkins University Press, 1961.

———. "J. P. Kennedy's *Quodlibet*: Whig Counterattack." *American Quarterly* 13 (September 1961): 84–92.

———. "*The Red Book*, 1819–1821: A Satire on Baltimore Society." *Maryland Historical Magazine* 51 (September 1956): 175–87.

———. "*Swallow Barn*: John P. Kennedy's Chronicle of Virginia Society." *Virginia Magazine of History and Biography* 68 (July 1960): 317–30.

Brown, Sterling. *The Negro in American Fiction*. Repr. New York: Arno Press, 1969.

Davis, Richard Beale. "Literary Tastes in Virginia Before Poe." *William and Mary Quarterly*, 2d ser. 19 (January 1939): 55–68.

———. "The 'Virginia Novel' Before *Swallow Barn*." *Virginia Magazine of History and Biography* 71 (July 1963): 278–93.

Ellison, Rhoda Coleman. "An Interview with Horse-Shoe Robinson." *American Literature* 31 (November 1959): 329–32.

Gaines, Francis Pendleton. *The Southern Plantation: A Study in the Development and Accuracy of A Tradition*. New York: Columbia University Press, 1924.

Gwathmey, Edward M. *John Pendleton Kennedy*. New York: Thomas Nelson, 1931.

Langley, Harold D. "John Pendleton Kennedy," *American Secretaries of the Navy*. Vol. 1. Ed. Paolo E. Coletta. Annapolis: Naval Institute Press, 1980.

Moore, John Robert. "Kennedy's *Horse-Shoe Robinson*: Fact or Fiction?" *American Literature* 4 (June 1932): 160–66.

Osborne, William S. "John Pendleton Kennedy: A Study of His Literary Career." Ph.D. diss., Columbia University, 1960.

————. "John Pendleton Kennedy's *Horse-Shoe Robinson*: A Novel with 'Utmost Historical Accuracy.' " *Maryland Historical Magazine* 59 (September 1964): 286–96.

Parrington, Vernon Louis. "John Pendleton Kennedy, A Southern Whig." *The Romantic Revolution in America, 1800–1860*. Vol. 2 of *Main Currents in American Thought*. New York: Harcourt, Brace, 1927.

Pretzer, Wallace Louis. "Eighteenth-Century Literary Conventions in the Fictional Style of John Pendleton Kennedy (1795–1870)." Ph.D. diss., University of Michigan, 1963.

Ridgely, J. V. *John Pendleton Kennedy*. New York: Twayne, 1966.

————. "John Pendleton Kennedy." *Antebellum Writers in New York and the South*. Ed. Joel Myerson, Vol. 3 of *Dictionary of Literary Biography*. Detroit: Gale Research, 1979.

Tomlinson, David O. "John Pendleton Kennedy: An Essay in Bibliography." *Resources for American Literary Study* 9 (Autumn 1979): 140–70.

Tuckerman, Henry T. *The Life of John Pendleton Kennedy*. New York: G. P. Putnam, 1871.

——————————— DAVID KIRBY ———————————

Grace King
(1852–1932)

Taken together, Grace King's stories and novels paint a sweeping mural of suffering and transcendence in the South during and after the American Civil War.

BIOGRAPHY

Grace Elizabeth King was born 29 November 1852 in New Orleans, the daughter of William Woodson King and Sarah Ann Miller King. As an adult, Grace King was fond of thinking of her early childhood in terms of a comfortable family life and the pleasant rigors of convent schooling. But the Civil War put a period to the ease and tranquillity she enjoyed as the daughter of a prosperous New Orleans lawyer, and as a child of nine, she watched from a window as residents of the port city burned bales of cotton, broke open barrels of whiskey and poured their contents into the gutters, and otherwise prepared to surrender to Union troops in late spring 1862. The King family was able to escape to the family plantation, where they sat out the conflict in comparative safety, but the period following the war was hard, and when they returned to New Orleans, it was to a small house in a poor neighborhood; years passed before the family was able to regain anything like the social and economic status they had enjoyed before the war.

The King children studied at home and at the different French-language schools in New Orleans; Grace herself attended the Institut St. Louis that she described in her first published story, "Monsieur Motte." She was determined to make her way as a writer, and eventually succeeded, even though her long and successful career had its beginning in a chance encounter. In 1885 Richard Watson Gilder, then editor of the *Century Illustrated Magazine*, asked King the reason for the rancor that so many New Orleanians seemed to feel for the popular author George Washington Cable and his writings. King told Gilder that Cable had painted unsavory portraits of her fellow citizens in order to please a Northern audience. Gilder replied, "If Cable is so false to you, why do not some of you write better?" King was stung by this response, but she went to bed that evening with the resolve to meet Gilder's challenge. The result was "Monsieur Motte," which appeared in the January 1886 number of the *New Princeton Review*.

King's stories and novels gained her a wide and admiring readership. She lived to see her fiction compared to that of Nathaniel Hawthorne, William Dean Howells, Theodore Dreiser, Willa Cather, and the French realists; her friends included Julia Ward Howe, Charles Dudley Warner, and Samuel Clemens. As a young woman, King began a series of trips abroad that continued throughout her life and allowed her to combine professional interests with pleasure; on one such trip to England, she was asked to speak to the young women of Newnham College, Cambridge, on the subject of Sidney Lanier and his work. But it is with France that King had the greatest affinity; as her biographer Robert Bush has pointed out, because of the French Creole education King had had in her native New Orleans, she was one of the few nineteenth-century Americans fully prepared to understand and appreciate French culture. In her travels King heard Ernest Renan lecture at the Sorbonne and saw Alexandre Dumas *fils* in the audience of the Théâtre d'Art. She met the most noted women of letters in Paris, including Madame Blanc and the Baronne de Bury, and frequented their salons. Like many provincials, King was a great cosmopolitan—because she was home somewhere, she was home everywhere.

Grace King never married. One recurring note in her fiction is the inadequacy of men, who often seem defeated and helpless in the face of war and its aftermath, and while it would be too easy to suggest a direct connection between the traumatic experiences of King's childhood and her lifelong celibacy, it is striking nonetheless that her memoirs and personal papers contain very few references to any sort of affair of the heart. Henry James is our greatest example of the writer-priest who recoiled from the idea of physical passion and instead poured everything into his work. King, too, renounced the conjugal life, although some of her best writings are painstaking dissections of the relationships between men and women. She died on 12 January 1932.

MAJOR THEMES

As Robert Bush has pointed out, the losses and suffering the King family felt during the war and the Reconstruction period were the major factors in determining Grace King's character; had she not felt the poverty and indignation that she did, King might never have written a line. The war is always present, explicitly or implicitly, in King's fiction. For example, the heroine of her first published story, "Monsieur Motte," is a young girl named Marie Modeste, who has been orphaned by the war, and everything that happens to her is a consequence of this. Marie attends a young ladies' boarding school in New Orleans, and the story involves the school's annual celebration, when proud parents come to see their daughters collect the prizes they have won. Since Marie has no parents, a mysterious uncle has been providing for her education; Marie has not seen this uncle since she was four, and when he does not appear at the celebration, she learns that he, too, has been long since dead and that for the past few years her schooling has been paid for by Marcélite, the school's humble hairdresser. King wrote three more sketches involving the same characters and published the whole as *Monsieur Motte* (1888), a thoroughly padded "novel" in which Marie Modeste marries someone very much like herself, a young man who has lost his parents and has been raised largely by a faithful female servant.

Throughout King's fiction men often betray the main character, either by deserting her or by dying (as in the case of Marie Modeste's father and uncle), and that character is often saved by a woman, usually a poor one. These themes, present already in King's rather pleasant and innocuous first story, are often treated with harrowing emotionality. A story called "A Quarrel With God" is set in an asylum for elderly ladies. The proprietor is one Madame B _____ , who has set up her establishment so that war widows and others will have a place where they can be cared for during their declining years. In doing so, Madame B _____ is motivated by the starvation death of a certain Madame M _____ , who is a basic character type in King's fiction, namely, the widow of a Confederate soldier and someone who has lost everything she had because of the war. In other words, death forms the very foundation of Madame B _____ 's asylum, and death is part of its daily life. Still, the ladies are shocked when a Mademoiselle Herminie is taken ill. For Mademoiselle Herminie sinks into despair so profound that she has a "quarrel with God" and gives up the practice of her religion. In a world where the men are unreliable and the women are good-hearted but poor, the only real recourse is to God, and Mademoiselle Herminie's heresy thus threatens the moral well-being of everyone in Madame B _____ 's establishment.

As in "Monsieur Motte," help comes from an unexpected quarter, and the true heroine of the story turns out to be Florestine, a servant. It is she who orchestrates the comings and goings of the doctor and the priest, although, since Mademoiselle Herminie is clearly dying, there is more work for the latter than the former. Florestine is concerned that the priest will not be in sympathy for the impenitent old woman. So she tells him of all the suffering the dying woman has undergone; as might be expected, there is much male wickedness in Herminie's history, including the suggestion that her mother died of syphillis acquired congenitally from her own father. Convinced there are genuine causes for Herminie's woe, the priest treats her sympathetically, and she revives just long enough to perform her religious duties and die within the bosom of the church.

There is much talk of the nature of God in this story; in a startling comparison, Florestine says that God is like a plantation owner, at once compassionate to his charges yet preoccupied with his own affairs. In fact, there is really only one basic male figure in King's fiction, whether he is called God, Master, Husband,

Father, or, in some of the stories, Knight Errant. In keeping with the tradition of chivalry, which the South is said to have borrowed from the novels of Sir Walter Scott, King's women sometimes see their men as knights. And even when they do not, the men often oblige by adopting the code of the Knight Errant anyway as they ride off to attempt impossible tasks—typically, the defeat of superior Union forces—and come home when they please, if at all. No matter what mask the male figure assumes, his relation with King's basic female character, the Wife/Daughter/Slave/Princess, is almost always the same. For though she is bound to him intimately, still he may put himself at a distance from her without warning and sometimes permanently.

The themes of male perfidy and female solidarity are given their fullest treatment in King's novel *The Pleasant Ways of St. Médard* (1916). Of King's three full-length novels, *The Pleasant Ways* is easily her best, probably because it describes events that King knew firsthand. The novel is a fictionalized version of the King family's return to New Orleans after the war and the years of privation they suffered before regaining some semblance of social and economic status. There are many differences between what actually happened to the King family and the events of the novel; for example, the children in *The Pleasant Ways* are much younger than the King children were at that time. Nonetheless, the book uses personal experience in a way that strikes responsive chords in others; as King said in a letter to the writer Edward Garnett, "Every woman who lived during Reconstruction says it is her own story."

In an introduction to the novel, King recalls the role reversal of the sexes that occurred as a result of the Civil War. Before the war, the typical household was set up according to a strict pattern, notes King. There was the warrior/father, virtually a God in the temple of his own home; the Mary-like mother, the sure intermediary between the God-like father and his subjects, a saintly creature who is in many ways stronger than the father yet wise enough to hide her strength; the children and servants, largely faceless creatures who will be buffeted this way and that by the storm forces of war but who will prove to be resilient in the end, like the mother but not the father, who will be turned on his head, his temple desecrated and his followers scattered. The father who was once a minor deity becomes a beggar and an outlaw. Only divine providence can restore him to his rightful place, but this prospect seems doubtful. After all, the father's aloof God scorned him in wartime, because there is no masculine solidarity as there is solidarity between women in King's fiction.

Part of the father's difficulty in *The Pleasant Ways* is that defeat in war has robbed him of his competitive instinct in the peacetime world. He is a lawyer, but not a very good one, and although King seems somewhat hesitant in her expression of the idea, it is clear before long that an unworldly father is an unworthy father. A worthy father is money-minded and mercantile; at least he can take care of his family. To make matters worse, the father in *The Pleasant Ways* falls sick with a debilitating and persistent fever. The novel's plot meanders and dozens of minor characters are introduced, mainly to reinforce the idea that when the world goes awry through masculine incompetence, it is usually a woman who sets it right again. Some of King's stock characters appear, such as the shrewd but sympathetic female servant who shields her incompetent superiors from the world's cruelty. In one scene, the family sees an old gentleman who looks like Robert E. Lee but is not; in an instant, the South's hero of heroes is reduced to mere mortal status.

In the end, the family is saved when circumstance and the connivance of friends combine to make the recently recovered yet still ineffectual father the executor of an enormous estate, one that will generate fees for years. All of the novel's villains—carpetbaggers, scalawags, most public officials, some businessmen, fever and other illness, and pessimism in general—are trounced by a coalition of dutiful parents (but mostly mothers), faithful friends, and patient physicians, with a good deal of aid from God, who seems to have become more attentive to the characters' plight at last. The ending is sufficiently, if not totally, plausible. Though order is restored, the main impression the reader brings away is that *The Pleasant Ways of St. Médard* is King's personal expression of the anger and embarrassment felt by a generation of Southerners. It would take another event on the same scale to drive thoughts of the Civil War from King's mind; Robert Bush, her biographer, quotes from a letter King wrote in 1914: "The great war in Europe has at last driven our little Civil War & its losses from my mind & given us other news to think about." In *Memories of a Southern Woman of Letters* (1932), which appeared after her death, King wrote that "the past is our only real possession." Certainly her own memory of the postbellum period and the opposite parts played in it by men and women became the bedrock of her subsequent thought and art.

SURVEY OF CRITICISM

Like other minor authors, Grace King has been treated rather evenly by critics over the years, neither neglected nor ballyhooed. As literary criticism has become more sophisticated, King has finally come to be appreciated for what she really is—a writer who provides a unique angle of vision into the psychology of the American woman and who presents a portion of the Southern experience that is not found in the work of better-known authors.

Of the studies that appeared during King's lifetime, one of the most gratifying to her personally was Charles W. Coleman, Jr.'s "The Recent Movement in Southern Literature," which appeared in *Harper's*, 74 (May 1887): 837–55. The article includes discussions and portraits of King, George Washington Cable, Joel Chandler Harris, Thomas Nelson Page, Lafcadio Hearn, and others. The section on King merely identifies her as a local colorist of grace and charm, but if the critical remarks are not particularly penetrating, still, wrote King afterward, "for a young writer . . . to be included in *Harper's* pages was equivalent to the presentation of a débutante at Court."

Of the early twentieth-century critics to take notice of King, the most distinguished was Fred Lewis Pattee. In *A History of American Literature Since 1870* (1922), Pattee calls the appearance of "Monsieur Motte" in the *New Princeton Review* "another step in the development of the short story. It was as distinctively French in its atmosphere and its art as if it had been a translation from Maupassant, yet it was as originally and peculiarly American as even [Cable's] *Madame Delphine*, which in so many ways it resembles." The page and a half that Pattee gives to King and her work in *The Development of the American Short Story* (1923) includes a concise and accurate statement on King's affinity with the French. Pattee notes her strengths and shortcomings, comments briefly on *Monsieur Motte* and *Balcony Stories*, and observes:

No other native American short-story writer has been so thoroughly French. Her tales are like well-made translations from the school of Flaubert and Daudet. Like Norris and Garland, she affected veritism: it was in the air of the times; she had learned of Zola to tell the Truth, but not after the manner of Zola. Cable she believed had romanticized New Orleans beyond toleration and misrepresented it: she would present the charming side of her people, their pride, their uniqueness, their distinction, their lovable unselfishness. If romance came into her tales it would be only because romance in New Orleans was the Truth. . . .

In the several decades following her death, it was commonplace for literary critics to cite King as a representative if minor local colorist and social historian of the postwar South. Thus her writings are mentioned (even if relatively few new points are made about them) in such standard general works as Jay B. Hubbell's *The South in American Literature, 1609–1900* (1954); Edmund Wilson's *Patriotic Gore: Studies in the Literature of the American Civil War* (1962); Warner Berthoff's *The Ferment of Realism: American Literature, 1884–1919* (1965); and Jay Martin's *Harvests of Change: American Literature, 1865–1914* (1967). King is mentioned briefly in the first edition of the authoritative *Literary History of the United States*, ed. Robert E. Spiller, Willard Thorpe, et al. (1946). Her work is given expanded coverage in the revised fourth edition (1974), which singles out the five long stories collected in *Tales of a Time and Place* for cautious praise, noting that they "displayed a distinguished style, a prose deliberate and cool, illuminated with splashes of color, and filled at the end with climactic passages of action. Both here and in later works Miss King carefully avoided controversial matters, stepped softly, and sought everywhere to tone down the more garish, but always more interesting, portraits which Cable had drawn" (p. 858).

Thanks to Robert Bush in the early 1970s, King's work received something like the attention it deserves. A series of articles culminated in an authoritative biography by Bush, *Grace King: A Southern Destiny* (1983). Bush's study of King's life has been complemented by the first full-length critical study of King's writing, David Kirby's *Grace King* (1980).

Elisabeth S. Muhlenfeld had written that "the very interesting New Orleans writer Grace King has been badly neglected by scholars'' (in a review of the two dissertations on King in *American Literary Realism* 8 [Autumn 1975]: 295). The Bush and Kirby books have helped to fill this gap, but work still needs to be done. Other critics have mentioned King's relation to the dominant literary movements of her time and place, Realism and local color, but it remains for someone else to develop fully the connection. Another fruitful area to explore is that of the similarities and differences between King and other contemporaries who were female or Southern or both.

BIBLIOGRAPHY

Works by Grace King

Monsieur Motte. New York: A. C. Armstrong, 1888.
Jean Baptiste le Moyne, Sieur de Bienville. New York: Dodd, Mead, 1892.
Tales of a Time and Place. New York: Harper, 1892; repr. New York: Garrett Press, 1969.
Balcony Stories. New York: Century, 1893; repr. New York: Gregg Press, 1968.
New Orleans: The Place and the People. New York and London: Macmillan, 1895.
De Soto and His Men in the Land of Florida. New York: Macmillan, 1898.
The Pleasant Ways of St. Médard. New York: Henry Holt, 1916.
Creole Families of New Orleans. New York: Macmillan, 1921.
La Dame de Sainte Hermine. New York: Macmillan, 1924.
Memories of a Southern Woman of Letters. New York: Macmillan, 1932.
Grace King of New Orleans: A Selection of Her Writings. Ed. Robert Bush. Baton Rouge: Louisiana State University Press, 1973.

Studies of Grace King

Bush, Robert. ''Charles Gayarré and Grace King: Letters of a Louisiana Friendship.'' *Southern Literary Journal* 7 (Fall 1974): 100–131.
———. ''Grace King (1852–1932).'' *American Literary Realism* 8 (Winter 1975): 43–49.
———. ''Grace King and Mark Twain.'' *American Literature* 44 (March 1972): 31–51.
———. *Grace King: A Southern Destiny*. Baton Rouge: Louisiana State University Press, 1983.
———. ''Grace King: The Emergence of a Southern Intellectual Woman.'' *Southern Review* 13 (Spring 1977): 272–88.
———. Introduction to *Grace King of New Orleans*. Baton Rouge: Louisiana State University Press, 1973.
Kirby, David. *Grace King*. Boston: Twayne, 1980.
Muhlenfeld, Elisabeth S. ''Grace King.'' *American Literary Realism* 8 (Autumn 1975): 295–96.
Pattee, Fred Lewis. *The Development of the American Short Story*. New York: Harper, 1923.
———. *A History of American Literature Since 1870*. New York: Century, 1922.
Vaughan, Bess. ''A Bio-Bibliography of Grace Elizabeth King.'' *Louisiana Historical Quarterly* 17 (October 1934): 752–70.

JANE S. GABIN

Sidney Lanier
(1842–1881)

Sidney Lanier is the only American poet of stature who was also a professional musician; in this fact lies the key to his reputation. His later work, wedding poetic expression and musical concepts, broke away from typical nineteenth-century patterns and created a highly original verse form. Lanier was also a composer, teacher, and scholar. Despite all these accomplishments, Lanier has never been accorded more than minor literary status. This, in large part, is because an early death cut short his career just at the point where it was most promising.

The life of Sidney Lanier is an odyssey from a small Southern city to the great cultural centers of the nation; from a law desk in a Macon, Georgia, office to a prominent place in a major professional orchestra; from an aesthetically restrictive tradition to an existence totally imbued with the arts. It is also a series of thwarted plans, shattered hopes, and incomplete projects. Lanier came from a genteel tradition that scorned following the arts as a profession; he spent most of his life dreaming of breaking with this tradition and entering artistic circles. But when he finally decided to do so, he was able to reach only slightly beyond the periphery, for he then had only seven years to live.

Yet it is remarkable that Lanier managed to do so much in so little time. He played first flute in the Peabody Conservatory orchestra; accepted numerous other musical engagements; delivered popular lectures on Shakespeare and on the English novel; wrote numerous essays on music and on literature; wrote editions for children of legendary classics; composed works for piano, voice, and flute; wrote a highly praised study of English prosody; and in the midst of all these activities wrote dozens of poems, some of which are among the most beautifully original in American literature.

BIOGRAPHY

Lanier was born on 3 February 1842 in Macon, Georgia, where the Lanier home on High Street now serves as headquarters of the Middle Georgia Historical Society. Mid–nineteenth-century Macon was a prosperous commercial center, and the Laniers shared in the general affluence. Lanier showed an aptitude for music at an early age, but neither he nor anyone else entertained the thought of his actually becoming a musician. Music in the South of that time was considered the domain of women and of the European men who gave lessons or who visited the city as guest performers.

Lanier entered Oglethorpe University in nearby Milledgeville in 1857 for a general liberal arts education; very likely it was assumed that he would follow his father into the practice of law. An honor student, Lanier also engaged in sports and debating. By this time, his interest in music had developed into a passion, and he would sometimes play his flute until falling into a deep reverie. He was true, however, to the code of his time and region in rejecting any thought of a musical career. After graduation in 1860, he worked at Oglethorpe as a tutor and considered an academic career, even dreaming of going to Germany for graduate studies.

But then the war broke out, and in July 1861 Lanier joined the Macon Volunteers, serving in the signal corps and then on a blockade runner. His ship was captured, and he was imprisoned for several months at a federal camp in Point Lookout, Maryland; here he contracted the tuberculosis that was to kill him seventeen years later. He was released in 1865 and, though gravely ill, walked most of the way home to Macon. He found his city profoundly changed by the war, and his own existence severely hampered by ill health and economic worries.

Lanier spent several months trying to recover his health and then began working at various positions—hotel clerk, tutor, headmaster—in order to support himself. For a while he worked at his father's small law office, but found the work unrewarding. He wrote several songs and poems and completed a Civil War novel, *Tiger-Lilies*. A sense of duty and the hold of tradition kept him at his law desk, but his desire to work as a professional musician increased. In general, this was a depressing period of poor health, unstimulating work, and nagging financial problems. The one bright spot was his marriage in 1867 to Mary Day of Macon.

During these years Lanier sampled various tastes of a richer musical life. He made several trips to New York on business and in search of medical care, and there attended many concerts. In fall 1872 he went to San Antonio, Texas, hoping to find relief in its drier climate. There he found a large community of immigrant Germans, including many musicians, and the atmosphere of German culture, part of which was an embracing love of music, seems to have been more beneficial to Lanier than the weather. He participated in musical groups and turned his hand to composition.

Encouraged by his success in this community, Lanier decided to seek a career in New York, the musical center of the country. "An impulse, simply irresistible," he wrote to his brother, "drives me into the world of poetry and music." Lanier's family, especially his wife, encouraged him, and in fall 1873 he headed north.

He did not have much luck in New York, probably because he underestimated the competition from the many established and aspiring musicians in the city. Contemporary accounts attest to Lanier's skill as a flute player; but he was largely self-taught, and was now trying to compete with conservatory-trained artists. When he stopped in Baltimore to visit a friend, he played for Asger Hamerik, the young Danish-born conductor of the orchestra of the new Peabody Conservatory. The result of this informal audition, at which Lanier played one of his own compositions, was Hamerik's offer of the position of first flute. Lanier's acceptance and his decision to remain in Baltimore marked the turning point in his life and career.

A popular figure in Baltimore artistic circles, Lanier was invited to play with several other groups in addition to his regular appointment with Peabody orchestra. Reviews always praised his playing, audiences loved him, and he was treated as a peer by the conservatory faculty. Lanier found Baltimore exciting and hospitable, joining several clubs and musical organizations. At this point, he still considered himself primarily a musician, though he was also writing a substantial amount of poetry; when he joined the Wednesday Club, he aligned himself with its musical rather than literary section.

Artistically, Lanier was maturing, in part because of the influence of Hamerik, who introduced his orchestra and audience to many new works by contemporary composers such as Berlioz, Tchaikovsky, and Wagner. Here, for the first time, Lanier was exposed to "programme-music," in which specific literary, natural, and emotional concepts were translated into tone. Programme-music complemented his idea that poetry should create mental images through the manipulation of sound. Although not everyone in the audience was ready to accept some of this "avant-garde" music, Lanier was thrilled. He enjoyed the challenge of playing and attempted some composition of programmatic music. He did not, however, publish any of this music; the only musical composition he published during his lifetime is a sentimental song, "Little Ella" (1867).

But Lanier continued to write poetry; in fact, by 1874 he was more interested in composing verse than music. The beginning of his national reputation as a poet can be dated from the 1874 publication of "Corn" in *Lippincott's*. His new stature prompted the Atlantic Coast Line Railroad, whose offices were in Baltimore, to commission him to write a railway travelers' guide to Florida. The pay was more than double Lanier's orchestral salary, and he needed to support his wife and sons, still in Georgia. The book, published in 1875, was a financial success, but to Lanier it was, as he said, "like a wound. . . . I did not wish ever to appear before the public again save in the poetic character." He would, however, have to write several more such works to make ends meet. They were always a source of pain to him, and the work strained his ever-precarious health.

A more prestigious opportunity came shortly afterward when Lanier was asked by the U.S. Centennial Commission to write a cantata for the opening ceremonies of its exhibition in Philadelphia. The cantata, with music by Dudley Buck of Connecticut (the Commission, in its spirit of reconciliation, wished the work to be a joint project between a Southerner and a Northerner), was performed on 10 May 1876. This *Centennial Meditation of Columbia* was for Lanier the culmination of a total aesthetic experience in which lyrics and music were mutually suggestive of the ideas presented.

Also in 1876, Mary Day Lanier moved north with their sons. Until now, the financial exigencies of living in Baltimore had made it impossible for Lanier to uproot his family. Although this situation, which lasted three years, was personally less than happy, the extensive, detailed, and loving correspondence that resulted is a valuable record of Lanier's experiences, which scholars would not have otherwise.

Lanier's first book of poems was published in 1877; it was the only volume of his poetry to appear during his lifetime, though many of his poems were published in various periodicals. By the end of 1877, Lanier's activities had shifted from the primarily musical to the primarily literary. After giving a successful series of private lectures, popularly called "parlor classes," Lanier was invited to deliver 24 lectures at the Peabody Institute as part of its 1878 "Shakespere [sic] course." Although the long hours of research and preparation were a great strain on Lanier's health, the joy of the work was its own compensation. This course further enhanced Lanier's academic reputation, and the following spring he was invited to join the faculty of the newly established Johns Hopkins University, something he had hoped for since the institution's founding in 1876.

Lanier's first set of lectures was open to the public, and his reputation was such that twice as many tickets were requested for the opening lecture as could be distributed. Lanier's lectures included some exalted thoughts on literature, typical of his idealistic view of the role of the arts: "I believe that it is the business of literature to keep the line of men touching shoulders as we move up through the darkness; I believe that the Poet is specially in charge, here below, to convert learning into Wisdom." During this period Lanier wrote his most musical poetry and published *The Science of English Verse*. But while the academic life was fulfilling for Lanier, his strength was declining rapidly. By the beginning of 1881 he could walk only with difficulty and had to deliver his lectures from a chair.

In summer 1881 the Laniers went to the mountains of North Carolina in search of relief; there, in a little house near Tryon, Lanier died on 7 September. He is buried in Baltimore, his grave marked by a stone with a quotation from his poem "Sunrise": "I am lit with the Sun." To his last days Lanier was characteristically optimistic, planning new books and artistic projects.

MAJOR THEMES

Lanier's work reveals a lasting concern with several themes: the unity of poetry and music; music as a symbol of human harmony ("Music is Love in search of a word" from *The Symphony* in his most-quoted phrase); the conflict between spiritual Art and materialistic Trade; the power of Nature; social problems; strong religious belief; and the progress of science. These concerns are embodied in various forms of verse (including some dialect poetry), academic essays, fiction, travel writing, and the retelling for young readers of classic medieval works. In fact, as Jack De Bellis has noted, part of Lanier's struggle was "to find the proper form in which to write." Lanier's energies were diffused into many areas, but the worlds of poetry and music compelled his strongest endeavors and produced his strongest works.

The most creative periods of Lanier's poetic life—and the happiest in his personal life—were those in which he was musically most active. Lanier's friends were, in the main, musical, not literary. He can hardly be said even to have brushed shoulders with the popular literary giants, such as Whitman or Longfellow, who were his contemporaries. But he found in enthusiastic applause for his flute playing compensation for rejection slips for his poetry. His writing often came under harsh attack from those who did not understand the form of poetry he was trying to create, but his musical performances never received an unfavorable review.

Lanier's position as a literary innovator, as a creator of a very individual musical verse, is the result of his exposure to innovation in musical composition, particularly nineteenth-century programme-music. Therefore, his early poems are simpler in style, following the song concept, whereas his late works reflect the influence of larger musical forms, the blending of voices, lines, and timbres characteristic of the symphony. Lanier's mature poems are freer in structure, rich in imagery, and as deliberately designed in sound as they are in meaning. This innovation, while securing his reputation, has also drawn negative criticism. In his desire to create musical verse, Lanier penned some overwrought and cumbersome lines, such as these from "Sunrise":

> The wave-serrate sea-rim sinks, unjarring, unreeling,
>   Forever revealing, revealing, revealing,
> Edgewise, bladewise, halfwise, wholewise,—'tis done!
>   Good morrow, lord Sun!

But the same efforts also resulted in the sensuous and melodic verse for which Lanier is most favorably noted. These lines are from "The Marshes of Glynn":

> Sinuous southward and sinuous northward the shimmering
>   band
> Of the sand-beach fastens the fringe of the marsh to
>   the fold of the land.
> Inward and outward to northward and southward the
>   beach-lines linger and curl
> As a silver-wrought garment that clings to and follows
>   the firm sweet limbs of a girl.

Although Lanier was not the only American poet to attempt to create musical verse, he was the only one who was also a professional musician; his poetry is therefore unique because it is the only American poetry whose musical qualities are determined by intense practical experience.

Lanier's literary output falls into several genres, the most significant of which is his verse. Second in importance are his essays on music and literature, which attest to his wide reading in classical and English literature and to the energy with which he tried to absorb all he could about early and contemporary composers. *The Science of English Verse* (1880) is a significant contribution to the study of prosody. His only novel, *Tiger-Lilies* (1867), is a youthful romantic-philosophical treatise set against the Southern mountains and the Civil War, in which characters passionately hold forth on Lanier's most cherished topics: love, nature, literature, music, science, and the conflict between good and evil. These subjects engaged Lanier for the rest of his life. A guidebook to Florida (1876) is a lesser work, though a carefully written one, interesting today for the contrast it provides with the picture of Florida after a century of development; there is also a chapter "For Consumptives," touching in its gallant optimism and pathetic in its medical ignorance. Additional literary projects Lanier had to undertake in order to support his family were the editing for young readers of classic tales of chivalry; only the prefaces to these books are Lanier's original work. Finally, Lanier's prodigious output of letters must be considered by any reader wishing a thorough understanding of the man and poet, for they constitute a fascinating record of his personal life and artistic maturation.

Although his possible further accomplishments can only be wistfully speculated, the final analysis of Lanier as a poet and musician is that he has endured because of more than substantial talent. As a musician he was praised not only by friendly local critics and colleagues but also by internationally known performers. Lanier's poetry is still—but not always—included in new anthologies of American literature. He remains on the periphery of our literature, largely ignored by the average student. Rich, image-laden poetry, intertwined with philosophy, is not popular; and it would seem that his exemplary and valiant life is no longer used as an inspirational model.

Yet Sidney Lanier continues to intrigue readers and critics who find in him a striking originality; whatever the shortcomings of his poetry, they are compensated for by the freshness of thought and expression with which he approached his subjects. He chose to follow no school, no safe and established practices, no patterns except his own. He may have sung alone at times, but he was distinctly heard.

SURVEY OF CRITICISM

Only a few of Lanier's contemporaries had a genuine appreciation of his art and understood all the sacrifices that lay behind each poem. Yet, as in the case of other artists whose lives were similarly bitter, he became the object of adulation after his death. Praise of Lanier and his work, sometimes bordering on the extravagant, expectedly increased after 1881, and through the 1940s magazines and newspapers were filled with the words of his worshipers. These evaluations range from scholarly critiques of his work to ecstatic tributes bespeaking the existence of a virtual Lanier cult. Among scholars, his reputation has increased steadily since the 1930s and in the last two decades there has been renewed interest in Lanier and his works.

The first wave of writings about Lanier, during the first three decades after his death, includes reviews of the 1884 volume of his poetry edited by Mary Day Lanier and tributes by those who knew him, the latter tending toward the hagiographic. All accounts agree on Lanier's personal goodness and decency and testify that he was loved by many. In addition to those who admired Lanier's life, there were those who saw in Lanier a symbol of Old South chivalry. But these images and ideas faded over the years, and by the 1930s Lanier was being attacked by the New Critics. Robert Penn Warren's "The Blind Poet: Sidney Lanier" (1933) was refuted by Aubrey Harrison Starke's "The Agrarians Deny a Leader," in turn criticized by John Crowe Ransom in "Hearts and Heads" (both in 1934).

Yet Lanier's supporters prevailed, and the following years saw Lanier scholarship culminate in the publication of the *Centennial Edition of the Works of Sidney Lanier* (1945), edited by Charles R. Anderson. These ten volumes are crucial to Lanier studies, containing Lanier's published and unpublished works and his correspondence. A critical introduction precedes each volume; volume 6 includes a lengthy bibliography of all writings by and about Lanier as of 1945. Jack De Bellis's *Sidney Lanier, Henry Timrod, and Paul Hamilton Hayne: A Reference Guide* (1978) provides an extensive annotated and cross-referenced bibliography of writings about Lanier from 1868 to 1976, including anonymous reviews and books and articles in which Lanier is discussed.

Continued interest in Lanier is attested to by the reprinting of several critical works and the appearance of new ones. The definitive biography by Aubrey Harrison Starke (1933) was reprinted in 1964. The concordance to Lanier's poetry, edited by Philip Graham and Joseph Jones in 1939, was reissued in 1969. Individual volumes of Lanier's works have also been reprinted since the late 1960s. Among the recent critical appraisals are: Edd Winfield Parks, *Sidney Lanier: The Man, The Poet, The Critic* (1969); Lewis Leary, "The Forlorn Hope of Sidney Lanier" (1971); Jack De Bellis's *Sidney Lanier* (1972); Louis D. Rubin, Jr., "The Passion of Sidney Lanier" (1976); the introductory section on Lanier in De Bellis's 1978 *Reference Guide*; and Jane S. Gabin, *A Living Minstrelsy: The Poetry and Music of Sidney Lanier* (1985).

BIBLIOGRAPHY

Works by Sidney Lanier

The Centennial Meditation of Columbia. New York: G. Schirmer, 1876.
Florida: Its Scenery, Climate, and History. Philadelphia: J. B. Lippincott, 1876.

Tiger-Lilies. New York: Hurd and Houghton, 1876.

Poems. Philadelphia: J. B. Lippincott, 1877.

The Boy's Froissart. New York: Charles Scribner's Sons, 1879.

The Boy's King Arthur. New York: Charles Scribner's Sons, 1880.

The Science of English Verse. New York: Charles Scribner's Sons, 1880.

The Boy's Mabinogion. New York: Charles Scribner's Sons, 1881.

The Boy's Percy. New York: Charles Scribner's Sons, 1882.

The English Novel. New York: Charles Scribner's Sons, 1883.

Poems of Sidney Lanier. Edited by his Wife. New York: Charles Scribner's Sons, 1884.

Music and Poetry. New York: Charles Scribner's Sons, 1898.

Bob: The Story of Our Mocking-Bird. New York: Charles Scribner's Sons, 1899.

Letters of Sidney Lanier. New York: Charles Scribner's Sons, 1899.

Retrospects and Prospects. Descriptive and Historical Essays. New York: Charles Scribner's Sons, 1899.

Shakespeare and His Forerunners. New York: Doubleday, Page, 1902.

Poem Outlines. New York: Charles Scribner's Sons, 1908.

The Centennial Edition of the Works of Sidney Lanier. 10 vols. Ed. Charles R. Anderson et al. Baltimore: Johns Hopkins University Press, 1945.

Studies of Sidney Lanier

Chase, Gilbert. *America's Music: From the Pilgrims to the Present*. New York: McGraw-Hill, 1966.

De Bellis, Jack. *Sidney Lanier*. New York: Twayne, 1972.

————. *Sidney Lanier, Henry Timrod, and Paul Hamilton Hayne: A Reference Guide*. Boston: G. K. Hall, 1978.

Gabin, Jane S. *A Living Minstrelsy: The Poetry and Music of Sidney Lanier*. Macon, Ga.: Mercer University Press, 1985.

Graham, Philip and Joseph Jones. *A Concordance to the Poems of Sidney Lanier*. Austin: University of Texas Press, 1939.

Leary, Lewis. "The Forlorn Hope of Sidney Lanier." *Southern Excursions: Essays on Mark Twain and Others*. Baton Rouge: Louisiana State University Press, 1971.

Lenhart, Charmenz. *Musical Influence in American Poetry*. Athens: University of Georgia Press, 1956.

Lorenz, Lincoln. *The Life of Sidney Lanier*. New York: Coward-McCann, 1935.

Mims, Edwin. *Sidney Lanier*. New York: Houghton, Mifflin, 1905.

Parks, Edd Winfield. *Sidney Lanier: The Man, The Poet, The Critic*. Athens: University of Georgia Press, 1969.

Ransom, John Crowe. "Heads and Hearts." *American Review* 2 (1934): 544–71.

Rubin, Louis D., Jr. "The Passion of Sidney Lanier." *William Elliott Shoots a Bear: Essays on the Southern Literary Imagination*. Baton Rouge: Louisiana State University Press, 1976.

Short, John Saulsbury. "Sidney Lanier, 'Familiar Citizen of the Town.' " *Maryland Historical Magazine* 35 (June 1940): 121–46.

Starke, Aubrey Harrison. "The Agrarians Deny a Leader." *American Review* 2 (1934): 455–73.

————. *Sidney Lanier: A Biographical and Critical Study*. Chapel Hill: University of
   North Carolina Press, 1933; repr. New York: Russell and Russell, 1964.
Warren, Robert Penn. "The Blind Poet: Sidney Lanier." *American Review* 2 (1933):
   27–45.

WILLIAM E. LENZ

Augustus Baldwin Longstreet (1790–1870)

The literary reputation of Augustus Baldwin Longstreet rests upon *Georgia Scenes, Characters, Incidents, &c., in the First Half Century of the Republic*, published in Augusta, Georgia, at the *States Rights Sentinel* office in 1835. The first volume of Southwestern humor to reach a national audience, *Georgia Scenes* was an immediate success; its eleven nineteenth-century editions testify to the growing popularity of regional American literature. As a repository of the attitudes, values, customs, and speech in the antebellum Old Southwest, *Georgia Scenes* is an invaluable resource. Longstreet chronicled the history of a region in transition, recapitulating an American pattern of rural to urban development that repeated itself in the South and West throughout the nineteenth century. The initiator of a tradition of Southwestern humor that includes William Tappan Thompson, Thomas Bangs Thorpe, Johnson Jones Hooper, Joseph Glover Baldwin, George Washington Harris, Richard Malcolm Johnston, and extends to William Faulkner and Flannery O'Connor, he pioneered the use of frontier materials and oral tale-telling techniques in loose literary forms. An amateur author like many of the Southwest humorists, he was also a lawyer, judge, politician, preacher, editor, temperance advocate, family man, and president of four colleges. An intensely moral man of quick enthusiasms and many interests, he appears to have been surprised by and unable to repeat his early literary success.

BIOGRAPHY

Augustus Baldwin Longstreet was born on 27 September 1790 in Augusta, Georgia, to William and Hannah Randolph Longstreet, former residents of New Jersey who joined many Americans in moving to the Old Southwest following the Revolution in search of the "flush times." His father was an inventor—he applied steam engines to a riverboat and the cotton gin, both ventures proving financially unremunerative—a gentleman of culture, and a speculator in land. The young Longstreet first attended local schools before enrolling at Dr. Moses Waddel's school at Willington, South Carolina, in 1808. After graduation he followed in the footsteps of family friend John C. Calhoun (the famous Southern "War Hawk") by entering Yale in 1811 (as a junior). Upon receiving his degree in 1813, Longstreet completed his formal education during a year of legal studies in Litchfield, Connecticut, at the school conducted by Judges Tapping Reeve and James Gould. Admitted to the Georgia bar on 26 May 1815, he rode the Richmond County, Georgia, circuit as a lawyer. A contemporary of Longstreet, W. H. Sparks, vividly described nineteenth-century circuit-riding:

Our circuit consisted of seven counties, and the ridings were spring and fall, occupying about two months each term. In each courthouse town was a tavern or two. These houses of entertainment were not then dignified with the sonorous title of hotel. The proprietors were usually jolly good fellows, or some staid matronly lady, in black gown and blue cap, and they all looked forward with anxious delight to the coming of court week. Every preparation was made for the judge and lawyers. Beds were aired and the bugs turned out. . . . The room usually appropriated to the Bench and Bar was a great vagabond-hall, denominated the ball-room, and for this purpose appropriated once or twice a year. Along the bare walls of this mighty dormitory were arranged beds, each usually occupied by a couple of the limbs of the law, and sometimes appropriated to three. If there was not a spare apartment, a bed was provided here for the judge. . . . Here assembled at night the rollicking boys of the Georgia Bar, who here indulged, without restraint, the convivialities for which they were so celebrated. Humor and wit, in anecdote and repartee, beguiled the hours. . . .

Longstreet's experiences during this period provided the material for *Georgia Scenes*.

It was while riding the circuit that Longstreet met and on 3 March 1817 married Frances Eliza Parke, the daughter of well-to-do parents in Greensboro, Georgia. The couple moved in with the Parke family for a year, a common arrangement, and then purchased a 600-acre farm nearby where Longstreet raised horses and cultivated fruit trees. Their first child—Alfred Emsley, born in July 1820—died at age four; only two daughters of the Longstreets' eight children survived to maturity. A devoted father and husband, Longstreet was greatly affected by these tragedies and by the increasingly delicate health of his wife. In 1827 the Longstreets converted to the Methodist Church. They moved to a plantation outside Augusta, Georgia, where Longstreet briefly served as a preacher; throughout his life he cherished moral principles and insisted on the necessity of religious faith.

In 1821 Longstreet was elected representative to the Georgia State Assembly from Greene County, and in 1822 he was elected judge of the Superior Court of Ocmulgee District. In 1827, having lost a bid for reelection—the anti–states' rights faction had risen to power, and Longstreet was throughout his life a staunch states' rights supporter—he ended his political career to begin a law practice with William W. Mann in Augusta, Georgia. Mann later became literary editor of *Southern Field and Fireside*, which published serially Longstreet's moralistic novel, *Master William Mitten*.

Longstreet began in 1830 to write the stories and anecdotes for which he was locally celebrated. His first sketches appeared in 1833 in the Milledgeville *Southern Recorder*, a weekly, in the following order: "The Dance," "The Song," "The Horse-Swap," "The Turf," "The Fight," "The Turn-Out," "The Character of a Native Georgian," and "The Gander Pulling." Becoming in 1834 the owner-editor of the weekly Augusta *States Rights Sentinel*, Longstreet published his strong political opinions under the ironic editorial pseudonym "Bob Short," while he continued to use the pen names "Hall" and "Baldwin" to indicate authorship of the sketches appearing there. These included "The 'Charming Creature' as a Wife," "The Militia Company Drill" (by "Timothy Crabshaw"—O. H. Prince), "The Mother and Her Child," "The Fox Hunt," "The Wax-Works," "The Debating Society," "A Sage Conversation," "Dropping to Sleep" (not included in *Georgia Scenes*), "Georgia Theatrics," "The Ball," "An Interesting Interview," and "The Shooting-Match." Several other stories later appeared in the Augusta *Mirror* (1838) and the *Magnolia* (1843); together with selections from *Georgia Scenes*, these were published posthumously by Longstreet's nephew, Fitz R. Longstreet, as *Stories with a Moral* in 1912.

In 1835 the *States Rights Sentinel* published *Georgia Scenes, Characters, Incidents, &c., in the First Half Century of the Republic*, "By a Native Georgian," making Longstreet's literary reputation. Immensely popular, it forms, as Bernard De Voto contends, "the frontier's first permanent work." The *Sentinel* went through a printing of nearly four thousand, while the Harper and Brothers "Second Edition" of 1840, published in New York under the author's name with an introduction and illustrations by E. H. Hyde, quickly sold 8,000 copies. Nine subsequent editions of *Georgia Scenes* appeared within the century.

Longstreet's other literary efforts included a pamphlet entitled *Letters on the Epistle of Paul to Philemon or the Connection of Apostolical Christianity with Slavery* (1845), a series of letters "from 'Georgia' to 'Massachusetts' " on the slavery question (collected in book form in 1847 as *A Voice from the South*), the novel *Master William Mitten* (the first five chapters appeared serially in 1849; the whole novel appeared serially in the *Southern Field and Fireside* in 1859; it was published in book form in Macon, Georgia, in 1864 and 1889), an antiwar tract, *Shall South Carolina Begin the War?* (1861), and the posthumous *Stories with a Moral* (1912).

In 1839 Longstreet accepted the presidency of the newly established Emory College, a position he held until 1848. Yale awarded him an honorary doctor of laws in 1841. He assumed the presidency of Centenary College in Jackson, Louisiana, after he failed to receive an anticipated appointment at the University of Mississippi, but he resigned within a year in disappointment. He was then elected to the presidency of the University of Mississippi, where he served until 1856. At that time Longstreet was appointed to the presidency of South Carolina College, a position he filled until the Civil War virtually emptied the campus in 1861.

The Longstreets retired to Oxford, Mississippi, where their house was burned by Northern troops. They then moved to Oxford, Georgia, and later to Columbus, Georgia, returning to Oxford, Mississippi, following the termination of hostilities. Longstreet died peacefully in Oxford, Mississippi, on 9 July 1870.

MAJOR THEMES

"With *Georgia Scenes*," writes Franklin J. Meine, "Longstreet established a pattern that had a profound influence on all subsequent humorous writers of the South." In fact, Meine argues, *Georgia Scenes* formed the "corner-stone" of Southwestern humor. The first collection of stories from the Old Southwest to reach a national audience, it dramatically demonstrated that life in the Old South was of interest to New Yorkers as well as to Virginians. Kimball King argues that it earned Longstreet "a permanent place in American regional literature." Longstreet's achievement, wrote Arthur Palmer Hudson in 1936, was that he had the "wit to realize that something old in talking might look new in writing." Experimenting with the boxlike structure of the dramatic frame, incorporating long stretches of local dialect, and picturing sharply visualized figures of regional character in his sketches, Longstreet was one of the first Southern writers to blend the art of oral story-telling with more traditional literary models. The frame technique establishes a comic, aesthetic distance between the author's narrative personae, "Hall" and "Baldwin," and his dialect-speaking characters; the reader joins the cultured narrator in laughing at the rude talk and crude manners of the country folk he describes. The structure also insists on an even greater moral distance, one not always apparent in oral tales, that suggests the moral alignment of author, audience, and narrator in contrast with the comically antisocial prancing, snorting, and swearing vernacular characters. As Longstreet contended in the preface to the 1840 "Second Edition," the sketches "consist of nothing more than fanciful *combinations* of *real* incidents and characters; and throwing into those scenes . . . some personal incident or adventure of my own, real or imaginery, as it would best suit my purpose; usually *real* but happening at different times and under different circumstances from those in which they are here represented." Nevertheless, he continued, "I have not always taken this liberty. Some of the scenes are as literal as the frailties of memory would allow them to be." Longstreet's faithful descriptions formed an exciting record of backcountry life, bringing to the attention of Americans new literary subjects within less formal literary structures. Throughout *Georgia Scenes* appears the influence not only of the periodical and familiar essay (in their *Spectator* and *Salmagundi* forms) but also of the frontier tradition of story-swapping. In his emphasis upon real events and real speech, Longstreet in part sets the stage for the local color and Realist movements of the later nineteenth century. Aware of some resistance to his transcriptions of rude language, he admitted the problem and attempted to address it in his preface: "I cannot conclude these introductory remarks, without reminding those who have taken exceptions to the coarse, inelegant, and sometimes ungrammatical language, which the writer represents himself as occasionally using, *that it is language accommodated to the capacity of the person to whom he represents himself as speaking*" (Longstreet's emphasis). The admonition certainly implies the intention to correct misconceptions about the author's ability to write the King's English, but the ambiguous rhetoric serves to blur rather than sharpen distinctions. Ignorance of the implications of using frontier materials and oral narrative techniques led Longstreet into tortured syntax, uncertain aesthetics, and occasionally urgentlemanly ethics.

Edgar Allan Poe, whose judgments of contemporary literary works were usually incisive if not always judicious, reviewed *Georgia Scenes* for the *Southern Literary Messenger* in 1836:

The author, whoever he is, is a clever fellow, imbued with a spirit of the truest humor, and endowed, moreover, with an exquisitely discriminative and penetrating understanding of *character* in general, and of Southern character in particular. . . .
Seriously—if this book were printed in England it would make the fortune of its author.
. . . Seldom—perhaps never in our lives—have we laughed as immoderately over any book as over the one now before us.

"Altogether," he concluded, "this very humorous, and very clever book forms an aera in our reading."

The nineteen sketches that comprise *Georgia Scenes* (all, with the exception of "The Militia Company Drill," written by Longstreet) fall into roughly two categories for the modern reader. The first group of conventional pieces derives its humor from the amused observations of an Addisonian narrator. "The Debating Society" makes much of the inflated, pseudo-legalistic nonsense contrived by two law students to befuddle their classmates. "The 'Charming Creature' as a Wife" satirizes the pretensions of fashionable, neglectful, self-absorbed "ladies." "The Song" pillories Americans who, like Miss Aurelia Emma Theodosia Augusta Crump—taught to sing by Madame Piggisqueaki—favor foreign entertainments to native fare. "The Mother and Her Child" pokes fun at the smothering behavior of females. And "The Ball" ridicules the social types Mr. Boozle, Mr. Noozle, Mr. Flirt, Miss Gilt, and Miss Rino.

The second set of tales focuses directly on frontier subjects and presents images in sharp contrast to those popularized by romantic writers of the plantation school such as John Esten Cooke. In the first story of *Georgia Scenes*, "Georgia Theatrics," the narrator begins with an extended description of a particular locale, the "Dark Corner" of Lincoln County, on 10 June 1809:

I believe it took its name from the moral darkness, which reigned over that portion of the county, at the time of which I am speaking. If in this point of view, it was but a shade darker than the rest of the county, it was inconceivably dark. If any man can name a trick, or sin, which had not been committed at the time of which I am speaking, in the very focus of the county's illumination, (Lincolnton), he must himself be the most inventive of the tricky, and the very Judas of sinners. (p. 5)

"Hall," Longstreet's narrator, separates himself stylistically from the moral wilderness of Lincoln; his tone is at once detached, amused, and condescending. As an analogue to the reader (and to the author), he represents the values of civilization and culture. These are suddenly shattered by the shouts of a backwoodsman:

"Boo-oo-oo! Oh, wake snakes, and walk your chalks! Brimstone and —— fire! Don't hold me, Nick Stoval! The fight's made up, and let's go at it! —— my soul, if I don't jump down his throat and gallop every chitterling out of him, before you can say 'quit'! . . . Enough! My eye's out!'' (p. 2)

The narrator, who rushes to the aid of the supposed victim, discovers that he has only overheard one man's rehearsal of a fight: " 'You needn't kick before you're spurr'd. There a'nt nobody there, nor ha'nt been nother. I was jist seein' how I could 'a' *fout*' " (p. 3). As Poe commented, "The whole anecdote is told with a raciness and vigor which would do honor to the pages of Blackwood."

"Georgia Theatrics" suggests several points. First, as the lead piece in *Georgia Scenes*, it sets the tone, style, and point of view of the author. Second, it captures the raw idiom of frontier dialect and locates it within a narrative frame designed to control and defuse it for an educated, cultured audience. Third, although the violence here is only theatrical, it also implies that real violence might readily occur in its most sensational form; it is, after all, a rehearsal for a real fight. Last, in the self-deprecating portrait of an overly fastidious narrator, the tale suggests that there is a value to rough country ways perhaps separate from and unavailable to the schoolmasterish narrator "Hall," who at the conclusion is left staring at the earth trying to make sense out of what he has just witnessed. Perhaps in Dark Corners frontier skills are required.

"The Fight" delivers in grotesque specificity the violence only implied in "Georgia Theatrics." Poe noted that "this article would positively make the fortune of any British periodical": "although involving some horrible and disgusting details of southern barbarity [it] is a sketch unsurpassed in dramatic vigor, and in the vivid truth to nature of one or two of the personages introduced." Ransy Sniffle, an ancestor of William Faulkner's Flem Snopes, acts as the go-between who arranges for his vicarious pleasure the fight between Billy Stallings and Bob Durham. "Hall," once again the narrator, recounts the particulars from a safe distance:

Bill presented a hideous spectacle. About a third of his nose, at the lower extremity, was bit off, and his face so swelled and bruised that it was difficult to discover in it anything of the human visage, much more the fine features which he carried into the ring. . . . I deemed it impossible for any human being to withstand for five seconds the loss of blood which issued from Bob's ear, cheek, nose, and finger, accompanied with such blows as he was receiving. (pp. 50–51)

Although Stallings and Durham recover and shake hands, and despite the narrator's insistence that "such scenes of barbarism and cruelty . . . are now of rare occurrence" (p. 52), the realistic descriptions of frontier violence reveal Longstreet's own fears concerning the leveling process of Jacksonian democracy. In "The Fight" Americans seem to be either snakes like Sniffle or brutish animals like Stallings and Durham. The narrator, at best, appears ineffectual.

"The Horse-Swap"—like "The Gander Pulling," "The Turn-Out," "The Turf," and "The Shooting-Match"—immortalizes a ritualized country custom. Here "Hall" transcribes the wild boasts of the Yellow Blossom from Jasper, a half-man, half-horse, half-alligator who repeatedly insists he is "perhaps a *leetle*, jist a *leetle*, of the best man at a horse-swap that ever trod shoe-leather" (p. 15). The humor is that of the archetypal "biter bit" motif, in which the "screamer" proves to be the second best man at a horse-swap to the deadpan Pete Ketch's first. The only violence in the tale is rhetorical, the only casualty the Yellow Blossom's inflated ego. As in the aforementioned rural activities, the good-natured competition of homespun types suggests qualities and values that Longstreet admired and embraced: competitiveness, cleverness, self-confidence, self-assertiveness, verbal skill, wit, daring, fair-mindedness, and perseverance.

Ned Brace, the only character to figure in more than one sketch, embodies potentially less attractive but probably equally typical values in "The Character of a Native Georgian" and "A Sage Conversation." A prankster reminiscent of Henry Junius Nott's Thomas Singularity, Ned Brace derives great pleasure from aberrant, antisocial behavior (he poses as a mute, drinks coffee and tea together in one cup, discomforts a traveling Frenchman) and from confounding gossiping matrons with a long story of two men who marry and raise a parcel of children (they are widowers).

The twentieth-century reader may find the conversation between two drunks in "An Interesting Interview" and the practical joke of "The Wax-Works" to be strained and interminable, and the modern reader may also recognize in sketches attitudes toward blacks, women, and foreigners that he or she finds repugnant. These attitudes, were, nonetheless, characteristic not only of Longstreet's fiction but also of much humor of the Old Southwest. Victimization—often broad and physical, racist and sexist—was and still remains the stock-in-trade of oral humor. Longstreet clearly viewed life as hierarchical, with blacks, women, and Frenchmen on a level beneath educated gentlemen. Overcultivated fops he considered un-American. Poor whites like Ransy Sniffle he presented as beneath contempt, though robust figures like Billy Stallings and Bob Durham claimed his respect. His ideal would combine the strength and physical vigor of the natural man with the masculine virtues of education and culture. Longstreet appeared ambivalent about the transformation he witnessed in the South, believing like James Fenimore Cooper in a blend of rural and urban attributes. That he was not always certain how or whether this could be brought to pass is evident in *Georgia Scenes*.

SURVEY OF CRITICISM

Any survey of criticism of *Georgia Scenes* rightly begins with Poe's 1836 review in the *Southern Literary Messenger*. The praise Poe offers *Georgia Scenes* is echoed by nineteenth-century critics from James Wood Davidson in *Living Writers of the South* (1869) to George M. Hyde in the *Bookman* in 1897; Hyde concluded that *Georgia Scenes* marked "the beginnings of realism in our country" and is "American humor writ large." Both critics agreed that *Master William Mitten* was, in Davidson's words, "the author's Moscow." In 1891 Oscar P. Fitzgerald published the first biography of Longstreet, and it is from this admiring and subjective appraisal that later scholars have drawn many details of Longstreet's life, a necessity resulting from the loss of records through fire.

The twentieth century witnessed a flurry of interest in Longstreet and in Southern writing. Samuel Albert Link's *Pioneers of Southern Literature* (1903) and Carl Holliday's *A History of Southern Literature* (1906) located Longstreet within a Southern literary tradition of humorists whose work culminated in realism, a claim repeated by Vernon Louis Parrington in his influential *Main Currents in American Thought* (1927). In 1925 Jennette Tandy added a brief analysis of Longstreet in *Crackerbox Philosophers in American Humor and Satire*. John Donald Wade's *Augustus Baldwin Longstreet: A Study of the Developments of Culture in the South* (1924) formed a critical benchmark; Wade's analysis of Longstreet as both a writer and a cultural type set the standard for future evaluation. The introduction to Franklin J. Meine's *Tall Tales of the Southwest, 1830–1860* (1930) charted Longstreet's influence on Southwestern writers; Walter Blair's *Native American Humor (1800–1900)* (1937) discussed Longstreet's importance to the development of American humor; Jay B. Hubbell's *The South in American Literature, 1607–1900* (1954) summarized Longstreet's career within a broad cultural context.

Bruce R. McElderry, Jr.'s modern edition of *Georgia Scenes* in 1957 ushered in a new era of Longstreet criticism. Kenneth S. Lynn explored one legacy of Longstreet in *Mark Twain and Southwestern Humor* (1959); Thomas W. Ford examined "Ned Brace of *Georgia Scenes*" (1965); and Kenneth Silverman developed the political significance of "Longstreet's 'The Gander Pulling' " (1966). In 1969 M. Thomas Inge edited a new edition of John Donald Wade's *Augustus Baldwin Longstreet*; Literature House issued a reprint of *Georgia Scenes* with an introduction by Clarence Gohdes; and Joseph H. Harkey's "A Note on Longstreet's Ransy Sniffle and Brackenridge's *Modern Chivalry*" appeared. The year 1972 saw the publication of C. Hugh Holman's *The Roots of Southern Writing*, Merrill Maguire Skaggs's *The Folk of Southern Fiction*, and Gerald J. Smith's "Augustus Baldwin Longstreet and John Wade's 'Cousin

Lucius' ''; Skaggs contends that Longstreet's sketches suggest an enduring American ideal in the plain, honest farmer. M. Thomas Inge, in *The Frontier Humorists* (1975), reprinted seminal essays by Meine, Wade, and Blair, together with his own fine introduction, Poe's 1836 review of *Georgia Scenes*, and an early essay on Longstreet by Wade; also included are an excellent checklist of criticism and a thorough bibliography of Southwestern humorists. Sylvia Jenkins Cook argued in *From Tobacco Road to Route 66* (1976) that Longstreet presented condescending portraits of poor whites. Recent articles on Longstreet include Alan Gribben's ''Mark Twain Reads Longstreet's *Georgia Scenes*'' (1978), William E. Lenz's ''Longstreet's *Georgia Scenes*: Developing American Characters and Narrative Techniques'' (1981), and James B. Meriwether's ''Augustus Baldwin Longstreet: Realist and Artist'' (1982). Most recently, Kimball King's Twayne Series volume, *Augustus Baldwin Longstreet* (1984), presents a thorough and thoughtful review of Longstreet's career and literary reputation as well as an annotated bibliography of secondary works. King summarizes current scholarly opinion in concluding that Longstreet's fame securely rests on four things *Georgia Scenes* accomplished: the successful adaptation of the techniques of the Southern oral tradition to literary forms; the depiction of rural Georgia folk in a realistic environment; the exploration of Southern culture in transition from agrarian to urban values; and the national popularization of a regional literature.

BIBLIOGRAPHY

Works by Augustus Baldwin Longstreet

Page numbers given in the text for *Georgia Scenes* refer to the 1957 McElderry edition; quotations from Longstreet's preface are from the Harper and Brothers 1840 ''Second Edition.''

Georgia Scenes, Characters, Incidents, &c., in the First Half Century of the Republic. By a Native Georgian. Augusta: Printed at the S. R. Sentinel Office, 1835. Subsequent editions: New York: Harper and Brothers, 1840, 1842, 1846, 1850, 1854, 1857, 1858, 1860, 1897. Atlanta: Franklin P. P., 1894. New York: Sagamore Press, 1957. Upper Saddle River, N.J.: Literature House, 1969. Savannah: Beehive Press, 1975.

Letters on the Epistle of Paul to Philemon, or the Connection of Apostolic Christianity with Slavery. Pamphlet printed in Charleston, 1845.

A Voice from the South: Comprising Letters from Georgia to Massachusetts, and to the Southern States. Baltimore: Western Continent Press, 1847.

Master William Mitten; or, A Youth of Brilliant Talents Who Was Ruined by Bad Luck. Serial publication: *Southern Field and Fireside,* 28 May to Nov. 1859. Book publication: Macon: Burke, Boykin, 1864; Macon: J. W. Burke, 1889.

Stories with a Moral Humorous and Descriptive. Ed. Fitz R. Longstreet. Philadelphia: John C. Winston, 1912.

Studies of Augustus Baldwin Longstreet

Blair, Walter. *Native American Humor, 1800–1900*. New York: American Book, 1937.

Cook, Sylvia Jenkins. *From Tobacco Road to Route 66: The Southern Poor White in Fiction*. Chapel Hill: University of North Carolina Press, 1976.

Davidson, James Wood. *The Living Writers of the South*. New York: Carleton, 1869.

Fitzgerald, Oscar P. *Judge Longstreet: A Life Sketch*. Nashville: Methodist Episcopal Church, South, 1891.

Ford, Thomas W. "Ned Brace of *Georgia Scenes*." *Southern Folklore Quarterly* 29 (1965): 220–27.

Godhes, Clarence. Introduction to *Georgia Scenes*. Upper Saddle River, N.J.: Literature House, 1969.

Gribben, Alan. "Mark Twain Reads Longstreet's *Georgia Scenes*." *Gyascutus: Studies in Antebellum Southern Humorous and Sporting Writing*. Ed. James L. W. West III. Atlantic Highlands, N.J.: Humanities Press, 1978.

Harkey, Joseph H. "A Note on Longstreet's Ransy Sniffle and Brackenridge's *Modern Chivalry*." *Western Pennsylvania Historical Magazine* 52 (1969): 43–45.

Holliday, Carl. *A History of Southern Literature*. New York: Neale, 1906.

Holman, C. Hugh. *The Roots of Southern Writing: Essays in the Literature of the American South*. Athens: University of Georgia Press, 1972.

Hubbell, Jay B. *The South in American Literature, 1607–1900*. Durham, N.C.: Duke University Press, 1954.

Hudson, Arthur Palmer, ed. *Humor of the Old Deep South*. New York: Macmillan, 1936.

Hyde, George M. "Old Times in Georgia." *Bookman* 6 (1897): 67–69.

Inge, M. Thomas, ed. *The Frontier Humorists: Critical Views*. Hamden, Conn.: Archon Books, 1975.

King, Kimball. *Augustus Baldwin Longstreet*. Boston: Twayne, 1984.

Lenz, William E. "Longstreet's *Georgia Scenes*: Developing American Characters and Narrative Techniques." *Markham Review* 11 (1981): 5–10.

Link, Samuel Albert. *Pioneers of Southern Literature*. Nashville: Methodist Episcopal Church, South, 1903.

Lynn, Kenneth S. *Mark Twain and Southwestern Humor*. Boston: Little, Brown, 1959.

McElderry, Bruce R., Jr., ed. Introduction to *Georgia Scenes*. New York: Sagamore Press, 1957.

Meine, Franklin J. Introduction to *Tall Tales of the Southwest, 1830–1860*. New York: A. A. Knopf, 1930.

Meriwether, James B. "Augustus Baldwin Longstreet: Realist and Artist." *Mississippi Quarterly* 35 (1982): 351–64.

Parrington, Vernon Louis. *Main Currents in American Thought*. New York: Harcourt, Brace, 1927.

Poe, Edgar Allan. Review of *Georgia Scenes*. *Southern Literary Messenger* 2 (1836): 287–92. Reprinted in Inge, pp. 85–93.

Rourke, Constance. *American Humor: A Study of National Character*. New York: Harcourt, Brace, 1931.

Silverman, Kenneth. "Longstreet's 'The Gander Pulling.' " *American Quarterly* 18 (1966): 548–49.

Skaggs, Merrill Maguire. *The Folk of Southern Fiction*. Athens: University of Georgia Press, 1972.

Smith, Gerald J. ''Augustus Baldwin Longstreet and John Wade's 'Cousin Lucius.' ''
    Georgia Historical Quarterly 61 (1972): 276–81.
Tandy, Jennette. *Crackerbox Philosophers in American Humor and Satire*. New York:
    Columbia University Press, 1925.
Wade, John Donald. *Augustus Baldwin Longstreet: A Study of the Developments of Culture
    in the South*. New York: Macmillan, 1924; repr. with Introduction by M. Thomas
    Inge. Athens: University of Georgia Press, 1969.

JON C. MILLER

Robert Munford
(ca. 1737–1783)

Robert Munford's two plays—*The Candidates* and *The Patriots*—are among the most significant belletristic achievements of the American Colonial and Revolutionary periods. Their themes are particularly American; and Munford himself is a careful, independent thinker. He is an artist well aware of his medium and well able to manipulate its conventions.

BIOGRAPHY

We possess little biographical material concerning Munford's life. Only a few letters have come to light. Most of what we know is the result of Rodney Baine's careful search of public records. Hence, we know much more of the public man than we do of the private man, still best known through his published work.

Family was the first determiner of position in aristocratic Virginia society, and the Munfords had done well in the eighteenth century. The dramatist's grandfather had married well—a Kennon; had been William Byrd II's overseer, attorney, protégé, and friend; had acquired substantial landholdings; and had become a Burgess. Perhaps of significance to his grandson's poem "Answer to 'The Winter Piece,' " he quarrelled with Robert Bolling of Chellowe's grandfather. Munford's father also married well—a Bland; also continued the Byrd connection; and also became a Burgess. But he was unfortunate financially. His brother-in-law reports that he became a "sot," that he had had to sell off most of his estates, and that he used his wife "very ill." He died in 1745 leaving his son, the future dramatist, who was born about 1737, a birthright consisting largely of family connections.

Young Robert, taken in by his uncle William Beverley, spent some time at the Beverley plantation and, in 1750, was taken by the Beverleys to England to be enrolled with their son in Beverley School and then in Wakefield Grammar School. These schools provided Munford with a formal education uncommon among the Virginia gentry—one which by itself would have been an entrée into that society. Wakefield in particular developed literary interests and classical skills in such Virginians as Robert Bolling and Richard Henry Lee. Munford's desire to translate Ovid was perhaps born here. Beverley's Memorandum Book also makes clear that Munford was at least introduced to the English theatre in 1750.

Meanwhile, his mother married George Currie, a Scot of more ability than position. Under his direction Munford's finances improved. Munford's feelings toward his stepfather are perhaps reflected in his defense of the Scottish merchants in *The Patriots*. Beverley died in 1756, leaving no provision for Munford, who returned to Virginia to continue his education in the law office of his cousin Peyton Randolph. These studies were interrupted by service in the French and Indian War as an officer in William Byrd III's regiment. Munford probably saw little fighting, but two letters to his uncle Theodorick Bland reveal his sense of duty and his sense of humor. Nevertheless, the experience labeled Munford for the rest of his life as a military man who had seen actual service. The Duquesne campaign over, Munford finished his legal studies, took possession of family estates in Southside Virginia (1760), and married his cousin Anna Beverley.

A sparsely settled frontier, the Southside was peopled by those "on the make." Landholdings were small; the social structure fluid. The deferential order characteristic of the Tidewater had not developed. While family land led Munford to the Southside, he must have hoped that in this unsettled area he might establish himself more firmly and more rapidly. Here his lack of finances, though improved by a dowry, would be less noticeable; here his family background and education would be more rare and perhaps more marketable. If such were his thinking, he was not mistaken; for in 1764 he was listed as one of the major land and slave holders in St. James Parrish. In 1765 he was made county lieutenant, appointed county agent, and elected to the House of Burgesses for the newly formed Mecklenburg County.

Munford's contemporaries Edmund Pendleton and Paul Carrington later recalled that Munford was a leader of the "hot and giddy" members who passed Patrick Henry's anti–Stamp Act Resolutions in Munford's first session as a Burgess. This affront to the ruling oligarchy must have been difficult for Munford, whose relatives Richard Bland and Peyton Randolph were opposed. Munford's feelings during the Robinson-Chiswell affairs are not known. It is tempting to identify him as the R. M. who attacked Chiswell's attorney in the 10 October 1766 *Virginia Gazette*. This letter, which involved the publishers in a libel suit, perhaps because even then the author was not known, articulates a position easy to associate with Munford. By attacking Wayles, the author directs blame away from Munford's relatives the Randolphs. At the same time, he remains firmly sided with those pressuring the ruling oligarchy.

Whatever Munford's position, the election of his cousin Peyton Randolph to the speakership and Virginia's post–1766 harmony curtailed his radical activity. Financial difficulties perhaps further contributed to his conservatism, increasingly apparent as the Revolution approached. Munford's Southside environment, emotionally and geographically close to that part of North Carolina where the War of the Regulation was being played out, undoubtedly sensitized him to the dangers involved in the willingness of some of the anti-Chiswell group to arouse class antagonism and incite popular political activity. Deplored in both of his plays, such activity is clearly attacked in *The Candidates*, which probably dates from the early 1770s, although it could have been written at any time during the decade. The approaching Revolution exacerbated leveling tendencies in the Southside, and the events of 1774 and 1775 made clear the precariousness of Munford's position. In 1774 Munford signed the first Association and chaired a meeting during which Mecklenburgers asserted their loyalty to the king but denied the power of Parliament to tax them; but William Van Shreeven and Robert Scribner find Munford's attendance at the First Convention unlikely, arguing that he and his fellow Burgesses were replaced in a special election by two candidates whose campaigns attacked the two Burgesses as being too aristocratic. Nor was Munford one of the county's 21 Committee of Safety members. As his 20 April 1775 letter to William Byrd asserts, however, he continued as a Burgess to work to restore Virginians to "a due Sense of the Obligation both of Duty and Alligiance that bind them to their Sovereign and to the Preservation of civil Order." The irony that this letter was written just hours before Dunmore seized the colony's powder suggests that events were outstripping Munford. Certainly he was closely tied to Tories Byrd and John Randolph and to neutral Robert Beverley. When the Burgesses finally adjourned, Munford, once Mecklenburg's leading man, was now its county lieutenant only. This enforced leisure allowed Munford to write *The Patriots*, which deals with events occurring in 1777, and the "Devil" poems, which seem to date around 1779, when one was published. "A Revolutionary Song" is clearly a wartime piece also.

As the war progressed, so did Munford's rehabilitation. After their early zeal, Mecklenburgers evidently determined a moderate could be a patriot; and Munford was elected to the House of Delegates in 1779. Here Munford's military experience led to his being assigned prominent roles in matters dealing with military preparedness. It was not a good time for such jobs. In 1780 Lincoln surrendered at Charleston, the Virginia militia disgraced itself at Camden, and the state itself was invaded. Surviving Munford letters to Generals Greene and Gates and service at Guilford Courthouse show Munford to have been actively engaged in the war effort, but a 1780 letter to Munford from Mordecai Gist shows that Virginia and perhaps even Munford himself were blamed for the deteriorating military situation. Certainly after 1779 Munford's House assignments were more trivial.

Despite the good marriages made by his two daughters—Elizabeth to Richard Kennon and Ursula Anna to Otway Byrd, to whom she took "a clever little fortune"—and the financial ability to provide for a Fitzhugh nephew whose Tory father had cut him off, the 1780s do not seem to have been a happy time for

Munford. He suffered from gout in 1781. In 1782 and 1783, he entered the public record for drinking and swearing. In 1783 his fellow magistrates asked that he be removed from their number. He died in December 1783.

MAJOR THEMES

Because Munford's plays are so firmly grounded in the issues and typical events of the Southside, they seem to suggest certain tensions in Munford's own life. Certainly his own family and its connections as well as his education introduced him to the aristocratic values typical of both Virginia's ruling oligarchy and the heroes of his own plays. These values and the social structures they represented were not securely in place in the Southside, and Munford himself lacked the personal resources that assured Tidewater aristocrats their power. In this fluid environment, the approach of the Revolution and the war itself exacerbated tensions between the old aristocratic tradition and the emerging democratic one.

Whatever Munford personally felt about this conflict, his two plays not only describe the threat that the new democratic feelings posed to the traditional order but also suggest the final replacement of that order and its representatives by new values and men. Because of this tension and because their heroes are aristocrats, the plays chronicle victories that seem empty. The heroes are outsiders moving through antagonistic environments much like spectators. Things happen to them more than they make things happen. Their victories are more often the result of outside forces than of their own efforts. In *The Candidates*, Wou'dbe's election is assured only by the practically deus ex machina appearance of Worthy, who seems to embody the personal and social position for which Munford's other heroes yearn. Matters have so deteriorated by the period of *The Patriots* that the protagonists cannot even communicate their positions to those around them. At the play's end, the protagonists, unchanged and misunderstood, are integrated into the play's world for no better reasons than they had been excluded from it. One senses that finally Munford found himself more tolerated than understood in his own Southside world.

This is not to say that Munford was Tory, neutral, or pacifist. His personal life and his plays demonstrate that he was none of these. But he was in 1775 a reluctant revolutionary loathe to sever all ties with England. Gordon S. Wood's description of Whig thinking is a useful measure of Munford's. Wood writes that "few Whigs in 1776 were yet theoretically prepared to repudiate the belief in the corporate welfare as the goal of politics or to accept divisiveness and selfishness as the normative behavior of men." In fact, "the solution to the problems of American politics seemed to rest not so much in emphasizing the private rights of individuals against the general will as it did in stressing the public rights of the collective people against the supposed privileged interests of their rulers." A society was made strong by the "virtue" of its people—"frugality, industry, temperance, and simplicity." "The virile martial qualities—the scorn of ease, the contempt of danger, the love of valor—were what made a nation great.'' Leadership should be above personal and private concern. "Disinterested,'' it could best serve the public good.

Munford seems to agree with much of this view. Wou'dbe's willingness in *The Candidates* to "enslave" himself for the privilege of serving the people implies his concern for the common good as does his refusal, when he is questioned at the barbecue, to serve any special interest, even his own. In *The Patriots* the heroes' repeated expressions of concern for their country and their defense of the Scots suggest the same stance. "Disinterest" and the need for public virtue are central themes in both plays. On the other hand, Munford does see selfishness and intemperance as characteristic of much human behavior. Lack of self-knowledge and self-control abounds in *The Candidates*; *The Patriots* criticizes the common misunderstanding, misapplication, and abuse of military virtues. Because the general will is so easily corruptible, people need to be protected from themselves and their fellows; but Munford, as a spokesman for minority and individual rights, does not argue for stronger individual voices (Trueman's "I hate these little democracies"). Instead, he harkens back to an old answer: the need for a strong, disinterested leadership—one prepared to lead by its social position, its education, and its virtue.

In *The Candidates* there is danger that an electorate capable of intemperance and self-interest will not do as it "ought,'' will not show its "judgment" and "spirit of independence,'' and will elect the wrong candidate. In *The Patriots* the wrong candidates have been elected. As Gordon S. Wood points out in *The Creation of the American Republic 1776–1787* (1969), the Revolutionary Committees, set up to establish the common good and to intimidate individuals differing from that definition of good, were sanctioned by classical Whig theory. Munford attacks the democratically elected committee not only because its leadership is selfish, hypocritical, and stupid, but also because its party-based definition of the common good is too narrow. Munford's fear of the radical Whigs was not uncommon among American patriots. Indeed, the satiric "Creed of a Rioter'' (1776) by North Carolina leader James Iredell almost reads as a gloss of *The Patriots*. The difficulty of Munford's position, and Iredell's, is suggested by the fact that neither of their pieces was published at the time of their writing. What we know of Iredell suggests both the Meanwell and Trueman roles and that of Skip.

When Wou'dbe complains in *The Candidates* to himself that he must electioneer "to gain an honour that is justly thine,'' he reveals in that "justly'' the sense of order and the class attitudes that underlie both plays. Munford's heroes believe themselves entitled to a special place in their society. They are men of wealth who, despite Pickle's "feast or famine'' remark in *The Patriots*, are able to distribute the largess expected of an aristocratic leadership by a deferential populace. Education also sets these men apart. Although their speech is often easy, it has none of the dialectal qualities Munford often uses to distinguish those less "fitten.'' It is perhaps a measure of democracy's progress that we almost agree with Brazen's "I hate your high flown speeches Mr. Trueman" and with Smallhope's "don't preach your damned proverbs here." As these epithets suggest, more than diction separates the speech of Munford's heroes from that of most of their listeners.

A cornerstone of Edmund Burke's conservatism is the idea that "circumstances (which some gentlemen pass for nothing) give in reality to every political principle its distinguishing colour, and discriminating effect." Munford's plays turn on the same epistemology. Wou'dbe can admire Sir John Toddy while "he confine[s] himself to his bottle and dogs" and can "despise" him as a candidate. Similarly, he refuses to make easy promises to the electorate, and at the barbecue, he decides each issue on its own merit. Indeed, the very premise of the election is to select the "ablest" individual, "to refuse a coxcomb—choose a man." Party, as a coalition dedicated to a set of specific ideas, does not exist. Candidates scramble to ally themselves loosely to those perceived to be the worthiest. War, however, demanded collective action, simplification, and commitment to an unknown future.

Munford's discomfort with "party" and with the "generalizing" habit of mind it requires is so clearly drawn in *The Patriots* that one suspects he is indirectly answering the generalizing of Thomas Paine's propaganda in the first *Crisis* paper (Munford's opening, "In times like these," echoes Paine's; both works define Patriot and Tory). Abstractions in *The Patriots* are constantly being undone by the particular. Isabella's patriotism forces her to argue that scars and amputations are beauty spots; Skip's, to assert that "No soldiers ought to be hurt." Labels obscure truths from party men. Because Flash is a soldier, the committee thinks him brave. For them all the Scots are enemies. In the irrationality of this either-or world, Munford has created a kingdom of dullness where "anyone who disapproves of men and measures" is labeled a Tory. The careful distinctions of Meanwell and Trueman fall on uncomprehending ears and lead to danger. Still they refuse to tack about as Trueman testifies; "Whenever the conduct and principles of neither [Whig nor Tory] are justifiable, I am neither; as far as the conduct and principles of either correspond with the duties of a good citizen, I am both."

Duty, dignity, and disinterest are also important values to Munford's heroes. Countering Worthy's defense of the retired life in *The Candidates*, Wou'dbe argues that "it is surely the duty of every man who has abilities to serve his country to take up the burden and bear it with patience." Self-aggrandizement is not even a possible motive; for Wou'dbe ties disinterest to duty: "to secure a seat in our august senate, 'tis necessary a man should be either a slave or fool . . . for begging a troublesome and expensive employment." Similarly, Meanwell states that real patriots "are industrious in the public service, but claim no glory to themselves." Even Captain Paunch's worthiness in not accepting a drink from those he will not vote for is acclaimed to stem from "a very disteress [*sic*] motive." Proper speech is only one mark of dignity; Munford's heroes consistently refuse to make spectacles of themselves. Real patriots are "mild" and "secretly anxious for their country." They do not bawl against tyranny, but serve their country. Wou'dbe will neither strip nor brawl because such activities, whatever their personal effect, undercut the high office to which the candidates aspire.

Although Munford never relegates virtue or vice to a single class, the world in which his heroes move is much less concerned with virtue than they are. Virtue and social order were major concerns in Virginia after the Robinson-Chiswell scandals; but in Munford's swirl of elections, barbecues, committees, and courts, chaos is a constant possibility. Order depends not only on the strength of a society's leadership but also on the quality of its yeomanry. Each must know its place and work within it. Self-knowledge, honesty, and social responsibility are necessary foundations of Munford's social order. Well-spoken, thoughtful, and independent, Captain Paunch in *The Candidates* is an exemplar for the lesser gentry. He knows his place: "Sir John . . . is no fitter for that place than myself"; and, as his final speech makes clear, he is willing to do as he "ought." The Heartfrees in *The Patriots* offer a similar example to the yeomanry. They know they are "plain and simple," and neither they nor their friends "stand upon finery." Ignorance, hypocrisy, and selfishness are enemies to this order because they misperceive, mask, or ignore it.

Always sensitive to the symbolic values of the conventions he employs, Munford points up the danger of irrationality by counterpointing two feasting scenes in *The Candidates*. Traditionally, the comic feast is a social communion celebrating order and renewal, and these values are readily apparent in the exquisite courtesy practiced at Wou'dbe's election breakfast. The contrast this offers to the barbecue is striking. The barbecue's very purpose is antihumane. People are commodities, votes to be bought; yet it is the people themselves who demand the event. Significantly, Paunch refuses to attend. Image after image suggests the variety of man's ignorance and selfishness. The scene begins with jealousy. Intemperance and violence intervene. The degrading climax is reached in Sir John's and Joan's drunken and unconscious parody of an impotent, bestial love. The every-man-for-himself values expressed here constantly threaten to disintegrate the fragile social order.

Munford uses a similar counterpointing in *The Patriots*. In this play, ignorance and selfishness are rendered more dangerous by the hypocrisy with which they are cloaked and by the fact that their representatives are in power. Trueman notes that Brazen "is fully resolved that nobody shall tyrannize over him, but very content to tyrannize over others." Juxtaposition of the "judgment" scenes clarifies the situation's inhumanity. The very names of the Committee members suggest their lack of temperance, and although Munford does not refer to the commercial motivation that lay beneath much persecution of the Scots, malicious and hypocritical ends motivate much of the Committee's harassment of Meanwell and Trueman. In defense of his own attitude toward the Scots, Trueman argues that the unhappy must be treated with kindness: "meanness dwells with oppression, and cowardice with insult." Although his argument has no effect upon the

Committee, who find the Scots guilty because they are Scots, the principles set forth by Trueman clearly guide Meanwell's humane handling of the irresponsible Pickle. For Munford, the common good demands attention to individuals as individuals.

One wishes that Munford had written the scene depicting Trueman's dispute with Brazen over "the doctrines of a state of nature and liberty without restraint," for such a scene might have provided one of the limits of Munford's thinking. Clearly he was nervous about democratic principles. At the same time he was committed to the American cause in ways that some of his friends and relatives were not. More clearly than many, Munford saw social changes inherent in the Revolution harmful to himself and his class. Although Trueman is married at play's end, his marriage does not mean, as it does in other eighteenth-century comedies, integration into and mastery over environment. He knows himself still to be at odds with his world's prevailing values, and he himself to be virtually powerless.

SURVEY OF CRITICISM

Although literary critics have labeled Munford's plays "the best written in America prior to the performance of Tyler's *The Contrast*" and historians have found *The Candidates* to be "one of the best documents on elections in eighteenth century Virginia," Munford and his plays have received significant attention only recently. Surprisingly, *A Collection of Plays and Poems* (1798), issued in a small posthumous volume from Petersburg by Munford's son, seems to have attracted no attention for almost 50 years in a nation eager to declare its cultural independence. The book's present scarcity suggests that it was never easily available. Rodney Baine details the circuitous routes by which individual copies have entered major collections and demonstrates that many early scholars were introduced to the plays *via* an imperfect copy in the Philadelphia Library Company. The use of this copy (lacking a title page and bound with other plays) has led to the misattributions and contributed to the host of ghost editions (e.g., 1776, 1792, 1796) that continue to plague Munford scholarship. Another probable reason for Munford's early neglect rests in the argument, most recently reiterated by Michael Kammen, that "between 1783 and about 1820 the young republic underwent an anxious quest for cultural cohesion. Those who wrote our history during those decades were either personally inclined or felt socially obliged to minimize the existence of divisiveness among earlier Americans and to maximize the distinctive coherence of our moral character as it emerged from the crucible of the Revolution." Perhaps because Munford's themes often seemed to run counter to the emerging democratic myths that celebrated the courage and common sense of the common man, his book was from the beginning in little demand.

Interest in William Munford's own posthumously published translation of *The Iliad* and Nathaniel Beverley Tucker's charges of sectional favoritism on the part of Northern anthologists stimulated Rufus Wilmot Griswold in 1850 to discuss Robert Munford briefly in his article on William. He alludes mysteriously to Munford letters ''to be found in collections relating to the time . . . written with grace and vigor.'' In *The Candidates* Munford ''exposes to contempt the falsehood and corruption by which it was frequently attempted to influence elections.'' This severity modern historians have often underplayed. Griswold also suggests *The Patriots* was written ''with an eye to some instance in Virginia''—a tack which Baine, Richard R. Beeman, and Jon C. Miller have pursued in discussing both plays.

George O. Seilhamer's notice of *The Patriots* exhibits the problems caused by the Philadelphia copy of the play. Without the title page Seilhamer posits a Philadelphia edition, making no mention of the author nor taking any notice of *The Candidates*. Nonetheless, by using the battles, Seilhamer dates the play, which he judges to be ''a very poor comedy'' but ''more like a play than any of its predecessors.'' A man of his time, Seilhamer finds the underplot ''coarse,'' but is still able to see that politically the play written in defense of moderate Whigs gives ''a very fair picture of the period.''

Although Arthur Hobson Quinn is clearly working from a ''good'' copy of Munford's book, he cites a Philadelphia edition of *The Patriots* and compounds Seilhamer's error by dating it 1776. Using the death of Botetourt, he dates *The Candidates* (1770–75); and he initiates the ''Ralpho'' debate, writing that Ralpho is ''probably the first Negro character in American drama.'' His reading of *The Patriots* (''decidedly pacificist'') well indicates why the play was not successful in the early National period.

Serious Munford scholarship began in 1948–49 with the publication of the two plays in the *William and Mary Quarterly*, making them easily available for the first time. Editors Jay B. Hubbell and Douglas Adair, noting that social criticism lay at the heart of both plays, point directly to the historical importance of *The Candidates* to students of Virginia politics. They place the play squarely in the traditional version of the aristocratic Tidewater society. ''The best men . . . the Worthys (Munford complains) are too often tempted to refuse office . . . partly because they know they can win too easily.'' Munford is identified not with Wou'dbe but with Worthy, who is seen as a realistic portrayal of the Virginia gentleman. These assumptions allow the editors to conclude that ''Munford's satire of 'the people' is neither sharp nor angry. . . . Given the right candidates to choose among they can be trusted to choose well.'' Later Hubbell seems to modify these positions in his *History*, where he argues that two such gentlemen as Wou'dbe and Worthy are unbeatable, but cites Wou'dbe's bitter lines at the end of Act I. He also refers to Jefferson's 1814 description of the difficulties Virginia's first families are having in being elected to office, but he does not suggest that Munford might be describing the same phenomena in the Southside years earlier. By pointing out that Ralpho does not use dialect, he calls Quinn's supposition into question.

The strain of trying to read Munford's plays in terms of the Tidewater's deferential society peeks through Courtlandt Canby's "Introduction to *The Pa-triots*." Munford's "message for the times" is to be found in Meanwell's speech, "I hope my zeal. . . ." Here Canby discovers "the strength of the American tradition of individual freedom under the law" and "a lesson for our over-zealous witch-hunters and congressional investigating committees." Noting that the play possesses "a new note of self-righteous indignation," Canby minimizes the play's tensions by defining its central conflict to be that between the foreign minority and the lesser gentry. Placed between these two factions are two con-servative gentlemen, representatives of a class whose power "social and political was immense." For Canby, the play makes clear that the Revolution encroaches upon but never really weakens this power. To argue that Munford's "conservative sense of decorum and his aristocratic dislike of the multitude" blinded him to the good the Committees of Safety might do misses the point that this "en-croachment" victimized Munford, separating him from the source of power, just as his protagonists are, and that some of Munford's indignation stems from his isolation. Canby further simplifies political themes by not acknowledging fully the important differences implicit in his remark that "as a class the gentle-men of Virginia . . . espoused the cause of independence—some reluctantly and late, some like Jefferson, with early enthusiasm. . . ." That such a conclusion refuses to recognize real differences is made clear by Hubbell's response to Canby's tentative supposition that the "slight improvement in *The Patriots*—suggests that both plays may actually have been staged." Hubbell writes that *The Patriots* "though it has every appearance of having been written for the stage could hardly have been publicly produced in this country until after Mun-ford's death" because of its political content.

Historians seemed most immediately excited by the publishing of the plays. Carl Bridenbaugh makes Munford an important member of the "hot Burgesses" from the Piedmont who were seeking power in 1765 at the expense of the Tidewater delegates: "No greater mistake can be made than to regard the Pied-mont gentlemen of 1765 as coming from humble walks of life. . . . They were cultivated gentlemen, eager to exercise their talents and they resented the Tide-water monopoly of the best offices." Their success in achieving power for themselves and, hence, for their sections insured that there would be no real challenge to the rule of gentlemen. Three more historians have used *The Can-didates* to support various arguments that posit the stable, hierarchical society Bridenbaugh describes. Charles Sydnor drew heavily from the play to create his classic account of an eighteenth-century Virginia political process that was at once deferential and democratic: "The function of the gentry was to provide candidates and often a measure of guidance as to which of these candidates to elect. The function of the rank and file . . . was to decide which of the several gentlemen to send to the House of Burgesses." Similarly, Daniel J. Boorstin argues that Virginians accepted "that the ruling planters of good family had a prescriptive right to become ruling Burgesses, always, of course, provided they had earned the good opinion of their less substantial neighbors. . . . This security of social position bred a wholesome vigor of judgment which made the Virginia House of Burgesses a place for deliberation and discussion rarely found in modern cultures." Boorstin, without reference to Munford, who consistently seems aware of the fundamental antitheses between aristocratic and democratic, concludes that such leaders were not "the first flower of the national spirit" but the last "flower of the aristocracy." The turmoil of the war spelled the decline of the aristocracy. For Edmund S. Morgan there is greater pressure on the social order; but the election in *The Candidates* demonstrates that Virginia politics was a "compound of social deference and demagoguery. But demagoguery in this particular election failed; and the social prestige that suceeded could not have operated so powerfully unless the small planters . . . were persuaded that their interests would be well served by big men." Aristocrats could win popular elections because all Virginians perceived "a common identity based on common interests."

Indispensable is Baine's excellent book, which is, as its title suggests, largely a biographical, historical study. As noted above, Baine has discovered most of what we know about Munford's biography. Equally important is his description of life in the Southside (Susan L. Bracey's book is also valuable in this way). The stream of people and events that Baine has recovered provides an important context for the plays. Much that had seemed merely eccentric or comic Baine shows to have been particularly or typically drawn from Munford's environment. The specifically literary problems he attacks tend to be those that can be solved historically. He relates the plays to English traditions; he elucidates topical allusions; he dates the plays convincingly. On both historical and literary grounds, he disposes of the claim that Ralpho is the first comic black character (see also David May's edition of *The Disappointment* for a similar discussion of Raccoon). Treated less extensively, but more fully and more sensibly than elsewhere, are such important topics as structure, language, and theme.

Norman Philbrick draws heavily upon Baine and Canby, but his emphasis on Munford's hatred of excess, his recognition of the complexity of Munford's intellectual position (which he does not define narrowly), and his insistence upon the artistic quality of *The Patriots* are significant. Kenneth Silverman's brief treatment is noteworthy for the important preception that "*The Candidates* shows the electorate to be credulous, bribable, and stupid, and Munford seems not so much confident that southern noblesse oblige will supply leaders as uneasy over democratic tendencies." Walter J. Meserve's readings are traditional. *The Candidates* is "optimistic," and "the best candidates triumph all too easily." As does Baine, he praises Munford's use of the three-pronged love plot in *The Patriots*. Because nothing has been published dealing specifically with Munford's poetry, the notes to Miller's edition remain their fullest treatment. J. A. Leo Lemay's article provides helpful background to "Answer to a Winter Piece."

Recent work by Richard R. Beeman and Rhys Isaac has argued that the deferential society depicted by earlier historians was under substantial stress in such outlying regions as Munford's Southside. These two have described a society there moving toward "the cavalier-gentry ethos," but never completing that process. The confident aristocratic stability was never established in this area. Munford's training and upbringing had instilled in him a firm sense of the proper ordering of social and political relationships, but that order was all too frequently obscured in the turbulent world of the Virginia Southside. Thus for Beeman, "the triumph of Worthy and Wou'dbe, when viewed in the conflicting contexts of Munford's own genteel code of values and of his particular world, seems more a description of the way Munford thought things *ought to be* than a description of the way things actually were."

Much good work has been done to help us understand Munford, but the focus has been upon the background. Munford's art and his thought are worthy of being brought to the fore.

BIBLIOGRAPHY

Works by Robert Munford

"The D____l to M____ ____M____, of Meck____ ____g." Dixon and Nicholson's
    Virginia Gazette, 21 August 1779.
*A Collection of Plays and Poems By the Late Col. Robert Munford, of Mecklenburg
    County, in the State of Virginia*. Petersburg: William Prentis, 1798.
"Robert Munford's *The Candidates*." Ed. Jay B. Hubbell and Douglas Adair. *William
    and Mary Quarterly*, 3d ser., 5 (April 1948): 217–57.
"Robert Munford's *The Patriots*." Ed. Courtlandt Canby. *William and Mary Quarterly*,
    3d ser., 6 (July 1949): 437–503.
"*A Collection of Plays and Poems By the Late Col. Robert Munford, of Mecklenburg
    County, in the State of Virginia*: A Critical Edition." Ed. Jon C. Miller. Ph.D.
    diss., University of North Carolina, Chapel Hill, 1979.

Studies of Robert Munford

Baine, Rodney. *Robert Munford, America's First Comic Dramatist*. Athens: University
    of Georgia Press, 1973.
Beeman, Richard R. *The Evolution of the Southern Backcountry: A Case Study of Lu-
    nenburg County, Virginia—1746–1832*. Philadelphia: University of Pennsylvania
    Press, 1984.
————. "Robert Munford and the Political Culture of Frontier Virginia." *Journal of
    American Studies* 12 (August 1978): 169–83.
Beeman, Richard R. and Rhys Isaac. "Cultural Conflict and Social Change in the Rev-
    olutionary South: Lunenburg County, Virginia." *Journal of Southern History* 46
    (November 1980): 525–50.
Boorstin, Daniel J. *The Americans: The Colonial Experience*. New York: Random House,
    1958.
Bracey, Susan L. *Life by the Roaring Roanoke: A History of Mecklenburg County,
    Virginia*. Mecklenburg County: Mecklenburg County Bicentennial Commission,
    1977.

Bridenbaugh, Carl. *Myths and Realities: Societies of the Colonial South*. Baton Rouge: Louisiana State University Press, 1952.

Griswold, Rufus Wilmot. *The Poets and Poetry of America*. Philadelphia: Carey and Hart, 1850.

Hubbell, Jay B. *The South in American Literature, 1607–1900*. Durham: Duke University Press, 1954.

Kammen, Michael. *A Season of Youth: The American Revolution and the Historical Imagination*. New York: Knopf, 1978.

Lemay, J. A. Leo. "Robert Bolling and the Bailment of Col. Chiswell." *Early American Literature* 6 (Fall 1971): 99–142.

Meserve, Walter J. *An Emerging Entertainment: The Drama of the American People to 1828*. Bloomington: Indiana University Press, 1977.

Morgan, Edmund S. *American Slavery, American Freedom: The Ordeal of Colonial Virginia*. New York: W. W. Norton, 1975.

Pendleton, Edmund. *The Letters and Papers of Edmund Pendleton 1734–1803*. Ed. David J. Mays. Charlottesville: University Press of Virginia, 1967.

Philbrick, Norman. *Trumpets Sounding: Propaganda Plays of the American Revolution*. New York: Benjamin Blom, 1972.

Quinn, Arthur Hobson. *A History of the American Drama from the Beginning to the Civil War*. New York: F. S. Crofts, 1946.

Seilhamer, George O. *History of the American Theatre: During the Revolution and After*. Philadelphia: Globe Printing House, 1889.

Silverman, Kenneth. *A Cultural History of the Revolution. Painting, Music, Literature, and the Theatre in the Colonies and the United States From the Treaty of Paris to the Inauguration of George Washington*. New York: Thomas Y. Crowell, 1976.

Sydnor, Charles. *Gentlemen Freeholders*. Chapel Hill: University of North Carolina Press, 1952.

Van Schreeven, William J. and Robert L. Scribner. *Revolutionary Virginia, The Road to Independence*. Vol. 2. Charlottesville: University Press of Virginia, 1975.

Wood, Gordon S. *The Creation of the American Republic, 1776–1787*. Chapel Hill: University of North Carolina Press, 1969.

——————————— ALLISON R. ENSOR ———————————

Mary Noailles Murfree
[Charles Egbert Craddock]
(1850–1922)

Mary Noailles Murfree, whose pen name was Charles Egbert Craddock, was one of the foremost Southern local color writers of the late nineteenth century. As soon as her first and probably best book, *In the Tennessee Mountains* (1884), appeared, reviewers began to compare her with local color writers of other sections, particularly the West's Bret Harte and New England's Sarah Orne Jewett, and with those who had already established themselves in the South, George Washington Cable and Joel Chandler Harris. The publication of *The Prophet of the Great Smoky Mountains* (1885) led many to believe that here was a new power to be reckoned with, one whose work would endure, one who might come to be ranked with Hawthorne as a novelist. The reviewer for *Catholic World* was hardly alone in predicting that the author would "win a place among the best of our American writers of fiction." The tremendous excitement generated by the revelation that Craddock was not "a strapping six-foot Tennessean" but a "delicate looking lady" (both phrases are from a Boston *Herald* account) could but add to the fame of this Tennessee novelist and short story writer.

Time, however, has not been kind to Murfree's reputation. Though she can hardly be challenged as one of the foremost interpreters of the life of the Tennessee mountaineer, she clearly failed to live up to her early promise. The stories and novels with which her career began were her best; in them she depicted the mountain scenery, the people, their language, and the kind of incidents that might occur in such a place. There was not a great deal more that she could say, but she went on saying it year after year, book after book. She eventually turned to other settings and times, but these attempts were never so successful as her initial stories and novels.

College anthologies of American literature have banished Murfree from their pages, finding her inferior to Harte, Jewett, Mary Wilkins Freeman, Cable, and other local colorists. Her reputation has clearly been surpassed by that of her fellow nineteenth-century Tennessean, George Washington Harris, and his humorous creation Sut Lovingood. But Murfree's work inevitably appears in anthologies of Southern literature and in some collections of local color or regional fiction; the story almost always chosen to represent her is the final one from *In the Tennessee Mountains*, "The 'Harnt' That Walks Chilhowee." A number of Murfree's 25 books have been reprinted, mostly in the 1960s and 1970s, though none has appeared in paperback, a fairly clear indication that present-day publishers judge her appeal to be limited. It remains to be seen whether the feminist movement, which has so enhanced the reputations of other nineteenth-century women writers, will aid Murfree also, though it may be doubted whether all her books put together contain as many feminist texts as Kate Chopin's *The Awakening* or Freeman's "The Revolt of Mother." Nevertheless, Murfree portrays a number of strong and admirable, though idealized, women who are willing to pursue the courses of action that seem best to them, regardless of how many men may think them out of their senses, or as one of her characters might say, "teched in the head."

BIOGRAPHY

Mary Noailles Murfree was born 24 January 1850 at Grantland, a 1200-acre estate on Stone's River near Murfreesboro, Tennessee, a town whose name had been changed earlier to honor her great-grandfather. Murfreesboro had served at one time as the state capital and stood on the main route between Nashville and Chattanooga, a circumstance that led to its being the site of an important Civil War battle in which the Murfree property was ravaged—as described in Murfree's novel *Where the Battle Was Fought* (1884).

Though permanently lamed by a fever and partial paralysis that struck her in childhood, Murfree was able to travel and to obtain a good education, first at the Nashville Female Academy and afterwards at the Chegary Institute in Philadelphia, a young women's finishing school that she and her sister Fanny attended shortly after the Civil War.

More significant for Murfree's fiction was the education she received from her experience in the mountains, first in the Cumberlands and later in the Great Smokies. The Murfree family spent some fifteen summers at Beersheba Springs, in Grundy County, south of McMinnville, then a popular resort. The big white frame hotel perched at the top of the mountain, overlooking the valley hundreds of feet below, was to appear in several Murfree novels and stories, beginning with "The Dancin' Party at Harrison's Cove." Experiences at Beersheba taught Murfree a good deal about the mountains and their people, though her knowledge was necessarily somewhat superficial and that of an outsider. The Murfrees also traveled further eastward, reaching another popular watering place, Montvale Springs, in Blount County, south of Maryville. Montvale lies at the foot of Chilhowee Mountain, which appears in several Murfree stories, most notably "The 'Harnt' That Walks Chilhowee." From there Murfree seems to have made excursions to Tuckaleechee Cove, Cades Cove, and Gregory's Bald—the last two now part of the Great Smoky Mountains National Park. This section of the Smokies appears often in Murfree's stories. Maryville and its fellow county seat town of Sevierville apparently appear as Shaftesville and Colbury in the fiction, whereas the more distant metropolis of Knoxville takes the name of Glaston.

If Murfree ever had any romantic involvement, that fact has not been passed on to posterity. The accounts of her life make it appear that she found entire satisfaction in the companionship of her also unmarried sister and in her devotion to writing. Murfree turned to writing in her twenties, with the encouragement of her father, who is supposed to have said, "Mary, stop sewing. Anyone that can write has no business sewing." The story is also told that on one occasion when her father had read a story aloud Murfree observed that she could have written one as good, and he challenged her to do so.

Murfree's original ventures in print bore little resemblance to the work that made her famous. The May 1874 *Lippincott's* carried her "Flirts and Their Ways," based on observations from the years in Nashville social circles and signed with the masculine pseudonym R. Emmet Dembry. A similar sketch entitled "My Daughter's Admirers," also bearing the Dembry signature, appeared in the July issue of the magazine, an issue containing a story set in western North Carolina, one that included a fair amount of mountain dialect—Rebecca Harding Davis's "The Yares of the Black Mountains."

Murfree must have been aware of the Davis story, as she must also have known that writers in various sections of the country were beginning to win fame with their stories of the people and places where they lived. Why should Tennessee not have a representative among these regional writers? And what was the most picturesque element in Tennessee? Surely it was the mountaineer. He had, after all, made some appearance in literature already: in the Sut Lovingood stories of George Washington Harris, in Sidney Lanier's novel *Tiger-Lilies*, and in Mark Twain and Charles Dudley Warner's *The Gilded Age*.

Murfree, having decided on the new direction her writing would take, submitted to *Appleton's* two Tennessee mountain stories, "Taking the Blue Ribbon at the County Fair" and "The Panther of Jolton's Ridge." Both were accepted, but the journal ceased publication before they could appear. Thus the opportunity of first publishing a Murfree mountain story fell to the more prestigious *Atlantic Monthly*, which in May 1878 printed "The Dancin' Party at Harrison's Cove," under the pseudonym of Charles Egbert Craddock, a name Murfree continued to use for the remainder of her career. Her editors at the *Atlantic* understood that the Craddock name was a pseudonym; all their correspondence from the author had been signed "M. N. Murfree."

Over the next several years the *Atlantic* published seven more mountain stories, concluding with the two-part "Drifting Down Lost Creek." At the same time Murfree was turning out a series of mountain stories tailored for young people: these ran in *Youth's Companion*, beginning with "On a Higher Level," in 1879. In addition, Murfree was evidently working on a novel about the effect of the

Civil War on Murfreesboro (*Where the Battle Was Fought*) and perhaps on a long, never published book to be called *Allegheny Winds and Waters*, in which mountain, Civil War, and Mississippi material all had a place. In the meantime, the Murfrees had moved to St. Louis, where they remained until 1890, after which they returned to Murfreesboro.

After eight mountain stories had appeared in the *Atlantic*, the time seemed right for issuing them in book form. Accordingly, *In the Tennessee Mountains* was published by Houghton, Mifflin in April 1884. Reaction was generally favorable, as reviewers likened the stories to those by Joel Chandler Harris and George Washington Cable. Little if any mention was made of George Washington Harris, of Sidney Lanier, or of Sherwood Bonner's *Dialect Tales*, Tennessee mountain stories that had appeared in 1883. The critical verdict of later years has been that *In the Tennessee Mountains*, seen at the time as only an indication of great things to come, was in fact Murfree's best. The book had the charm of novelty; the public had not yet begun to count the number of times the moon rose over the mountains or become annoyed with Murfree's lengthy scenic descriptions and overly pedantic narration. The Tennessee mountains were virtually unknown to the readers of the *Atlantic* and *Youth's Companion*, and the new collection delighted readers with a glimpse of the place and of those who lived there and the strange way in which they talked—so at variance with the narrator's prose. If the author liked to do a little moralizing here and there, as in the often-quoted conclusion to "The 'Harnt' That Walks Chilhowee," so much the better.

Those who read and reviewed *In the Tennessee Mountains* and *Where the Battle Was Fought* (published some two months later) were under the impression that they were the work of a man named Craddock. Only the *Saturday Review* voiced the suggestion that "Mr. Craddock writes in a feminine spirit. He seems mostly concerned to show that women are much the best half of humanity. . . . " But there was a crescendo of curiosity about the author. Who was he? Where did he get his knowledge of the mountain folk? Eventually the report got into print that the author was M. N. Murfree. The family decided it was time to reveal the truth. Murfree, in company with her sister and father, journeyed to Boston and in March 1885 told Thomas Bailey Aldrich, then editor of the *Atlantic*, news he could hardly believe: Charles Egbert Craddock was a woman. Most accounts of what followed indicate that there was a sensation in the literary world, comparable only to the revelation of the sex of George Eliot.

The excitement over at last learning the identity of the mysterious Craddock could only help the sales of Murfree's first mountain novels, the juvenile *Down the Ravine* (May 1885) and *The Prophet of the Great Smoky Mountains* (September 1885). *The Prophet* had, in fact, been running serially in the *Atlantic* at the time of Murfree's trip to Boston. With its story of a tormented mountain preacher, Hiram Kelsey, and of Rick Tyler's struggle with the law and his unsuccessful attempt to gain the love of Dorinda Cayce, the novel proved a critical success and is now seen as one of Murfree's best, perhaps the best, rivaled only by *In the Clouds* (1886) and *In the "Stranger People's" Country* (1891).

For a number of years following 1885 Murfree continued to write stories and novels set in the Tennessee mountains. After *The Juggler* (1879), her thirteenth book, she shifted to a different Tennessee subject, the relations between whites and Indians in the early frontier days. The Macmillan publishing company was partly responsible for the shift, having invited her to contribute something to its series Stories from American History. After a great deal of research, Murfree produced *The Story of Old Fort Loudon* (1899), a novel based on the brief existence of a colonial outpost in eighteenth-century Tennessee (located on the Little Tennessee, southwest of Maryville and Knoxville), which had surrendered to the Indians in 1760. *The Bushwhackers* (1899), *A Spectre of Power* (1903), *The Frontiersmen* (1904), and *The Amulet* (1906) make similar use of Cherokee Indian material. Other attempts to move still further from the familiar mountain material are *The Champion* (1902), a story for young people apparently set in St. Louis, and two novels set in Mississippi, *The Fair Mississippian* (1908) and *The Story of Duciehurst* (1914). Murfree's father had owned plantations in Mississippi, and she was able to draw on memories of them for some of her settings. Murfree did not stay away from the mountains permanently, but came back to them in *The Windfall* (1907) and in her last mountain novel, *The Ordeal* (1912). Reviewers were to a large extent unimpressed. It was becoming more and more obvious that Murfree's best work was well behind her. Certain critics had long urged her to write about something other than the mountains, but when she did, the results were not satisfying; when she returned to the subject of the mountains, her work was no better.

Murfree's career, which had begun so brilliantly and had produced eighteen novels and seven collections of short stories, was coming to a disappointing and unhappy close. The last pieces to be published in Murfree's lifetime ran in *Youth's Companion*. A final novel, *The Erskine Honeymoon*, was dictated to Fanny Murfree and then published in a Nashville newspaper, though never in book form. One last gesture of recognition came from the University of the South at Sewanee, Tennessee, when it awarded Murfree an honorary doctorate. She was too ill to be present to accept, however, and she died soon afterwards, in Murfreesboro, on 31 July 1922. The obituary printed in the New York *Times* contained only four lines.

MAJOR THEMES

Murfree's central subject was the Tennessee mountains and their inhabitants. Though she showed in such books as *The Champion*, *The Fair Mississippian*, and *The Story of Duciehurst* that she could write of other locales, it was her depiction of the scenery and people of the Cumberlands and especially of the Great Smoky mountains that made her famous, appearing as it did in book after book and story after story from "The Dancin' Party at Harrison's Cove" in 1878 to *The Ordeal* in 1912.

Murfree uniformly depicted the mountains as grand and imposing, more like the Rockies than the actual mountains of Tennessee. Furthermore, they are pictured as they might appear to an enraptured outsider—rather than to the characters of the fiction, who are customarily unmoved by the scenic grandeur around them. The moutaineers themselves are almost always of the poorest sort, ignorant, knowing little of the outside world, superstitious, obsessed by religion. From time to time a mountain character, especially a young unmarried woman, rises above the rest, but by and large the portrait of the mountaineer is none too favorable—certainly not as favorable as it might have been had Murfree portrayed a wider variety of mountain types and brought her stories nearer to the time of their writing, that is, after the coming of the industrial revolution. Murfree would doubtless have been more accurate if she had depicted differences in speech and customs of mountaineers living in different sections and if she had not insisted on the unchanging nature of the mountaineers' existence. There is no Murfree character who really stands out or is sharply differentiated from others of the same type. The types are there—lovely young girls, pathetic mountain women, bad men, preachers, moonshiners, lawmen—but not the striking individual creations that one looks for in fiction.

The plots in which Murfree involves her characters have all too much sameness in them, as similar plot devices are repeated over and over. Among her most familiar are (1) a love interest, usually between a mountain girl and an outsider or between a mountain girl and some fugitive from justice, often wrongfully accused; (2) the heroism of some young, lovely, unmarried girl who does some remarkable deed, usually to help someone who may be thoroughly unappreciative; (3) the commission of some crime or supposed crime and attempts of the law to apprehend the criminal; (4) some supernatural manifestation, which turns out to have a natural explanation, though the mountaineers may not accept it; and (5) the relationship of the mountains to the outside world, whether the nearby valley towns or the greater cities beyond.

One of Murfree's most persistent stories is that of the young mountain girl wise and determined beyond her sisters. Several appear in the first collection, *In the Tennessee Mountains*—Celia Shaw, Selina Teade, Clarsie Giles, Cynthia Ware. Many another can be found in the novels, among them Dorinda Cayce of *The Prophet of the Great Smoky Mountains*, Alethea Sayles of *In the Clouds*, and Litt Pettingill of *In the "Stranger People's" Country*. Frequently the girl is in love with some outsider, a man who is a stranger to the mountains and their ways. Such love is almost always doomed to disappointment, as in "The Star in the Valley," in which Reginald Chevis, though "touched in a highly romantic way by the sweet beauty of this little woodland flower," leaves her behind and only later learns that she died soon after. Selina Teake, in "The Romance of Sunrise Rock," fares no better. She too dies an early death and only afterwards does John Cleaver realize that she loved him instead of his friend

Fred Trelawney. By contrast, Cynthia Ware, the protagonist of "Drifting Down Lost Creek," is not in love with an outsider but a fellow mountaineer, Evander Price, who is (like many Murfree characters) falsely accused of a crime and sent to the state penitentiary. Cynthia, the only one who believes in Price's innocence, puts forth an immense effort to set him free, eventually presenting a petition to the governor of Tennessee on the day he visits Sparta. Price is freed, but ten years pass before he comes home to the mountains, married to a woman "far superior to himself in education and social position" with whom he cannot really be happy. He gives Cynthia only "a fragmentary attention," hardly a surprise in view of his total unconcern as to who had obtained his pardon. When he does get around to considering it, Cynthia never crosses his mind. Such is her reward for all her love and concern.

Clarsie Giles is unique among the young women of *In the Tennessee Moun-tains*: in "The 'Harnt' That Walks Chilhowee" her kindness and compassion are shown not to the man she loves but to the supposed ghost of Reuben Crabb. She shows the same determination that we see in Cynthia Ware—"she air mightily sot ter hevin' her own way," says her father—and is even willing to risk a jail sentence for aiding Crabb. She does not, however, marry either Crabb or Simon Burney, an elderly suitor who magnanimously takes Crabb into his home, but Tom Pratt—a fact that is given the reader in an offhanded manner near the story's end.

In *The Prophet of the Great Smoky Mountains* Dorinda Cayce is the object of the affection of three men: Rick Tyler, a fugitive; Hiram Kelsey, the "prophet"; and Amos James, son of the miller. Though she loves Tyler, she has much feeling for Kelsey, and when Tyler refuses to testify in the parson's behalf, she rejects him, saying that she won't marry any man who isn't good. Alethea Sayles, of *In the Clouds*, loves the scamp Mink Lorey and tries to help him, but without success. Litt Pettingill, of *In the "Stranger People's" Country*, falls in love with the outsider Shattuck, an archaeologist who seeks to open the graves of the "leetle people." But he leaves her and forgets his promise and never returns to the mountains.

Shattuck is one of a number of Murfree characters who are outsiders in the world of the mountaineer—as was Murfree herself. Among the notable outsiders in the first collection of stories are Reginald Chevis of "The Star in the Valley" and John Cleaver and Fred Trelawney in "The Romance of Sunrise Rock." Mr. Kenyon, the hero of "The Dancin' Party at Harrison's Cove," is, like the others spending the summer at the New Helvetia Springs, an outsider though better acquainted with the mountains than Chevis, Cleaver, and Trelawney. Often the outsider is initially contemptuous of the mountaineer, as when Chevis looks at Celia Shaw with "pity for her dense ignorance, her coarse surroundings, her low station." What he does not see at the time are the "moral splendors" of the girl, which are to be manifested in her journey to warn the Peels that they are about to be murdered by her father and others. When Chevis sees the courage of the girl, he discovers that "despite all his culture, his sensibility, his yearnings toward humanity, he was not so high a thing in the scale of being; that he had placed a false estimate upon himself.'' In similar fashion the narrator of ''The Romance of Sunrise Rock'' tells us that Cleaver's ''position in life was as false as it was painful. But the great human heart was here, untutored though it was, and roughly accoutred.'' Ordinarily the outsider comes to understand the depth of character possessed by at least some of the mountaineers; he recognizes that there is a ''common humanity''—Murfree's phrase in ''The Star in the Valley''— which binds them together. Perhaps the most notable instance of the rejection of the outsider occurs in *In the "Stranger People's" Country* where Shattuck has the ''capacity to enter into the feelings of the mountaineers, to meet them, despite the heights of his learning and his social position, without effort and without affectation'' but is nevertheless not allowed to open the graves of the pygmies and narrowly escapes being killed. Other notable outsiders are Kenneth Kenniston, the architect of *His Vanished Star* who tries to build a hotel for summer guests, and Lucien Royce of *The Juggler*, a sleight-of-hand performer who pretends unconvincingly to be a mountaineer.

Another aspect of the conflict between the mountaineers and the outside world lies in the often-described ill feeling between the former and the people of the valley towns closest to them. When someone like Rufus Chadd in ''Election-eering on Big Injun Mounting'' goes from one society to another, the mountaineers are disgusted that he should ''git tuk up with them town ways, an' sot hisself ter wearin' of store-clothes.'' Occasionally the mountain people who venture out into the wider world are delighted, as when Evander Price of ''Drifting Down Lost Creek'' seems ''mighty glad ter git shet o' the mountings'' and declares that ''one year in the forge at the Pen war wuth a hundred years in the mountings.'' But, as Murfree says in the same story, more often they find ''a foreign world, full of strange habitudes and alien complications.'' When Cynthia Ware makes her journey from Lost Creek to Sparta (one of Murfree's few actual town names), she feels ''sifflicated'' by the denser atmosphere. Similarly, Narcissa Hanway of *The Mystery of Witch-Face Mountain* recalls ''the suffocating experience of one visit to the metropolitan glories of the little town in the flat woods known as Colbury,'' with its ''muddy streets, the tawdry shops, the jostling, busy-eyed people.''

One constant reason in Murfree's fiction for interaction between the mountain and valley people is the law, disobeyed by someone in the mountains and enforced by a sheriff or deputy from the county seat town in the valley. Time and again such characters as Rick Tyler in *The Prophet of the Great Smoky Mountains* or Mink Lorey in *In the Clouds* flee from the law, are caught and imprisoned, and then escape. Much of ''Electioneering on Big Injun Mounting'' turns on this theme as Rufus Chadd, formerly a mountain man himself, prosecutes so many mountaineers that one remarks, ''Ef it hedn't been fur this term a-givin' out he would hev jailed the whole mounting after a while!'' In the end, however, he forbids the prosecution of Isaac Boker, who had attacked him, and so wins the approval of the mountain people—and the next election.

Finally, there is the subject of religion. Though not especially prominent in *In the Tennessee Mountains*, it becomes a major subject in the novels *The Prophet of the Great Smoky Mountains* and *The Despot of Broomsedge Cove*. In the first story collection there are various references to the circuit rider, but no preachers actually appear. Mr. Kenyon of "The Dancin' Party at Harrison's Cove" is taken to be a preacher, and when he appears at the Harrison house, the assumption is that he has come "to stop the dancing and snatch the revelers from the jaws of hell." In truth, he is but a lay reader in the Episcopal church and does not share the mountain belief that dancing is a great sin. In *The Prophet of the Great Smoky Mountains* the preacher, Hiram Kelsey, is the title character. The admiration in which he is held by some may be sensed in the observation of one mountain man: "I 'low ez a man what kin ride a beastis an' read a book all ter wunst mus' be a powerful exhorter, an' mebbe ye'll lead us all ter grace." Those present when Kelsey breaks up a gander pulling have somewhat less regard for him, though, and the mountaineers reject him entirely when he confesses his loss of faith and proclaims that "Hell an' the devil hev prevailed agin me." Kelsey, arrested on a charge of helping the outlaw Rick Tyler escape, is imprisoned but eventually released, only to die at the hands of the Cayces, who believe that they are killing Micajah Green, the sheriff. Murfree presumably intends the reader to see Kelsey's substitutionary death as paralleling Christ's, though some have thought her source as much Charles Dickens as the Bible. Teck Jepson, the "despot," has no doubts about religion. Like other Murfree characters, he believes that the scenes of the Old Testament occurred in the mountains of East Tennessee, and as Cratis Williams observes, Jepson symbolizes "the triumph of cruel and inhuman religion over all other social forces in a community riddled with superstition and ignorance."

Superstition is indeed strong in many of Murfree's characters, as witness their fears about "the t'other mounting"—that something bad will happen to anyone who goes there—and their belief in the "harnt that walks Chilhowee every night o' the worl'." In the latter instance, the supposed ghost of Reuben Crabb turns out to be no harnt ("haint" is perhaps closer to the actual word for a ghost or spirit) but simply a starving man trying to avoid prosecution for a crime he did not commit. *In the Clouds* offers two false ghosts: the idiot boy Tad Simpkins, presumed to have drowned, and that of the mysterious "herder" seen from time to time on Thunderhead. Mink Lorey is in fact killed in the belief that he is the "harnt" he had pretended to be a short time earlier.

SURVEY OF CRITICISM

Relatively little has been written about Murfree since her death. Several M.A. theses were written in the late 1920s and 1930s, particularly by women who were able to consult Murfree's sister Fanny. The only recent work by graduate students appearing to be of consequence lies in two dissertations, that of Cratis D. Williams at New York University in 1961, which offers extensive summary and critical discussion of Murfree's work in the context of other Appalachian fiction, and Reese M. Carleton's on realistic, romantic, and romanticistic elements in Murfree's fiction, done at Wisconsin in 1976. Martha H. Pipes has edited Williams's dissertation for publication in the *Appalachian Journal* (1975–76) as *The Southern Mountaineer in Fact and Fiction*.

Only two book-length studies of Murfree have been published. The first, by Edd Winfield Parks, grew out of his dissertation at Vanderbilt in 1932 and appeared nine years later. Though helpful in establishing biographical facts about Murfree—especially her relationship with editors and publishers—it is less critical than one might wish. Criticism is largely confined to one chapter, "The Novels as Literature," in which some of the later novels get no more than a paragraph or so. Parks is not especially favorable to Murfree, finding her mind and art static, her observation of people limited. Her works, he says, have "with some justice been largely forgotten." He speculates that her reputation would have been much higher had she stopped writing after her first few books. Nevertheless, Parks does conclude that the best of Murfree's work is "too rare ever to be quite abandoned."

The second book on Murfree, Richard Cary's, appeared in 1967 in the Twayne United States Authors Series. It treats in detail many of the stories and novels (not merely those set in the Tennessee mountains), taking them according to subject and type rather than chronologically. This procedure is at times a little disconcerting, as when *Where the Battle Was Fought* (1884) is discussed after *The Ordeal* (1912) because they are classified under different headings. Cary finds Murfree "among the most eminent" of local color writers but suggests that she might have done better in the kind of manners writing she did for *Lippincott's* under the Dembry pseudonym.

An occasional study of the novel devotes a chapter or long section to Murfree's work, as does Alexander Cowie's *The Rise of the American Novel* (1948), which speaks of "undeniably excellent local color and her fine discernment of psychological detail" but finds her lacking in "breadth and weight." She has "skill and accuracy" but emphasizes background so much that human affairs are neglected. In the end Cowie concludes that she "excelled only in a limited milieu and with a comparatively simple plot."

Only a few significant articles have been published on Murfree. A particularly negative one by Durwood Dunn takes Murfree to task for her "lack of any real insight into the daily lives of the people" and finds it unfortunate that Murfree's misconceptions helped shape an enduring image of Appalachia. Dunn, a historian, finds that Murfree "failed in many important respects to depict accurately" the mountaineers and denounces her "simplistic distortions and selective perceptions." Perhaps the feminist movement will bring forth more writing on Murfree. There has been one such article pointing out how "unliberated" "Craddock's girls" are. The omission of Murfree from such works as *The Norton Anthology of Literature by Women* may, however, be significant.

One of the most useful tools for working with Murfree is Carleton's extensive bibliography of primary and secondary sources in *American Literary Realism*. Carleton provides brief annotation for every review, article, chapter, or book concerning Murfree from the time she began writing to the early 1970s. Still needed are an annotated edition of Murfree's letters and modern editions of at least her best novels and story collections. The only modern edition of any consequence has been that of *In the Tennessee Mountains* with an introduction by Nathalia Wright.

BIBLIOGRAPHY

Works by Mary Noailles Murfree

In the Tennessee Mountains. Boston: Houghton Mifflin, 1884. Ridgewood, N.J.: Gregg Press, 1968. Introd. by Nathalia Wright; Knoxville: University of Tennessee Press, 1970.

Where the Battle Was Fought. Boston: James R. Osgood, 1884.

Down the Ravine. Boston: Houghton Mifflin, 1885.

The Prophet of the Great Smoky Mountains. Boston: Houghton Mifflin, 1885.

In the Clouds. Boston: Houghton Mifflin, 1886.

The Story of Keedon Bluffs. Boston: Houghton Mifflin, 1888.

The Despot of Broomsedge Cove. Boston: Houghton Mifflin, 1889.

In the "Stranger People's" Country. New York: Harper, 1891.

His Vanished Star. Boston: Houghton Mifflin, 1894.

The Phantoms of the Foot-Bridge and Other Stories. New York: Harper, 1895. New York: Garrett Press, 1969.

The Mystery of Witch-Face Mountain and Other Stories. Boston: Houghton Mifflin, 1895. New York: Garrett Press, 1969.

The Juggler. Boston: Houghton Mifflin, 1897.

The Young Mountaineers. Boston: Houghton Mifflin, 1897. Freeport, N.Y.: Books for Libraries Press, 1969.

The Bushwhackers and Other Stories. Chicago: Herbert S. Stone, 1899. Freeport, N.Y.: Books for Libraries Press, 1969.

The Story of Old Fort Loudon. New York: Macmillan, 1899. Upper Saddle River, N.J.: Gregg Press, 1970.

The Champion. Boston: Houghton Mifflin, 1902.

A Spectre of Power. Boston: Houghton Mifflin, 1903.

The Frontiersmen. Boston: Houghton Mifflin, 1904. Freeport, N.Y.: Books for Libraries Press, 1970.

The Storm Centre. New York: Macmillan, 1905.

The Amulet. New York: Macmillan, 1906.

The Windfall. New York: Macmillan, 1907.

The Fair Mississippian. Boston: Houghton Mifflin, 1908.

The Ordeal: A Mountain Romance of Tennessee. Philadelphia: Lippincott, 1912.

The Raid of the Guerilla and Other Stories. Philadelphia: Lippincott, 1912.

The Story of Duciehurst: A Tale of the Mississippi. New York: Macmillan, 1914.

The Erskine Honeymoon. Nashville (Tenn.) *Banner*, 29 December 1930–3 March 1931.

" 'The Visitants from Yesterday': An Atypical, Previously Unpublished Story from the

Pen of 'Charles Egbert Craddock.' '' Ed. Benjamin Franklin Fisher IV. *Tennessee Studies in Literature* 26 (1981): 89–100.

Studies of Mary Noailles Murfree

Byrd, Eva Malone. "The Life and Writings of Mary Noailles Murfree." M.A. thesis, University of Tennessee, 1937.

Carleton, Reese M. "Conflict in Direction: Realistic, Romantic, Romanticistic Elements in the Fiction of Mary N. Murfree." Ph.D. diss., Wisconsin, 1976.

———. "Mary Noailles Murfree (1850–1922): An Annotated Bibliography." *American Literary Realism* 7 (1974): 293–378.

Cary, Richard. *Mary N. Murfree.* New York: Twayne, 1967.

Dunn, Durwood. "Mary Noailles Murfree: A Reappraisal." *Appalachian Journal* 6 (1979): 197–205.

Ensor, Allison. "The Geography of Mary Noailles Murfree's *In the Tennessee Mountains.*" *Mississippi Quarterly* 31 (1979): 191–99.

Harris, Isabella. "Charles Egbert Craddock as an Interpreter of Mountain Life." M.A. thesis, Duke University, 1933.

———. "The Southern Mountaineer in American Fiction, 1824–1910." Ph.D. diss., Duke University, 1948.

Lanier, Doris. "Mary Noailles Murfree: An Interview." *Tennessee Historical Quarterly* 31 (1972): 276–78.

Mooney, Mary S. "An Intimate Study of Mary Noailles Murfree, Charles Egbert Craddock." M.A. thesis, George Peabody College, Nashville, 1928.

Nilles, Mary. "Craddock's Girls: A Look at Some Unliberated Women." *Markham Review* 3 (1972): 74–77.

Parks, Edd Winfield. *Charles Egbert Craddock (Mary Noailles Murfree).* Chapel Hill: University of North Carolina Press, 1941.

Shuman, R. Baird. "Mary Murfree's Battle." *Tennessee Studies in Literature* 6 (1961): 33–37.

Spence, Eleanor B. "Collected Reminiscences of Mary N. Murfree." M.A. thesis, George Peabody College, Nashville, 1928.

Taylor, Archer. "Proverbs and Proverbial Phrases in the Writings of Mary N. Murfree (Charles Egbert Craddock)." *Tennessee Folklore Society Bulletin* 24, no. 1 (1958): 11–50.

Warfel, Harry. "Local Color and Artistry: Mary Noailles Murfree's *In the Tennessee Mountains.*" *Southern Literary Journal* 8 (1970): 154–63.

Williams, Cratis D. "The Southern Mountaineer in Fact and Fiction." Ph.D. diss., New York University, 1961.

———. *The Southern Mountaineer in Fact and Fiction.* Ed. Martha H. Pipes. *Appalachian Journal* 3 (Autumn 1975): 8–61; 3 (Winter 1975): 100–62; 3 (Spring 1976): 186–261; 3 (Summer 1976): 334–92.

Wright, Nathalia. "A Note on the Setting of Mary Noailles Murfree's 'The 'Harnt' That Walks Chilhowee.' '' *Modern Language Notes* 62 (1947): 272.

HARRIET R. HOLMAN

Thomas Nelson Page
(1853–1922)

Most readers consider Thomas Nelson Page the quintessence of nineteenth-century Southern romanticism, an apologist for the Old South. His significant contributions in opening the national market to Southern writers have not been clearly recognized.

BIOGRAPHY

A son of John and Elizabeth Burwell Nelson Page, Thomas Nelson Page was born 23 April 1853 at his Nelson grandparents' home some 40 miles north of Richmond, but any meaningful understanding of his life must begin three generations earlier with Governor Thomas Nelson, whose heroic public service reduced his family to straitened circumstances. As a wealthy Yorktown merchant, he guaranteed the money payment for labor to build fortifications at Yorktown, and himself directed cannonfire against his own home, which the British had commandeered for headquarters. Neither Virginia nor Congress ever paid him for either. Before his death the Nelsons had retired to rural obscurity north of Richmond among the clay hills of Hanover County, where his widow declined a visit from Lafayette in 1826 because she could not receive him in the style to which both were accustomed. The family treasured remembrance of a pretty daughter whose one white cotton dance frock was varied by ribbons bought for her by a slave who caught fish to pay for them. Out of such family memories Page evolved the protective and ingenious servants and noble owners of his fiction.

The upland soil at Oakland Plantation could not support all the family and the slaves who worked it. Somebody had to bring in money, and John Page practiced law in the rural community.

Long before Tom Page learned to read from the family Bible, he was used to hearing his father and William Nelson arguing the intent of the Founding Fathers on states' rights. Even earlier, his first clear memory was of being deposited in the middle of his nurse's snowy-counterpaned bed while she complained to his mother that being a slave was hard. Mrs. Page agreed, but added that the responsibilities of the master were hard too. Each must work faithfully in the station to which he was called, as St. Paul taught.

Except for two Nelson cousins from Mt. Air a mile away, Tom Page's companions were the slave boys on the place, his own brothers being five years older and five younger. As soon as he learned to read, he tried to share this new skill with "the boys," but he could never convince them such knowledge was desirable. Something of the otherwise happy relationship appears in *Two Little Confederates* (1888). Significantly, the book has never been out of print. The adult blacks who influenced him most were Carpenter William, the "head man," second in authority only to his uncle William Nelson, and Unc' Balla Brooks, the carriage driver whose skills the boy believed grander than Jehu's.

On his eighth birthday the boy saw William Nelson ride off to war with a sweeping bow and a flourish of his plumed hat to the Oakland ladies while his father marched away with a gun on his shoulder. Neighbors had elected him an officer, but he would not accept because, knowing his opposition to secession and war, they might not place full confidence in his leadership.

For Tom Page the war years shaped both the writer and the man. They taught him more than compassion and pity and the poignance of separation and grief. When John Page's body-servant Ralph came to Oakland for news and supplies and others returned briefly to the community, they brought news of the battles audible at Oakland and tales of individual heroism and gallantry. Once the boy accompanied his uncle the Rev. Dr. Robert Nelson to visit his father, by then Major John Page, in camp at Fredericksburg. (There he learned the unmistakable stench of death, which he long afterwards recognized when he led a Red Cross relief party into the Abruzzi Mountains above Rome following an earthquake in 1915.) In consequence, Tom Page knew Virginia campaigns as personal history long before they were written down, and he hated war and every form of strife enough to be lifelong a dedicated peacemaker. Forty years after the Civil War, that detailed knowledge helped make Page a valued consultant on American War College field trips through the Virginia battlegrounds.

John Page returned from war fiercely determined that his sons should have an education. He sent Tom to construe Latin while he kept stray cattle out of the cornfields planted by his father and his uncles. At Washington College from 1869 to 1872 during the presidency of Robert E. Lee, Tom lived in the home of his uncle the Reverend Dr. William Nelson Pendleton, professor of mathematics and formerly Lee's chief of artillery. So, as officers who had served under Lee and Pendleton came to talk with them, in that place Page had unusual exposure to history, though he lacked training in the systematic thoroughness and documentation now expected of historians.

John Page contrived to send his son for the year 1873–74 to the law school at the University of Virginia, which, like Oakland, became an abiding influence on Page's activities and outlook. He went in fall 1876 to practice law in Richmond and enjoy its brisk social life, where his family name, his affability, and gifts as raconteur opened doors for him.

He was writing constantly—obituaries, addresses for local occasions, and news accounts, the most memorable the unfortunate report he and A. C. Gordon made on Emerson's address at the University of Virginia. The university had invited Emerson to speak in 1876, the nation's centennial year that also ended Reconstruction. But the old man was already failing, his voice did not carry, and he seems to have been confused by the questions the young men asked. They considered him rude. Their adverse newspaper report attracted national comment, in effect nullifying the university's efforts at national conciliation.

His writing attracted more favorable attention when as part of the prolonged centennial observance he wrote, and *Scribner's Monthly* published, an article on Yorktown (October, 1881). His letterbooks and office records of that time (University of Virginia) show scenarios and dramatis personae suggesting that he was either dreaming of or writing costume novels, but what he sent with the Yorktown article was a short story in dialect. The editors liked it enough to pay for it, though they could not be sure that their readers were ready to accept the late war as history or the death of a slave-owning Confederate as subject of pathos and tragedy. So "Marse Chan" lay in Scribner vaults until April 1884, when it was published in *Century Magazine*.

With its appearance Page was established overnight as a writer and as persuasive spokesman for a South long denied access to the national media. The magnitude of that achievement is hard now for a reader lacking familiarity with the press of Page's time to comprehend; any reunion of Confederate veterans or noticeable effort to erect a memorial to fallen Confederates, at Gettysburg for example, was likely to evoke thunder in the halls of Congress and vituperative letters to editors. With Page's stories, however, popular imagination seized on the idea of a golden Southern past of chivalrous men, selfless women, and contented slaves devoted to their masters. For a generation magazine editors continued to ask for "another Marse Chan."

While he was trying to supply the requests of editors, business continued to take him far from Richmond, first to the mines opening in the Cumberland Mountains beyond Charlottesville, then to Colorado, and finally in search of capital to London, where his reputation had preceded him. Interesting as he found Edmund Gosse's discreet literary lunches, a happy afternoon with Rudyard Kipling, lively political evenings with the T. P. O'Connors, the heady company of notables assembled at Augustin Daly's Green Room suppers, he found Mrs. Francis Jeune's salons more to his purpose as authors commingled with judges, dons, journalistic firebrands, members of Parliament, artists, bankers, the squirearchy, military men, merchants, and theater people. Mrs. Jeune's mix of stimulating individuals from all walks of life established the pattern for his own hospitality from Richmond to Rome, adding texture and richness to the outwardly quiet years of his life. For, though he spoke for the Old South, Thomas Nelson Page was very much part of the bustling New South.

His brief idyllic marriage to Anne Seddon Bruce ended with shattering impact when she died in 1888. Her death turned him for a time from writing and the lyceum circuit, which in the nineteenth century was the surest way for a writer in America to make money. Sam Clemens generously kept Page's Baltimore engagement at that time.

Page's stage presence and his mellifluous voice added charm to the message underlying his stories: that the Confederacy had not been the exclusive domain of Simon Legrees and slaves living in degradation. The one-night engagements showed him contemporary America from Wisconsin to New England and Florida. Some of the money he made went for a stained glass window and some into a more lasting memorial: he founded and stocked Richmond's first free library, the Rosemary, in remembrance of his wife.

In 1892 at a series of private readings in the baronial affluence of Chicago's West Side, Page met the widowed sister-in-law of Marshall Field, Florence Lathrop Field. At their first meeting, tradition says, he told her that he was going to marry her. They were married a year later with the Oakland family in attendance and began their honeymoon on a private train. At the time of her marriage Florence Field gave Henry Field's collection of Impressionist paintings as nucleus of Chicago's Museum of Modern Art.

By then Page could afford to give full time to writing. To his wife, privately educated in France and accustomed to the excitements of Paris and Chicago, neither Richmond nor the rural seclusion of Charlottesville offered promise of a full life. They agreed instead on the cultural and social life of Washington.

The new work habits changed Page's style. The early work belongs essentially to the tradition of the storytellers and raconteurs among whom he grew up. To be sure, he wrote them first, but he read them aloud again and again, smoothing them effectively before any editor saw them. Even the framework form of the early fiction suggests the storyteller's traditional beginning, and most of the early stories conclude, like a raconteur's story, with a word or an action revealing the very essence of character. That what transpired seemingly more often happened than developed, that they were tales rather than short stories, did not greatly matter to him or to his readers.

But when Page turned to novels, both his shift from the oral tradition and this weakness in plotting became obvious to editors if not to readers caught up in the romantic aura of another time irrevocably beyond their reach. Before his remarriage he had written *On Newfound River* (1891), which not even an extensively revised version (1906) made memorable. He next turned his attention to *Red Rock* (1898), a long novel on the Civil War as he had known it behind the lines and to the troubled times that followed.

Red Rock remained a best-seller for two years. What readers saw in it was an engrossing novel that epitomized for them and established forever, for better or for worse, the romantic idea of the Confederate South at mid–nineteenth century as a superior region of chivalrous strength, nobility, and beauty.

Red Rock essentially marks the end of Page's Southern fiction. That writing had made him independently wealthy. As the first writer to break the editorial taboo against Southern material and writers from the old Confederacy—Mark Twain hardly counts because, as William Dean Howells observed, he was thoroughly reconstructed—Page's example encouraged editors to open up the literary market to other Southern writers. Their letters to Page make it clear that they looked to him as a trailbreaker. And in the process he had accomplished much toward the reconciliation between the sections. It had always been his concern. His was a pleasant and courteous voice among bitter diatribes. If, as the witticism goes, Margaret Mitchell finally won the war, Page had certainly mapped the terrain and done the early staff work for her. It was no happenstance that Page was asked to write *The Peace Cross Book* (1899) for the Cathedral of SS Peter and Paul.

With the encouragement of Charles Scribner, Page turned to contemporary material, the opening up of mines in the Virginia mountains. (It should be noted that he was interested in the developing conservation movement.) Set in Virginia's Cumberland Mountains, *Gordon Keith* (1903) shows young civil engineers bringing roads and industry to a people time forgot. Though Page had changed his subject matter, his way of seeing his material did not change. His heroes remained inherently superior, his heroines marvelously passive, his villains simply evil, and the chasms separating social classes deep. His introduction of a stock character beloved by twentieth-century writers, the good-hearted prositute, does nothing to alter the impression of stagey unreality. The book-buying public made *Gordon Keith* a best-seller, but for readers eight decades later the novel remains an unsuccessful application of a romantic angle of vision to the materials of realism. Though critics were not hostile, they were not impressed, and Page turned his attention in other directions.

Early in this century, when the first wave of urban unrest among the blacks crowded into Southern cities began to emerge, S. S. McClure, who knew sensational material wherever he encountered it, asked Page to write a series of articles for *McClure's Magazine*. With some revision they became *The Negro: The Southerner's Problem* (1904). It indicates clearly enough his limited perception of masses of humanity. His perceptions and sympathies were with individuals.

By this time Page was supporting an astonishing list of pensioners and beneficiaries including indigent blacks who had never belonged to his family and women who had nowhere to turn when a change of administration in Washington put them out of work. With habitual generosity Florence Page met community needs by providing both a visiting nurse and a lending library for Hanover County and York Harbor.

While he produced a steady stream of essays, local color anecdotes, and short fiction, Page tried again, as he had been trying ever since the heady excitement of Green Room suppers with Ada Rehan and Augustin Daly, to write a play or to dramatize some of his well-known Southern short stories. Those efforts inevitably failed for two reasons: his stories, like his personal life, contain little of the conflict that creates dramatic tension, and Page made the mistake of trying to write for the stage of Dickens and Daly after Ibsen had changed both the theatre and the audience.

With the approach of 1909, the centennial year for Lee, Page produced two small studies of Lee, *Robert E. Lee, the Southerner* (1908) and *Robert E. Lee, Man and Soldier* (1911). Neither Page nor Scribner claimed they were history; perhaps they deserve consideration now as the sort of acclaim the men who served under Lee wanted history to accord their leader, their protective reaction to the streams of villification still appearing in the press.

By this time his essays and articles on antebellum Virginia, including those collected as *The Old Dominion: Her Making and Her Manners* (1908), had earned Page the reputation of being knowledgeable about the details of daily living in Virginia's plantation past, so that when the committee working to restore Mt. Vernon needed specifics for an eighteenth-century kitchen, they turned to him. The house at Oakland burned, and though Page rebuilt it and scoured second-hand shops to replace the old-fashioned eighteenth-century furniture lost in the blaze, he continued to regret the loss of virgin oaks and Governor Nelson's Elzevirs; on a motor visit to Concord, he had been shocked to find Emerson's library smaller than the one lost at Oakland.

Some years in their travels the Pages arranged to meet Florence's brother Barbour Lathrop, a global plant explorer. Sometimes they accompanied Helen and Bryan Lathrop, her brother who handled her investments and was generous patron to the Chicago opera. Sometimes they went alone—to London, Paris, Portugal, Spain, Venice, Florence, Rome, and in 1912 by chauffeur-driven car across North Africa. Usually Page kept journals, three of which were published (1969–71) by Henry Field. Of all these experiences probably the only recognizable reflection in his fiction is the Monte Carlo background of "A Goth" (1907).

Scribner began publishing the Plantation Edition of Page's work in 1906 and issued the eighteenth volume in 1912, including a big novel on Chicago, *John Marvel, Assistant* (1909). The novel incorporated corrupt city officials, railroad strikes, and irresponsible misuse of wealth. Samuel Gompers, Ida Tarbell, David Graham Phillips, Vachel Lindsay, Carl Sandburg, or Jane Addams could have told him to leave such matters to people who understood them better. Carrie Chapman Catt or Ellen Glasgow could have disposed of his gentlewomen in terse language. But always, as in stories of war and its aftermath, his concern centered on victims of conflict and greed, and the public, loving it all, made the novel a best-seller.

Beyond the shortcomings obvious to better-informed readers of a later time, *John Marvel, Assistant* is of literary interest because it shows more clearly than even *Gordon Keith* the kind of satirical portraiture Page learned from Thackeray.

Perhaps the finality of a collected edition or perhaps his long struggle with magazine editors unwilling for him to break away from his old local color material influenced his decision in 1910 to give up writing in favor of public affairs. Page wanted to make a difference in the world. Since early in his practice as a lawyer, he had lobbied on both state and national concerns. A devout and automatic Democrat, possessing charm and social grace, he had easy access to every president from Grover Cleveland to Theodore Roosevelt and Taft. He saw Woodrow Wilson's election as a signal of real peace at last in the old sectional animosities. When Wilson appointed Page Italian ambassador, he and his wife went to Rome in 1913 with a high sense of service. After Italy declared war, Sir Rennell Rodd, the British ambassador, reported that Page always could tell him what would happen next.

Trying to counter Italian newspaper attacks on America, Page found an effective ally in an Italian-speaking aviator, Fiorello La Guardia, who as New York congressman had enlivened Page's dinners with talk of the future of aviation. Now he flew by day and made pro-American speeches by night. Once, in a lovely small irony of history, New York's "Little Flower" flew the author of "Marse Chan" above the rout at Caporetto that set aflame Ernest Hemingway's imagination.

The inevitable frustrations of wartime increased for Page when at the Paris Peace Conference he was denied access to anyone who could reach any policymaker in his own government.

Back in Washington, at Scribner's request he produced a light book for the popular market, *Washington and Its Romance* (1923), and when the Page-Barbour Foundation at the University of Virginia, endowed by Florence Page, asked him to initiate a series of lectures, he delivered three on Dante. They were published as *Dante and His Influence* (1922). At the same time he was working on a novel discarded twenty years earlier on the aftermath of war and Reconstruction in South Carolina. Page returned from collecting background oral history in South Carolina to find his wife unexpectedly dying. He continued to work on the novel, but it remained unfinished when he died suddenly at Oakland, 1 November 1922. His brother completed the novel, renamed *The Red Riders* for publication (1924). No shaper of history, Page was very much a man of his times; he saw history unfold and knew men who shaped it. Tom and Florence Page are buried in Washington's Rock Creek Cemetery.

MAJOR THEMES

Perception of the central theme of Page's Southern work has changed with the years since "Marse Chan" and "Meh Lady." For the first half century it was seen as defense of the Old South and the Confederacy. Then as the old animosities diminished into shared national concerns, it became more evident as a conscious effort to reconcile North and South; in *Red Rock* unadmirable characters were not only the Northerners; low-caste Southerners complicated life for Page's high-born Blairs and Carys. Page obviously intended the detestable Leech as an antidote for Harriet Beecher Stowe's Simon Legree. He was, in effect, saying that these people and this life could not have merited all the charges of Abolitionist rhetoric. *Red Rock* was not polemic. It pleaded no causes; it pointed no finger of blame. It did, however, break new ground in American war fiction because it presented war as damaging to all people of goodwill, even those not helpless. Though some die-hard Abolitionists grumbled in print at this account sympathetic to the plight of Southerners, no one saw that Page wrote of war in a new way in American fiction, not of its impact on an individual or a group, but of a region undergoing war. It is tempting to attribute this development to the Tolstoy he and Florence were reading together, but the idea had been implicit in his early stories and a Scribner's editor, Robert Underwood Johnson, had seen the symbolic union of Northerner and Southerner in "Meh Lady." Now a hundred years later it is clear that Page's central theme was peace because war inflicts loss on all men of goodwill.

Noblesse oblige, the old belief that privilege and opportunity confer responsibility, informs his characters from the letter-writer of "Marse Chan" to the heroic railroad man of "Run to Seed" and Hampton's Red Shirts of *Red Riders*. This responsibility in Page's world implied family loyalty and the group's superior claims over the individuals, most obviously in *The Old Gentlemen of the Black Stock* (1897). It automatically extends to the protection of women, whom he believed inherently less capable than white males. The unlovely obverse of chivalry shows most clearly when he writes of twentieth-century women in this genteel tradition, in *Gordon Keith*, *Land of the Spirit*, and *John Marvel, Assistant*; for the reader of the plantation stories tends to accept uncritically the convention of the protected position of the ladies of the household.

One corollary of his belief in the absolute decisiveness of heredity—the unchanging nature of class, so obvious in his fiction—ran counter to convictions he expressed in his journals as he traveled through Europe. Page believed as firmly as Stowe in the natural inferiority of blacks, even those exhibiting exceptional qualities of ingenuity, like Billy, or persistence, like "Ole 'Stracted." Except in *The Negro: The Southerner's Problem* and a few of *Pastime Stories*, blacks received from Page the same tolerant amusement he bestowed on children.

SURVEY OF CRITICISM

From the beginning, in approval or bitter attack, Page criticism has more often shown the critic's perception of Page as apologist for the plantation South and the Confederacy than as writer of fiction. See, for example, Thomas Wentworth Higginson, "The Case of the Carpet-Baggers," *Nation* 58 (March 2, 1899): 162–63, and Carlton McCarthy, *Typical Virginia* (Richmond: J. L.

Hill, 1894). Even so careful a scholar as Fred Lewis Pattee pointed out that Page's villains were Northerners, but failed to note that Page carefully balanced against them benevolent non-Southerners like the Welches in *Red Rock*. Southern-sympathizing readers, as a flood of letters to Page attest, were equally concerned with what they perceived as Page's message favorable to their status and beliefs. Only Arthur Hobson Quinn, from first review to *A History of American Fiction and Critical Survey* (1936), accorded Page dispassionate literary judgment.

The emergence of Page as part of a distinctive Southern literature early caught the attention of William Malone Baskervill and his colleagues at Vanderbilt. They sought him out and fostered his talent. Long before publication of Baskervill's *Southern Writers: Biographical and Critical Studies* (1902–3) they confirmed in him his agrarian tendencies and his conviction that the Civil War should never have been fought. Edwin Mims's *The Advancing South: Stories of Progress and Reaction* (1926) deals with these ideas. When W. J. Cash (1942) recognized similarities between Page and the Vanderbilt Agrarians, he understandably assumed that Page influenced them. He erred; for they shared the same tradition as Baskervill, Mims, and their Vanderbilt colleagues.

In the last half century as studies in American literature have proliferated, Page has received some attention from scholars. Harriet R. Holman used that portion of the Page family's huge collection of papers in the manuscript department of the Duke University Library for the background of her *The Literary Career of Thomas Nelson Page, 1884–1910* ([1948], 1978); and when more became available at the University of Virginia, she published journals and letters that show him thoughtfully cosmopolitan. A study by his grandson, the distinguished archaeologist Henry Field, *Thomas Nelson Page: A Memoir of Thomas Nelson Page* (1978), reinforces that perception. Page's influence on Faulkner was pointed out by Edward Stone (1962). In the satiric portraits of exploiters, fashionable society, and venial clergymen of *Gordon Keith* and *John Marvel*, Kimball King has seen Page's awareness of declining idealism in the twentieth century (1965).

The most detailed literary evaluation of Page's work has been provided by Theodore L. Gross in the Twayne United States Authors volume *Thomas Nelson Page* (1967), though the book errs on some biographical facts and has not always escaped the tendency of Page critics to substitute historical consideration for literary. Gross's lack of depth of background in his subject unfortunately leads him on occasion to attribute to flaws in Page's judgment or craftsmanship what a better-informed critic would have seen as a record of social or psychological changes, as, for example, the psychology of the defeated men in "Burial of the Guns." The critic was irritated less by the writer and the writer's handling of his material than by his own failure to comprehend other days, other ways. For to use Gross's phrase, in fiction and essay Page wrote the epitaph of a civilization.

BIBLIOGRAPHY

Works by Thomas Nelson Page

Marse Chan: A Tale of Old Virginia. New York: Charles Scribner's Sons, 1885.
In Ole Virginia: or Marse Chan and Other Stories. New York: Charles Scribner's Sons, 1887.
Two Little Confederates. New York: Charles Scribner's Sons, 1888.
Elsket, and Other Stories. New York: Charles Scribner's Sons, 1891.
On Newfound River. New York: Charles Scribner's Sons, 1891. rev. 1906.
The Burial of the Guns, and Other Stories. New York: Charles Scribner's Sons, 1894.
Pastime Stories. New York: Harper and Brothers, 1894.
The Old Gentleman of the Black Stock. New York: Charles Scribner's Sons, 1897.
Social Life in Old Virginia Before the War. New York: Charles Scribner's Sons, 1897.
Red Rock; A Chronicle of Reconstruction. New York: Charles Scribner's Sons, 1898.
The Peace Cross Book, Cathedral of SS. Peter and Paul, Washington. New York: R. H. Russell, 1899.
Gordon Keith. New York: Charles Scribner's Sons, 1903.
Bred in the Bone. New York: Charles Scribner's Sons, 1904.
The Negro: The Southerner's Problem. New York: Charles Scribner's Sons, 1904.
The Novels, Stories, Sketches and Poems of Thomas Nelson Page. The Plantation Edition. New York: Charles Scribner's Sons, 1908–12. 18 vols. Reissued Grosse Pointe, Mich.: Scholarly Press, 1968.
The Old Dominion: Her Making and Her Manners. New York: Charles Scribner's Sons, 1908.
Robert E. Lee, the Southerner. New York: Charles Scribner's Sons, 1908.
John Marvel, Assistant. New York: Charles Scribner's Sons, 1909.
Robert E. Lee, Man and Soldier. New York: Charles Scribner's Sons, 1911.
The Land of the Spirit. New York: Charles Scribner's Sons, 1913.
Italy and the World War. New York: Charles Scribner's Sons, 1920.
Dante and His Influence. New York: Charles Scribner's Sons, 1922.
Washington and Its Romance. New York: Doubleday, Page, 1923.
The Red Riders. New York: Charles Scribner's Sons, 1924.

Studies of Thomas Nelson Page

Baskervill, William Malone, ed. *Southern Writers: Biographical and Critical Studies*. 2 vols. Nashville: Methodist Episcopal Church, South, 1902–3, 2: 120–51.
Cash, W. J. *The Mind of the South*. New York: Knopf, 1942.
Field, Henry. *Thomas Nelson Page, A Memoir of Thomas Nelson Page*. Miami: Field Research Projects, 1978.
Fusco, Jeremiah N. *Diplomatic Relations Between Italy and the United States, 1913–1917*. New York: Carlton Press, 1970.
Gross, Theodore L. *Thomas Nelson Page*. New York: Twayne, 1967.
Holman, Harriet R., ed. *John Fox and Tom Page as They Were*. Miami: Field Research Projects, 1969.

————. *The Literary Career of Thomas Nelson Page, 1884–1910*. Miami: Field Research Projects, 1948, 1978.

King, Kimball. Introduction. *In Ole Virginia*. Chapel Hill: University of North Carolina Press, 1969.

Longest, George C. *Three Virginia Writers; Mary Johnston, Thomas Nelson Page, and Amélie Rives Troubetzkoy: A Reference Guide*. Boston: G. K. Hall, 1978.

Mims, Edwin. *The Advancing South: Stories of Progress and Reaction*. Garden City, N.Y.: Doubleday, Page, 1926.

Page, Roswell. *Thomas Nelson Page: A Memoir of a Virginia Gentleman*. New York: Charles Scribner's Sons, 1923.

Rubin, Louis D., Jr. "The Other Side of Slavery in Thomas Nelson Page's 'No Haid Pawn.' " *Studies in the Literary Imagination* 7 (Spring 1974): 95–99.

C. MICHAEL SMITH

Edward Coote Pinkney
(1802–1828)

In a brief time, Edward Coote Pinkney lived an extraordinarily varied life and demonstrated considerable poetic promise. Once popular as a poet of Cavalier charm, he is still considered an important poet of the antebellum South.

BIOGRAPHY

Edward Coote Pinkney, whose father was a prominent diplomat and U.S. attorney general, was born in London 1 October 1802 and was educated at Baltimore College and St. Mary's College in Baltimore. When he was fourteen, he joined the U.S. Navy as a midshipman and sailed aboard the *Washington*, which carried his father to a diplomatic post at Naples. For the next three years he served on naval vessels in the Mediterranean and learned about southern European culture. His subsequent naval career, marked by rebellious outbursts directed at his commanding officers, led to a court-martial for disrespect at one point and a commendation for bravery at another.

After his father's death in 1822, he left the navy and returned to Baltimore to live. There he fell in love with Mary Hawkins, to whom several of his poems are addressed. After being spurned by her, he married Georgia McCausland in 1824. His life continued to be punctuated by hot-tempered outbursts. One example was his encounter with the eccentric literary figure John Neal. Because Neal's novel *Randolph* (1823) included an unflattering characterization of Edward's father, Pinkney challenged Neal to a duel, and when Neal refused the young poet distributed handbills proclaiming his antagonist "unpossessed of courage to make satisfaction for the insolence of his folly."

By 1823 he had written a number of lyrics including several poems that are still frequently anthologized and had completed his most ambitious poem, *Rodolph: A Fragment* (1823), published by Joseph Robinson in Baltimore and dedicated to Georgia McCausland. Despite the poem's unevenness, it received some favorable notices, including a review in the *North American Review*. The reviewer acknowledged the poem's obscurity but praised the "highly poetic vein" running throughout.

In 1825 Joseph Robinson published Pinkney's only collection, *Poems*. In this slender volume were previously published poems, an expanded version of "Rodolph: A Fragment," and some poems not published before. The 1825 volume met with substantial success but did little to solve the practical problems of making a living and supporting a family. Without the navy to provide a livelihood, Pinkney turned to law, but was unsuccessful. He also accepted the title of professor at the fledgling University of Maryland, but received no remuneration. He turned again to his nautical training and traveled to Mexico to offer his services to the Mexican navy. Turned down in Mexico, he returned to Baltimore in ill health.

Despite his illness, he found a new opportunity waiting for him in Baltimore. He accepted the position of editor of a newspaper, *The Marylander*, founded to support John Quincy Adams. On 5 December 1827 *The Marylander* began twice-weekly publication. As Pinkney described in his prospectus, the paper would "zealously advocate the re-election of the illustrious statesman, John Quincy Adams to the Presidency of the United States."

Pinkney's newspaper vigorously attacked Andrew Jackson, published other pieces, and reprinted poetry and prose by such authors as Thomas De Quincey, Sir Walter Scott, Robert Southey, and Thomas Carew. Also included were some of Pinkney's own poems. Political commentary and invective predominated, however, and attracted the attention of Adams's opponents including Stephen Simpson, editor of a Jacksonian publication. Pinkney, hot-blooded to the last, challenged Simpson to a duel.

As winter moved toward spring 1828, Pinkney's health, uncertain since his trip to Mexico, continued to decline. Finally, on 11 April 1828, he died, only twenty-six years old.

MAJOR THEMES

Most of Pinkney's poems are love songs or lyrics in praise of a woman and her beauty. The love theme is clearly evident in his most famous poem, "A Health," which elicited Poe's praise in "The Poetic Principle" for its "poetic elevation" and "brilliancy and spirit." Pinkney casts this poem in the form of a toast. It begins:

> I fill this cup to one made up of loveliness
>   alone,
> A woman, of her gentle sex the seeming paragon;

The final quatrain repeats these lines and ends with a couplet that gives the poem a wistful closing:

> Her health! and would on earth there stood some
>   more of such a frame
> That life might be all poetry, and weariness a
>   name.

The poem is generally thought to be addressed to Pinkney's wife.

"Serenade," an earlier poem probably written to Mary Hawkins, may best demonstrate the playfulness and skill with figures that mark Pinkney's love poetry. The images of night/day, dark/light, blindness/sight, and sleep/waking are cleverly sustained and summed up in the final four lines:

> Nay, Lady, from thy slumbers break
>   And make this darkness gay,
> With looks whose brightness well might make
>   Of darker nights a day.

Pinkney's love poetry occasionally turned to expressions of sadness and torment at unrequited or lost love. "A Picture Song" laments the lost love of Mary Hawkins. Beginning with praise for a picture of the lady, Pinkney turns to a lament:

> The sportive hopes, that used to chase their
>   shifting shadows on,
> Like children playing in the sun, are gone—
>   forever gone;

Also lamenting Mary Hawkins's rejection of him is Pinkney's poem "Lines: From the Port-Folio of H _____ ." The poem begins:

> We met upon the world's wide face,
>   When each of us was young
> We parted soon, and to her place
>   A darker spirit sprung.

Pinkney's love laments lead into another prominent theme in his modest poetic output—the passing of time. The two themes are interwoven: love can conquer time, but when love is lost the pain of time becomes more prominent. As "On Parting" states, "our pleasant moments fly / On rapid wings away / While those recorded with a sigh, / Mock us by long delay." The search for freedom from time is explicit in "The Voyager's Song," inspired by Ponce de León's quest for the fountain of youth. It is hinted at in the frequently anthologized "Evergreens," which describes evergreen trees as shadows against the hills in summer that emerge in winter as "bright hopes to-morrow." The theme turns to a melancholy meditation on death in his later poem, "The Grave," which describes a once beautiful woman now "Buried in this narrow cave."

Though love and loss are dominant in Pinkney's verse, he attempted to explore other themes, enough to suggest that had he lived he might have developed a much greater range. Examples of these attempts to break away from the pattern of short love lyrics can be found as early as "Rodolph: A Fragment," which seems to echo Byron in places while it explores deranged states of mind in others. The poem also reflects the mood of gothic romance popular at the time. Another theme Pinkney addressed was the patriotic call for freedom. His "Prologue," delivered at the Greek Benefit in Baltimore in 1823 to support the struggle for independence from Turkish rule, is a powerful expression of support for "A struggling nation's strife for liberty."

Despite the occasional forays into other themes, Pinkney's principal subject is love, and his attitude toward his theme is more often playful than serious. His best poems remain the light lyrics and toasts such as "A Health," "Serenade," and the several poems entitled "Song."

SURVEY OF CRITICISM

The most significant early review in establishing Pinkney's reputation appeared in the *North American Review* in 1825. In it, F. W. P. Greenwood criticizes Pinkney's obscurity but praises a number of the poems and indicates that the promise of the earlier version of "Rodolph" is realized in this second volume. According to Greenwood, "Some of the small pieces in this very small volume are really exquisite." In the same review, two of the lines of Pinkney's "Italy" are described as "Grand poetry," and "A Health" is praised for its "ardent and at the same time respectful and spiritual passion." The only negative comments are reserved for Pinkney's occasional obscurity and his Byronesque cynicism and "gloom and moodiness."

With this good notice and with Poe's subsequent label of "the first of American lyricists," Pinkney was included in various nineteenth-century anthologies. Evert A. and George L. Duyckinck's *Cyclopaedia* in 1856 includes a biographical sketch, excerpts from "Rodolph: A Fragment," and five poems. The Duyckincks describe Pinkney as "a writer of exquisite taste and susceptibility." Even "Rodolph" is praised as "a poem of power and worth."

Not all the nineteenth-century critical assessments were positive, however. An article in *The Poets and Poetry of America* (1842) questioned the morality of Pinkney's verse. Echoing some of the criticism of "Rodolph" in the *North American Review*, the author faults Pinkney for his "selfish melancholy and sullen pride; dissatisfaction with the present, and doubts in regard to the future life."

Despite such occasional negative reaction, a flowering of appreciation arose at the turn of the century. Praise from Eugene L. Didier in *Harper's* (1882) and the *New York Times* (1902) spurred a resurgence of popular interest, whereas Charles Hunter Ross's article in the *Sewanee Review* (1896) laid the groundwork for a scholarly reassessment. Wrightman F. Melton followed with an article in the *Library of Southern Literature* in 1907 in which he describes Pinkney as "our Petrarch or Carew, standing near the head of the limited list of American Cavalier lyricists." Melton developed this theme further in articles in the *South Atlantic Quarterly* (1912) and *Modern Language Notes* (1913). The portrayal of Pinkney in the Cavalier tradition continued with J. P. Simmons's article in the *South Atlantic Quarterly* (1929).

In 1926 Thomas Olive Mabbott and Frank Lester Pleadwell published the work on Pinkney that has never been superseded, *The Life and Works of Edward Coote Pinkney*. The biographical portion includes copious quotations and reprintings from letters and other documents and is painstakingly referenced. The authors mediate among the varying accounts of Pinkney's life and allow his verse to stand on its own without detailed analysis.

Since 1930, Pinkney has received little critical attention but has continued to be represented in anthologies of Southern literature. Richard Beale Davis, C. Hugh Holman, and Louis D. Rubin, Jr.'s *Southern Writing, 1585–1920* includes four poems, whereas Thomas Daniel Young, Floyd C. Watkins, and Richmond Croom Beatty's *The Literature of the South* has nine. Rubin's *The Literary South* places less emphasis on Pinkney but still includes two of his poems. Most frequently anthologized are "Serenade," "A Health," "Song" ("We break the glass"), "Song" ("Day departs this upper air"), and "The Voyager's Song."

With this representation Pinkney continues to occupy a place as a minor poet who had considerably more promise than his short life allowed him to develop. He stands as an intriguing figure, a hot-blooded embodiment of the *coda duello* in biographical accounts, a Cavalier poet of some ingenuity in critical assessments. No longer as popular as he was during the New South era when the mythology of the antebellum South was refined and embraced, he still deserves a place among the early American poets for his possible influence on Poe and for his few finely crafted lyrics.

BIBLIOGRAPHY

Works by Edward Coote Pinkney

Rodolph, A Fragment. Baltimore: Joseph Robinson, 1823.
Poems. Baltimore: Joseph Robinson, 1825. Repr. New York: Arno Press, 1972. (See also Mabbott and Pleadwell, listed below.)

Studies of Edward Coote Pinkney

Didier, Eugene L. "Pinkney: First of American Lyricists." *New York Times*, 11 January 1902, p. 27.
———. "The Social Athens of America." *Harper's* 65 (1882): 20–36.
Duyckinck, Evert A. and George L. Duyckinck. *Cyclopaedia of American Literature*. Vol. 2. New York: Charles Scribner, 1856.

[Greenwood, F. W. P.] Review of *Poems by Edward C. Pinkney*. *North American Review*
     21 (1825): 369–76.

Griswold, Rufus Wilmot, Ed. *The Poets and Poetry of America*. Philadelphia: Parry and
     McMillan, 1842.

Hubbell, Jay B. *The South in American Literature, 1607–1900*. Durham, N.C.: Duke
     University Press, 1954.

Mabbott, Thomas Olive and Frank Lester Pleadwell. *The Life and Works of Edward
     Coote Pinkney*. New York: Macmillan, 1926.

Melton, Wrightman F. "Edward Coote Pinkney." *The Library of Southern Literature*.
     Vol. 9. Ed. Edwin Anderson Alderman, Joel Chandler Harris, and Charles William
     Kent. Atlanta: Martin & Hoyt, 1909.

———. "Edward Coote Pinkney." *South Atlantic Quarterly* 11 (1912): 328–36.

———. "The Influence of Petrarch upon Edward Coote Pinkney." *Modern Language
     Notes* 28 (1913): 199–200.

Ross, Charles Hunter. "Edward Coate [*sic*] Pinkney." *Sewanee Review* 4 (1895–96):
     287–98.

Simmons, J. P. "Edward Coote Pinkney—American Cavalier Poet." *South Atlantic
     Quarterly* 28 (1929): 406–18.

ERIC W. CARLSON

Edgar Allan Poe
(1809–1849)

The most important writer to emerge from the Old South, Edgar Allan Poe helped to create the modern literary imagination. He steered art away from the didactic to artistic integrity—both in the example of his fiction and poetry and in his powerful critical pronouncements.

BIOGRAPHY

Edgar Allan Poe's life was relatively brief and embattled. Born in Boston 19 January 1809, he was orphaned before the age of three by the death in Richmond 8 December 1811 of his mother, Elizabeth Arnold Poe, a talented actress of English birth. His father, David Poe, Jr., a mediocre actor of Irish descent, had earlier deserted his family; a heavy drinker, he died two days after his wife. Edgar was taken in by John and Frances Allan; his older brother William Henry and his younger sister Rosalie were cared for in other homes. Circumstances and heredity thus early affected the child Edgar, not the least being his adoption by the childless Allans—Mr. Allan being as stern and matter-of-fact as his wife was overaffectionate. From 1815 to 1820 Allan, a prosperous merchant, visited briefly in Scotland, the land of his birth, and then tended to business affairs in England. During this time, "Master Allan," as Edgar was called, attended several schools, including Dr. John Bransby's classical academy at Stoke Newington, near London. After the Allans' return to Richmond, Edgar attended private schools and began writing verse. As a youth, he was a strong swimmer and enjoyed shooting, skating, and the broad jump. Throughout these years, Edgar enjoyed full social and educational status as Allan's son, though not legally adopted. The Allans attended church and theatre regularly and summered in the mountains. Allan inherited the fortune of an uncle in 1825, a year in which he had faced financial difficulties.

At sixteen, Poe became "engaged" to Sarah Elmira Royster, an engagement broken by her parents after Poe entered the University of Virginia in February 1826. Poe was well liked and a very good student, especially in the classical and romance languages. As was common among his fellow students, he sometimes overindulged in drinking and in gambling. When his allowance failed to cover the cost of books and clothes, Poe turned to playing cards for money. The subsequent "debts of honor," which Allan refused to pay, led to Poe's withdrawing from the University. Added to this disappointment was the discovery that his engagement to Sarah no longer held. After a quarrel with Allan over the debts, Poe set off by boat for Baltimore and Boston, where he found employment as clerk and reporter; and then, 26 May, he enlisted in the army as "Edgar A. Perry" and was stationed at Fort Independence in Boston Harbor.

In 1827 Poe's first book, *Tamerlane and Other Poems* "By a Bostonian," was published by a young printer. It went unnoticed. On 1 January 1829 Poe was promoted to the highest noncommissioned rank of sergeant major. After Frances Allan died on 28 February, Poe was partially reconciled with Allan. On 15 April he received an honorable discharge from the army and moved to Baltimore to live with his aunt, Mrs. Maria Clemm, and her daughter, Virginia. There, in December, a second volume of his poems, *Al Aaraaf, Tamerlane, and Minor Poems*, came off the press and was favorably noticed by John Neal of the Boston *Yankee*. In a final effort to regain Allan's goodwill and as a step to a possible military career, Poe entered West Point on 1 July 1830. There he delighted in amusing his fellow cadets with verses lampooning the officers. Poe's comment in a letter—"Mr. A. is not very often sober"—did not help his cause when Allan saw it. When Allan remarried in October 1830, Poe rightly surmised that there would be neither reconciliation nor inheritance, and purposely forced his own dismissal from West Point by breaking regulations. Determined to resume his writing, Poe moved in February 1831 to New York, where his third book, *Poems*, appeared—a volume that contained the introductory "Letter to Mr. B _____ " and three of his best poems: "To Helen," "The City in the Sea," and "Israfel." Six poems, in all, were new; others were much revised. Despite a review and a notice, the volume sold to only a few subscribers.

Having thus served his apprenticeship as a poet, with three slender volumes and some remarkably fine poems to his credit, Poe was discouraged by lack of recognition. By May he was back in Baltimore, living with Mrs. Clemm, eight-year-old Virginia, his grandmother Elizabeth Poe, and his brother, William Henry, who died 1 August. Turning to the short story as a more salable commodity, Poe began his apprenticeship in 1831 by writing five tales for a contest sponsored by the Philadelphia *Saturday Courier*. Although none of the stories won—all but "Metzengerstein" were comic satires—they were published during 1832 in the *Courier*. In 1833 Poe lived at the Amity Street house in Baltimore. In that year he conceived of his "Tales of the Folio Club," a mildly Chaucerian project under which each author of eleven tales would be satirized—he and his tale both. The eleven consisted of the five *Courier* tales plus six others, only two of which ("Lionizing" and "Epimanes") are clearly satires. When he found no publisher, Poe submitted several to another contest in which his "MS. Found in a Bottle" won a prize of $50. In the poetry competition, "The Coliseum" took second place. Both tale and poem were published in the sponsoring Baltimore *Saturday Visiter* for October. In January 1834 "The Visionary" (later called "The Assignation") appeared, unsigned, in *Godey's Lady's Book*, Poe's first in a magazine of wide circulation. When John Allan died 27 March 1834, Poe learned that he was not mentioned in the will, though several legitimate and illegitimate children were. Earlier in the year, Poe had visited Allan's home, only to be ordered to leave by Allan, who was very ill.

In March 1835 John Pendleton Kennedy, a judge in the *Visiter* contest, helped Poe to an assistant editorship with the *Southern Literary Messenger (SLM)*, published by Thomas W. White in Richmond. From December 1835 he served as an editor; during that time the *SLM* became the leading critical magazine in the South, its circulation increasing from 500 to over 3,500. To the *SLM* Poe contributed poems and tales, new and old, and over 80 reviews, including two of high praise for Dickens. By January 1837, however, his low salary of $10 per week and disagreements over editorial freedom led to Poe's resignation. In search of a new position, Poe moved to New York with Mrs. Clemm and Virginia, his cousin, whom he had married on 16 May 1836, when she was not quite fourteen. When Poe could find no editorial work, Mrs. Clemm took in boarders, and Poe published poems and stories, among them "Ligeia," and continued writing *The Narrative of Arthur Gordon Pym*, two installments of which had been printed in the *SLM*, until it was completed and published as a novel in July 1838. In England, where it was pirated, it sold better than in his country. Still hoping to "live by literary labor," Poe had moved with his family to Philadelphia but found conditions there no better—so bad, in fact, that the Poes lived on bread and molasses for weeks at a time. In a letter to the secretary of the navy, 19 July 1838, Poe begged for a clerkship "by land or sea," but in vain. When he had seriously considered turning to lithography or printing for a livelihood, an old friend, Lambert A. Wilmer, came to his rescue with a poem welcoming Poe back to literary life. Shortly afterwards, two other friends published three of his major tales, "Ligeia" among them.

In 1839 Poe received $50 for lending his name as author to *The Conchologist's First Book*, a manual. In May be became coeditor with William Burton of the latter's *Gentleman's Magazine*, writing most of the reviews and one feature a month, the most notable being "The Fall of the House of Usher" and "William Wilson." Late in the year *Tales of the Grotesque and Arabesque* appeared (dated 1840), consisting of 25 tales in two volumes. The reviews were few, the sales poor. *The Journal of Julius Rodman* was serialized from January to June 1840. In May, Burton discharged Poe for excessive drinking; later they became friends again. Poe's plans for a critical magazine of his own, to be called *The Penn Magazine*, received no support. In 1841 George Graham bought *Burton's Magazine*, retitled *Graham's Magazine*, which Poe edited from April 1841 to May

1842 at a salary of $800, with responsibility for reviews and an occasional "feature." For the April issue Poe wrote "The Murders in the Rue Morgue," often considered the first detective story. Other notable Poe tales followed: "A Descent into the Maelstrom," "The Island of the Fay," and "Eleonora." Poe's hopes revived for a clerkship in the federal government and for support of *The Penn Magazine* through appeals to James Fenimore Cooper, William Cullen Bryant, Washington Irving, John Pendleton Kennedy, and others. Both came to naught.

When in January 1842 Virginia almost died from the effects of a ruptured blood vessel, Poe's personal life took on a darker tone. A meeting with Charles Dickens brought none of the hoped-for benefits. For Poe as writer, however, the year was productive: "Masque," "Oval Portrait," "The Pit and the Pendulum," "Marie Roget," "Landscape Garden," "The Conqueror Worm," and a review of Hawthorne's *Twice-Told Tales* came from his pen. A two-volume collection, *Phantasy Pieces*, failed to be published. When Poe resigned from *Graham's* in May, his successor was Rufus Wilmot Griswold. In the next year Poe contributed "The Tell-Tale Heart," "Lenore," and "Rationale of Verse" to *The Pioneer*, a new magazine, which failed after three issues. In March he tried again for a government job in Washington and for subscriptions to *The Stylus*. Still drunk from a spree, his cloak inside out, he called on President Tyler for his interview; after this fiasco, friends put him on the train for Philadelphia. Although he continued writing poems, reviews, and tales, Poe was reduced to borrowing from Griswold and James Russell Lowell. But with the publication in June of his $100 prize-winning and widely reprinted story "The Gold Bug," Poe became instantly famous as a "popular author." In July *The Prose Romances of Edgar A. Poe*, the first of a projected pamphlet series, was published; it reprinted "The Murders in the Rue Morgue" and "The Man That Was Used Up." The series was not continued. Beginning a new career, Poe lectured on "Poetry of America" in Philadelphia; Wilmington, Delaware; and Newark. In January 1844 he repeated this lecture at Baltimore and at Reading, Pennsylvania. In April the Poes moved to New York. "Balloon Hoax" appeared on 13 April and was reprinted the next day. *Doings of Gotham* consisted originally of seven newsletters, May-June 1844. "The Literary Life of Thingum Bob" satirized Graham and other editors. In November Poe began writing short commentaries called "Marginalia" to fill up columns.

Thomas O. Mabbott, the preeminent Poe scholar, called 1845 Poe's annus mirabilis. On 29 January "The Raven" was published in the *Evening Mirror*, with a brief introduction by N. P. Willis that became famous. The poem was immediately reprinted and even parodied, a sure sign of success. In *Graham's Magazine* for February, James Russell Lowell contributed the first essay-length appreciation of Poe as writer, praising him as "the most discriminating, philosophical and fearless critic upon imaginative works who has written in America." It was Lowell, too, who paved the way for Poe's joining the *Broadway Journal* as editor. In it Poe reprinted his poems and tales; for it he wrote over

60 literary essays and reviews; his new stories were minor. From his pen also came a long essay on Elizabeth Barrett (Browning) and five articles charging Longfellow with "plagiarisms"—a regrettable controversy known as "the Longfellow War." This year also marked Poe's entry into society in the sense that he attended Anne Lynch's famous soirees in Greenwich Village, where he read "The Raven" with a quiet intensity. Poe was known as a fascinating, brilliant conversationalist. In one of his lectures on "The Poets of America," he praised Frances Sargent Osgood's poems. A subsequent meeting of Poe and Mrs. Osgood developed into a two-year romantic literary companionship. In business, however, Poe was not so lucky. With borrowed money, he bought the *Broadway Journal*. The 25 October masthead read: "Edgar A. Poe, Editor and Proprietor." The *Journal* attracted such contributors as Thomas Holley Chivers, William Gilmore Simms, Philip Pendleton Cooke, and even a "Walter Whitman," whose "Art Singing and Heart Singing" was printed in the 29 November issue. Poe and Whitman met once at the office of the *Journal*. By the end of the year, however, it was losing money; the 3 January 1846 issue was its last.

With the help of Evert A. Duyckinck, *Tales*, a selection of twelve stories, was published in June 1845; and in November *The Raven and Other Poems*. In October Lowell invited Poe to read a new poem at the Boston Lyceum. Instead, after an oration by Caleb Cushing of two and a half hours, Poe spoke for twenty minutes on poetry and then read "Al Aaraaf" to an understandably baffled and unappreciative audience. Though T. W. Higginson and a few others were spellbound by Poe's musical voice, the performance was harshly criticized by the Boston *Transcript*. Poe replied that he had been drunk (not true) and had hoaxed his listeners with verses written at the age of ten (also not true, of course).

The year 1846 was difficult for Poe: his illness, as well as Virginia's, coupled with lack of steady employment and a fixed place of residence, caused severe economic hardship and mental depression. When Poe was able to settle down with his family and Catterina, the cat, in the Fordham Cottage, Marie Louise Shew, for whom Poe later wrote a poem (now lost), came to help care for Virginia, whose health had worsened. In spite of these difficulties, Poe produced "The Philosophy of Composition," "The Cask of Amontillado," "Marginalia," and reviews, as well as "The Literati of New York City" satires. His reputation, damaged by the Lyceum incident, was not enhanced by the lawsuit that grew out of Poe's attack on Thomas Dunn English in "The Literati" and the latter's countercharge that Poe was a forger and "an assassin in morals." "As regards the *Stylus*," he wrote to an admirer, "that is that grand purpose of my life, from which I have never swerved for a moment."

After a series of harrowing relapses, during each of which Poe despaired of her life, Virginia died of tuberculosis on 30 January 1847. When Poe fell seriously ill, Mrs. Clemm and Mrs. Shew helped him recover. Dr. Valentine Mott thought Poe might have suffered from a brain lesion earlier in life, sometimes associated with faces twisted like Poe's in his late photographs. His literary output was reduced to revisions of the Hawthorne review and "The Landscape Garden," plus two poems, one being "Ulalume." The next year, his literary work was concentrated on the lecture "The Universe," reworked into the long essay published as *Eureka*. To raise capital for *The Stylus*, he also read his lecture "The Poetic Principle" (not published until 1850) to a Providence audience of 1,600, so he claimed. Poems of this period include "The Bells" and two inspired by romantic friendships: "For Annie," which may relate to Poe's recovery from an overdose of laudanum in Boston after visiting Mrs. Charles (Annie) Richmond in Lowell; and "To Helen" ("I saw thee once") out of Poe's relationship with Sarah Helen Whitman, a forty-five-year-old widow in Providence, who had agreed to an engagement conditional on his leaving the bottle alone. Three months later, when Poe called on her after drinking, the engagement was called off. At this time Poe's letters to his lady friends are masterpieces of rhetoric. Out of the Whitman-Poe relationship came not only the second poem entitled "To Helen," but also Mrs. Whitman's slender volume, *Edgar Poe and His Critics* (1860), a sympathetic defense of Poe's character and achievement.

That Poe was aware of the deeper causes of his occasionally excessive drinking is borne out by his own comments, especially during Virginia's five-year illness. "My enemies referred the insanity to the drink rather than the drink to the insanity . . . it was the horrible never-ending oscillation between hope and despair which I could not longer have endured without the total loss of reason." Still, it is not clear how much of Poe's indulgence is attributable to his agonizing fear that Virginia would die.

His final year, 1849, saw Poe productive again, writing chiefly for the Boston *Flag of Our Union*, more for its pay scale than its quality. In it appeared "For Annie," "Landor's Cottage," "Hop-Frog,' "Von Kempelen and His Discovery," "Eldorado," and "To My Mother." "The Bells" (expanded version) and "Annabel Lee" appeared posthumously. From mid-July Poe enjoyed two months in Richmond with old friends and new, and delighted in the company of Susan Archer Talley, eighteen, and his former youthful fiancée, Elmira Royster Shelton, now a widow, who accepted Poe's proposal of marriage. But the record of the next seven days is not clear. On 26 September, seemingly in fair health, he boarded a boat for Baltimore, where he arrived on the 28th presumably. A week later, on 3 October, election day, he was found outside a polling place in a semiconscious, delirious state. Mabbott rejects the idea that Poe was the victim of election-day violence. Brought to the hospital by Dr. Snodgrass and Henry Herring, Poe's uncle by marriage, he remained delirious or unconscious, with some moments of consciousness near the end. His death on 7 October 1849 was attributed to "congestion of the brain." No death certificate was required.

In the words of Mabbott, the story of Poe's life is "a sad chronicle, but it is not a tragedy. A man who accomplished what he wished in his chosen fields of poetry and romance won a victory."

MAJOR THEMES

In the work of every artist or writer, certain images, characters, and plots develop into motifs, symbols, and patterns of plot and character. The recurrence of such elements, with associated themes, makes it possible to identify three major phases or perspectives in the development of Poe's version of man. First, a brief period from 1827 to 1831, is marked by an Edenic pastoralism in the form of "dreams" or "memories" of a lost Paradise or Golden Age. Second, from 1831 to 1841, more or less, an existentialist vision of the human condition is manifest both on the cosmic and the psychocultural levels of experience. Third, from 1835 to 1839 in the fiction, and from 1841 to 1849 in the criticism and the poetry, "psychal transcendentalism" becomes Poe's central and climatic vision of man. Although usefully distinguished, these periods are not mutually exclusive; sometimes thematic overlaps occur from one period to the next.

In the early "dream" poems of 1827, the vision or "memory" comes as a "holy dream" of an "evergreen and radiant Paradise . . . the circumscribed Eden" of the poet's making. In *Eureka*, youth is said to be "peculiarly haunted by such dreams; yet never mistaking them for dreams," that is, for mere illusory wishes. The reality and power of these dreams lie in the dynamic ideal life-values embodied as themes in these poems—as, for example, in "Al Aaraaf," the unfinished cosmic allegory of man's effort to achieve salvation through his recovered power of insight and imagination, his sense of beauty and harmony. The most romantic of these Jungian dream poems—"Evening Star," "A Dream," "Dreams," "A Dream within a Dream"—exalt the values of Beauty, Innocence, Joy, and Love as more real than mundane existence. The elemental forces within the psyche imply the potential for harmony of self with nature, with the "soul," and with "God." In "A Dream within a Dream," the theme of carpe diem gives voice to the feeling that the golden moments, love included, must add up to more than moments, and until the speaker finds some continuity or pattern or meaning in experience, he will remain without Hope.

An acute sense of loss is reflected in the haunting melancholy and at times in the demonic despair of the narrator, in "Tamerlane," "The Lake: To _____ ," and "Alone." The dream ideal of love and loyalty may be threatened or destroyed by passion, ambition, harsh circumstances, and passing time. But the deeper dream power, latent in the unconscious even if temporarily suppressed, remains as an indwelling "memory" of what life once was and can once again become. This "oceanic" feeling of childhood's "glory and dream" Wordsworth described as "related to unknown modes of being" confronting the poet.

During the transition year 1831, the intermediate version of "Romance" describes the major change in Poe's outlook on his life as a poet: the rejection of romantic rhetoric and the commitment to face "the eternal Condor years" of heavy burdens, griefs, and sorrows. That serious poetry demands nothing less than such heartfelt conviction is conveyed also in "Israfel." "To Helen" acts out and resolves in two brief stanzas a drama of psychic conflict; the "lost" psychic mariner comes "home" to his Psyche (soul) with a heightened sense of being reunited with a "holy" ideal. The classical qualities of Helen's name, face, hair, lamp, and statue-like appearance interweave to form a composite symbol of classical, ideal beauty. Although she may have been initially inspired by Mrs. Stanard, "the first purely ideal love of my soul" (in Poe's words),

Helen is less a real person than a symbolic construct of Hellenism, the "Holy-Land" of the poem. Few readers have realized how fundamentally this poem represents Poe's view of the "lost" soul in search of self-reintegration.

The year 1831 also marked a radical change from the psychal landscape of pastoral innocence, joy, and beauty to one of restless disharmony and anxiety. For a decade (to 1841) a number of poems and tales reflect a preoccupation with the existentialist theme of angst, death, and the cosmic Void. In "The Valley of Unrest" nature's restlessness symbolizes the unease that has come over the formerly smiling, quiet valley since the "wars" forced the inhabitants to evacuate. The grieving lover of the dead Irene ("The Sleeper") finds in her beauty and composure qualities essential to his inner peace, perhaps to his very will to live. Similarly, Lenore represents the highest, incomparable innocence and worth as well as beauty and love. In "The City in the Sea" the scene shifts again to the symbolic cosmos of the sea: within its silent, "hideously serene" depths hovers the beautiful arabesque city, destined to disappear into the nothingness of Hades (not a Christian hell of the damned). Why does Hell do this city reverence? Even there it is worshiped for its beauty, as suggested by lines 15–23. In "Silence—A Fable" (1837), God, if not "dead," is "silent": the spirit of man can face up to the storms of life, even its desolation, but not the terrifying silence that implies the total absence of life and purpose. This theme was repeated in "Sonnet—Silence." The silence is not of natural death but of the Void, best imagined in our time by the "nuclear winter" that probably would follow a nuclear conflict. These poems belong to "the literature of silence," part of Poe's contribution to what Robert M. Adams entitles *NIL: Episodes in the Literary Conquest of Void in the Nineteenth Century* (New York, 1966).

Further examples are the sea tales. "MS. Found in a Bottle" (1833), the earliest of these, dramatizes the theme of death-in-the-Void; silence gives way to the roaring, bellowing, and thundering of the ocean as the ship goes down, surrounded by "the blackness of eternal night." The finality of death in the existentialist boundary situation—without exit, without hope—is qualified by the positive counterthemes of "discovery," awe, and wonder. The new feeling or "entity" added to the narrator's soul turns out to be the power of a higher mode of knowledge that, coupled with the "curiosity to penetrate the mysteries of these awful regions," triumphed over his despair as the ship rushed to its doom. Whereas death here is the price of the "discovery," in "The Descent into the Maelstrom" (1841) the protagonist survives to experience a revelation that transforms the black walls and the abyss into a "wonderful manifestation of God's power" and the moonlight into "a flood of golden glory." But this insight does not lessen the narrator's overpowering sense that Man is at the mercy of an indifferent Universe, that God is a God of power, not love. Confronted by that stark fact, Man responds with his will to know, his will to survive, and his courage to be. Thus in his peak experience the psychic mariner's feeling of terror is transformed into an illuminative discovery of the Unconditional as transcendent power and beauty. In the early 1840s such existentialist themes also appear, in varying degree, in "The Pit and the Pendulum," "The Masque of the Red Death," "The Conqueror Worm," and "The Premature Burial." In the last named, "all was void, and black, and silent, and Nothing became the universe. Total annihilation could be no more." But in "The Pit and the Pendulum" the will to live is rewarded by the outstretched hand of General Lasalle. Otherwise, the hero is condemned by Time, the Abyss, and man's inhumanity to man. In "The Masque" the ebony clock tolls hourly the mortality theme as the pleasure-mad masqueraders whirl madly on, indifferent to Time and Death.

Thus, between 1831 and 1841 (or 1844), Poe's writings depict the Spirit of Man confronted by death—death as finality or death as "discovery." Shortly thereafter, during the early and mid–1840s, came the murder tales, which have identified Poe with the pathological and the psychotic, and hence, to some earlier readers, as lacking in "heart," "humanity," or "soul." Allen Tate, for instance, stated that Poe was well ahead of his time as "the conscious artist of an intensity which lacked moral perspective." But these tales have also been labeled "tales of conscience." Overtly violent and sadistic, they have undercurrents that are moral and psychological, inward and spiritual. Their terror is "not of Germany but of the soul," as Poe insisted in his preface to *Tales of the Grotesque and Arabesque*. To a degree, they represent a "search for the self beyond the ego." D. H. Lawrence, Tate, and others have recognized Poe as anticipating the Jamesian and Joycean hero, as discovering the dissociation and disintegration of the modern personality. Does it follow that Poe himself had no moral perspective? On the contrary, a strong moral consciousness speaks through these studies of the demonic self and the pathology of crime and confession.

True, the tales themselves do not reveal the root causes of the disorientation. But "The Colloquy of Monos and Una" (1841) provides a major clue. In that essay-dialogue Poe sets forth a cultural and psychological diagnosis of his day as a time of "diseased commotion, moral and physical." He sees "man's general condition at this epoch" as marked by "general misrule" resulting from false ideas about "universal equality"; he deplores the "huge smoking cities" and other blotches of ugly industrialization. Most serious of all, to him it was a sick society in which the "leading evil, Knowledge" (abstract rationalism), together with the mechanical arts, had led to "the blind neglect" of "Taste" (sensibility, imagination) and the domination of "harsh mathematical reason." In another essay Poe describes the "World of mind" as a delicate harmony of intellect, taste, and moral sense. When "taste alone could have led us gently back to beauty, to Nature, and to Life," it was too late for "the majestic intuition of Plato" to correct the imbalance. In Emerson's words (*Nature*, 1836), "The reason why the world lacks unity is because man is disunited with himself." Man is "a god in ruins," a condition he later described as "a crack in nature" between "intellect and affection."

Beginning in 1839 with "William Wilson," Poe composed six major tales of demonic compulsion, the last being "The Cask of Amontillado" in 1846. These are more than murder tales or tales of horror for horror's sake; the horror, as in

Conrad's Kurtz, is inward and spiritual, and leads to moral self-destruction. Each of the protagonists ultimately suffers the retribution of his conscience as embodied in the second William Wilson, the second black cat, and in more subtle ways, as the "imp" or moral sense, compelling the murderer to confess or subconsciously reveal his guilt. In "The Imp of the Perverse" (1845) Poe theorizes on "the spirit of the Perverse," which he does not equate with any "intelligible principle," for it is "occasionally known to operate in furtherance of good," as in the dramatic conclusions of these tales. Even in "The Tell-Tale Heart" and "The Black Cat," where the narrators are clearly psychotic, the "imp" of conscience asserts itself. Without such confession (self-knowledge) man has no identity; he is doomed to a life of restlessly losing his true self among the faceless masses—the theme of "The Man of the Crowd." Although there is no overt confession in "The Cask of Amontillado," is not Montresor's telling of his story 50 years after the event a kind of irrepressible confession, an attempt to unburden his soul? When, at the end, he says "My heart grew sick on account of the dampness of the catacombs. I hastened to make an end of my labour," the reader senses that it was more than the dampness that sickened his heart. And the concluding "*In pace requiescat*!" applies to Montresor as well as Fortunato.

Poe's third, central and culminating vision of man may be labeled "psychal transcendentalism." It is the most pervasive of his three major perspectives, being expressed in his essays, in *Eureka*, in "Mesmeric Revelation," in his letters, in his poems, especially in late poems, and in his tales, notably a cluster of symbolic stories published between 1835 and 1839. Poe referred to "Mesmeric Revelation" (1844) as a "somewhat detailed" article of his "Faith," that faith being his vision of a possible "ultimate life" of heightened perception and creative power—the life of the "angelic imagination," as Allen Tate entitled his essay-study of Poe's philosophic perspective. Through the "painful metamorphosis" of death, the individual is transformed from the life of the "ordinary" sense into a state of "nearly unlimited perception" and "unlimited comprehension," as happens to Monos when he is "born again." In 1846 a short marginalia essay on "psychal fancies" describes certain "sleep-walking" moments of creative insight as being "supernal to the Human Nature." However rare they might be, to Poe they seem "Common to all mankind." In "The Poetic Principle" such "psychal impressions" became the essence of the "Poetic Sentiment"—the unquenchable thirst for not merely "the Beauty before but a wild effort to reach the Beauty above . . . of which *through* the poem or *through* the music, we attain to but brief and indeterminate glimpses." When artistic experience offers the Self such a transcendence of the Ego, the individual will feel an "identity with God" or "the universal Ens." The concluding paragraph to *Eureka, An Essay on the Material and Spiritual Universe*, implies an ideal transcendental unity of man, nature, and God.

The theme of psychal transcendence is most successfully dramatized in the symbolic arabesques, a group of visionary tales published between 1835 and

1839. These early dates suggest that this theme was first realized by Poe in his fiction, slightly later in his colloquies, and finally in his essays and late poems. As tales of psychic conflict, they are, in the words of the poet Richard Wilbur, "the best things of their kind in our literature," a judgment that has not been questioned. More than "Moral allegories" because of psychedelic forces at work, they are really psychomoral. (In Poe's time the words *moral* and *moral energy* related to the conative or volitional faculty, as distinguished from the intellectual and moralistic. Poe's "moral sense," therefore, connotes a deep, dynamic willing, vitality, and creativity, especially when joined by "taste" or "poetic intellect" to "intellect.") Although "Berenice" and "Morella," both 1835, stand as independent works of art, they anticipate "Ligeia" (1838) to such a degree in character, conflict, and theme that the earlier two seem to be études of the tale that Poe regarded as his best. In "Ligeia" specific mention is made of "the many mysteries of the transcendentalism in which we were immersed" and the "assumptions and aspiration which mortality had never before known." The theme of will is given prominence in the epigraph attributed to Joseph Glanvill, much of which Ligeia repeats in her final outcry of protest. Similarly, after a series of opium-induced visions during which Ligeia seems to revive and the narrator's soul to awaken, the climactic transformation occurs: with a shriek of recognition he witnesses the resurrection of Ligeia with her black hair, her full, black, wild eyes, his "lost love," the LADY LIGEIA! Symbolically, through his persistent and intense willing, he has recovered the "spiritual" Ligeia depths in himself. (The "meaning" of Ligeia is carefully conveyed in the symbolic portrait of her near the beginning.)

In "The Fall of the House of Usher" (1839), Poe's best-known serious gothic or neogothic narrative, Madeline's function parallels that of Ligeia, Roderick that of Ligeia's husband, and the narrator adds to the complexity of the story as a reliable witness of the action and the psychomoral conflict. As poet, painter, and musical artist, Roderick symbolizes creative sensibility of the most "arabesque" quality. His repressed will, or "moral energy," takes its revenge on Roderick and thus the whole Usher "house" as well. In these tales, the cause of the disintegrating conflict lies with the male characters, not the women. The women in Poe's poems generally manifest a transcendent quality of beauty (as in Helen), or of love and loyalty (Annabel Lee, Lenore, Annie, Ulalume). By contrast, the men are lost, unloving, lacking in insight. These symbolic character differences link the tales of psychic conflict to the late poems. In "The Raven," for example, the narrator's final resignation points up his sense of loss and ineradicable grief.

When, near the end of *Eureka*, Poe claimed that "each soul is, in part, its own God—its own creator," he summed up the Emersonian faith in each individual's psychal capacity for realizing his "proper identity" (individuated selfhood) and his "identity with God" (the transcendental connection with the "universal Ens"—or "Over-Soul"). These two "identity" themes are sometimes too subtly fused to be readily apparent; but once the reader is sensitized to Poe's outlook on life and art, he becomes aware that the theme underlying most of Poe's serious work is a positive one: the search for psychal unity through a reintegration of the divided self. Further expressions of this theme in the late poetry and prose include "Eleonora" (1841), "The Island of the Fay" (1841), "The Domain of Arnheim" (1847), "Ulalume" (1847), "For Annie" (1849), and "Eldorado" (1849).

Many of Poe's early tales were satires, either burlesque or grotesque. Judging by his introduction to "The Folio Club" (1833), Poe's satiric purpose would take the form of parody, caricature, humorous mockery, a great deal of verbal wit and byplay, some of it subtle, some of it a sort of rhetorical slapstick—all of it mainly for the reader's amusement, with the Chaucerian intent of exposing the teller as well as the tale. Five of the eleven tales, however, are serious rather than satiric: "Metzengerstein," "MS. Found in a Bottle," "The Assignation," "Shadow—A Parable," and "Silence—A Fable." A greater consistency and a better guide to Poe's genre intentions can be had in the preface and table of contents to *Tales of the Grotesque and Arabesque*, where the two modes are clearly alternated. Despite Poe's overuse of artifice and exaggeration, of caricature and implausible situation, of sophomoric puns, strained coinages, and other verbal trickery, his comic fiction often effectively lampoons the literary and social fashions of his time, including some of his own fictional devices. The best example is "How to Write a Blackwood Article," and its companion-piece illustration, "A Predicament" or "The Scythe of Time." Some critics consider the comic fiction to be an integral part of Poe's work, revealing his "vision of dehumanized man," "the deadness of society," the cruelty of the "ins" toward the "outs," the inadequacy of conventional idealism, etc.

Closely related to the satires are the hoaxes, of which "The Facts in the Case of Monsieur Valdemar" became the most notorious, and "The Balloon Hoax" the purest. "The Unparalleled Adventure of One Hans Pfaall" is the most sustained imaginary moon voyage, but its satire is weak and overdone by comparison with the social satire of New York fashion and of Democracy in "Mellonta Tauta," also an impossible mixture of social criticism and balloon journey. In addition to these advances in science fiction, Poe applied his analytical mind to the mystery story, or tale of ratiocination. A few of the detective stories are the first and the best of their kind. In the first, "The Murders in the Rue Morgue," the narrator's prefatory lecture on method uses the psychology of association to justify Dupin's intuitive powers of mind reading. In "The Purloined Letter," Dupin has raised analysis to an intuitive art, in contrast to the plodding, merely logical procedures of the unimaginative Parisian police. The superiority of the poetic intellect—he is a poet as well as a detective—makes Dupin a seer, a hero of the imagination, whose intuitions are disciplined by both observation and introspection. Thus the theme of transcendental insight appears again, where it is least expected. No new themes emerge from "The Mystery of Marie Roget" and "Maelzel's Chess Player," but "The Gold-Bug" is notable not only as Poe's great cryptographic tale but as a dramatic example of how imaginative insight can find treasure of great value. It is LeGrand's intuitions that enable him to follow the clues in the secret coded message, complete with invisible ink, symbols, and cryptogram. The theme lies in this excitement of intellectual discovery rather than in the unearthed treasure itself. Like Dupin, LeGrand too has a Bi-Part Soul, both creative and resolvent.

Beginning as a first-person participant-witness serialized adventure story, *The Narrative of Arthur Gordon Pym* was turned into a novel, published in 1838. As science fiction it is an imaginary exploration into the unknown and uncharted Southern regions, somewhat based on Poe's reading about Antarctic expeditions. Pym is almost constantly subjected to shipwreck, accident, ambush, and treachery in an unpredictable, deceitful human and natural world, a preparation for the ultimate revelation and theme: the awesome mystery of human destiny, as symbolized in the concluding paragraphs.

In the broadest sense of the term, Poe's nonfiction prose includes his literary essays, reviews, lectures, letters, and social and philosophical writings, including *Marginalia*. Some of his ideas about society, democracy, progress, literature, etc., are expressed through his satires and hoaxes, as already noted. In the preceding pages, more important essays, under whatever guise (*Eureka*, "The Colloquy of Monos and Una," etc.) have been related to themes in the poetry and fiction.

In his critical theory Poe sharply distinguished the poetic function from didactic moralizing (the "Didactic Heresy"). Truth in art must be suggested through the "under current of meaning," not directly stated. The poet's "silent analytical promptings" will guide him to rely on "a suggestive indefinitiveness of meaning, with the view of bringing about a definitiveness of vague and therefore of *spiritual* effect." For Poe, as with most poets, this theory of the *vague*, this "atmosphere of the mystic," gave a new functional emphasis to sound-values, evident in his dramatic, impressionistic tales as well as in his lyric and dramatic poems—the rich patterns of rhymes, alliteration, assonance, repetend, tone, and melody. The poet must have both creative imagination ("the poetic principle") and craftmanship to shape the poem into a harmonious whole. To offset the notion that poetry is composed by "a species of fine frenzy," in "The Philosophy of Composition" he deliberately overstated the case for conscious craft as if every element and effect were preconceived and calculated. In his reviews of Hawthorne's *Twice-Told Tales*, he places major emphasis again on "a certain unique or single *effect*" through "the one pre-established design"—the "unity of impression" conveyed by an integration of tone, style, characters, symbol, plot, and theme.

Poe's insistence that a poem or a tale must be brief, or the necessary unity of effect will be lost, reflects not only his aesthetic of sustained intensity in artistic experience but also his work and outlook as a "magazinist." He welcomed the trend away from the quarterlies to the magazine, the latter being more responsive to the need for "the curt, the condensed, the pointed, the readily diffused." In his critical theory he gave original emphasis to the responsibility of the critic to deal more with the poem as poem in terms of its poetic qualities, its form and function, and less with history, biography, or philosophy. The ideal critic should also be objective in his analysis, even to the point of being unsparingly negative, when necessary, as Poe was in his "tomahawk' reviews. Genuine criticism should avoid both "the cant of generality" and "the cant of critical Boswellism."

SURVEY OF CRITICISM

Two days after Poe's death, the infamous "Ludwig" obituary by Rufus Wilmot Griswold was published; it was Griswold's "Memoir" in the 1850–56 edition of Poe's works. As a consequence, Poe's reputation as person and author suffered almost irreparable damage for years to come. (Before his death, there had been discriminating and laudatory appreciations of Poe's writing by John Neal, Louis Tasistro, James Russell Lowell, Margaret Fuller, Martin Tupper, Philip Pendleton Cooke; shortly after his death, tributes by N. P. Willis and Evert Augustus Duyckinck.) In Europe, beginning in the 1850s Poe's achievement was championed by Charles Baudelaire, and in the following decades by Fyodor Dostoevsky, Stéphane Mallarme, Algernon Charles Swinburne, Johann August Strindberg, Edmund Gosse, and William Butler Yeats.

In 1909, the centennial year, an essay by George Bernard Shaw praised Poe as "the finest of fine artists" and as the poet-rebel against American materialism. But it was not until 1924 (just before and after), the 75th anniversary of Poe's death, that modern criticism of Poe began with the publication of germinal essays by D. H. Lawrence, Paul Valery, William Carlos Williams, and Edmund Wilson—only to be followed in the 1930s by the radically diverse appreciations of Aldous Huxley, Constance Rourke, George Saintsbury, Marie Bonaparte, and Yvor Winters. The insights of the former group seem to have been ignored or missed completely by Huxley, Bonaparte, and Winters. Thereafter, it was not until 1948–51 that another breakthrough in Poe criticism occurred with lectures and essays by T. S. Eliot, W. H. Auden, and Allen Tate. Eliot described the "puzzling'| but "immense" effect of Poe's prose, poetry, and poetics on three generations of French writers, whose response impressed Eliot with "the importance of his [Poe's] *work* as a whole." Auden soon followed with an introduction to *Edgar Allan Poe: Selected Prose and Poetry* (1950) in which he surveyed Poe's work, giving special praise to the little-read *Eureka* and *Pym*, "one of the finest adventure stories ever written." Tate's lecture "The Angelic Imagination" attempted to define "what I think I have seen in Poe that nobody else has seen"—the "philosophic perspective" implicit in the three colloquies, especially the psychic disintegration caused by the conflict between the angelic intellect or reason and feeling or moral sense. Many of these essays are reprinted in collections edited by Eric W. Carlson, Robert Regan, and David B. Kesterson.

Parallel to the critical studies, many biographies appeared. Griswold's "Ludwig" letter and "Memoir" brought forth articles and books in defense of Poe, among them Sarah Helen Whitman's *Edgar Poe and His Critics* (1860), John H. Ingram's *Edgar Allan Poe* (1880), and George Edward Woodberry's *Life* (1885; rev. ed., 2 vols., 1909).

With the publication in 1902 of *The Complete Works of Edgar Allan Poe*, ed. James A. Harrison, in 17 vols.—the Virginia Edition—a definitive text became available for the first time. But the life and letters in volumes 1 and 17 did not satisfy biographers intrigued by the "enigma" of Poe. In the 1920s new biographies appeared in quick succession. Those by Hervey Allen and Mary E. Phillips were conventional and highly factual, not critical or interpretive; those by Joseph Wood Krutch (1926) and Marie Bonaparte (1933, English tr. 1949) read Poe's life and work in terms of Freudian psychology, Bonaparte's psychoanalytical treatment representing an extreme that would eventually stimulate a telling refutation by Roger Forclaz in two articles in *Revue des Langues Vivantes* 36, nos. 3, 4 (1970). In 1941 came Arthur Hobson Quinn's *Edgar Allan Poe: A Critical Biography*, still the only full-scale, reliably documented, scholarly life-and-letters. Killis Campbell's *The Mind of Poe* (1933) remains an authoritative source, as do the biographical essays of James Southall Wilson, Floyd Stovall, and Thomas O. Mabbott (whose "Annals of Poe's Life" is one of the best recent chronologies). Frances Winwar's romantic, William Bittner's simplified, and Edward Wagenknecht's selective approaches were counterbalanced by Sidney P. Moss's detailed studies of Poe's literary battles and libel suits. In 1978 two popular biographies appeared, one by Wolf Mankowitz, the English novelist and playwright, the other by Juliana Symons, the poet and mystery writer. Both reflect a deplorable journalistic bias against academic scholarship; as a result both are not only factually inaccurate but interpretively unbalanced and warped, trusting to Marie Bonaparte for clues to the Poe enigma.

Meanwhile, John Carl Miller published two volumes of his selections from the John Ingram collection. The first, *Building Poe Biography*, prints 86 letters from Ingram's correspondence with Maria Clemm, Annie Richmond, and others, along with other material on Ingram. The second, *Poe's Helen Remembers*, contains the correspondence between Ingram and Sarah Helen Whitman, plus ten Ingram essays on Poe, 1874–78, thus revealing Poe's reputation in the 1870s. But the most documentary record is the 1978 dissertation by Dwight R. Thomas (Pennsylvania), who constructed a detailed chronology, "Poe in Philadelphia, 1838–1844," along with a directory of associates and correspondents of that time and place. At the opposite extreme, the poorly documented biographical study is represented by John E. Walsh's *Plumes in the Dust*, which tries unconvincingly to make a case for Fanny Fay's being the daughter of Poe and Frances Sargent Osgood. Far better than anything since Mabbott's "Annals" is G. R. Thompson's 30,000-word monograph on Poe in the *Dictionary of Literary Biography*. In attempting to show the interrelations among Poe's literary and journalistic writings, Thompson seeks to define the underlying patterns, oppositions, "binaries," and paradoxes, concluding that Poe's "works and his career are brilliant records of that inconclusive quest," the quest for unity. A highly recommended critical survey of Poe biographies from Quinn's (1941) through 1980 is Alexander Hammond's "On Poe Biography: A Review Essay," *ESQ* 28 (3d Quarter 1982): 197–211. In his conclusion Hammond broadly defines the need for a literary or critical biography of Poe that will interweave his intellectual and aesthetic concerns with "the inner tracings of his personality" and its impact on his professional career. In so doing, the biographer-critic will attempt to establish a baseline from which, by a kind of literary parallax, to measure the angle of Poe's vision. Such was the value of the early essays by D. H. Lawrence, Edmund Wilson, and William Carlos Williams and the academic contributions by Killis Campbell, Floyd Stovall, and Geoffrey Rans. These were complemented by a biblical scholar, William Mentzel Forrest, whose *Biblical Allusions in Poe* (1928) provided a solid philosophical and literary analysis of Poe's ideas and style. Unfortunately, probably because of the connotations of its narrow title, it is one of the most neglected valuable works on Poe.

Complementary to Forrest's volume and essays by Lawrence, Wilson, and Williams, in the early 1950s, Auden, Tate, Edward H. Davidson, and Richard Wilbur laid the groundwork for a criticism disciplined by knowledge of Poe's vision. Following them came a record number of first-rate studies dealing with Poe, at least in part: Jay B. Hubbell's *The South in American Literature* (1954), Patrick F. Quinn's *The French Face of Edgar Poe* (1957), including his germinal essay on *Pym*, Harry Levin's *The Power of Blackness* (1958), exploring the "blackness" theme in *Pym* and the tales; Stephen Mooney's "Poe's Gothic Waste Land" and Charles Sanford's "Edgar Allan Poe," both applying a cultural context to clarify Poe's symbolic intent (and both reprinted in Eric W. Carlson's *Recognition*). Wilbur's half dozen essays on Poe—three of them reprinted in *Responses* (see Bibliography)—are models of insight and analysis. His "hypnagogic" interpretation, as presented in "The House of Poe' (1959) and the long introduction to Poe in *Major Writers in America*, has been supplemented by the concept of the "gnostic soul" in his essay on *Pym* (the Godine edition, 1973). Wilbur has closely studied the symbolic intentions of Poe's cosmic myth (in *Eureka* and the colloquies) and his epistemology (in "psychal fancies," "The Poetic Principle"). This perspective approach was followed also in *Poe: A Critical Study* (1957) by Edward H. Davidson, who added a special emphasis on Poe's sense of himself as a social outcast, his romantic solipsism, his invention of a new poetic language, and his treatment of death, eros, and horror. Among anthologists of Poe's writings, Eric W. Carlson, in his *Introduction to Poe: A Thematic Reader* (1966), defined the evolving patterns of Poe's ideas on life and art, suggesting that a study of those patterns precede the reading of the poems and the tales, thus justifying the parallel grouping by genre and theme as a much-needed stimulus to reader realization.

Carlson continued to apply the parallactic "perspective" approach in his 1969 MLA paper, "Poe's Vision of Man" (in *Papers on Poe*, ed. Richard P. Veler), "Poe on the Soul of Man" (1973), and *Poe's "The Fall of the House of Usher"* (Charles Merrill casebook, 1971). In 1967 Carlson edited *The Recognition of*

Edgar Allan Poe: Selected Criticisms since 1829, a chronological gathering of reviews, letters, essays, poems, and lectures, both favorable and unfavorable, ending with James Gargano's perceptive and much-reprinted essay, ''The Question of Poe's Narrators'' (1963). Similar, though less generous, selections were made by Robert Regan and by David B. Kesterson.

Other notable contributions of this time include Stovall's *Edgar Poe the Poet: Essays New and Old on the Man and His Work* (1969), the fruit of many years of research on Poe; Robert D. Jacobs's *Poe: Journalist & Critic* (1969), which, beginning with Poe's Southern imagination as ''matrix,'' traces the development of Poe's theory of poetry, and in chapters 11 and 18, his transcendental epistemology and neoplatonic metaphysic. Burton R. Pollin collected the results of his indefatigable investigation of sources into *Discoveries in Poe* (1970), as did Jean Alexander of historical French criticism of Poe in *Affidavits of Genius* (1971). But the early 1970s mainly gave birth to new approaches and insights in criticism: Richard P. Benton in *New Approaches to Poe*, Stuart G. Levine's *Edgar Poe: Seer and Craftsman*, which saw Poe as both a transcendental thinker and skilled entertainer; Daniel Hoffman's *Poe Poe Poe Poe Poe Poe Poe* suggested the seven faces or facets of Poe's achievement; Richard P. Veler's edition of *Papers on Poe: Essays in Honor of John Ward Ostrom* (1972) presented a wide range of viewpoints in its seventeen contributions by as many Poe scholars; Richard M. Fletcher's *The Stylistic Development of Edgar Allan Poe* (1973), by contrast, left much to be desired. Carl L. Anderson's *Poe in Northlight: The Scandinavian Response to his Life and Work* (1973) came as a welcome report on the long-standing interest in Poe on the part of Strindberg, Hanson, and others. W. T. Bandy edited Baudelaire's essays on Poe in 1973, and in the following year two of the foremost Poe scholars in France and Switzerland had their dissertations published in French: Roger Forclaz, *Le Monde d'Edgar Allan Poe* (1974) and Claude Richard, ed., *Edgar Allan Poe: Journaliste et Critique* (1978). Of the total 962 + i-xxxvi pages, Richard's main text (596 pp.) consists of a detailed discussion of Poe's career as a reviewer and editor, followed by two long chapters on the development of his literary tastes—major sources among essayists, novelists, and poets—and his aesthetics of beauty, imagination, poetry, and tale. Though Jacobs's volume of the same title appeared in 1969, Richard notes that he had completed work on his study by then; nevertheless, he manages a long annotation in his bibliography (p. 708) in which he states that Jacobs's *Poe* is the most important work on the subject. Richard is especially impressed by the last two chapters, notably the excellent analysis of *Eureka* as the logical culmination of Poe's thought process.

When G. R. Thompson's *Poe's Fiction: Romantic Irony in the Gothic Tales* (1973) appeared, it received negative reviews because of its narrow and tendentious argument. It begins with a mistaken definition of the problem, the claim that Poe criticism suffers from a literal gothicism, when in fact by 1972 nearly 30 years of significant criticism had discovered new symbolic dimensions in Poe's writings. Thompson ignored this achievement of the mainstream critics:

Tate, Wilbur, Mooney, Davidson, Jacobs, P. Quinn, Gargano, Stovall, and others—none of them "Gothicist critics." Although Thompson can be lucid and perceptive, he rides his thesis beyond plausibility by twisting the plain sense of some statements of Poe's, by ignoring as basic documents "The Poetic Principle," "psychal fancies," the major poems, and the important concluding dozen paragraphs in *Eureka*, and by giving a badly distorted interpretation of "Ligeia," "Usher," "Mesmeric Revelation," *Eureka*, and the colloquies. To hold that *Eureka* is "Poe's most colossal hoax" flies in the face of overwhelming evidence to the contrary, and to refer to "Mesmeric Revelation," which Poe called a "somewhat detailed" statement of his faith, as "a parody on the beatitudes of the psychal mystics" (p. 260) is as absurd as the final labeling of Poe as an "Absurdist" whose main purpose was to "delude" and "hoax" the reader through the Germanic formula application of "delusive irony," parody, and satire. (As used here, the terms "Romantic Irony" or "Transcendental Irony" are not to be found in Poe.)

Edgar Allan Poe: A Phenomenological View by David Halliburton is the first (and to date only) comprehensive reading of Poe's work in terms of such "unfolding" intentions and concerns as power and powerlessness, victimization, confrontations, and "above all, the need for transcendence and affirmation." The cosmic vision of *Eureka* comes as a sublime culminative affirmation that the universe is God. This emphasis on a positive, transcendent will places Halliburton's critique in the mainstream of Poe criticism. Halliburton is especially insightful in his section on "Tales About Women" as embodying vitality, the will to live, and primal wholeness. These ontological themes are found also in "Usher" and the landscape tales or sketches, the colloquies, and the poems.

Another fine study in the further clarification of the visionary Poe is David Ketterer's *The Rationale of Deception in Poe* (1979). Despite its misnomer of a title and its mistaken conclusion, this work traces the pervasive pattern and theme of the "arabesque" as synonymous with transcendence in subsuming death, horror, and the "grotesque." Most of Ketterer's examples of "deception" are forms of indirection ("the half-closed eye") and not calculated gullings of the reader. In one of the most original and intricately analytical treatises, *American Hieroglyphics: The Symbol of the Egyptian Hieroglyphics in the American Renaissance* (1980), John T. Irwin examines the impact of the decipherment of the Rosetta Stone in the 1820s on Emerson, Thoreau, Whitman, Hawthorne, Melville, and especially Poe. *Eureka*, half a dozen tales, and *Pym* are mined for evidence of the "journey" quest, cannibalism and sacrifice, symbolic death and rebirth, doubling, writing self/written self, the return to oneness, and the ultimate certainty, among other motifs. In the closing philological note of *Pym*, the textual quest for certainty is seen as a death wish. As the writing self within the story, Pym is necessarily blind to the final meaning of the story insofar as it requires a closure synonymous with death, whereas, "the narrative of one's own life is always unfinished."

The opposing views of Poe as either a visionary or an ironist were deliberately joined in a debate between Patrick Quinn and G. R. Thompson over the meaning of the imagery and structures and the reliability of the narrator in "The Fall of the House of Usher," as published in *Ruined Eden of the Present: Hawthorne, Melville, and Poe*, eds. G. R. Thompson and Virgil L. Lokke (1981). Quinn seems to have much better of the argument here. In *The Naiad Voice: Essays on Poe's Satiric Hoaxing* (1983), Dennis W. Eddings offers a reprinting of fourteen journal articles (1954–77) by various hands and a concluding plea for the dubious notion that Poe's comic satires and hoaxes are integral to and unified with Poe's serious work, thus blurring the distinction between the comic satire and the serious Gothic fiction. A far more representative selection is to be found in the *Poe-Purri* issue of *University of Mississippi Studies in English*, edited by Benjamin Franklin Fisher IV (1982), with useful incomplete, short surveys of Poe criticism by Benton and Fisher; papers by Richard Wilbur on "Poe and the Art of Suggestion"; Kent Ljungquist on the picturesque; David Hirsch on "Metzengerstein"; James Gargano on "Usher"; John E. Reilly on Sarah Helen Whitman; Joan Dayan on "Landor's Cottage"; to cite a few—each critic a specialist on his subject.

In Poe studies, specialization has increased, with both good and bad results. As noted above, the fallacy of the "Romantic Irony" and "hoaxing" thesis lies in the claims that Poe's perspective was one of "duplicity" toward his reader and that an absurdist irony and satire characterize both his comic and his serious gothic fiction. But this modish preoccupation has shifted to new approaches in literary criticism generally, each of which has its proponents in Poe studies: fantasy in Poe's work, as presented in papers at conferences in Florida and California (the latter published in *Bridges to Fantasy*, edited by George E. Slusser, Eric S. Rabkin, and Robert Scholes, 1982) and in *Survey of Modern Fantasy Literature*, edited by Frank N. Magill (1983); Poe's use of the supernatural, by J. Gerald Kennedy and Barton Levi St. Armand in *The Haunted Dusk* (1983); the Jungian interpretation, as in *The Unsounded Centre* (1980) by Martin Bickman; Gnosticism, alchemy, as well as Jungian psychology, in the readings of Poe by St. Armand; the "picturesque" in Poe's landscapes as studied by Kent Ljungquist, Dayan, Edward Pitcher; Poe's humor and style, by Donald Stauffer; Poe's use of enclosure in his fiction by Leonard Engel; Poe's impressionism and "modernism," as expounded by Kronegger, Stauffer, and Carlson; in addition, special studies of Poe's text and its revisions by Benjamin F. Fisher IV, of *Pym* by Richard Kopley and by Douglas Robinson (review of *Pym* criticism, *Poe Studies* 15:47–54) and in Richard Benton's symposium; of *Eureka* by Dayan and in a symposium by Benton; of the early poems, by Robert Jacobs and G. R. Thompson; of "Usher" by Gargano and others. The reader-response theory has been applied to Poe by Joan Dayan, David Saliba, and Judith Sutherland in *The Problematic Fictions of Poe, James, & Hawthorne* (1984), but less so than in the "structuralist" approach of Derrida and Lacan to "The Purloined Letter," first reported by Barbara Johnson at the English Institute and reviewed by Donald Pease in *Poe Studies* 16:18–23, along with a survey of recent Poe criticism in France by Henri Justin, *Poe Studies* 16:25–31. The most recent deconstructionist critiques are by Jefferson Humphries in *Metamorphoses of the Raven* (1985) and by Louis A. Renza in "Poe's Secret Autobiography" (*The American Renaissance Reconsidered*, 1985). On these publications, more specific data, bibliography and evaluation may be found in *Poe Studies* (Washington State University), in the *Poe Studies Association Newsletter*, in the Poe chapter of the annual *American Literary Scholarship*, and in *Critical Essays on Edgar Allan Poe*, ed. Eric W. Carlson (Boston: G. K. Hall, 1986).

BIBLIOGRAPHY

Works by Edgar Allan Poe

For Poe's works as published in his lifetime under his supervision, see initial "Biography" section. See also Charles F. Heartman and James R. Canny, *A Bibliography of First Printings of the Writings of Edgar Allan Poe*. rev. ed. Hattiesburg, Miss.: Book Farm, 1943.

Books Published During Poe's Life

Tamerlane and Other Poems. By a Bostonian. Boston: Calvin F. S. Thomas, 1827.
Al Aaraaf, Tamerlane, and Minor Poems. Baltimore: Hatch & Dunning, 1829.
Poems by Edgar A. Poe. Second Edition. New York: Elam Bliss, 1831.
The Narrative of Arthur Gordon Pym. New York: Harper and Brothers, 1838.
Tales of the Grotesque and Arabesque. 2 vols. Philadelphia: Lea and Blanchard, 1840.
The Raven and Other Poems. New York: Wiley and Putnam, 1845.
Tales by Edgar A. Poe. New York: Wiley and Putnam, 1845.
Eureka: A Prose Poem by Edgar A. Poe. New York: Putnam, 1848.

Editions

Works of Edgar Allan Poe, with Notices of his Life and Genius. Ed. Rufus Wilmot Griswold. 4 vols. New York: J. S. Redfield, 1850–56.
The Works of Edgar Allan Poe. Ed. E. C. Stedman and G. E. Woodberry. 10 vols. Chicago: Stone and Kimball, 1894–95.
The Complete Works of Edgar Allan Poe. Ed. James A. Harrison. 17 vols. New York: Thomas Y. Crowell, 1902. Known as the "Virginia Edition."
Doings of Gotham, as described in a series of letters to the editors of the Columbia Spy [1844], *together with various editorial comments and criticisms by Poe now first collected*. Comp. Jacob E. Spannuth with an introduction by Thomas Olive Mabbott. Pottsville, Pa.: Jacob E. Spannuth, 1929.
The Letters of Edgar Allan Poe. Ed. John Ward Ostrom. 2 vols. Cambridge: Harvard University Press, 1948; republished with three supplements, Gordian Press, 1966; fourth supplement, *American Literature* 45 (January 1974): 513–36. See also Ostrom's "Revised Checklist of the Correspondence of Edgar Allan Poe" in *Studies in the American Renaissance: 1981*, pp. 169–225.
The Poems of Edgar Allan Poe. Ed. Floyd Stovall. Charlottesville: University Press of Virginia, 1965.

Collected Works of Edgar Allan Poe. Ed. Thomas Olive Mabbott. 3 vols.; 1, *Poems* (1969); 2–3, *Tales and Sketches* (1978). Cambridge: Belknap Press of Harvard University Press, 1969–78.

Collected Writings of Edgar Allan Poe. Vol. 1, *The Imaginary Voyages: The Narrative of Arthur Gordon Pym, The Unparalleled Adventure of One Hans Pfaall, The Journal of Julius Rodman.* Ed. Burton R. Pollin. Boston: Twayne, 1981. Vol. 2, *The Brevities of Edgar Allan Poe.* New York: Gordian Press, 1985.

Selections from the Critical Writings of Edgar Allan Poe. Ed. F. C. Prescott. New York: Holt, 1909. Repr. with new preface by J. Lasley Dameron and new introduction by Eric W. Carlson. New York: Gordian Press, 1981.

Edgar Allan Poe: Poetry and Tales. Ed. Patrick F. Quinn. New York: Library of America, 1984.

Studies of Edgar Allan Poe

Bibliographies

Dameron, J. Lasley and Irby B. Cauthen, Jr. *Edgar Allan Poe: A Bibliography of Criticism 1827–1967.* Charlottesville: University Press of Virginia, 1974.

Ebans, Mary G. *Music and Edgar Allan Poe: A Bibliographical Study.* Baltimore: Johns Hopkins University Press, 1939.

Hyneman, Esther K. *Edgar Allan Poe: An Annotated Bibliography of Books and Articles in English, 1827–1973.* Boston: G. K. Hall, 1974.

Pollin, Burton R. "More Music to Poe." *Music and Letters* 44 (Oct. 1973): 391–404. "Music and Edgar Allan Poe: A Second Annotated Checklist." *Poe Studies* 15 (June 1982): 7–13.

Indexes and Concordances

Booth, Bradford A. and Claude E. Jones. *A Concordance to the Poetical Works of Edgar Allan Poe.* Baltimore: Johns Hopkins University Press, 1941.

Dameron, J. Lasley and Louis Charles Stagg. *An Index to Poe's Critical Vocabulary.* Hartford, Conn.: Transcendental Books, 1966.

Pollin, Burton R. *Dictionary of Names and Titles of Poe's Collected Works.* New York: Da Capo Books, 1968.

———. *Poe, Creator of Words.* rev. and augmented ed. Bronxville, N.Y.: Nicholas T. Smith, 1980.

———. "Poe's Word Coinage: A Supplement." *Poe Studies* 16 (Dec. 1983): 39–40.

———. *Word Index to Poe's Fiction.* New York: Gordian Press, 1982.

Reilly, John E. *A Calendar and an Index to the Ingram Poe Collection at the University of Virginia.* 2d ed., 1986.

Biographies

Allen, Hervey. *Israfel: The Life and Times of Edgar Allan Poe.* 2 vols. New York: Doran, 1926.

Bittner, William. *Poe: A Biography.* Boston: Little, Brown, 1962.

Bonaparte, Marie. *The Life and Works of Edgar Allan Poe: A Psychoanalytic Interpretation.* Trans. John Rodker. London: Imago, 1949. French ed., Paris, 1933.

Griswold, Rufus Wilmont. "Memoir of the Author." *The Works of the Late Edgar Allan Poe*. New York: J. S. Redfield, 1850. 3, vii-xxxix.

Ingram, John H. *Edgar Allan Poe: His Life, Letters and Opinions*. 2 vols. London: John Hogg, 1880.

Krutch, Joseph Wood. *Edgar Allan Poe: A Study in Genius*. New York: Knopf, 1926.

Mabbott, Thomas O. "Annals of Poe's Life." *Collected Works of Edgar Allan Poe*. Cambridge: Belknap Press of Harvard University Press, 1969–78. 1, 527–72.

Mankowitz, Wolf. *The Extraordinary Mr. Poe*. New York: Summit Books (Simon & Schuster), 1978.

Miller, John Carl, ed. *Building Poe Biography*. Baton Rouge: Louisiana State University Press, 1977.

———. *Poe's Helen Remembers*. Charlottesville: University Press of Virginia, 1979.

Moss, Sidney P. *Poe's Literary Battles: The Critic in the Context of His Literary Milieu*. Durham: Duke University Press, 1963.

———. *Poe's Major Crisis: His Libel Suit and New York's Literary World*. Durham: Duke University Press, 1970.

Phillips, Mary E. *Edgar Allan Poe, the Man*. 2 vols. Chicago: John C. Winston, 1926.

Quinn, Arthur Hobson. *Edgar Allan Poe: A Critical Biography*. New York: D. Appleton-Century, 1941; New York: Cooper Square, 1970.

Symons, Julian. *The Tell-Tale Heart: The Life and Works of Edgar Allan Poe*. New York: Harper & Row, 1978.

Thomas, Dwight R. "Poe in Philadelphia, 1838–1844: A Documentary Record." Ph.D. diss., University of Pennsylvania, 1978.

Thompson, G. R. "Edgar Allan Poe." *Antebellum Writers in New York and the South*. Ed. Joel Myerson. Vol. 3 of *Dictionary of Literary Biography*. Detroit: Gale Research, 1979, pp. 249–97.

Wagenknecht, Edward. *Edgar Allan Poe: The Man Behind the Legend*. New York: Oxford University Press, 1963.

Walsh, John E. *Plumes in the Dust: The Love Affair of Edgar Allan Poe and Fanny Osgood*. Chicago: Nelson Hall, 1980.

Whitman, Sarah Helen. *Edgar Poe and His Critics*. New York: Rudd & Carleton, 1860; New Brunswick: Rutgers University Press, 1949; New York: Gordian Press, 1981.

Winwar, Frances. *The Haunted Palace; A Life of Edgar Allan Poe*. New York: Harper, 1959.

Woodberry, George Edward. *The Life of Edgar Allan Poe, Personal and Literary*. 2 vols. Boston: Houghton Mifflin, 1909.

Critical Studies

Alexander, Jean, ed. *Affidavits of Genius. Edgar Allan Poe and the French Critics, 1847–1924*. Port Washington, N.Y.: Kennikat, 1971.

Allen, Michael. *Poe and the British Magazine Tradition*. New York: Oxford University Press, 1969.

Alterton, Margaret. *The Origins of Poe's Critical Theory*. Iowa City: University of Iowa, 1925.

Anderson, Carl L. *Poe in Northlight: The Scandinavian Response to His Life and Work*. Durham: Duke University Press, 1973.

Bandy, W. T., ed. *Edgar Allan Poe, sa vie et ses ouvrages* by Charles Baudelaire. Toronto: University of Toronto Press, 1973.

Benton, Richard P., ed. *New Approaches to Poe: A Symposium*. Hartford, Conn.: Transcendental Books, 1970.

———. *Poe as Literary Cosmologer: Studies on Eureka. A Symposium*. Hartford, Conn.: Transcendental Books, 1975.

Bickman, Martin. *The Unsounded Centre: Jungian Studies in American Romanticism*. Chapel Hill: University of North Carolina Press, 1980.

Buranelli, Vincent. *Edgar Allan Poe*. rev. ed. Boston: Twayne, 1977.

Cambiaire, Celestin. *The Influence of Edgar Allan Poe in France*. New York: G. E. Stechert, 1927.

Campbell, Killis. *The Mind of Poe and Other Studies*. Cambridge: Harvard University Press, 1933.

Carlson, Eric W., ed. *The Recognition of Edgar Allan Poe: Selected Criticism Since 1829*. Ann Arbor: University of Michigan Press, 1966.

Davidson, Edward H. *Poe: A Critical Study*. Cambridge: Harvard University Press, 1957.

Eddings, Dennis W., ed. *The Naiad Voice: Essays on Poe's Satiric Hoaxing*. Port Washington, N.Y.: Associated Faculty Press, 1983.

Fagin, N. Bryllion. *The Histrionic Mr. Poe*. Baltimore: Johns Hopkins University Press, 1949.

Fisher, Benjamin Franklin IV, ed. *Poe at Work: Seven Textual Studies*. Baltimore: Edgar Allan Poe Society, 1978.

———, ed. "Poe-Purri:" Edgar Allan Poe Issue of *University of Mississippi Studies in English*. n. s. 3 (1982).

Fletcher, Richard M. *The Development of Edgar Allan Poe*. The Hague: Mouton, 1973.

Forclaz, Roger. *Le Monde d'Edgar Allan Poe*. Berne: Herbert Lang; Frankfurt: Peter Lang, 1974.

Forrest, William Mentzel. *Biblical Allusions in Poe*. New York: Macmillan, 1928.

Halliburton, David. *Edgar Allan Poe: A Phenomenological View*. Princeton: Princeton University Press, 1973.

Hammond, Alexander. "On Poe Biography: A Review Essay." *Emerson Society Quarterly* 28 (3d Quarter 1982): 197–211.

Harris, Laurie Lanzen, ed. *Nineteenth-Century Literary Criticism*, Vol. 1. Detroit: Gale Research, 1981.

Hoffman, Daniel. *Poe Poe Poe Poe Poe Poe Poe*. Garden City, N.Y.: Doubleday, 1972.

Humphries, Jefferson. *Metamorphoses of the Raven: Literary Overdeterminedness in France and the South Since Poe*. Baton Rouge: Louisiana State University Press, 1985.

Hyslop, Lois Boe and Francis E. Hyslop, Jr., eds. *Baudelaire as a Literary Critic*. Introd. and trans. by the authors. University Park: Pennsylvania State University Press, 1964.

Irwin, John T. *American Hieroglyphics: The Symbol of the Egyptian Hieroglyphics in the American Renaissance*. New Haven: Yale University Press, 1980.

Jacobs, Robert D. *Poe: Journalist & Critic*. Baton Rouge: Louisiana State University Press, 1969.

Kesterson, David B., ed. *Critics of Poe*. Coral Gables: University of Miami Press, 1973.

Ketterer, David. *The Rationale of Deception in Poe*. Baton Rouge: Louisiana State University Press, 1979.

Levin, Harry. *The Power of Blackness: Hawthorne, Poe, Melville*. New York: Knopf, 1958.

Levine, Stuart G. *Edgar Poe: Seer and Craftsman*. Deland, Fla.: Everett/Edwards, 1972.

Link, Franz H. *Edgar Allan Poe: Ein Dichter zwischen Romantik und Moderne*. Frankfurt am Main: Atheneum Verlag, 1968.

Ljungquist, Kent. *The Grand and the Fair: Poe's Landscape Aesthetics and Pictorial Techniques*. Potomac, Md.: Scripta Humanistica, 1984.

Magill, Frank N., ed. *Survey of Modern Fantasy Literature*. Englewood Cliffs, N.J.: Salem Press, 1983.

Parks, Edd Winfield. *Edgar Allan Poe as a Literary Critic*. Athens: University of Georgia Press, 1964.

Phillips, Elizabeth. *Edgar Allan Poe: An American Imagination—Three Essays*. Port Washington, N.Y.: Kennikat Press, 1979.

Pollin, Burton R. *Discoveries in Poe*. Notre Dame, Ind.: University of Notre Dame Press, 1970.

Quinn, Patrick F. *The French Face of Edgar Poe*. Carbondale: Southern Illinois University Press, 1957.

Rans, Geoffrey. *Edgar Allan Poe*. Edinburgh and London: Oliver and Boyd, 1965.

Regan, Robert, ed. *Poe: A Collection of Critical Essays*. Englewood Cliffs, N.J.: Prentice-Hall, 1967.

Richard, Claude, ed. *Edgar Allan Poe: Journaliste et Critique*. Paris: Klincksieck Press, 1978.

Slusser, George E., Eric S. Rabkin, and Robert Scholes, ed. *Bridges to Fantasy*. Carbondale: Southern Illinois University Press, 1982.

Stovall, Floyd. *Edgar Poe the Poet: Essays New and Old on the Man and His Work*. Charlottesville: University Press of Virginia, 1969.

Sutherland, Judith L. *The Problematic Fictions of Poe, James, and Hawthorne*. Columbia, Mo.: University of Missouri Press, 1984.

Thompson, G. R. *Poe's Fiction: Romantic Irony in the Gothic Tales*. Madison: University of Wisconsin Press, 1973.

Thompson, G. R. and Virgil L. Lokke, eds. *Ruined Eden of the Present: Hawthorne, Melville, Poe: Critical Essays in Honor of Darrel Abel*. Lafayette, Ind.: Purdue University Press, 1981.

Veler, Richard P., ed. *Papers on Poe: Essays in Honor of John Ward Ostrom*. Springfield, Ohio: Chantry Music Press at Wittenberg University, 1972.

Walsh, John. *Poe the Detective: The Curious Circumstances Behind "The Mystery of Marie Roget."* New Brunswick, N.J.: Rutgers University Press, 1968.

Wilbur, Richard. "The House of Poe." *Anniversary Lectures 1959*. Washington, D.C.: Reference Department of the Library of Congress, 1959; repr. in *Recognition of Edgar Allan Poe*, ed. E. W. Carlson.

———. Introduction and Notes to *Poe*. The Laurel Poetry Series. New York: Dell, 1959.

———. *Responses: Prose Pieces, 1953–1976*. New York: Harcourt Brace Jovanovich, 1976. Includes "Edgar Allan Poe," 1962; "The Poe Mystery Case," 1967; "The Narrative of Arthur Gordon Pym," 1973.

Irwin Russell
(1853–1879)

In his brief and self-consuming race towards death, Irwin Russell created the small body of poems that make his place in Southern literature as the explorer of Negro dialect poetry, a genre that previously existed only in scattered poems. Russell's development of his subject, the black man—and sometimes woman—caught in a limbo somewhere between slavery and freedom, earned him the approval of Joel Chandler Harris and Thomas Nelson Page.

BIOGRAPHY

The tragicomic romance of doomed youth found in fragmentary letters and recollections of Irwin Russell chronicles adventures at times heroic, at times pathetic and absurd. This hero of a romance, dying young out of it, is a boy who comes easily and early by his talent, but who despite ambition—to write a "Negro novel," to explore the black imagination and character in drama, prose, and poetry—never finds the strength of body and will necessary to realize his dreams.

Russell's childhood is a collection of adversities. His physician father could not keep his three-month-old child from yellow fever; his mother, a former teacher, was a woman of delicate health who nursed in Irwin a love of books and a spirit that rebelled against the heavy shade of her protection. He never resolved the mingled guilt and affection he felt towards his family.

Russell's life appears as a thread snipped early, but frayed from the beginning. While a small child he blinded himself in one eye with a fork. Elizabeth Allen Russell could not shadow him everywhere, although she kept him from rough play, exercise, and fresh air. As a young man he appeared slight, hollow chested, and myopic. With his false teeth clicking and the "scattered tufts" of a beard he once cultivated, Russell must have cut an odd figure, although his friends praised his charm, sweetness, and the "magnetic" lights of those dim eyes.

Most of Russell's childhood was spent in Port Gibson, Mississippi, where he was born 3 June 1853, although from later that year until the Civil War he lived in St. Louis. The child who read Milton at six grew up to be a mischievous and emotional young man. His lively pen ensnared young ladies who had met him only on paper. He fell in love twice, but never married; after parting with his first love, he was later to see her dying of yellow fever. Love, poetry, and adventure stirred him. The poet who would toss off a poem with, alas, little or no revision was the same young man who would impulsively "go West" only to return quickly under the pressure of hardship and ill health. Once he ran away, not to sea but to a sailors' boardinghouse. He was known as wayward, moody, and a "victim" of alcohol. The other side of his coin was kindness, a love of poetry and banjo music, and a fondness for fun. His most famous and costly prank was an invitation, signed with a false name, to suffragette Mary Walker. Dr. Walker arrived in Port Gibson clad in trousers and flowering hat, followed by an admiring troop of children, one thumping on a drum.

During these years a whirlwind of interests tossed him. At the University of St. Louis he was reported brilliant in "higher mathematics" and the "science of navigation." He returned home, read law, and was admitted to the bar by a special act of the legislature. He was only nineteen. He never brought a case to court; the law was not "congenial" to his spirit. Instead he made many false starts, but late in 1877 turned back to the law. The next summer when the yellow fever epidemic of 1878 devastated Port Gibson, it came for Russell as something to which he could devote himself. None of the pathos and comedy of Russell's life can take away from the simple heroism of a man, still almost a boy, who fed and comforted the ill and dying, dug graves for a family of children, or sat up with a dead baby all night because the mother feared to think of it lying alone. When the fever died away, 350 people in Port Gibson and the surrounding county were dead.

Russell broke from home after the epidemic and attempted to establish himself in New York. Before the fever, Russell tried printing and wrote a "farce comedy," now lost. From Port Gibson he had published poems in *Scribner's Monthly*, but in New York he became a frequent contributor, encouraged by Richard Watson Gilder and Underwood Johnson. Johnson and Henry C. Bunner of *Puck* cared for Russell when he grew ill—already an alcoholic, Russell had been weakened by his labor during the epidemic.

After only six months in New York, Russell determined to return south. The trip once again meant trials and near tragedy for him. In strained health he worked his way to New Orleans as a steamer's coal heaver. The now rootless man earned a place on the New Orleans *Times* staff with an account of his trip south. Alone in New Orleans, he refused to ask for help from his friends or family, who did not know how ill stress and drinking had made him. Dr. William McNab Russell had died during his son's absence, and Mrs. Russell and her daughters had departed for California, one of the many goals in the West that Irwin Russell never reached.

The creative and the destructive twined equally in his character, and both were present in his final days. He spoke of his own life then as a "romance," one in which the love of mother, a girl, and friends was not enough to save him from himself. He had made of his life a book, one which now hastened its readers to the inevitable and necessary close. He died, worn out, under the care of his poor Irish landlady. With a final bit of poignancy Russell would have loved, some say that letters arrived from his mother and sweetheart, but that he was already delirious, rushing towards death. The romance was over, two days before Christmas 1879, but once again, Russell could not rest easy. Buried in New Orleans, his body was later removed to St. Louis.

MAJOR THEMES

Russell's expressed ambitions centered on his conception of the uniqueness and value of the black character, a territory of life Russell saw as unplowed ground. His published and unpublished work also contains album pieces and occasional poems; "Irish" dialect poems; comic and serious ballads; tales of yellow fever; narratives that mock pedants, scholars, lawyers, and politicians; imitations of Burns and Herrick; and late lyrics that reveal a submission to death and anonymity, reminding the reader of his Catholic faith and ill health. But Russell's best poems are those dealing with black figures.

In his introduction to Russell's poems Joel Chandler Harris praised the happy delineation of "the old-fashioned, unadulterated negro, who is still dear to the Southern heart." Before his death Russell was fired with the wish to create what he called the "Negro novel," never written. His comedy has been lost. Letters reveal his conception of a black people filled with unregarded virtues, and at whose vices a reader may smile. But the poems Harris called a "perfect" picture of black life remain; they display a curious vision.

Russell once wrote in a letter that the black soul must find its way to freedom, and the black people he describes in poems are caught somewhere between plantation life and independence. These good-humored types still show deference to the white man, although they are capable of impudence and a kind of innocent scoundrel's behavior, ready to dupe a white boy with a dog or a white man with a bale of cotton ballasted with rocks. The white man is still master of situations and detects all subterfuge. Still the black man goes on laughing at "gemmen" who reel in spades and hearts instead of fish, or at "Norvern" folks who don't know just how good possum and gumbo can be. There is a kind of genial family feud between the former slave and the old master, who may fill a stick with gunpowder to tease his unreconstructed and childlike neighbor for stealing from his woodpile. In these poems if there is anyone injured it is not the cartoon black man, further blackened by soot from the explosion of this harmless "joke," but Russell's aging black people who do not know what to do with freedom, or the old master, now ruined, who remains a source of pride to his ex-slave. There are new dangers, and from within; a black version of Polonius will warn his adventurous son against life on the river and "low-minded roustabout niggers." These shrewd but superstitious children, lovers of music and dance, are familiar stereotypes.

Russell thought his types "Original in act and thought, / Because unlearned and untaught," as he wrote in his best-known poem, "Christmas-Night in the Quarters," a poem in couplets that juxtaposes white admiration of simple virtues with dialect voices. In this and other poems a distinct voice for black characters is established, one dependent on exaggeration, paradox, homely metaphor, and aphorism for its exposé of black wisdom and innocence.

The comparisons made between black and white, earthly and heavenly life suggest the ambiguities present in Russell's portrait of blacks caught between freedom and chains. His black preachers evoke an Eden that is a garden of the soul, guarded by an "oberseer" angel. The Jordan lies just beyond a sleep, and angels fly from its borders to the soul, lifting it from a world the white man still oversees to the heavenly realm of the "Mahsr."

SURVEY OF CRITICISM

A glance at Russell's plentiful publications in *Scribner's*, *St. Nicholas*, *Puck*, and other magazines shows that he was regarded as one of that perennial and hopeful variety, the promising young writer. Although Russell's output was slim, Joel Chandler Harris thought enough of his dialect poems to launch the 1888 posthumous *Poems* with an introduction that praised Russell's "bold and striking" poems. Russell's reputation increased after his death, his poems finding place in William P. Trent's *Southern Writers*; Joel Chandler Harris and Edwin A. Alderman's *Library of Southern Literature*; Stark Young's *Southern Treasury*; Richard Beale Davis, C. Hugh Holman, and Louis D. Rubin, Jr.'s *Southern Writing*; and many other collections.

Appreciation of Russell's work has proved modest but steady, focusing on the poet's places among his contemporaries. Critical surveys such as Thomas Daniel Young, Floyd C. Watkins, and Richmond Croom Beatty's *The Literature of the South* link Russell with Harris and Thomas Nelson Page, and assert that the poet was the first to realize the literary potential of his subject. Many writers note Russell's connection to Harris; Jay B. Hubbell clarifies Russell's relation to Page in *The South in American Literature*. Beyond surveys and anthologies are a number of shorter works that declare him the pioneer in Negro dialect poetry. A corrective to this view is L. Moody Simms, Jr.'s placement of Russell in company with Poe, Simms, Kennedy, and others. Going beyond the depiction of black characters, Simms turns to the issue of dialect and reminds his readers that Thomas Dunn English, Sherwood Bonner, and Sidney and Clifford Lanier were Russell's predecessors in Negro dialect poetry. Yet in his interest in and exploration of this genre Russell surpassed these writers.

A reader of critical comment devoted to Russell discovers little worth dwelling on. Not only are there few efforts to elucidate Russell's interests and relation to his peers, but the life itself is obscured by gossip and legends. Dates, events, and motivations are described variously, especially where they concern the self-destructive passages of the poet's life. Most biographical sketches turn back and add little to Charles C. Marble's early recollections in *The Critic*, although John S. Kendall's report of Russell in New Orleans is useful. A reader who wishes to piece together the life, unpublished work, and the early appreciation of Russell should turn to Laura D. S. Harrell's bibliographic checklist.

BIBLIOGRAPHY

Works by Irwin Russell

Poems. New York: Century, 1888.
Poems. New York: Century, 1888. [The second edition contains an additional poem, "Going."]
"The Unpublished Verse of Irwin Russell." Ed. Alfred Allen Kern. *South Atlantic Quarterly* 11 (1912): 244–50.
Christmas Night in the Quarters. Kansas City, Mo.: W. O. Graham, Art Craft, 1913.
Christmas Night in the Quarters and Other Poems by Irwin Russell with an Introduction by Joel Chandler Harris and an Historical Sketch by Maurice Garland Fulton. New York: Century, 1917.

Studies of Irwin Russell

Baskervill, Willliam Malone. *Southern Writers: Biographical and Critical Studies*. Vol. 1. Nashville: Methodist Episcopal Church, South, 1897.
Harrell, Laura D. S. "A Bibliography of Irwin Russell, with a Biographical Sketch." *Journal of Mississippi History* 8 (1946): 3–23.
Holman, Harriet R. "Irwin Russell (1853–1879)." *A Bibliographical Guide to the Study of Southern Literature*. Ed. Louis D. Rubin, Jr. Baton Rouge: Louisiana State University Press, 1969.
Kendall, John S. "Irwin Russell in New Orleans." *Louisiana Historical Quarterly* 14 (July 1931): 321–45.
Kern, Alfred Allen. "Biographical Notes on Irwin Russell." *Texas Review* 2 (October 1916): 140–49.
Marble, Charles C. "Irwin Russell." *The Critic: A Weekly Review of Literature and the Arts* n.s. 10 (27 October 1888): 199–200 [accompanied by an unsigned review, "Irwin Russell's Poems," pp. 200–201] and (3 November 1888): 213–14.
Musgrove, Maggie Williams. "Memories of Irwin Russell and His Home in Port Gibson." New Orleans *Daily Picayune*, 2 June 1907, sec. 3, p. 11.
Nott, William G. "Irwin Russell, First Dialect Author." *Southern Literary Messenger* 1 (December 1939): 809–14.
Schuman, R. Baird. "Irwin Russell's Christmas." *Mississippi Quarterly* 15 (1962): 81–84.

Simms, L. Moody, Jr. "Irwin Russell and Negro Dialect Poetry: A Note on Chronological Priority and True Significance." *Notes on Mississippi Writers* 2 (Fall 1969): 67–73.

Webb, James Wilson. "Russell, Irwin: 1853–1879." *Lives of Mississippi Authors, 1817–1967*. Ed. James B. Lloyd. Jackson: University Press of Mississippi, 1981, pp. 397–98.

———. "New Biographical Material, Criticism, and Uncollected Writings of Irwin Russell." M.A. thesis, University of North Carolina at Chapel Hill, 1940.

Weber, W. L. "Irwin Russell—Firstfruits of the Southern Romantic Movement." *Mississippi Historical Society Publications* 2 (1889): 15–22.

MARY ANN WIMSATT

William Gilmore Simms
(1806–1870)

A generous, impetuous, outspoken, and volatile man; a planter, politician, and vigorous proponent of Southern concerns; Willliam Gilmore Simms epitomizes the literary and cultural life of the antebellum South. From 1825 to 1870 he produced poetry, fiction, drama, histories, biographies, essays, and orations in great quantities, meanwhile actively engaging in Southern politics, editing Southern newspapers and magazines, befriending fellow writers North and South, and tirelessly promoting Southern literature in all its branches. The author of nearly 80 books, with perhaps 20 more volumes of uncollected writing, he remains the chief exemplar of the literary vocation in the South before 1865.

Simms's work has slipped from public gaze, and few academicians know about his career; yet he is an author whose life and literary productions are well worth bringing back into view. Much of his personal energy, humor, and charm found their way into his writing, which, viewed as a whole, presents a lively and detailed picture of Southern civilization from the late seventeenth century through the Civil War.

BIOGRAPHY

William Gilmore Simms was born in Charleston, South Carolina, on 17 April 1806, to a mother with ties to Virginia gentlefolk and a father who had immigrated to South Carolina from Ireland during boyhood. Simms's mother died in childbirth when he was not yet two, and his father, declaring in a memorable phrase that Charleston was for him ''a place of tombs'' (Trent, p. 4), left South Carolina to become a cavalry officer under Andrew Jackson. After many adventures, he made his way to Mississippi, where he built up a reasonably prosperous plantation and remained for the rest of his life.

The boy Simms was reared in Charleston by his maternal grandmother, Jane

Miller Singleton Gates, who had lived through the Revolutionary War and who nourished Simms's imagination by her tales of it, ghosts, his family, and the proud Carolina past. In fact, Mrs. Gates, with her lively storytelling powers, may be credited with starting her grandson on the road to authorship. She also, by Simms's testimony, mismanaged his inheritance and stinted his education. He attended the city schools, which he called "worthless and scoundrelly" (Trent, p. 5), and the College of Charleston, which he entered at about the age of ten and where he remained for nearly two years, reading medicine and studying languages. The family, though comfortable, was not wealthy; and his grandmother took him out of school when he was twelve to apprentice him to a druggist, hoping thereby to prepare him for a career in medicine.

From his upbringing in Charleston, and particularly from his grandmother, Simms acquired a strong sense of tradition, a respect for Southern culture, an abiding commitment to low-country or Tidewater values, and an overwhelming interest in the Revolutionary War. From his grandmother he also apparently inherited an imperious disposition and in personal relationships a tendency to obtuseness that would cause him some trouble in later life. These features of his personality were crossed and made complex by elements deriving from his father—a Celtic temperament, merry and despondent by turns; enormous verbal fluency and a flair for many kinds of literary expression; impatience; rebelliousness; a tendency toward restless dissatisfaction with his circumstances; and perhaps an inability to judge his talents wisely. Such contrasting qualities of the boy's nature help explain some causes of his misfortunes in mature professional life and suggest some bases in personality for the diversity of his writing.

Simms's father, once settled in Mississippi, tried to persuade his son to move there, but the ten-year-old boy chose to remain with his grandmother. He later made several trips to the Gulf South, a fact that affected the many books he wrote. The first and most important of these trips came in 1824–25, when, as a youth of eighteen, he spent several months with his father exploring wild and primitive Indian territory on horseback, at times traveling several hundred miles beyond the Mississippi River. His father urged him to remain in the region, promising financial success and a seat in Congress while predicting that Charleston Simms's talents would be "poured out like water on the sands" (Trent, p. 17). But Simms was apparently already engaged to Anna Malcolm Giles, a Charleston girl he had known for some years, and so he returned there to marry in 1826. His father died in 1830, and the following year Simms returned to Mississippi to settle the estate, thereby viewing the Gulf South near the beginning of the flush times and storing up impressions for his later writing about it.

By his middle twenties Simms had already been exposed to two great regions of the South, the low country or Tidewater—civilized, patrician, elegant—and the Gulf or lower South in its pioneer and settlement stages. Throughout his life he would amplify these experiences through reading, travel, and reflection as he drew repeatedly upon them for his writing. They formed the basis for his mature view of Southern culture; they sinewed his histories, biographies, poems, essays, and orations; and they gave rise to the two major streams of his fiction—romances, tales, and short novels, from *The Yemassee* to *The Cassique of Kiawah*, set in the low country and tracing its development from the seventeenth century through the Revolution and the antebellum period; and novels and tales, from *Guy Rivers* to *Voltmeier*, describing the settlement of the Gulf and mountain South.

Simms, who had meanwhile left the druggist's shop for law, had, in 1827, been admitted to the bar. He had also begun to write in earnest. From about the age of eight onward, he had turned out poetry, drama, and short fiction in profusion, publishing some of his early productions in Charleston magazines (*The Album* and the *Southern Literary Gazette*) that he edited or helped to edit. His first publication in book form was the stately couplet poem called *Monody, on the Death of Gen. Charles Cotesworth Pinckney* (1825), which commemorates the scion of a Carolina family that had figured prominently in the Revolutionary War. Hard on the heels of this book came further volumes of poetry showing the young author's astonishing fluency and his wide range of subjects and verse forms—*Lyrical and Other Poems* (1827), *Early Lays* (1827), *The Vision of Cortes, Cain, and Other Poems* (1829), *The Tri-Color* (1830), and *Atalantis. A Story of the Sea* (1832). Revealing his debt to John Milton, Alexander Pope, William Collins, William Wordsworth, Lord Byron, Sir Walter Scott, and William Cullen Bryant, these books contain topographical poems in the eighteenth-century manner, sprightly love lyrics, meditative blank verse, and galloping stanzas on Scripture and ancient foreign history. *Atalantis*, in particular, was well received; and by the early 1830s Simms, who had gradually abandoned law in order to write, was headed toward popular authordom. By the end of that decade, he had become a committed professional man of letters subject to vicissitudes of the economy, vagaries of the book trade, and inevitable shifts in literary taste. In the most active years of his professional life, he first hoped to conquer, and finally fought to stay alive in, a mixed and perilous book market that witnessesd the steady expansion of readership and consequently of the literary canon, with some attendant cheapening and lowering of literary taste.

Simms's numerous and varied works of the 1830s may be seen as an attempt to blend personal experience with knowledge gained from reading and travel. He tried to synthesize this knowledge in culturally sanctioned and marketable forms of verse, sketches, tales, and romances. After *Atalantis*, he published *Martin Faber* (1833), a short novel in the criminal-confession vein, and *The Book of My Lady* (1833), a self-styled *melange* of poems, sketches, and stories aimed at the gift-book trade. During the remainder of the decade, though he issued two further collections of stories and an important book of poems, he concentrated on long romances of currently popular types—historical novels about the Revolution, books about the settlement of the Gulf South, and fiction on foreign themes, chiefly Spain under the Moors and Spanish explorers in America. Among these works were *Guy Rivers* (1834) and *Richard Hurdis* (1838), his first two Border Romances, set in Georgia and Alabama respectively; *The Yemassee* (1835), his tale of a tragic Indian uprising in colonial Carolina; *The Partisan* (1835) and *Mellichampe* (1836), Revolutionary War Romances depicting the early stages of the struggle in Carolina; *Pelayo: A Story of the Goth* (1838), and *The Damsel of Darien* (1839), his first two novels on Spanish subjects. He also brought out an important collection of poems, *Southern Passages and Pictures* (1839), whose title suggests his affection for his region. The success of his first novels prompted him to claim exuberantly to a friend, ''The Alps may be passed but Rome's beyond them, and I shall not be satisfied short of a . . . classically well-built residence in the Eternal City!'' (*Letters* 1:59). The 1830s, in fact, show his total commitment to belles lettres during what would prove to be the last period in which genteel popular writing of the sort he had trained himself to produce could flourish.

Simms's wife had died in 1832, leaving him a daughter, Augusta, to rear. After several years of widowhood, in 1836—secure in the financial success of his fiction—he married Chevillette Eliza Roach, the daughter of a wealthy Carolina landholder with strong English leanings. He thereby gained a wife whose wit, elegance, and composure helped to balance his Irish ebullience and to temper the sometimes unbridled enthusiasm of his social conduct. His alliance with the stable, prosperous Roach family broadened his political and social influence while securing for him the life of a typical Southern planter household, teeming with friends, relatives, and children (he and Chevillette had fourteen in all, though only five lived to adulthood).

Throughout the 1830s and 1840s Simms was also making valuable friends whose literary and political interests matched or challenged his—Bryant, Melville, Cooper, James Kirke Paulding, and Washington Irving, among others, in the North; Nathaniel Beverley Tucker, John Reuben Thompson, James Henry Hammond, and many others in the South. He and Hammond whetted each other's political interests; and, in the middle 1840s, Simms—six feet tall, with steely blue-gray eyes, a man of power, commanding presence, and proven oratorical talent—served in the state legislature, narrowly losing the race for lieutenant governor. Generous, affectionate, and assiduous in his promotion of Southern literature, from the 1840s on he befriended dozens of Southern writers, established and aspiring—among them Poe, Henry Timrod, Richard Henry Wilde, John Esten Cooke, and Paul Hamilton Hayne. He also, in the middle 1840s, became a vocal participant in the Young America–Knickerbocker wars, helping to promote the cause of native literature while making, in the process, a permanent enemy of his one-time supporter, the powerful Lewis Gaylord Clark of the *Knickerbocker Magazine*—who thereafter denounced his writing and peppered him in print with insults.

Even as Simms's political and domestic fortunes flourished, his literary prospects were beginning to decline. Late in the preceding decade there had occurred the Panic of 1837, which altered the course of the book market on which he had eagerly fixed his hopes for wealth and fame. The recession, which lasted well into the 1840s, made the publication of long fiction economically unprofitable; and it was in the writing of such fiction that Simms had made his first real name and in which he was determined to continue. Romances such as he wrote were further harmed by a flood of cheaply printed and bound books and by mammoth weekly newspapers that pirated works by British authors. Hence at the time when he might have consolidated his fame as a popular author and attained some measure of literary maturity, he was forced away from his major field, and indeed from concentration on imaginative writing, into increasingly miscellaneous, often superficial endeavors that at times resembled hackwork. The 1840s were productive years for him, but the work he did during them was not calculated to inspire his orderly development as a writer nor to give him the discipline of form and style that he needed in fiction and verse.

The decade began auspiciously enough for Simms with the rollicking *Border Beagles* (1840), his third Border Romance and the one most filled with comic backwoods types. Still following the standard forms of popular fiction as they had existed in the 1830s, he brought out his third Revolutionary War Romance, *The Kinsmen*, in 1841. The book, retitled *The Scout* in the 1854 edition, describes the war in the South Carolina upcountry; its sales, as he remarked in a letter, were poor. Hence after *Confession* (1841), a domestic novel of love, attempted seduction, and revenge, and *Beauchampe* (1842), a two-volume work based on the famous Kentucky Tragedy, he published no more long fiction until the 1850s.

Instead he turned to history (*The History of South Carolina*, 1840), orations (*The Social Principle*, 1843), biography (lives of Francis Marion, 1844; Captain John Smith, 1846; and the Chevalier Bayard, 1847), social and literary criticism (*Views and Reviews*, 1845), and poetry (*Donna Florida*, 1843; *Areytos*, 1846; and *The Cassique of Accabee*, 1849). Particularly important for his writing in the next decade were his short fiction and his work with periodical literature as editor, contributor, and reviewer. In fiction, he produced a lively tale of city life (*The Prima Donna*, 1844), ghostlore (*Castle Dismal*, 1844), and his final novel in the Border Romance series, *Helen Halsey* (1845); he also brought out *The Wigwam and the Cabin* (1845), a collection of stories showing humorous and tragic elements in low-country and backwoods life. His fiction introduced him to the profit and the discipline of short forms, encouraged him to be freer and more fanciful than he was able to be in the highly conventionalized long romance, and developed veins of macabre fantasy and sprightly humor in his writing.

Meanwhile, his editorship of the *Magnolia* (1842–43), the *Southern and Western* (1845), and the *Southern Quarterly Review* (1849–55) exposed him, as the chief book reviewer for these journals, to entertaining varieties of nineteenth-century realism—Southern or Southwestern humor, flourishing in book form through such popular volumes as *Major Jones's Courtship*, and social fiction, particularly the novel of manners, as it emerged from the pens of Edward Bulwer-Lytton and William Makepeace Thackeray. Simms, who noted these literary strains with interest, found abundant material for them in Southern life, and he used them with grace in his novels of the 1850s.

That in the 1850s he could return to long novels at all was one happy result of the improving economy, to which the book market had responded. After hitting its low point in 1843, it had gradually recovered; and long fiction became more salable. But its complexion had changed significantly. The literary marketplace at mid-century was more open, more varied, more receptive to miscellaneous kinds of writing and to short fiction than it had been when Simms became a professional author in the 1830s; and after two decades of steadily expanding readership, it was less controlled by genteel taste and less dominated by literary forms associated with the upper and upper-middle classes. The dignified historical romances that Simms had learned to write as a young man had given way to sentimental and domestic fiction and, in Hawthorne's and Melville's hands, to a kind of romance that subordinated history to psychological, metaphysical speculation.

Simms's novels and novelettes of the 1850s show his response to the altered market. In one way or another, each of these works reveals his striving to incorporate new modes of realism in fiction as he had learned to construct it. In particular, he developed with some skill the manners and humor strains he had noted in the 1840s. Hence his fourth Revolutionary War Romance, *Katharine Walton* (1851), a satiric treatment of socialite Charleston during British occupation, and the short novel *The Golden Christmas* (1852), a comedy of nineteenth-century manners set in the Carolina low country, show the legacy of the British social fiction he was then describing in the *Southern Quarterly Review*. A companion volume to *The Golden Christmas*, *As Good as a Comedy* (1852)— a brisk short novel laid in middle Georgia—makes a bold move into the Southern humorists' camp. Simms's last three Revolutionary War Romances—*The Sword and the Distaff* (1852; retitled *Woodcraft* in the 1854 edition), *The Forayers* (1855), and *Eutaw* (1856)—use social comedy and backwoods humor in approximately equal measure as they portray the conclusion of the war in Carolina. *The Cassique of Kiawah* (1859), a satiric slap at seventeenth-century Charleston, shows his new blend of manners comedy, backwoods humor, and romance at its best. Though relatively unknown, this novel, with its pictures of Indians, pirates, socialites, and sharpsters, represents the climax of his career as a writer of long fiction.

As Simms may in part have realized, the 1850s saw the apex of his popularity, a fact confirmed by the appearance of the Uniform Edition of his works brought out by Justus Starr Redfield, a prominent New York publisher. *The Forayers* and *Eutaw* were published for the first time in the Redfield edition, which also contained revised versions of earlier Revolutionary

War novels and of Border fiction; *Vasconselos* (1853), Simms's last romance on Spanish themes; *Poems Descriptive, Dramatic, Legendary and Contemplative* (1853), an assemblage of poetry written over a period of twenty years; and *Southward Ho!* (1854), a collection of tales. Together with other works—notably two plays with contemporary settings, *Norman Maurice* (1851) and *Michael Bonham* (1852)—the edition shows the versatile Simms's great productivity at mid-century, and it represents the high point of his reputation. The 1850s also saw his growing immersion in the politics of sectional strife, an occupation that would repeatedly deflect him from imaginative writing.

From the 1830s on, Simms had ardently defended Southern culture and social institutions, including slavery. As editor of the Charleston *City Gazette*, he had opposed the Nullification movement; but as the strife between North and South grew sharper in the 1840s and 1850s, he began openly to advocate secession. He published a long screed (first written in the 1830s) in the influential collection of essays, *The Pro-Slavery Argument* (1852) and in the following year issued a pamphlet, *South-Carolina in the Revolutionary War*, that shows his growing sectional bias. In 1856 he made a protracted speaking tour of the North that was ruined when he antagonized audiences by his impassioned defense of his homeland. Hurt and puzzled by newspaper attacks, he returned to Carolina and to energetic political activity, writing long letters to Southern friends in Congress and making plans for the defense of Charleston harbor. He heard the guns of war in Charleston from his plantation 70 miles away in Barnwell District; and, year by year, he suffered the devastations that civil conflict brought to the region he called his "poor dear old Carolina" (*Letters* 5:242). He described the war graphically in letters; and he treated it in a number of poems, in the framing story of his dialect novel, *Paddy McGann* (serialized 1863), in the moving, vigorous *Sack and Destruction of the City of Columbia, S.C.* (1865), and in the anthology *War Poetry of the South* that he compiled and edited during 1866.

With the deaths of two favorite little sons in 1858 and a son and daughter during 1861, Simms had sustained grievous family losses; but the greatest blow he had to endure in a life marked increasingly by tragedy came in 1863, when his beloved Chevillette died suddenly, leaving him with several children to support. At the end of the war, hoping to regain some degree of fame and financial security, the aging, impoverished author renewed his contacts with Northern friends and publishers. But the book market, affected by the war, had moved even further away from the sort of writing he was equipped to do. Once again he was forced into all manner of miscellaneous projects (an edition of *Mother Goose* the most surprising) and into newspaper editing, short fiction, and periodical publication.

Desperately writing to support his family, Simms overburdened himself with work, accepting contracts in 1868 for three novels to be written at the same time. He had serialized a last story of the Revolution, *Joscelyn*, during 1867;

for his new novels, he turned to the Appalachian Mountains—the only important region of the South he had not yet fully treated in his fiction—for material. From trips to the area in the 1840s, and especially from the two weeks he had spent in 1847 camping with professional hunters, he was well prepared to write about mountain life; and, in fact, he had already drawn upon his experiences for an essay and some lectures in the 1850s. Now he mined them in earnest for his Mountain fiction—"The Cub of the Panther" (serialized 1869), *Voltmeier* (serialized 1869), "How Sharp Snaffles Got His Capital and Wife" (1870), and "Bald-Head Bill Bauldy" (in manuscript until publication in 1974). Marked by comic and sinister strains of folk material, acerbic social commentary, realistic pictures of mountain people, and freewheeling backwoods humor, these works are somewhat different, in tone and structure, from the fiction Simms had earlier produced. Less optimistic and romantic, less florid and fulsome, than his previous writing, they show his recognition, as his nineteenth-century biographer William P. Trent remarked, that the day of the romancer was over and that of the realist dawning. They also anticipate, in their emphasis upon the lives of plain people in picturesque settings, the local color writing that would shortly capture public fancy.

Though Simms did not regain the reputation he had enjoyed in the heady days of the 1830s, he succeeded in providing for his family through his writing, and he even achieved some comfort and security in his final years. He continued to aid and encourage friends, relatives, and younger writers, as he had done for decades; they, in turn, sustained and cherished him. But the enormous strains he had put upon his once robust constitution by working on three novels at the same time while bearing heavy family and plantation responsibilities finally took their toll. Drained, enfeebled, apparently stricken with cancer, he made his last public appearance in Charleston during May 1870 and died in the city on 11 June of that year. He had survived, and gamely, the wrecking of his world, his fame, his South; his life, in large measure, had reflected and epitomized the fading fortunes of his section.

MAJOR THEMES

Though Simms is sometimes called a Southern firebrand who helped bring on the Civil War, as late as 1842 he styled himself an "ultra-American" (*Letters* 1:319), and up through the 1840s he viewed himself as a national writer committed to advancing the cause of native literature. In this role he spoke emphatically about the historical conditions of American culture and pushed for a national literature grounded in its facts. Until well past mid-century his writing was extremely popular in the North, which had been somewhat quicker than the South to recognize and praise his talent. Northern reviewers commended his "truly American romances" (New York *Mirror* 13:239); Northern publishers, notably the Harper brothers, issued his books; he spent several months of most years in the North arranging for their publication; and he had numerous influential friends in the literary circles of New York City. For the first twenty years of his career, his subjects and themes are those of national American literature—the Indian, the Negro, the differences among the sections, the Revolutionary War, the frontier, the problem of national destiny, and heroic passages from foreign history. He discusses these and other subjects in *Views and Reviews*, issued in 1845—whose full title, it may be noted, is *Views and Reviews in American* (not simply "Southern") *Literature, History and Fiction*.

Views and Reviews is a summary of the work Simms had done between 1825 and 1845, a forecast of the writing he would shortly do, and an index to several of his dominant themes. In it, he argues vigorously for a national literature based on native materials; to that end he sets forth, as he says in a chapter heading, the "epochs and events of American history, as suited to the purposes of art in fiction." His four main periods of American history are (1) the era of French, Spanish, and English exploration from the sixteenth century to the founding of Jamestown, (2) the century and a half from Jamestown's beginnings to the reign of George III, (3) the preliminaries to the Revolutionary War and the war itself, and (4) the opening of the Gulf South and Middle Western frontiers.

Many Simms pieces usually seen as peripheral to the main body of his writing fall readily into place if viewed within the categories he develops in *Views and Reviews*. He portrays, for example, the first of his four periods, that of foreign exploration, in *The Vision of Cortes*; in *Book of My Lady* pieces such as "Vasco Nunez" (about Balboa); in *The Damsel of Darien*, set on the isthmus of Central America and likewise about Balboa; in those parts of the *History of South Carolina* that describe Spanish and French explorers; in the *Views and Reviews* essay "Cortes and the Conquest of Mexico"; in *Donna Florida*, which treats Ponce de León; in *Vasconselos*, which treats De Soto; in *The Lily and the Totem*, which depicts French Huguenots in Florida; and in other essays, stories, and poems. The second period that Simms notes in *Views and Reviews*, stretching from 1607 to the 1760s, forms the basis for poems about the New England Indian leader King Philip of Massachusetts; the biography of Captain John Smith and poems connected to it in subject, such as "The Forest Maiden," about Pocahontas; *The Cassique of Kiawah*, set in late seventeenth-century Charleston; *The Yemassee*, set in early eighteenth-century Carolina; and a romance planned but never published about the French and Indian Wars that would have dealt with the middle years of the eighteenth century.

Simms's third period, the preliminaries to the Revolution and the war itself, is portrayed in the eight Revolutionary War Romances from *The Partisan* to *Joscelyn*; in tales such as "Grayling" in *The Wigwam and the Cabin*; in biographies and biographical sketches of Francis Marion, Nathaniel Greene, William Moultrie, Thomas Sumter, and other military leaders; in poems, essays, and a play about Benedict Arnold and John André; and in verse about such foreign heroes of the Revolution as Lafayette. His fourth and last period, from the conclusion of the war to the mid–nineteenth century, is shown in poetry about the War of 1812 and in a series of works about the pioneer and settlement phases of the Gulf South—"Notes of a Small Tourist," a group of newspaper letters describing his trip to the region in 1831; the four main Border Romances, from *Guy Rivers* to *Helen Halsey*; works related to them in setting and subject, such as *Confession*, *Beauchampe*, and *Charlemont*; poems showing the squalor of frontier life, such as "The Indian Village" and "The Western Emigrants"; and the essay in the second series of *Views and Reviews* called "The Humorous in American and British Literature," which commends the indigenous humor of the rural South. Also representing this fourth period are two large groups of his writing, culminating in *The Golden Christmas* and "Sharp Snaffles," that set forth the general social outlines of the South between 1830 and 1860. In one group he stresses the patrician element in Southern society, centering on Charleston and the surrounding plantations and portraying them by the methods of the novel of manners; in the other, he surveys small-town and rural Southern life in the Carolina countryside, the Gulf South backwoods, and the Appalachian Mountains, handling his material by the methods of Southern or Southwestern humor.

Typicallly enough for an author of the Romantic era, Simms in much of this writing stresses patriotism, freedom, individualism, and the necessity of revolution in the establishment of liberty and political independence. He develops these themes through works set in medieval Spain, Spanish America, colonial America, France during the Revolution, and Greece during the nineteenth-century wars of independence. He uses as representative heroes such diverse historical figures as Cortez, Balboa, Ponce de León, Daniel Boone, the eighth-century Spanish Basque leader Pelayo, and the Indians Pocahontas, William McIntosh, and King Philip. As antitheses to these figures, he develops traitors, antiheroes, and hero-villains such as the biblical Cain, Roderick the Goth, and Count Julian of Spain; British officers such as Lord Cornwallis and "Bloody Banastre Tarleton"; Benedict Arnold, and the "Reverend Devil" John Murrell, archcriminal of the early nineteenth-century Gulf South.

Simms's poetry also shows the influence of the British and American Romantic movements. In it he develops such standard themes of the period as fame, ambition, passion, hope, fulfillment, destiny, and conquest; he also treats the lure of foreign places, forgetfulness, idleness, and escape. Throughout his verse he uses familiar Romantic symbols suggesting his fascination with many aspects of nature—the seasons, perhaps particularly spring; trees, night, the wind, and flowers, seen alternately as emblems of hope, solitude, and despair; stars, representing desire and aspiration; and the sea, a pervasive element in his writing, which may function as an enchanted, demonic realm as in *Atalantis*, a background for tempestuous passions as in "Apostrophe to Ocean" and "The Plank," or a free-flowing, halcyon domain that is contrasted to the corrupt mainland, as in *The Cassique of Kiawah*. Love is a dominant concern of his poetry, as it is of the poetry of many ages; his love poems range from graceful conventional verses written for a lady's album through whimsical personifications of "Wisdom, Love, and Folly" to delicate statements of personal feeling for his wife Chevillette. His poetry, in general, bears witness to the fertility, beauty, freshness, and consolation that he, like other writers of the Romantic period, found in nature.

Described broadly, the outlook of this self-styled "ultra-American" shifted in the 1850s from a national to a regional perspective because of two developments in the 1840s, the sharpening sectional conflict and the faltering book market, the latter forcing Simms to seek Southern instead of Northern publishers for his writing; hence he turned his eyes toward his fellow Carolinians in a way he had not when he was enjoying the tributes of Northern presses in the 1830s. Despite his growing involvement with his section, he continued to argue, in essays written for the Young America movement and in such books as *The Wigwam and the Cabin*, for a national literature based on regional materials. To that end he wrote four long articles pleading for an international copyright law, argued forcefully for the use of graphic realism in polite literature, and praised without stint what he called the "rare, racy, articulate, native humour" (*Views and Reviews* 2:178) of Augustus Baldwin Longstreet and kindred comic writers. But his increasing attention to the kinds of Southern subjects that form the real basis of his writing is worth probing a little further, for it tells us a good bit about his knowledge of Southern history and culture and his views of issues that are still prominent in the literature of the South.

In the main body of his writing, Simms lovingly portrays Southern civilization in several eras and of many aspects—the colonial, Revolutionary, and antebellum periods, the Tidewater, Gulf, and Mountain South, the Southern agricultural system, Southern military leaders, Southern politics, the Southern class hierarchy, and, inevitably, slavery. His devotion to the region was so great that it has led one or two twentieth-century commentators on his work to believe that he consciously set out to create an epic picture of the South; and, while it is hardly necessary to see his books in quite this way, it is nevertheless true that the South, historically considered, is both the genesis and the informing principle of his best writing. That writing is deeply rooted in depictions of Southern social classes; accurate, detailed descriptions of plantation architecture, landscaping, and crops; portrayals of such ethnic groups inhabiting the region as Germans, Dutch, and French; close observations of Southern flora and fauna; and lively disquisitions on proud old Carolina names. These relatively unobtrusive details, no less than the wars and other major public events that go to form the larger structures of his writing, ground his work firmly in the Southern culture of his and other times.

It was, in fact, in his devotion to his homeland, despite the aspersions he was fond of casting on her, that Simms finally and decisively took his stand. "I am a Southron, sir," claims a character in his early novel *The Partisan*, "one of a people not apt to suffer wrong to their friends or kindred, without resenting or resisting it" (ch. 27). Simms, an "ultra-American" who was also a "born Southron" (*Letters* 1:319), fervently resented Northern criticism of his beloved Southland: he bitterly attacked Lorenzo Sabine's inaccurate account of Southern Tories in *The American Loyalists* (1847); and he heaped coals on the North's head in his disastrous lecture tour of 1856.

Thus, while in moments of extreme despair Simms cried that Charleston had "never smiled" (Trent, p. 239) on any of his labors, he was also capable of declaiming, on the eve of the Civil War, that "Charleston is worth all New England" (*Letters* 4:315). His great allegiance to Southern culture, his long immersion in Southern history, his delight in Southern landscape, and his abiding love for his "poor dear old Carolina" engendered in his writing the qualities that twentieth-century critics call central to Southern literature: a strong consciousness of history, a deep commitment to place and region, an interest in class hierarchies, and a pervasive consciousness of human imperfectibility in a flawed yet exhilarating world.

SURVEY OF CRITICISM

Though Simms, who was proud and sensitive, complained frequently about the lack of attention paid his writing, he in fact received copious, generous attention in the notices, reviews, and review essays that poured from the presses during his lifetime. The response of critics North and South to his work, despite a few dissident voices, was loud and favorable, though it faltered with the book trade in the 1840s and again in the 1860s, when relative neglect foreshadowed his obscurity in the late nineteenth and early twentieth centuries. The criticism leveled against him, as by Lewis Gaylord Clark in the *Knickerbocker Magazine* and Cornelius Felton in the *North American Review*, was motivated in the main by literary politics or by a failure to appreciate his kind of writing and his particular talents. But Evert Duyckinck, Charles Fenno Hoffman, Rufus W. Griswold, and Poe, at one time or another, all praised him warmly; a host of anonymous reviewers lauded his poetry, novels, histories, and other works for their vigorous creativity; and a commentator in a New York newspaper (1867), noting his Irish qualities, celebrated his "ease, eloquence, grace, and fire." The appearance of the Redfield edition gave rise to the glowing tributes of Paul Hamilton Hayne in *Russell's Magazine* (1857), John Esten Cooke in the *Southern Literary Messenger* (1859), and J. Quitman Moore in *De Bow's Review* (1860). Simms's reputation, on the eve of the Civil War, seemed secure.

But the situation changed with the war, Simms's death, the advent of realism and naturalism, and inevitable shifts in popular taste. John William DeForest's charge in *The Nation* (1868) that romancers of Simms's stripe were "ghosts" and Howells's remark in *Harper's Magazine* (1892) that Simms's historical romances, while energetic, were "non-marketable, . . . old-fashioned wares" (85:154) serve as indications of the new attitude, though Howells, at least, had some understanding of Simms's writing. Scarcely the same can be said for other critics of the postwar period, who poked fun at what they called Simms's "feeble" poems or condescendingly claimed that his work was more respected than read. Hayne, it is true, praised Simms at length in "Ante-Bellum Charleston" (1885); joining in the praise was Edward F. Hayward, writing in the *Atlantic Monthly* during 1889; whereas Samuel A. Link in *Pioneers of Southern Literature* (1896) commended Simms's role in helping to create the antebellum Southern literary tradition. But the attitude of DeForest and Howells crystallized, so to speak, in the work of William P. Trent, who wrote the first (and to date only) book-length biography of Simms.

Trent's *William Gilmore Simms* (1892) remains a testament to the industry and the biases of this confirmed New Southerner, who lived, ironically, in two bastions of the Old South—Richmond, Virginia, and Sewanee, Tennessee. For his volume, Trent did much admirable spadework: he assiduously read Simms's books, interviewed his descendants, and drew upon his correspondence. But with his narrow, intolerant view of antebellum Southern culture and Simms's role in it, and with his uncomprehending dislike of the romance that Simms espoused, Trent produced a book that, though intermittently sympathetic, is circumscribed in treatment, unreliable in judgment, and unhappily flippant in tone. Until near our time, it influenced critics in unfortunate ways, leading zealous proponents of Simms to overstate their case while fueling the anti-Southern stance of other writers.

The period between Simms's death and Trent's biography represents the lowest stage that Simms's reputation reached; the period between Trent's biography and Vernon Louis Parrington's *Main Currents in American Thought* (1927) was little better. Scattered short and favorable assessments of Simms's writing sank before such flaccid surveys as that of Carl Van Doren in the *Cambridge History of American Literature* (1917) and of John Erskine, who in *Leading American Writers* (1910) denounced Simms's melodrama; derided his humor; and, in a trite reprise of Trent, maintained that the Southern social system undermined Simms's talent. Ignorance and misconceptions about Simms's writing reigned until the appearance of *Main Currents*, a volume whose enthusiastic chapter on Simms started the upswing in his fortunes that has been visible ever since.

Like Trent, Parrington soundly castigated Charleston for alleged neglect of Simms, and he also charged that its "social and economic romanticism" benumbed Simms's "strong instinct for reality" (2:136). But he praised Simms's sweep, his vigor, his lively dialect speakers, and his humor. With a firm intuitive grasp of Simms's fundamental strengths, he identified the great vitality and creative drive beneath the conventionalized surfaces of Simms's writing, though his limited critical vocabulary did not let him give these features precise formal definition. He overpraised Simms, and he distorted Simms's work by failing to acknowledge the primacy of its romantic features; but his exuberant tribute to the South Carolinian's writing helped to offset Trent's often unenlightened detractions.

The two decades between 1929 and 1950, when serious modern scholarship on Simms began, were characterized by much uncomprehending commentary and a few sensible observations. Typical of the former was the comment of Stanley J. Kunitz and Howard Haycraft in *American Authors 1600–1900* (1938) that Simms was the chief "Almoster" of his time; typical of the latter was the reasonably judicious survey, in *American Fiction* (1936), by Arthur Hobson Quinn, who claimed that Simms could not satisfactorily be classified as either a realist or a romancer and who assessed his work more thoughtfully than other students of fiction in this period such as Carl Van Doren and Van Wyck Brooks. Alexander Cowie's introduction to *The Yemasse* (1937) gave detailed treatment to Simms's writing and literary theories. But informed, comprehensive scrutiny of Simms did not really start until the late 1950s, with the work of C. Hugh Holman and Jay B. Hubbell and the appearance of the hefty five-volume set of Simms's letters.

Holman, in a series of trenchant studies beginning with his University of North Carolina doctoral dissertation in 1949, investigated Simms's involvement with the Revolutionary War; Simms and the British dramatists; Simms, Scott, and Cooper; and Simms and the South. These studies, which range over many aspects of Simms's work, are unquestionably the genesis of modern scholarly interest in him. The chief drawbacks to Holman's reasoned, searching inquiries are his tendency to prefer historical over literary criteria and his inclination to rate Simms's imaginative writing somewhat lower than it usually merits. But he was the first scholar seriously to apply rigorous methods of contemporary scholarship to Simms.

Simms scholarship in the 1950s was also greatly helped by Hubbell's long chapter on the South Carolinian in *The South in American Literature* (1954). Hubbell, it appears, had read more of Simms's writing than anyone save Holman and Trent, and he was the first writer since Trent to attempt a comprehensive picture of Simms's career as it was affected by developments in the antebellum period. Treating Simms's life, his literary relationships, his social and political stances, and much of his writing, Hubbell was sympathetic and judicious in his treatment, though old-fashioned in approach even for his time. Like Parrington, he helped correct Trent's views, and he pointed to the fact that critics since Trent had not read as much Simms as Trent had—a fact that remains true down to the present day of general treatments of antebellum literature that touch on Simms.

Meanwhile, the five thick volumes of *The Letters of William Gilmore Simms* (1952–56), ably edited by Mary C. Simms Oliphant, Alfred Taylor Odell, and T. C. Duncan Eaves, put before readers for the first time the full record of Simms's hopes, ambitions, triumphs, disillusionments, and tragedies, together with pictures of what Holman in a review called "the precarious economics of professional authorship" (*American Quarterly* 10:182), North-South literary relationships, and sociocultural patterns in the South between 1830 and 1870. More than any other event in the history of Simms scholarship, the letters inspired careful investigations of his writing, life, and career. Meticulously annotated, they are a storehouse of biographical, bibliographical, genealogical, and publishing lore. Their factual information is, on the whole, more trustworthy than their interpretive stance, at least as exemplified by Donald Davidson's controversial introductory essay that opens *Letters* I. A long polemic marred by flabby literary judgments, Davidson's screed is more a belated rear-guard action in his Agrarian-based warfare with the North than a solid introduction to Simms's writing. A. S. Salley's lengthy biographical essay in the same volume is more factual and judicious than Davidson's piece, though it is thin on Simms's life after about the middle 1830s.

The 1950s also saw the beginning of important inquiries into previously neglected aspects of Simms's writing. At least since John Esten Cooke, commentators on Simms had tended to emphasize his Revolutionary War and Border romances while slighting other branches of his writing. In the 1950s, however, with the record of Simms's multitudinous activities brought into view by the *Letters*, scholarship ventured down other avenues. John C. Guilds, in his Duke University doctoral dissertation (1954) and also in a series of careful articles appearing in the 1950s and 1960s, examined Simms's editing of such Carolina magazines as *The Album*, the *Cosmopolitan*, and the *Southern Literary Gazette*. And J. Wesley Thomas in "The German Sources of William Gilmore Simms" (1957) surveyed the chief European influence on Simms's novels and short fiction in what remains one of the more unusual approaches to his art.

Simms scholarship of the 1960s continued to open new veins in the many publications of the author. The 1960s, in fact, were boom times for Simms scholarship, as important new books and reprints that kept him before an academic audience appeared. Edd Winfield Parks in 1961 brought out his detailed study, *William Gilmore Simms as Literary Critic*, a shorter version of which became part of Parks's *Ante-Bellum Southern Literary Critics* issued the following year. The year 1961 also saw the publication of William R. Taylor's *Cavalier and Yankee*, a spirited treatment of American character and the Old South with a long chapter "Revolution in South Carolina" that centers on Simms. Concerned with political and social thought, it contains keen, if occasionally misguided, analyses of some major Simms novels and essays, and it stimulated considerable commentary in the 1960s and thereafter. In 1962 appeared the Twayne volume *William Gilmore Simms* by J. V. Ridgely, who, treating chiefly the Revolutionary War and Border romances, claimed that Simms consciously tried to create a myth of the Old South, a view challenged by later commentators.

Also testifying to swelling interest in Simms during the 1960s were two editions of *The Yemassee* with long introductions, one by C. Hugh Holman (1961), the other by J. V. Ridgely (1964), a reprinting of *Woodcraft* with an introduction by Richmond Croom Beatty, and an edition of *Views and Reviews, First Series* (1962) with an excellent introduction by Holman. In addition, the decade saw studies by Holman of Simms and the American Renaissance, by Moffitt L. Cecil and Hugh Hetherington of Simms's most famous comic character, Porgy, and by Mary Ann Wimsatt of Simms and Irving. But the most important event in Simms studies since the publication of the *Letters* in the middle 1950s was the appearance in 1969 of his Mountain romance *Voltmeier*, with an introduction and notes by Donald Davidson and Mary C. Simms Oliphant. Simms's last long novel, whose only previous appearance had been as a magazine serial during 1869, *Voltmeier* began the Centennial Simms textual edition edited by John C. Guilds and James B. Meriwether—an enterprise, now unfortunately stalled, that greatly enhanced modern scholarly scrutiny of Simms.

Interest in Simms continued to rise in the 1970s, as further Centennial Simms volumes appeared—*As Good as a Comedy* and *Paddy McGann* (1972), with introduction and notes by Robert Bush; *Stories and Tales* (1974), with introduction and notes by John C. Guilds; and *Joscelyn* (1975), with introduction and notes by Stephen E. Meats. In 1972 Guilds published a long article on Simms and the *Magnolia*, the most important periodical Simms edited besides the *Southern Quarterly Review*; in 1973 Jon L. Wakelyn brought out *The Politics of a Literary Man*, a painstaking study but one that badly distorts Simms's imaginative writing by construing it as political allegory and that overemphasizes Simms's role in the politics of his state.

Holman's *The Roots of Southern Writing* (1972) contains several previously published essays on Simms. Other studies of the 1970s include Charles S. Watson's chapter in *Antebellum Charleston Dramatists* (1976); a reissue, with annotations, of the Revolutionary War novels (including *Joscelyn*), edited by James B. Meriwether and Stephen Meats (1976); Holman's chapter on the Revolutionary War fiction in *The Immoderate Past* (1977); and studies by Miriam Shillingsburg of his writing about the Appalachians; by James E. Kibler, Jr., of his use of mountain folklore, by Mary Ann Wimsatt of his social comedy and of Porgy, by Betty Jo Strickland of his short stories; and by Louis D. Rubin, Jr., of his blacks. Perhaps the most significant scholarship of this busy decade were two books by Kibler—a listing of *Pseudonymous Publications of William Gilmore Simms* (1976), proving that Simms used an incredible 218 pen names, and an exhaustive study, *The Poetry of William Gilmore Simms: An Introduction and Bibliography* (1979), which brought an important area of Simms's writing back into view. Keen Butterworth's surveys of Simms's writing and career in *First Printing of American Authors* (1977) and in *Antebellum Writers in New York and the South* (1979), with their stress on the immensely fluent author's great body of writing, fittingly closed the decade by suggesting that comprehensive treatments of Simms's oeuvre were in order.

The 1980s, with their straitened circumstances for scholarly publishing, have seen a slight falling off in studies of Simms, though there are signs that work may be picking up again. Early in the decade appeared the extremely useful *William Gilmore Simms: A Reference Guide* (1980), compiled by Butterworth and Kibler; there were also Wimsatt's studies of his realism and romance and his backwoods humor, Shillingsburg's treatment of him as a "Southron," and Charles S. Watson's edition of *Woodcraft* (1983) and his essay on Simms's Appalachian fiction. Especially notable among the productions of the 1980s was the sixth volume of *Simms's Letters* (1982), which collects correspondence that had turned up since the first five volumes came out 30 years ago, and *The History of Southern Literature* (1985), edited by Louis D. Rubin, Jr., with a long chapter by Wimsatt surveying Simms's poetry, drama, criticism, and fiction. Perhaps the additional set of *Letters* and the *History* together will stimulate new inquiries into Simms, as the older *Letters* and the Centennial Simms volumes did in previous years. In progress at present (1986) are two biographies, at least two critical studies, and an edition of Simms's poetry.

Despite the important work done since 1950, Simms scholarship is still virtually in its youth: the field is large, open, and inviting to scholars willing to explore the life and writing of this energetic, dedicated, outspoken author who in his time was a tireless supporter of Southern literature and the leading symbol of Southern literary activity. We badly need authoritative scholarly editions of his writings; studies of rare, late, or neglected novels; investigations of his poetry, drama, and short fiction; scrutinies of his nonfiction; and a comprehensive critical biography—still the main desideratum in the Simms field after more than a century of work.

BIBLIOGRAPHY

Works by William Gilmore Simms

Monody, on the Death of Gen. Charles Cotesworth Pinckney. Charleston, S.C.: Gray and Ellis, 1825.

Early Lays. Charleston, S.C.: A. E. Miller, 1827.

Lyrical and Other Poems. Charleston, S.C.: Ellis and Neufville, 1827.

The Vision of Cortes, Cain, and Other Poems. Charleston, S.C.: James S. Burges, 1829.

The Tri-Color; or the Three Days of Blood, In Paris. With Some Other Pieces. London: Wigfall and Davis, 1830. [Evidence suggests the volume was actually printed in Charleston.]

Atalantis. A Story of the Sea. New York: Harper, 1832.

The Book of My Lady. A Melange. Philadelphia: Key and Biddle, 1833.

Martin Faber; The Story of a Criminal. New York: Harper, 1833.

Guy Rivers: A Tale of Georgia. New York: Harper, 1834.

The Partisan: A Tale of the Revolution. New York: Harper, 1835.

The Yemassee. A Romance of Carolina. New York: Harper, 1835.

Mellichampe. A Legend of the Santee. New York: Harper, 1836.

Pelayo: A Story of the Goth. New York: Harper, 1838.

Richard Hurdis; or, The Avenger of Blood. A Tale of Alabama. Philadelphia: Carey and
     Hart, 1838.

The Damsel of Darien. Philadelphia: Lea and Blanchard, 1839.

Southern Passages and Pictures. New York: George Adlard, 1839.

Border Beagles; A Tale of Mississippi. Philadelphia: Carey and Hart, 1840.

The History of South Carolina. Charleston, S.C.: S. Babcock, 1840.

Confession; or, The Blind Heart. A Domestic Story. Philadelphia: Lea and Blanchard,
     1841.

The Kinsmen: or The Black Riders of Congaree. A Tale. Philadelphia: Lea and Blanchard,
     1841. [Retitled *The Scout* in the Redfield edition.]

Beauchampe, or The Kentucky Tragedy. A Tale of Passion. Philadelphia: Lea and Blan-
     chard, 1842. [First volume revised and republished as *Charlemont or The Pride
     of the Village. A Tale of Kentucky.* New York: Redfield, 1856.]

Donna Florida. A Tale. Charleston, S.C.: Burges and James, 1843.

The Social Principle: The True Source of National Permanence. An Oration. Tuscaloosa,
     Ala.: [Erosophic] Society, 1843.

Castle Dismal: or, The Bachelor's Christmas. New York: Burgess, Stringer, 1844.

The Life of Francis Marion. New York: Langley, 1844.

The Prima Donna: A Passage From City Life. Philadelphia: Louis A. Godey, 1844.

The Sources of American Independence. An Oration. Aiken, [S.C.]: [The Town] Council,
     1844.

Helen Halsey: or, The Swamp State of Conelachita. New York: Burgess, Stringer, 1845.

Views and Reviews in American Literature, History and Fiction. First and Second Series.
     New York: Wiley and Putnam, 1845.

The Wigwam and the Cabin. First and Second Series. New York: Wiley and Putnam,
     1845.

Areytos; or, Songs of the South. Charleston, S.C.: John Russell, 1846.

The Life of Captain John Smith. New York: Geo. F. Cooledge, 1846.

The Life of the Chevalier Bayard. New York: Harper, 1847.

The Cassique of Accabee. A Tale of Ashley River. With Other Pieces. Charleston, S.C.:
     John Russell, 1849.

*Katharine Walton: or, The Rebel of Dorchester. An Historical Romance of the Revolution
     in Carolina.* Philadelphia: A. Hart, 1851.

Norman Maurice; or, The Man of the People. An American Drama. Richmond, Va.:
     Jno. R. Thompson, 1851.

As Good as a Comedy: or, The Tennesseean's Story. Philadelphia: A. Hart, 1852.

The Golden Christmas: A Chronicle of St. John's, Berkeley. Charleston, S.C.: Walker,
     Richards, 1852.

Michael Bonham: or, The Fall of Bexar. A Tale of Texas. Richmond: Jno. R. Thompson,
     1852.

*The Sword and The Distaff; or, "Fair, Fat, and Forty," A Story of the South, at the
     Close of the Revolution.* Charleston, S.C.: Walker, Richards, 1852. [Retitled
     Woodcraft in the Redfield edition.]

Poems Descriptive, Dramatic, Legendary and Contemplative. New York: Redfield, 1853.

*South-Carolina in the Revolutionary War: Being a Reply to Certain Misrepresentations
     and Mistakes of Recent Writers, in Relation to the Course and Conduct of this
     State.* Charleston, S.C.: Walker and James, 1853.

Vasconselos: A Romance of the New World. New York: Redfield, 1853.

Southward Ho! A Spell of Sunshine. New York: Redfield, 1854.
The Forayers: or, the Raid of the Dog-Days. New York: Redfield, 1855.
Eutaw: A Sequel to the Forayers. New York: Redfield, 1856.
The Cassique of Kiawah: A Colonial Romance. New York: Redfield, 1859.
Sack and Destruction of the City of Columbia, S.C. Columbia, S.C.: Daily Phoenix, 1865.
Ed. *War Poetry of the South*. New York: Richardson, 1866.
The Letters of William Gilmore Simms. Vols. 1–5, ed. Mary C. Simms Oliphant, Alfred Taylor Odell, and T. C. Duncan Eaves. Columbia: University of South Carolina Press, 1952–56. Vol. 6, ed. Mary C. Simms Oliphant and T. C. Duncan Eaves. Columbia: University of South Carolina Press, 1982.
The Yemassee: A Romance of Carolina. Ed. C. Hugh Holman. Boston: Houghton Mifflin, 1961.
Views and Reviews in American Literature, History and Fiction. Ed. C. Hugh Holman. First Series. Cambridge, Mass.: Harvard University Press, 1962.

Volumes in *The Centennial Edition of the Writings of William Gilmore Simms*, ed. John C. Guilds, James B. Meriwether, and Keen Butterworth:

Voltmeier or The Mountain Men. Introduction and Notes by Donald Davidson and Mary C. Simms Oliphant. Vol. 1. Columbia: University of South Carolina Press, 1969.
As Good as a Comedy: or The Tennesseean's Story and *Paddy McGann; or The Demon of the Stump*. Introduction and notes by Robert Bush. Vol. 3. Columbia: University of South Carolina Press, 1972.
Stories and Tales. Introduction and notes by John C. Guilds. Vol. 5. Columbia: University of South Carolina Press, 1974.
Joscelyn: A Tale of the Revolution. Introduction and notes by Stephen E. Meats. Vol. 16. Columbia: University of South Carolina Press, 1975.

Studies of William Gilmore Simms

Butterworth, Keen. "William Gilmore Simms: 1806–1870." *First Printings of American Authors*. Ed. Richard Layman. Vol. 1. Detroit: Gale Research, 1977.
——. "William Gilmore Simms." *Antebellum Writers in New York and the South*. Ed. Joel Myerson. Vol. 3 in *Dictionary of Literary Biography*. Detroit: Gale Research, 1979.
Butterworth, Keen and James E. Kibler, Jr. *William Gilmore Simms: A Reference Guide*. Boston: G. K. Hall, 1980.
Cecil, Moffitt L. "Symbolic Patterns in *The Yemassee*." *American Literature* 35 (January 1964): 510–14.
Cooke, John Esten. "William Gilmore Simms, Esq." *Southern Literary Messenger* 28 (May 1859): 355–70.
Duyckinck, Evert A. and George L. Duyckinck, eds. "William Gilmore Simms." *Cyclopaedia of American Literature*. Vol. 2. New York: Charles Scribner, 1855.
Felton, Cornelius C. Review of *The Wigwam and the Cabin* and *Views and Reviews*. *North American Review* 63 (October 1846): 357–81.
Griswold, Rufus W. *The Poets and Poetry of America*. Philadelphia: Carey and Hart, 1842.

Guilds, John C. "Simms as Editor and Prophet: The Flowering and Early Death of the Southern *Magnolia.*" *Southern Literary Journal* 4 (Spring 1972): 69–92.

———. "William Gilmore Simms and the *Southern Literary Gazette.*" *Studies in Bibliography* 21 (1968): 59–92.

Hayne, Paul Hamilton. "Ante-Bellum Charleston." *Southern Bivouac* 1 (October 1885): 257–68.

Hayward, Edward F. "Some Romances of the Revolution." *Atlantic Monthly* 64 (November 1889): 627–36.

Hetherington, Hugh W. *Cavalier of the Old South: William Gilmore Simms's Captain Porgy.* Chapel Hill: University of North Carolina Press, 1966.

Holman, C. Hugh. *The Immoderate Past: The Southern Writer and History.* Athens: University of Georgia Press, 1977.

———. *The Roots of Southern Writing: Essays on the Literature of the American South.* Athens: University of Georgia Press, 1972. Collects the following essays on Simms previously published in journals: "William Gilmore Simms's Picture of the Revolution as a Civil War"; "The Influence of Scott and Cooper on Simms"; "Simms and the British Dramatists"; "William Gilmore Simms and the 'American Renaissance.' "

Hubbell, Jay B. "William Gilmore Simms." *The South in American Literature, 1607–1900.* Durham, N.C.: Duke University Press, 1954.

Kibler, James E., Jr. *The Poetry of William Gilmore Simms: An Introduction and Bibliography.* Spartanburg, S.C.: Reprint Company, 1979.

———. *Pseudonymous Publications of William Gilmore Simms.* Athens: University of Georgia Press, 1976.

———. "Simms' Indebtedness to Folk Tradition in 'Sharp Snaffles.' " *Southern Literary Journal* 4 (Spring 1972): 55–68.

Link, Samuel A. "William Gilmore Simms: The Novelist, the Poet." *Pioneers of Southern Literature.* Nashville: Barbee and Smith, 1896.

Moore, J. Quitman. "William Gilmore Simms." *De Bow's Review* 29 (December 1860): 702–12.

Parks, Edd Winfield. *William Gilmore Simms as Literary Critic.* Athens: University of Georgia Press, 1961. Revised as part of *Ante-Bellum Southern Literary Critics.* Athens: University of Georgia Press, 1962.

Parrington, Vernon Louis. "William Gilmore Simms: Charleston Romancer." *Main Currents in American Thought.* Vol. 2. New York: Harcourt, Brace, and Company, 1927.

Poe, Edgar Allan. Review of *The Wigwam and the Cabin. Broadway Journal* 2 (4 October 1845): 190–91.

Quinn, Arthur Hobson. *American Fiction: An Historical and Critical Survey.* New York: D. Appleton-Century, 1936.

Ridgely, J. V. *William Gilmore Simms.* New York: Twayne, 1962.

Shillingsburg, Miriam J. "From Notes to Novel: Simms's Creative Method." *Southern Literary Journal* 5 (Fall 1972): 89–107.

———. "The Southron as American: William Gilmore Simms." *Studies in the American Renaissance* (1980): 409–23.

Strickland, Betty Jo. "The Short Fiction of William Gilmore Simms: A Checklist." *Mississippi Quarterly* 29 (Fall 1976): 591–608.

Taylor, William R. "Revolution in South Carolina." *Cavalier and Yankee: The Old South and American National Character*. New York: Braziller, 1961.

Thomas, J. Wesley. "The German Sources of William Gilmore Simms." *Anglo-German and American-German Crosscurrents*. 3 vols. 1, ed. P. A. Shelley et al. Chapel Hill: University of North Carolina Press, 1957.

Trent, William P. *William Gilmore Simms*. Boston: Houghton Mifflin, 1892.

Wakelyn, Jon L. *The Politics of a Literary Man: William Gilmore Simms*. Westport, Conn.: Greenwood Press, 1973.

Watson, Charles S. "Simms and the Beginnings of Local Color." *Mississippi Quarterly* 35 (Winter 1981–82): 25–39.

———. "William Gilmore Simms." *Antebellum Charleston Dramatists*. Tuscaloosa, Ala.: University of Alabama Press, 1976.

Wimsatt, Mary Ann. "Realism and Romance in Simms's Midcentury Fiction." *Southern Literary Journal* 12 (Spring 1980): 29–48.

———. "Simms and Irving." *Mississippi Quarterly* 20 (Winter 1966–67): 25–37.

———. "Simms and Southwest Humor." *Studies in American Humor* 3 (October 1976): 118–30.

———. "William Gilmore Simms." *The History of Southern Literature*. Ed. Louis D. Rubin, Jr., et al. Baton Rouge: Louisiana State University Press, 1985, pp. 108–17.

Charles Henry Smith
["Bill Arp"]
(1826–1903)

Bill Arp is remembered as the jester of the Confederate States of America during the Civil War. His popularity in the South continued into the twentieth century, as he mellowed into the rustic philosopher in newspaper columns, particularly in the Atlanta *Constitution*, after the Reconstruction and during the subsequent years of the New South. He was the journalistic creation of a Georgia lawyer named Charles Henry Smith. Smith's literary achievement is not great—nor did he mean it to be—but it is a human and humorous expression of the Southern psyche during the traumatic years of 1860 to 1903.

BIOGRAPHY

A belligerently loyal Georgian, Charles H. Smith was the son of Asahel Reed Smith, a Yankee schoolteacher and merchant, and of Caroline Maguire Smith, the daughter of an Irish linen merchant. Charles's writing showed as much Yankee wit as Southern humor, and he probably derived part of it from his father. His father arrived in Georgia about 1817. He went to work for a Savannah grocer; then he found a job as a teacher. Caroline Maguire was one of his pupils in Liberty County, some 30 or 40 miles from Savannah. Her mother and father had died in a yellow fever epidemic in Charleston when she was seven. In 1823, when she was sixteen, she married A. R. Smith.

Charles, one of ten children, was reared in comparatively comfortable middle-class surroundings. He was born 15 June 1826 in Lawrenceville, Georgia, some twenty miles northeast of Atlanta, where his father was a partner in a general store. His home life instilled in him the Democratic partisanship and the Presbyterian faith that he held throughout his life. He went to school at the Gwinnet County Manual Labor Institute, which his father had helped found; and he entered

Franklin College, which later became the University of Georgia, as a sophomore in 1844.

Though he left college a few months short of a degree—to help his ailing father in the store—his college experience was crucial. There he met the future political giants Alexander Stephens, Robert Toombs, and Joseph H. Lumpkin, as well as the poet Henry Timrod. There, in debate, he formed views on slavery and the Southern cause that he argued throughout his life. There he received the education that served him well in law, politics, and literature. There he achieved the polish necessary for him to marry into one of the wealthy families of the region.

Charles began married life on 7 March 1849 with his sixteen-year-old bride, Mary Octavia Hutchins, the daughter of Judge Nathan Lewis Hutchins, who, according to his son-in-law's account, owned a plantation on the upper Chattahoochee with over a hundred slaves. Three of the slaves, including the faithful Tip who figured in the Bill Arp letters, were given to the bride as a wedding present; and others were added from time to time, somewhat to the embarrassment of Smith, who did not want the care of them. Octavia's pampered home life and finishing-school education might seem ill-suited for the life she led with Charles Smith; but like many other Southern wives, she brought up a family of ten children despite the privations of the Civil War and the Reconstruction; and she outlived her septegenarian husband.

After two or three months of study under his father-in-law, Judge Hutchins, Smith was conditionally admitted to the bar and permitted "to ride the circuit at the tail of the procession." The semiannual sessions of the circuit courts were a gala feature in the life of backcountry Georgia in antebellum times. As the court moved from town to town, the judge and the lawyers rode together, ate and drank together, and roomed in the same local taverns. It was a time for the exchange of jokes and yarns that had been saved up for the preceding six months, and a time for some of the most brilliant minds of the South to display their wit. From these colleagues, Smith learned a great deal about law and politics and more about human nature.

In 1851 the Smiths moved to Rome, a western settlement in what had recently been Cherokee territory. As the partner of Judge J.W.H. Underwood, Smith soon became a respected citizen of the town. He took part in the organization of a chamber of commerce, was on the board of education, played flute in a fire company band, and was repeatedly elected alderman. In 1856, although he felt cramped for lack of ready money, he valued his house—the gift of his father-in-law—at $12,000; and he owned other property. "My assets are abundant and increase continually but still I am embarrassed," he wrote.

Smith's growing family was the center of his life. Two children had been born in Lawrenceville, and eleven more were born in Rome between 1851 and 1873, all but three surviving to adulthood. In addition, during the 1860s, two cousins grew up in the family as Smith's wards. The children learned to work and play together and to help each other grow up. With the flute and piano playing of Charles and Octavia, and the singing of the children, the family held its own musical evenings and dances. Partly because of Octavia's aristocratic restrictions on outside acquaintances, they maintained a certain social self-sufficiency.

Such was the background of the man who created Bill Arp. A mild, smooth-featured man of middle age, he was of medium height and tended toward stoutness. A great black beard and mustache offset a dome-like head, already mostly bald. He did not look like a comedian, his manner in public was usually dignified and reserved, and only the gentleness of his eye and an occasional inward smile betrayed the humor beneath. Yet he was already becoming known among his cronies in Rome as one of the choicest wits in a town that prided itself on its wags and eccentrics.

The Bill Arp letters were begun in the odd moments of the author's busy wartime career. The first letter came spontaneously from his pen, and he quickly accepted the suggestion of an illiterate local joker, the "original" Bill Arp, that he sign his name to it. Thereafter, Smith often had the original in mind as he wrote. "I tried to write as he would, could he have written at all," said the author in 1866. "His earnest, honest wit attracted my attention, and he declares to this day that I have faithfully expressed his sentiments." But there can be no doubt that Smith's own sentiments came out as he experienced the troubles and trials of war.

Most of Smith's Civil War service was spent in the odious roles of procuring supplies for the armies and of trying cases of treason against the Confederacy. "I killed as many of the Yankees as they killed of me," he is said to have remarked. In 1861 he was a private in the Rome Light Guards and reportedly a member of the Cherokee Artillery, Phillips's Brigade. But he did not see active duty until he joined the staff of General Francis Bartow as commissary for the Second Brigade, with the rank of major, Second Corps, of the Army of Northern Virginia. After the general's death at Bull Run, Smith served in the same capacity under General George Thomas Anderson, Third Brigade, First Division. In 1863 he was a first lieutenant in the Forrest Artillery Company.

During Sherman's advance through Georgia, Smith joined his family, now "runagees," finally leaving them in comparative safety at the Hutchins plantation, after a circuitous route to Alabama and back. For a while he held a special commission from Jefferson Davis as Judge Advocate in Macon, but the court was broken up by Wilson's raiders, and Smith returned to his family. In January 1865 the family once again took up residence in Rome, having to begin again with nothing to live on and the community to rebuild. The return home was briefly described in the Bill Arp letters:

I shall not allude to it now, only to remark that our coming back was not so hasty as our leaving. It was in the dead of winter, through snow and through sleet, over creeks without bridges and bridges without floors, through a deserted and desolate land where no rooster was left to crow, no pig to squeal, no dog to bark, where the ruins of happy homes adorned the way, and ghostly chimneys stood up like Sherman's sentinels a-guarding the ruins he had made.

The experience was never forgotten—nor forgiven.

In Rome, Smith managed a store for a while, as he had with his father before his marriage. There was virtually no civil government in Georgia and no work for a Confederate lawyer. With the meagerest of supplies, he undertook to trade with customers who needed everything and had no money to pay. His writing probably helped a little, for the Bill Arp letters had become very popular in the South and were printed and reprinted in Atlanta, Nashville, Richmond, and elsewhere. In 1866 he contributed occasionally to the *Metropolitan Record* in New York, and that paper published his first book, *Bill Arp, So Called*, the same year. His financial situation was improved when he was elected to the Georgia Senate, which met in Milledgeville, in December 1865. As a senator, he voted for the ratification of the Thirteenth Amendment and was a member of committees on enrollment, the judiciary, finance, banks, the lunatic asylum, and the deaf and dumb asylum. But, when the Reconstruction Act abolished the Georgia government, he returned to the practice of law in Rome, with Joel Branham, Jr., as partner.

He was active in local politics in Rome, as mayor during the period of military government in 1867, and, for several years, as the leader of what was dubbed by its enemies "the Smith Ring." The mayoralty campaign of 1871 almost came to violence because of the invective of the Rome *Courier*, which opposed Smith's candidacy, although "the Ring" obviously had the support of the majority, including the local foundry workers. The feud with the *Courier* was a long-standing one. Smith is said to have owned and edited the Rome *Commercial* for a while during this period, and it is likely that his motive was to oppose the *Courier*. The editor of the *Commercial* at the time of the 1871 election was probably Smith's young friend Henry W. Grady.

Violence was certainly in the air in the Georgia of Reconstruction times. Floyd County, of which Rome was the seat, was a center of Ku Klux Klan activity from its beginning. Smith's daughter Marian reported much later an experience she had as a child when she unexpectedly entered the parlor one night: "On the sofa were the strangest things, white and long and some holes in them that looked like eyes. I only had a glimpse for Mamma saw me and quick I was put out of the room, Mamma telling me that I must not speak of what I saw for it would get Papa into trouble."

By 1877 the partisan strife and violence had somewhat diminished in north Georgia, and Smith seemed to have lost interest in politics and law. In October he dissolved his partnership with Branham to move to a farm five miles north of Cartersville in Bartow County. It was a good farm, though hilly; the farmhouse stood high and afforded a splendid view of the verdant north Georgia countryside. The red Etowah River ran not far away, and Indian relics were still to be found on the hillsides. Smith was enthusiastic about farming: it could satisfy his American craving for a rural retirement, and it also promised to bring him closer to the old antebellum ideal of the country gentleman. He wrote in the Bill Arp letters, "It's a wonder to me that everybody don't go to farming. There is no profession that gives a man such freedom, such latitude, and such a variety of employment as farming." But Smith was not especially successful at farming. His first year was a trial. "It took all available means to pay for the farm and stock it and add a few rooms to a two room house," he wrote in 1878. "The Rent Corn was purchased with the farm and so we lived on corn—for 4 months we had no flour nor rice nor sugar nor coffee nor butter and only 2 qts. of milk a day." He remained at Fontainebleau, as he called it, for ten years—long enough for his youngest children, Carl and Jessie, to have the advantages of a rural childhood and for the rest of the family to be grown and independent.

Meanwhile, he began in 1878 to contribute Bill Arp letters to the Atlanta *Constitution*, soon to become one of the most powerful and progressive newspapers in the South. His first contributions brought him only five dollars a week, but he continued, with occasional intermissions, for the remainder of his life. The pay from the *Constitution* became the mainstay of his life, and it was supplemented by income from his books and his lectures. It is estimated that Smith wrote more than two thousand Arp letters between 1861 and 1903, probably more than two-thirds of them for the Atlanta paper. Their popularity persisted; at its height they were appearing in over seven hundred weekly newspapers according to one commentator—although, of course, Smith received no royalties for the reprinting.

In the same year that he began writing for the *Constitution*, "Bill Arp" became a professional lecturer. He had previously spoken now and then in Rome and Cartersville, but on 25 June 1878 he delivered "A Cousin in Berlin" in Atlanta as the first of many scheduled lectures throughout the South. From then until 1902, he lectured well over 300 times in Georgia, Virginia, the Carolinas, Florida, Alabama, Tennessee, Kentucky, Louisiana, Mississippi, Arkansas, and Texas, and at least once as far north as New York City and as far northwest as Kansas City. When he spoke in Charleston, South Carolina, in 1884, the state legislature adjourned to let him use its hall; and he was accompanied onstage by the governor, ex-governor, judges of the South Carolina Supreme Court, president of the Senate, and speaker of the House. The Atlanta *Constitution* announced one of his lectures, 4 August 1888: "Bill Arp will lecture at Chautauqua tonight. This bare assertion ought to be sufficient to insure him an audience of a thousand people."

As for his books, there were five collections of Arp letters, each one repeating some or all of the letters in the preceding volume. Following *Bill Arp, So Called* in 1866, he published *Bill Arp's Peace Papers*, 1873; *Bill Arp's Scrap Book*, 1884; *The Farm and the Fireside*, 1891; and *Bill Arp: From the Uncivil War to Date*, 1903—the last three with Atlanta publishers. The final volume was the most complete and contained some straight autobiographical chapters not previously published. A posthumous Memorial Edition of it contained in addition a biographical sketch by his daughter Marian Smith. He also wrote a textbook, *A School History of Georgia*, published in Boston in 1893, in which he attempted to set the record straight for the benefit of the rising generation using such emotionally stacked terms as the following: "This was known as the 'Reconstruction Period,' and the people were so galled and oppressed by these overbearing tyrants that to this day the 'Reconstruction Period' is regarded with almost as much horror as the war itself." It was, however, his first book, *Bill Arp, So Called*, that was most remembered.

Smith spent his last years in Cartersville at The Shadows, a handsome house surrounded by roses and shade trees where he had retired in 1887. He was by no means inactive, however; he continued to write and to lecture. He was a vice president of the Rome Exposition in 1888, and he made occasional trips to visit the families of his scattered children or to attend the Cotton States and International Exposition in Atlanta in 1895. His last Bill Arp letter, published in the *Constitution* on 9 August 1903 recounted again the adventures of the Smith family as refugees from Sherman's march through Georgia; and its incoherence indicated a sad deterioration in the author's mental powers.

Marian Smith recalled his last days: "The day came when he grew too feeble to walk in his garden, or to read or write as he had always done. Then he would totter out to his chair on the porch and with his 'far-glasses' on wait patiently for the coming of his little grandchildren. His mind, grown childlike, craved their companionship." Charles Henry Smith died in Cartersville on 24 August 1903, following an operation for the removal of gallstones. He was mourned by thousands of readers of the Atlanta *Constitution* and by those who still remembered his wartime letters. As Cartersville's "first citizen," he was buried on 26 August while the townspeople suspended all local activities for the funeral.

Occasional newspaper articles about him have appeared in the South since his death. There are historical markers at his birthplace in Lawrenceville and near his farm north of Cartersville, and a bronze plaque commemorates him in the Cartersville Presbyterian Church, of which he was an elder. Occasional scholarly articles have been written about "Bill Arp," and he is sometimes included in collections of American humor. Otherwise, his fame resides in the frequent mention he received in books and memoirs of the Civil War.

MAJOR THEMES

Charles Henry Smith's right to remembrance lies in the truth of his picture of life in upper Georgia. In many ways he was a representative citizen of his region and of the larger South. The Bill Arp letters, basically autobiographical, were a diary of the place and time. But they were heightened by humor and a sensitiveness to representative details that transcended autobiographical fact.

If many of Bill's beliefs and attitudes are unacceptable today and even contrary to the facts as we know them, they are nevertheless valid as the sincere reflections of a genial Southern observer. He left on record not only the realities but the myth. Since the Bill Arp letters were not begun until 1861, and since Smith had only a recent claim to Southern gentility, the picture of the antebellum South was reminiscent and often colored by myth. Like many Southerners, Smith continued to look back nostalgically to an Old South that he had only partially experienced and that in reality had only a partial existence. Bill Arp's antebellum Georgia was, therefore, an amalgam of sentiment and realistic detail, containing a literary truth beyond literal truth. To understand that truth is to comprehend the everyday forces and motivations that made the South what it was and is.

Bill Arp's greatest popularity and most lasting fame came from the letters he wrote during the Civil War and at its conclusion. Henry Grady, editor of the Atlanta *Constitution*, said: "I doubt if any papers ever produced a more thorough sensation than did the letters written by Major Smith during the war." His success derived from his expression of the feelings of the people. He did not concern himself with battle strategy, statistics of dead and wounded, observations in the field, or political issues. His concern was the hopes and fears, the boasts and complaints, the ideals and disillusionments of the ordinary Southerner. In his preface to *Bill Arp, So Called*, Smith wrote

These letters may be worthy of preservation as illustrative of a part of the war—as a side-show to the Southern side of it—an index to our feelings and sentiments. . . . At the time they appeared in the press of the South, these sentiments were the silent echoes of our people's thoughts, and this accounts in the main for the popularity with which they were received. Of course they contain exaggerations, and prophecies, which were never fulfilled; but both sections were playing "brag" as well as "battle," and though we could not compete with our opponents in the former, yet some of us did try to hold our own.

The Civil War came much closer "home" to the Southerner than to the Northerner. In Georgia, where there was little actual fighting until Sherman's devastating march in 1864, the war nevertheless affected every aspect of ordinary life from government to daily bread. Besides shortages, inflation, and the fear of cavalry raiders, both Yankee and Confederate, Georgia life was punctuated by conscriptions that were continually more inclusive, and by the financial frauds that always accompany a war effort. These were the things that Bill Arp talked about; but, most of all, he spoke of the indomitable spirit of the average Georgian who faced these difficulties.

The years of Reconstruction in Georgia were a time of bitterness, disillusion, and frustration. To Georgians, the national government seemed fickle and vindictive. The old order in the South had collapsed, and nobody was sure how to start over. The state government seemed to exist or to fall according to the whims of Northern lawmakers who were fighting among themselves. The physical and economic destruction of the war left the problem of producing the essential commodities. Free Negro labor was unreliable, and many of the whites had been casualties of the war. In addition, the prices for agricultural products slumped, so that the small farmer, who still made up most of the population, could at best earn little more than a living. Political corruption seemed to be the order of the day on both national and state levels, and money that should have gone to the welfare of the people went into the pockets of grafters.

The Bill Arp letters of the Reconstruction period were the most bitter he ever wrote. Many of them were published in *Bill Arp's Peace Papers* in 1873, but not reproduced in the later collections of Arp letters. They were evidently put into the book with very few changes from the original newspaper versions— even the comic misspellings were not changed as they were in Smith's other volumes—and they still convey some of the heat with which they were written.

If the sentiments which bubble up in this volume dont soot sum foaks, they will be gratyfide to see what a fool a man can make of himself without tryin. If a man dont like another man, its a cumfort to see him do that, and I've always thought it was a luvly trait in my carakter that I was disposed to gratify the wishes of all my Ameriken brethren— excep sum.

Nearly all the Bill Arp letters written after 1877 were first printed in the Atlanta *Constitution*. From the appearance of the one on 17 May 1878, Smith contributed a letter a week, with occasional lapses, until 9 August 1903. The character of these letters was clearly different from that of the earliest ones. The overall approach was good-natured and sentimental rather than satiric, and the subject matter was farm and home life rather than war and politics. When politics were mentioned, it was with a comparatively disinterested air. Even the language became more literary and at times genteel. The timely satirist had become the country sage.

As a sentimental country sage, Bill Arp still had a lot to contribute to our understanding of a time and a place and a culture. Joel Chandler Harris once spoke of the eccentricities of character and manners that abounded in nineteenth-century Georgia:

Every settlement had its peculiarities, and every neighborhood boasted of its humorist,— its clown, whose pranks and jests were limited by no license. Out of this has grown a literature which, in some of its characteristics, is not matched elsewhere on the globe; but that which has been preserved by printing is not comparable, either in volume or merit, with the great body of humor that has perished because of the lack of some one industrious enough to chronicle it.

One of the chroniclers of this body of humor was Charles H. Smith, who did his share both in volume and merit. The Bill Arp letters recorded the feelings and opinions of their time, but they went deeper than that. They presented with remarkable accuracy the pronunciations, vocabulary, idiom, and phrasing of the people. They were rich in folk sayings, superstitions, and anecdotes; and they contained plentiful allusions to current games, customs, and songs. They were a repository of dialect and folklore.

SURVEY OF CRITICISM

Scholarly studies of Charles Henry Smith (Bill Arp) are basically three: Walter Blair's account in *Native American Humor* (1937); Anne M. Christie's doctoral dissertation, "Charles Henry Smith, 'Bill Arp' " (1952); and James C. Austin's *Bill Arp* (1969). Blair's work is the beginning of any serious study of the crackerbox humorists, and its dozen or so pages on Bill Arp are basic. Christie's dissertation is the most thorough biographical and bibliographical study, including references to manuscript material and to newspaper publications. Virtually all of the Bill Arp papers were published originally and republished in newspapers. Christie has tracked down most of these publications, including many not reprinted in book form. She also lists Smith's lectures. Austin, relying on the previous sources, presents Bill Arp in a literary, historical, linguistic, and folkloristic context. His book includes a chronological table of Smith's life and a selective annotated bibliography.

Otherwise, there have been references in newspapers and magazines to Bill Arp from the 1860s to the 1960s. But there have been few scholarly studies. The following bibliography will explain itself, but there are a few notes to be added. Anne M. Christie's article in *Civil War History* (1956) is a fine brief assessment of the Bill Arp letters. Wade H. Hall, in his *Reflections of the Civil War in Southern Humor* (1962), shows Bill Arp in the context of his times and place. Margaret Gillis Figh contributed three articles on folklore and dialect in the Bill Arp letters (1948, 1949, 1950). James Austin and Wayne Pike applied modern knowledge of dialect geography in "The Language of Bill Arp" (1973). Walter Blair and Raven I. McDavid, Jr., in *The Mirth of a Nation* (1983), interpreted Arp's bad grammar, bad spelling, and pronunciation. There is honorable mention of Bill Arp in Jesse Bier's *The Rise and Fall of American Humor* (1968) and in Walter Blair and Hamlin Hill's *America's Humor* (1978).

SELECTED BIBLIOGRAPHY

Works by Charles Henry Smith

The Majority of the Bill Arp letters originally appeared in the Atlanta *Southern Confederacy*, 1861 ff., and the Atlanta *Constitution*, 1878–1903. Manuscript letters by Smith are listed in Joseph Jones, ed., *American Literary Manuscripts* (Austin, Texas, 1960). Additional letters are in the collections of Professor Anne May Christie and of various of Smith's descendants.

Bill Arp, So Called. New York: Metropolitan Record Office, 1866.
Bill Arp's Peace Papers. New York: Carleton, 1873.
Bill Arp's Scrap Book: Humor and Philosophy. Atlanta: J. P. Harrison, 1884.
The Farm and the Fireside: Sketches of Domestic Life in War and in Peace. Atlanta: Constitution, 1891.
A School History of Georgia. Boston: Ginn, 1893.

"Have American Negroes Too Much Liberty?" *Forum* 16 (October 1893): 176–83.
Bill Arp: From the Uncivil War to Date. Atlanta: Byrd, 1903.

Studies of Charles Henry Smith

Aubrey, George H. "Charles Henry Smith (Bill Arp)." *Men of Mark in Georgia.* Ed. William J. Northen. Atlanta: A. B. Caldwell, 1911.

Austin, James C. *Bill Arp.* New York: Twayne, 1969.

Austin, James C. and Wayne Pike. "The Language of Bill Arp." *American Speech* 48 (Spring-Summer 1973): 84–97.

Bier, Jesse. *The Rise and Fall of American Humor.* New York: Holt, Rinehart and Winston, 1968.

Blair, Walter. *Native American Humor, 1800–1900.* New York: American Book, 1937.

Blair, Walter and Hamlin Hill. *America's Humor: From Poor Richard to Doonesbury.* New York: Oxford University Press, 1978.

Blair, Walter and Raven I. McDavid, Jr. *The Mirth of a Nation: America's Great Dialect Humor.* Minneapolis: University of Minnesota Press, 1983.

Branham, Joel. *The Old Court House in Rome.* Atlanta: Index, 1921.

Brantley, Rabun L. *Georgia Journalism of the Civil War Period.* Nashville: George Peabody College for Teachers, 1929.

Budd, Louis J. "Gentlemanly Humorists of the Old South." *Southern Folklore Quarterly* 17 (December 1953): 232–40.

Christie, Anne M. "Charles Henry Smith, 'Bill Arp': A Biographical and Critical Study of a Nineteenth Century Georgia Humorist, Politician, Homely Philosopher." Ph.D. diss., University of Chicago, 1952.

———. "Civil War Humor: Bill Arp." *Civil War History* 2 (September 1956): 103–19.

Cooper, Cornelia E. "Bill Arp: The Cherokee Philosopher." *Georgia Magazine* 8, no. 6 (April-May 1965): 12–15.

Cunyus, Lucy J. *The History of Bartow County, Formerly Cass.* Cartersville, Ga.: Tribune, 1933.

Dutcher, Salem. "Bill Arp and Artemus Ward." *Scott's Monthly Magazine* 1–2 (June 1866): 472–78.

Figh, Margaret Gillis. "Folklore in Bill Arp's Works." *Southern Folklore Quarterly* 12 (September 1948): 169–75.

———. "Tall Talk and Folk Sayings in Bill Arp's Works." *Southern Folklore Quarterly* 13 (December 1949): 206–12.

———. "A Word-List from 'Bill Arp' and 'Rufus Sanders.' " *Publication of the American Dialect Society* 13 (April 1950): 3–11.

Ginther, James E. "Charles Henry Smith, Alias 'Bill Arp.' " *Georgia Review* 4 (Winter 1950): 313–21.

———. "Charles Henry Smith, the Creator of Bill Arp." *Mark Twain Journal* 10, no. 1 (Summer 1955): 11–12, 23–24.

Hall, Wade H. *Reflections of the Civil War in Southern Humor.* Gainesville: University of Florida Press, 1962.

———. *The Smiling Phoenix: Southern Humor from 1865 to 1914.* Gainesville: University of Florida Press, 1965.

Hubbell, Jay B. *The South in American Literature, 1607–1900.* Durham, N.C.: Duke University Press, 1954.

Kesterson, David B. "The Literary Comedians and the Language of Humor." *Studies in American Humor* n.s. 1 (June 1982): 44–51.

McIlwaine, Shields. *The Southern Poor White from Lubberland to Tobacco Road*. Norman: University of Oklahoma Press, 1939.

Massey, Mary Elizabeth. *Refugee Life in the Confederacy*. Baton Rouge: Louisiana State University Press, 1964.

Mott, Frank Luther. *American Journalism*. New York: Macmillan, 1962.

Nixon, Raymond B. *Henry W. Grady: Spokesman of the New South*. New York: Alfred A. Knopf, 1943.

Rutherford, Marjory. "Homey Philosophy, Which Early Georgians Wrote." Atlanta *Journal and Constitution*, 26 October 1953.

Smith, Marian Caroline. "The Home Life of Bill Arp." *Bill Arp: From the Uncivil War to Date*, by Charles Henry Smith. Memorial Edition. Atlanta: Hudgins, 1903.

———. *I Remember*. Jacksonville, Fla.: Ambrose, 1931.

Tandy, Jennette. *Crackerbox Philosophers in American Humor and Satire*. New York: Columbia University Press, 1925.

Trent, William Peterfield. "A Retrospect of American Humor." *Century* 63 (November 1901): 45–64.

Watterson, Henry, ed. *Oddities in Southern Life and Character*. Boston: Houghton, Mifflin, 1883.

Weber, Brom. "The Misspellers." *The Comic Imagination in American Literature*. Ed. Louis D. Rubin, Jr. New Brunswick, N.J.: Rutgers University Press, 1973, pp. 127–37.

Wiggins, Robert Lemuel. *The Life of Joel Chandler Harris from Obscurity in Boyhood to Fame in Early Manhood*. Nashville: Methodist Episcopal Church, South, 1918.

JENNIFER R. GOODMAN

Captain John Smith
(1580–1631)

Among the earliest Southern writers, Captain John Smith remains a figure of unquestioned importance and controversy. The influence of his primary vision of America on later authors has led to his being considered the first truly American writer. Smith's works have contributed to literature, history, legend, science, geography, and ethnology. These eyewitness accounts of the reactions of the Jamestown settlers to the New World have become vital sources for the understanding of the American colonial experience and imagination.

BIOGRAPHY

John Smith was born at Willoughby by Alford, in Lincolnshire, England, probably in 1580, for we know he was baptized 9 January 1580. He was the eldest son of George Smith, a yeoman farmer who was a tenant of Lord Willoughby de Eresby. This useful family connection was to maintain its importance throughout Smith's career as a soldier, explorer, and author.

By his own account, Smith's adolescent years were enlivened by a struggle to escape from his comfortable agricultural surroundings. He records an attempt to run away to sea at age thirteen, proabably inspired by the exploits of the great Elizabethan sea dogs. In 1595 he went from the school he had attended at Louth to an apprenticeship to Thomas Sendall, a merchant of King's Lynn. After George Smith died in 1596, John Smith inherited his father's Lincolnshire property.

Receiving this modest legacy did not quell Smith's interest in foreign adventures; on the contrary, he is next heard of serving in the Netherlands with a Captain Joseph Duxbury, a distant connection of Lord Willoughby. In 1599 Smith attended the second son of Lord Willoughby, Peregrine Bertie, on his journey from England to join his brother in France. Smith returned by way of

Scotland in 1600, with letters of introduction to the court of James VI, but abandoned the project and returned home without encountering the future monarch of England, having "neither money nor meanes to make him a Courtier."

On his return to Lincolnshire, Smith became acquainted with Theodore Paleologue, a Greek riding master in the service of the Earl of Lincoln. It seems to have been Paleologue who aroused Smith's interest in military service against the Turks in Eastern Europe. Smith left England once more in 1601 with this intention, and after an erratic and painful progress across France, with detours by sea across the Mediterranean and through Italy, he reached Vienna and joined the Imperial Army there under the Count of Modrusch. He was promoted to be captain of 250 horse after distinguishing himself at the siege of Limbach by means of his knowledge of long-distance signaling methods. In 1602 Smith's campaigns in Hungary and Transylvania came to their climax with his victorious duels against three Turks in succession outside a besieged town. For this feat, Captain Smith was rewarded a pension from the Prince of Transylvania, Zsigmond Bathory, together with the right to display three Turks' heads on his coat of arms, and the title of gentleman. Later in the same year, Smith was captured by the Turks and sold as a slave. He escaped after being sent first to Constantinople, and was then forced to work as a serf somewhere along the Don River. Smith journeyed back to Western Europe by way of Muscovy and Poland. On reaching the territory of the Holy Roman Empire once more, he succeeded in obtaining payment for his services in the army, as well as a certificate from Zsigmond Bathory attesting to his military prowess and the grant of the coat of arms. Then Smith continued his travels through Germany, France, Spain, and North Africa.

By 1605 Captain Smith had returned to England again and had become involved with Bartholomew Gosnold in planning a colonizing expedition to Virginia. The three ships and roughly a hundred colonists embarked for America in December 1606. Some unspecified disagreement between Smith and at least one of the aristocratic members of the group apparently led to the Captain's spending thirteen weeks under arrest, although he was to be designated as one of the governing council of the colony when the ships reached Virginia. The fleet arrived in the West Indies in March 1607 and entered Chesapeake Bay late in April to found the settlement named Jamestown. Smith was appointed supply officer to the colony in September. By this time he had begun to make notes about the colonists' experiences.

Late in the year 1607, Smith was captured by local Indians and taken to their chief, Powhatan. According to Smith's now-famous account of events, he was saved from execution by Powhatan's young daughter, Pocahontas, and was adopted into the tribe as Powhatan's son before being returned to Jamestown.

In May 1608 Smith sent his personal narrative of the Jamestown colony to England. Written as a personal letter rather than a public statement, it was later printed as *A True Relation*. After exploring Chesapeake Bay and the Potomac, Smith was elected president by the governing council of the colony. As a leader, the Captain distinguished himself by his firm and intelligent attitude towards the natives, his energetic activity in investigating their surroundings and obtaining supplies, and his disgust at the sloth of many of the gentlemen colonists. The map and valuable description of the area and its natives that Smith sent to England late in the same year bear witness to his energy and observation; they appeared in 1612 as part of *A Map of Virginia*. Smith's experiences at Jamestown ended abruptly when he was burned in a gunpowder explosion. He returned to England in 1609, much to the relief of many of the less active settlers.

In 1610–11, while searching for a new field of action, Captain Smith revised his materials on the Virginia colony and published them in 1612 in the thorough and perspicacious *A Map of Virginia*. Smith's association with the Reverend Samuel Purchas, Hakluyt's successor as publicist of the British colonies in the New World, dates at least from this period.

Smith sailed for America a second time in March 1614 with two ships, on a whaling and fur-trading venture off the coast of Maine. His explorations of the coast he named New England developed into plans for a colony in the Massachusetts Bay area, territory he found especially promising. On his return to England, the Plymouth Company named Smith Admiral of New England.

This was, frustratingly, Smith's last visit to the North American continent, although he struggled to return throughout the remainder of his life, and directed much of his writing to that end. In 1615, on embarking for New England a second time, he was captured by a French pirate and ignominiously adandoned by his own ship; he wrote *A Description of New England* while confined aboard the French ship. Smith's 1617 expedition was canceled after being delayed for three months in Plymouth harbor by adverse winds. Other attempts failed similarly in 1618–19 and 1622.

Smith's remaining years were divided between these abortive colonizing expeditions and his remaining publications. *New Englands Trials* (1620; augmented in 1622) was first written as a memorial to Francis Bacon, then Lord Chancellor; it is emphatically a work of colonial promotional writing. Smith's major work, *The Generall History* (1624), combined his own writing with earlier accounts and the testimony of other eyewitnesses to produce a connected account of the Virginia venture. Of his later writings, *An Accidence* (1626), revised and augmented as *A Sea Grammar* (1627), was, remarkably, the first basic manual of naval terminology and practice in the English language. *The True Travels* (1630) recounted the events of Smith's rather improbable career once more; he had already offered Purchas much of the same material for his *Pilgrimes*. The *Advertisements* (1631) provided Smith's final words of advice to the colonists of the new world, present and future.

Although the specific details of Smith's life during these final years are unknown, references in his works and other documents connected with him indicate that he had developed an acquaintanceship that included Sir Samuel Saltonstall, Sir Robert Cotton, John Tradescant, and the poets John Donne and John Taylor. Smith died on 21 June 1631 at the age of fifty-one. The cause of his death has not been recorded. He was buried at St. Sepulchre's Church in London; although his original memorial tablet was burned in the Great Fire of London, a replica is visible today, with a text based on the copy from Stow's *Survey of London*.

MAJOR THEMES

As a writer, John Smith remains of first importance for his influential descriptions of the new American continent, its natives, and the early English settlements here, together with his encouragement and advice for future settlers. His works fall under many categories: travel or migration literature, history, autobiography, scientific or ethnological observation, promotional pamphlets, and works of instruction. His chief work remains the *Generall History of Virginia*, a narrative providing valuable early information about the Jamestown colony and its surroundings.

One of the major difficulties for modern critics in evaluating John Smith as a historical source has been the fact that he cannot be regarded under any circumstances as an objective professional historian. Except on the rarest occasions, Smith is a solidly personal writer with vigorous opinions reporting his own highly colored experiences. His candid and emphatic views make his work lively to read; he puts the stamp of a forceful personality on his most straightforward works of instruction. This feature becomes the source of both his most enduring contributions to the literature and legend of America, and the greatest problems for his critics.

The *Generall History* set out to be a comprehensive account of English colonization in the New World. It collects material published by Smith himself earlier, as well as appropriate sections of Hakluyt's *Voyages* and manuscript materials made available by Samuel Purchas to record earlier voyages, together with the most recent news of New England. The *Generall History* has been regarded since its publication as an invaluable historical source. It has also been seen as a somewhat idiosyncratic production. Smith's work, here as elsewhere, is frank, opinionated, frequently and necessarily self-justifying, and strongly committed to its subject, reflecting very clearly its author's own character as well as the circumstances under which he wrote.

Among his shorter works—pamphlets, really, rather than full-length books—*The Accidence* and *The Sea Grammar* are important as the earliest manuals of everyday seagoing language and basic practice in the English language. They should be classified among the popular Jacobean works of self-improvement, and fall rather outside the main body of Smith's writings.

The *True Travels*, written at the request of Sir Robert Cotton the antiquary for a separate account of Smith's eventful European past, reworks the account Smith gave in Purchas's *Pilgrimes* into a volume of travel and chivalric adventures in Europe and Asia. Again, this was a popular genre with the seventeenth-century public, as Smith and his publishers undoubtedly recognized.

Smith's first composition, *A True Relation*, and his later *Map of Virginia* were probably regarded by his contemporaries as short travel pieces as well as early accounts of doings at the Virginia settlement. The *Description of New England, New Englands Trials*, and the *Advertisement* were enthusiastic works of promotion for the American colonies at the same time that they were valuable sources of information for future settlers; Smith objected that the Puritans who settled Massachusetts found it less expensive to buy his books than to hire their author as a guide to the expedition. *A Map of Virginia* in particular has been praised for Smith's acute observations of the geography and inhabitants of the area surrounding Jamestown; it is still important today as the only source describing the customs, appearance, and language of the Indians of Tidewater Virginia at this early period. The *Advertisement*, Smith's last work, is famous for its generous commendation of the latest Puritan settlement in New England; Smith clearly had no idea of the religious biases of the group he was praising. His final words of advice to future colonists are remarkable for their tolerance and breadth of outlook.

All of Smith's writings are valued today for their author's detailed observations. His interest in exact numbers, names, and locations allows Smith to give an uncommonly vivid picture of his surroundings and to present his opinions with force. Smith's opposition to the Jamestown settlers' preoccupation with tobacco and gold, his insistence on the primary need for agricultural self-sufficiency, and his interest in timber, furs, fishing, and eventually wine-making as useful American products reveal him as a sensible if not prophetic advocate of the New World. Jacobean in the liveliness of their prose, Smith's works are characteristic of nobody but their author in their sincerity, specificity, and vivid presentation of personal triumphs and frustrations.

SURVEY OF CRITICISM

The study of John Smith's writings has tended to focus primarily on the question of whether the Captain can be relied on as a reporter of events. Thomas Fuller's *Worthies of England* (1660) first challenged Smith on the grounds that he was the sole reporter of many of his important exploits. Later in the century Henry Wharton's life of Smith in Latin reestablished him as a respectable witness, at least as far as its author was concerned. The debate was renewed in the nineteenth century by Charles Deane and by Henry Adams, then a young historian searching for a controversial subject in the wake of the Civil War. Since then, the efforts of a series of historians working in the United States, England, and throughout Europe have succeeded in reasserting Smith's essential veracity. Laura Polanyi Striker, Bradford Smith, and Philip L. Barbour have been particularly instrumental in this effort.

The most thorough account of Smith's life is Barbour's *The Three Worlds of Captain John Smith*; since its appearance in 1964, all students of Smith have been deeply indebted to it. The biographical writings of Bradford Smith and Laura Polanyi Striker are still well worth consulting.

The sensational possibilities of Smith's career, with his controversial position as a historian and his central role in American legend, have given rise to a number of very unreliable popular biographies as well. These are perhaps best regarded as witnesses to the importance of the Captain as a figure in folklore rather than as sources of biographical information.

As a writer Smith has been much less studied than he deserves. Everett H. Emerson's is the one extended study to attempt a characterization of Smith as an author. Bradford Smith and Philip Barbour devote some attention to Smith's writing as part of their biographies. Jennifer Robin Goodman's brief study of Smith and Percy G. Adams's comments on him emphasize in different ways the connections between travel and imaginative writing in Smith's works. The thrust of recent criticism, led perhaps by Emerson, is directed toward the attempt to give Smith greater credit as a master of narrative writing. Consideration of the practical aims that induced Smith to become an author seems now to be giving way to interest in his writings as enjoyable prose compositions. This shift in critical attitudes towards Smith from the strict concern for historical fact to an appreciation of his lively talents as narrator can only enhance his position as one of the most important of the early Southern authors.

Publication in 1986 of the three-volume *The Complete Works of Captain John Smith*, edited by Philip L. Barbour et al., should spark new interest in Smith as a writer. The introductions, textual notes, chronologies, and annotations in this splendid edition should provide ample opportunities for students and scholars to look with fresh eyes on Smith's works and to reexamine his importance as an early chronicler of the strange New World.

BIBLIOGRAPHY

Works by Captain John Smith

The first collected edition was *Captain John Smith, President of Virginia, and Admiral of New England. Works. 1608–1631*, published in two volumes and edited by Edward Arber (Birmingham, England: English Scholar's Library Edition, 1884). A. G. Bradley reprinted Arber's edition as *Travels and Works of Captain John Smith, President of Virginia, and Admiral of New England, 1580–1631* in two volumes (Edinburgh, Scotland: John Grant, 1910), with new biographical and critical introductions. These editions have been superseded by the three-volume edition published in 1986: *The Complete Works of Captain John Smith (1580–1631)*, edited by Philip L. Barbour et al., and published for the Institute of Early American History and Culture, Williamsburg, Virginia, by the University of North Carolina Press, Chapel Hill.

A True Relation of such occurences and accidents of noate as hath hapned in Virginia. London: Printed for John Tappe, by W[illiam] W[elby], 1608.

A Map of Virginia. With a Description of the Countrey, the Commodities, People, Government and Religion. Oxford: Joseph Barnes, 1612.

A Description of New England: Or the Observations and discoveries, of Captain John Smith. London: Humfrey Lownes, for Robert Clerke, 1616.

New England Trials. Declaring the successe of 26 Ships. London: William Jones, 1620.

New Englands Trials. London: William Jones, 1622. (Enlarged by 12 pages.)

The Generall History of Virginia, the Somer Isles, and New England. . . . London, 1623. A four-page advertisement.

The Generall History of Virginia, New-England, and the Summer Isles. . . . London: Printed by J[ohn] D[awson] and J[ohn] H[aviland] for Michael Sparkes, 1624.

An Accidence (for the Sea), or The Pathway to Experience. London: Printed for Jonas Man and Benjamin Fisher, 1626.

"John Smith of his friend Master John Taylor and his Armado." In John Taylor, *An Armado*. London, 1627.

A Sea Grammar, With the Plaine Exposition of Smith's Accidence for young Sea-men, enlarged. London: John Haviland, 1627.

"In the due Honor of the Author Master Robert Norton, and his Worke." In Robert Norton, *The Gunner*. London, 1628. (These two poems are reprinted in "Two 'Unknown' Poems by Captain John Smith," ed. Philip L. Barbour, *Virginia Magazine of History and Biography* 75 (1967): 157–58.

The True Travels, Adventures, and Observations of Captaine John Smith, In Europe, Asia, Africa, and America, from Anno Domini 1593 to 1629. London: John Haviland for Thomas Slater, 1630.

Advertisements For the unexperienced Planters of New-England, or any where. Or, The Path-way to experience to erect a Plantation. London: John Haviland, 1631.

Captain John Smith's America: Selections from His Writings. Ed. John Lankford. New York: Harper and Row, 1967.

Studies of Captain John Smith

Adams, Percy G. *Travel Literature and the Evolution of the Novel*. Lexington: University of Kentucky Press, 1984.

Andrews, Matthew Page. *The Soul of a Nation: The Founding of Virginia and the Projection of New England*. New York: Charles Scribner's Sons, 1943.

Barbour, Philip L. *The Three Worlds of Captain John Smith*. Boston: Houghton Mifflin, 1964.

Dunn, Richard S. "Seventeenth-Century English Historians of America." *Seventeenth-Century America*. Ed. James Morton Smith. Chapel Hill: University of North Carolina Press, 1959.

Eames, Wilberforce. "Bibliography of Captain John Smith." *Bibliotheca Americana: A Dictionary of Books Relating to America*. 29 vols. Ed. Joseph Sabin et al. New York: Bibliography Society of America, 1868–1937. Repr. New York: BSA, 1927. 20: 218–63.

Emerson, Everett H. *Captain John Smith*. New York: Twayne, 1971.

Glenn, Keith. "Captain John Smith and the Indians." *Virginia Magazine of History and Biography* 52 (1944): 228–48.

Goodman, Jennifer Robin. "The Captain's Self-Portrait: John Smith as Chivalric Biographer." *Virginia Magazine of History and Biography* 89 (January 1981): 27–38.

Rozwenc, Edwin C. "Captain John Smith's Image of America." *William and Mary Quarterly* 3d ser., 16 (1959): 26–36.

Smith, Bradford. *Captain John Smith: His Life and Legend*. Philadelphia: J. B. Lippincott, 1953.

Striker, Laura Polanyi. "The Hungarian Historian, Lewis A. Knopf, on Captain John Smith's *True Travels*: A Reappraisal." *Virginia Magazine of History and Biography* 66 (January 1958): 22–43.

———, trans. *The Life of Captain John Smith, English Soldier*, by Henry Wharton (1685). Chapel Hill: University of North Carolina Press, 1957.

Striker, Laura Polanyi and Bradford Smith. "The Rehabilitation of Captain John Smith." *Journal of Southern History* 28 (1962): 474–81.

Vaughan, Alden T. *American Genesis: Captain John Smith and the Founding of Virginia*. Boston: Little, Brown, 1975.

GERALD M. GARMON

John Reuben Thompson
(1823–1873)

Of the writers who helped shape American literature in the nineteenth century, John Reuben Thompson was far more important than his present reputation would suggest. He was an accomplished editor, journalist, essayist, reviewer, letter writer, poet, and conversationalist who knew many of the best writers of his time and helped to create a sense of purpose and unity in American letters.

BIOGRAPHY

John Reuben Thompson was born in Richmond, Virginia, on 23 October 1823. His father was from New Hampshire and had married Sarah Dyckman of New York before moving to Richmond (ca. 1818) to open a hat, cap, and fur store. They lived in rooms above the shop, where John Reuben was born. The Thompsons with their three children, John, Susan, and Sarah, were a happy, close family. John started school in Richmond, then spent a year, 1836, at a preparatory school in East Haven, Connecticut, then returned to finish at the newly opened Richmond Academy, from which he was graduated in 1840. The following fall he entered the University of Virginia, where he was an indifferent student; however, he was graduated in July 1842 with a major in chemistry and a reputation as an accomplished linguist. He entered the law offices of James A. Seddon, and in 1844 returned to Charlottesville and earned a Bachelor of Law degree. He set up a law practice in Richmond but showed more interest in society and literature than in law.

Unhappy at the practice of law, Thompson determined to make his way as a writer. On the basis of vague hopes and vaguer expectations, he began to look for a place on a magazine. Thus, when his friend B. B. Minor determined to sell the *Southern Literary Messenger*, Thompson, with his father's backing, purchased it for $2,500.

Thompson remained editor of the *Southern Literary Messenger* for thirteen years, from 1847 to 1860. While he was editor, he worked tirelessly to establish a reading public in the South; to increase his public's taste in reading; to create a larger, more stable group of American writers; to cement relations between the writers of North and South; and to encourage young writers. Among his contributors and literary contacts were Henry Wadsworth Longfellow; Donald Grant Mitchell (Ik Marvel); Sarah Whitman; Thomas Dunn English; Thomas Bailey Aldrich; his close friends Philip Pendleton Cooke and his brother, John Esten Cooke; William Gilmore Simms; and Edgar Allan Poe.

Thompson's name is mentioned rarely today, and when it is, it is usually in connection with those of Poe and Rufus Griswold. In summer 1848—a year after Thompson had taken over the *Messenger*—Poe returned to Richmond. Thompson was told by a stranger that Poe had been "several days at a tavern in the lower section of the city; and his friends ought to look after him." Thompson found Poe and offered him the use of the *Messenger* office for the duration of his stay there. Poe left Richmond in September, and between that time and his return in June 1849, he wrote at least six letters to Thompson. Poe spent much of his time during his 1849 stay in the *Messenger* office, and as he was leaving in September he said to Thompson, "By the way, you have been very kind to me—here is a little trifle that may be worth something to you." He handed Thompson a small roll of paper with the verses of "Annabel Lee" written on it. Poe went from Richmond to Baltimore, and there he died on 7 October.

In the November *Messenger*, Thompson published his tribute to Poe, whom he regarded as a friend, and praised his strengths as a writer and his contributions to literature and, in particular, to the *Messenger*. He ended with a conciliatory note, but one that has since been much misunderstood: "That he had many and sad infirmities cannot be questioned. Over these we would throw in charity the mantle of forgetfulness. The grave has come between our perception and his errors, and we pass them over in silence. They found indeed a mournful expiation in his alienated friendships and his early death." These are the most negative words Thompson ever published on Poe, but because of his acquaintance with Griswold and an unsigned essay published in the *Messenger* in 1850 by John Moncure Daniel—during the interim editorship of John Esten Cooke—Thompson has been placed in the Griswold circle and has been frequently slighted by Poe scholars for that reason.

Later, in 1859, Thompson presented a lecture, which he repeated often over the rest of his life, titled "The Genius and Character of Edgar Allan Poe." Its purpose, ostensibly, was the "sincere desire of arriving at a juster estimate of Poe." And it is probably from this time, with the aid of Mrs. Whitman, that Poe's reputation began its recovery to respectability.

In 1860 Thompson left the *Messenger* and accepted an editorship of the

Southern Field and Fireside in Augusta, Georgia, at a great increase in salary. But Thompson was already suffering from consumption, which was irritated by hot weather, and after a particularly debilitating summer, he resigned and returned to Richmond in November. He was still looking for a new position when the Civil War began. Since his health made him unfit for military duty, he became a journalist, and some time in the early months of the war he became assistant to the Secretary of the Commonwealth of Virginia. Thompson also helped with the state library, issued the official war news, and wrote occasional speeches for the governor of Virginia. Much of his writing at this time was as war correspondent to the Memphis *Daily Appeal* and the London *Index*, the Confederate organ in England. He was also writing more poetry.

But the steady strain and work weakened Thompson's health, and in June 1864 he departed Richmond to join the staff of the London *Index*, of which he later became editor. While in London, Thompson renewed his acquaintance with William Makepeace Thackeray and met his daughter Anne—later Lady Richie. Between these two grew a warm friendship. Another friendship developed between Thompson and Thomas Carlyle, who sided with the Southern cause. When the *Index* closed in 1865, Thompson stayed on in London writing for the *Standard*, *Blackwood's*, the *Cosmopolitan*, and other periodicals there as well as for the Louisville *Journal* and the New Orleans *Crescent Monthly* and the *Picayune*. Then he was contracted to write a book-length memoir by Heros Van Borcke, former chief of staff of General J.E.B. Stuart. Busy as he was, Thompson made numerous friends among the writers and artists of London; among the more famous friendships he cultivated were those with the Brownings, John Everett Millais, Holman Hunt, Charles Dickens, Wilkie Collins, and Alfred, Lord Tennyson—at whose home Thompson spent a long weekend—but even this attractive society and reasonably stable employment could not keep Thompson from going back home to see what damage the war had done.

Yet back in the United States Thompson could find no work and wandered about between Richmond and New York for three desperate years before William Cullen Bryant, editor of the New York *Evening Post*, hired him in 1868 as his first literary editor. Thompson remained in New York until his death on 30 April 1873. He was a close friend to Bryant and well liked by his colleagues, one of whom, Watson R. Sperry, wrote that Thompson was a "Rebel to be loved. . . . Mr. Thompson had a big man's beard, a delicate body, and a sensitive feminine nature. He was a bit punctilious, but kindness itself."

MAJOR THEMES

Thompson's achievement as a critic and editor—and with him the jobs were inseparable—was considerable. He possessed the necessary attributes, none of them brilliant but all competent and useful. He had endurance, despite his struggle with consumption. He kept the *Messenger* going longer than any other magazine in the country at that time except the *Knickerbocker*, which was a year older.

He endured, and he was tactful. He was not temperamentally suited to the kind of criticism he called the "tomahawk" or "slashing," the kind at which Poe excelled. Thompson praised almost everything, Southern and Northern; praise came naturally to him. He carried with him for most of his life a disposition to think the best of people and events. But he did have prejudices, as all men do. He preferred the South and supported whatever its authors produced; yet he did not sacrifice the literary independence of the *Messenger* for the popularity that a more thoroughgoing sectionalism would have brought him. He refused, for example, to let the *Messenger* become the voice of politics of any kind; though he did write a thoroughly "slashing" review of *Uncle Tom's Cabin*, his attack was primarily on literary grounds.

He admired the moral tone. He singled out Hawthorne as one "attuned to all that is good in nature." He was influenced by the New York force field known as the genteel tradition: Richard Henry Stoddard, Edmund Clarence Stedman, Thomas Bailey Aldrich, and Bayard Taylor. He was unoriginal and classic in his search for form and idea that have their origin in works already esteemed. As a critic he looked backward and seemed often incapable of understanding the value of what was new in works of genius. Yet he was forced to deal with and seemed genuinely to admire the rough and crude humor of the Southwest humorists; nor did he agree with the genteel tradition in its refusal to recognize change.

In poetry he attempted nothing new or original, but he had a broad, genial, and compassionate view of man, which, if it did not inspire, often moved his readers to pity or laughter. One of his strengths was humorous poetry, and at his best he approached the comic genius of Lord Byron, but he lacked Byron's bite. Much of his poetry was magazine verse on public occasions, such as his "Sonnet on the Death of Zachary Taylor" or on the death of his friend "Philip Pendleton Cooke." They are solid, workmanlike, conventional poems, durable and at times touching, topical, appealing, and immediate. At times he could turn a graceful phrase, but he lacked depth of thought and any mastery of subtle prosody. All of his poetry was characterized by the hackneyed and cumbersome poetic diction of the eighteenth century. Still, well into the twentieth century his popular and conciliatory war poems, including "Ashby," "The Burial of Latane," "Lee to the Rear," and "Music in Camp," were commonly included in anthologies of historical verse.

SURVEY OF CRITICISM

Understandably, little has been written about Thompson in recent times, though his name appears often in works on Poe where the intention is without exception to minimize Thompson's influence on Poe's reputation. C. M. Graves's essay, "Thompson, the Confederate," is a biographical sketch. John Rodney Miller's dissertation for the University of Virginia is the only comprehensive work on Thompson, but it, too, is largely biographical and accepts the traditional interpretation of Thompson and his work. Gerald M. Garmon's biography for the Twayne Series is the only published book on Thompson.

BIBLIOGRAPHY

Works by John Reuben Thompson

Across the Atlantic. New York: Derby and Jackson, 1857. [Based on Thompson's European journey in 1854, this book was burned before it could be issued. The only copy is in the University of Virginia Library.]
The Poems of John R. Thompson. Ed. John S. Patton. New York: Scribner's, 1920. [With the exception of one poem, which appears in Garmon's book, all of Thompson's known poetry is collected here.]
The Genius and Character of Edgar Allan Poe. Richmond: Whitty and Rindfleish, 1929.
Letters and Papers in the Thompson Collection, University of Virginia Library.
"Some Unpublished Letters of John R. Thompson and Augustin Louis Taveau." Ed. David K. Jackson. *William and Mary Quarterly* 16 (April 1936): 206–21.
"A Southern Response to Mrs. Stowe: Two letters of John R. Thompson." Ed. Henry T. Manierre. *Virginia Magazine of History and Biography* 49 (January 1961): 83–92.

Studies of John Reuben Thompson

Andrews, J. Cutler. *The South Reports the Civil War*. Princeton, N.J.: Princeton University Press, 1970.
Bagby, George W. *John Daniel's Latch Key: A Memoir of the Late Editor of the Richmond Examiner*. Lynchburg, Va.: J. P. Bell, 1868.
Beaty, John O. *John Esten Cooke, Virginian*. New York: Columbia University Press, 1922.
Cooke, John Esten. "John Reuben Thompson." *Hearth and Home*, December 20, 1873.
Garmon, Gerald M. *John Reuben Thompson*. Boston: Twayne, 1979.
Graves, Charles Marshall. "Thompson, the Confederate." *Lamp* 30, no. 3 (October 1904): 181–90.
McCabe, William Gordon. "John R. Thompson." *Library of Southern Literature*, vol. 13. Ed. Edwin A. Alderman and Joel Chandler Harris. Atlanta: Martin & Hoyt, 1907–1910.
Miller, Joseph Rodney. "John Reuben Thompson: His Place in Southern Life and Literature." Ph.D. diss., University of Virginia, 1930.

William Tappan Thompson
(1812–1882)

William Tappan Thompson was one of the most popular humorists in America during the middle of the nineteenth century. Editions of *Major Jones's Courtship*, his best-known book, were often read until they fell apart. Although Thompson is no longer widely read, a few of his fictional letters and sketches are worth remembering as notable examples of humorously realistic writing.

BIOGRAPHY

Little is known about William Tappan Thompson's ancestry. His father, David Thompson, was a Virginian; and his mother, Catherine Kerney, was a native of Dublin, Ireland, who emigrated to America with her father after the 1798 Irish revolution against the British. Shortly before the outbreak of the War of 1812, David and Catherine Thompson moved to the Connecticut Western Reserve, settling in Portage County, Ohio. Here their son William Tappan was born 31 August 1812 in the recently founded town of Ravenna. Thompson spent his first years in this frontier village and nearby Brimfield. His mother died when he was eleven, and at the age of fourteen he decided to leave home to earn his own living. Not long afterwards his father also died.

Thompson went to Philadelphia and eventually obtained a job on the *Daily Chronicle*, probably as a printer's devil. During his three-year stay in the city, he attended plays and even joined an amateur theatrical company. In the process he developed an interest in the stage that in future years led him to write his own plays. Through the influence of relatives or friends, he became the private secretary of James D. Westcott, who had recently been appointed by President Andrew Jackson as secretary for the Territory of Florida. Thompson also planned to read law under his new employer.

Thompson and Westcott arrived in Tallahassee in 1830. At this time the capital of the territory was a colorful small town on the Southern frontier. During his four years as Westcott's assistant, Thompson observed exciting events and eccentric characters that he later portrayed in his first sketches. He heard stirring accounts of duels fought by prominent men. At least twice he traveled with Westcott to the Seminole reservation in central Florida to help pay a government annuity to the Indians. On one occasion he represented the governor in an unsuccessful attempt to apprehend desperadoes who had robbed an Indian chief living on the Apalachicola River. Through these and other experiences, Thompson gained firsthand knowledge about frontier life and formed a lasting attachment to the South.

In 1834 he left Florida and went to Augusta, Georgia, where he arranged to read law under Augustus Baldwin Longstreet. He also worked in the printing office of the *States Rights Sentinel*, a newspaper recently purchased by Longstreet. The Judge, as Longstreet was affectionately known, soon achieved fame as the author of *Georgia Scenes* (1835), a collection of realistically humorous sketches first published in Georgia periodicals. Undoubtedly, Longstreet had a significant influence on Thompson. Several of Thompson's earliest sketches resemble those in *Georgia Scenes* in both subject matter and style.

During part of 1836 Thompson served in the Florida Seminole Indian War with the Richmond Blues, a volunteer unit from Augusta. He wrote several letters about the campaign for anonymous publication in the *States Rights Sentinel*. After his return to Augusta, this paper also carried his first published sketch, "The Seminole Dance. An Extract from the Journal of a Private Secretary," based upon a visit he had made to the Seminole reservation while working under Westcott. ("The Seminole Dance" is an uncollected sketch. See: *States Rights Sentinel* [Augusta, Ga.] 3 [8 July 1836]: 2.)

On 12 June 1837 Thompson married Caroline Love Carrie of Augusta. They eventually had ten children, but only four lived to be adults. Thompson was devoted to his wife and dedicated the 1872 edition of *Major Jones's Courtship* to her with these words: "To my wife, the dear companion, who blessed the morning, cheered the noon, and brightens the evening of my life, I dedicate this volume."

In May 1838 he and another veteran of the Richmond Blues established the *Augusta Mirror*, a semimonthly magazine featuring literature and the arts. A number of Thompson's writings first appeared in this periodical, including the novelette *John's Alive; or, The Bride of a Ghost* and the five sketches later gathered under the title "Recollections of the Florida Campaign of 1836."

Financial problems forced Thompson to merge the *Augusta Mirror* with the *Family Companion and Ladies' Mirror*, a monthly magazine published in Macon, Georgia, by Benjamin F. Griffin and edited by his wife, Sarah. Thompson's first Major Jones letter appeared in the June 1842 issue of the magazine. He wrote this humorous dialect letter as a satire of the sentimental language used in many of the literary periodicals of that time.

After a sharp disagreement with the Griffins, Thompson left the *Family Com-*

panion in August 1842 to become editor of the Madison, Georgia, *Southern Miscellany*, a newspaper published by Cornelius R. Hanleiter. To increase the circulation of this country weekly, Thompson began publishing a series of humorous letters from Major Jones, after first revising and reprinting the initial letter that had appeard in the *Family Companion*. In 1843 he collected the first sixteen letters, and Hanleiter published them in a pamphlet under the title *Major Jones's Courtship*. In 1844 Carey and Hart, a Philadelphia company, published a second enlarged edition that had 26 letters and included illustrations by F.O.C. Darley. The 1847 edition contained all 28 of the Major Jones letters that were ever collected.

The *Southern Miscellany* experienced financial difficulties, and in February 1844 Hanleiter could no longer afford to retain his editor. Thompson returned to Augusta and soon afterwards gathered eight of his sketches into a volume entitled *Chronicles of Pineville*, which Carey and Hart published in 1845. Later that year he went to New York to supervise publication of William A. Hotchkiss's *A Codification of the Statute Law of Georgia* (1845). While in New York, he entered into a partnership with Park Benjamin, a poet and former editor of the *New World*, to establish a weekly family newspaper in Baltimore. The first issue of this paper, the *Western Continent*, appeared in January 1846; but within a few months Benjamin resigned, since he and Thompson disagreed over editorial policies. While editing this paper, Thompson published a new series of Major Jones letters and collected 22 of them in *Major Jones's Sketches of Travel, Comprising the Scenes, Incidents, and Adventures in His Tour from Georgia to Canada* (1848). He also wrote an introduction for a series of pro-slavery letters submitted to the *Western Continent* by A. B. Longstreet and published them in *A Voice from the South: Comprising Letters from Georgia to Massachusetts, and to the Southern States* (1847). Thompson continued as editor of the paper, and briefly as sole proprietor, until 1848, when he sold his interest.

During his years in Baltimore, Thompson wrote a dramatic adaptation of the first fifteen Major Jones letters entitled *Major Jones's Courtship; or Adventures of a Christmas Eve, a Domestic Comedy, in Two Acts* (1850). He also wrote two other plays, *The Live Indian* and a dramatic version of Oliver Goldsmith's *The Vicar of Wakefield*, neither of which was ever published.

In December 1849 Thompson returned to Georgia and joined John M. Cooper in founding a daily newspaper in Savannah. The first number of the *Daily Morning News*, as the paper was known, appeared on 15 January 1850. With the exception of a brief period at the end of the Civil War and immediately afterwards, Thompson served as editor of the paper until his death 32 years later.

When Confederate batteries opened fire on Fort Sumter, Thompson took a train to Charleston and witnessed part of the bombardment. He served as an aide-de-camp to the Adjutant and Inspector General of Georgia during 1862 and helped to organize state militia units for recruitment into the Confederate Army. Throughout the war he vigorously supported the Southern cause in his editorials. When General William Tecumseh Sherman's army entered Savannah in December 1864, Thompson left the city with the retreating Confederate soldiers and spent the remainder of the war as a private foot soldier.

After the war Thompson and his family experienced many hardships. He had no job, he was ill, and his family was nearly destitute. He wrote a sketch, *Truth at the Bottom of a Well, or How Billy Williams Escaped from the Deserters*, which was published as a pamphlet in 1865. He hoped that the sketch would sell well enough to contribute to the family income. Eventually, he accepted a position as associate editor of the Savannah *Daily Herald*, a newspaper established in the old offices of the *Daily Morning News* by Samuel W. Mason, a Union journalist.

In 1867 Thompson traveled to Europe to tour the Paris Exposition and take notes for a new book to be entitled "Major Jones in Europe." He sent several letters describing his travels to the *Daily News and Herald*, the new name of Mason's paper; but he never completed the proposed book. He also negotiated with a London publisher for an English edition of *Major Jones's Courtship*, but the sudden appearance of a pirated version of the book ruined the market for an authorized publication.

Thompson became editor of the *Daily News and Herald* in June 1868 when Mason sold his interest in the paper to John Holbrook Estill, a young Savannah businessman. Later that year the paper was renamed the Savannah *Morning News*. With Thompson's editorial expertise and Estill's energy and business skills, the *Morning News* prospered.

Joel Chandler Harris joined Thompson's staff in 1870, beginning as a writer of humorous paragraphs. He later became assistant editor and sometimes wrote the lead editorials when Thompson was out of town. Harris wrote a number of letters, articles, and poems for the *Morning News* before leaving in 1876 for a position on the Atlanta *Constitution*.

In 1872 D. Appleton and Company of New York published a revised edition of *Major Jones's Courtship*, to which Thompson had added thirteen humorous sketches. T. B. Peterson and Brothers of Philadelphia later published *Rancy Cottem's Courtship* (1879), a book created by adding a revised version of *Truth at the Bottom of a Well* to the thirteen sketches included in the Appleton edition of *Major Jones's Courtship*.

Thompson was deeply involved in politics in the years following the Civil War. He was a delegate to the National Democratic Convention in New York in 1868. During summer 1877 he participated in a convention in Atlanta to draft a new constitution for Georgia. In 1879 he was seriously considered as the nominee for Congress from his congressional district, when the incumbent died, but the convention nominated another man.

Thompson was not well during his final years. He had yellow fever during the severe 1876 epidemic in Savannah and never fully recovered his health. He died 24 March 1882 at his home on Columbia Square in Savannah. His funeral was held at Trinity Methodist Church, and he was buried in Laurel Grove Cemetery. Tributes to him appeared in papers throughout the South and other parts of the nation. The next year his daughter, Mary Augusta Wade, gathered several of his uncollected writings and had them published under the title *John's Alive; or, The Bride of a Ghost, and Other Sketches* (1883).

MAJOR THEMES

Many of Thompson's sketches and fictional letters provide a humorously realistic portrait of rustic life in the antebellum South. Although colorful characters, comic incidents, homespun sayings, and humorous dialect are the most noticeable features of these writings, significant themes and ideas are also present. Common sense as a standard of conduct is a pervasive theme throughout his work. Much of his humor arises from the portrayal of characters who lack common sense. In his later fiction a defense of the South and its institutions is an important motif. Early in his career Thompson also wrote editorial articles to encourage the growth of Southern letters as a means of protecting the South and promoting its interests. He believed that this literature should be realistic rather than sentimental, and he followed this concept in his own writing. Another theme concerns the pathos and suffering that underlie the surface reality of characters and events in his fictional world. Although much of Thompson's work has a lighthearted, comic viewpoint, a somber, more serious perspective is sometimes evident.

Thompson presents common sense and morality as standards for the conduct of individuals and communities. Departures from these standards are targets for his humor and, occasionally, his satire. He depicts homespun common sense in opposition to affectation and foolish extremes. Often the characters in his sketches, through a lack of practical sense, become victims of their own naïveté or foolishness, exposing themselves to the jokes, and sometimes the cruelty, of pranksters.

Thompson's spokesman for common sense and morality is Major Joseph Jones of Pineville, Georgia. He is the central character in *Major Jones's Courtship* (1843), *Major Jones's Sketches of Travel* (1848), the play *Major Jones's Courtship; or Adventures of a Christmas Eve* (1850), and the unpublished fragment "Major Jones in Europe" (ca. 1867). The Major embodies the best American qualities from a rural Southern viewpoint. He represents the middle-class farmer who has practical sense, honesty, and integrity, even though he sometimes falls victim to practical jokers or makes a fool of himself. To some extent he resembles Seba Smith's Major Jack Downing in his outspoken independence, but Major Jones is not so exclusively concerned with politics as is his New England counterpart. The Major is a planter who owns a few slaves and works in the fields with them. Although lacking in formal education, he is familiar with Shakespeare and a few other writers. His spelling and grammar are atrocious, but he enjoys writing long gossipy letters to his editor friend, Mr. Thompson. He is an advocate for old-fashioned virtue, moderation, conservatism, and patriotism. Through this character Thompson voiced many of the conservative values of middle-class

Southerners. The pungent language and dialect in which these views were expressed gave the Major's letters a broad appeal among this class of readers.

Thompson portrays a lack of common sense in *Chronicles of Pineville*. The virtues of homespun wisdom explicitly proclaimed in *Major Jones's Courtship* are largely implied by their absence in this collection of sketches. The setting is Pineville, the Major's village, but the Major himself appears in only one sketch, "The Mystery Revealed." Most of the sketches focus upon a colorful individual who appears foolish as a result of naïveté, pretentiousness, or overindulgence in some vice, such as drinking.

Chronicles of Pineville is significant as one of the earliest and most thorough realistic portrayals of a Southern community in American humorous writing. Each sketch contributes to a composite portrait of a backwoods village. But Thompson is selective in his details, and the resulting picture is incomplete. Women, children, blacks, and prosperous farmers rarely appear. Instead, most of the sketches feature male characters who are presented as amusing curiosities. In the preface to the book, Thompson states that additional education would eventually form the citizens of such backwoods communities into a great people, making them more respectable but also less interesting. He wished to paint the people in the rural South before time could efface their distinctive characteristics. In this respect he anticipates the local color writers of the next generation.

Some of Thompson's most effective sketches are those that blend humor and pathos with a realistic depiction of vivid characters. "Boss Ankles, the Man What Got Blowed up with a Sky-Racket," "The Duel," and "The Fire-Hunt" have these characteristics. In these sketches the humor is derived at the expense of the main character. This individual becomes the victim of his own folly, and the other characters are amused by his discomfiture, sympathizing only to a limited degree. The narrator remains aloof, relating the story in an unsentimental manner while relishing the humor of the situation. In one sense the central characters deserve being made into laughingstocks because of their foolish or inept behavior, but their punishment also seems somewhat extreme. In "The Fire-Hunt," for example, Samuel Sikes is a persistently unlucky poor white who enjoys illegal nighttime hunting. He is such an inveterate hunter that he neglects his farming and provides a meager living for his nagging wife and "five or six little tallow-faced" children. He persuades the narrator to accompany him on a fire-hunt and accidentally shoots his own mule, mistaking the mule's shining eyes for those of a deer. This misfortune is only the latest in a long string of bad luck, and the conclusion of the sketch implies that the fortunes of Sam and his family will never improve. In "Boss Ankles" Boss is a semiliterate "schoolkeeper" who puts on airs about his limited educational attainments and drinks excessively. Major Ferguson Bangs in "The Duel" is normally a sensible man, but when drunk, he becomes a braggadocio and provokes quarrels. Boss and Major Bangs both become the victims of practical jokes that are carried too far by their fellow townsmen. In these three sketches Thompson satirizes human weaknesses, but he counterbalances the humor by revealing the anguish of the protagonists. He also presents a mischievous side to human nature, showing how people sometimes enjoy the suffering of less fortunate individuals. These sketches and others, such as "The Burglars of Iola" and "How to Kill Two Birds with One Stone," show not only the boisterous humor and surface realism of the backwoods South but also the folly, cruelty, deceit, and pathos inherent in the human condition. Although the perspective is predominantly comic, a dark underside gives greater depth and complexity to these writings.

As the controversy between the North and South became more intense, Thompson used Major Jones as a spokesman for Southern views. Consequently, a significant theme in *Major Jones's Sketches of Travel* (1848) is a defense of the South and its institutions. On his trip to the North and Canada, the Major praises Yankee ingenuity and technology, but he attacks the abolitionists and criticizes the living conditions of free blacks in Northern cities. He claims that slaves in Georgia are materially better off than free blacks in Pennsylvania. He also charges that Northerners are just as racially prejudiced as Southerners and that the abolitionists are misleading blacks with ideas about equality.

After the Civil War Thompson continued to defend the South in "Major Jones in Europe" (ca. 1867). In this unfinished book Major Jones describes his travels in England, but his thoughts occasionally revert to the defeated condition of the South. The people and scenes that he encounters sometimes remind him of the war and the confused situation at home. Upon seeing a statue of Charles I in London, for example, he recalls the English civil war and the turmoil following its conclusion. It is clear, however, that, in describing this conflict, he is really thinking about the American Civil War and its aftermath. In this description he indirectly attacks the North and the Reconstruction policies imposed upon the South. He observes, though, that England eventually recovered from its civil war with a restoration of constitutional government, and he hopes that America may have a similar recovery.

Thompson's defense of the South included promoting the growth of Southern literature. In several editorials and reviews published in the *Augusta Mirror* and the *Southern Miscellany*, he expressed his ideas on literature in general and Southern writing in particular. He questioned why a literary magazine could not be sustained in the South and concluded that in literature, as in other matters, Southerners were too dependent upon the North. Southern writers, he believed, should create a bold, original literature of their own. He stated that the writings of fashionable authors in the North were filled with sickly sentimentalism as a result of dwelling too much on the titled nobility of Europe. Southern literature, though still in its infancy, was different, promising to be "staunch republican, when grown." He wrote that Southern institutions "favor the growth of a purely American literature, in the same degree that they favor practical republicanism and the inculcation of true democratic sentiment" (Untitled editorial, the *Augusta Mirror* 2 [25 July 1840]: 207). A vigorous domestic literature would protect Southern institutions and advance the conservative interests of education and morals.

Thompson advocated a literature that was practical, moral, and realistic; and he shaped his own stories and sketches to exemplify these ideals. Most of his fiction was directed against affected sentimentality, the antithesis of these values. He modeled his first stories upon Longstreet's *Georgia Scenes*, a collection of realistic sketches he greatly admired. He wrote his first Major Jones letter in reaction to the sentimental language popular at that time in literary periodicals, prefacing the letter with editorial comments attacking such writing.

To some extent, however, Thompson eventually undercut his artistry by using his fiction for nonliterary purposes. He deliberately shaped *Major Jones's Courtship* as an epistolary novel focusing upon the Major's courtship, marriage, and family life. The Major's homespun observations on politics and such social matters as women's bustles and men's beards do not impede the narrative flow or detract from the realistic presentation of his character. In later writings, though, the more Thompson used the Major as a spokesman, the less convincing he became as a character creation in his own right. Sometimes in *Major Jones's Sketches of Travel* and to a greater degree in "Major Jones in Europe," the distinction between the Major as a separate character and Thompson as an editor speaking his own views is blurred. Occasionally, Thompson almost completely drops the Major's dialect to write a passage resembling an editorial. The use of the Major to defend the South and comment on other prominent issues of the day reveals the journalistic nature of much of Thompson's writing. After he had become editor of the Savannah *Daily Morning News*, he became almost totally absorbed in politics and wrote little fiction. This preoccupation perhaps explains why he never completed "Major Jones in Europe." During Reconstruction the crucial political issues required his full attention as an editor.

Thompson is a limited writer who rarely deals with the greatest themes of literature. His characters have little complexity, and many of his sketches are simply comic portraits or moral pieces without depth. Thompson, nevertheless, is a significant minor writer. Although he was chiefly interested in depicting the surface reality of rural life in antebellum Georgia, he accomplished this aim with skill. He is one of a group of nineteenth-century Southern writers who pioneered in the use of realistic dialect. His Major Jones is a vivid, original character in American literature. A few sketches in *Chronicles of Pineville* and elsewhere have genuine literary merit, revealing fundamental truths about human nature through a balanced combination of humor, realism, and pathos. His literary criticism and the example of his own fiction helped define the course of realistic Southern writing.

SURVEY OF CRITICISM

The most important scholarly work on Thompson thus far is Henry Prentice Miller's "The Life and Works of William Tappan Thompson" (1942), a University of Chicago dissertation, only portions of which have been published. This thoroughly researched dissertation contains the most complete biography, critical analysis, and bibliography now available. All subsequent Thompson scholarship relies to some extent upon this study. Miller introduces his dissertation with a short biography of Thompson. In the remainder of his work, he provides a careful analysis of Thompson's fiction and plays, although he devotes more attention to *Major Jones's Courtship*. He briefly discusses the uncollected sketches, including the unpublished manuscript of "Major Jones in Europe." The bibliography offers a comprehensive list of Thompson's fictional writings and records manuscript materials examined.

Miller published a chapter of his dissertation under the title "The Background and Significance of *Major Jones's Courtship*" (1946). This article provides an in-depth analysis of Thompson's best-known book, discussing major influences, the characters, the dialect, the humorous techniques, and the influence of the volume upon later writers. Miller also published a revised appendix from the dissertation as "The Authorship of *The Slaveholder Abroad*" (1944). This brief article offers evidence that one of Thompson's Augusta friends, Ebenezer Starnes, rather than Thompson himself, is the author of *The Slaveholder Abroad* (1869).

Walter Blair's *Horse Sense in American Humor* (1942) focuses upon *Major Jones's Sketches of Travel*, pointing out the Major's horse-sense ideas about such subjects as Whig politics, the education of women, mechanical inventions, patriotism, and slavery. Blair notes that Thompson tends to use the Major as a mouthpiece whenever the subjects of patriotism and slavery appear. He considers *Major Jones's Courtship* as little more than a series of amusing yarns about courtship and marriage with only a few ideas.

A useful brief survey of Thompson's fiction is the article written by Paul R. Lilly, Jr., for *American Humorists, 1800–1950* (1982). Lilly states that Thompson's chief contribution to American humor is the creation of the character Major Jones. He perceives the Major as unique in Southern humor, since other writers were less likely to use colloquial speech to support traditional values.

Another worthwhile study is Robert L. Phillips's 1971 dissertation on the narrative method of Augustus Baldwin Longstreet, William Tappan Thompson, Richard Malcolm Johnston, and Joel Chandler Harris. Phillips states that Thompson's use of a fictional narrator allowed him to be realistic when he wished and to withdraw from a realistic depiction of the South when this step seemed prudent. His realism, on the one hand, and his refusal to portray all aspects of the South realistically, on the other, Phillips claims, is the distinction between the novel and the romance.

Articles on more limited aspects of Thompson's work include D. M. McKeithan's "Mark Twain's Letters of Thomas Jefferson Snodgrass" (1953), Herbert Shippey's "William Tappan Thompson as Playwright" (1978), and David C. Estes's "Major Jones Defends Himself: An Uncollected Letter" (1979–80). McKeithan states that Mark Twain, in writing the Snodgrass letters, was influenced by Thompson's *Major Jones's Sketches of Travel*. He points out correspondences between Twain's letters and Thompson's book. Shippey examines two holograph manuscripts of the dramatized version of *Major Jones's Courtship*, discussing the background for the writing and performance of the play, as well as Thompson's techniques of revision. Estes offers background information on an uncollected Major Jones letter entitled "Reply to 'Pardon Jones,' of the N. O. 'Pic.,' " originally published in the *Southern Miscellany* in 1844 and shortly afterwards reprinted in W. T. Porter's *Spirit of the Times*. The text of the letter follows Estes's introduction.

Presently, the most thorough biography is the unpublished first chapter of Miller's dissertation. In preparing this account, Miller had access to letters and other papers of the Thompson family. He also scanned existing files of the periodicals that Thompson edited. Brief biographical sketches are contained in Jay B. Hubbell's *The South in American Literature, 1607–1900* (1954) and in *Humor of the Old Southwest* (1975), edited by Hennig Cohen and William B. Dillingham. Portions of Thompson's life are covered by several other works. John Donald Wade's *Augustus Baldwin Longstreet: A Study of the Development of Culture in the South* (1924) has some information on Thompson's association with Longstreet in Augusta, Georgia, during the latter half of the 1830s. Gertrude Gilmer's "A Critique of Certain Georgia Ante Bellum Literary Magazines Arranged Chronologically, and a Checklist" (1934) summarizes Thompson's editorial career on the *Augusta Mirror*, the *Family Companion and Ladies' Mirror*, and the *Southern Miscellany*. A more in-depth study of the same periodicals and Thompson's editorship of them may be found in Bertram H. Flanders' *Early Georgia Magazines: Literary Periodicals to 1865* (1944). The best account of Thompson's later editorial activities is given by Carl R. Osthaus in "From the Old South to the New South: The Editorial Career of William Tappan Thompson of the Savannah *Morning News*" (1976).

After Miller's dissertation, the most useful bibliographic work on Thompson's writings is George R. Ellison's "William Tappan Thompson and the *Southern Miscellany*, 1842–1844" (1970). This article includes a chronological list of Thompson's fiction that appeared in the *Southern Miscellany* from 5 April 1842 to 4 March 1844. In *Early Georgia Magazines* Flanders mentions fiction by Thompson published in the *Augusta Mirror*, the *Family Companion and Ladies' Mirror*, and the *Southern Miscellany*.

A number of manuscript letters and other materials pertaining to Thompson's life survive, although most of these items are still in the possession of his descendants. The library of Georgia College in Milledgeville, Georgia, has two manuscript versions of the dramatic adaptation of *Major Jones's Courtship*, in addition to a few letters and a family scrapbook. Selected items from a more extensive collection of original papers are on microfilm at the South Carolinian Library of the University of South Carolina in Columbia.

Thompson's letters, uncollected fiction, and selections from his nonfiction writings need to be collected. A full-length biography is also needed. Publication of these items may reveal that Thompson is a more versatile writer than has been previously supposed. His significance in the history of Southern journalism and Georgia politics may also be more clearly perceived. Until these materials are published, scholars cannot fully assess his position in American literature.

BIBLIOGRAPHY

Works by William Tappan Thompson

Major Jones's Courtship: Detailed, with Other Scenes, Incidents and Adventures, in a Series of Letters, by Himself. To Which Is Added, The "Great Attraction!" Madison, Ga.: C. R. Hanleiter, 1843.

Major Jones's Courtship: Detailed, with Other Scenes, Incidents, and Adventures, in a Series of Letters, by Himself. Second Edition, Greatly Enlarged. Philadelphia: Carey and Hart, 1844.

Chronicles of Pineville: Embracing Sketches of Georgia Scenes, Incidents, and Characters. Philadelphia: Carey and Hart, 1845.

John's Alive; or, The Bride of a Ghost. Baltimore: Taylor, Wilde, 1846.

"Introduction" to [Augustus Baldwin Longstreet]. *A Voice from the South: Comprising Letters from Georgia to Massachusetts, and to the Southern States.* Baltimore: Western Continent Press, 1847.

Major Jones's Sketches of Travel, Comprising the Scenes, Incidents, and Adventures in His Tour from Georgia to Canada. Philadelphia: Carey and Hart, 1848.

Major Jones's Courtship; or Adventures of a Christmas Eve, a Domestic Comedy, in Two Acts. Savannah, Ga.: Edward J. Purse, 1850.

Truth at the Bottom of a Well, or How Billy Williams Escaped from the Deserters. Augusta, Ga.: Printed at the Constitutionalist Office, 1865.

Major Jones's Courtship: Detailed, with Other Scenes, Incidents, and Adventures, in a Series of Letters by Himself. Revised and Enlarged. To Which Are Added Thirteen Humorous Sketches. New York: D. Appleton, 1872.

Rancy Cottem's Courtship. Detailed, with Other Humorous Sketches and Adventures. Philadelphia: T. B. Peterson, [1879].

John's Alive; or, The Bride of a Ghost, and Other Sketches. Philadelphia: David McKay, 1883.

Studies of William Tappan Thompson

Blair, Walter. *Horse Sense in American Humor.* New York: Russell & Russell, 1942, pp. 107–22.

Blair, Walter and Hamlin Hill. *America's Humor: From Poor Richard to Doonesbury.* New York: Oxford University Press, 1978, pp. 184–86.

Cohen, Hennig and William B. Dillingham, eds. *Humor of the Old Southwest.* 2d ed. Athens: University of Georgia Press, 1975, pp. 121–41.

Davidson, James Wood. *The Living Writers of the South.* New York: Carleton, 1869.

Ellison, George R. "William Tappan Thompson and the *Southern Miscellany*, 1842–1844." *Mississippi Quarterly* 23 (Spring 1970): 155–68.

Estes, David C. "Major Jones Defends Himself: An Uncollected Letter." *Mississippi Quarterly* 33 (Winter 1979–80): 79–84.

Flanders, Bertram H. *Early Georgia Magazines: Literary Periodicals to 1865*. Athens: University of Georgia Press, 1944.

Gilmer, Gertrude. "A Critique of Certain Georgia Ante Bellum Literary Magazines Arranged Chronologically, and a Checklist." *Georgia Historical Quarterly* 18 (December 1934): 293–334.

Holbrook, Laura Doster. "Georgia Scenes and Life in the Works of William Tappan Thompson." M.A. thesis, University of Georgia, 1967.

Lilly, Paul R., Jr. "William Tappan Thompson (Major Joseph Jones)." *American Humorists, 1800–1950*. Ed. Stanley Trachtenberg. Vol. 11 of *Dictionary of Literary Biography*. Detroit: Gale Research, 1982. Part 2, pp. 485–90.

McKeithan, D. M. "Mark Twain's Letters of Thomas Jefferson Snodgrass." *Philological Quarterly* 32 (October 1953): 353–65.

Miller, Henry Prentice. "Ante-Bellum Georgia Humor and Humorists." *Emory University Quarterly* 5 (June 1949): 84–100.

———. "The Authorship of *The Slaveholder Abroad*." *Journal of Southern History* 10 (February 1944): 93–95.

———. "The Background and Significance of *Major Jones's Courtship*." *Georgia Historical Quarterly* 30 (December 1946): 267–96.

———. "Enter Major Jones." *Emory University Quarterly* 4 (December 1948): 232–38.

———. "The Life and Works of William Tappan Thompson." Ph.D. diss., University of Chicago, 1942.

Osthaus, Carl R. "From the Old South to the New South: The Editorial Career of William Tappan Thompson of the *Savannah Morning News*." *Southern Quarterly* 14 (April 1976): 237–60.

Phillips, Robert L., Jr. "The Novel and the Romance in Middle Georgia Humor and Local Color: A Study of Narrative Method in the Works of Augustus Baldwin Longstreet, William Tappan Thompson, Richard Malcolm Johnston and Joel Chandler Harris." Ph.D. diss., University of North Carolina at Chapel Hill, 1971.

Shippey, Herbert. "William Tappan Thompson as Playwright." *Gyascutus: Studies in Antebellum Southern Humorous and Sporting Writing*. Ed. James L. W. West III. Atlanta Highlands, N.J.: Humanities Press, 1978, pp. 51–80.

Suttler, Bernard. "William Tappan Thompson." *Men of Mark in Georgia*. Ed. William J. Northen. Atlanta: A. B. Caldwell, 1911. 3, 16–20.

Thompson, Maurice. "An Old Southern Humorist." *Independent* 50 (20 October 1898): 1103–5.

Wade, John Donald. *Augustus Baldwin Longstreet: A Study of the Development of Culture in the South*. New York: Macmillan, 1924, pp. 151, 165–67, 194–96, 204–5, 208, 239–40, and 285.

EUGENE CURRENT-GARCIA

Thomas Bangs Thorpe
(1815–1878)

Thomas Bangs Thorpe, Louisiana's transplanted Connecticut Yankee, probably worked harder and more felicitously than any other writer of his time to publicize the pristine grandeur and allure of the antebellum Southwestern frontier. Although he is famed today chiefly for his magnificent tall tale "The Big Bear of Arkansas," Thorpe wrote six books and nearly 200 essays, tales, and sketches, most of them dealing with life in the South and West, which were published in prominent nineteenth-century magazines.

BIOGRAPHY

The eldest of three children, Thorpe was born in Westfield, Massachusetts, on 1 March 1815 to Rebecca Farnham and Thomas Thorp (the original spelling of the surname). His father, a zealous but frail Methodist circuit-riding minister, gave the infant a middle name to honor Nathan Bangs, the presiding elder of his district. During the next few years the family moved several times—to Middletown and New Haven in Connecticut, then to New York, where Thomas, Senior, died on 18 January 1819, a few days before the birth of his third child. Shortly thereafter Rebecca took her young children to live with her parents in Albany, but by the late 1820s she returned with them to New York. There Thomas Bangs received the bulk of his primary and secondary education.

Among the leading literary figures in New York at that time, Washington Irving clearly exerted the strongest influence upon young Thorpe; he not only admired Irving's *Sketch Book* and the *Knickerbocker History* but also sought to reproduce characters and scenes from these works while studying figure painting with a local offbeat artist, John Quidor, who also painted fire engine panels for a living. By the early 1830s Thorpe and his close friend Charles Loring Elliott, another of Quidor's students, were both bent on becoming professional artists, submitting their paintings for exhibit at the Academy of Fine Arts, and seeking aid and advice from their elders toward furthering their careers. Lack of funds, however, crushed Thorpe's hopes of continuing his art studies abroad; instead, a poor second choice for him at seventeen was to be enrolled at Wesleyan University in Middletown, where he fulfilled two pleasant but undistinguished years of academic study from 1834 to 1836. Poor health and still slender family resources—his mother having earlier remarried and borne another daughter to Charles Albert Hinckley, a widowed bookbinder from Maine—prompted Thorpe to heed the advice of several friendly Southern classmates who urged him to visit their gentler native climate, both to recuperate and perhaps even gain a livelihood from his portrait painting.

Traveling overland in winter 1837, Thorpe eventually established himself in the Baton Rouge environs of Louisiana, the Feliciana parishes where he quickly found friends among affluent cotton planters such as Bennett Barrow of St. Francisville, who introduced him to the more agreeable hedonistic aspects of their life-style: hunting, fishing, horse racing, and bibulous social festivities. Soon acclimated to this gregarious society, by 1838 Thorpe had also married a young woman from Maine named Anne Maria Hinckley (probably an older daughter of his mother's second husband); and together they planned to raise a family while he carried on a threefold career as portraitist, newspaper editor, and yarn-spinning essayist, devoting both brush and pen to his depiction of scenes and characters in the lush territory of the Mississippi Delta. With his artist's eye keyed to the picturesque tradition of John James Audubon and the Hudson River School of painters—and with enthusiasm as ardent as theirs—Thorpe recorded the wonders and mysteries of a large portion of America's still unspoiled wilderness; and in his many tales and sketches he strove to dramatize the impact upon the settlers of its trackless forests and teeming wild life.

As a young husband of twenty-four, Thorpe quickly discovered that while portrait painting alone would not support a family in Louisiana, writing about his experiences there might help to pay the bills. Luckily, his promising literary career was launched when his first published sketch, "Tom Owen, the Bee-Hunter," appeared in a popular New York sporting weekly, the *Spirit of the Times*, on 27 July 1839. During Thorpe's visit to New York a year later, the *Spirit*'s genial editor, William Trotter Porter, not only encouraged him to continue writing similar humorous pieces about the strange backwoods characters and events he knew but also introduced him to Lewis Gaylord Clark, editor of the fashionable *Knickerbocker Magazine*, whose enthusiasm also kindled Thorpe's desire to become a professional writer. He fulfilled that aim by writing during the 1840s, after returning to St. Francisville with his wife and daughter, nearly 50 more miscellaneous pieces, most of which also appeared first in the *Spirit*, though a few were also published in the *Knickerbocker* and several other magazines. Included among those in the *Spirit* was the most famous of all his writings, "The Big Bear of Arkansas" (27 March 1841), which Porter promptly recognized as a masterpiece and subsequently used with great success as the title story in his own first collection of Southwest frontier yarns, most of them drawn from the *Spirit*'s files. Published in 1845 by the Philadelphia firm of Carey and Hart as one in a new series called the Library of Humorous American Writers, Porter's excellent little anthology was illustrated by the highly regarded Felix O. C. Darley. Among its 21 separate pieces was another, "Stoke Stout, of Louisiana," attributed to Thorpe "or Patterson his partner," and the book was given a full title to suggest its broad appeal: *The Big Bear of Arkansas, and Other Sketches, Illustrative of Characters and Incidents in the South and South-west.*

Although Thorpe's writings about the backwoods did not gain nationwide fame until after Porter's anthology appeared, his sketches had become familiar to readers of the *Spirit* throughout the early 1840s because Porter reminded them each time he published another that it was from the author of "Tom Owen, the Bee-Hunter" and "The Big Bear of Arkansas." By 1843 at least fifteen more of Thorpe's pieces appeared in the *Spirit*, several of which (such as "A Piano in Arkansas," "The Disgraced Scalp-Lock," and "The Devil's Summer Retreat, in Arkansas") were frequently reprinted in later collections until as recently as the 1970s. In July 1843 Thorpe also began writing a hilarious burlesque series entitled "Letters from the Far West," which poked sly fun at another writer's sobersided reports of a fantastic hunting expedition financed by a wealthy Scotsman, Sir William Drummond Stewart. Signed "P.O.F." and written in the typically tall-tale hyperbole of a naive Irish narrator, the twelve "Letters" appeared originally in Thorpe's own Louisiana newspaper, the Concordia *Intelligencer*, but were quickly snapped up by Porter and reprinted in the *Spirit*.

During the next five years Thorpe's varied newspaper work led in turn to his major literary achievement, the authorship of six full-length books. His first, *The Mysteries of the Backwoods; or Sketches of the Southwest*, was a collection of sixteen of the pieces originally published in the *Spirit* while Thorpe was editing the *Intelligencer* and serving as postmaster at Vidalia, Louisiana. Largely through Porter's influence, the book appeared in 1846 as Number 4 in Carey and Hart's series of humorous literature; yet, except for revised versions of "Tom Owen, the Bee-Hunter" and "A Piano in 'Arkansaw'," this book contained very little humor. Nor was it meant to; rather, Thorpe's aim was "to give those personally unacquainted with the scenery of the Southwest, some idea of the country, its surface and vegetation." So despite Darley's graphic illustrations among the accounts of buffalo hunting, turkey shootings, alligators, and wildcats, the book lacked the much broader appeal of both Porter's recent anthology containing "The Big Bear of Arkansas" and J. J. Hooper's rollicking *Adventures of Simon Suggs*.

Disappointed over lagging sales of *The Mysteries*, Thorpe promised Carey and Hart to work up another volume of purely humorous sketches, but he soon undertook instead what he felt to be a more promising literary endeavor. After leaving Vidalia in July 1845, he had tried unsuccessfully to edit and manage two New Orleans newspapers, the *Commerial Times* and the *Daily Tropic*; and at the outbreak of the Mexican War in April 1846 he hoped to capitalize on that event as a war correspondent. His eyewitness reports of General Zachary Taylor's campaign, which had first appeared as letters in the *Tropic*, Thorpe carefully revised and then persuaded Carey and Hart to publish, along with his own drawings of camp and battlefield scenes, in two small books entitled *Our Army on the Rio Grande* (1846) and *Our Army at Monterey* (1847). These, however, proved to be even less successful than *The Mysteries*; so that when the publishers refused to handle the third projected volume of his Taylor trilogy, Thorpe appealed to another one, D. Appleton and Company. In 1848 Appleton published over his old pen name of Tom Owen, the Bee-Hunter *The Taylor Anecdote Book*, an undistinguished yet popular miscellany containing a brief biographical sketch of Taylor together with a potpourri of short but amusing war anecdotes, most of them designed to enhance Taylor's "presidential" image. But this book, too, though well received in the North, added little to Thorpe's literary fame and even less to his hopes for a political appointment.

After 1848, publication of Thorpe's essays and sketches about the Southwest virtually ceased until he returned to New York with his family in 1854. But during those six remaining years in Louisiana he kept on painting, writing, and hoping as a loyal Whig to gain some desirable post as a reward for his efforts on Taylor's behalf. When he moved back to Baton Rouge from New Orleans early in 1848, Thorpe's failure as a publisher of two other newspapers the previous year (the *Louisiana Conservator* and the *Daily National*) had strengthened his resolve to support Taylor's candidacy to the utmost. Besides his biographical sketch in the *Anecdote Book*, he contributed other laudatory statements to the Baton Rouge *Gazette* that were also noted in the New York press; and soon after Taylor's election he also began a full-length oil painting of the president. Completed long after Taylor's death, the portrait was purchased by the Louisiana Legislature in 1852 for $1,000. This was to be Thorpe's sole financial reward for his stalwart support of Taylor and the Whig Party; for he had declined the post as register of the Land Office at New Orleans that Taylor had offered him instead of the foreign assignment he coveted. And when he ran for the office of state superintendent of schools in 1852, he was roundly defeated in the December general election that swept Franklin Pierce into the presidency.

That defeat may have climaxed a number of circumstances that prompted Thorpe's reluctant decision to abandon his comfortable home in Louisiana. Toward the end of the 1840s, while working on the Taylor portrait, he had produced several paintings that drew favorable notice in the North, and besides his vigorous political editorials in the *Gazette* he had contributed occasional articles to the national magazines, notably his "Incidents in the Life of Audubon," published in *Godey's Lady's Book* in May 1851. During a summer visit to New York in 1852, he had also begun negotiations for publishing a new, completely revised and expanded edition of his humorous sketches and backwoods mysteries. But his most important project following his defeat in the December election was that of establishing a contract—during a second visit to New York—with the Harper brothers for an extensive series of illustrated articles on the South to be published in *Harper's New Monthly Magazine*. When the first one, "Sugar and the Sugar Regions of Louisiana," appeared in November 1853, Thorpe was enthusiastically hailed as the South's most successful interpreter to offer Northern readers a "true idea of Southern life." As a prelude to more than 30 others that *Harper's* would publish to the end of Thorpe's life, the article must have convinced him that henceforth greater security for himself and his family was to be found in New York, not in Louisiana. Nevertheless, the move took its toll; within a year ill health had weakened all of them, and on 4 October 1855 Thorpe's wife died at age thirty-six, not long after the birth of their third child, Dordie Rebecca.

The articles Thorpe began writing for *Harper's* in the winter of 1853–54 appeared fairly regularly thereafter, seventeen in all from the end of the year until October 1856. Primarily factual, they provided a faithful if somewhat idealized image of the South's social and economic life as well as of its scenery and wildlife. Meanwhile, Thorpe's most ambitious tribute to his adopted homeland was likewise emerging in his two major books: *The Hive of "The Bee-Hunter,"* an expanded version of his earlier yarns and sketches, and *The Master's House*, a romantic novel dealing with the explosive issue of slavery.

In *The Hive*, published by Appleton in spring 1854, Thorpe finally succeeded in bringing together under his own name the best of all his magazine writings on the Southwest, including "The Big Bear of Arkansas." Subtitled *A Repository of Sketches, Including Peculiar American Character, Scenery, and Rural Sports*, the entire work was painstakingly revised and given, in Thorpe's preface, a renewed emphasis upon both the romantic wonders of nature and the realistic peculiarities of Western characters. Contemporary reviewers promptly hailed the author as one of the nation's foremost literary figures—"a bright and captivating American humorist, an effective stylist, and a discerning and truly creative reporter of scenery, social customs, and character in the Southwest"—and soon representative samples of the humorous sketches in *The Hive* were being included in such popular anthologies as Halliburton's *Traits of American Humor* and the Duyckincks' *Cyclopaedia of American Literature*. Later in the year when T. L. McElrath of New York published Thorpe's novel, it too was well received in the North: appearing at first under the pseudonym "Logan," *The Master's House; A Tale of Southern Life* was recognized as an honest, though flawed, work of reform fiction resembling that of Harriet Beecher Stowe's notorious *Uncle Tom's Cabin*. A third edition of the novel, published the following year, acknowledged Thorpe's authorship, but the reviewers noted that its literary quality was inferior to that of his humorous sketches.

From 1855 until the onset of the Civil War, Thorpe's literary, journalistic, and political activities in New York varied considerably. Although he produced no more full-length books, his self-illustrated nature essays were appearing frequently in *Harper's* and occasionally in the *Knickerbocker*. As a disaffected Whig, he may have contributed in 1855 to a scandalous volume entitled *A Voice to America*, issued by the rabidly nativist American (Know-Nothing) Party. In fall 1857 he joined the editorial staff of *Frank Leslie's Illustrated Newspaper*; that year he also married Jane Fosdick and began the study of law, which he practiced leisurely for the next two years. During this period his close associates in New York included his longtime friends, Charles Loring Elliott, the artist; Henry William Herbert ("Frank Forester"), a popular contributor to Porter's *Spirit of the Times*; and Porter himself. Beside writing several articles for George Ripley and Charles Dana's *New American Cyclopedia* and exhibiting some of his paintings at the National Academy of Design, early in 1859 Thorpe also bought a part-interest in the *Spirit*, a few months after Porter's death. Thereafter, until the *Spirit* succumbed to the hostilities of the war in 1861, he wrote for its pages more than twenty essays and editorial commentaries on the National Academy of Design and on art and "A Search for the Picturesque."

During the war years Thorpe's energies were directed first toward recruiting volunteers for the Union cause. After the capture of New Orleans in April 1862, he was commissioned as colonel under General Benjamin Franklin Butler to supervise the distribution of food and shelter to destitute families, to repair the levees, and to clean up the city's streets and canals in order to prevent a recurrence of the dreaded yellow fever plague. Later Thorpe worked closely with Governor Michael Hahn while serving on the Constitutional Convention, which had been called to adopt a new body of laws for implementing President Lincoln's emancipation policies and his plans for the education and possible enfranchisement of the freedmen. In the general election of 5 September 1864, which approved the new state constitution, Thorpe also ran for one of the seats on the General Assembly allotted to the Second Orleans District, but once again he lost his bid for public office. The next month he sailed for New York aboard the U.S. Mail Steamship *Evening Star* and never returned to the South.

Reestablished in his Brooklyn residence after the war, Thorpe again took up, along with Republican Party political work, his painting and journalism, off and on submitting landscapes to the National Academy of Design and numerous articles to the newspapers and magazines. In fall 1868 upon the death of his lifelong friend Elliott, the painter, he wrote a long obituary for the *Evening Post* that was later reissued as a separate pamphlet, *Reminiscences of Charles L. Elliott, Artist*. Shortly thereafter Thorpe also received the political plum he had long sought, a post in the New York Customhouse that he held till he died. Occasionally during those last ten years he wrote and published many more essays: nearly a dozen long ones for *Harper's* and, following the establishment of *Appleton's Journal* in 1869, about 30 shorter illustrated ones for that prestigious magazine, several of which were reprinted in a huge two-volume collection, *Picturesque America* (1872), edited by William Cullen Bryant. Within the single year 1873–74 Thorpe also wrote twenty or more weekly columns on "Art and Drama" for still another popular magazine, *Forest and Stream*; and during his last five years he wrote eighteen short essays, chiefly on painters and paintings of the century, for a well-paying private magazine, *Baldwin's Monthly*. His last essay, "American Pictures," appeared in it just a short time before his death on 20 September 1878.

MAJOR THEMES

The keynote to Thorpe's contribution to the literature of mid–nineteenth-century America was first struck in the short preface with which William T. Porter introduced the 21 tales in his collection, *The Big Bear of Arkansas, and Other Sketches*. "A new vein of literature," Porter began, "as original as it is inexhaustible in its source," had recently burgeoned in the weekly offerings of the *Spirit of the Times*. It was being written by a robust group of contributors who were familiar with the "thrilling scenes and adventures" among the early settlers and "squatters" of the backwoods; familiar, too, with "their strange language and habitudes, and [their] peculiar and sometimes fearful characteristics." Chief among this new group, each of them noted for their courtesy and their fondness of storytelling, Porter named Thorpe, whose "sketches of the men and manners of the great valley of the Mississippi . . . have been read and admired wherever our language is spoken."

Most of these contributors to the *Spirit*, Porter concluded (after naming among seventeen others Audubon, Timothy Flint, Caroline Kirkland, and Albert Pike), were "endowed with a keen sense of whatever is ludicrous or pathetic, with a quick perception of character, and a knowledge of men and the world; more than all, they possess in an eminent degree the power of transferring to paper the most striking and faithful pictures with equal originality and effect." Obviously, the key terms in Porter's eulogy of the *Spirit*'s galaxy of stars are "thrilling scenes and adventures," "original characters," "strange language," and "whatever is ludicrous and pathetic." These underscore Thorpe's major themes and the source of his appeal to his own and later generations of readers. His attitudes and biases, as well as his associations, political preferences, and literary competency, fit neatly into the stereotype of the Southern Whig gentleman described by Hennig Cohen and William P. Dillingham, the editors of *Humor of the Old Southwest*, as "a man of education and breeding who felt deeply and spoke with conviction . . . [who] was convinced that if the nation was to be saved from chaos and degradation, only the honor, reasonableness, and sense of responsibility of gentlemen—Whig gentlemen—could save it."

Moreover, the Southern Whig gentleman, whether a native son like J. J. Hooper or a transplant like Thorpe, felt strongly protective toward the South, its institutions, folkways, and its archaic social system. This fact helps to explain both the transiency of much of Thorpe's voluminous writings and the permanence of a small portion of them. Time has altered the mood as well as the perspective from which modern artists or writers and their audience contemplate the wonders of nature, either in the Southwest or elsewhere in the United States. Thus the strong influence of Washington Irving's fondness for the picturesque, echoed in the opening statement of Thorpe's preface to *Mysteries of the Backwoods*, has faded into limbo. We can no longer "bow," as he did, with quite the same "wonder and awe" before exhibitions of nature in the "vast primitive forests, . . . beautiful prairies, and . . . magnificent rivers" of that region. Neither can we respond as enthusiastically as he to most of the "thrilling scenes and adventures" he encountered there—the buffalo and grizzly bear hunts, turkey shootings, and what he originally called "piscatory archery." Much of what he found wonderful, ludicrous, or pathetic in these activities no longer quickens our imagination. Except for the massacre at the Alamo, military skirmishing on the Rio Grande seems as remote as Yorktown or Bunker Hill.

Thorpe's three books on Zachary Taylor's exploits, like his *Mysteries of the Backwoods*, therefore offer little excitement to readers of the late twentieth century. They are dated, as even much of Washington Irving's prose is dated, their appeal limited chiefly to the interests of literary specialists in American studies. So too is that of Thorpe's novel on slavery, *The Master's House*, one of the sixteen longer works of fiction published between 1852 and 1855 in response to Harriet Beecher Stowe's explosive *Uncle Tom's Cabin*. With varying intensity, most of these books sought to refute Stowe's three main charges against slavery: it provoked cruel treatment of the slaves, forcibly separated their families, and deprived them of religious instruction.

Unlike the other conventional Southern rebuttals, however, *The Master's House* did not flatly deny these charges or attempt to portray slavery as a benign institution offering greater care and protection to families of black workers than free laboring men and women, white or black, enjoyed under the North's laissez-faire economic system. On the contrary, through several violent episodes in its loosely constructed plot, Thorpe exposes a number of serious social ills fostered by the South's slave system: for example, the indolence, haughtiness, and proneness to hot-tempered dueling among the aristocratic planter class, whom Thorpe most admired; the brutality and callousness toward all blacks on the part of arrogant overseers and slave traders; the failure of the church to condemn cruelty toward helpless slaves; and the breakdown of legal sanctions against such treatment resulting from the political manipulation of ignorant poor whites in the courtroom and at the ballot box. Thus as a tendentious novel, *The Master's House* develops a deeply felt but ambivalent theme: a passionate love for the South's alleged philanthropic social ideals as embodied in the character of the hero, Graham Mildmay; yet a cry for needed reform that appears to corroborate rather than refute the message of *Uncle Tom's Cabin*. Though contemporary reviewers casually dismissed *The Master's House* as a novel of little artistic merit, they noted approvingly that in its shambling sketches of local scenery and characters Thorpe had presented the South's peculiar society and its social usages with greater fidelity to actual conditions than Stowe had achieved. They saw, too, that despite its stylistic flaws the book displayed both moral passion and powerful touches of humor, satire, and a prophetic if ambiguous realism. They saw, in short, that Thorpe's literary fame would depend ultimately not on his skill as a novelist but on the artistry displayed in the best of his humorous sketches in *The Hive of "The Bee-Hunter."*

SURVEY OF CRITICISM

The critical judgment of Thorpe's peers has been sustained through more than a century of America's literary development. For present-day scholars and critics agree, as they did, not only that *The Hive of "The Bee-Hunter"* marks the "high point" of Thorpe's long career, but also that "The Big Bear of Arkansas," his major story in it, is a literary masterpiece comparable to the best of Boccaccio's and Chaucer's tales. Despite its brevity and seeming artlessness, this story has become a literary touchstone, a standard-bearer against which other tales of its genre are judged and compared; its title, in fact, has given the frontier humorists as a group their name, "The Big Bear School." What makes "The Big Bear" itself so unique, according to Walter Blair, is its artful blend of contrasting styles, narrators, and modes of characterization. It is a story within a story, introduced in the staid, almost stuffy language of a gentleman passenger aboard a Mississippi River steamboat, who sets the stage for the appearance of Jim Doggett, the Big Bear himself. But once Jim announces his presence with typical frontier hyperbole and greets the motley crowd of his fellow passengers, his personal ebullience and zestful eloquence soon transform their bemused displeasure into respectful attention.

Expostulating volubly at his own pace and in his own pungent vernacular, Doggett first primes his entranced auditors with a dazzling rodomontade on the natural wonders of his native state, where mosquitoes as well as beets and bears are both superabundant and gargantuan. Someone then challenges him to demonstrate his vaunted skill as a bear hunter by recalling a particular hunting experience, and his response is the tale of a great "unhuntable bear" that he had pursued for years but finally shot from a squatting position while engaged in his habitual morning's defecation. A combination of the earthy and the fantastic, Thorpe's story is perfectly told; for as scholarly critics are quick to point out, embedded at the heart of this delightful yarn, yet so artfully concealed, is "the oldest joke in the world—the joke of being caught with one's britches down." Small wonder that the original narator is so captivated by the mystery associated with Doggett's account of the great bear's death that he concludes the story in a tone of reverential awe. "The Big Bear of Arkansas" clearly brought its author such fame that nearly a century after his death, Thorpe's biographer Milton Rickels could firmly place his writings "among the finest productions of the frontier humorists and realists."

Aside from the broadly favorable recognition that Thorpe's humorous writings received from his own contemporaries, little further serious critical attention was paid to them until the twentieth century. From 1840 on, however, the influence of the *Spirit of the Times* was crucial to the spread of Thorpe's subsequent literary reputation. As its editor, Porter had not only encouraged him to keep on writing humorous sketches such as "Tom Owen" and "The Big Bear" but also touted these two works so enthusiastically that by mid-century they had reappeared with added luster in the literary anthologies of both England and the United States, Griswold's, Halliburton's, the Duyckincks', and the London *Bentley's Miscellany*. Again, in 1859 when Thorpe became part-owner of the *Spirit* after Porter's death, he was reintroduced to a new generation of readers as one who had "inaugurated a new style of writing . . . [and helped bring together] the most truly original and genuine American humor that the literature of the country can boast." And as if by design, in May and June of the following year the *Spirit* published in an anonymous two-part essay its most serious formal attempt to analyze the substance of frontier humor, to account for its universality, and to commend Thorpe among several others for having embodied in his writings "most of the peculiar traits and oddities, fun, humor, and wit on the Southwestern United States."

Renewed interest on this level of critical study in both frontier humor generally and in Thorpe's contribution to it was stimulated by the pioneering scholarship of Constance Rourke, Franklin J. Meine, and Walter Blair in the 1930s. In the wake of Meine's *Tall Tales of the Southwest* (1930) and Blair's more comprehensive *Native American Humor* (1937), a spate of articles and books followed one another during the next four decades, the titles of which are listed in the bibliography of Hennig Cohen and William Dillingham's second edition of *Humor of the Old Southwest* (1975) and in that of *The Frontier Humorists* (1975), edited by M. Thomas Inge.

Among the earlier articles dealing chiefly with Thorpe's own significance, his close ties with Porter and the *Spirit*, and with the artistic quality of his individual writings, important information is contained in each of the following: Walter Blair's "The Technique of The Big Bear of Arkansas," originally published in the *Southwest Review* (1943) but revised and reprinted in *The Frontier Humorists* as " 'The Big Bear of Arkansas': T. B. Thorpe and His Masterpiece," and refurbished once more in Walter Blair and Hamlin Hill's *America's Humor* (1978); Eugene Current-Garcia, " 'Mr. Spirit' and *The Big Bear of Arkansas*" (1955), " 'York's Tall Son' and His Southern Correspondents" (1955), and "Thomas Bangs Thorpe and the Literature of the Ante-Bellum Southwestern Frontier" (1956); Barrie Hayne, "Yankee in the Patriarchy: T. B. Thorpe's Reply to *Uncle Tom's Cabin*" (1968); John F. McDermott, "T. B. Thorpe's Burlesque of Far West Sporting Travel" (1958); Milton Rickels, "Thomas Bangs Thorpe in the Felicianas, 1836–1842" (1956); and Arlin Turner, "Seeds of Literary Revolt in the Humor of the Old Southwest" (1956).

The most fully researched book-length study of Thorpe is the biography by Rickels, *Thomas Bangs Thorpe: Humorist of the Old Southwest* (1962), which contains a detailed bibliography of all of Thorpe's known publications. Valuable additional information on his literary associations is also available in Norris W. Yates's *William T. Porter and the "Spirit of the Times"* (1957) and in Richard Boyd Hauck's *A Cheerful Nihilism: Confidence and "the Absurd" in American*

Humorous Fiction (1971). Among other recent studies that place Thorpe within the total context of American humorous writing, one of the most enjoyable is the work already mentioned, *America's Humor*, by Walter Blair and Hamlin Hill. But important variant discussions of the subject are also to be found in James M. Cox's "Humor of the Old Southwest" in *The Comic Imagination in American Literature* (1973), edited by Louis D. Rubin, Jr.; in J. A. Leo Lemay's "The Text, Tradition, and Themes of 'The Big Bear of Arkansas' " (1975); and in Neil Schmitz's "Tall Tale, Tall Talk: Pursuing the Lie in Jacksonian Literature" (1977).

With such a wealth of critical analysis as this devoted to Thorpe's major literary endeavors during the last few decades, one might assume that little more need be expected. But if the vigorous deconstructionist implications expressed in the last two essays listed above signalize a new trend, then a contrary assumption may be equally valid.

BIBLIOGRAPHY

Works by Thomas Bangs Thorpe

The Mysteries of the Backwoods; or Sketches of the Southwest: Including Character, Scenery, and Rural Sports. Philadelphia: Carey and Hart, 1846.

Our Army on the Rio Grande. Being a Short Account of the Important Events Transpiring from theTime of the Removal of the "Army of Occupation" from Corpus Christi, to the Surrender of Matamoros; with Descriptions of the Battles of Palo Alto and Resaca de la Palma, the Bombardment of Fort Brown, and the Ceremonies of the Surrender of Matamoros: With Descriptions of the City, etc. etc. Philadelphia: Carey and Hart, 1846.

Our Army at Monterey. Being a Correct Account of the Proceedings and Events which Occurred to the "Army of Occupation" Under the Command of Major General Taylor, from the Time of Leaving Matamoros to the Surrender of Monterey with a Description of The Three Days' Battle and the Storming of Monterey: The Ceremonies Attending the Surrender: Together with the Particulars of the Capitulation. Philadelphia: Carey and Hart, 1847.

The Taylor Anecdote Book. Anecdotes and Letters of Zachary Taylor. New York: D. Appleton, 1848.

The Hive of "The Bee-Hunter," A Repository of Sketches, Including Peculiar American Character, Scenery, and Rural Sports. New York: D. Appleton, 1854.

The Master's House; A Tale of Southern Life. New York: T. L. McElrath, 1854.

Studies of Thomas Bangs Thorpe

Bain, Robert. "Thomas Bangs Thorpe." *Antebellum Writers in New York and the South*. Ed. Joel Myerson. Vol. 3 of *Dictionary of Literary Biography*. Detroit: Gale Research, 1979, pp. 335–39.

Blair, Walter. *Native American Humor, 1800–1900*. New York: American Book, 1937.

————. "The Techniques of The Big Bear of Arkansas." *Southwest Review* 28 (Summer 1943): 426–35.

Blair, Walter and Hamlin Hill. *America's Humor: From Poor Richard to Doonesbury*. New York: Oxford University Press, 1978.

Callow, James. *Kindred Spirits: Knickerbocker Writers and American Artists, 1807–1855*. Chapel Hill: University of North Carolina Press, 1967, pp. 9–10, 171, 235.

Cohen, Hennig and William B. Dillingham, eds. *Humor of the Old Southwest*. Boston: Houghton Mifflin Company, 1964, pp. ix–xxviii passim. 2d ed. Athens: University of Georgia Press, 1975.

Cox, James M. "Humor of the Old Southwest." *The Comic Imagination in American Literature*. Ed. Louis D. Rubin, Jr. New Brunswick, N.J.: Rutgers University Press, 1973, pp. 101–12.

Current-Garcia, Eugene. " 'Mr. Spirit' and *The Big Bear of Arkansas*." *American Literature* 27 (November 1955): 332–46.

————. "Thomas Bangs Thorpe and the Literature of the Ante-Bellum Southwestern Frontier." *Louisiana Historical Quarterly* 39 (1956): 199–222.

————. " 'York's Tall Son' and His Southern Correspondents." *American Quarterly* 7 (Winter 1955): 371–84.

Hauck, Richard Boyd. *A Cheerful Nihilism: Confidence and "the Absurd" in American Humorous Fiction*. Bloomington: Indiana University Press, 1971, pp. 40–76.

Hayne, Barrie. "Yankee in the Patriarchy: T. B. Thorpe's Reply to *Uncle Tom's Cabin*." *American Quarterly* 20 (Summer 1968): 180–95.

Inge, M. Thomas. *The Frontier Humorists: Critical Views*. Hamden, Conn.: Archon Books, 1975.

Lemay, J. A. Leo. "The Text, Tradition, and Themes of 'The Big Bear of Arkansas.' " *American Literature* 47 (November 1975): 321–42.

McDermott, John F. "T. B. Thorpe's Burlesque of Far West Sporting Travel." *American Quarterly* 10 (Summer 1958): 175–80.

Meine, Franklin J., ed. *Tall Tales of the Southwest: An Anthology of Southern and Southwestern Humor, 1830–1860*. New York: Alfred A. Knopf, 1930, pp. xv–xxxii.

Rickels, Milton. "A Bibliography of the Writings of Thomas Bangs Thorpe." *American Literature* 29 (May 1957): 171–79.

————. *Thomas Bangs Thorpe, Humorist of the Old Southwest*. Baton Rouge: Louisiana State University Press, 1962.

————. "Thomas Bangs Thorpe in the Felicianas, 1836–1842." *Louisiana Historical Quarterly* 39 (1956): 169–97.

Schmitz, Neil. "Tall Tale, Tall Talk: Pursuing the Lie in Jacksonian Literature." *American Literature* 48 (January 1977): 471–91.

Simoneaux, Katherine G. "Symbolism in Thorpe's 'The Big Bear of Arkansas.' " *Arkansas Historical Quarterly* 25 (Fall 1966): 240–47.

Turner, Arlin. "Seeds of Literary Revolt in the Humor of the Old Southwest." *Louisiana Historical Quarterly* 39 (1956): 143–51.

Weber, Brom. "American Humor and American Culture." *American Quarterly* 14 (Fall 1962): 503–7.

Yates, Norris W. *William T. Porter and the "Spirit of the Times": A Study of the Big Bear School of Humor*. Baton Rouge: Louisiana State University Press, 1957.

Henry Timrod
(1828–1867)

Henry Timrod is generally considered second only to Sidney Lanier among Southern poets of the nineteenth century. Despite his slim output, his designation of "Poet Laureate of the South" still fits, making his poetry interesting for anyone who would understand the intellectual and emotional climate of the South before, during, and after the Civil War.

BIOGRAPHY

"I have achieved so little! I thought to have done so much!" These pathetic words of the dying Timrod epitomize his life and, perhaps, the antebellum South as well. Henry Timrod was born in Charleston, South Carolina, on 8 December 1828 to a home with some literary pretentions. His father, who died when Timrod was only ten, had published a volume of poems (his "Ode to Time" was praised by Washington Irving). In 1846 Timrod attended the University of Georgia for a year, and acquired such a taste for the classics that at one time he intended to seek a professorship in classics. His desire to write a translation of Catullus is instructive, since it may explain his energetic interest in perfecting many types of verse. Yet Byron and Shelley also intrigued him, though later he took Wordsworth and Tennyson to be his mentors because of their ethical and aesthetic aims. He tutored after leaving the University of Georgia, but teaching dulled his poetic sensibility, whose subjects at this early stage included, like those of his father, birds, young women, and local events. Like his father, he studied law, but also found it unconducive to poetic inspiration, and in the 1850s he began to work on local newspapers in Charleston and elsewhere hoping to create a nest egg for marriage. (He did not marry until 1864.)

Although he was not a successful journalist, the training forced his attention to the concrete details of life, and, later, to the tragic details of suffering when he worked briefly as a war correspondent. But before the ravages of war, Timrod found that journalism introduced him to such writers of similar temperament as Paul Hamilton Hayne (his lifelong friend and eventual editor of his collected poetry); William Gilmore Simms, an established man of letters; and several professors and writers who clustered about the Charleston library or John Russell's Bookstore. They would help to buttress his belief in the ability of feeling to stimulate the ethical sense.

For a South increasingly isolated from Northern and European developments in poetic form, Romanticism was a breath of fresh air. When *Russell's Magazine* was formed in the late 1850s with Hayne as editor, Timrod had a platform for the first time; most issues contained at least one of his poems. Additionally, his essay "The Literature of the South" advocated a poetry in line with Wordsworth's feeling for the familiar and Tennyson's evocation of moral power. Another essay, "A Theory of Poetry," challenged Poe's assertion that poetry was essentially subjective and reasserted Timrod's preference for its ethical foundation. Though Timrod could turn these theories only occasionally into successful poems, he nevertheless remained an energetic advocate of what poetry ought to be. Readers of *Russell's* must have noted the discrepancy between Timrod's poetry and the direction he seemed to promote for the literature of the South. They surely wanted more of "The Arctic Voyager," which appeared in the first issue of *Russell's*, a poem whose situation, stance, and language recalled Tennysonian idealism.

By the end of the 1850s, then, Timrod had shown a vigorous talent in the craft of verse, an awareness of exciting directions in poetry, and an eagerness to translate Wordsworth and Tennyson to the Southern scene. Yet he was not instinctively a Romantic poet. His nature poetry was commonplace, and his love poems were written more to test his wit than to reply spontaneously to other promptings of his heart. His heart would speak, however, in defense of the South and for peace during the tragic times approaching as he published his only volume, *Poems*, in 1860. If "The Arctic Voyager" haunted him from childhood, as he said, perhaps because of the subject's moral earnestness, and if he could not go to the arctic as a Southern Ulysses, the arctic adventure could come to him in service to the Confederacy. He served two terms of duty: in 1861 as a war correspondent, and in 1862 when he participated in the retreat from Shiloh, having reenlisted after a bout with the tuberculosis that was to kill him. "Ethnogenesis" and "The Cotton Boll" of 1861 contain sufficient vision to certify the passion underlying the Southern cause, in their depiction of a "birth of a nation" and the spiritual power resident in the concrete reality of cotton as a commercial product, a way of life, and an emblem of the purity of the Southern Cause. Ironically, this shy, sensitive, absentminded young classics tutor was called upon to bear the "lyre of Tyrtaeus," which, as he said, was "the only one to which the Public would listen now." Yet Timrod was capable of recognizing the practical limits of the King Cotton myth. Like Lanier, he would admit that Southern emotion had overwhelmed its better judgment. But, unlike Lanier, Timrod made this judgment in 1862 when he recognized that King Wheat was as strong as King Cotton. His impassioned anger toward the North turned, in his poetry, to hatred of war itself, and for this he earned Tennyson's title of "The Poet Laureate of the South," an improvement upon H. T. Thompson's "Laureate of the Confederacy." The very war that appeared to Timrod to turn him from those things he felt he was born to write had given him his voice.

The war provided him with vigorous poems unlike anything he had ever written, though they may have been vaguely suggested in his "graveyard" poetry, to which he would return when the South's painful Reconstruction became his own personal tragedy after the war. Absorbed in his powerful calls to arms and his touching pleas for peace are the dignity of Tennyson's moral world and the moving simplicity of Wordsworth's. Yet those poems also contained the language of "Southern chivalry." These different influences supplied a special tension to his work.

He was not to strum his elegiac lyre for long. When Columbia was burned in February 1865, his journalistic livelihood was also destroyed, and enormous burdens on his family may have contributed to the death of his infant son eight months later. The hardships surely accelerated his early death. His postbellum life is a depressing record of stillborn projects—from attempts to publish in notable Northern magazines (where he was anathema), to attempts to write for nearly moribund newspapers, including a scheme to regenerate the defunct Columbia *Daily South Carolinian*. Most pathetically, his plan to publish an expanded volume of verse in London collapsed, and, it has been said, during those strenuous preparations he experienced a hemorrhage that bloodied the proof sheets of the aborted 1862 edition.

From his son's death came the anguished "Our Willie" and its companion "A Mother's Wail." Together they align his personal calamities to the general Southern horror and make Timrod's most moving poems. Meanwhile, he was, along with Hayne and Simms, the subject of an unfair attack by a Northern critic. More disturbing was Sidney Lanier's hasty and ungenerous accusation that Timrod had little feeling for the craft or technique of poetry. His illness also estranged him from Simms. Timrod had fallen so low that he told Hayne he would gladly consign all his poems to oblivion for $100.

Perhaps fortunately, he had undertaken no major projects in his last years. Even so, like Lanier he felt that his great work was still ahead of him, after a long artistic apprenticeship. Timrod quoted on his deathbed a stanza from his early "A Common Thought" to his sister Emily, despairing at not having used his life more productively than he had. More than a century later, however, we may be grateful that his unlucky life produced some poetry with some uncommon thoughts.

In February, 1864, Timrod married Katie Goodwin, an Englishwoman whose brother had married Timrod's sister Emily. Plagued by a need for money and by ill health, Timrod spent his last years, as he wrote to Hayne, in "beggary, starvation, death, bitter grief, [and] utter want of hope." He died in Columbia, South Carolina, on 7 October 1867.

MAJOR THEMES

Timrod did his memorable work during the brief period from 1861 to 1867. The common theme uniting his war poetry and his elegiac poetry is the sense of affirmation in the face of catastrophe. His resilient spirit forced him again and again to start over, first when war approached and he contracted the rampant fever to rally round the flag; later when he recognized the unacceptable horror of the war and sought peace with no regard to Southern victory; and finally when he found the will to withstand his personal loss in his son's untimely death. Only in these events did the poetry of Timrod find a focus for his belief that emotion could elevate moral sentiments. In a real sense, his themes chose him.

It may be ironic that the first and last poems of Timrod's, poems of death, enclose so many other poems about death, for he intended at first to turn his art toward an evocation of other Romantic subjects, particularly those that could aid in educating the moral feelings of his readers. His 1843 extravagant parody of Charles Wolfe's poem on the death of a tutor initiates his career; his pious tribute to a departed friend, Harris Simons, terminates it. These conventional stances enclose four richer poems about mortality written for formal occasions that reach beyond the pious platitudes of the "Graveyard School."

The first occasion was the consecration of Magnolia Cemetery in Charleston in 1851. Death will not triumph here, Timrod asserts in his "Hymn," because "stars and sunlight" will sparkle through the funeral bowers, which are both "grave and garden." The events of war, of course, made mortality less decorative. In "The Unknown Dead" (1864) the rain itself is like a spadeful upon a coffin; nature does not mitigate the fact of death. But in the end grief gives way to hope as the "lover's bower" leaves Nature "Oblivious of the crimson debt" and laughs with April grace. Two years later Timrod would offer an "Ode" for the decoration of Confederate graves in the same cemetery he had helped to consecrate, and he would again insist that the "brave martyrs" for their "defeated valor" occupy holy ground. The formal elegy thus relies on the stock language of graveyard poetry, but when Timrod responded to his personal loss, he used vigorous imagery.

"Our Willie" (1866) is written from the personal anguish of the death of his son, who, born on Christmas Day, 1864, seemed to offer special hope. But by the next Christmas Willie was dead. Timrod uses the frame of two Christmases to emphasize the bitterness of the child's short life and to incorporate religious meanings. He had nearly blasphemed, the narrator admits, when he celebrated Willie's arrival rather than Christ's: "it scarcely seemed a sin to say / That they rang because that babe was born, / No less than for the sacred day." But the cherubs who adore Jesus ironically prefigure the angel Willie would become by the following Yule. They also reveal that Willie came from another world and brought unutterable truth with him. The flame that had lit his "crystal dome" bore a Wordsworthian truth from his previous life, for he was a "little wide-eyed seer'' who spoke with a ''murmur like a mystic speech.'' The transcendental emphasis supplies the speaker with a degree of awe that enables him to withstand the furious fact of the child's painfully brief existence.

''A Mother's Wail'' of a month later was a continuation and development of ''Our Willie,'' but with two additional strategies that purified the pain. Timrod wrote from the mother's point of view, projecting his imagination into the kinds of anguish a woman would feel. Though the poems share the common images of the mystic babe and the lamp of life, ''A Mother's Wail'' diminishes the importance of the transcendent to focus upon a figurative realization of the loss. The babe is a ''single rose-bud in a crown of thorns,'' a ''lamp'' that burned ''with the lustre of the moon and stars'' ''whence I looked forth upon a night of storm!'' The gothic landscape becomes transmuted in the startling metaphor ''Earth drinks the fragrant flame.'' The mother then recalls nursing her baby: ''that warm, wet, eager mouth, / With the sweet sharpness of its budding pearls!'' Sentimentality aside, the details are touching. She recalls the living boy around her neck, the grave ''chilled beneath the moon,'' and the cherub ''wearing roses of mystic bliss.'' The transcendent image is the least credible for her, however. In these two poems the spiritual and the realistic encompass man's capability to withstand and understand the terror of mortality. Joined by a common grief, the husband and wife remain painfully isolated by what unites them. In the alembic of his own pain, Timrod had learned to explore the theme of death with an original voice.

''A Mother's Wail'' provides a realistic portrait of a woman, yet it stands in relief against Timrod's other treatments of women. For, true to Southern chivalry, Timrod espoused the chivalric theme of ''Frauendienst'' (lady service) offering himself as a knight for his lady-love. In his war poetry, the theme of Frauendienst translates into service to the South, as the theme of mortality in the ''graveyard poetry'' gives way to a sense of the carnage of war. His early poetry showed an eagerness to pose as a gallant. In ''Madeline'' (1852) he would like to be the angel Raphael and follow Madeline. A sonnet from 1857 warns his lady of illusions. Elsewhere he brings roses, ''like a great lip bitten through,'' or lays tribute at her feet as a ''vassal.'' He courts his future wife ''Kattie'' (1861) with the same imagery, musing about her English origin in his reverie about ''the Court of St. James.''

Timrod's most interesting use of the Frauendienst theme, though, lodges in his use of the feminine ''spirit of nature'' in ''A Vision of Poesy'' (1859), one of his most ambitious poems. The narrator's mother tells him that when he was born a ''Lady'' was dimly seen leaving the room, and this news sends him on a quest into sublime nature, for he knows he has had a purer previous existence. There he meets the Vision of Poesy, who informs him that final meanings are glimpsed only after death. Like Tennyson's Galahad, he promises to keep pure and remain ''mailed in the Truth.'' In Part 2 the narrator admits the vision has not returned, and with the world he awaits ''the genuine bard'' whose songs are ''riddles.'' In a visionary moment, the speaker sees that the ''real poet spheres /

Worlds in himself.'' This use of the feminine spirit of nature is an imaginative
leap beyond anything Timrod had accomplished in his traditional lady-service
poems. As an American Wordsworth, Timrod thus explored the intimations of
his own creativity. Yet the poem treats the recollections as part of lady-service,
and so the poet appears to fail since he does not actuate his high aspirations.
The mixture of themes does not draw the poem into a focus, and it remains an
interesting effort to analyze a Romantic idea of the poetic process within an
ethical context.

The lady-service theme blends with the ''graveyard theme'' in Timrod's most
complex theme, war and peace. Although he said in ''Retirement'' (1857) that
he would like to find a separate peace (''to wars, / Whether of words or weapons
we shall be / Deaf''), nevertheless within three years he wrote the South's most
stirring calls to arms. ''Ethnogenesis,'' written during the meeting of the first
Southern Congress in 1861, asserted that nature itself shall serve this ''nation
among nations'' as if it were a knight doing lady-service: ''The very sun / Takes
part with us''; with yellow blossoms as ''her fairy shield''; and the blue sky of
June ''azure banner to the wind.'' The cotton ''snow of Southern summers''
will offer the same impediment to the North that Russia had to Napoleon, should
the Yankees ''fling down their mortal gage.'' Northern ''Charity'' whets a
dagger's edge, and it is so unknightly that it leaves the poor to starve and ''turns
some vast philanthropy to gold.'' The South has ''Truth without a stain.'' Avert-
ing his eyes from slavery, Timrod says the South has laws that give ''Not the
mean right to buy the right to live, / But life, and home, and health!'' The courtly
South wants from the ''redder sea'' merely ''hushed murmurs of a world's
distress,'' so that even the Arctic will feel Southern warmth. Southerners read
and admired Scott's novels of chivalry. Apparently Timrod borrowed chivalric
images from him.

The image of cotton as knightly purity is extended to a vision of the South's
material power in ''The Cotton Boll'' (1861). The narrator idly examines a boll
and finds in its fibers bands that ''Unite, like love, the sea-divided lands.'' A
veil is lifted from his eyes and ''the landscape broadens'' seemingly ''Against
the Evening Star!'' The ''small charm'' enables him to look down from ''some
great temple of the Sun.'' He asks stars and sun to attest to the truth that ''No
fairer land hath fired a poet's lays.'' The ''mighty commerce'' of cotton ''hushes
hungry lips,'' reviving the ''half-dead dream of universal peace.'' A Miltonic
simile compares Cornwall miners who toil calmly while a storm rages overhead,
to his industrious ''woof / of song'' that ignores the ''bruit of battles.'' Timrod
begs the ''sacred fields of peace'' be spared the stain of blood. The poet's vision
has spun a dream of peace in which knightly virtue would conquer the unchar-
itable ''Goth,'' as the fibers of the boll will ameliorate the life of all men. Thus
cotton, the economic support for the Confederacy, reflects the virtues of the
South.

Only a month after writing ''The Cotton Boll'' Timrod recorded that he felt
such torpor that he was like a banner in the rain, beaten into the bloody clay.

He roused himself, however, to write two of the most vibrant poems inspired by the Civil War. "A Cry to Arms" (1862) entreats the woodsmen to lay aside the "bloodless spade" and the tradesmen to burn their books. Using the long-ago coined images of "tyrant" and "martyr"—worn smooth by Jefferson and the Romantic poets—Timrod asserts that the patriot "might brain a tyrant with a rose." Blending these images with Frauendienst, he explains that the example of women should lead men to place their "lines of steel / Beneath the victor's arch." Four days later he wrote "Carolina," wherein the imagery of Revolutionary days is revived: the "despot treads thy sacred sands," but before the tyrant can fall, science, trade, and art must fill the fields with spears, and "Ten times ten thousand men must fall." "Assured in right, and mailed in prayer," Carolina will fling down the gauntlet to the "Huns." "Ripley" continued the same blend of Revolutionary and chivalric imagery when this hero of Vera Cruz is called to "wield / The weapon of a tyrant's doom." It is unlikely that Timrod had any specific "tyrant" in mind—the language was loaded enough to stir the required patriotism.

With the siege of Charleston, however, such chauvinism gave way to recognition of the horrors of war, and when Timrod faced life through his own pain, he wrote well. In "Charleston" (December, 1862) Timrod strengthened his imagery with new metaphors: "a thousand guns lie couched . . . / Like tigers in some Orient jungle crouched." Not heroes but ordinary "grave and thoughtful men" may "wield the patriot's blade / As lightly as the pen." Instead of men taking courage from lady-service, the maidens "have caught the strength of him / Whose sword she sadly bound." No longer unimpeachably on the side of the just, God has inscribed Charleston's "doom." By Christmas Timrod would pray so earnestly for peace that Tennyson is said to have remarked that the poet deserved to be called "Poet Laureate of the South." Charleston sits beneath an "Arctic noon" little interested in the mirth of the holiday, thinking instead of Christ "who died to give us peace." The formerly militant fields imaged as spears are now sites to be blessed by peace, as are the "whirring marts." Yet four months later in "Spring," Timrod called upon "the hills" to "crush the tyrants and the slaves," with a million soldiers, apparently no longer with peace in their hearts.

Of course, it would be difficult to expect Timrod to replace his sectional love with national love, but his reliance upon the imagery of chivalry transmitted his sincerity through outmoded language. "The Unknown Dead" describes the men as "martyrs," and in "Carmen Triumphale" (1863) the foes are "false recreants in all knightly strife" who "fought as tyrants fight." As in "Ode" (1866), the valor of the "martyrs" has made Magnolia cemetery holy.

Clearly, Timrod struggled with personal desires for peace and a determination to speak for the public passions of the South. His use of trite imagery to express the horror of the Civil War is only one indication of the unresolved tension within him between his private humanity, enhanced by his Romantic sensitivity, and his need to articulate the public passion, rooted in his neoclassic training and his admiration for ethical poetry. Because Timrod found no satisfying solution to these competing elements within him, his poetry after the war reflects this tension.

Yet this tension in Timrod obliquely explains the direction that Southern writing would take in the next century. At first fixated upon romanticized images of the Old South, Southern writing would explore the public passion of the South's tragedy. Old times there would not be forgotten; they would be sentimentalized. As richer imaginations took their stand on the Southern tragedy, old times would be apprehended in all their richness and mythologized. The Southern Renascence would carry forward the work Timrod had in part begun. If he did not write better than he did, it is greatly to his credit that, considering his situation, he wrote so well. From the early poems to "A Mother's Wail" he traveled a great distance. When a journey is undertaken, no one can know completely the difficulty of the passage. Despite his weaknesses as a poet, in his way Timrod made his personal journey to the Arctic and may stand as a Southern Ulysses.

SURVEY OF CRITICISM

Edd Winfield Parks wrote the best introduction to the life and works in *Henry Timrod* (1964). The various introductions, listed below, provide additional biographical and critical assessments of Timrod as a poet and critic. In *Sidney Lanier, Henry Timrod and Paul Hamilton Hayne: A Reference Guide* (1978), Jack De Bellis lists and annotates the most pertinent biographical and critical appraisals.

Because Timrod was the Poet Laureate of the Confederacy, his reputation suffered after the Civil War. Timrod's best poems came from the excitement and agony of the war, though he had published a slender volume before the hostilties began. Paul Hamilton Hayne, Timrod's friend and fellow Southern poet, did his best to keep Timrod's work before the public by gathering *The Poems of Henry Timrod* in 1873. But the job of pointing out Timrod's achievements as poet and critic largely fell to such twentieth-century editors and commentators as Edd Winfield Parks; Guy Cardwell, Jr.; Jay B. Hubbell; and others.

Though these commentators have some difficulty placing Timrod in the antebellum or postbellum period, most agree that he wrote his best poems between 1861 and 1866. As a critic, Timrod has not yet received sufficient recognition for his insights, especially in his essay "Literature and the South," first published in *Russell's Magazine* in August 1859.

BIBLIOGRAPHY

Works by Henry Timrod

Poems. Boston: Ticknor and Fields, 1859.
The Poems of Henry Timrod. Ed. Paul Hamilton Hayne. New York: E. J. Hale, 1873.

Katie. New York: E. J. Hale, 1884.

Poems of Henry Timrod. Memorial Edition. Boston: Houghton Mifflin, 1899.

The Last Years of Henry Timrod, 1864–1867. Ed. Jay B. Hubbell. Durham: Duke University Press, 1941.

The Essays of Henry Timrod. Ed. Edd Winfield Parks. Athens: University of Georgia Press, 1942.

The Uncollected Poems of Henry Timrod. Ed. Guy Cardwell, Jr. Athens: University of Georgia Press, 1942.

The Collected Poems of Henry Timrod. Ed. Edd Winfield Parks and Aileen Wells Parks. A Variorium Edition. Athens: University of Georgia Press, 1965.

Studies of Henry Timrod

De Bellis, Jack. *Sidney Lanier, Henry Timrod and Paul Hamilton Hayne: A Reference Guide*. Boston: G. K. Hall, 1978, pp. 107–37.

Green, Claude B. "Henry Timrod." *Antebellum Writers in New York and the South*. Ed. Joel Myerson. Vol. 3 of *Dictionary of Literary Biography*. Detroit: Gale Research, 1979, pp. 339–42.

———. "Henry Timrod and the South." *South Carolina Review* 2 (May 1970): 27–33.

Hubbell, Jay B. *The South in American Literature, 1607–1900*. Durham, N.C.: Duke University Press, 1954, pp. 466–74.

Parks, Edd Winfield. *Henry Timrod*. New York: Twayne, 1964.

Rubin, Louis D., Jr. "Henry Timrod and the Dying Light." *Mississippi Quarterly* 11 (Summer 1958): 101–11.

Thompson, Henry. *Henry Timrod: Laureate of the Confederacy*. Columbia, S.C.: That State, 1928.

Wauchope, George A. *Henry Timrod: Man and Poet*. Columbia, S.C.: University Press, 1915.

DONALD R. NOBLE

George Tucker
(1775–1861)

Novelist, biographer, statistician, economist, lawyer, congressman, historian, teacher, planter, gentleman—George Tucker was all these and more—a prolific antebellum Southern writer whose nonfiction has been rediscovered by modern historians, but whose literary work is still largely neglected.

BIOGRAPHY

George Tucker was born in Bermuda on 20 August 1775. The Tucker family had been important to Bermudians for almost 200 years, and George was educated in a "Latin school" under tutors imported from England, and by the lawyer Josiah Meigs, who later became professor of natural philosophy at Yale and the president and founder of the University of Georgia. Tucker then read law in the office of George Bascomb and was tempted to pursue a career in law in Bermuda, but chose rather to emigrate to America where his financial and political ambitions would find greater scope. Tucker had important connections in America: his kinsman, St. George Tucker, was a wealthy landowner, judge, and professor of law at the College of William and Mary; Thomas Tudor Tucker was a physician, a congressman from South Carolina, and later treasurer of the United States.

In July 1795, shortly after the death of his mother, Tucker sailed to Philadelphia. After enjoying a brief holiday in what was then the capital of the United States, he traveled to Williamsburg seeking St. George Tucker. The judge was in western Fluvanna County presiding over one of the courts under his jurisdiction. Tucker caught up with him there, borrowed much-needed funds, and took his kinsman's advice: he returned to Williamsburg to enroll in the College of William and Mary.

Williamsburg, no longer the capital city of Virginia, was in decline, with a population of only 1,200; but Tucker, always a convivial man who knew how to find or make a good time, enjoyed the five years he lived there. He made a constant social round with professors, judges, physicians, retired planters, and selected students from the college. These refined and intelligent people enjoyed musical evenings, amateur theatricals, witty conversation, and the other diversions for which the Tidewater aristocracy has long been noted.

His studies were not very rigorous, and after spending only one year instead of the required two as a general student and then another studying law, he was graduated in 1797 *ex speciali gratia*. He had even found time in summer and fall 1796 to take an extended trip to New York and Philadelphia, where his letters of introduction obtained for him meetings with John Jay, the governor of New York, and George Clinton, the ex-governor, and then, on his way home in November, a brief and much desired meeting with George Washington in Philadelphia.

Although he enjoyed his travels, Tucker was eager to return to Williamsburg, for he was successfully courting the charming and wealthy Mary Byrd Farley, a great-granddaughter of William Byrd II. Tucker and Farley were married in October 1797 and immediately traveled to Bermuda, presumably to improve the bride's health, for she was seriously ill, probably with tuberculosis. The Tuckers returned to Williamsburg to what should have been a pleasant and affluent existence, but Mary Tucker died on 25 May 1799. Because of technicalities in her will, Tucker never inherited all that he thought was intended for him, in spite of twenty years of litigation. In summer 1800 Tucker moved to Richmond to practice law and make his way in politics.

Richmond, the capital, was a bustling city of 5,000, and Tucker moved easily in its society. In February 1802 he married Maria Ball Carter, the great-niece of George Washington. Tucker was a great success in Richmond literary circles as well. In 1801 he published his *Letter ... on ... the Late Conspiracy of the Slaves*, in which he advocated the purchase of a section of land west of the Mississippi where blacks could be settled. (Over the years, Tucker's attitude towards slavery would change and his ''solutions'' would vary.) Throughout his residence in Richmond, he published both essays and verse, often anonymously, in various newspapers and magazines. His verse was ''occasional'' or love poetry or satirical in the manner of Swift. His essays, often satirical, were on local politics and social events.

What Tucker did not manage successfully, however, was his professional and financial life. He had not mastered the law, was a poor public speaker, and was successful only in the unchallenging post of commissioner of bankruptcy, a post some influential friends obtained for him. Meanwhile, he was using up his capital in lavish entertaining, real estate speculation, poor investments, and constant and unsuccessful gambling. His expenses also increased with the birth of Daniel George on 23 November 1802 and Eleanor Rosalie on 4 May 1804. By 1806 Tucker had dissipated a considerable fortune, had lost his reputation for honesty in a scandal involving a lottery held for the Richmond Academy, had narrowly avoided a duel over a minor political argument, and had shown himself to be incompetent at his chosen profession. He needed a new start.

In fall 1806 Tucker moved his family to the home of his wife's parents in Frederick County in the Shenandoah Valley. He economized, worked hard at his profession, and after two years was able to buy Woodbridge in Pittsylvania County to the south. Here he became a respected member of the community and, after two unsuccessful attempts at the state legislature, was elected in 1816. He had written in 1811 his pamphlet *A Letter, to a Member of the General Assembly . . . on the Navigation of the Roanoke . . .* , which had brought him some public attention, and in 1813 wrote a series of essays, "Thoughts of a Hermit," which were published in Philadelphia in *Port Folio* in 1814 and 1815. His financial life was improving too, and by 1818 he had sold Woodbridge and his other holdings and established himself in Lynchburg, where he became a trustee of the Lynchburg Female Academy, a vestryman in St. Paul's Episcopal Church, and in 1819 a member of the United States Congress. As Tucker wrote to St. George in a letter dated 9 October 1808: if he had only moved sooner, he "should have been so much more advanced in . . . profession, so many thousands richer in purse, and so many years younger in health and ambition."

At this point matters looked most promising, but Tucker's life was always to go up and down. His father-in-law had moved to Culpepper County and overextended himself financially. Despite the efforts of Tucker and others, the Charles Carter estate was sold at public auction, with Tucker able to arrange for the purchase of some of Carter's possessions and slaves. Tucker established the Carters on his smaller estate, Deerwood, for the rest of their lives.

An undistinguished congressman, Tucker served three terms, usually siding with the Jeffersonian Republicans, but spent too much time in expensive entertaining and unsuccessful gambling. He was also distracted by the births of his fifth and sixth children, Lelia in October 1810 and Harriet in May 1813, and by the sudden death of Harriet in 1816 and of their eldest, Rosalie, in 1814. He also worried over the mental stability of his only son, Daniel, who was later institutionalized and who died in Philadelphia in 1838.

Tucker's third term in Congress ended in 1825. In December 1824 he received a most flattering and attractive proposal: Thomas Jefferson, accepting the recommendations of Joseph C. Cabell and James Madison, offered Tucker the post of professor of moral philosophy at the new University of Virginia with lifetime tenure, rent-free housing, and a guaranteed annual income of $1,500. It may be that his ever-potent family connections were operating here again, or perhaps Madison and Cabell had read and admired his *Essays on Various Subjects of Taste, Morals, and National Policy* (1822), a gathering of the *Port Folio* essays of 1814–15.

One would think Tucker accepted immediately, but this was not the case, for he had just finished his first novel and had high hopes of becoming a professioal author. He wrote back to Cabell on 1 January 1825 that he had recently completed a novel, *The Valley of Shenandoah; or, Memoirs of the Graysons*, in only two months. James Fenimore Cooper, he had heard, earned $5,000 from each of his novels, so Tucker was unwilling to tie himself down to a university position if he could gain wealth and fame as a professional novelist. Unfortunately, critics and readers ignored *The Valley*; Tucker made nearly nothing by it and wrote to both Cabell and Jefferson in February accepting the post and explaining his delay by saying that he had been seriously considering remaining in public life and had also distrusted his qualifications for a professorship.

Disappointed though he was in its reception, Tucker had reason to be hopeful over *The Valley*'s prospects. This novel, perhaps the first important novel ever written by a Virginian, has literary merit. In it Tucker portrays the collapse of a distinguished Shenandoah Valley family, the Graysons. Because of financial mismanagement, high living, and the recently deceased Colonial Grayson's overgenerous cosigning of friends' notes, the Grayson estate must be sold at public auction. Louis Grayson is deceived and seduced by a callow New Yorker, James Gildon; and Edward Grayson, the son and now sole protector of the family, is killed in a fight over the family honor. Mrs. Grayson lives out her remaining years a poor, childless widow. Tucker paints a faithful, informed portrait of life on a Valley plantation—slavery, plantation management, the influx and social rise of the "Dutch" (Germans), and much more.

Tucker moved with his family to their quarters on the Lawn in spring 1825 and was to spend twenty years at the University of Virginia. He was immediately voted chairman of the faculty, perhaps because, at fifty, he was its oldest member. He had also been a Virginian for 30 years, and he was one of only two professors who had been educated in America. The duties of chairman were rather like those of a modern university president.

His teaching duties as professor of moral philosophy included lectures on what were then called the mental sciences—ethics, logic, etc.—and he later added courses in political economy, rhetoric, and belles lettres. He worked hard at his studies, having little formal education in these areas, and, from contemporary accounts, was well regarded as a teacher, although some remarked upon his aloofness and his social snobbery, and others complained that his lectures were boring and poorly delivered. Apparently Tucker never developed into a proficient public speaker. Life at the university must have been quite pleasant; Tucker and his colleagues were a distinguished, amiable group and entertained one another with dinners and conversation.

In February 1823 his second wife, Maria, died, and finding solitude unbearable, Tucker courted and married Louisa A. Thompson of Baltimore in December 1828. They lived together happily until her death in 1858.

While at the University, Tucker found time to write only two more novels. He published his second novel, *A Voyage to the Moon*, in 1827 under the pen name Joseph Atterley. This novel, a Swiftian satire, is a simple, Jules Verne–like tale of a trip to the moon by means of an antigravity stone. Joseph Atterley is taken to the moon by a Hindu wise man named Gurameer; on the leisurely trip they discuss a range of matters of interest to Tucker—race, politics, the effect of climate on cultural development, and so on. Once there, they travel widely and comment on the excesses of women's fashions—they cover themselves with feathers—dietary fads, "projectors" of all sorts and, of course, lawyers and physicians. The reader is never allowed to forget that the folks back home on earth are guilty of the same kinds of foolishness.

A Century Hence, written in 1841 but not published until 1977, is somewhat similar. Set in 1941, this epistolary novel tells the story of a romantic misunderstanding that causes Henry Carlton, a high-born young man, to take a trip around the world to sooth his wounded heart. He is accompanied by an older friend, Caspar Bentley, and they write back of their adventures and observations. Tucker can thus embed his prophecies—political, racial, technological—in a credible plot.

In the fields of biography, history, economics, statistics, and philosophy, however, Tucker's pen was indefatigable. With his friend and colleague, Dr. Robley Dunglison, he wrote and published a weekly magazine, *The Virginia Literary Museum*, beginning in June 1829 and continuing for one year. Tucker contributed more than 75 essays to the *Museum*. He also found time to write *The Laws of Wages, Profits and Rent Investigated*, *The Life of Thomas Jefferson* . . . in two volumes, and *Public Discourse on the Literature of the United States*, all published in America in 1837. In 1842 he published *Essay on Cause and Effect*, and in 1843 both *Progress of the United States in Population and Wealth in Fifty Years, as Exhibited by the Decennial Census* and *Public Discourse on the Dangers Most Threatening to the United States*. In 1845, the year of his retirement, he published his tribute to an old colleague, *Memoir of the Life and Character of John P. Emmet, M.D., Professor of Chemistry and Materia Medica in the University of Virginia*.

During his tenure in Virginia, Tucker found little opportunity for travel. The one real exception was his three-month trip to England in 1839. To his great disappointment he found English society too stratified and reserved; this experience in some small measure checked his steady movement to the right politically. He had been distressed by the excesses of Jacksonian democracy and over the years had moved from being near-Jacobin to a supporter of Henry Clay. England also demonstrated to Tucker the dangers of overpopulation and reinforced his interest in the dismal predictions of Thomas Malthus.

Tucker was seventy years old when he freed his five slaves and retired to Philadelphia to enjoy the cultural and intellectual life of the city and continue his writing. He completed a four-volume *History of the United States* (1856–58), *Political Economy for the People* (1859), and *Essays, Moral and Metaphysical* (1860). He was a well-known figure in his later years but, sadly, was often respected more for the number and variety of his books than for their merit. Henry S. Randall remarked that Tucker's trying to understand the personality of Jefferson was like "ice trying to understand fire."

Tucker was also terribly perplexed by the growing sectional rift. He was a staunch nationalist; in spite of his strong attachments to the South and his increasingly firm belief that abolition would be a tragedy, he was no secessionist. Tucker spent the harshest months of each winter visiting in the South and in January 1861 was in Mobile, Alabama, about to embark on his return voyage to Virginia when he was struck on the head by a falling bale of cotton. He was taken to the home of his daughter in Richmond, and there he died 10 April 1861.

MAJOR THEMES

Since George Tucker was the author of some 23 books and pamphlets and more than 150 articles, essays, and poems over a period of 63 years, it is evident that he expressed himself on a number of subjects. But in his fiction and non-fiction, he returned repeatedly to certain themes.

His most enduring subject was his adopted home, Virginia. Tucker often depicted at great length the Virginia society he loved, praising its virtues, satirizing its faults, and issuing warnings of what the future would hold if certain changes were not implemented. *The Valley of Shenandoah*, his best novel and his best book, is an extended description of life on a Valley plantation. He evokes the natural beauty of the place, describes the various kinds of agriculture and industry, and shows how the residents—white and black—live, labor, and amuse themselves. Tucker draws portraits of the Scotch-Irish, who are "hardy, restless, brave, and enterprising." They are valuable trailblazers, warriors, and legislators who promote education, but, alas, they are improvident and often overextend themselves financially and end up bankrupt with their estate sold at auction to pay the Jewish moneylender. The "Irish" then go west to Kentucky to start this cycle over and thus ironically help to settle the new nation.

He depicts the Germans as the opposite. They devote themselves to industry, sobriety, and thrift, have well-kept farms and well-managed businesses; but they contribute little to the commonwealth by remaining clannish, aloof, and often ignorant. They take little notice of public affairs, the arts, or education.

Tucker, himself a perennially improvident man, admired the "Irish" but devoutly wished they would adopt some of the financial responsibility of the "Dutch." Since he had suffered so from imprudence, it is a constant theme in his work, and in *The Valley* the loss of the family fortune is a contributing factor to Louisa's seduction and the ruin of all the Graysons.

A major concern of Tucker, as it was with a great many thinking Southerners, was slavery. His pamphlet . . . *on* . . . *the Late Conspiracy of the Slaves* (1801) underestimates the seriousness of the Richmond revolt led by a slave named Gabriel Prosser, but contains an extended criticism of the institution. Tucker felt that slavery unsettled society through the constant threat of rebellion and retarded the growth of industry because half the men work unwillingly and the other half not at all. Tucker warned that the birthrate among slaves was much higher than among whites and that the situation could only grow worse. He believed that "transportation" was impractical and cruel, but did suggest that slaves be emancipated and moved to a section of land west of the Mississippi, to be bought from Spain. As it then stood, slave labor kept wages low and drove white labor west over the mountains. Since he believed that a nation could achieve economic and cultural heights only with a dense and hardworking population, slavery in 1801 stood in the way of all Tucker's hopes for America. St. George Tucker, always an influence on him, had written *A Dissertation on Slavery* (1796) advocating emancipation and declaring that all humans have "natural rights." In 1801 Tucker seemed to agree.

His position changed. In 1824 in *The Valley*, he shows the terrible cruelty of the slave auction, with humans up for sale and families threatened with separation; but he apologizes for slavery in general by asserting that most masters are kind, if only out of self-interest. He has Edward Grayson admit slavery is "evil," "checks the growth of our wealth—is repugnant to . . . justice—. . . inconsistent with its principles—injurious to its morals—and dangerous to its peace," but he insists that there is no "cure."

In his nonfiction from 1824 to 1841, Tucker prophesies that slavery will die a natural death, but in *A Century Hence* (1841) we are told slavery still exists in some Southern states in 1941. By the 1850s Tucker was writing in favor of slavery, using the arguments that slavery helped to develop "leadership qualities" among Southern whites, that slaves were induced to work hard through rewards and family loyalty, not punishment, and that slaves were better treated than Northern laborers. As the Civil War approached, Southern writers were expected to defend the institution even if, like Tucker, they were anti-secessionists.

Besides having interests in politics and social questions, Tucker was also a lifelong statistician and economist.The focus of his interest was the question of population, for him a two-edged sword. On the one hand, Tucker believed that man's highest achievements could only come from cities, cultural centers, and a high density of population in general. He applauded immigration and lamented western migration because it thinned out the seaboard colonies, thus retarding their cultural and economic growth. At various times, Tucker took the Whiggish position of advocating the construction of canals and other improvements.

Early in his career, Tucker wrote anti-Malthusian essays and what we might call antiromantic essays, asserting that the noble savages are simply savage, not noble. Tucker always associated population density with industrialization, wealth, progress, the creation of an aristocratic class, and thus more rapid progress in all the arts. Although he came to America as a Jeffersonian Republican, Tucker was shortly no kind of egalitarian. He saw the landed aristocracy as the repository of man's highest virtues, and he accepted easily that the masses of men in a highly industrialized society would be poor wage-slaves, who constituted some danger and whose political rights needed to be limited. Later in his life, he began to think Thomas Malthus more correct. In *A Century Hence*, especially, he illustrates the horrors of overpopulation in England, Egypt, and other places, but felt that the vastness of America would absorb almost any amount of population.

Tucker was throughout his life a student of the eighteenth-century Scottish, common sense school of philosophy. He read especially Dugald Stewart, Thomas Reid, and Thomas Brown and often wrote essays refuting idealism and skepticism. Tucker was a thinker whose opinions were sometimes changing, sometimes contradictory. But he was, in any case, a man thinking.

SURVEY OF CRITICISM

There have been only two studies of the work of George Tucker. Tipton R. Snavely's *George Tucker as Political Economist* (1964) is a specialized work, little concerned with Tucker's fiction. Snavely devotes chapters to Tucker's theories on rent, profits, wages, tariff, etc. *George Tucker: Moral Philosopher and Man of Letters* (1961), by Robert Colin McLean, is the more general and better book, with a long biographical sketch and chapter-length essays on Tucker's main concerns. McLean has a complete bibliography of Tucker's work and materials, unpublished studies and books and articles he found valuable in the preparation of his book. Useful also are the introductions to recent editions of *The Valley of Shenandoah* (1970) and *A Century Hence* (1977), both by Donald R. Noble, Jr.

BIBLIOGRAPHY

Works by George Tucker

"By a Citizen of Virginia." *Letter to a Member of the General Assembly of Virginia, on the Subject of the Late Conspiracy of the Slaves with a Proposal for Their Colonization*. Baltimore: Bosnal & Niles, 1801. 2d ed. Richmond, Va.: H. Pace, 1801.

"By Citizen of Pittsylvania." *A Letter to a Member of the General Assembly of North Carolina on the Navigation of the Roanoke and Its Branches*. Richmond: John O'Lynch, 1811.

Anonymous. *Letters from Virginia, Translated from the French*. Baltimore: Fielding Lucas, Jr., 1816.

Recollections of the Life of Eleanor Rosalie Tucker. Addressed to Her Surviving Sister by Their Father. Lynchburg, Va. [James Boyce], 1818.

Speech of Mr. Tucker, of Virginia, on the Penetration of Slavery in Missouri. Delivered in the House of Representatives of the United States February 25, 1820. [Washington, D.C.: n.p., 1820].

"By a Citizen of Virginia." *Essays on Various Subjects of Taste, Morals, and National Policy*. Georgetown, D.C.: J. Milligan, 1822.

To the Freeholders of the Counties of Campbell, Pittsylvania, and Halifax. Lynchburg, Va.: n.p., 1824.

"By a Citizen of Virginia." *The Valley of Shenandoah; or, Memoirs of the Graysons.* 2 vols. New York: C. Wiley, 1824. 2d ed. New York: O. A. Roorbach, 1828. Repr. Chapel Hill: University of North Carolina Press, 1970.

"Joseph Atterley." *A Voyage to the Moon: With Some Account of the Manners and Customs, Science and Philosophy, of the People of Morosofia and Other Lunarians.* New York: E. Bliss, 1827.

The Laws of Wages, Profits and Rent Investigated. Philadelphia: Carey & Hart, 1837.

The Life of Thomas Jefferson, Third President of the United States, with Parts of His Correspondence Never Before Published, and Notices of His Opinions on Questions of Civil Government, National Policy, and Constitutional Law. 2 vols. Philadelphia: Carey, Lea & Blanchard, 1837; other ed. London, 1837, 1838.

Public Discourse on the Literature of the United States. Charlottesville, Va.: n.p., 1837.

"By a Virginian." *Defence of the Character of Thomas Jefferson Against a Writer in the New York Review and Quarterly Church Journal.* New York: W. Osborn, 1838.

Theory of Money and Banks Investigated. Boston: C. C. Little and J. Brown, 1839. 2d ed., Boston: C. C. Little and J. Brown, 1839.

Essay on Cause and Effect. Philadelphia: n.p., 1842.

Progress of the United States in Population and Wealth in Fifty Years, as Exhibited by the Decennial Census. Boston, New York, Philadelphia, Washington, D.C.: Little & Brown, 1843.

Public Discourse on the Dangers Most Threatening to the United States. Washington, D.C.: n.p., 1843.

Memoir of the Life and Character of John P. Emmet, M.D., Professor of Chemistry and Materia Medica in the University of Virginia. Philadelphia: C. Sherman, 1845.

An Essay on Cause and Effect; Being an Examination of Hume's Doctrine, that We Can Perceive No Necessary Connexion Between Them. Philadelphia: Lea & Blanchard, 1850.

Progress of the United States in Population and Wealth in Fifty Years, as Exhibited by the Decennial Census, with an Appendix, Containing an Abstract of the Census of 1850. New York: Press of Hunt's Merchant's Magazine, 1855.

A History of the United States from Their Colonization to the End of the Twenty-Sixth Congress, in 1841. 4 vols. Philadelphia: J. B. Lippincott, 1856–58.

Essays, Moral and Metaphysical. Philadelphia: C. Sherman, 1860.

Political Economy for the People. Philadelphia: C. Sherman, 1859. 2d ed. Philadelphia: C. Sherman, 1860.

A Century Hence; Or, a Romance of 1941. Ed. and intro. by Donald R. Noble, Jr. Charlottesville: University Press of Virginia, 1977.

Studies of George Tucker

Helderman, Leonard C. "A Satirist in Old Virginia." *American Scholar* 6 (Autumn 1937): 481–97.

———. "A Social Scientist of the Old South." *Journal of Southern History* 2 (May 1936): 148–74.

Hubbell, Jay B. *The South in American Literature, 1607–1900.* Durham, N.C.: Duke University Press, 1954, pp. 216–17, 243–55.

McLean, Robert Colin. *George Tucker: Moral Philosopher and Man of Letters*. Chapel Hill: University of North Carolina Press, 1961.

Noble, Donald R. Introduction to *The Valley of Shenandoah; or, Memoirs of the Graysons*, "By a Citizen of Virginia." Chapel Hill: University of North Carolina Press, 1970.

————. "*A Century Hence*: George Tucker's Vision of the Future." *Virginia Cavalcade* 25 (Spring 1976): 184–91.

Snavely, Tipton R. *George Tucker as Political Economist*. Charlottesville: University Press of Virginia, 1964.

Nathaniel Beverley Tucker
(1784–1851)

Primarily known as a jurist, a professor of law, and an ardent secessionist, Nathaniel Beverley Tucker also contributed to the growing literature of the Old South three novels that not only depict the physical aspect of the region but also reveal the mind of a staunch defender of its slave-based social structure.

BIOGRAPHY

Beverley Tucker (his first name was seldom used) was born on 6 September 1784 at Matoax, Virginia, the fourth child of St. George Tucker and Frances Bland Tucker. In an increasingly class-conscious and patriotic society, his parentage was auspicious. His father, a member of the old Bermuda gentry, had emigrated to Virginia in 1771 to study law at the College of William and Mary in Williamsburg. He also saw wartime service during the American Revolution. His fortunes began to ascend when in 1778 he married a widow, Frances Bland Randolph, whose husband had left her several considerable estates, as well as three sons. The youngest and most noted of these, John Randolph—he later added the aristocratic "of Roanoke" to his name—was thus the half-brother of Beverley Tucker. This politically active but highly eccentric figure would come to exercise a powerful force on his younger kinsman.

Tucker attended William and Mary and studied law with his father and others; he was licensed to practice in 1806. In 1809—after some opposition from his father—Tucker married Mary (known as Polly) Coulter, sister of a law tutor. He served with a militia company during the War of 1812 but saw no action, and he emerged from the war without the military distinction and the chance for advancement that he had coveted.

His law practice had not prospered during this early period of his marriage, and he began to think that his prospects might improve if he moved to the West.

After considerable exploration in the region, he finally settled with his family in the promising frontier country of Missouri. His gamble quickly paid off. In December 1817 he was appointed to the Northern Circuit Court of Missouri; his case load, however, was heavy, and he was soon embroiled in the sectional quarrels that accompanied the application of Missouri for admission to the Union. Tucker at once engaged in a pamphlet war that turned on complex constitutional issues. At the center, of course, was the problem of slavery. Was Missouri, as the first state whose boundaries lay entirely beyond the Mississippi River, to be free or slave territory? Tucker and several cohorts argued the states' rights view— that the original Union had been a compact into which sovereign states freely entered. Thus, if the federal government tried to impose restrictions on the entry of a new state against the will of that state, it violated the basic principles upon which the nation had been founded.

The Missouri Compromise of 1820, which admitted Missouri as slave territory and Maine as free and set up conditions for the addition of new states, brought a temporary calm. But the debate hardened Tucker in his opposition to a central government that could threaten all he held dearest: a structured, paternalistic, agrarian, and slave-based South. Implicit in this view was the recourse to secession if such a way of life came under outside attack.

Tucker stayed in Missouri for several more years, dreaming of a "new Virginia" of the West, in which he and other wealthy planters could enjoy their hierarchical status. This ideal society was not to be, but Tucker had other successes. He was appointed a federal judge, and took advantage of his position to uphold the supremacy of the bench in a state that retained much of its frontier spirit. But Tucker was always restive; Virginia was still his real home, and it appeared not to have noticed to a proper degree his status in the West. Family tragedies also made life in Missouri less alluring. In fall 1827 his beloved wife Polly died of complications during pregnancy; in 1828 he married her niece, Eliza Naylor, a consumptive who succumbed to her disease only five months later. In a rather surprising move, he now courted the lively and pretty Lucy Ann Smith, daughter of a Virginia-born retired army general who had settled in west-central Missouri. Lucy was seventeen, Tucker a rather physically battered forty-six; nonetheless they were married in 1830. The marriage was happy and fecund; by 1848 Lucy had borne her husband seven children.

But if domestic content was now restored for Tucker, the national scene promised nothing but profound discontent and disruption. In 1832 South Carolina took the extreme step of declaring tariff laws null and void—precipitating the Nullification Crisis. Though Tucker could not support the tactics of South Carolina's champion, John C. Calhoun, he was outraged by the proclamation of President Andrew Jackson, which denied any validity to the doctrine of state sovereignty. It was Tucker's excuse to return to Virginia, and he immediately went home to weather the crisis. He waged a newspaper campaign and even went to the White House to meet with Jackson and argue his case. Henry Clay's compromise tariff bill again defused the explosive situation between North and

South, but Tucker was not appeased. He now felt that his real role resided in
wielding his pen closer to the centers of power. Returning with his family from
Missouri to Virginia in June 1833, he learned of the death of his old mentor,
his kinsman John Randolph. While awaiting the settlement of the Randolph
estate, Tucker received perhaps the most gratifying news of his life: he had been
elected to the chair of law at William and Mary. St. George Tucker's son was
coming home to stay at last.

As a teacher of constitutional law, Tucker now emerged as an important
influence on a generation of students whom he tutored in the doctrine of states'
rights. As Tucker's recent biographer, Robert J. Brugger, has observed: "Several
of his students carried the lessons they learned to the Virginia secession convention in the spring of 1861"—a full ten years after Tucker's death. But in
1834 Tucker was also emerging as a man of letters. He had through most of his
career published articles on social, economic, and political issues; now he began
to contribute reviews on literary and other topics for the *Southern Literary
Messenger*, recently founded by Thomas W. White in Richmond. He also unexpectedly turned to a form lately made popular by William Alexander Caruthers,
William Gilmore Simms, John Pendleton Kennedy, and others—the Southern
romance. Both of Tucker's ventures into the genre appeared in 1836: *George
Balcombe*, based in part on Tucker's experiences in Missouri; and *The Partisan
Leader*, a rather wild work set in the future that predicted the secession of
Virginia. A third but more domestic tale, "Gertrude," appeared as a serial in
the *Southern Literary Messenger* in 1844–45.

For the remainder of his life, Tucker carried on animated correspondence with
the chief political leaders and men of letters of the South—Simms, Poe, Edmund
Ruffin, Thomas R. Dew, James Henry Hammond, and Abel P. Upshur, among
many others. Both Poe and Simms quickly recognized the importance of Tucker's
contributions to a growing Southern literature. Poe had early praised not only
Tucker's fiction but also his poetry, and Simms frequently prodded Tucker for
contributions to his *Southern Quarterly Review*. Tucker was undeniably pleased
by his reception as a literary man, but he never lost sight of his primary goal:
Southern separatism. In 1841 he emerged again as a politician by publishing a
series of articles attacking Henry Clay and the reestablishment of the national
bank. He also somehow found time to issue three books on law and political
science.

Tucker's final service to the cause of secession was as a delegate to the
Nashville Convention of 1850. Though Tucker misread the mood of the convention—it was more conciliatory toward the North than he had expected—he
fervently pressed for separatism and even for the establishment of a Southern
empire that would extend into the Caribbean. It was his last major effort to stir
his fellow Southerners into quick action, but it failed.

In the immediate aftermath of the convention, Tucker visited James Henry
Hammond at his South Carolina plantation; he was pleasantly received but became disappointed by the lukewarm response to his heated opinions. Indeed,

disappointment darkened the rest of Tucker's life. The South simply was not ready to join in his vision of its exalted future. He felt ill, listless, weary. At the close of the academic term of 1851, he tried salt baths in Gloucester County and felt restored enough to write Hammond, once again urging him to take on leadership on the South's behalf. One more trip remained to him. In July Simms, on his way to see his publishers in the North, stopped by Williamsburg; the pair then visited Washington, Harpers Ferry, and the Virginia springs. But Tucker returned from the expedition exhausted; on 26 August 1851 he died. His family buried him in Williamsburg's Bruton Parish Church; an obelisk by the grave commemorated him as a jurist and law professor who was "descended from the best blood of Virginia." He could have—and may have—written the epitaph himself.

MAJOR THEMES

Like many others of his place and class, Tucker drew his notions of the literary craft from the lofty pronouncements of such Scottish periodicals as the *Edinburgh Review* and *Blackwood's*. Inevitably, too, he took as model for his historical romances the popular tales of Sir Walter Scott, which sketched a broad background of a past era and showed the effects of changing times upon a set of fictional characters. Most important, Tucker insisted that a tale must have a didactic purpose—an obvious attempt to counter the oft-repeated charge that fiction was, by self-definition, a "lie." In his romances he generally produced an effect of verisimilitude in the depiction of those areas whose history and physical aspect he knew from firsthand experience. He also accurately conveyed the fear felt by many Southerners that the federal government had become a despotism intent, in the service of Northern commercial interests, on destroying the Southern way of life. His characters, therefore, are largely types who carry moral messages: the "good" are clearly good and the "bad" are appropriately reprehensible. Tucker's overriding theme in fiction was that which informed his position in the legal and moral spheres—the preservation of a civilization in which Virginia had taken the lead since earliest colonial days.

Tucker was not the only novelist who saw the value of his state as an exemplar for the whole American experiment—but he was by far the fiercest. Preceding him had been William Wirt, whose *Letters of the British Spy* (1803) had turned the Jamestown settlement into primary legend, and his kinsman George Tucker, whose *The Valley of Shenandoah* (1824) was one of the earliest of a rising crop of plantation novels. Tucker was also surely aware of the more recent work of William Gilmore Simms and John Pendleton Kennedy, whose careers started with his own in the 1830s.

Tucker's strengths as a polemicist and his weaknesses as a craftsman in plotting and characterization are both exhibited in the first of his three works of fiction, *George Balcombe* (1836). The story is a welter of narrative lines, but it centers on the misfortunes of a young Virginian, William Napier, who tells his own tale. It opens in Missouri with the meeting of Napier and George Balcombe, a fellow Virginian and William and Mary graduate, who is now a prosperous (and platitudinous) planter in the West. Napier discovers that he has been done out of his rightful inheritance of his father's property in Virginia by a scoundrel named Montague. The bulk of the tale essentially is the pursuit of Montague and the recovery of Napier's estate in the Tidewater region, where the story ends in a joyful reunion with the old family slaves. Almost any scribbler of the period could have cobbled together such a melodrama; what makes *George Balcombe* worth recovering is its genre pictures of Missouri life (such as a revival meeting) and its discursive treatment of some of Tucker's pet themes: slavery, states' rights, the proper relationships between husband and wife, the messy confusion of Missouri courts, and above all the power (and duty) of the Virginia gentleman to bring about the triumph of justice.

George Balcombe was well received, particularly by the *Southern Literary Messenger*, which published a long review by Poe in its January 1837 issue. Most of the notice consists of plot summations and long quotations from the text—a practice not uncommon in the period—but there is no doubt that the *Messenger* was aiming to please. Tucker was now a valued contributor—and Poe slyly revealed the authorship of the anonymously published novel in his final paragraph—but one need not suspect mere sycophancy in his praise. "[W]e are induced to regard it," he summed up, "upon the whole, as *the best* American novel. There have been few books of its particular kind, we think, written in *any* country much its superior. . . . Talent of a lofty order is evinced in every page of it." Five years later Poe would repeat this judgment in his *Marginalia*.

After this strong beginning, Tucker next published a work that is at once his most curious and most characteristic. Called *The Partisan Leader: A Tale of the Future*, it was issued in Washington in 1836; however, its title page carried the spurious date of 1856 and the byline of "Edward William Sidney." It does indeed tell a tale, though a rather cloudy one; more basically it is a tract—perhaps the most fire-snorting piece of secessionist propaganda issued before the 1850s. Tucker saw an immediate danger to the South in the ambitions of Martin Van Buren, and the urgency of his warning is such that it all but overthrows the narrative vehicle. The presumed protagonist is introduced in the opening pages but is dropped until nearly the close; the narrator is brought in as a new character at the very end of the book, and he cuts off the story without managing to bring any of its actions to a conclusion. But as polemic the book carries emotive weight. Tucker sets the internal time of the action in 1849; Van Buren is about to run for his fourth term, and Virginia is facing disaster. The lower states have already left the Union and formed a Southern Confederacy—not, as might be expected, because of the issue of slavery but because they have continued their strong stand against the tariff. The North is being run by the tyrannical Van Buren, who directs his loathsome schemes from the sanctity of his Washington "mansion." In between stands Virginia; having delayed in joining its sister states, it now faces occupation by Van Buren's troops. By the end of the book, the Virginia forces, under the leadership of Colonel Douglas Trevor, a U.S. Army officer who has now seen the light, have launched guerilla warfare against the president's men. But, surprisingly, we learn in the closing pages that Trevor has become Van Buren's prisoner in Washington. What will be the fate of the noble Partisan Leader? No reader can doubt that the partisan cause eventually will triumph, but Tucker gives the book's closing words to the narrator, who has been putting together a history of the rebellion. Here is his final message:

I have been interrupted in my narrative. I have hesitated whether to give this fragment to the public, until I have leisure to complete my history. On farther reflection, I have determined to do so. Let it go forth as the first *Bulletin* of that gallant contest, in which Virginia achieved her independence; lifted the soiled banner of her sovereignty from the dust, and once more vindicated her proud motto, which graces my title page,—SIC SEMPER TYRANNIS!

Some recent critics of the book have tended to see it less as straight prophecy and more as a campaign tract in an election in which, should he win, Van Buren would carry on the anti-South policies of Andrew Jackson. There seems to be some evidence for this view in light of the fact that several members of the Trevor family are lightly disguised portraits of Tucker's own kinsmen. (Tucker himself may be represented by the character of "Mr. B——.") Moreover, a review of *The Partisan Leader* by Abel P. Upshur (probably done with Tucker's collaboration) emphasized the present political message rather than its visionary tone. (And perhaps not so coincidentally, it appeared in the same issue of the *Southern Literary Messenger* as Poe's review of *George Balcombe*.) But the continued life of the book indicates that it was indeed read as a forecast of the South's future. In 1861 the book was reissued in New York with the tantalizing blurb "A Key to the Disunion Conspiracy." An "explanatory introduction" informed the reader that he would "learn from the following pages that the fratricidal contest into which our country has been led is not a thing of chance, but of deliberate design, and that it has been gradually preparing for almost thirty years." In 1862 a Richmond publisher also resurrected the book, giving it a different emphasis as "A Novel, and an Apocalypse of the Origin and Struggles of the Southern Confederacy." What both sides appear to have recognized was Tucker's one true bit of prophecy—that the successful assertion of states' rights would inevitably lead to the breakup of the Union.

When he was negotiating with his Washington publisher for the issuance of *The Partisan Leader,* Tucker wrote that, should the work prove popular, he might continue the story by adding a volume every month of his life. In fact, some eight years passed before he returned to fiction. His final effort, ''Gertrude; An Original Novel,'' was published in serial installments in the *Southern Literary Messenger* between September 1844 and December 1845. It was Tucker's most ''magazinish'' piece—pious, moralistic, domestic, sentimental, and clearly directed to women readers. Certainly its plot was one with which they could more readily identify than with the manly and martial posturings of *The Partisan Leader*. Gertrude, a poor Virginia country girl, is packed off to a Washington townhouse, where she will be less of a burden to her family. Gertrude and her stepbrother, a virtuous lawyer, have already acknowledged their love for each other; but in the capital city Gertrude attracts the unwanted attention of a wealthy South Carolina planter now serving as a congressman. Much of the plot deals with the machinations of Gertrude's mother, a cold and mercenary figure, to bring off this desirable match—despite Gertrude's own determination to remain faithful to her country lover. Tucker had probably intended no more than the sort of love story so necessary for the fortunes of a struggling magazine. Inevitably, though, his strong didactic strain mingled with the romantic flow. No reader—no matter how engrossed with Gertrude's interrupted happiness—could have missed the point that a Southern girl could become a mere pawn in the power politics of the federal capital, particularly if her mother supported arranged marriages. Tucker even inserted his own economic views in discussing the fate of Gertrude's stepfather, who loses his fortunes in the collapse of a "wildcat" bank. But above all else, "Gertrude" is a portrait of true Southern Womanhood—as Tucker viewed it. Secure in the sanctity of his own marriage, and proud of his daughters, he limned the Woman as the warm center of a home in which she was to exhibit the Christian virtues of tenderness, self-sacrifice, and total obedience. This was hardly a quirky view of womanhood in this period, but Tucker managed to give it a touch of Southern flavoring. The Southern home, dominated by a strong but just father and given moral direction by a faithful wife who recognized God's plan for her without ever questioning it, was the bedrock of its ideal social system.

Tucker would write no more fiction; he had a bare six years of life left, and his time was burdened by what was for him much more important work. In this he was typical of the attitude toward belles lettres in the Old South. Creative writing that smelt of "professionalism" was anathema to the true gentleman. In such a situation we may be grateful that Tucker took up the form of the romance at all. For—crude in plot and in characterization as they so often are— these three books can still give us more of a sense of the idealistic dream of a perfected Southern society than do his "serious" writings. Tragic though this dream proved to be, it is now a part of our national record; in Tucker's fictions we have one man's record of how it came into being.

SURVEY OF CRITICISM

Like the work of most writers of the Old South, Tucker's works went into eclipse in the years following the Civil War. As a man of considerable prominence, he was not, of course, neglected by historians of the South or by biographers of men in whose lives he had figured. He was also occasionally remembered in encyclopedia articles and in Southern literary histories that began to appear around the turn of the century. But his recovery as a man of letters has been the work of twentieth-century critics. In 1927 Vernon Louis Parrington included Tucker in a chapter on "The Older Plantation Mind" in his classic *Main Currents in American Thought*. He saw the centrality of *The Partisan Leader* to the "mind" he was discussing, though he was forced to call the book "quite the absurdest in the library of the Old South."

Following Parrington, other academic critics soon turned their attention to Tucker. In 1947 Norma Lee Goodwin presented "The Published Works of Nathaniel Beverley Tucker" as an M.A. thesis at Duke University; and in 1952 Percy Winfield Turrentine completed a massive doctoral dissertation at Harvard, which is particularly valuable for its inventory of Tucker's many scattered writings. Arthur Wrobel focused more specifically on Tucker's literary theories in " 'Romantic Realism': Nathaniel Beverley Tucker" in *American Literature* (1970); his study centers on the vexed question of "realism" in fiction and argues that, "despite his good intentions toward realism, Tucker failed just as his contemporaries did, and a study of his fiction and critical prejudices reveals why the writing of a truly realistic literature was postponed." Wrobel also contributed the entry on Tucker to the *Dictionary of Literary Biography*, Vol. 3.

A thorough and well-written scholarly analysis is Robert J. Brugger's *Beverley Tucker: Heart Over Head in the Old South* (1978). Brugger made full use of Tucker's many writings and delved deeply into manuscript holdings. His study takes account of Tucker's romances, but his scope is broad: "to sharpen our understanding of the Old South, especially its intellectual life, by examining carefully one man's experience in that society." For Brugger, Tucker's "life story is useful as microcosmic history, suggesting how certain young Southerners matured and gained a moral sense in this period, became acquainted with ideas, and developed habits of thinking. Tucker offers a case study in the growth of states' rights, proslavery persuasion, his later extremism providing a refracted view of the ideology he shared with many other men who were less visible."

The fullest biographical treatment is also the most recent: Beverley D. Tucker's *Nathaniel Beverley Tucker, Prophet of the Confederacy, 1784–1851* (1979). The author, a kinsman of his subject, draws upon materials collected by Turrentine (see above) and manuscript holdings in the library of the College of William and Mary. It fills in many details about the whole Tucker clan and quotes liberally from the letters of his subject. Reviewing this biography in the *Southern Literary Journal* (Spring 1980), Lewis Leary concludes with a comment that might well stand for current opinion on Beverley Tucker: "He is now remembered as a curiously contentious and prophetic man whose vision of secession came true. Brave, vain, relentlessly stubborn, he is a large, ultimately tragic figure from our troubled past."

BIBLIOGRAPHY

Works by Nathaniel Beverley Tucker

A Lecture on the Study of the Law. Richmond: T. W. White, 1834.
George Balcombe. A Novel. 2 vols. New York: Harper and Brothers, 1836.

The Partisan Leader: A Tale of the Future. "By Edward William Sidney." "Printed for
the Publishers, by James Caxton, 1856." [Washington: Duff Green, 1836.]
"Gertrude: An Original Novel." *Southern Literary Messenger* 10 (September, November,
December, 1844); 11 (March, April, May, June, July, November, December,
1845).
A Series of Lectures on the Science of Government. Philadelphia: Carey and Hart, 1845.

[A listing of Tucker's other numerous papers may be found in Turrentine's dissertation,
cited below, and in Brugger's study, pp. 261–64.

Studies of Nathaniel Beverley Tucker

Brugger, Robert J. *Beverley Tucker: Heart Over Head in the Old South.* Baltimore: Johns
Hopkins University Press, 1978.
Hubbell, Jay B. *The South in American Literature, 1607–1900.* Durham, N.C.: Duke
University Press, 1954.
Parrington, Vernon Louis. *Main Currents in American Thought.* Vol. 2. New York:
Harcourt, Brace, 1927.
Tucker, Beverley D. *Nathaniel Beverley Tucker, Prophet of the Confederacy, 1784–
1851.* Tokyo: Nan'un-do, 1979.
Turrentine, Percy Winfield. "Life and Works of Nathaniel Beverley Tucker." Ph.D.
diss., Harvard University, 1952.
Wrobel, Arthur. "Nathaniel Beverley Tucker." *Antebellum Writers in New York and the
South.* Ed. Joel Myerson. Vol. 3 of *Dictionary of Literary Biography.* Detroit:
Gale Research, 1979.
———. " 'Romantic Realism': Nathaniel Beverley Tucker." *American Literature* 42
(November 1970): 325–35.

CARL R. DOLMETSCH

St. George Tucker
(1752–1827)

St. George Tucker is better known today as "the American Blackstone" than a a belletrist because his extant literary efforts, comprising some 210 poems, 29 Addisonian essays, and three completed plays plus some dramatic fragments, mostly remain unpublished manuscripts, the main body of which is in the Tucker-Coleman Collection of Swem Library at the College of William and Mary. When these manuscripts at last see print, Tucker will be appreciated as a pivotal figure in a circle of Jeffersonian Virginian writers, including William Wirt, the Munfords, Francis Walker Gilmer, George Tucker (a cousin), and others, who can instructively be compared to their contemporaries, the Knickerbocker Group and the Connecticut Wits. These so-called Virginia Wits shaped the literary tastes and traditions of much of the antebellum South.

BIOGRAPHY

Tucker was born at The Grove, Port Royal, Bermuda, the youngest of six children of Henry and Anne (Butterfield) Tucker, on 10 July (29 June, Old Style) 1752. Following a grammar school and tutorial education, he came to Virginia with his brother, Nathaniel, in 1772 to study at William and Mary College and thereafter to prepare for the bar under George Wythe. Excepting brief visits to his native island between 1773 and 1785, some of them on smuggling voyages for the American rebels, Tucker remained in the Old Dominion for the rest of his long life, distinguishing himself successively as a planter-lawyer, an innovative professor at his alma mater, and on the bench of Virginia's highest court and the federal district court, where many of his decisions and opinions set enduring precedents for the then infant American judiciary system. He served as a militia officer in the final campaign of the Revolutionary War, suffering a slight wound at Guilford Courthouse and participating in the siege of Yorktown, during which he kept a journal that has been an important source for historians. His patriotic verses penned between 1775 and 1781 and reflecting, in several instances, his battle experiences are among his salient early literary achievements.

Although he was a delegate to the Annapolis Convention (September 1786), which prefigured the 1787 Constitutional Convention, Tucker was dissatisfied with the compromises reached at Philadelphia and, like his friend Jefferson, he remained a "strict constructionist" and a foe of centralization in the federal system. An early and frequent advocate for ending chattel slavery, Tucker published in 1796 (in *Dissertation on Slavery . . .*) a proposal that children born of slaves in Virginia beyond a specified date should be freed upon reaching adulthood and either employed for wages by their mothers' owners or released to seek such work elsewhere. Unfortunately, the Virginia Assembly, to whose members he sent copies of his *Dissertation*, chose to ignore it completely.

St. George Tucker's rapid ascent in public life was owed in some measure to his prudent successive marriages to widowed heiresses in the plantation oligarchy. His first wife, Frances Bland Randolph, whom he married in 1778, died in 1788, and three years later he wedded Lelia Skipwith Carter, who lived until 1822. All together these marriages produced eight children, four of whom did not survive infancy. The most distinguished of them were Henry St. George and Nathaniel Beverley, both of whom followed their father's profession and were also writers. Among his several stepchildren was the irascible John Randolph of Roanoke, whom Tucker reared and educated.

Although the possibility of becoming a professional writer scarcely existed for Tucker, he came by literary inclinations naturally. The Bermuda Tuckers were, so to say, a "writing clan." Among the manuscripts in the Tucker-Coleman Collection are verses St. George as a student received from siblings back home. Nathaniel, his next-older brother who eventually settled in medical practice in England and Scotland, where he died in 1807, composed and published while still in Williamsburg a lengthy pastoral ode, *The Bermudian*, and in 1783 he wrote a curious allegorical verse drama of the American Revolution, *Columbinus: A Mask*, which he hoped would become a kind of national *Festspiele* "to be presented annually on some public occasion, such as a meeting of Congress or at the time of some public ceremony." Both works profoundly influenced the form and substance of much that St. George himself wrote, even many years later.

What St. George Tucker published of his own imaginative creations during his lifetime represents what might without exaggeration be called the tip of a literary iceberg. Although a perfectionist who withheld anything of which he was unsure (some of his unpublished verses, for example, exist in several revised versions), it is clear that he did not intend concealment. He sought publication whenever and wherever possible, but such opportunities were unavailable in Williamsburg after 1781, and books had to be sent to New York, Philadelphia, or Richmond to see print. Moreover, writing was for him an avocational interest, to be pursued only when he had leisure from his judicial or other duties, which was neither often nor at regular intervals. There were thus a few periods in his life characterized by frequent and sometimes intense literary activity punctuated by long intervals during which he apparently wrote nothing of a belletristic nature even while he continued to write (and occasionally saw published) essays on jurisprudence and to keep a notebook of sporadic scientific (mainly astronomical) observations and plans and drawings for such inventions as a semaphore (or beacon light) system to telegraph messages up and down the eastern seacoast of the United States and a primitive water closet that could be emptied from outside.

Tucker's first period of poetic endeavor coincided roughly with the Revolutionary War era (1775–81), during which he composed a dozen or so patriotic verses that appeared in contemporary newspapers or later, in 1790 and 1792, in Carey's *American Magazine*, and a long verse allegory, *Liberty, A Poem on the Independence of America* (published 1788) plus a few others that have only recently been published. In 1786 he published a 65-stanza ballad, *The Knights & The Friars*, but neither this nor *Liberty* has been reprinted, and originals are exceedingly rare. In 1790 or 1791 appeared, probably from a Philadelphia printer, a curious anthology of which a unique copy, lacking title page and interleaved with a journal by Margaret Lowther Page, survives in the Tucker-Coleman Collection, containing six of Tucker's earliest *vers de société* written in some instances a decade earlier as well as "The Belles of Williamsburg," a collaborative effort with John Page and Dr. James McClurg that has wrongly been considered (and widely reprinted) as Tucker's most characteristic poem.

His next productive interlude of composition came during the mid–1790s with his anti-Federalist satires by "Jonathan Pindar," the first fourteen of which appeared between June and September 1793 in Freneau's *National Gazette* (and were falsely attributed to the editor even by later scholars such as Vernon Louis Parrington). These, together with a second set of pseudonymous mock odes with glosses by "Christopher Clearsight" (William Giles), were published in book form in 1796. During this latter year, he made his first sustained excursions into dramatic writing and the Addisonian essay, the results of which still remain unpublished.

Throughout the later years of Tucker's tenure in the chair of "Law and Police" (1790–1803) established by Jefferson for his old mentor, George Wythe, and in which Tucker was the second incumbent, he was absorbed in his five-volume redaction of *Blackstone's Commentaries*, a work that endured as a standard text for Virginia lawyers and others for more than a century. A few weeks after resigning his William and Mary professorship (in December 1803) amid controversy over his teaching methods, he became a judge on the Virginia Supreme Court of Appeals, the duties of which left him little leisure for writing during the next seven years. He resigned this post in March 1811 with the resolve to retire from public life—a resolution he was able to keep for only two years. Tucker's most intensive period of writing coincided with the onset and progress of the War of 1812. The emotions Tucker felt in this second American conflict with Great Britain recalled those sentiments he had felt and expressed some 30 years earlier, and he not only engaged in the writing of new poems, plays, and essays, but he also revised and gathered for an abortive collected edition many of his works from the Revolutionary War era. Among the many other pieces he completed during the years 1811–15, almost all of them still unpublished, is a very ambitious long poem replete with notes for its numerous topical allusions, entitled *"Carmen Seculare*, an Ode for the Fourth of July 1784,"* offering a kind of verse history of the War for Independence. Tucker had worked on this poem at sporadic intervals for nearly three decades, and he seems to have considered it his masterpiece. None of his literary manuscripts dates from later than December 1819 although his poem "Resignation," written in 1807, was published in 1823 in a London magazine (*The Mirror of Literature, Amusement and Instruction*), where it was widely admired by, among others, Tucker's erstwhile archfiend, John Adams.

In January 1813 President Madison appointed Tucker judge of the Federal District Court of Eastern Virginia, a position he held with great esteem until ill health forced him to retire in December 1825. His second wife having died in 1822, he spent the final months of his retirement at the home of a stepson-in-law, Joseph C. Cabell, at Warminster, in the mountains of western Virginia, and it was there that he died and was buried, 10 November 1827.

MAJOR THEMES

St. George Tucker's writings are infused with the kind of patriotic fervor one often encounters in the expression of immigrants who have prospered and achieved distinction in their adopted land. Love of the land—of the Commonwealth of Virginia and the new nation he preferred to call "Columbia" rather than "America"—is the overriding theme of Tucker's *oeuvre* in all of its forms, but especially in his poems and plays. The Revolutionary War provided Tucker the most exciting and personally fulfilling period in his long life. In later years he fondly invoked that era as America's Golden Age to be enshrined in the hearts of the young as a source of strength to the republic that was ever in danger of forgetting and forsaking its revolutionary ideals. He was a true pedagogue, and his intended audience was almost always a younger generation of readers and theatergoers.

In political matters, Tucker was an uncompromising Jeffersonian anti-Federalist, and, like Jefferson's, the mind that is revealed in his topical prose shows a thorough familiarity with the ideas of the French *philosophes* as well as those of the Scottish Enlightenment. He was so fond of the writings of Henry Bolingbroke, and of appropriating Bolingbroke's thoughts to inform his own work, that he needed warning from his friend William Wirt of the dangers of unconscious plagiarism. His literary models—Joseph Addison, William Shenstone, Jonathan Swift, William Cowper, and, to a lesser degree, Robert Burns, Thomas Gray, and Oliver Goldsmith—illustrate the "colonial lag" in American culture and taste at the time of the Republic's founding, and he remained a staunch

Anglican Deist long after the Presbyterian and Baptist ascendancy in Virginia had rendered that religious viewpoint unfashionable, even slightly odious.

Tucker's ardent patriotism is inseparable from his commitment to the ideals of individual freedom, egalitarianism, and local autonomy, which he believed to be inherent in the new American as opposed to the old European way of life. This theme is most clearly and fully expressed in his 270-line *Liberty, a Poem on the Independence of America* (1780–81, 1788), an allegorical verse history of the progress of the goddess, Liberty, from her birthplace in Ancient Greece through Switzerland, the Netherlands, and Britain, and thence to "Columbia's rising states." Here at last Liberty may reign supreme, but only if the newly independent nation remains mindful of history and vigilant against the double threat of encroaching tyranny and internal discord. All of Tucker's other patriotic poems, several of his essays, and two of his plays contain variations or particularizations of the central theme in *Liberty*.

Tucker thought he saw the serpent of tyranny as well as that of discord (which he called "faction") lurking in the policies and machinations of the Federalists, especially following the reelection of Washington in 1792, and he used all the powers of satire at his command to lampoon their leadership—Adams, Hamilton, Jay, Henry Knox, Fisher Ames, and others—in the *Probationary Odes of Jonathan Pindar, Esq., A Cousin of Peter's, and Candidate for the Post of Poet Laureat to the C.U.S.* (1793, 1796), a work that deserves at least as much recognition and critical scrutiny as the contemporaneous collaborative effort of the Connecticut Wits, *The Anarchiad*. His specific targets in these verses were Alexander Hamilton's policies in funding the national debt (including assumption by the central government of the states' debts), the national bank, the "Citizen Genet" affair, and finally, the Jay-Grenville Treaty, which pledged American neutrality in the Anglo-French conflicts. In his choice of pseudonym, "Jonathan Pindar," the poet was capitalizing upon the popularity of the London satirist John Wolcot ("Peter Pindar"), whose odes were directed against the British king and the Pitt ministry. "Jonathan" was a symbolic American name of the Early National period, somewhat equivalent to our "Uncle Sam" of today. The *Probationary Odes*, however, express a particularly Southern, Francophile viewpoint rather than a widely held national one of that day.

Perhaps as many as a third of Tucker's 200-odd poems (many of which exist in more than one manuscript version) fall into that somewhat ambiguous category, *vers de société:* occasional verses for a friend's or family member's wedding, for Christmas or another holiday, or even cleverly rhymed gossip. They are light, whimsical, somewhat old-fashioned pieces in a graceful, neoclassical manner that employs such mythical soubriquets as Chloe, Sylvia, and Cynthia. A few are more private, more deeply felt. One such is "To Sleep" (dated 24 January 1788) lamenting the death of the poet's first wife, Frances. Another is his valedictory "Resignation" (on the *ubi sunt* theme), and yet others are moralistic meditations such as "A Fable":

> I dreamed last night, the debt of nature paid,
> I, cheek by jowl, was by a Negro laid;
> Provoked at such a neighborhood, I cried,
> "Rascal! begone. Rot farther from my side."
> "Rascal!" said he, with arrogance extreme,
> "Thou are the only rascal here, I deem;
> Know fallen tyrant, I'm no more thy slave!
> Quaco's a monarch's equal, in the grave."

Ballads and humorous rhymed anecdotes, some of which might be regarded as crude and coarse today, form another sizable group of Tucker's versifying efforts. His first publication outside of newspapers was *The Knights and The Friars: An Historical Tale; After the Manner of John Gilpin* (1786), an "Americanization" of a verse tale with a very similar title by Richard Jodrell, published a year earlier in London. A mock ballad (Jodrell's had been in couplets), it tells a lugubrious tale of what supposedly happened to the corpse of a libertine monk. Other works of a similar vein include "Numps and Robin" (1788), recounting the Rabelaisian manner in which a country bumpkin is duped on his wedding night. One of his best comic efforts is the mock-heroic "To Col. Lovelace of the British Guards" (1781), describing an incident at Guilford Courthouse in which, Falstaff-like, a British officer feigned death to avoid capture, much to his later embarrassment. Tucker's most ribald poem is a three-stanza mock-lament, "The Judge With a Sore Rump" (1819), in which a judge bewails a boil on his posterior when court cases keep him sitting on the bench all day.

Tucker's efforts at playwriting, none of which has yet reached the stage nor seen print, nevertheless deserve attention here. His earliest extant attempt is a 205-line pastoral colloquy, "Fairy Hill, a Rural Entertainment. Intended to be Adapted to Musick," which exists in three manuscripts, the earlist dated 7 May 1781 and the last July 1812. It is a strange hybrid, perhaps unique in the annals of American literature, involving three fairies (Puck, Oberon, and Titania) from *A Midsummer Night's Dream* plus others of Tucker's invention who cavort, sing, and declaim in the moonlight on the banks of the Schuylkill (near Philadelphia) about events in the closing campaign of the Revolutionary War. It ends hopefully with an "Ode to Peace."

In June 1789 Tucker began an anti-Federalist farce, "Up & Ride, or The Borough of Brooklyn," abandoning it in the second of what was evidently intended to be a three-act satire on "Daddy Vice" (John Adams), a character he salvaged for later use in his *Probationary Odes*. From the same period (ca. 1789–90) there is also a fragment of an "olio" (perhaps a short curtain-raiser or afterpiece), "The Profligate," adapted from material in Le Sage's *Gil Blas*, but only the opening scene was written. In Williamsburg during Christmas and New Year's 1796–97, however, Tucker completed a five-act farce, "The Wheel of Fortune," about speculative swindling in Northwest Territory lands (the Scioto

scandal was still fresh then) and political corruption in high places. He immediately sent the manuscript to John Page, then a congressman in Philadelphia,
in the hope his friend might persuade Thomas Wignell to stage it at the Chestnut
Street Theatre. When Wignell declined it, Tucker made some unavailing inquiries
about possible productions in Norfolk or Petersburg, but then abandoned his
efforts. It remains the most stageworthy and in most respects the most polished
of Tucker's dramatic compositions.

In autumn 1811, amid a growing crisis over the British navy's impressment
of American seamen in their long struggle with Napoleon, Tucker was urged by
his friend Wirt to take up the dramatist's pen again to whip up hawkish sentiment
against England. This he did gladly, finishing on 15 December 1811 a three-act
"medley" (musical melodrama), "The Times, or The Patriot Rous'd," which
very probably would have been staged in Richmond that season but for the tragic
fire that destroyed the Richmond playhouse with tremendous loss of life on
Christmas night 1811 (an event Tucker memorialized in an elegy for the victims).
This play is on the Romeo and Juliet theme, the "star-cross'd" lovers in this
instance being children of Virginian families (Trueman and Friendly) divided
by their pro- and anti-British leanings who are happily united against the common
foe in the denouement when Henry, the young hero, escapes from British shan-
ghaiers. Into "The Patriot Rous'd" Tucker wove nine of his patriotic poems
(most of them dating from the 1780s) that he intended to be set to music by
Peter Pelham or another Richmond composer and sung by various characters.
For the finale he asked for a grand chorus and a spectacular apotheosis of
Revolutionary War heroes (Washington, Franklin, Warren, Montgomery, Mercer, Greene, and others) "surrounded by a glory (with) Trueman and the rest
looking all the while as rapt in wonder and admiration." In March 1815, the
end of the War of 1812 prompted him to rough out a sequel, "The Patriot
Cool'd," in which the young hero returns Ulysses-like in disguise from the
Battle of New Orleans to joyous celebrations. The play lacks the dramatic tension
of "The Patriot Rous'd," and much of the material in this unrevised draft is
interpolated directly from local newspapers.

Since the serial essay as created by Joseph Addison and Richard Steele was
unquestionably the most popular literary genre in America throughout Tucker's
lifetime, it was only natural for him to turn his hand to this form too. What
seems incredible is that, owing to a series of adverse circumstances, so few
(perhaps only two) of his 30-odd familiar essays were ever published. His earliest
essay, in a manuscript dated 25 August 1796, is called "A Dream," but it might
more properly be designated "a nightmare." It is an apocalyptic vision of the
future of the United States as an expansionist, imperialist world power that
sprawls across the North American continent, then gobbles up Latin America
and extends itself across the Pacific, losing its democratic character and degen-
erating into oppressive monarchy without relinquishing republican forms. The
nation then begins to disintegrate internally from a kind of centrifugal unwiel-
diness and, finally, as the narrator of the dream awakens, is on the verge of

destruction in a war with a colossal "Kamchatkan" nation that has arisen on the ashes of the old Russian Empire! Some details that Tucker himself (or certainly his potential readers) must have thought fantastic to the point of absurdity in 1796 have proved frighteningly prophetic. What is clear is that, even seven years before the Louisiana Purchase, Tucker was wary of ideas that ere long would be subsumed in the phrase Manifest Destiny and would serve to exacerbate sectional strife.

Two years later, in the winter of 1798–99, Tucker began an abortive series for the Richmond *Examiner* entitled "The Dreamer," but he inexplicably broke off in the middle of the fourth number, and none of the essays was printed. What endures is a fascinating Swiftian allegorical history of the American Revolution and the founding of the federal government (Constitutional Convention, ratification debates, etc.) reminiscent of Jeremy Belknap's contemporaneous *The Foresters*. Perhaps the most interesting element of the "Dreamer" essays is Tucker's uses of Gotham and Gothamites as fictional names for America and its inhabitants several years before Irving (in the seventh *Salmagundi*) employed the same labels for the city and people of Manhattan.

In summer 1811 Tucker was solicited by William Wirt for contributions to a pseudonymous collaborative essay series then running under his aegis in the Richmond *Enquirer* under the general title "The Old Bachelor." During the next two months (August-September) Tucker sent Wirt 27 or 28 essays in which he assumed an astonishing variety of personae, ranging from an elderly sage to a grieving widow and even a flighty coquette in order to discourse on an equally astonishing variety of subjects: education, oratorical eloquence, dueling, the evils of slavery, gambling, partriotism, clothing fads, religion, astronomy, and much more. The essays Tucker headed "For the old Batchellor [*sic*]" contain some of his most inspired and most ingratiating writing. Unfortunately, only one of them was published: the 27th (and penultimate) essay in the *Enquirer* "Old Bachelor" series (17 December 1811), which was republished in book form in 1814.

The reason for Wirt's not including Tucker's contributions more fully along with his own and those of his other collaborators—Frank and Dabney Carr, Richard E. Parker, Dr. Louis Girardin, and David Watson—is quite simple. At the time Wirt asked Tucker to join the Old Bachelor circle, he already had a sufficient number of essays on hand to complete the projected first series and he was planning for a second series, which Thomas Ritchie, the *Enquirer* (and book) publisher, decided for some reason not to print. Tucker retrieved as many of his essays from Wirt as he could (four or five apparently were lost) and in late summer 1813 he integrated them into a projected scheme of his own to "revive and continue publication [of the series] under the title of the *Hermit of the Mountain*" (Letter, Tucker to Wirt, 12 September 1813). After writing an introductory essay for the series in which the character and literary lineage of the old Hermit (as the fictional successor to Wirt's supposedly deceased "Old Bachelor") and his *prodesse delectare* aims are established, Tucker broke off abruptly in the middle of his second "Hermit" essay on 26 September upon receiving news of his daughter's death, and he never resumed his project. His surviving manuscript essays show Tucker's command of every mode of the genre then in use. Dream vision and allegory—sometimes, but not always, combined in the same piece—were his favorites, but his efforts also include polemics, burlesques, character studies, cautionary tales, fables, Socratic dialogues, and the exotic Oriental tale. As in his other writings, Tucker appears in his esays an even-tempered humanitarian rationalist and a somewhat old-fashioned writer with a graceful, witty, and felicitous style.

In the same notebook, headed *Nugae* (legal Latin for "trivia"), in which he started his "Hermit of the Mountain" project, Tucker sketched several pieces on his astronomical observations and speculations that have recently been excerpted and discussed by Hans C. Von Baeyer (see Bibliography).

SURVEY OF CRITICISM

The paucity of Tucker criticism is the obvious consequence of his still almost submerged career as a writer, with its numerous unpublished manuscripts plus the lack of modern reprints of the work published during his lifetime. One may hope this situation will be remedied. When it is, Tucker's fully revealed oeuvre should furnish fresh grist for the scholar-critic's mill and even enable fresh reappraisals of the state of literary endeavor in Jefferson's Virginia, building upon the unfinished pioneer studies of the late Richard Beale Davis.

The only full-length biography of Tucker is by an admiring descendant, Mary Haldane Coleman, whose information was incomplete and sometimes inaccurate and whose appraisals of an illustrious ancestor are less than objective. Somewhat more scholarly, if necessarily brief, is the account of another descendant, the Reverend Dr. Beverley D. Tucker, in his monograph on St. George's novelist son, Nathaniel Beverley. Most other biographical accounts have been chiefly if not exclusively based on Coleman's.

Jay B. Hubbell, in his encyclopedic study of early Southern literature, was the first to give critical attention to Tucker's belletristic efforts, but he was then evidently unaware of the unpublished manuscripts in Williamsburg, and his four-page discussion lumps St. George with his brother, Nathaniel. In his quite thorough 33-page introduction to his selection of Tucker's poems (based largely on his 1954 Yale dissertation), editor William S. Prince is primarily concerned with providing information rather than criticism, and the same may also be said of the articles listed below by Prince and by Carl Dolmetsch.

Between 1971 and 1981 there were ten M.A. theses (in English literature and language) completed at the College of William and Mary, which included editions with critical commentary of "Old Bachelor" essays and one play ("The Times, or The Patriot Rous'd") in the Tucker-Coleman Collection manuscripts, and one M.A. thesis (in history) surveying Tucker's personal library and reading.

BIBLIOGRAPHY

Works by St. George Tucker

The Knights and The Friars: An Historical Tale. New York: Eleazar Oswald, 1786.

Liberty, A Poem on the Independence of America. Richmond: Augustine Davis, 1788.

A Dissertation on Slavery: With a Proposal for the Gradual Abolition of it, in the State of Virginia. Philadelphia: Matthew Carey, 1796.

Probationary Odes of Jonathan Pindar, Esq. Philadelphia: Benjamin Franklin Bache, 1796.

Blackstone's Commentaries: with Notes of Reference, to the Constitution and Laws, of the Federal Government of the United States; and of the Commonwealth of Virginia. 5 vols. Philadelphia: Birch and Small, 1803.

The Poems of St. George Tucker, of Williamsburg, Virginia, 1752–1827. Ed. William S. Prince. New York: Vantage Press, 1977. (71 poems, some reprinted but most from manuscript sources)

Studies of St. George Tucker

Coleman, Mary Haldane. *St. George Tucker: Citizen of No Mean City.* Richmond: Dietz Press, 1938.

Dolmetsch, Carl. "The Revolutionary War Poems of St. George Tucker." *Tennessee Studies in Literature* 26 (1981): 48–66.

———. "Tucker's 'Hermit of the Mountain' Essays: Prolegomenon for a Collected Edition." *Essays in Early Virginia Literature Honoring Richard Beale Davis.* Ed. J. A. Leo Lemay. New York: Burt Franklin, 1977, pp. 257–76.

Hubbell, Jay B. *The South in American Literature, 1607–1900.* Durham, N.C.: Duke University Press, 1954, pp. 149–53, bibliography 968–69.

Prince, William S. "St. George Tucker: Patriot Bard on the Bench." *Virginia Magazine of History and Biography* 103 (October 1976): 5–27.

Tucker, Beverley D. *Nathaniel Beverley Tucker: Prophet of the Confederacy, 1784–1851.* Tokyo: Nan'un-do, 1979, pp. 17–38 passim.

Von Baeyer, Hans C. "The Universe According to St. George Tucker." *Eighteenth Century Life* n.s. 6 (November 1981): 67–79.

Booker T. Washington (1856–1915)

Booker T. Washington was the most popular and most prolifically published Southern black writer of the early twentieth century. One of his autobiographies, *Up From Slavery* (1901), sold millions of copies, and his legacy to the post-Reconstruction development of ex-slaves is still a catalyst for debate among critics, historians, and scholars of Southern culture.

BIOGRAPHY

Booker T. Washington was born on 5 April 1856 to a slave cook named Jane who lived and worked for the Burroughs family in Franklin County, Virginia. His father was an anonymous white plantation owner who lived nearby. The lad was a slave himself for the first nine years of his life. During the arduous economic times of Reconstruction, his mother married Washington Ferguson, and in 1865 the family—including Booker's older brother, John, and his younger sister, Amanda—moved to Malden, West Virginia, where Ferguson had secured a job in a salt furnace. Here Booker first went to work in the sooty West Virginia coal mines. (Not knowing his true father's name, Booker took Ferguson's first name as his surname.) After a few years the young man obtained more prestigious employment as a houseboy for the wife of General Lewis Ruffner. Impressed with his industriousness, Mrs. Ruffner allowed Booker to attend (on a part-time basis) the local school which an itinerant black teacher, William Davis, had founded. Later he wrote of the general's wife: she "always encouraged and sympathized with me in all my efforts to get an education. It was while living with her that I began to get together my first library" (*Up From Slavery*, p. 45).

In fall 1872 Booker's family and several other members of the black community raised whatever money they could to send him to the Hampton Normal and Agricultural Institute in Virginia. At Hampton he came under the influence of the institute's founder, Samuel Chapman Armstrong, whom he later described as "the noblest, rarest human being that it has ever been my privilege to meet" (*Up From Slavery*, p. 54).

Washington graduated from Hampton in 1875 after completing studies in agriculture, academic subjects, and public speaking. But during his first trip home, after two years in college, he endured his first major trauma. His mother—who had fired his dreams with Bible stories, and who had resisted Ferguson's insistence that Washington could not be spared from the coal mines to attend school—died quietly one night shortly after his return from school. Washington had hoped to retire her from a life of poverty and slavish labor as soon as he finished school.

Before going to Tuskegee, Alabama, to begin a lifeling career as founder and president of Tuskegee Institute, Washington returned again to Malden, this time to work for several years as an itinerant teacher. There he was instrumental in state politics, organizing the first block black vote for a successful Republican gubernatorial candidate. There he established a library, a night school, and literary and debating societies.

In 1878 he moved to Washington, D.C., to enroll in an eight-month study program at the Wayland Seminary. Although he found the school's approach to education too liberal and theological studies unchallenging, he used the time to further his reputation as a public speaker. The next year General Armstrong invited him to return to Hampton, "partly as a teacher and partly to assume some supplementary studies" (*Up From Slavery*, p. 96). In addition to graduate studies and teaching responsibilities, Armstrong wanted Washington to be "housefather" to over 75 "wild and for the most part perfectly ignorant" Indian youths: "It was not long before I had the complete confidence of the Indians, and . . . their love and respect" (*Up From Slavery*, pp. 97, 98).

During Washington's tenure at Hampton, General Armstrong received a letter from a newly appointed Board of Commissioners who had been authorized by the Alabama state legislature to start an industrial school for ex-slaves to be located at Tuskegee. Tuskegee, the seat of Macon County, was in the heart of the Alabama black belt and was the home of an enterprising Negro leader named Lewis Adams, who first had the idea for the school. Adams took his plan to an ex-slave owner, W. F. Foster, who was campaigning for the Negro vote in his race for the legislature. The Board offered the presidency of the school to Washington, at the recommendation of General Armstrong.

Washington arrived in spring 1881 to face the devastating poverty of ex-slaves without the economic opportunity to enjoy their freedom. Sharecroppers, living in squalor, were growing cotton right up to their front doors because they needed funds to pay off debts to local stores for food and supplies. Washington went on foot to visit every black family in the town and countryside, convincing them to support a school of higher learning for their children. The dauntless optimist opened Tuskegee Institute with 30 students on 4 July 1881 in an old church and a broken-down shack, both of which he borrowed from local citizens. The new principal modeled the school mainly after the system at Hampton, but whereas his alma mater employed mostly white teachers, Washington always sought to employ black faculty as models of excellence and achievement.

In 1882 Washington married Fannie Smith, a girl from his hometown whom he had known all of his life and who had just graduated from Hampton. Unfortunately, she died two years later in May 1884, when their daughter, Portia, was less than a year old. The following year, Washington married his assistant principal, Olivia Davidson. Two years older than twenty-eight-year-old Washington, she had worked indefatigably to help raise funds for the school. Washington initiated his literary career as a tool in these fund-raising efforts. He did not have time to give extensive attention to the prose of his first book, *Black Belt Diamonds*, which Louis R. Harlan claims was selected and arranged by Victoria Earle Matthews, an ex-slave who became a New York journalist. By this time, Washington had secured a 100-acre abandoned plantation about a mile outside of Tuskegee on which he built a substantial classroom building, several dormitories, and a dining hall. He had fathered two sons (Booker Taliafero and Ernest Davidson) by his second wife, and in 1895 he had made his famous Atlanta Exposition Speech, catapulting him to national prominence as America's leading black spokesman. In the controversial Atlanta speech, Washington gave white Southerners the assurances of black separatism, promising that the black masses did not seek social or political equality and were willing to remain a servant class. The speech was hailed by most prominent white politicians, including President Grover Cleveland. Later that year, Washington was invited to address the Louisiana Constitutional Convention, and the following year he became the first black to receive an honorary degree from Harvard University. As if to solidify his fame and promise, President and Mrs. William McKinley, members of his cabinet and their families, along with the Alabama legislature, visited Tuskegee at Washington's invitation.

After the second Mrs. Washington died in 1889, Washington again remarried, this time to Margaret Murray of Macon, Mississipppi, who, after graduating from Fisk University in Nashville, had joined the Tuskegee faculty. By the time his next book, *The Future of the American Negro*, was published, Washington was an internationally known figure who had written for major American publications. But he still had to write *The Future* to raise personal funds and finances for Tuskegee. In the text, Washington lays down a blueprint for the betterment of black America, and although he evades salient political issues in future volumes, he addresses disfranchisement, recolonization of blacks in Africa, and emerging lynching laws.

Washington's next book looks to the coming century. J. E. MacBrady, a Chicago publisher, wrote the introduction for *A New Negro for a New Century*. The book includes essays by N. B. Wood, author of *The White Side of a Black Subject*, and Fannie Barrier Williams, wife of Chicago attorney Samuel Laing Williams, a lifelong Washington supporter. A certain amount of domestic peace now accompanied Washington's personal life. Margaret supervised the schooling of his three children, was the principal in charge of industrial education for the female students of Tuskegee, and held separate women's and children's meetings when her husband conducted the newly organized Negro Farmers' Conferences.

Washington made his first attempt at autobiography in *The Story of My Life and Work*, which appeared in 1900, a prolific year for the young writer. *Sowing and Reaping* and *Education of the Negro* were also published the same year. Thus in the space of two years, Washington had produced five books and numerous articles, admittedly with the aid of ghostwriters, advisers, and editors. In *The Story of My Life and Work*, Washington recounts his 1899 European tour. His fascination with European class divisions, and his association with several aristocrats (including Queen Victoria) during this and two subsequent tours, provide source material for all of his autobiographical works and for another major book, *The Man Farthest Down* (1912). In 1900 Washington also traveled to Africa to train Africans how to grow and interbreed American cotton with local varieties. He made subsequent trips to Africa and was a major influence behind America's African policy and certain foreign service appointments to this continent. The popularity of *The Story* widened Washington's political sphere. He had organized the National Negro Business League the year before and now used his popularity as a fulcrum to organize black business associations throughout the South.

In *Up From Slavery* (1901) Washington used in his writing the smooth, careful rhetoric that made his speeches famous. The public and press lavishly compared the book to Harriet Beecher Stowe's *Uncle Tom's Cabin* and Benjamin Franklin's *Autobiography*. With a circulation of more than 100,000, *Outlook* magazine serialized the autobiography from 30 November 1900 to 3 February 1901, and these segments started additional funding flowing into Tuskegee, even before the book was published. As the book began to reach an international audience, Washington was finally able to pull the college out of debt. Unlike most of his previous works, *Up From Slavery* was a critical success as well, with a favorable review from William Dean Howells to heighten its prestige.

The year 1901 saw the publication of *The Negro in Business, The Negro in the South*, and *Frederick Douglass*. But criticism of Washington was mounting in the black community. W.E.B. Du Bois had started the Niagara Movement, which led to the formation of the NAACP. Washington had made what seemed to be some ultraconservative statements about the 1906 Atlanta race riots, in which federal and state officials asked him to mediate. Also, he had had a personal and political breach with longtime associate T. Thomas Fortune. Fortune, along with other editors of black newspapers, especially William Monroe Trotter, began publicly castigating Washington. Trotter had led several anti-Washington protesters in a confrontation at a speaking engagement in Boston's African Methodist Episcopal Church in 1903. Police were called to disperse the hecklers, but the whole incident was labeled "The Boston Riot" in newspapers around the country. Most papers blamed Trotter and praised Washington for his self-control. In addition, Tuskegee, now a fully functioning institution with a much larger faculty, needed more of Washington's supervision. He insisted on maintaining an equal balance between academic and industrial training and on his strict control over every area of campus life. But a more sophisticated faculty resisted his paternal oversight.

Earlier in the same year, Washington encountered a hostile audience of 2,000 during an appearance at Gainesville, Florida. Certain whites were angry about the amount of money being donated to black institutions, especially Tuskegee, and about the idea of having a black man, however prominent, address a group of white people. State Superintendent of Education William Sheats introduced Washington by saying that although he could not name the greatest white American, he knew that Washington was the greatest Negro American. In complete rhetorical control, Washington said that blacks had to be taught "to lift common labor out of drudgery . . . to where it becomes beautiful"; he ended the speech, "I cannot believe that the Negro will ever appeal to the Southern white man in vain." The press lauded the speech as his most successful and diplomatic foray among volatile Floridians.

Washington returned to autobiography in *My Larger Education* (1911). The lengthy volume, ghostwritten by Emmett J. Scott and Robert Parks, was originally intended as a sequel to *Up From Slavery*. *The Story of the Negro* (1909) was not a literary nor a financial success, and it signaled a decline in Washington's popularity.

In 1911 Washington also suffered his most humiliating public exposure. Without making the usual arrangements for his travel to the North, he went to New York in mid-March to make a few church appearances. While there, he tried to locate Daniel C. Smith, an auditor for the college. When Washington found what he thought was Smith's address on West Sixty-Third Street, he was assaulted by a German named Henry Albert Ulrich, who said that Washington had been loitering around the apartment building for several weeks and had been making advances to Ulrich's girlfriend, a Mrs. Alvarez.

Hospitalized for several injuries, Washington charged Ulrich with felonious assault. The incident and the subsequent trial made headlines across the nation. The story was sensationalized because a white woman was involved and because many felt that Washington had no plausible explanation for being in a white neighborhood that late at night—a neighborhood which Smith did not live in at all. Many found Washington's explanations unbelievable, but others, including President Taft, supported the black leader. After several postponements of the trial, Ulrich was tried in November; he and Mrs. Alvarez still insisted that Washington had been caught "peeping through the keyhole to her apartment" and greeting her as "sweetheart." Ulrich was acquitted. Washington and his supporters were outraged because in addition to the injustice, immeasurable damage had been done to Washington's image of moral integrity.

The now elderly black statesman never recovered from the affront of the Ulrich episode. Thoroughly fatigued, he was urged by his friends and family to curtail his travels. But he continued to fulfill a heavy speaking schedule until fall 1915. While in the northeast, near the end of October, he had to be taken to a New York hospital. Told that he would die in a few hours, he begged to be taken to Tuskegee, saying, "I was born in the South, I have lived and labored in the South, and I wish to die and be buried in the South" (Mathews, p. 301). Friends placed him aboard an express train and he died a few hours after reaching Tuskegee on 14 November 1915.

MAJOR THEMES

In his first book, *Black Belt Diamonds* (1898), Washington sounded a call for hope and optimism among his people. With early cautious political savvy, he usually avoided discussions of racial incidents, although in one "gem" he did say: "Physical death comes to the one Negro lynched in a county, but death of the morals, death of the soul, comes to the thousands responsible for the lynching" (p. 98).

T. Thomas Fortune heavily edited Washington's first book that was not a collection of speeches, *The Future of the American Negro* (1899). Most chapters are parts of articles that Washington had previously written for the *Atlantic Monthly* and *Popular Science Monthly*. Washington succinctly stated his complete philosophy for "uplifting" the Negro race: industrial education first; then amicable relations with whites, especially in the South; next blacks were to display the enduring strength and optimism needed to gain full respect and participation in the economy; and only after those gains had been accomplished were they to enter politics. In *The Future*, Washington also praised the antebellum plantation system because it produced "colored men skilled in the trades." He wrote that he drew upon that system for his plan of industrial training at Tuskegee. The book includes an open letter to the Constitutional Convention of Louisiana in which Washington appeals for equalized voting tests. Further, he presents one of his rare discussions of Northern migration and recolonization of American blacks to Africa: "We want to impress upon the Negro the importance of identifying himself more closely with the interests of the South . . . [the eight million blacks in America are] almost a nation within a nation." He stressed that most of those blacks were concentrated in the South and that these numbers meant power. He constantly repeated these themes during most of his literary career.

Harlan believes that *The Story of My Life and Work* (1900), Washington's first autobiography, was intended to be read by blacks rather than by whites. After the Atlanta Exposition Address, Washington sent a collection of speeches to Walter Hines Page of Houghton Mifflin. Rejecting the collection, Page suggested that a narrative would probably be more salable. So Washington hired a young journalist named Edgard Webber to assist him in compiling a record of his life. Harlan insists that both the publisher and the ghostwriter were unfortunate choices. Webber had sent the book to a rather obscure subscription bookhouse, J. L. Nichols and Company in Illinois, without Washington's permission, while the author was away on a two-year fund-raising tour. Although it sold about

1,500 copies before the second printing, the book was actually an embarrassment to Washington, who later wrote that it was "chock full of typographical and aesthetic blemishes." The book did, however, gain the attention of certain publishers—S. S. McClure of *McClure's Magazine*, Henry Wysham Lanier and Walter Page of Doubleday, and Lyman Abbott, editor of the *Outlook*—to Washington's potential as a best-selling autobiographer. *The Story* appeared in three revised editions, two in 1901 and one posthumously in 1915. Washington's life before the birth of Tuskegee receives very cursory treatment in the first four chapters of the work; the rest is a merger of themes: the growth of Tuskegee; Washington's career as a black spokesman; his trips to Europe, Africa and the Caribbean; and the birth and the progress of the National Negro Business League.

Undoubtedly, Washington's best written, most critically acclaimed, and most popular book is *Up From Slavery*. In his lifetime the book in English and in translation had sold in at least nineteen foreign countries; it is still in print today. Serialized first in *Outlook* magazine, it was also a tremendous fund-raising instrument for Tuskegee. The zenith of Washington's expression of hope for all oppressed people, the book gave blacks their own Horatio Alger story; many ex-slaves wrote him that they had encountered many similar experiences. Harlan found the book a conscience-salve for whites, some of whom derived warm comfort from this evidence that a representative black man did not hate them.

Washington presented *Working With the Hands* in 1904 as a sequel to *Up From Slavery*. He had a two-part thesis for the book: (1) "Mere hand training, without thorough moral, religious, and mental education, counts very little. The hands, the head, and the heart together should be so corelated that one may be made to help the others"; and (2) "The effort to make an industry profitable should not be the aim of first importance. . . . teaching should be most emphasized. Our policy at Tuskegee is to make an industry pay its way if possible, but at the same time not to sacrifice the training to mere economic gain" (p. 504). The book is interspersed with photographs by the nationally famous photographer Frances Benjamin Johnston, whom Washington met through his connections with President Theodore Roosevelt.

Moving away from Tuskegee and his life as primary subjects, Washington in *The Negro in Business* (1907) demonstrated the viability of the National Negro Business League, which he founded. "My main object in preparing this volume has been to set forth some examples . . . that may serve to encourage other men and women of the race to go forward to win success in business directions."

Also in 1907, Washington joined W.E.B. Du Bois for a series of lectures sponsored by the Philadelphia Divinity School and funded by William Levi Bull as a lectureship of Christian sociology to discuss the "application of Christian principles to Social, Industrial, and Economic problems of the time." In the collected lectures subsequently titled *The Negro in the South*, Washington theorized that the three signs of Christianity are "clothes, houses, and work." He then synthesized these symbols with hallmarks of capitalism: "We should get the man to the point where he will want a house, where his wife will want carpet for the floors, pictures on the walls . . . to educate the children . . . to put money in the bank. When this state of development has been reached there is no difficulty in getting individuals to work six days during the week."

Washington's biographical treatment of Frederick Douglass (*Frederick Douglass*, 1907) uses a careful historical approach, exemplary for the author who, as an industrial educator, had not had extensive scholarly training. Never more than distant acquaintances, the two maintained an amiable professional relationship. Douglass gave a commencement address at Tuskegee in 1892; and after the older man's death on 20 February 1895, Washington joined others in raising funds to save the Douglass estate. Because Washington devoted four chapters to the mass experience of black people, both before and after slavery, rather than to Douglass's life, some felt that the book was merely a propagandistic attempt to summarize well-known current history. Certainly the text had none of the eruditely balanced Ciceronian rhetoric for which Douglass's narrative is so famous; the reader does, however, get views of Douglass's later life, which Washington was able to glean from interviews with S. Laing and Fannie Barrier Williams, Douglass's closest personal friends, and with Douglass's son, Major Charles R. Douglass.

The two-volume *The Story of the Negro* is a celebration of the black population's remarkable rise in the 40 years following Emancipation. The book traces the diaspora from Africa to America. Washington gives an overview of the status of free and slave Negroes before the Civil War. He then discusses various Northern abolitionists, the founding of early black churches, and the first black settlements in the North. The first volume ends with a summary of the contributions that blacks made to free themselves in the war effort. In the second volume, Washington gives a carefully cheerful view of Reconstruction, presenting the Negro as a workman and landowner and touting the rise of professional classes.

My Larger Education is the last installment of Washington's autobiographical offerings. Washington recounts valuable lessons that he learned through interaction with prominent whites. These included Presidents Taft, Roosevelt, and McKinley and such mentors as General Armstrong. It also recounts his association with other black leaders—J. E. Napier, register of the U.S. Treasury; William H. Lewis, assistant U.S. district attorney; and Whitfield McKinlay, the first black to serve in the collectorship of the port of Georgetown. The book details clashes with Northern blacks, whom he refers to as "the intellectuals and the Boston Mob . . . a small group of colored people" who wanted to assume leadership of the black nation simply because they lived in the North.

The Southern patriarch's last major work was *The Man Farthest Down*. A collection of travelogues, the book consists of his observations (and those of Robert E. Park, who edited the text) of the lowest classes in several European countries. Washington compares the social, political, industrial, agricultural, religious, and moral status of these poorest Europeans to blacks in America. He concludes that regardless of their ethnic backgrounds, those who comprised the most economically disadvantaged classes in Europe were always referred to as "the inferior race."

SURVEY OF CRITICISM

There is probably more continuous scholarship on Booker T. Washington than on most black writers in America. This popularity reflects the acceptability of his political ideologies to white people and to certain scions in the publishing industry. That same political stance has been an engima to historians of the black experience in the Reconstruction Era and to literary critics who grapple with Washington's vast influence. Collected first by the Library of Congress in 1958, 1,000 boxes of Washington's papers were finally organized, edited (by Louis R. Harlan) and published, beginning in 1972, in a fourteen-volume chronological production, twelve volumes of which are now in print. At least ten book-length biographies are available, as well as several other volumes on the history of Tuskegee in which Washington is the central character. Emma Lou Thornbrough and Hugh Hawkins have each edited collections of essays on Washington and on his impact on the contemporary black South. Most studies of the postbellum and antebellum South, of race relations in America, or of black American social and educational philosophies include Washington as a major figure.

Harlan's three-volume biography is now the most complete and up-to-date account of Washington's life. Basil Mathews's account gives a sympathetic view of the poverty that the young teacher encountered in rural Alabama and of the courageous inroads he made towards establishing a black middle class. It is clearly the best of several biased biographies. Harlan makes every effort to be objective, taking pains to elucidate Washington's "blind spots," particularly his often ruthless attacks against those clergymen, college administrators, or black newspaper editors who did not support him. Few biographers give a post–1960s African-American political perspective. Notable exceptions are Judith Stein, Francis Shaw, and Alfred Young. Few modern scholars have commented on the lingering presence of Washington's political and educational philosophies in black colleges and other facets of Southern thought and life. There has been little economic assessment of the failure of his agricultural-industrial pedagogy to withstand the collapse of the Southern agrarian economy.

Even so, there are scores of articles on Washington in state and regional organs; in literary and historical journals; and in journals on culture, education, and sociology. Articles by August Meier and Louis Harlan are indispensable for serious study of Washington and his era. Several scholars (Jacqueline James, Donald Colista, and Lawrence J. Friedman) are attempting to revise the general view that Washington played the accommodating politics of an Uncle Tom. Richard C. Potter and William W. Rogers and John K. Severn have valuable studies of Washington's run-ins with white Floridians. Emma Lou Thornbrough ("More Light on Booker T. Washington and the New York *Age*"), Michael

Goldstein, and Elliott M. Rudwick ("Race Leadership Struggle: Background of the Boston Riot of 1903") have written solid essays that explore Washington's influence in Northern black politics. Rudwick ("Booker T. Washington's Relation with the National Association for the Advancement of Colored People") and Thornbrough ("Booker T. Washington as Seen by His White Contemporaries") give additional accounts of Washington's poor relationship with other emerging black leaders. Another useful essay in this regard is Broadus N. Butler's "Booker T. Washington, W.E.B. Du Bois, Black Americans and the NAACP."

BIBLIOGRAPHY

Works by Booker T. Washington

Black Belt Diamonds: Gems from the Speeches, Addresses, and Talks to Students of Booker T. Washington. New York: Fortune and Scott, 1898.

The Future of the American Negro. Boston: Small, Maynard, 1899.

Education of the Negro. Albany, N.Y.: J. B. Lyon, 1900; 1904.

A New Negro For A New Century. With N. B. Wood and Fannie Barrier Williams. Chicago: American Publishing House, 1900.

Sowing and Reaping. Boston: L. C. Page, 1900.

The Story of My Life and Work. Naperville, Ill.: J. L. Nichols, 1900.

Up From Slavery: An Autobiography. New York: Doubleday, Page, 1901.

Character Building: Being Addresses Delivered on Sunday Evenings to the Students of Tuskegee Institute. New York: Doubleday, Page, 1902.

The Negro Problem: A Series of Articles by Representative American Negroes of Today. With W. E. Burghardt Du Bois, Paul Laurence Dunbar, Charles W. Chesnutt et al. New York: J. Pott, 1903.

Working With the Hands. New York: Doubleday, Page, 1904.

Tuskegee and Its People: Their Ideas and Achievements. New York: D. Appleton, 1905.

Putting the Most into Life. New York: T. Y. Crowell, 1906.

The Negro in Business. Boston: Hertel, Jenkins, 1907.

The Negro in the South: His Economic Progress in Relation to His Moral and Religious Development. With W. E. Burghardt Du Bois. Philadelphia: G. W. Jacobs, 1907.

Frederick Douglass. Philadelphia: G. W. Jacobs, 1907.

The Story of the Negro. 2 vols. New York: Doubleday, Page, 1909.

My Larger Education. New York: Doubleday, Page, 1911.

The Man Farthest Down: A Record of Observation and Study in Europe. With Robert E. Park. New York: Doubleday, Page, 1912.

The Story of Slavery. Dansville, N.Y.: F. A. Owen; Chicago: Hall & McCreary, 1913.

One Hundred Selected Sayings of Booker T. Washington. Montgomery, Ala.: Wilson, 1923.

Selected Speeches of Booker T. Washington. Ed. E. Davidson Washington. New York: Doubleday, Doran, 1932.

The Booker T. Washington Papers. 12 vols. Ed. Louis R. Harlan and Raymond W. Smochs. Urbana: University of Illinois Press, 1972–

Studies of Booker T. Washington

Boulware, Marcus H. *The Oratory of Negro Leaders: 1900–1968*. Westport, Conn.: Negro Universities Press, 1969.

Butler, Broadus N. "Booker T. Washington, W.E.B. Du Bois, Black Americans and the NAACP." *Crisis* 85 (August-September 1978): 222–30.

Colista, Donald. "Booker T. Washington: Another Look." *Journal of Negro History* 4 (October 1964): 240–55.

Drake, St. Clair. "The Tuskegee Connection: Booker T. Washington and Robert E. Park." *Society* 20 (May/June 1983): 82–92.

Du Bois, William Edward Burghardt. "Of Mr. Booker T. Washington and Others." *The Souls of Black Folk*. New York: New American Library, 1969.

Friedman, Lawrence J. "Life in the Lion's Mouth: Another Look at Booker T. Washington." *Journal of Negro History* 59 (October 1974): 337–51.

Gatewood, Willard. B. "Booker T. Washington and the Ulrich Affair." *Phylon* 30 (Fall 1969): 286–302.

Goldstein, Michael. "Preface to the Rise of Booker T. Washington: A View from New York City of the Demise of Independent Black Politics, 1889–1902." *Journal of Negro History* 62 (January 1977): 81–99.

Harlan, Louis R. "Booker T. Washington and the *Voice of the Negro*, 1904–1907." *Journal of Southern History* 45 (February 1979): 45–62.

———. *Booker T. Washington: The Making of a Black Leader, 1856–1901*. New York: Oxford University Press, 1972.

———. *Booker T. Washington: The Wizard of Tuskegee, 1901–1915*. New York: Oxford University Press, 1983.

Harlan, Louis R. and Pete Daniel. "A Dark and Stormy Night in the Life of Booker T. Washington." *Negro History Bulletin* 33 (November 1970): 159–61.

Hawkins, Hugh, ed. *Booker T. Washington and His Critics: Black Leadership in Crisis*. 2d ed. Lexington, Mass.: D. C. Heath, 1974.

Mathews, Basil. *Booker T. Washington: Educator and Interracial Interpreter*, Cambridge: Harvard University Press, 1948.

Patterson, Lillie. *Booker T. Washington: Leader of His People*. Champaign, Ill.: Garrard, 1962.

Potter, Richard C. "Booker T. Washington: A Visit to Florida." *Negro History Bulletin* 40 (September-October 1977): 744–45.

Rogers, William W. and John K. Severn. "Theodore Roosevelt Entertains Booker T. Washington: Florida's Reaction to the White House Dinner." *Florida Historical Quarterly* 54 (January 1976): 306–38.

Rudwick, Elliott M. "Booker T. Washington's Relations with the National Association for the Advancement of Colored People." *Journal of Negro Education* 29 (Spring 1960): 134–44.

———. "Race Leadership Struggle: Background of the Boston Riot of 1903." *Journal of American Education* 31 (Winter 1962): 16–24.

Scott, Emmett J. and Lyman B. Stowe. *Booker T. Washington: Builder of a Civilization*. Garden City, N.Y.: Doubleday, Page, 1916.

Shaw, Francis, "Booker T. Washington and the Future of Black Americans." *Georgia Historical Quarterly* 56 (Summer 1972): 193–209.

Spencer, Samuel, Jr. *Booker T. Washington and the Negro's Place in American Life*. Boston: Little, Brown, 1955.

Stepto, Robert B. *From Behind the Veil: A Study of Afro-American Narrative*. Urbana: University of Illinois Press, 1979.

Stokes, Anson Phelps. *A Brief Biography of Booker Washington*. Hampton, Va.: Hampton Institute Press, 1936.

Thornbrough, Emma Lou. *Booker T. Washington*. Englewood Cliffs, N.J.: Prentice-Hall, 1969.

————. "Booker T. Washington as Seen by His White Contemporaries." *Journal of Negro History* 53 (April 1968): 161–82.

————. "More Light on Booker T. Washington and the New York *Age*." *Journal of Negro History* 43 (January 1958): 34–49.

Walden, Daniel. "The Contemporary Opposition to the Political and Educational Ideas of Booker T. Washington." *Journal of Negro History* 45 (April 1960): 103–15.

White, Arthur O. "Booker T. Washington's Florida Incident, 1903–1904." *Florida Historical Quarterly* 51 (1973): 227–49.

Young, Alfred. "The Educational Philosophy of Booker T. Washington: A Perspective for Black Liberation." *Phylon* 37 (September 1976): 224–35.

Albery Allson Whitman
(1851–1901)

Albery Whitman was, in all likelihood, a black American poet to whom his color signified less—much less—than his conviction that he was born to be a poet. Before the advent of Paul Laurence Dunbar, he divided the honor of being regarded as the most eminent and popular of living black American poets only with Frances Ellen Watkins Harper. Now, by constantly increasing consensus, he is coming to share that honor with no one.

BIOGRAPHY

A mulatto, Albery Allson Whitman was born 30 May 1851 on a farm just outside the small town of Munfordville in central Kentucky. His parents were slaves as, consequently, was he. By his own testimony he went to work daily for long, arduous hours in his master's fields when he was scarcely larger than a toddler. Nevertheless, he unfailingly remembered his birthplace and its environs with affection. Indeed, he tends to rhapsodize, almost as much as Wordsworth, in his references to the locale of his earliest years. Nor does he speak harshly of his treatment there. Although anything but an apologist for slavery, he is, at no time, as bitter as many others in his allusions to the South's peculiar institution. Sheer chance had determined that he would never know bondage in the Deep South or labor as only one of a gang of virtually anonymous, often abused laborers sometimes driven as callously as cattle. It was easier, therefore, for him to forget slavery as it may have been at its worst. The relative mildness of his experience with slavery did not deceive him as to the proper residence of his own racial loyalties. He may not have been a David Walker, a tribune for black people, but he was immune to hating whites simply because they were

white. Nor did he pity himself because he was a Negro. Race, he felt, should
mean nothing, for good or ill, in the assessment of his worth as a human being.

Both of Whitman's parents died before the end of the Civil War—his mother
in 1862, his father in 1863. Whitman's personal confinement to the status of a
slave was brief. He was, de facto and de jure, emancipated about the time he
became fully orphaned. Free, he took to the road. First, he tested his new
independence in Louisville and, then, in Cincinnati. In Troy, Ohio, he held jobs
for several months each in a machine shop where plows were manufactured and,
later, as a construction worker on the railroad. But in Troy he also went to
school, if only for seven months. His brief exposure to formal education was
still, in his view, sufficient for him to essay school teaching, as he did, in
Carysville, Ohio, and in Kentucky near his birthplace. By no later than 1870
he had become a student at Wilberforce University. There he added only six
months to his schooling by others. More important, he became the protégé of
Daniel Alexander Payne, Wilberforce's founder and a bishop of the African
Methodist Episcopal Church. This association influenced Whitman's career
profoundly.

The 1870s launched Whitman on the two careers with which he was to be
ever afterward associated, preaching and the writing of poetry. Denomination-
ally, he espoused African Methodism. He first pastored an African Methodist
church in Springfield, Ohio; in 1871 his first book of poetry, *Essays on the Ten
Plagues and Other Miscellaneous Poems*, was published. In 1873 the long poem
Leelah Misled followed. Next, giving himself a capacious arena in which to
exercise his predilection for telling melodramatic tales and his matching propensity for writing verse often inordinately rich in rhythms, sibilants, and vowels,
he wrote the more than 5,000 lines of *Not a Man Yet a Man*, once thought to
be the longest poem ever written by a black American poet. It was published in
1877. In 1877 he also served as general financial agent for Wilberforce
University.

Among his contemporaries, Whitman achieved a wide and deserved renown
as a preacher with a histrionically effective manner. Thus, African Methodism
treasured him on two fronts. Not only did he serve his own church ably, but he
also helped to start and develop new churches. By the wish of his superiors in
African Methodism, his career became a sort of odyssey, leading him, for about
a score of years, to various towns in Ohio, Kansas, and Texas, either as the
new pastor for an old church or as a missionary extending African Methodism.

By the end of the 1890s Whitman was able to abandon his missionary role,
but the odyssey continued. Given the pastorate of St. Philip's in Savannah, he
expected, at least for an appreciable time, to remain in one place. Within a year
a storm and fire destroyed St. Philip's. Undaunted, Whitman immediately undertook to rebuild the edifice he and his congregation had lost. His bishop, in
which may well have been a fitting gesture of atonement to Whitman for the
precarious existence African Methodism had earlier forced upon him, transferred

him to Allen Temple in Atlanta, where his stay was to be as transitory as his residence in Savannah. On a visit to Anniston, Alabama, he contracted pneumonia. Borne back ill to Atlanta, within a month he was dead. He died in his home on 29 June 1901.

Whitman the poet was as indefatigable as Whitman the preacher. He followed *Not a Man* (to which, long as it was, he appended eighteen "miscellaneous" poems) with *The Rape of Florida*, another long poem. *The Rape* appeared in 1884. Whether or not *Not a Man* ever was (as is probable) the longest poem of Negro authorship, *The Rape of Florida* was the first poem in the Spenserian stanza written by an American black. It was reissued, somewhat revised, as *Twasinta's Seminoles, or The Rape of Florida* in 1885. With *Not a Man* and a collection of 23 lyrics called *Drifted Leaves*, it was reissued again in 1890. Whitman's pamphlet, *The World's Fair Poem*, containing the relatively short "The Veteran" and the much longer "The Freedman's Triumphant Song," appeared in 1893. *An Idyl of the South, An Epic Poem in Two Parts* was published in 1901, the year of his death. Like *The World's Fair Poem*, it was in ottava rima. In terms of the quality of art in both its narrative and its prosody, it was the best poem Whitman ever wrote.

Whitman was a troubadour as well as a poet. His chief black rival, Frances Ellen Watkins Harper, declaimed her poetry to audiences throughout the Eastern and Southern United States, thereby greatly widening the circle of people conscious of her name and literary activity. Whitman did likewise, as did his wife, Caddie, a beautiful octoroon. A master in the pulpit, Whitman recited his verses effectively. Charmed listeners undoubtedly responded also to Caddie's skilled delivery of her husband's lines and the spectacle of her own dazzling figure and face. At the Chicago World's Fair, as part of the same program, Whitman declaimed his own "The Freedman's Triumphant Song" and Caddie, his "The Veteran." Whitman and Caddie had two daughters, who later joined with their two step-sisters born to Caddie after Whitman's death to form a quartet famous as singer-dancers in vaudeville on two continents, America and Europe, especially in the 1920s and 1930s.

Unfortunately, Whitman's public successes were accompanied by a destructive addiction. Sincere though he was both as minister and poet, he loved to drink. Despite the protestations of his friends, even the protestation of Bishop Payne, he never found himself able to curb his passion for alcohol. His drinking complicated, as well as largely caused, his early death.

MAJOR THEMES

No copies of Whitman's *Essays on the Ten Plagues* survive. What *The Essays* might have told us about his theories of poetry or art is subject to speculation. But certain themes and situations appear regularly in his work. He was especially interested in characters of mixed blood and with situations of sexual violence. The stories he told were highly dramatic. *Leelah Misled* contains no Negro characters; Leelah is not only white and blond, but she also has the bluest of blue eyes. Her youthful beauty attracts the interest of McLambert, her social superior and an accomplished rake. But Leelah falls in love with McLambert with an intensity akin to that of Juliet for Romeo. McLambert, however, merely gratifies his philanderer's vanity with her and then, without remorse, abandons her. Thus, Whitman introduces into his poetry the old, frequently recurring, if not hackneyed, theme of sexual defilement of an innocent. It was a theme to which he returned repeatedly. It appears a second time, in *Not a Man*, somewhat uglier, as a white man rapes both an Indian chief's daughter and a lovely, helpless octoroon. The situation appears again in "The Octoroon," where it is the direct cause of the female protagonist's death. Leelah's sexual defilement, or anything having to do with Leelah or McLambert, encompasses little space in *Leelah Misled*, perhaps no more than one-tenth of the verses in the poem.

Few poets have ever been as discursive as Whitman. In *Leelah Misled* his many digressions range over an astounding diversity of topics. *Leelah Misled*, beyond its main theme, is a clotted jungle of barely articulated and randomly chosen mini-themes.

Not a Man begins in frontier Illinois, where Whitman juxtaposes the white settlement of Saville and a village of Sac Indians. Obvious in this juxtaposition is the influence of Rousseau and his doctrine of the noble savage uncorrupted by the degenerate culture of urban-oriented Europe. There dwells in Saville, however, at least one noble person, the twenty-year-old Rodney, of rugged strength and virtuous, valiant character, six feet, three inches tall, great hunter and woodsman supreme and, although "eighty-five percent Saxon," the black slave of Saville's leading citizen, Sir Maxey. Nanawawa is Chief Pashepaho's daughter. Sir Maxey has a daughter also, Dora. With absolutely no provocation, Saville's whites loot and destroy Chief Pashepaho's village, in the process raping and murdering Nanawawa. When the Indians retaliate, the whites flee, leaving Dora in the Indians' possession. Single-handedly, Rodney rescues Dora, not without conceiving for Dora an affection to which Dora replies with a similar sentiment for Rodney. Sir Maxey has proclaimed that any savior of his daughter would earn his daughter's hand. But Sir Maxey, aided by other whites, now arranges Rodney's sale to slave traders, who take Rodney south. In Florida, Mosher Aylor, Rodney's new master, imprisons Rodney on Aylor land when he discovers that Rodney and Leona, a very attractive slave girl, have fallen in love. With Leeona's help Rodney escapes from Aylor's custody. Although he fails to prevent Aylor from raping and impregnating Leeona, he does arrive upon the scene of Leeona's flight from Aylor's domain in time to kill, or scatter, the men and dogs who are pursuing her. The two lovers eventually reach the security of Sussex Vale in Canada. There they stay and raise a family. They are given a helping hand by Dora, who, somehow, also migrates to Sussex Vale. Moreover, Rodney and his two sons, who leave Sussex Vale during the Civil War to fight against slavery, stumble upon Aylor, now a Confederate officer who lies dying on a battlefield.

In *The Rape of Florida* (or *Twasinta's Seminoles*) the heroine, Ewald, is part Indian, part Spanish and, least of all, part Negro. Her father is the venerable Seminole chief, Palmecho; her lover and beloved, the young Seminole chief, Atlassa. The great Seminole chief, Oseola, has only a cameo appearance in the poem. But the principal plot of the work centers upon the perfidy of some whites who twice betray truce agreements to capture and hold Palmecho. In the end Palmecho, Atlassa, and Ewald, with fellow Seminoles, are chained by the whites who have coveted their lands and at last, through treachery, obtained them, and sent their captives to Santa Rosa in a part of Mexico now Texas. The captain of the ship conveying the Seminoles into forced exile is, whenever possible, a practicing humanitarian. He removes the chains from the Seminoles while they are aboard his ship, and they begin a second life for themselves.

"The Octoroon" presents another female protagonist who is beautiful and only slightly Negro. This heroine, named Lena, is owned by a man named Maury who discovers, to his horror, that his strikingly handsome son, Sheldon Maury, loves Lena (who loves Sheldon in return) and intends to treat her not as a concubine but as the woman of honor she is. The elder Maury sells Lena to an elderly army officer—a lecher and a drunkard, who attempts, as the elder Maury had expected and hoped, to despoil Lena. Lena withstands her new owner's assaults upon her chastity and escapes from him, but at such a cost to herself that her health is shattered. A distraught Sheldon finally discovers her in her hiding place, a woodsman's cottage. He comes too late. She dies a tragic talisman of the steadfastness of her own respect for her virtue and human dignity.

Titles tell much about Whitman's poetry. He was not given to the use of cryptic headings in the identification of anything he wrote. "The Veteran" is a poem about the old soldiers who fought in the Civil War. It evokes the crude, tribal notions of strength and honor and applies, with impartial fervor, to Confederate and Union survivors alike. "The Freedman's Triumphant Song" is, in its way, as banal as "The Veteran." "The Southland's Charms and Freedom's Magnitude" is an exercise in sectional conciliation. Its "Southland" is less baneful than the actual South in the 1890s appeared to many Negroes as they observed the ebb and flow of racism in their country.

Although Whitman's short lyrics touched upon an amazing and heterogeneous collection of subjects, only two of them were written in Negro dialect, as were, somewhat surprisingly, two or three of the Spenserian stanzas in *Not a Man* (in the humorous ballad "Solon Stiles," Whitman also affects German dialect). Whitman lyricizes over capital and labor in "The Great Strike," with a voice much more that of a capitalist than a labor leader; eulogizes, on the one hand, the black poet Joshua McCarter Simpson and, on the other, in "Ye Bards of England," such white poets as Chaucer, Shakespeare, and Byron; and hymns the praises not only of Grant and Custer, but also of Stonewall Jackson. Of all his lyrics his tribute to Stonewall Jackson had, by far, the most phenomenal success. Caddie recited it in opera houses around America, North and South, to highly receptive hearers and, most memorably, to both houses of the Mississippi legislature, jointly assembled, which approved of her performance with a demonstration roughly equivalent in vigor and glee to a sustained rebel yell. Even so, Whitman does not neglect, in his lyrics, themes traditional with lyric poets, as the beauties of nature or the tender emotions of the human heart. His lyric poems were like many of his digressions in his major poems. They provided him with opportunities to expatiate on many themes.

Whitman's long poems have been characterized as novels in verse. More perceptively, perhaps, they may be seen as plays, if not fully rendered plays. *Leelah Misled* and ''The Octoroon'' are domestic dramas. *Not a Man* and *The Rape* are Marlovian in what they attempt. Theirs, on a lesser scale, is the universe of Tamburlaine and Faustus. Whether in his domestic drama or his versions of Marlovian epic, Whitman persistently addresses his art to the twin subjects of human exploitation and human freedom. They are two sides of the same coin, the wrong and right of his study of the perplexities of the world.

Although not a single character in any of his longer poems is as dark as a mere mulatto, he does propagandize for Negro causes and relief. Yet he is never creative in his social vision. There is no espousal, or hint, of revolutionary thought anywhere in his work. Essentially, he was in agreement with the bourgeois masters of the Industrial Revolution; Whitman's concept of freedom was theirs. Freedom meant to him what it meant to the men of property who wrote the American Constitution. To those men America was ideally to be a land of opportunity wherein the best would get ahead and the rabble would fall by the wayside. Rugged individualism tempered with Christian charity and the maxims of such sages as Cicero and Plutarch approximately sufficed to govern all their reactions as to what should be in this world. Whitman was also a rugged individualist, a Christian, and a respecter of the West European cultural past. It would be an exaggeration to say that he completely eschewed racial protest. He speaks explicitly, at times, particularly in introductions, dedications, and some of his digressions, as a true believer in genuine universal brotherhood. There is also, obviously, racial protest in the very plots of all his longer poems other than *Leelah Misled*. But he has much more to say in his poetry about abstract freedom than about racial protest. He tends to emphasize the positive rather than the negative. Hence, he subordinates the theme of exploitation, whether of women or blacks, to the bigger, more comprehensive theme of what he would probably have called the Christian idea of heaven-inspired love.

There is yet a further word to be said about Whitman's themes. Although he was self-taught, his reading ranged widely, and he drew upon his reading for his verse.

The extensiveness of Whitman's vocabulary reflects his reading of other poets as he pursued his interest in poetry. In *Not a Man* he varies his verse with his picture of external circumstance. Saville is described in the couplet of Goldsmith's *The Deserted Village*; the Sac village, in the trochaics of Longfellow's *Hiawatha*. The hue and cry of Dora's capture and rescue appears in the verse form of Whittier's *Snow-Bound* and Longfellow's *Paul Revere's Ride*. Everything that happens in Florida happens in the verse form of Scott's *The Lady of the Lake*. And when at last Rodney and Leeona bask in the relative serenity of their existence in Sussex Vale in Canada, they do so in the dactyls of Longfellow's *Evangeline*. But the most significant fact, perhaps, about his versifying is the indication it seems to give of the catholicity of his tastes. That circumstances had withheld from him the kind of access to the cloisters of the learned bestowed upon many other poets only throws into higher relief the completeness of his commitment to art. Art, indeed, to him, was the breath of life. His recognition of that reality about himself speaks through all the discipline he imposed upon himself to be a poet. Like Keats, he found the search for beauty and the search for truth to be the same.

SURVEY OF CRITICISM

As visible as Whitman was while he lived, he has attracted attention for his contribution to Afro-American literature almost exclusively since the Harlem Renaissance. His stock is unmistakably on the rise. No longer do critics of Afro-American literature ignore him, and no longer does the tendency to treat him as a minor black writer continue. On the other hand, the social scientists, who seem to insinuate their presence into every aspect of the study of Afro-American culture, have, however generally insatiable their curiosity about things black, not yet discovered Whitman. There are, moreover, no book-length studies of Whitman.

In *To Make a Poet Black* (1939) by Saunders Redding, one of the abler and more authoritative studies of Negro literature, there is no treatment of Whitman nor even any mention of him. That name, at least, is cited by Sterling Brown in *Negro Poetry and Drama and The Negro in American Fiction* (1937); Brown includes a brief and somewhat critical entry of Whitman's work. But this entry is clearly not of the kind Brown would have given Whitman had Brown considered Whitman a figure of impressive stature in the history of black American literature. Whitman is recognized in that classic anthology of Negro literature, *The Negro Caravan* (1941), which Brown edited along with fellow specialists in Negro literature, Arthur Davis and Ulysses Lee. The single exhibit from Whitman's work is a fairly long excerpt from *Twasinta's Seminoles*. In *Dark Symphony* (1968), edited by James A. Emanuel and Theodore L. Gross, at the height of the influence of the Black Power Movement, Whitman is not present; Emanuel and Gross intended their anthology to be highly selective. They were swayed, too, by the prevailing winds of a highly tempestuous moment in America's history. "Selective" meant for them, therefore, largely accommodation to the doctrines of the new black aesthetic. One black writer in their anthology represents all the black writers of America antecedent to Chesnutt and Dunbar. That sole representative is Frederick Douglass. But Whitman, it would seem presently, may be expected, in the closing years of the twentieth century, to appear in as many anthologies of black American literature as Douglass.

Vernon Loggins in his pioneering study *The Negro Author* (1931) treats Whitman at some length. *The Negro Author* was originally Loggins's doctoral dissertation at Columbia where in the 1920s members of the faculty, including
those who directed doctoral dissertations, would have been unusual if they did
not stereotype Negroes. Indications exist in *The Negro Author* that Loggins
viewed himself as a friend of the American Negro. He may have been what he
thought he was. But he was certainly also enamored of the stereotypes of the
Negro palatable to the great majority of Columbia professors, as they were to
the rank and file of average Americans. Loggins summarizes Whitman, to use
Loggins's own qualifying adjective, as the "mockingbird" poet. He pays much
attention to Whitman's many imitations of other English and American poets.
About the quality of these imitations Loggins is no more approving than dis-
approving. Loggins suggests that imitation is a specifically racial trait. To Loggins, consequently, Whitman was a typical black poet. Imitating whites was a
thing Negroes were supposed to do, perhaps especially in the high arts, if only
because Negroes were not gifted enough, from the rude resources of their native
genius, to be as creative as whites, particularly where sophistication was required.
Loggins, accordingly, seems to assume that in Whitman he is encountering a
"mockingbird." On the other hand, Loggins does evince some concern for
estimating how good a "mockingbird" Whitman is.

William H. Robinson, Jr., in *Early Black American Poets* (1969), an anthology
he edited while he was still a colleague of Sterling Brown and Arthur Davis at
Howard University, casts an eye as critical as that of Loggins on Whitman's
faults. Yet, from Robinson emerges a reaction to Whitman quite more complex,
and less negative in its summary judgments, than that of Loggins. Robinson
declares, in effect, despite regrettable lapses in Whitman's poetry too numerous
to be ignored, that the poetry contains much newly minted gold. Kenney J.
Williams, in *They Also Spoke* (1970), views Whitman similarly. She does not
avert her eyes from Whitman's imitativeness, yet, like Robinson, emphasizes
Whitman's positive achievements: his ability to infuse adventurous narrative
with genuine excitement and to create characters who transcend stereotypes; his
ability to write verse with lyric beauty. Williams also notes that Whitman asserts
the special interests of his race. And Louis D. Rubin, Jr., in his essay which
opens a work prepared collaboratively with Blyden Jackson, *Black Poetry in
America* (1974), speaks even more forcefully. Rubin finds that Whitman's best
poetry compares favorably with the best American poetry of the "latter years
of the nineteenth century," and he proclaims Whitman, in his mastery of poetic
craft, probably the "most accomplished" of all black American poets who
immediately preceded Dunbar.

The best and fullest account of Whitman, either as a person or a poet, occurs
in Joan R. Sherman's *Invisible Poets: Afro-Americans of the Nineteenth Century*
(1974). In her reconstruction of Whitman's life Sherman uses exhaustively and
judiciously the previous literature of her subject. But she also improves her
portrait of Whitman with information gathered through her own research. She

has read all of Whitman's poetry with care. There is no better existing record than hers of the canon of Whitman's verse. Critically, she is of the same persuasion as Williams, Robinson, and Rubin, by no means insensitive to Whitman's penchant for mimicry, but insistent on the exceptional worth of his individual endowments as a poet and of his secure and relatively exalted place in the pantheon of black poets of America. Her work may be supplemented by two treatments of special issues connected with Whitman, Carl Marshall's "Two Protest Poems by Albery A. Whitman" (1975) and Charles E. Wynes's "Albery Allson Whitman—The 'Black Mocking Bird' (?) Poet" (1978). Marshall's work offers evidence to rebut the thesis that Whitman, the poet, skirted too widely the area of racial protest. Quite to the contrary, argues Marshall; in both *Not a Man* and *The Rape of Florida*, Whitman speaks out "strongly" as a Negro unhappy with American racism. The themes Whitman chooses in these two poems, with their emphasis on freedom, Marshall indicates permit him to disclose his opposition to American color caste. Whitman also finds means and occasions, Marshall adds, in the preliminary matter to both these poems, as well as in the profusion of verse within them, to articulate his racial protest. Wynes, to an extent that Marshall does not, reviews all of Whitman's poetry. He sees Whitman as both a born romantic and a born poet. He sees him also as an artificer of beauty. He alludes to Marshall's defense of Whitman as a poet of racial protest, albeit with a strong measure of skepticism about its absolute validity. Wynes believes that Whitman, as a social critic as well as a poet, played many roles and, therefore, dwelled in many partisan camps. He could be a W.E.B. Du Bois at one moment and a Booker T. Washington at some other time. He was, Wynes clearly implies, a mockingbird in other ways than writing poetry. The imitativeness of his verse Wynes concedes, even as much as Loggins. But Wynes writes mainly to argue against the notion that Whitman's imitativeness stifles his creativity. So much of a genuine poet was Whitman that no amount of imitating other poets could hide the truth that Whitman was, without help from any other poet, quite sufficiently a poet from the resources he received from himself, and himself alone.

BIBLIOGRAPHY

Works by Albery Allson Whitman

Essays on the Ten Plagues and Miscellaneous Poems, 1871(?).

Leelah Misled. Elizabethtown [Kentucky], 1873.

Not a Man and Yet a Man, with Miscellaneous Poems. Springfield, Ohio: Republic, 1877.

The Rape of Florida. St. Louis: Nixon-Jones, 1884.

Twasinta's Seminoles, or Rape of Florida. St. Louis: Nixon-Jones, 1885.

Not a Man and Yet a Man, Twasinta's Seminoles and Drifted Leaves. St. Louis: Nixon-Jones, 1890.

The World's Fair Poet: The Freedman's Triumphant Song, with "The Veteran." Atlanta: n.p., 1893.
An Idyl of the South, An Epic Poem in Two Parts. New York: Metaphysical, 1901.

Studies of Albery Allson Whitman

Brawley, Benjamin. *The Negro Genius.* New York: Dodd, Mead, 1937, p. 110.

Brown, Sterling. *Negro Poetry and Drama.* Washington, D.C.: Associates in Negro Folk Education, 1937.

Jackson, Blyden and Louis D. Rubin, Jr. *Black Poetry in America.* Baton Rouge: Louisiana State University Press, 1974, pp. 11–13.

Loggins, Vernon. *The Negro Author: His Development in America to 1900.* New York: Columbia University Press, 1931, pp. 336–41.

Marshall, Carl. "Two Protest Poems by Albery A. Whitman." *CLA Journal* 19 (September 1975): 50–56.

Robinson, William H., Jr. *Early Black American Poets.* Dubuque, Iowa: William C. Brown, 1969, pp. 193–225.

Sherman, Joan R. *Invisible Poets: Afro-Americans of the Nineteenth Century.* Urbana: University of Illinois Press, 1974, pp. 112–28.

Walden, Daniel. "Alberry [*sic*] Allson Whitman." *Dictionary of American Negro Biography.* Ed. Rayford W. Logan and Michael R. Winston. New York: W. W. Norton, 1982, pp. 650–51.

Williams, Kenny J. *They Also Spoke: An Essay on Negro Literature in America, 1787–1930.* Nashville: Townsend Press, 1970, pp. 138–44.

Wynes, Charles E. "Albery Allson Whitman—The 'Black Mocking Bird' (?) Poet." *Illinois Quarterly* 41 (Fall 1978): 40–47.

ELIZABETH DUNN

Richard Henry Wilde
(1789–1847)

Largely self-educated, Richard Henry Wilde became a lawyer, congressman, poet, biographer, and translator. Although he pursued the role of poet intermittently, he wanted most to be remembered for his work on Dante.

BIOGRAPHY

The sixth of twelve children of Richard and Mary Newett Wilde, Richard Henry Wilde was born in Dublin, Ireland, on 24 September 1789. In 1797 political pressures forced the family to move to Baltimore, Maryland, and after the senior Wilde's death in 1802, Mrs. Wilde and her six surviving children relocated to Augusta, Georgia. It was necessary for the young Wilde to work in the family store, but he spent his spare time studying under the tutorship of his well-educated mother, cultivating his love of languages.

In 1808 Wilde began studying law texts on his own and in 1809 was admitted to the bar. Wilde's law career in Augusta was successful, although it clashed mightily with his artistic interests. As he explained later to Hiram Powers, a passion for art "can't live in the atmosphere of Law and Commerce. It is like putting some innocent warm-blooded animal into carbonic gas."

Wilde was appointed attorney general of Georgia in 1811 and served as representative to the United States Congress six times from 1815 to 1835. He suffered a party defeat in his run for the 24th Congress, but accepted his respite from politics with relief, for now he would have time to pursue his first love—poetry.

Since his teens, Wilde had hoped to become a poet, and despite his concern about his "want of invention" and his realization that he was financially bound to a law career, he obeyed his better instincts and wrote hundreds of original poems and produced translations throughout his lifetime. An early poem, "The

Ocean Fight'' (1815), won a poetry contest, and at about the same time, Wilde began a nationalistic epic on Florida. He dropped the project, however, when his brother, James, the inspiration for the poem, was killed in a duel in 1815. Part of this long work, a poem known variously as "The Lament of the Captive" and "My Life Is Like the Summer Rose," is Wilde's most famous poem, partly because it involved him in a foolish plagiarism controversy that continued from 1819 until Anthony Barclay resolved it in 1871.

Although Wilde was bitter about the charges of plagiarism, his love of poetry and his desire to compose memorable verse did not wane. By 1827, the year of the death of his wife of eight years, Wilde had decided to work on another nationalistic poem—*Hesperia*—which, though incomplete at the time of Wilde's death, was prepared for publication by his son William and released posthumously in 1867 under Wilde's chosen pseudonym, Fitzhugh De Lancy, Esq.

Freed in 1835 from political obligations, Wilde sought the artistically stimulating atmosphere of Europe and found his heart's home in Florence, where he spent six years. His first literary project was a treatise exploring the reasons for the madness and imprisonment of Tasso, accompanied by Wilde's translations of Tasso's poems. The work appeared in two volumes in 1842 as *Conjectures and Researches Concerning the Love, Madness, and Imprisonment of Torquato Tasso*. A second project, incomplete and unpublished during Wilde's lifetime, is *The Italian Lyric Poets*, which Wilde envisioned as a series of biographical sketches with accompanying translations. Wilde also undertook another massive scholarly project while in Florence—*The Life and Times of Dante with Sketches of the State of Florence, and of his Friends and Enemies*. Initially overwhelmed by the amount of information he found on Dante, Wilde persisted with his characteristic determination and completed the first volume in 1842. It was for this work on Dante that Wilde most wanted to be remembered as an author.

In an 1842 letter to Hiram Powers, Wilde confessed: "I build upon it my hopes of 'being remembered in my life,' with my land's language—and of leaving to Posterity as Milton said, 'Something so written as that they would not willingly let it die.' " In the same letter, he stated that he rewrote every line of the biography "fifteen to Twenty times over," and believed that "most of the matter will be new even to the Italians themselves."

Finally, while in Florence, Wilde gathered most of his original poems and a few translations into a manuscript, *Poems, Fugitive and Occasional*, which contains over one hundred verses. Wilde was also instrumental in discovering a hidden portrait of Dante by Giotto, and he enjoyed the intellectual companionship of fellow artists Horatio Greenough, Charles Sumner, and Hiram Powers.

After depleted savings forced a reluctant Wilde to return to America in 1841, he eventually settled in New Orleans in 1843, where he again took up "the weightier matters of the Law." A dearth of sources caused Wilde to abandon work on the second volume of the Dante biography, but he spent his remaining years encouraging other artists in their careers, Hiram Powers in particular. Wilde's desire to improve the cultural and intellectual climate of New Orleans

led him to an active role in the founding of a law school at the University of
Louisiana (Tulane University), of which he was made professor of public, international, and constitutional law in 1846.

The yellow fever epidemic of summer 1847 claimed Wilde's life on 10 September. The Haynes Circle of Georgia in 1885 moved his body to the Poet's
Corner of Magnolia Cemetery outside Augusta and in 1896 erected a monument
in Wilde's honor, on which was engraved the first stanza from his still-popular
poem "The Lament of the Captive."

MAJOR THEMES

In keeping with the Southern desire for a nationalistic literature, Wilde's first
serious literary attempts were at poetry with America as his subject, such as his
projected Florida epic and *Hesperia*. But, like Irving and others, Wilde had
difficulty finding suitable poetic materials in America. In his dedication to *Hesperia*, he complained that America "Wants the objects and events which are
essential to poetry." To Wilde, a poet cannot simply describe objects in nature;
personal experiences and feelings must be associated with them, as he explained
in *Hesperia*:

> Could we our country's scenery invest
> With history, or legendary lore . . .
> As our descendants hence may do—
> We should—and then shall have—our poets too!

Believing that "Few write well, except from personal experience," Wilde si-
desteps regionalism and returns inevitably to the personal lyric. It is not surprising, then, that his best poem from the Florida work is "The Lament of the
Captive," in which the speaker, a lone hostage among the Indians, observes
that Nature mourns the loss of each rose and leaf but realizes despairingly that
"none shall thus lament for me!" Similarly, *Hesperia*, intended "merely to
sketch scenes and objects," became instead, Wilde admitted, "the depository
of thoughts inseparable from them in my mind." As a result, the verses "have
no plan"; they are instead a series of personal lyrics about places associated in
De Lancy's memory with the Marchesa Manfredina Di Cosenza, to whom the
work is fondly dedicated. Wilde's other poems, most of which are gathered in
Poems, Fugitive and Occasional, often exhibit what Edd Winfield Parks called
"Byronic attitudinizing" and are permeated by the stilted poetic diction of the
English Romantics. Wilde deals unoriginally with the themes of mutability and
the vanity of earthly wishes, as in "Solomon and the Genie" and in the untitled
poem beginning "Choose as thou wilt!"; with true love, as in "Forget Me Not"
and "At Night"; and with the theme of farewell, as in "On Leaving Florence"
and "Farewell to America." Many of Wilde's poems are plagued by an over-
fondness for exclamation and the repetitive refrain, but perhaps a few of these

problems arise from the fact that he intended some of his verses to be set to music and wrote them accordingly.

One of Wilde's strengths, which surfaces when his poems are read as a whole, is an interesting narrative voice whose personality is well-developed and sustained throughout the poems. Wilde's melancholy persona, whose only resemblance to the author himself appears in his doubts about his poetic ability, is reminiscent certainly of Byron, but is much more indebted to the Italians, as a glance at Wilde's translations in *The Italian Lyric Poets* easily demonstrates. The speaker of Wilde's poems yearns for a life filled with "Hope" and "Joy" but has repeatedly been betrayed by "the world's misjudging incredulity" or, more often, by fickle love. The persona's responses to the tortures of love and fate include escaping with sentimental memories of a pleasanter time and yearning for the safety of the grave. Sounding in these instances rather melodramatic and affected, Wilde's persona exhibits a distinctively sincere voice when he adopts a fierce stoicism in the face of the world's reproaches. In the poem beginning "It was a just reproof," the speaker summons pride to hide his pain, refusing to "play woman with my tongue" and deciding instead to don the "garb Indifference." In a similar poem beginning "I have deceived myself!," the poet, awakening bitterly from his "proud hopes of high dominion," declares that he is "Conquered, but not subdued" and vows to endure "Prometheus-like in this, as in the rest." Wilde's poems arouse in the reader a sense of a quietly saddened man who masks the loss of his ideals with effusive exclamations and impassive silences.

Perhaps Wilde's greater significance lies in his lifelong devotion to poetry and the arts, which sets him apart from the typical antebellum lawyer-poetaster who wrote a poesy or two as a token gesture to culture. In his love for literature, Wilde is allied with William Gilmore Simms's "Sacred Circle," a spiritual companionship that Simms himself acknowledged in an 1842 letter to Wilde, in which he encouraged Wilde to persevere in his poetic endeavors as an escape from and an affront to politics.

SURVEY OF CRITICISM

Simms was not the only contemporary to admire Wilde's verse. His poems, when he agreed to publish them, appeared in such reputable magazines as the *Southern Literary Messenger* and *Knickerbocker*; both Washington Irving and James Kirke Paulding promoted Wilde's scholarly works in the *Knickerbocker*. Rufus Griswold included several of Wilde's poems in his *Poets and Poetry of America*, pronouncing them "graceful and correct." Griswold also published excerpts from one of Wilde's congressional speeches and from his review of Campbell's *Life of Petrarch* in *The Prose Writers of America* (1847), praising Wilde's elegance and scholarship and regretting "that his whole attention was not given to letters." In 1857 Longfellow paid his tribute to Wilde when he included eighteen of Wilde's translations of Tasso in his *Poets and Poetry of*

Europe. In 1865 Wilde was ranked the sixth best American poet by E. C. Stedman.

Wilde's reputation as a poet has declined in recent years, with the general tendency being to see his poetry as sentimental and affected. Carl Holliday in *A History of Southern Literature* (1906) declares flatly that Wilde "failed of great results," and Jay B. Hubell in *The South in American Literature 1607–1900* finds "little poetic development" in Wilde's verse. Lewis Parke Chamberlayne in *The Library of Southern Literature* focuses on what he sees as Wilde's inability to develop fully a theme, unite his ideas, or bring "fire" to his verses. Parks too agrees that Wilde's poems do not develop well, with words seeming to pile up on one another.

Wilde's readers have a higher regard for his prose than for his original verse, but they praise his abilities as a translator. In the only full-length published study of Wilde, Edward L. Tucker follows critical consensus, declaring that most of Wilde's poems are highly affected and insincere, and seeing his best work in his translations.

Apart from J. Chesley Mathews's study of the influence of Dante on Wilde's poetry and Douglas C. Gronberg's comments on the previously unnoticed fictional editor of *Hesperia*, recent scholars have concentrated on unearthing facts about Wilde's life—his role in the Cumming-McDuffie duels, his illegitimate son, and the identity of the Marchesa to whom *Hesperia* is dedicated (now accepted to be Mrs. Ellen Adair White-Beatty).

Wilde's "Lament of the Captive," "Sonnet to Lord Byron," and "To the Mocking-Bird" are the few individual poems that have been commented upon (and still only cursorily). More attention should be given to Wilde's other poems, particularly in light of his knowledge of the Italian and English lyricists, his frustration in the face of the Southern hostility to literary pursuits, and his preoccupation with the tragic contrast between the ideals of the past and the harsh realities of the present.

BIBLIOGRAPHY

Works by Richard Henry Wilde

"The Lament of the Captive." *Analectic Magazine* 13 (1819): 352.

Conjectures and Researches Concerning the Love, Madness, and Imprisonment of Torquato Tasso. 2 vols. New York: Alexander V. Blake, 1842.

Hesperia, A Fragment. Boston: Ticknor & Fields, 1867.

Poems, Fugitive and Occasional. In *Richard Henry Wilde: His Life and Selected Poems*. Edward L. Tucker. Athens: University of Georgia Press, 1966, pp. 117–99.

The Italian Lyric Poets. Preface and translations in Tucker, *Richard Henry Wilde*, pp. 203–49. Biographical introductions in an unpublished manuscript, Library of Congress.

The Life and Times of Dante with Sketches of the State of Florence, and of his Friends and Enemies. Unpublished manuscript, Library of Congress.

"The Letters of Richard Henry Wilde to Hiram Powers." Ed. Nathalia Wright. *Georgia Historical Quarterly* 46 (1962): 296–316; 417–37.

"Richard Henry Wilde in New Orleans: Selected Letters, 1844–1847." Ed. Edward L. Tucker. *Louisiana History* 7 (1966): 333–56.

Studies of Richard Henry Wilde

Barclay, Anthony. *Wilde's Summer Rose: or the Lament of the Captive. An Authentic Account of the Origin, Mystery, and Explanation of Hon. R. H. Wilde's Alleged Plagiarism*. Savannah, Ga.: n.p., 1871.

Graber, Ralph S. "New Light on the Dedication of Richard Henry Wilde's *Hesperia*." *Georgia Historical Quarterly* 44 (1960): 97–99.

Gronberg, Douglas C. "The Problem of the Pseudonym and the Fictional Editor in Richard Henry Wilde's *Hesperia: A Poem*." *Georgia Historical Quarterly* 66 (1982): 549–54.

Jones, Charles C., Jr. *The Life, Literary Labors and Neglected Grave of Richard Henry Wilde*. Augusta, Ga.: n.p., 1885.

Mathews, J. Chesley. "Richard Henry Wilde's Knowledge of Dante." *Italica* 45 (1968): 28–46.

Parks, Edd Winfield. "Richard Henry Wilde: Expatriate." *Ante-Bellum Southern Literary Critics*. Athens: University of Georgia Press, 1961, pp. 51–59.

Starke, Aubrey H. "The Dedication of Richard Henry Wilde's *Hesperia*." *American Book Collector* 6 (1935): 204–9.

———. "Richard Henry Wilde: Some Notes and a Check-List." *American Book Collector* 4 (1933): 226–32; 285–88; 5 (1934): 7–10.

Tucker, Edward L. *Richard Henry Wilde: His Life and Selected Poems*. Athens: University of Georgia Press, 1966.

Wright, Nathalia. "Richard Henry Wilde on Greenough's Washington." *American Literature* 27 (1956): 556–57.

——————— LYNNE P. SHACKELFORD ———————

Augusta Jane Evans Wilson
(1835–1909)

Augusta Jane Evans Wilson was one of the most talented domestic sentimental writers of the nineteenth century. She fulfilled the demands of the genre with her idealized characters and religious didacticism, but she transcended its limitations by incorporating philosophical and aesthetic discussions in her romances.

BIOGRAPHY

Augusta Jane Evans was born on 8 May 1835 in Columbus, Georgia, to parents from old, distinguished Southern families. Shortly after the founding of Columbus in 1828, her father, Matthew Ryan Evans, had left his family's South Carolina plantation to establish a dry goods firm in the new town. There he made friends with the leading citizens, met and married Sarah Skrine Howard, and built his new bride an elegant white-columned mansion. He also began acquiring a vast tract of land in Alabama. Matt was a charming gentleman and a loving husband and father, but a foolhardy speculator. His financial ups and downs cast a shadow over his daughter's childhood—so much so that as an adult, despite having earned a literary fortune of over $100,000, she always kept $100 on her person for security. To compensate for the family's embarrassing financial difficulties, Evans's mother provided her daughter with intellectual stimulation. She told Augusta stories of great writers, encouraged her interest in history and geography, and recited poetry to her, especially verses from William Cowper's *The Task* and James Thomson's *The Seasons*. Augusta proved an enthusiastic, capable pupil. She was blessed with a photographic memory, which in later years enabled her to fill her books with erudite quotations.

In 1845, after Matt declared bankruptcy, the family moved west. They made an arduous journey in a covered wagon to Houston and then settled in San Antonio, which, after the outbreak of the Mexican War in 1846, became a major depot for military supplies and a gathering place for American troops. Tense relations with the Mexicans, fear of raids by the increasingly hostile Comanches, and homesickness for Southern life made the family eventually dissatisfied with Texas.

In 1849 the Evanses returned east, this time settling in Mobile, Alabama, where Matt had heard the building of the Mobile & Ohio Railroad would cause an economic boom. Unfortunately, problems seemed inescapable for the family, which by this time included eight children. First, a fire burned the house they had rented and many of their possessions. Next, Matt suffered ill health, resulting in a loss of salary. In the hope of alleviating the family's financial woes by earning money as a writer, Augusta Evans undertook her first novel.

Confiding only in the loyal slave Minervy, who supplied her with oil for her lamp, Evans labored secretly over her manuscript each night until the early morning hours. On Christmas Day 1854 she presented her father with the complete work entitled *Inez: A Tale of the Alamo.* Inspired by the strong anti-Catholic feeling she had developed in Texas and the military unrest she had witnessed, Evans portrays in her book the heroism of those who fought in the Texas War of Independence and the villainy of a Jesuit who, serving as a spy for the Mexican leader Santa Anna, tries to thwart the cause. With a donation to cover the cost of an edition from a mysterious benefactor, probably the young novelist's uncle and namesake, Augustus Howard, Harper published *Inez* in 1855. *Inez* showed the expected limitations of an adolescent novel in its unsuccessful attempt to integrate historical adventure with romance and its overzealous attack upon the Catholic Church. It revealed, however, its author's willingness to indulge in complex theological and philosophical speculation—a challenge she handled more competently in her second novel.

As a young woman in her early twenties, Evans began to question the tenets of the Evangelical Protestantism that her mother had taught her. Unable to reconcile science and faith, Evans embarked upon an intensive reading program, which included works by Thomas Carlyle, Johann Goethe, Samuel Taylor Coleridge, William Wordsworth, Alfred Tennyson, John Stuart Mill, and Ralph Waldo Emerson. She sought a rational explanation of the mysteries of the universe, but ultimately concluded that Truth transcends Reason and returned to the orthodox Methodism of her youth, vowing to "combat scepticism to the day of my death, and if possible, to help others to avoid the thorny path I have trod ere I was convinced of the fallibility of human Reason." The result of that vow was the highly autobiographical *Beulah.* In her second novel, Evans charts the speculations of her title character, who, after reading Poe's *Eureka,* finds herself puzzled about the universe and God. Troubled explorations of Thomas De-Quincey, Richter, Emerson, Kant, and others lead Beulah to confusion, then to desperation, and finally to the promised land of Christian peace, as signified by her name.

Initially the manuscript met rejection from Appleton. Evans, accompanied by her cousin, Colonel John W. Jones, traveled to New York to try other firms.

She took the novel to J. C. Derby of Derby and Jackson, who offered it to his family for judgment. They approved the novel enthusiastically, and in 1859 Derby and Jackson published it. Within one year, it sold over 20,000 copies, establishing its author as a prominent sentimentalist and enabling her to purchase a house for her family. *Beulah* also brought Evans attention from a pious young Yankee editor named James Reed Spaulding, who in 1860 proposed. They became engaged, but the relationship broke up when the two could not resolve their sectional disagreements.

By summer 1859, Evans had turned her attention from metaphysics to politics. Her trip to New York had forced her to acknowledge strong differences between the North and the South about slavery and states' sovereignty. In October and November 1859, the Mobile *Daily Advertiser* published a series of articles comparing Northern and Southern literature. They were unsigned, but the ideas expressed and the style seem to confirm that they were written by Evans. The thesis of the series was that Northern literature is written out of commercial motives and is sensationalistic, whereas Southern literature reflects the cultural and moral idealism of its people. With the election of Lincoln in 1860, Evans became an ardent propagandist, proudly declaring, "I am an earnest and uncompromising Secessionist." When the Confederacy was formed in 1861, she devoted herself wholeheartedly to the Southern cause. She advised influential Southern politicians and military leaders, published articles supporting the Confederacy, served as a volunteer nurse, and established in Mobile an army hospital, named Camp Beulah.

Perhaps the most important of Evans's wartime activities was the novel she worked on from June 1862 to March 1863, much of it written while she nursed the sick at Camp Beulah. The manuscript, entitled *Macaria*, was published by West and Johnson in Richmond in 1863, using coarse wrapping paper—the only material available at the time. The author also managed to smuggle a copy by a blockade runner to Derby in New York. He arranged with J. B. Lippincott for a Northern edition, which was published in 1864.

Dedicated "To the Brave Soldiers of the Southern Army" *Macaria* celebrates the Southern victories in the Civil War, particularly the battles at Bull Run and Manassas, for which General P.G.T. Beauregard provided details. It also evaluates the strengths of the Confederate government and discusses potential dangers facing the South. Filled with idealized portraits of kind, aristocratic Southerners and stereotyped faithful slaves who protect their mistresses and follow their masters into battle, the novel offers a Southern response to Harriet Beecher Stowe's *Uncle Tom's Cabin*. So effective was *Macaria* as propaganda that General G. H. Thomas of a Yankee army in Tennessee forbade his troops to read it and burned copies that he confiscated. Southerners read *Macaria* eagerly. In fact, the legend arose that the life of a Confederate soldier was saved when the book, which he had hastily put into his breast pocket upon being called to battle, stopped a bullet from piercing his heart.

At the end of the war Evans was burdened with family problems. The Evanses' slaves had been freed, and the family was virtually destitute. Moreover, her father's health was declining, and her favorite brother, Howard, had returned home with a war wound that left his arm and shoulder paralyzed. Dissatisfied with the medical treatment Howard was receiving in Mobile, Evans took her brother to New York to see a specialist. There she visited her friend and publisher Derby, who to her astonishment revealed that he had held for her a large sum of money made from the Northern sales of *Macaria*. The money was a great boon, but realizing that it would not last long, Evans decided to write another novel in the domestic sentimental tradition of *Beulah*.

That novel, *St. Elmo*, published in 1866, became a best-seller of the nineteenth century. According to its publisher, it reached over one million readers only four months after publication. *St. Elmo* covers the career of the orphaned Edna Earl—from a childhood spent with her poor, uneducated grandfather to her upbringing by the aristocratic Murray family, and finally to her emergence as a successful writer of didactic literature. It also portrays the heroine's changing reactions to St. Elmo Murray, a Byronic hero whose dissipation evokes Edna Earl's repugnance until he repents, becomes a minister, and earns her hand in marriage. Simultaneously titillated by St. Elmo's passion for Edna Earl and uplifted by Evans's depiction of the redemptive power of Christianity, the public regarded the book as a major cultural phenomenon. Steamboats, railway coaches, hotels, and several villages were named after the novel, while a number of children were christened for its hero and heroine. There was a "St. Elmo" punch, a "St. Elmo" cigar, and even in later years a "St. Elmo" camellia in honor of the author. The novel so captured the public's imagination that Charles Henry Webb thought it deserved a parody, which he entitled *St. Twel'mo, or the Cuneiform Cyclopedist of Chattanooga*. Webb offered humorous renditions of Evans's purple-patch style and attributed his heroine's vast knowledge to the fact that she had swallowed a dictionary.

After the publication of *St. Elmo*, the most notable event in Evans's life was her marriage to Colonel Lorenzo Madison Wilson on 2 December 1868. Colonel Wilson owned the beautiful estate of Ashland, only a quarter of a mile from the Evans home. The two families had been friends for years, but it was only after the death of Mrs. Wilson in 1862 that Evans began to realize the many interests she shared with the Colonel, particularly a fondness for gardening. Despite a 28-year difference in their ages, Augusta and Colonel Wilson were extremely compatible. Together they made Ashland a showplace; its Spanish moss-covered live oaks and colorful varieties of azaleas and camellias were renowned among the Mobilians, as were their hothouses and collection of domestic fowl.

Augusta Evans Wilson managed her new household efficiently, yet she still found time for her vast correspondence and for novel writing. In 1869 her publisher, George W. Carleton, who had taken over Derby's firm, issued *Vashti; or, Until Death Us Do Part*, paying its author the remarkable sum of $15,000 to obtain the copyright. The book portrays the plight of its title heroine, who discovers that her husband married her only for money. Since Wilson did not believe God sanctions divorce, Vashti must endure her horrible life until she dies of a broken heart. In the early 1870s, Wilson took a hiatus from writing at the request of her husband, who was concerned that she was exhausting herself by purusing too many interests. By 1875, however, she had completed *Infelice*, a melodramatic tale of a suffering actress. Her seventh novel, *At the Mercy of Tiberius*, did not appear until twelve years later, for Wilson began suffering from such severe bouts of hay fever that she was often unable to write or read for months at a time. In its focus upon a murder trial, *At the Mercy of Tiberius*, which she declared was her favorite book, pursued a different type of plot from her previous works. Her heroine Beryl permits herself to be convicted falsely of murder to protect her brother, who she assumes is guilty. Finally both Beryl and her brother are absolved of guilt when the discovery of a photograph reveals there was no murder; the victim was electrocuted by a bolt of lightning.

After the death of Colonel Wilson on 7 October 1891, Wilson decided that she could not remain at Ashland: the memories of the happy times with her husband would be too painful. She closed the estate and spent her last years residing with her brother Howard in a large house in Mobile. In 1902, despite failing eyesight and a weak heart, she surprised the public with yet another romance, *A Speckled Bird*. In this work she portrays a woman who, after being deserted by her husband, becomes involved with a group of labor protesters and consequently loses both her femininity and her Christian faith. *A Speckled Bird* reveals Wilson's belief in the inevitable downfall of a woman who enters the spheres of business and politics. Her final publication, appearing in 1907, was a small volume entitled *Devota*. In this book a woman must decide whether to marry the governor of the state, a man she once rejected. After the death of Howard Evans on 5 June 1908, Augusta never fully recovered from her grief. She died of a heart attack on 9 May 1909, one day after her seventy-fourth birthday. She is buried beside her brother Howard at Magnolia Cemetery in Mobile.

MAJOR THEMES

Augusta Evans Wilson owes a literary debt to Charlotte Brontë's *Jane Eyre*. She favors orphaned heroines who through keen intellect, indomitable self-reliance, and Christian fortitude not only survive "the slings and arrows of outrageous fortune," but also fall in love with and reform Rochester-like heroes. Her major theme is that only through steadfast Christian faith can one achieve enduring happiness. Thus in her romances she assigns appropriate rewards and punishments to her characters. Those who selflessly accept Christian doctrine receive wealth, blissful marriages, or, at the very least, satisfaction in a life well lived. Those who forsake Christ's teachings and succumb to temptation face loveless marriages and often ignominious deaths—that is, unless they reform by the last chapter. What prevents Wilson from being merely one of what Hawthorne termed "a d _____ d mob of scribbling women" is the sincerity with which she professes her Christian beliefs. She movingly portrays human suffering—physical, emotional, and mental—and is convincing in her formula for securing happiness: intellectual stimulation, independence, and love—all achieved through trust in God's wisdom and gratitude for His gifts.

Wilson believed that Christian faith must be tested, and thus her characters confront a variety of tribulations. Her protagonists are either introduced as orphans or become so as the narrative progresses. They endure poverty and take such positions as a teacher or a governess to survive. Their lack of wealth or social status, in turn, leads to public scorn from insufferable snobs. Even their charitable acts bring suffering; a recurring event in her novels is the heroine's tireless nursing of the ill until she contracts their disease or collapses from exhaustion. Noteworthy examples of suffering abound in Wilson's works. Near death herself when her nemesis May Chilton purposely fails to give her needed medicine, Beulah, an orphan, faces the death of her only sister, humiliation at being termed a "beggarly orphan," and prolonged mental anguish when she cannot reconcile Christianity and rationalism. *St. Elmo* opens with the death of the heroine's only relative, her grandfather, and her subsequent leaving home in Tennessee for Columbus, Georgia, where, at the age of twelve, she intends to make her way in the world. As if Edna Earl's plight were not difficult enough, she is injured in a train wreck on the way. Perhaps the greatest suffering in Wilson's novels is endured by Beryl Brentano in *At the Mercy of Tiberius*. Beryl is sentenced to five years in prison for a murder she did not commit. Wilson seemed to believe both morally and literarily that suffering builds character.

Alleviation from suffering for Wilson's protagonists comes first through intellectual stimulation. From childhood on, her major characters are bookworms, eagerly borrowing volumes from those fortunate enough to possess well-stocked libraries. Reading enables them to transcend the deprivations of their lives. Her characters are also eloquent, able to present impassioned political speeches, as in the case of *Macaria*'s hero, Russell Aubrey, or to recite apt literary quotations, as Edna Earl so often does in *St. Elmo*. The talents of her characters are impressive. Russell becomes a statesman and military leader of the Confederacy. Irene Huntingdon, the beautiful heiress in *Macaria*, is an enthusiastic student of astronomy and can discourse on its history from the Chaldean shepherds to Sir Isaac Newton. Beryl is an artist, winner of an award for a Christmas card she designed; and Beulah and Edna Earl are published authors. In fact, duplicating the career of her creator, Edna Earl publishes several books that the critics condemn but the public loves. Commitment to knowledge is an essential trait of Wilson's protagonists; it is, in part, what makes their lives worth living.

A second ingredient in her prescription for happiness is independence. As with Jane Eyre, her protagonists succeed because they believe in themselves. Many of her major characters are taken into the homes of wealthy families or befriended by kind mentors. These characters insist that they do not wish to take advantage of those who help them and adamantly refuse offers of money or adoption. Believing self-respect comes from self-sufficiency, they work for a living—sometimes damaging their health. One of the best exemplars of this stubborn independence is Beulah, who forsakes the sumptuous mansion of Dr. Guy Hartwell for a small room in a boardinghouse and a job as a schoolteacher. Another example is Beryl, who not only rejects legal counsel and defends herself at her murder trial, but also refuses the inheritance of her grandfather's estate and instead gives it to his adopted son. Free from pecuniary motives, Wilson's protagonists value their integrity and self-sufficiency far more than any material possessions.

The most important way in which Wilson's characters attain happiness is in giving and receiving love. They are devoted to their parents or the memory of them, protective of their siblings, and compassionate towards the poor, the handicapped, and the lonely. But the kind of love Wilson most strongly emphasizes is romantic love. She believes in the concept of soul mates: each of her major characters can love only one ideal person, a person equally intelligent, strong-willed, and courageous. According to Wilson, one should never marry solely because of physical attraction or desire for wealth or social prestige. When such marriages occur in her works, the results are disappointing, sometimes even tragic, as with Vashti and many of her minor characters. Moreover, Wilson advises that the decision of whom to marry must never be impulsive or influenced by the opinions of others. Although the heroines of her most popular novels receive several proposals from attractive men, they refuse, as they say, to perjure their souls by agreeing to a wrong marriage. For example, Irene Huntingdon accepts being disinherited by her father rather than submitting to the socially strategic union he has arranged. Similarly, Edna Earl rejects proposals from a handsome young aristocrat, a leading literary critic in New York, and an English nobelman because she feels merely friendship towards these men, not love.

The romances that Wilson favors are those demonstrating the validity of Lysander's observation in *A Midsummer Night's Dream* that "the course of true love never did run smooth." They often seem doomed to disaster or to be highly improbable. Interfering parents, scheming relatives, ardent suitors, and man-hungry flirts provide obstacles, as do the unsavory or unhappy pasts of many of her male characters and the unrealistically high ideals of some of her heroines. Even political circumstances may conspire against the lovers. In *Macaria* the Civil War interrupts the relationship between Russell and Irene. He dies in battle; she never marries, preferring to visit his grave the rest of her life. Wilson is at her best when she assumes the role of a matchmaker whose matches at first appear to be mismatches. In *St. Elmo* she pairs the saintly Edna Earl with a misanthropic hero whom she loathes throughout most of the novel. Beulah's intended is a man whom she originally perceived as a father figure, and Beryl is wedded to the prosecuting attorney responsible for her imprisonment. Wilson obviously relishes manipulating her readers' emotions—from an anxious witnessing of the clash of wills between seemingly irreconcilable lovers to a cathartic relief at the long-awaited first kiss or passionate declaration of love.

The ultimate consequences of these ostensibly perverse pairings in Wilson's romances are that the heroines find the comfort and security so long denied them, and the heroes receive spiritual redemption. For example, Lennox Dunbar, stirred by unprecedented feelings of tenderness when he comes to know Beryl, moves beyond the cynicism of the law court and the superficialities of the drawing room to become a caring individual. The most dramatic conversion in Wilson's canon is that of St. Elmo Murray, who, realizing Edna Earl can never love an infidel, repents of his former dissipations and becomes a pastor. In most of Wilson's romances the heroine is a moral instructor, teaching the male characters the evil of alcohol, the virtue of chastity, and the power of prayer.

Religion was clearly the primary motive for Wilson as a novelist; however, it did not prevent her from addressing political and social issues. *Macaria* is her most direct piece of political propaganda. With its references to "Yankee Egyptic bondage" (p. 300), "the Cain-cursed race of New England" (p. 373), and "the glittering coils of the Union boa-constrictor, which writhed in its efforts to crush the last sanctuary of freedom" (p. 333), the novel makes explicit its author's support of Southern secession. *A Speckled Bird*, another work with a political focus, displays a conservative's distrust of labor unions and strong support of capitalism.

Also conservative is Wilson's attitude toward the proper role of women—an issue she addresses in many of her novels. To the twentieth-century reader, Wilson seems paradoxical. She forcefully defends her heroines' right to develop their minds and talents so that they may support themselves financially; yet she concludes that no goal in life is more sacred than to be a loving and, to a large degree, submissive wife. As happy as her heroines are in marriage, they weaken and pale as characters. And it seems significant that their married life is usually covered only within the last few pages of the novels. Nowhere in Wilson's works is the heroine's change more pronounced than in the concluding paragraphs of *St. Elmo*. On her wedding day, the formerly assertive and independent Edna Earl, whose literary genius has been acclaimed by admiring readers, follows unquestioningly her husband's will, as he advises:

"To-day I snap the fetters of your literary bondage. There shall be no more books written! No more study, no more toil, no more anxiety, no more heartaches! And that dear public you love so well, must even help itself, and whistle for a new pet. You belong solely to me now, and I shall take care of the life you have nearly destroyed in your inordinate ambition." (p. 489)

Edna Earl's last action in the novel is to gaze "reverently" into her husband's face. One wonders if Wilson herself could have so willingly sacrificed her writing if Colonel Wilson had issued such an ultimatum.

Christian values, sentiment, tradition—these are the keystones of Wilson's novels, and her goal was, as she herself defines it in a letter to her friend J.L.M. Curry, "that with the blessing of God, my 'labor will not be in vain,' and that I may be the humble instrument of doing some good, of leading some soul safely to God."

SURVEY OF CRITICISM

The novels of Augusta Jane Evans Wilson have been far more acclaimed by the reading public than by serious scholars. Reviews of her works fall into one of two categories: those that rhapsodize about her imaginative power and inspiring moral messages and those that rail against her erudition and artificial style. A typical example of the first kind of criticism is John Shirley Ward's 1867 review of *St. Elmo* published in *Scott's Magazine* of Atlanta:

With a fancy bold and fervid—with an imagination as warm and luxurious as the breath of the orange groves of her own sunny land—with a taste cultivated and refined by a thorough knowledge of classical and modern belles-lettres—with a genius as versatile as De Stael's and as spiritual as Hannah More's—we are ready to crown her Queen Regnant of Southern Literature.

On the other hand, another 1867 review of *St. Elmo* published in *De Bow's Review* gives a quite different assessment:

Bombast weakens the force of her arguments, pedantry mars the effect of the most thrilling scenes, and so overdrawn and unnatural are the characters introduced that they fail to live, move, and have their being, remaining to the end but the creations of an ill-regulated and heated fancy.

In general, those reviewers who judged a novel by its didacticism were impressed with Wilson's romances, whereas those who sought technical expertise or favored realism were not.

Much of what has been written about Wilson falls under the heading of personal reminiscence. Her friend and frequent correspondent Mary Forrest published a biographical sketch of her in *Women of the South Distinguished in Literature* (1860). The publisher J. C. Derby's account of Wilson in *Fifty Years among Authors, Books and Publishers* (1884) has special interest. Derby recalls his first meeting with Wilson, especially the reactions of her cousin, Colonel John W. Jones, who confessed that he had been prepared to hurl a book at Derby from one of the publisher's shelves if he had not accepted the manuscript of *Macaria*. Derby also reveals how he and J. B. Lippincott interceded on her behalf to secure royalties from Michael Doolady, an unscrupulous publisher who had acquired a copy of *Macaria* and printed an unauthorized edition.

Two of the best critical sketches of Wilson appear in Alexander Cowie's *The Rise of the American Novel* (1948) and Jay B. Hubbell's *The South in American Literature, 1607–1900* (1954). In his chapter entitled "Domestic Sentimentalists and Other Popular Writers," Cowie begins with a delightfully satirical receipt for the typical domestic novel and then provides brief evaluations of thirteen writers, including Wilson. He notes the "unwholesome" suppressed eroticism in her books but praises her inventive plots and flexible prose style, concluding,

"She was a first-rate writer of a second-rate type of fiction" (p. 434). Hubbell provides a comprehensive biographical sketch and an assessment of the critical reception of Wilson's novels.

The major study of Wilson's life and works is William Perry Fidler's *Augusta Evans Wilson 1835–1909: A Biography* (1951). Conducting his research thoroughly, Fidler interviewed Wilson's niece, Lily Bragg; combed the files of the author in the Department of Archives and History in Montgomery, Alabama; and published a letter requesting information about Wilson in a newsmagazine and several Southern newspapers—a letter that led to several hundred responses. The result of Fidler's diligent research is a book that not only chronicles the major events in Wilson's life but also captures her personality.

With the critical disfavor that the domestic sentimental genre has evoked in recent decades, there seems little likelihood of many future studies of Augusta Evans Wilson's works. But Alfred Habegger, in *Gender, Fantasy, and Realism in American Literature* (1982), reexamines nineteenth-century domestic and sentimental fiction to trace its influence on the rise of realism. Habegger, who argues that this genre reveals cultural fantasies and conflicts, discusses *St. Elmo, Beulah*, and *Macaria* in his study. Perhaps Habegger's cultural and historical criticism may renew interest in Wilson's work.

BIBLIOGRAPHY

Works by Augusta Jane Evans Wilson

Inez: A Tale of the Alamo. New York: Harper, 1855.

Beulah. New York: Derby and Jackson, 1859.

Macaria; or, Altars of Sacrifice. Confederate edition. Richmond: West and Johnson, 1863. Northern edition. New York: J. B. Lippincott, 1864.

St. Elmo. New York: G. W. Carleton, 1866.

Vashti; or, Until Death Us Do Part. New York: G. W. Carleton, 1869.

Infelice. New York: G. W. Carleton, 1875.

At the Mercy of Tiberius. New York: G. W. Dillingham, 1887.

A Speckled Bird. New York: G. W. Dillingham, 1902.

Devota. New York: G. W. Dillingham, 1907.

Studies of Augusta Jane Evans Wilson

Alderman, Edwin A. and Joel Chandler Harris, ed. *A Library of Southern Literature*. Atlanta: Martin and Hoyt, 1907. 13: 5841–64.

Brewton, W. W. "*St. Elmo* and *St. Twel'mo*." *Saturday Review of Literature* 5 (22 June 1929): 1123–24.

Brown, Herbert Ross, *The Sentimental Novel in America: 1789–1860*. Durham, N.C.: Duke University Press, 1940, pp. 189–90, 329, 335–36, 339–40, 348.

Cowie, Alexander. *The Rise of the American Novel*. New York: American Book, 1948, pp. 430–34.

Derby, J. C. *Fifty Years among Authors, Books and Publishers*. New York: G. W. Carleton, 1884, pp. 389–99.

Fidler, William Perry. *Augusta Evans Wilson 1835–1909: A Biography*. University: University of Alabama Press, 1951.

———. "The Life and Works of Augusta Evans Wilson." Ph.D. diss., University of Chicago, 1947.

File of Augusta Evans Wilson. Department of Archives and History. Montgomery, Alabama.

Forrest, Mary (Mrs. Julia Deane Freeman). *Women of the South Distinguished in Literature*. New York: Derby and Jackson, 1860, pp. 328–32.

Habegger, Alfred. *Gender, Fantasy, and Realism in American Literature*. New York: Columbia University Press, 1982, pp. 16–17, 19, 26, 35, 111, 120, and the notes on 306, 309, 318.

Hubbell, Jay B. *The South in American Literature, 1607–1900*. Durham, N.C.: Duke University Press, 1954, pp. 610–16.

Maurice, A. B. "*St. Elmo* and Its Author." *Bookman* 16 (September 1902): 12–14.

Moses, Montrose J. *The Literature of the South*. New York: Thomas Y. Crowell, 1910, pp. 330–37.

Pattee, Fred Lewis. *The Feminine Fifties*. New York: Appleton Century, 1910, pp. 67, 120, 125.

Rutherford, Mildred. *The South in History and Literature: A Hand-book of Southern Authors from the Settlement of Jamestown, 1607, to Living Writers*. Atlanta: Franklin-Turner, 1906, pp. 568–72.

William Wirt
(1772–1834)

Preeminent in the long line of literary lawyers who flourished during the first third of the nineteenth century stands William Wirt, best known for his biography of Patrick Henry, which included the famous "give me liberty or give me death" speech. Wirt, himself one of the greatest orators of his day, is also important for carrying on the eighteenth-century tradition of the familiar essay, a genre in which he excelled.

BIOGRAPHY

Wirt's career from poor orphan boy to candidate for president of the United States restated the early American dream, the success story of Benjamin Franklin and others who rose to high political posts by dint of industry and canny attention to their business or calling.

William Wirt, born in Bladensburg, Maryland, on 8 November 1772 was the youngest of six children of a Swiss father (who may have been an indentured servant) and a German mother. Both parents died before he was eight years old, and Wirt was raised by his uncle Jasper and his very religious wife, both of whom had been born in Switzerland. At an early age he was sent to a classical school in nearby Georgetown, where he boarded in a small log house with a Quaker named Schoolfield. Transferred to another similar school in Charles County, about 40 miles from Bladensburg, he advanced as far as Caesar's *Commentaries* with only "a single application of the ferrule" (Cruse, *Letters,* 17). When his new schoolmaster, Hatch Dent, died, Wirt was again uprooted and sent to a school run by a Presbyterian clergyman, the Rev. James Hunt. He remained in this school four years, studying Latin, Greek, geography, mathematics, and a little astronomy. Hunt, a Princeton graduate, had a good library, and here at the age of twelve or thirteen young Wirt was reading *Guy of Warwick* (a fourteenth-century verse romance), Tobias Smollett's *Peregrine Pickle*, the English dramatists, Alexander Pope, Joseph Addison, and Horne's *Elements of Criticism*. At Hunt's school, where he remained until 1787, the boys were permitted to attend court trials at the Montgomery Courthouse, some four miles distant. There was plenty of opportunity to practice oratory in Hunt's school. Thus the young boy's liking for spread-eagle oratory, the law, and the classics arose naturally and early. After the breakup of Hunt's school, Wirt served for two years as tutor in the household of Benjamin Edwards, in whose library he had further access to works by Greek and Roman authors.

About this time, suffering from a pulmonary complaint, he was advised to go south for the winter. He traveled by horseback to Augusta, Georgia, staying with his married sister until the spring, when he returned to Maryland to study law with William P. Hunt, the son of his old schoolteacher. He also studied with a Thomas Swann (who later became U.S. district attorney in Washington, D.C.). Wirt was licensed to practice law in Virginia in autumn 1792, when he was twenty years old.

As a young trial lawyer, Wirt showed little sign of becoming one of America's greatest orators. A friend described him as tongue-tied: "his ideas seemed to outstrip his power of expression . . . he clipped some of his words sadly; his voice, sweet and musical in conversation, grew loud and harsh, his articulation rapid, indistinct and imperfect" (Cruse, *Letters*, 36). Wirt himself said, "My pronunciation and gesture at this time were terribly vehement. I used sometimes to find myself literally stopped, by too great rapidity of utterance" (Kennedy, *Memoirs*, I, 86).

Possibly these early forensic difficulties helped determine his liking for literature. At any rate, when he was a young lawyer his library, according to his own admission, consisted only of a copy of Blackstone, two volumes of *Don Quixote*, and *Tristram Shandy*. John Pendleton Kennedy, Wirt's friend and biographer, thinks that Wirt was also reading *Tom Jones* and *Roderick Random* and other classics during this period. The result was that, although the law became for him "the ladder of preferment," a passion for literature came to rival it as "the Tantalus cup" of his life (Kennedy, *Memoirs*, I, 48).

Wirt's success in the law during the first two years of his practice led to his acquaintance with Dr. George Gilmer of Pen Park (near Monticello), a friend of Jefferson, Madison, and Monroe and widely known for his classical learning. Marriage to Mildred Gilmer and residence at Pen Park and Rose Hill brought Wirt into social contact with some of the best lawyers as well as some of the most prominent families in Virginia. His appetite for literature received an added edge from his father-in-law's library, where he read Francis Bacon, Boyle, John Locke, Thomas Hooker, and John Milton.

After the death of his wife (17 September 1799), Wirt moved to Richmond, became clerk in the Virginia House of Delegates, and further increased his friendship with Madison. Here, too, he met John Taylor of Caroline. But although Patrick Henry also was then a member of the House, Wirt never met or even saw him. (Henry died a few months after his election.) In 1802 Governor Monroe appointed Wirt to one of the three new chancery court positions. He moved to Williamsburg and for a while contemplated migrating to Kentucky, where he had heard he could make more money. But finally he let himself be persuaded by Littleton Waller Tazewell to go to Norfolk (in the winter of 1803–4), where he shared Tazewell's law practice. On 7 September 1802 he married Elizabeth Gamble, by whom he eventually had twelve children. This marriage to the daughter of Colonel Gamble of Richmond, a wealthy merchant and a Federalist, marked the end of Wirt's early development as a lawyer.

In August 1803, when his wife was expecting their first child, Wirt began a new period of his development—as a writer. *The Letters of the British Spy*, which appeared anonymously in Samuel Pleasants's Richmond newspaper (entitled *The Virginian Argus*) during September and October, was a series of essays in the Addison tradition. The essays attracted considerable interest—by their title—and by their anonymity. They purported to be by an English gentleman who for the past six months had been living in Richmond under an assumed name and enjoying his incognito status. "There is something of innocent roguery in this masquerade, which I am playing," writes Wirt, "that sorts very well with the sportiveness of my temper. To sit and decoy the human heart from behind its disguises: to watch the capricious evolutions of unrestrained nature, frisking, curvetting and gambolling at her ease with the curtain of ceremony drawn up to the sky—Oh! it is delightful!" (Cruse, *Letters*, 100). Readers of these *Letters* suspected that they were written either by an Englishman of rank corresponding with a friend in London or by an American intent on entertaining Richmond. Moreover, the thinly veiled allusions to such contemporaries as Edmund Randoph, James Monroe, John Marshall, and John Wickham roused interest.

These essays, two of which were written by George Tucker, were collected in book form and underwent ten editions during Wirt's lifetime. The popularity of this book, writes Kennedy, "had scarcely a parallel in any work, in the same department of letters, which had at that date, been attributed to American literature" (Kennedy, *Memoirs*, I, 105). He praises the "polished and elegant style" and states the chief topic as "a dissertation on eloquence and the illustration of it by a picture of the leading lawyers of Virginia" (Kennedy, *Memoirs*, I, 106). Although *The British Spy*, historically speaking, made Wirt's reputation, Kennedy notes that by 1850 this book was "but little read" (Kennedy, *Memoirs*, I, 107). Something of a tempest in a teapot, *The British Spy* made Wirt a few enemies, but these were not long lasting.

Although Wirt managed to maintain his anonymity for some time after the appearance of *The British Spy*, in a letter from Norfolk (16 January 1804) to his close friend Dabney Carr he says he will not deny the "brat" to be his own (Kennedy, *Memoirs*, I, 108). In a letter to his wife in October 1830 Wirt amusingly tells of an encounter with John D. Burke. Burke had told him that although he considered Wirt to have considerable literary talent, he did not regard it of sufficiently high order to enable him to have written *The British Spy*. Burke, too, thought the essays "elegantly written" (Davis, *Letters*, xx-n).

But Wirt himself was always modest about his literary ability. He referred to these essays as "bagatelles" in this same letter to his wife. Self-critically he deprecated—on the occasion of the second edition—both the mind and style of the author: "The letters bespeak a mind rather frolicksome and sprightly than thoughtful and penetrating; and therefore a mind qualified to amuse, for the moment, but not to benefit either its proprietor, or the world, by the depth and utility of its researches" (Kennedy, *Memoirs*, I, 112).

The British Spy was indebted to the Addison tradition for more than style. Addison had used the device of a foreign visitor commenting on English manners and mores. So had Goldsmith in his *Citizen of the World*, as had Montesquieu earlier in his *Persian Letters*. Poe, whom Wirt later befriended, pointed out another possible source—Giovanni Paolo Marana's *Letters Written by a Turkish Spy Who Lived Five and Forty Years at Paris* (1687). And there were others, too, such as George Littleton's *Letters from a Persian in England* (Davis, *Intellectual*, 104). Although following a well-worn literary path for his overall formal design, Wirt nevertheless was original in what he had to say.

What he did have to say concerned, besides the decay of eloquence in Virginia, such topics as the unequal distribution of property in Virginia; the hypocrisy of pretending to honor democracy while silently honoring the son of a visiting English lord; the illegal seizure of land once owned by the Indians; the Virginians' passion for wealth; low pay for the professors at William and Mary, who were fed "like a band of beggars, on the scraps and crums [*sic*] that fall from the financial table"; (Cruse, *Letters*, 194) as well as the dissipation of the students there; infidelity in religious belief, a corrupting foreign influence imported from William Godwin in England; the state of the Virginia bar, which is treated satirically; the need for public education; and admiration for *The Spectator*. It is obvious that Wirt, now a young lawyer, was a man with a sensitive social conscience rather than a genteel writer seeking only to amuse. He had developed sufficient literary skill to know that with the particular audience he was addressing it was necessary to soften his social criticism by putting on the cloak of a visiting foreigner (with aristocratic connections) from a country that had once been the prime enemy of his readers.

In the following year (1804) Wirt again appeared in print, this time with an essay "On the Condition of Women," a sentimental tale of a deserted woman. The essay was second in a collection of ten constituting *The Rainbow* (first series). Wirt had joined with nine other writers, all followers of Jefferson, to form the Rainbow Association, directed by the Scottish schoolmaster James Ogilvie, who wrote the first essay, "On the Utility of Miscellaneous Essays." These anonymous essays had first been published in the Richmond *Enquirer* from 11 August to 20 October 1804. (Only the first series was collected; the second series also appeared in the same newspaper, and Ogilvie began a third there with an essay on luxury.) The unsigned manuscript of Wirt's essay is in the Maryland Historical Society Collection of Wirt papers, edited for microfilm by John B. Boles.

Wirt was now managing to find more time for his literary pursuits. Writing from Norfolk to Dabney Carr on 8 June 1804, he says he has been reading Johnson's *Lives of the Poets*. "I have contracted an itch for biography," he explains. "Do not be astonished, therefore, if you see me come out with a very *material* and splendid life of some departed Virginia worthy,—for I meddle no more with the living. Virginia has lost some great men, whose names ought not perish. If I were a Plutarch, I would collect their lives for the honour of the state and the advantage of posterity" (Kennedy, *Memoirs*, I, 116).

Six months later we find him reminding Judge Tucker of an earlier letter in which he had asked Tucker for information on Patrick Henry in "conversation and debate, judicial and political." Wirt had wished to discover:

the colour of his [Henry's] eyes, a portrait of his person, attitudes, gestures, manners; a description of his voice, its tone, energy, and modulations; his delivery, whether slow, grave and solemn, or rapid, sprightly and animated; his pronunciation, whether studiously plain, homely, and sometimes vulgar, or accurate, courtly and ornate,—with an analysis of his mind, the variety, order and predominance of its powers; his information as a lawyer, a politician, a scholar; the peculiar character of his eloquence &c., &c., for I never saw him. (Kennedy, *Memoirs*, I, 122–23)

During this same period he wrote to his wife: "I hope to immortalize the memory of Henry and to do no discredit to my fame." He recalled that from early youth he had resolved "to profit by the words of Sallust, who advises that if a man wishes his memory to live forever . . . , he must either *write* something worthy of being read, or *do* something worthy of being written and immortalized in history" (Kennedy, *Memoirs*, I, 133).

But other events were to delay the progress of Wirt's famous biography. First, the trial of Aaron Burr in 1807, in which Wirt played a major part by assisting the attorney general, demanded his close attention. Although the jury found Burr not guilty of treason, Wirt's conspicuous role in the prosecution—especially his eloquent defense of the immigrant Herman Blennerhasset (upon whom Burr's lawyers had attempted to shift a major part of the blame)—won him great popularity in Richmond, where the trial took place. Second, at approximately the same time the *Leopard-Chesapeake* naval affair had posed a threat of war, Wirt, who held the rank of major in the militia, set about raising a legion to fight the British, whose ships had been stopping, searching, and impressing sailors aboard American vessels. In his letter to Dabney Carr (Richmond, 9 July 1807) he thought war was inevitable and wrote that he and Carr were to be made colonels in two of the four regiments proposed. By the second of September, however, a turn of events—the British withdrawal of ships near the American coast, in response to Jefferson's proclamation—caused Wirt to abandon this plan.

As a consequence of his new fame, resulting largely from the Burr trial, Jefferson invited Wirt to run for the House of Representatives. Wirt's letter of 14 January 1808 makes clear his reason for declining—the economic necessities of his increasingly large family. He was nonetheless elected in 1808 (without campaigning) to the state legislative body—the Virginia House of Delegates—as representative from Richmond. He served until 1810. As a legislator he followed Jefferson's administration, championing a protection policy for American domestic manufacturers. He also wrote the report of the special committee considering French and British belligerents against the United States.

During the year 1810, Kennedy tells us, Wirt came to the defense of Madison against his political detractors with a few essays entitled *The Centinel*:

These papers were written in a different style from his former political compositions; were more free of that ambitious declamation which may be noticed in some portions of the letters of One of the People [1808]. His object in this change was to mislead the public as to the author; but the public, accustomed to the flavour of his pen, were not deceived by the assumed disguise, and he became as well known for these essays as for the former. (Kennedy, *Memoirs*, I, 254–55)

Probably Wirt's most important series of familiar essays, *The Old Bachelor*, now began appearing in the Richmond *Enquirer*. Late in 1810 he had been publishing in this paper a series called *The Sylph*, but in December he abandoned it for the new series. The central character, the old bachelor Dr. Robert Cecil, bore some resemblance to Addison's Roger de Coverley, but was more enthusiastic and more sentimental, traits that characterized Wirt himself. Twenty-eight numbers of *The Old Bachelor* entertained the readers of the *Enquirer* from 22 December 1810 to 11 December 1813; five more, in 1814. All 33 essays were published in book form in 1814 in Richmond. There was a later edition in Baltimore in 1818.

Wirt did not write all of these essays, being assisted by his friends Richard E. Parker, Dabney Carr, and Dr. Frank Carr (whom Wirt repeatedly calls a "rascal," apparently for his failure to send in copy), Louis Hue Girardin, Major David Watson, and George Tucker. St. George Tucker and Francis W. Gilmer might also have contributed. Contributors to *The Old Bachelor* used a great variety of pseudonyms—Obadiah Squaretoes, Galen, John Truename, Alfred, Melmoth, Richard Vamper, Peter Schryphel, Stephen Micklewise, and Romeo in Number 20, Diogenes and Susannah Thankful in Number 27. Jay B. Hubbell attributes the name of Arthur O'Flannegan to Wirt himself in Number 15. He thinks Wirt responsible for writing all or part of the following numbers: 1, 9, 12, 13, 14, 17, 18, 19, 20, 30, 31, and 32 (Hubbell, *WMQ* 23: 149n., 150).

In some ways the year 1817 brought to a climax Wirt's literary development, for it signaled the publication of his long delayed biography of Patrick Henry, on which his more recent literary reputation so largely, but unfairly, depends.

Wirt lists some of his main sources for the *Sketches of the Life and Character of Patrick Henry* in the preface to his book: Jefferson, St. George Tucker, Nathaniel Pope, Judge Winston (who had married Patrick Henry's widow and who was himself a first cousin of Henry's), Judge John Tyler, Judge Spencer Roane (Henry's son-in-law), Judge William H. Cabell, Governor Page (who had prepared "a pretty extended sketch" of Patrick Henry's life), the files of newspapers from 1765 to the close of the Revolutionary War, original letters, court records, and state archives (Wirt, *Henry*, 3). In addition, a host of other sources are indicated in the footnotes. Since Wirt had never seen or heard Henry he had to depend on secondhand reports, which he found often contradictory. He apparently wrote several drafts and submitted large parts of the manuscript to Jefferson, St. George Tucker, and others.

The actual writing of the biography proved difficult. It was "up hill all the way, and heavy work," he writes to Dabney Carr. It was much like "attempting to run, tied up in a bag," he adds in the same letter of 20 August 1815 (Kennedy, *Memoirs*, I, 344). A few days earlier he had informed St. George Tucker that he had completed 96 pages and intended 300. "O. Brains, Brains! Help me out of this scrape, and if ever I tax you again with such another task, 'Spit in my face, and call me horse!' " he writes to Tucker. "I foresee that Patrick will be the ruin of my literary name," he dolefully complains (Tyler, *WMQ*, 22: 250). At one time he thought that he might never be able to finish the work. To Jefferson he writes, "I propose, at present, to prepare it and leave the manuscript with my family" (Kennedy, *Memoirs*, I, 302). Plagued with professional interruptions, he finally completed it after having worked on the book off and on for over twelve years.

The *Sketches of the Life and Character of Patrick Henry* was generally well received, although the critic for the *North American Review* thought the author had spent too much time on unimportant aspects of the history of the period. Kennedy found it dissappointing in spite of its good style and clear, flowing narrative. John Adams liked it and offered Wirt congratulations on his new cabinet post of attorney general, which he had just received from Monroe. John Taylor of Caroline called it a "splendid novel" (Kennedy, *Memoirs*, II, 63). Wirt thought about revising it, but never did.

From 13 November 1817, the date of his assuming the office of attorney general, a post he retained for the next twelve years—longer than any other incumbent—his legal duties overshadowed his literary publications. As attorney general he wrote three large volumes of legal opinions and effected numerous reforms in that office. Besides, he was participating actively in many important law trials, such as the Dartmouth College case of 1819; the Bank Trials in Bel Air, Maryland, where he opposed his old antagonist William Pinkney; and the steamboat case of 1824. In fact, as one writer put it, Wirt "participated in almost every litigation of national significance from the Callender trial in 1800 to the Cherokee cases of 1831–1832" (Boles, *Papers*, Film 1, p. 1). Harvard gave him a Doctor of Laws degree in 1824. (The College of New Jersey at Princeton had given him the same degree earlier—in September, 1816.) Jefferson tried to lure Wirt away from his government post in 1826 by offering him a position as professor of law *and* president of the University of Virginia, which Wirt declined. That Wirt's reputation as an orator had reached a high point in this year may be seen in his being selected to deliver the memorial oration (before both houses of Congress) honoring Jefferson and Adams.

After resigning as attorney general in 1829, Wirt moved to Baltimore and continued his law practice, defending Judge James H. Peck in that important impeachment case of 1830 and being involved in the Cherokee Indian cases of 1831–32. His interest in literary matters, however, had not waned, for there is a record of his having addressed a literary society at Rutgers College in 1830.

He had acquired land in Florida and had planned to colonize a group of German immigrants there in 1833. But the Germans, once arrived in Wirtland, deserted after only three months and the plan failed.

Wirt's acceptance of the Anti-Masonic Party's nomination for President in the election of 1832 amounted to a miscalculation. During his earlier life he had actually been a Mason. In accepting the nomination he had hoped for support by the Whigs, because of his and their dislike of Jackson. But the Whigs backed Clay, a friend of Wirt's, and Jackson swept the country. (Wirt won only the state of Vermont.)

He died of erysipelas in Washington on 18 February 1834 while attending a session of the U.S. Supreme Court. Both houses of Congress adjourned for his funeral, which was also attended by the president and vice president, the Supreme Court, and the diplomatic corps. After 1834 Wirt's memory lived on in the William Wirt Societies or "Literary Institutes" in a number of American cities, at one of which Poe once spoke (Davis, *Intellectual*, 385).

MAJOR THEMES

Wirt's major theme was the passing glory of an earlier age in Virginia, the age of Patrick Henry. His biography of Henry is probably his best work. It is admirably adapted to illustrate this theme of a passing heroic age, an age of rationalism, one attuned to nature. For Wirt, Patrick Henry is above all an orator with a great *natural* gift, a perfect representative of classical ideas of sublimity. Longinus uses frequent examples from Demosthenes to explain and delineate this idea, and Wirt takes particular pains to exhibit Henry as more like Demosthenes than Cicero. Specific traits of characterization that Wirt emphasizes are Henry's voice, his distinct articulation, his wide range of emotional appeal (from comedy to tragedy), his tone of mild persuasion, his vehemence in arousing an audience, his appropriate gestures. But above all Wirt stresses Patrick Henry's "*strong natural sense*" of human nature—and reminiscent of Aristotle's definition of *rhetoric*—of "what was needed in particular situations" (Wirt, *Henry*, 425). Thus he pictures Henry as a backwoods orator, a yeoman farmer, the champion of the poor, and spokesman for the common man.

Needless to say, this picture appealed to the romantic sense of his readers, not only because it adverted to an earlier age of men transcendently gifted by nature but also because it provided a model for the new, popular democracy that Andrew Jackson was to usher in. It is ironical, of course, that Wirt was no friend of Jackson, either tempermentally or politically. But like Franklin, Wirt was so much a representative man of his age that almost anything he said or wrote, given his great popularity, found relatively easy acceptance. The following description of Patrick Henry as a young man illustrates his closeness to the frontier and at the same time shows the classical style that Wirt used:

His person is represented as having been coarse, his manners uncommonly awkward, his dress slovenly, his conversation very plain, his aversion to study invincible, and his faculties almost entirely benumbed by indolence. No persuasion could bring him either to read or work. On the contrary, he ran wild in the forest, like one of the *aborigines* of the country, and divided his life between the dissipation and uproar of the chase, and the languor of inaction. (Wirt, *Henry*, 6)

But Wirt could also employ a more romanticized—almost Homeric—style when he aimed at giving the reader some notion other than that of the young savage, as we see in the following, depicting Patrick Henry in the grandeur of his power:

He rose like the thunder-bearer of Jove, when he mounts on strong and untiring wing, to sport in fearless majesty over the troubled deep—now sweeping in immense and rapid circles—then suddenly arresting his grand career, and hovering aloft in tremulous and terrible suspense—at one instant, plunged amid the foaming waves—at the next, reascending on high, to play undaunted among the lightnings of heaven, or soar towards the sun. (Wirt, *Henry*, 426)

In mild persuasion, it [Henry's voice] was as soft and gentle as the zephyr of spring; while in rousing his countrymen to arms, the winter storm along the troubled Baltic, was not more awfully sublime. (Wirt, *Henry*, 413)

When he hobbled, it was like the bird that thus artfully seeks to decoy away the foot of the intruder from the precious deposit of her brood; and at the moment when it would be thought that his strength was almost exhausted, he would spring magnificently from the earth, and tower above the clouds. (Wirt, *Henry*, 253)

Along with his sense of the passing glory of Virginia and the decline of eloquence, Wirt reveals in this book a strong didactic sense, perhaps best seen in its dedication: "To the young men of Virginia." As a young man Wirt had been a tutor to Ninian Edwards; in later life he became the close adviser and teacher of numerous law students who, under his direction, read in his large library of law books—some 480 items of which are listed in the papers of the Maryland Historical Society Collection. Patrick Henry, then, as Wirt presents him, was not only a backwoods model for the commoners who were beginning to constitute the new, popular democracy, but also a model of the young "natural aristocrats'' that Adams and Jefferson hoped for. Wirt pulls no punches in describing Henry's defects—his laziness and his lack of learning are certainly not held up for emulation. Rather, Henry's transcendent powers as orator; his courteous treatment of opponents; his courage, particularly when facing what Cicero called a ''hostile'' audience; his logic and common sense; his sense of justice; his stance as champion of the poor—these are the qualities Wirt cherishes and would instill in the young.

Thus he felt that education was necessary to correct the state of society—education not only for the privileged but as well for the poor. The ninth letter of *The British Spy*, for example, begins with the spy's casting his eye over Virginia and observing ''the very few who have advanced in the theatre of public observation, and the very many who will remain forever behind the scenes.'' Although the subject of this essay seems to be Wirt's faith that genius will prevail against malice and envy—Chatham is his example—there occurs an interesting reversal at the end of the essay, where he reflects on the waste of talent in the western part of Virginia—because of the lack of education there. In the ''Apology'' interposed between this essay and the tenth letter, he hopes that his miscellaneous remarks might be of use to the ''many literary young men . . . growing up in Virginia.'' In his person he excuses himself to any who have taken offense—on grounds that his deficiencies have been imposed on him by *Nature* and by his ''rustic education.''

The need for education is also an important theme in *The Old Bachelor*, which followed *The British Spy* by almost a decade. In the ''Advertisement'' to this later series the subject had been announced as eloquence, but only a few essays explored that theme. The series had didactic goals.

Wirt's effort to instruct the rising generation sometimes misled him into sentimentalism. His description of the suffering young wife who dies following the desertion of her husband in the second essay of *The Rainbow* (first series) might be cited, as well as the *ubi sunt* motif in the fourth and sixth letters of *The British Spy*, where he seems to pine for Pocahontas, Captain John Smith, and other figures of the past. But there is another theme that emerged in Letter IV: his sense of injustice at the Indians' being dispossessed of their lands.

The real theme of *The British Spy*, however, seems, as in his biography of Henry, still to be his favorite topic of eloquence, which is treated variously in Letters III, VII, and VIII and, a little later, in *The Rainbow* (second series) with his essay ''On Forensic Eloquence.''

Ostensibly, the decay of eloquence in legal oratory in Virginia since the death of Patrick Henry is the subject of the third *British Spy* letter. But this decay is not limited to Virginia or the United States, for it is caused by a widespread deficiency in ''general knowledge, failure to acquire the habit of close and solid thinking,'' and ''lack of originality'' (Cruse, *Letters*, 133). *Civilization*, he says, has ''interwoven with society a habit of artificial and elaborate decorum, which deters the fancy from every bold enterprise and buries nature under a load of hypocritical ceremonies'' (Cruse, *Letters*, 133). He contrasts Demosthenes with

Cicero; the former has "more fire and less smoke than Tully" (Cruse, *Letters*, 136). Defining eloquence as a form of *sympathy*, he proceeds to offer a rather mystical view of it (from Bacon's *Advancement of Learning*) as transmission "without mediation of the senses" of a kind of spiritual intercourse. How does it happen, he asks, that one speaker puts us to sleep, "benumbing all the faculties of our soul," while another awakens and arouses us "like the clanguor of the martial trumpet"? The one speaker will bring down "my powers exactly to the level of his," he explains; but the other will descend "like an angel of light, breathe new energy into my frame, dilate my soul with his own intelligence, exalt me into a new and nobler region of thought, snatch me from the earth . . . and rap me to the seventh heaven" (Cruse, *Letters*, 139).

His description of Patrick Henry's delivery exemplifies this lofty conception of eloquence:

> I am told that his general appearance and manners were those of a plain farmer or planter of the back country; that, in this character, he always entered on the exordium of an oration; disqualifying himself, with looks and expressions of humility so lowly and unassuming, as threw every heart off its guard and induced his audience to listen to him, with the same easy openness with which they would converse with an honest neighbour: but, by and by, when it was little expected, he would take a flight so high, and blaze with a splendour so heavenly, as filled them with a kind of religious awe, and gave him the force and authority of a prophet. (Cruse, *Letters*, 144–45)

He accounts for the paucity of the surviving reports on Henry's orations by "the stenographer's having never attempted to follow him, when he arose in the strength and awful majesty of his genius" (Cruse, *Letters*, 146).

In the seventh letter Wirt (through his persona of the spy) gives us a different portrait of the natural orator—the blind preacher James Waddell, whom he says he had heard during an excursion into the Blue Ridge Mountains one Sunday morning in Orange County, where he attended a rural church service. Listening to him, he says, "Never before did I completely understand what Demosthenes meant by laying such stress on *delivery*" (Cruse, *Letters*, 199). He likens the blind preacher to Homer, to Ossian, to Milton and is especially struck by the preacher's quotation from Rousseau: "Socrates died like a philosopher, but Jesus Christ, like a God!" (Cruse, *Letters*, 198). On reaching Richmond, the spy discovers that no one there knew Waddell. "Is it not strange," he asks, "that such a genius as this, so accomplished a scholar, so divine an orator, should be permitted to die in obscurity, within eighty miles of the metropolis of Virginia?" And he finds this a conclusive argument that the Virginians either have no taste for great oratory or have no love for "genuine exalted religion" (Cruse, *Letters*, 202–3). He then launches an attack on infidelity in religious belief, attributing it to foreign influence rather than native backsliding and naming Godwin, whose brand of atheism and anarchy he particularly disliked, as a corrupter of the youth.

Letter VIII contains satire of some of the leading lawyers of Virginia, whom

Wirt discusses without naming. He criticizes their "extreme prolixity," the "exuberant fondness for literary finery" of one member of the bar, although he approves the same member's "extensive reading" and being "a fine *belles-lettres* scholar" (Cruse, *Letters*, 214). Praising the ingenuity and wit of one lawyer, he says this man "never brandishes the Olympic thunder of Homer, but . . . seldom, if ever, sinks beneath the chaste majesty of Virgil" (Cruse, *Letters*, 218). Of this same man he reports that he is so quick at shifting his position when in danger of being beaten in argument, that he is like Proteus, "and the courts are disposed to doubt their senses even when he appears in his proper shape" (Cruse, *Letters*, 218–19).

Ever well balanced and judicious in his criticism, Wirt carried this same attitude into his political views. Throughout his life he was a liberal Republican. He defended Madison in *The Centinel* essays, and although he tended to side with the French instead of the British, he nevertheless distrusted Napoleon. In his letter to Dabney Carr (15 February 1814) he says, "As for Napoleon, I care no more for him . . . than I do for any other tornado that is past" (Kennedy, *Memoirs*, I, 329). He no longer worries that Napoleon might invade America; he wonders what effect his reverses might have on British obstinacy towards America. Will France share the same fate as Poland?

As for monarchy, Wirt had made his position on that clear during the Burr trial, when he announced, "I hate monarchy with all its mysteries, as I do the mysterious movements of those who are lovers of monarchy" (Kennedy, *Memoirs*, I, 156). But at the same time, despite his admiration for republican government, he can also remark, as he does in the eighth letter of *The British Spy*, that "many well meaning men" "smitten with the love of republican simplicity and honesty" have "fallen into a ruggedness of deportment, a thousand times more proud, more intolerable and disgusting, than Shakespeare's foppish lord with his chin new reaped and pouncet box" (Cruse, *Letters*, 216).

Although he believed strongly in the virtues of the democratic republican society, he evidenced in his own character and writing the aristocratic concept of noblesse oblige. He wrote to William Pope (Richmond, 5 August 1803): "Good men only deserve to be rich, because they only are disposed to employ their wealth for the good of the world." He was aware, however, that "things in general take a different turn, and that none grow rich but the selfish and the sordid" (Kennedy, *Memoirs*, I, 100). Since at this time he himself had suffered from the low pay with which Virginia then rewarded its public servants, he objects that "in a republic, public economy is an important thing, but public justice is still more important" (Kennedy, *Memoirs*, I, 99).

For politicians whose chief interest was mere survival in office Wirt had only contempt, especially for those who always knew which way the wind was blowing and let it sway them. An honest public servant, he tells William Pope, might sometimes have to offend the people, giving as example a Roman consul who disobeyed an order of the Roman government in order to pursue Hannibal and drive him from the country. "Hannibal was vanquished,—Rome was saved, and a triumph was decreed for the disobedient victor. What member of our Assembly,'' he asks, ''is like this consul?'' (Kennedy, *Memoirs*, I, 100).

Since Wirt's main publishing career as a writer spanned a relatively short period from 1803 to 1817, he deserves more than a little credit for his accomplishments. He revived Longinus's concept of the sublime or elevated style in oratory, vivifying it in a biography that will forever remain a glorious part of the American tradition, a book that keeps alive the memory of a man Jefferson called ''the greatest orator who ever lived'' (Wirt, *Henry*, 36). In addition, largely during this brief period of fourteen years, through his *Letters of the British Spy, The Rainbow*, and *The Old Bachelor*, Wirt managed to express themes and ideas of interest not only to readers of his day but also to those of ours. He worked with skill and charm in the genre of the familiar essay during a time when it functioned as social criticism as well as amusement, during a time when neoclassical influence began to dwindle and give way to an age of a new and less genteel kind of democracy.

SURVEY OF CRITICISM

Twentieth-century scholarship on William Wirt has been scanty. Richard Beale Davis, Jay B. Hubbell, and a few others have done excellent pioneer work. Joseph Clarke Robert of Richmond is still at work on what promises to be the definitive biography of Wirt, part of which has already been published in his outstanding ''William Wirt, Virginian''—to date the most informative and best written of all research on Wirt.

Davis's monumental *Intellectual Life in Jefferson's Virginia, 1790–1830* presents an outstanding picture of Wirt—probably the best to date—against the large historical backdrop of the period. Since Wirt was so much a man of his time, this approach gains immeasurable value. Wirt's importance in this period may be seen by the fact that Davis's index contains more entries for him than for any other single figure with the exception of Jefferson and Madison. Davis does not exaggerate Wirt's ability as a writer in his discussion of all his published work and his voluminous correspondence with friends—such as Dabney Carr, the Gilmers, and the Tuckers. Neither, on the other hand, does he undervalue Wirt's oratorical powers and the commanding place he held in the age of Webster, Pinkney, and other such giants (Davis, *Intellectual*, 382–85).

Davis's conclusion is that although Wirt's writings were well known throughout the United States, his ''real fame was as a lawyer and an orator'' and that his literary and legal skills ''inextricably fused in his reputation'' (Davis, *Intellectual*, 383). This judgment is sound and seems to account for the difficulties so many other commentators have encountered in trying to assess Wirt's literary power. One must treat the whole man, as Davis does, calling Wirt ''widely read but no intellectual,'' ''self-educated, eager,'' and ''genial.'' His fondness for classical allusions, his sententiousness, ''his tendency to the high flown or flowery'' (Davis, *Intellectual*, 383) —all defects of which he was conscious and tried to eliminate—permeate, says Davis, his numerous surviving legal papers and occasional addresses.

Much, but possibly not enough, of Wirt's companionable, genial, and fun-loving nature can be gleaned from Kennedy's biography, since it consists so largely of letters to friends. Until Robert's work appears, Kennedy's book still remains the standard biography.

Among the shorter twentieth-century studies, that of Hubbell on Wirt's familiar essays in *The British Spy, The Rainbow*, and *The Old Bachelor* pioneered in identifying the contributors to two of these series. Davis's illuminating note on Wirt's friendly treatment of Poe and the possibility that Wirt may have known Poe's mother—he was a good friend of two members of her acting company at the time of her final visit to Richmond—gives an interesting and well-documented sidelight.

John B. Boles's fine editing for microfilm (24 rolls) of the approximately 8,000 Wirt papers in the Maryland Historical Society library collection provides new access to aspects of Wirt's career that have been neglected in the past. Although many of these are legal and administrative, this collection also contains unpublished letters and some of his verse as well as manuscripts of several essays. Boles lists some of the other principal collections—such as that of the Library of Congress, the National Archives, and various university libraries. With the availability of this abundant material, it is hoped the neglect of this representative author will begin to be repaired.

BIBLIOGRAPHY

Works by William Wirt

The Letters of the British Spy. Richmond: Samuel Pleasants, Jr., 1803.
The Rainbow, first series, with others. Richmond: Ritchie and Worsley, 1804.
The Old Bachelor, with others. Richmond: Enquirer Press, 1814.
Sketches of the Life and Character of Patrick Henry. Philadelphia: James Webster, 1817.
Introduction to *The Letters of the British Spy by William Wirt, Esq*. Ed. Richard Beale Davis. Chapel Hill: University of North Carolina Press, 1970, pp. vii-xxii.
A Guide to the Microfilm Edition of the William Wirt Papers, 1786–1873. Ed. John B. Boles. (Manuscript 1011 in Maryland Historical Society Library Collection) Baltimore: Maryland Historical Society, 1971.

Studies of William Wirt

Cauble, Frank P. "William Wirt and his Friends: A Study in Southern Culture, 1772–1834." Ph.D. diss., University of North Carolina, 1933.
Cruse, Peter Hoffman. "Biographical Sketch of William Wirt." *The Letters of the British Spy*. 10th ed. New York: J. and J. Harper, 1832, pp. 9–91.

Davis, Richard Beale. "The Influence of William Wirt." *Francis Walker Gilmer: Life and Learning in Jefferson's Virginia*. Richmond: Dietz Press, 1939.

———. *Intellectual Life in Jefferson's Virginia, 1790–1830*. Chapel Hill: University of North Carolina Press, 1964; Knoxville: University of Tennessee Press, 1972.

———. *Literature and Society in Early Virginia, 1608–1840*. Baton Rouge: Louisiana State University Press, 1973.

———. "Poe and William Wirt." *American Literature* 16 (November 1944): 212–20.

———, ed. *Correspondence of Thomas Jefferson and Francis Walker Gilmer, 1814–1826*. Columbia: University of South Carolina Press, 1946.

———, et al., eds. *Southern Writing, 1585–1920*. New York: Odyssey Press, 1970.

Diehl, George West. "The Rise and Development of Southern Oratory." M.A. thesis, University of Richmond, 1917.

Dobie, Armistead M. "William Wirt." *Library of Southern Literature*. Ed. Edwin A. Alderman, Joel Chandler Harris, and Charles W. Kent. Atlanta: Martin and Hoyt, 1910. 13: 5903–08.

Fulton, Maurica Garland. *Southern Life in Southern Literature: Selections of Representative Prose and Poetry*. New York: Ginn, 1917.

Gilmer, Francis W. *Sketches of American Orators*. Baltimore: n.p. 1816.

Griswold, Rufus W. *Prose Writers of America*. 4th ed. Philadelphia: A. Hart, 1852.

Guy, Mr. and Mrs. John H., ed. "Letters from Old Trunks." *Virginia Magazine of History and Biography* 48 (1939): 147–52.

Hubbell, Jay B. *The South in American Literature, 1607–1900*. Durham, N.C.: Duke University Press, 1954, pp. 234–42, 972–74.

———. "William Wirt and the Familiar Essay in Virginia." *William and Mary Quarterly* 2d ser., 23 (April 1943): 136–52.

Kennedy, John Pendleton. *Memoirs of the Life of William Wirt, Attorney-General of the United States*. 2 vols. rev. ed. Philadelphia: Lea and Blanchard, 1850.

Lillich, Richard B. "William Wirt: The Literary Lawyer." *Speaker* 40 (May 1958): 30–41.

Manly, Louise. *Southern Literature From 1579 to 1895*. Richmond: B. F. Johnson, 1895.

Matthews, William. "William Wirt." *Magazine of American History* 13 (1885): 108.

Page, Thomas Nelson. *The Old South*. 1892. Repr. New York: Negro Universities Press, 1969, pp. 67–68.

Parks, Edd Winfield. *Ante-Bellum Southern Literary Critics*. Athens: University of Georgia Press, 1962.

Parrington, Vernon L. "William Wirt." *Main Currents in American Thought*. New York: Harcourt, Brace, 1927. 2: 30–35.

Pattee, Fred Lewis, ed. *John Neal's American Writers*. Durham, N.C.: Duke University Press, 1937, pp. 183–84.

Robert, Joseph Clarke. "William Wirt, Virginian." *Virginia Magazine of History and Biography* 80 (October 1972): 387–441.

Rubin, Louis D., Jr. *The Literary South*. New York: John Wiley, 1979.

Taylor, William R. "William Wirt and the Legend of the Old South."*William and Mary Quarterly* 3d ser., 14 (1957): 477–94. Repr. in *Cavalier and Yankee* (New York: Braziller, 1961); pp. 67–94.

Thomas, Frederick William. *John Randolph of Roanoke, and Other Sketches of Character, Including William Wirt*. Philadelphia: A. Hart, 1853.

[Tyler, Lyon G.] "William Wirt's Life of Patrick Henry." *William and Mary College Quarterly Historical Magazine* 22 (April 1914): 25–57.

Wellford, B. Randolph. "Check-List of the Editions of Wirt's *The Letters of the British Spy.*" *Secretary's News Sheet* of the Bibliographical Society of the University of Virginia, no. 31, pp. 10–16.

Index

Compiled by Nancy West

Note: *Italicized* page numbers refer to main author entries.

Aaron, Daniel, 104
Abbott, Lyman, 508
Abner Daniel (Harben), 214
Abolitionist Movement, 46
Abridgement of the Publick Laws of Virginia, An ... (Beverley), 39, 41
Absalom, Absalom!, xi, 9
Accidence, An (J. Smith), 429, 430
"Account of a Negro Boy, An" (Byrd), 56
Act for Establishing Religious Freedom (1779), 269
Adair, Douglas, 331
Adams, Henry, 199, 431
Adams, John, 5, 6, 268–69, 273, 287, 289, 360, 495, 497
Adams, Percy G., 67, 70, 432
Adams, Robert, 372
Adams, Wirt, 75
Addams, Jane, 353
Addison, Joseph, 495
Address to the People of St. Helena Parish (Elliott), 206, 208
Addums, Mozis. *See* Bagby, George William
Adventures in His Tour from Georgia to Canada (W. T. Thompson), 442
Adventures of Huckleberry Finn (Twain), 12, 146, 148, 149, 151, 152, 157, 158, 222
Adventures of Tom Sawyer, The (Twain), 12, 145, 149, 151, 158
Advertisements for the Unexperienced Planters (J. Smith), 2, 429–31

Agrarians, 237
"Al Aaraaf" (Poe), 369, 371
Al Aaraaf, Tamerlaine, and Minor Poems (Poe), 366
Alabama Journal (Montgomery), 251
Albert, Franky, 118
Album, The, 397, 409
Alchemy, 383
Alderman, Edwin A., 209, 392
Aldrich, Thomas Bailey, 339, 436, 438
Alexander, Jean, 381
Alexander, Phebe, 86
Alida, 221
Allan, Frances, 365, 366
Allan, John, 187, 365
Allegheny Winds and Waters (Murfree), 339
Allen, Hervey, 379
Almost Persuaded (Harben), 213, 215–16
"Alone" (Poe), 371
Alta California, 145
Amacher, Richard E., 36
Ambrose, Paul, 289
America, 134
American Anti-Slavery Society, 46
American Authors, 1600–1900, 408
American Claimant, An (Twain), 146, 152
American Fiction, 408
American Fugitive in Europe, The (Brown), 48, 49
American Literary Realism, 159

American Loyalists, The, 406
"American Pictures" (Thorpe), 458
American Renaissance, 224
American Revolution, 48, 170, 196
American Social Science Association, 77
American Turf Register and Sporting Magazine, 207
Amulet, The (Murfree), 340
Anarchiad, The, 496
Anderson, Carl L., 381
Anderson, Charles A., 209
Anderson, Charles R., 247, 309
Anderson, Frederick, 159
Anderson, George Thomas, 418
Andre, John, 404
Andrews, Kenneth R., 158
Andrews, William L., 52, 116
Andros, Edmund, 38, 56
"Angelus, The" (Chivers), 125
"Annabel Lee" (Poe), 436
Ann Boyd (Harben), 215
"Anniversary, An" (Hayne), 244
Another Secret Diary (Byrd), 59, 60, 63, 65
"Answer to a Winter Piece" (Munford), 333
"Ante-Bellum Charleston" (Hayne), 407
Anthony, Aaron, 191, 192
"Apology for Fools, An" (Bagby), 23
"Apostrophe to Ocean" (Simms), 404
Appeal, 260
Archer, Captain Gabriel, 2
"Arctic Voyager, The" (Timrod), 465
Areytos (Simms), 399
Argus and Commercial Herald (Knoxville), 222
Arms, George, 141
Armstrong, Regina, 282
Arnavon, Cyrille, 140
Arner, Robert D., 70, 172
Arnold, Benedict, 404
Arnold, Matthew, 243
"Arolio" (Hayne), 244
Arolio: A Legend of the Island of Cos (Hayne), 241
Arp, Bill. *See* Smith, Charles Henry
Art of Slave Narrative, The, 52
"As from the Grave" (Twain), 148
As Good as a Comedy (Simms), 400, 410
"Ashby" (J. Thompson), 438
"Ashley at the Battery, The" (Hayne), 243
"Aspects of the Pines" (Hayne), 244
"Assignation, The" (Poe), 376
Atala (Chivers), 119, 121

Atalantis. A Story of the Sea (Simms), 397, 404
"Atala's Prayer" (Chivers), 120
At Fault (Chopin), 134–36
"Athénaïse" (Chopin), 138
Atlanta . . . (Chivers), 124
Atlanta *Constitution*, 16, 212, 228–31, 416, 420–23
Atlanta Exposition Speech, 18
Atlantic Monthly, 17, 108, 109, 145–46, 338, 339
"At Night" (Wilde), 526
At the Mercy of Tiberius (Wilson), 534–35
Auden, W. H., 378, 380, 407
Audubon, John James, 453, 458
Augusta *Mirror*, 314, 441, 446, 449
Auld, Hugh, 192–94, 200
Auld, Thomas, 192, 194
Austin, James C., 424
Autobiography (Jefferson), 272
Autobiography of Mark Twain, The (Twain), 157
"Awake from Thy Slumbers" (Chivers), 122
Awakening, The (Chopin), 18, 133–35, 138, 140, 337

Bacon, Francis, 429
Bacon, Nathaniel, 3, 93
"Bacon and Greens" (Bagby), 24, 26
Bacon's Rebellion, 7
Baer, Florence E., 236
Baezhold, Howard G., 158
Bagby, George William ["Mozis Addums"], 20–28, 10, 90; bibliography, 27–28; biography, 20–25; criticism of, 27; major themes, 25–27. Works: "An Apology for Fools," 23; "Bacon and Greens," 24, 26; "Canal Reminiscences," 26; "Cornfield Peas," 26; "Fishing in the Appomattox," 21; "Getting Married," 24; "Good Eating," 21, 24; "History uv the Waw, by Mozis Addums," 27; "A Horrible Scrape," 24; *John Brown and Wm. Mahone . . .* , 25; "John M. Daniel's Latch-Key," 24, 26; "The Letters of Mozis Addums to Billy Ivvins," 22; *The Letters of Mozis Addums to Billy Ivvins*, 11; "The Local Takes a Turn on the Ice," 21–22; "Meekins's Twinses," 27; Mozis Addums," 26; *Mozis Addums' New Letters*, 11; "My Uncle Flatback's Plantation," 21; "The Old Virginia Gentleman," 21, 24, 26; *Original Letters of Mozis Addums to Billy Ivvins*, 22;

"The Politican," 24; "The Sacred Furniture Warehouse," 21; "An Unrenowned Warrior ...," 23; "Uv Wimmin," 27; "The Virginia Editor," 22; "The Virginia Negro," 24; "What I Did with My Fifty Millions," 27; "Yorktown and Appomattox," 25

Bailey, Harriet, 190

Bain, Robert, 69, 225

Baine, Rodney, 323, 331, 333

Bair, John G., 253

Bair, Rowdy G., 253

Baker, Houston A., 199–200

Balaam and His Master (J. C. Harris), 230, 233

Balboa, Vasco Nunez de, 7, 403–4

Balcony Stories (King), 18, 301

"Bald-Head Billy Bauldy" (Simms), 402

Baldwin, Joseph Glover, *29–37*, 10, 20, 312; bibliography, 36–37; biography, 29–31; criticism of, 36; major themes, 31–36. Works: "The Bar of the Southwest," 33; "The Bench and the Bar," 33; "California Flush Times," 30, 31, 34; "A Cool Rejoinder," 33; "An Equitable Set-Off," 33; "Examining a Candidate for License," 33; *Flush Times of Alabama and Mississippi*, 11, 29–32, 34, 35; "How the Times Served the Virginians," 33; *Party Leaders* ..., 30, 31, 32, 35; "Samuel Hele, Esq. ...," 33; "Simon Suggs, Jr., Esq. ...," 33; "Squire A. and the Fritters," 33

Baldwin's Monthly, 458

"Ball, The" (Longstreet), 314

"Balloon Hoax" (Poe), 368, 376

Bandy, W. T., 381

Banister, John, 39, 40

Banks, Will, 262

Banner of the South, 12

Barbour, Philip L., 431–32

Barclay, Anthony, 525

Barlow, Arthur, 2

"Bar of the Southwest, The" (Baldwin), 33

Barth, John, 2, 3

Bartlett, Louisa (Mrs. G. W. Cable), 76

Bartow, Francis, 418

Bascomb, George, 473

Baskervill, William Malone, 356

Bassett, John S., 68

Bates, John, 251

Bathory, Zsigmond, 428

Battle of Bull Run, 23

Baudelaire, Charles, 378, 381

"Baxter's Procrustes" (Chesnutt), 109

Bayard, Chevalier, 399

Bayou Folk (Chopin), 134, 136

Bearskin, Ned, 66

Beatty, Richmond Croom, 68, 159, 363, 392, 410

Beaty, John O., 180

Beauchampe (Simms), 399, 404

Beauchamp-Sharpe murder case, 119

Beaufort College, 205

Beauregard, P. G. T., 532

Bedford, William, 194

Beeman, Richard R., 331, 333

Bell, Landon C., 128

"Belles Demoiselles Plantation" (Cable), 17, 80

"Belles of Williamsburg, The" (St. G. Tucker), 494

"Bells, The" (Poe), 370

"Bench and the Bar, The" (Baldwin), 33

Benjamin, Park, 442

Bennett, Emerson, 91

Benton, Joel, 128

Benton, Richard P., 381, 383

"Berenice" (Poe), 375

Berkeley, Sir William, 170

Bermudian, The, 493

Bernard, W. B., 90

Berthoff, Warner, 140, 301

Bertie, Peregrine, 427

Beulah (Wilson), 14, 531, 532–33, 539

Beverley, Anna, 324

Beverley, Nathaniel, 7

Beverley, Peter, 39

Beverley, Robert, *38–43*, xi, 3, 69, 325; bibliography, 41–43; biography, 38–39; criticism of, 41; major themes, 39–41. Works: *An Abridgement of the Publick Laws of Virginia* ..., 39, 41; *The History and Present State of Virginia*, 3, 38–40

Beverley, William, 323

"Beyond the Potomac" (Hayne), 245

"Bibi" (Cable), 80

Bickley, R. Bruce, Jr., 236

Bickman, Martin, 383

Bier, Jesse, 424

"Big Bear of Arkansas, The" (Thorpe), 10, 34, 453–56, 584, 460

Bill Arp: From the Uncivil War to Date (C. H. Smith), 420

Bill Arp, So Called (C. H. Smith), 11, 419, 420, 422

Bill Arp's Peace Papers (C. H. Smith), 420, 423

Bill Arp's Scrap Book (C. H. Smith), 420

Birth-Day Song of Liberty (Chivers), 119, 125

Bishop and the Boogerman, The (J. C. Harris), 231, 234

Bittner, William, 379

Black, William, 243

Black Belt Diamonds (Washington), 504, 507

"Black Cat, The" (Poe), 374

Black Man, The . . . (Brown), 48

Blackmore, R. D., 243–44

Black Poet, The (Horton), 262, 266

Blackstone's Commentaries (St. G. Tucker), 494

Blackwood's, 437

Blair, James, 40, 65

Blair, Walter, 35, 157–58, 224, 282, 319, 424, 448, 461–62

Bland, Richard, 4, 324

Bland, Theodorick, 324

Blankenship, Russell, 86

"Blue Dave" (J. C. Harris), 233

Bohner, Charles H., 188, 292–93

Bolling, Robert, 324

Bonaparte, Marie, 378–79

Bonaventure (Cable), 77

Bonner, Henry C., 390

Bonner, Sherwood, 339, 392

"Bonny Brown Hand, The" (Hayne), 244

Book News, 135

Book of My Lady (Simms), 397, 403

Boone, Daniel, 64, 404

Boorstin, Daniel J., 332–33

Border Beagles (Simms), 399

Border fiction, 401

"Border States, The" (Kennedy), 289

Bordley, Thomas, 166–67

"Boss Ankles . . . " (W. T. Thompson), 445

Boucher, Jonathan, 4

"Bouquet, The" (Chesnutt), 113

Bowers, Claude G., 273

Boyd, William K., 67

Boyesen, H. H., 76, 82

Boykin, Mary Whitaker, 97

Boyle, Charles, 66

Boyle, John, 63

Bracey, Susan L., 333

Bradley, Sculley, 159

Bragg, Lily, 539

Branch, Edgar M., 156

Branham, Joel, Jr., 419

Bransby, John, 365

Brantley, Mary, 251

Bratten, Mary Jo, 181

Brawley, Benjamin G., 265

Bridenbaugh, Carl, 332

British Empire in America, The, 39, 57

Broadway Journal, 8, 368

Brodie, Fawn M., 273

Brönte, Charlotte, 242

Brookes, Stella Brewer, 235–36

Brooks, Van Wyck, 155, 408

Brown, Sterling, 293, 520, 521

Brown, William Wells, *44–54*, xi, 9, 273; bibliography, 53–54; biography, 44–48; criticism of, 52–53; major themes, 49–52. Works: *The American Fugitive in Europe*, 48, 49; *The Black Man* . . . , 48; "Celebrated Colored Americans," 48; *Clotel; or, The President's Daughter*, 9, 47, 50–52; *The Escape* . . . , 48, 50; *Experience*, 52; *Memoir*, 48; *My Southern Home*, 48; *The Narrative of William W. Brown, A Fugitive Slave*, 9, 46, 50, 52; *The Negro in the American Rebellion* . . . , 48; *The Rising Son*, 48; *St. Domingo: Its Revolutions and Its Patriots*, 48; *Three Years in Europe*, 47

Browne, Ray B., 157

Browne, William Hand, 277–78, 283

Browning, Elizabeth Barrett, 22, 369, 437

Browning, Robert, 243, 437

Bruce, Anne Seddon, 351

Brugger, Robert J., 485, 490

Bry, Theodore de, 168

Bryant, William Cullen, 368, 397, 398, 437, 457

Bryer, Jackson, 202

Buck, Paul, 15

Budd, Louis J., 158

Bulwer, Edward, 35, 186, 400

"Burglars of Iola, The" (W. T. Thompson), 446

"Burial of Latane, The" (J. R. Thompson), 438

"Burial of the Guns" (Page), 356

Burke, Edmund, 35, 327

Burke, Kenneth, 208

Burns, Robert, 222, 495

Burton, William, 367

Burton's Magazine, 367

Burwell, Major, 57

Burwell, Willie Anne Corbin Taylor, 184

Burwell Papers, 3

Bush, Robert, 217, 282, 297, 300, 301, 410
Bushwhackers, The (Murfree), 340
Busy Man's Bible, The (Cable), 78
Butcher, Philip, 82
Butler, Broadus N., 511
Butler, Samuel, 168
Butterfield, Stephen, 200
Butterworth, Keen, 8, 410–11
Bylow Hill (Cable), 78, 82
Byrd, Mary Horsmanden Filmer, 55
Byrd, Otway, 325
Byrd, Ursula, 39
Byrd, William I, 2, 3
Byrd, William II, *55–74*, xi, 3, 35, 40, 323,
  325; bibliography, 72–74; biography, 55–61;
  criticism of, 67–72; major themes, 61–67.
  Works: "An Account of a Negro Boy
  . . . ," 56; *Another Secret Diary*, 59, 60,
  63, 65; "Cavaliero Sapiente," 63; *A Dis-
  course Concerning the Plague*, 59; "Dr.
  Glysterio," 63; "The Female Creed," 63,
  70; *The History of the Dividing Line*, 3, 60–
  63, 69–71; "Inamorato L'Oiseaux," 59, 65,
  71; *A Journey to the Land of Eden*, 3, 60,
  64; *Letters*, 60, 63–66; *The London Diary*,
  59, 64, 65; *Neu-gefundenes Eden(?)*, 60;
  "A Poem Upon Some Ladies At Tunbridge
  1700," 57; *A Progress to the Mines*, 3, 60;
  Secret Diary, 57, 59, 61, 63–67, 69, 71;
  The Secret History of the Line, 3, 60, 61,
  63–67, 69, 71; "A Song," 63; *Tunbrigalia*,
  59; "Upon a Fart," 63
Byron, Lord, George Gordon, 35, 222, 397,
  438, 464
"By the Grave of Henry Timrod" (Hayne), 244

Cabell, James Branch, 19
Cabell, Joseph C., 475, 495
Cable, George Washington, *75–85*, xi, 16, 18,
  108, 115, 230, 231, 242, 336, 339; bibliog-
  raphy, 83–85; biography, 75–78; criticism
  of, 82–83; major themes, 79–82. Works:
  "Belles Demoiselles Plantation," 17, 80;
  "Bibi," 80; *Bonaventure*, 77; *The Busy
  Man's Bible*, 78; *Bylow Hill*, 78, 82; *The
  Cavalier*, 78, 81; *The Churches and Chari-
  ties of New Orleans*, 76; *The Creoles of
  Louisiana*, 77; *Dr. Sevier*, 77, 79; "The
  Entomologist," 82; *The Flower of the
  Chapdelaines*, 78; "The Freedman's Case in
  Equity," 77, 81; *Gideon's Band*, 78, 80;
  The Grandissimes, 17, 76, 80, 83, 115;
  "The Great South," 76; "Jean-ah Poque-
  lin," 17, 79; *John March, Southerner*, 17,
  77, 78, 81; *Kincaid's Battery*, 78, 81; "Lit-
  erature in the Southern States," 81; *Lovers
  of Louisiana*, 78; *Madame Delphine*, 17,
  76, 80; "My Politics," 79, 80; *The Negro
  Question*, 17, 79, 80, 81; *Old Creole Days*,
  17, 76, 79; "Posson Jone'," 17; "'Sieur
  George," 17; *The Silent South*, 17, 77;
  "The Story of Bras-Coupé," 17, 80;
  Strange True Stories of Louisiana, 77;
  Strong Hearts, 78, 82
Cable, Rebecca Boardman, 75
Cain, 404
Cairns, William B., 247
Caldwell, Erskine, 236
Caldwell, Joseph, 260
Calhoun, John C., 206, 313, 484
"California Flush Times" (Baldwin), 30–31,
  34
Calvert, Benedict Leonard, 166–67
Calvert, Charles, 166
Cambridge History of American Literature,
  407
"Cambyses and the Macrobian Bow"
  (Hayne), 245
Campbell, Killis, 379, 380
"Canal Reminiscences" (Bagby), 26
Canby, Courtlandt, 332, 333
Candidates, The (Munford), 5, 325–33
Cannon, Carl L., 70
Cantwell, Robert, 140
Cape Fear *Recorder*, 250
Captain and the Colonel, The (Chesnutt), 15,
  101, 103
"Captain Stormfield's Visit to Heaven"
  (Twain), 158
Cardwell, Guy A., 83, 471
Careless Husband, The, 70
Carew, Thomas, 360
Carey, Henry, 288
Carleton, George W., 533
Carleton, Reese, 345
Carlson, Eric W., 8, 380, 383–84
Carlyle, Thomas, 437
"*Carmen Seculare* . . . " (St. G. Tucker), 495
"Carmen Triumphale" (Timrod), 470
Carnegie, Andrew, 78
"Carolina" (Timrod), 470
Carolina Sports by Land and Water (Elliott),
  207–9
Carpet Bag, 30

Carr, Dabney, 499

Carr, Frank, 499

Carrie, Caroline Love, 441

Carrington, Paul, 324

Carter, Everett, 159

Carter, Maria Ball, 474

Carter, Robert "King", 3

Caruthers, William Alexander, *86–95*, xi, 7, 293; bibliography, 93–95; biography, 86–88; criticism of, 92–93; major themes, 88–92. Works: *The Cavaliers*, 87–89, 91, 92; "Excerpts from the Portfolio of an Old Novelist," 88; *The Kentuckian in New-York*, 87, 89, 90, 92; *The Knights of the Golden Horse-Shoe*, 7, 88, 89, 92, 93, 485; *The Virginia Cavaliers*, 7; *Westward Ho!*, 87

Caruthers Affair, The (Harben), 214

Cary, Richard, 345

Cash, W. J., 356

"Cask of Amontillado, The" (Poe), 369, 373

Cassique of Accabee, The (Simms), 399

Cassique of Kiawah, The (Simms), 397, 400, 403, 405

Castle Dismal (Simms), 399

Catesby, Mark, 65

Cather, Willa, 297

Catholic World, 336

Catt, Carrie Chapman, 353

Cavalier, The (Cable), 78, 81

"Cavaliero Sapiente" (Byrd), 63

Cavalier Poet, 182, 363

Cavaliers of Virginia, The (Caruthers), 87–89, 91–92

Cecil, Moffitt L., 410

"Celebrated Colored Americans" (Brown), 48

Celebrated Jumping Frog . . . , The (Twain), 145

Centenary College, 314

Centennial Edition of the Works of Sidney Lanier, 309

Centennial Meditation of Columbia (Lanier), 306

Century Hence, A (G. Tucker), 477, 479

Century Magazine, 17, 77, 296

Cervantes, Miguel, 222

Chamberlayne, Churchill Gibson, 27

Chamberlayne, Lewis Parke, 528

Champion, The (Murfree), 340

Chandler, Maybelle, 213

"Character of a Native Georgian, The" (Longstreet), 314, 318

Charlemont (Simms), 404

"Charleston" (Hayne), 243, 245, 419

"Charleston" (Timrod), 13, 470

Charleston *City Gazette*, 401

Charleston *Mercury*, 24

"Charming Creature as a Wife, The" (Longstreet), 314, 316

Chase-Ribaud, Barbara, 273

Chaucer, Geoffrey, 242, 460

Chesnut, James, Jr., 15, 97–101, 103

Chesnut, Mary Boykin, *96–106*, xi, 14; bibliography, 105–6; biography, 96–102; criticism of, 104–5; major themes, 102–4. Works: *The Captain and the Colonel*, 15, 101, 103; *A Diary from Dixie*, 14, 96, 102, 104; *Manassas*, 15, 101; *Mary Chesnut's Civil War*, 14, 15, 96, 101–5; *The Private Mary Chesnut: The Unpublished Civil War Diaries*, 96; *Two Years: or The Way We Lived Then*, 15, 101

Chesnutt, Andrew Jackson, 107

Chesnutt, Charles Waddell, *107–17*, xi, 15, 16, 18, 200, 520; bibliography, 116–17; biography, 107–10; criticism of, 116; major themes, 110–15. Works: "Baxter's Procrustes," 109; "The Bouquet," 113; *The Colonel's Dream*, 18, 109, 114, 115; "The Conjurer's Revenge," 11; *The Conjure Woman*, 18, 108, 110, 111; "The Goophered Grapevine," 18, 108, 110; "The Gray Wolf's Ha'nt," 111; "Her Virginia Mammy," 111, 112; "Hot-Foot Hannibal," 111; *The House Behind the Cedars*, 18, 108, 113, 115; *The Marrow of Tradition*, 18, 109, 114; "Mars Jeems's Nightmare," 111; "A Matter of Principle," 112; "The Sheriff's Children," 112, 113; "Sis's Becky's Pickaninny," 111; "Uncle Wellington's Wives," 112; "The Web of Circumstance," 112, 113; "The Wife of His Youth," 108, 111, 112; *The Wife of His Youth and Other Stories . . .* , 108, 111, 112

Chesnutt, Helen M., 116

Chevalier Merlin, The (P. P. Cooke), 187

Chilton, Edward, 40

Chilton, W. P., 252

"Chinese Serenade" (Chivers), 126

Chivers, Thomas Holley, *118–31*, xii, 6, 369; bibliography, 130–31; biography, 118–19; criticism of, 128–30; major themes, 119–28. Works: "The Angelus," 125; *Atala*, 119, 121; "Atala's Prayer," 120; *Atlanta . . .* , 124; "Awake from Thy Slumber," 122;

Birth-Day Song of Liberty, 119, 125; "Chinese Serenade," 126; *Concha*, 122; *Conrad and Eudora*, 119, 125; "Corn Shucking Song," 127; *Eonchs of Ruby*, 119, 122, 123–25, 129; "Isadore," 129; "Lament on the Death of My Mother," 129; *Les Natchez*, 119; "Lord Uther's Lament for Ella," 123; *The Lost Pleiad*, 121, 122, 125, 128; *Memoralia*, 119, 124; "The Mighty Dead," 123; *Nacoochee*, 119–21, 124, 128; "No More," 129; *Path of Sorrow*, 119, 120, 125, 126; "The Poet," 124; "Railroad Song," 126; "The Retrospect," 126; *Search After Truth*, 119, 120; "The Soaring Swan," 121; "To Allegra Florence in Heaven," 129; "The Virgil of Aiden," 122; *Virginalia*, 119, 124, 125

Chopin, Kate, *132–43*, xi, 16, 18, 337; bibliography, 141–42; biography, 132–35; criticism of, 140–41; major themes, 135–40. Works: *At Fault*, 134–36; "Athénaïse," 138; *Awakening, The*, 18, 133–35, 138, 140, 337; *Bayou Folk*, 134, 136; "Désirée's Baby," 137; "Emancipation: A Life Fable," 135; "If It Might Be," 134; *A Night in Acadie*, 134, 137, 138; "A Point at Issue," 134, 136; "A Respectable Woman," 137; "The Storm," 18, 140; "The Story of an Hour," 18, 137; "Wiser Than God," 134, 136; "Young Doctor Gosse," 135

Chopin, Oscar, 132

Christian Science (Twain), 155

Christie, Anne M., 424

Christmas Night in the Quarters (Russell), 14, 392

Chronicle of Aunt Minery Ann, The (J. C. Harris), 230

"Chronicle of Young Satan, The" (Twain), 148, 153

Chronicles of Pineville (W. T. Thompson), 442, 445, 447

"Churches and Charities of New Orleans, The" (Cable), 76

Cibber, Colley, 70

"City in the Sea, The" (Poe), 9, 366, 372

Civil War, 5, 11, 15, 48, 96, 104, 175–76, 179–81, 248, 282, 299, 300, 308, 351, 356, 402, 421–22, 431, 442, 470

Civil War (Chesnut), 15

Clark, Lewis Gaylord, 119, 398, 406, 453

Clasby, Nancy T., 200

Clay, Henry, 252, 477, 484, 485

Clemens, John Marshall, 144

Clemens, Olivia, 149

Clemens, Samuel Langhorne [Mark Twain. References to individual entries in the index will appear as "Twain."], *144–64*, xi, 2, 4, 10–13, 20, 77, 79, 82, 115, 222, 230, 235, 237, 279, 282, 297, 338, 352, 448; bibliography, 159–64; biography, 144–49; criticism of, 155–59; major themes, 149–55. Works: *Adventures of Huckleberry Finn*, 12, 146, 148, 149, 151, 152, 157, 158, 222; *The Adventures of Tom Sawyer*, 12, 145, 149, 151, 158; *An American Claimant*, 146, 152; "As from the Grave," 148; *The Autobiography of Mark Twain*, 157; "Captain Stormfield's Visit to Heaven," 158; *The Celebrated Jumping Frog ...*, 145; "The Chronicle of Young Satan," 148, 153; *Collected Letters*, 156; *A Connecticut Yankee in King Arthur's Court*, 146, 152, 153, 157, 159; "Corn Pone Opinions," 153; "The Death of Jean," 149; *Early Tales and Sketches*, 156; "Early Times," 148; *Extract from Captain Stormfield's Visit to Heaven*, 149; "The Facts Concerning the Carnival of Crime in Connecticut," 155; "A Family Sketch," 157; *Following the Equator*, 147, 157; *The Gilded Age*, 145, 146, 151; "Huck Finn and Tom Sawyer Among the Indians," 150; *The Innocents Abroad*, 145, 150, 151; "Jim Smiley and His Jumping Frog," 145; *King Leopold's Soliloquy*, 148; "Letters from the Earth," 149; *Letters from the Earth*, 153; *Life on the Mississippi*, 12, 145, 146, 151, 157; "Man's Place in the Animal World," 154; "The Man That Corrupted Hadleyburg," 12, 154; *Mark Twain's Autobiography*, 157; *The Mysterious Stranger*, 153, 156; "No. 44, The Mysterious Stranger," 148, 154; "Old Times on the Mississippi," 12, 144, 146, 149; *Personal Recollections of Joan of Arc*, 147; *The Prince and the Pauper*, 146, 150–52, 154; *Pudd'nhead Wilson*, 2, 12, 115, 147, 152, 154, 157; "Reflections on Religion," 153; *Roughing It*, 145, 150; "A Singular Episode," 157; "Those Extraordinary Twins," 154; *Tom Sawyer Abroad*, 147, 150, 157; "Tom Sawyer's Conspiracy," 148, 150; "To the Person Sitting in Darkness," 148; *The Tragedy of Pudd'nhead Wilson*, 147; *A Tramp Abroad*, 146–47, 152; "A True Story," 12;

"The War Prayer," 148; "What is Man?,"
    148, 153–54; *What is Man? . . .*, 154;
    "Which Was It?," 148
Clemm, Maria, 379
Cleveland, Grover, 354
Clinton, George, 474
"Closing In" (Hayne), 244
Clotel; or, The President's Daughter (Brown),
    9, 47, 50–52
Cobbs, John L., 266
Cocke, William Archer, 91
Coers, Donald V., 172
Cohen, Edward H., 172
Cohen, Henig, 253, 449, 458, 461
Coleman, Charles, W., Jr., 282, 300
Coleman, Mary Haldane, 500
"Coliseum, The" (Poe), 367
Colista, Donald, 510
Collected Letters (Twain), 156
Collection of Plays and Poems, A (Munford),
    330
College of Charleston, 396
College of William and Mary, 2, 268
Collins, Carvel, 181
Collins, Wilkie, 243, 437
Collins, William, 397
Collinson, Peter, 60, 65
"Colloquy of Monus and Una, The" (Poe),
    373, 377
Colonel's Dream, The (Chesnutt), 18, 109,
    114–15
Columbinus: A Mask, 493
Commager, Henry Steele, 273
Complete Works, The (Poe), 9, 379
Complete Works of Captain John Smith, The,
    432
Concha (Chivers), 122
Conchologist's First Book, The (Poe), 367
Confession (Simms), 399, 404
"Confessions of an Officeholder" (Kennedy),
    287
Congreve, William, 222
Conjectures and Researches . . . (Wilde), 525
"Conjurer's Revenge, The" (Chesnutt), 111
Conjure Woman, The (Chesnutt), 18, 108,
    110–11
Connecticut Yankee in King Arthur's Court, A
    (Twain), 146, 152, 157, 159
"Conquered Banner, The" (Ryan), 12
"Conqueror Worm, The" (Poe), 368, 373
Conrad, Joseph, 374
Conrad and Eudora (Chivers), 119, 125

Constitutionalist (Augusta), 11, 241
Coogler, J. Gordon, 11
Cook, Andrew, 165
Cook, Anne Bowyer, 165
Cook, Ebenezer, *165–73*, xi, 3, 4; bibliog-
    raphy, 172–73; biography, 165–67; criticism
    of, 171–72; major themes, 167–71. Works:
    "An Elegy on the Death of the Honorable
    Nicholas Lowe," 167; *ELOGY*, 165–57;
    "History of Nathaniel Bacon's Rebellion in
    Virginia," 167, 168, 170, 171; "In Mem-
    ory . . . ," 166; *The Maryland Muse*, 4,
    167, 171; *The Sot-Weed Factor*, 3–4, 165–
    72; *Sotweed Redivivus*, 167–69; "A Voyage
    to Maryland" (*The Sot-Weed Factor*), 168
Cook, Edward, 166
Cook, Sylvia Jenkins, 320
Cooke, John Esten, *174–83*, 7, 90, 92, 242,
    243, 398, 406, 409, 436; bibliography,
    182–83; biography, 174–77; criticism of,
    180–82; major themes, 177–80. Works: *El-
    lie*, 175; *Fairfax*, 181; *Hammer and Rapier*,
    176; *The Heir of Gaymount*, 7, 176; *Henry
    St. John, Gentleman*, 7, 175; *Her Majesty
    the Queen*, 176; *Leather Stocking and Silk*,
    7, 175, 181; *Life of Stonewall Jackson*, 176;
    Mohun, 7, 176, 179–80; *Pretty Mrs. Gas-
    ton*, 176; *Surry of Eagle's Nest*, 7, 176,
    179, 181; *Virginia: A History of the People*,
    176, 177; *The Virginia Comedians*, 7, 175–
    76, 178–79; *Wearing the Gray*, 176
Cooke, Philip Pendleton, *184–89*, 6, 175, 369,
    378, 436; bibliography, 188–89; biography,
    184–86; criticism of, 187–88; major themes,
    186–87. Works: *The Chevalier Merlin*, 187;
    The Crime of Andrew Blair, 186, 187;
    "Florence Vane," 184, 186; *Froissart Bal-
    lads, and Other Poems*, 185, 187; "Geof-
    frey Tetenoire," 187; *The Gregories of
    Hackwood*, 186, 187; *John Carper, the
    Hunter of Lost River*, 187; "The Last In-
    dian," 187; "The Master of Bolton," 187;
    "The Murder of Cornstalk," 187; "The
    Song of the Sioux Lovers," 187; *Two
    Country Houses*, 186
Cooley, Thomas, 159
"Cool Rejoinder, A" (Baldwin), 33
Cooper, James Fenimore, 63, 64, 89, 175,
    186–87, 212, 242, 291–92, 310, 368, 398,
    408
Cooper, John M., 442
"Corn" (Lanier), 13, 305

"Cornfield Peas" (Bagby), 26
"Corn Pone Opinions" (Twain), 153
"Corn Shucking Song" (Chivers), 127
"Cortes and the Conquest of Mexico"
 (Simms), 403
Cortez, Hernando, 404
Cosmopolitan, 409, 437
Cosway, Maria, 269, 271
Cottage of Delight, The (Harben), 216–17
Cotton, Robert, 429
"Cotton Boll, The" (Timrod), 13, 465, 469
Countryman, 228
Couser, G. Thomas, 199
"Cousin in Berlin, A" (C. H. Smith), 420
Cousins, Paul M., 236
Covey, Edward, 200
Cowie, Alexander, 89, 181, 345, 408, 538
Cowper, William, 495, 530
Cox, James M., 156, 462
Craddock, Charles Egbert. *See* Mary Noailles
 Murfree
Craft, Ellen, 47
Craft, William, 47
Craigie, William A., 89
Crane, Stephen, 231
Creation of the American Republic 1776–1787,
 The, 327
"Creed of a Rioteer," 327
Creoles of Louisiana, The (Cable), 77
Crime of Andrew Blair, The (P. P. Cooke),
 186–87
Crisis, 328
Crisis, The, 109
Crockett, David, 90
Cromwell, Elizabeth, 56
Cruse, Peter Hoffman, 287
"Cry to Arms, A" (Timrod), 13, 470
"Cub of the Panther, The" (Simms), 402
Current-Garcia, Eugene, 36, 224, 461
Currie, George, 324
Custis, John, 59
Cutting, Rose Marie, 67
Cyclopaedia of American Literature, 209

Daddy Jake the Runaway (J. C. Harris), 230,
 233
Daily Herald (Savannah), 443
Daly, Augustin, 350, 353
Damon, S. Foster, 128
Damsel of Darien, The (Simms), 7, 398, 403
"Dance, The" (Longstreet), 314
"Dancin' Party at Harrison's Cave, The"
 (Murfree), 337–38, 341, 342, 344

Dandridge, William, 62
Daniel, John Moncure, 436
Dante, 186
Dante and His Influence (Page), 354
Darby, John, 100
Darley, Felix O. C., 442, 454
Davidson, Donald, 409–10
Davidson, Edward H., 380, 382
Davidson, James Wood, 319
Davidson, Olivia, 504
Davis, Arthur, 52, 520, 521
Davis, Charles T., 199
Davis, Jefferson, 15, 98, 99, 418
Davis, Rebecca Harding, 338
Davis, Richard Beale, 4, 40, 67, 69–70, 172,
 293, 363, 392, 500
Davis, Varina, 98, 100
Davis, Warren R., 288
Dawson, William, 4
Day, Donald, 224
Dayan, Joan, 383
Deane, Charles, 431, 531
"Death of Jean, The" (Twain), 149
"Debating Society, The" (Longstreet), 314,
 316
De Bellis, Jack, 13, 309, 471
De Bow's Review, 91, 406
Defense of the Whigs (Kennedy), 289
Defoe, Daniel, 2
DeForest, John William, 406–7
Delaware College, 21
Dembry, R. Emmet, 338
Dennis, Mary Cable, 82
De Pietro, Thomas, 201
De Quincey, Thomas, 360
Derby, J. C., 532, 538
"Descent into the Maelstrom, A" (Poe), 368,
 372
Description of New England, A (J. Smith),
 429–31
Desired Woman, The (Harben), 215
"Désirée's Baby" (Chopin), 137
De Soto, Hernando, 403
Despot of Broomsedge Cove, The (Murfree),
 344
"Devil's Summer Retreat, The" (Thorpe), 454
Devota (Wilson), 534
De Voto, Bernard, 148, 155, 157, 254, 314
Dew, Thomas R., 485
Diary from Dixie, A (Chesnut), 14, 96, 102,
 104
Dickens, Charles, 21, 30, 35, 47, 222, 242,
 289, 344, 368, 437

DiCosenza, Marchesa Manfredina, 526
Didier, Eugene L., 362
Dillingham, William P., 253, 449, 458, 461
Discourse Concerning the Plague, A (Byrd),
  59
"Disgraced Scalp-Lock, The" (Thorpe), 454
Dissertation on Slavery (St. G. Tucker), 6,
  479, 493
Divine Event, The (Harben), 216
"Division of an Estate" (Horton), 9, 261, 265
Dixie Hart (Harben), 215
Dixon, Thomas, 109, 231
"Dr. Glysterio" (Byrd), 63
Dr. Sevier (Cable), 77, 79
Dodge, Mabel Mapes, 157
Dog and Gun . . . (Hooper), 251
Doings of Gotham (Poe), 368
Dolmetsch, Carl R., 6, 70, 500
"Domain of Arnheim, The" (Poe), 376
Donna Florida (Simms), 399, 403
Donne, John, 429
Dorr, Julia C. R., 247
Dorsey, Walter, 286
Dos Passos, John, 273, 289
Dostoevsky, Fyodor, 378
Douglass, Frederick, *190–204*, xi, 9, 18, 46,
  50, 520; bibliography, 202–4; biography,
  190–95; criticism of, 198–202; major
  themes, 195–98. Works: "The Heroic
  Slave," 194, 196, 198, 201; *Life and Times
  of Frederick Douglass*, 190, 195, 197, 198;
  My Bondage and My Freedom, 190, 194,
  195, 197, 198, 200, 201; *Narrative of the
  Life of Frederick Douglass . . .* , 9, 190,
  195–200
Douglass' Monthly, 194
Down the Ravine (Murfree), 339
Draper, Lyman C., 292
"Dream, A" (Poe), 371
"Dream, A" (St. G. Tucker), 498
"Dreamer, The (St. G. Tucker), 499
"Dreams" (Poe), 371
"Dream Within a Dream, A" (Poe), 371
Dreiser, Theodore, 231, 297
Drifted Leaves (Whitman), 516
"Drifting Down Lost Creek" (Murfree), 338,
  343
"Dropping to Sleep" (Longstreet), 314
Dryden, John, 40
Du Bois, W.E.B., 109, 508, 522
"Duel, The" (W. T. Thompson), 445
Duffy, Charles, 247

Duke, Maurice, 202
Dukesborough Tales (Johnston), 17, 277–80,
  282
Duke University Library, 356
Dulaney, Daniel, 4, 166
Dumas, Alexandre, 186, 297
Dunbury, Joseph, 427
Duneka, Frederick A., 153
Dunglison, Robley, 477
Dunn, Dorwood, 345
Duyckinck, Evert A., 362, 369, 378, 406
Duyckinck, George L., 362
Dyckman, Sarah, 435

"Early Educational Life in Middle Georgia"
  (Johnston), 279
Early Lays (Simms), 397
Early Tales and Sketches (Twain), 156
"Early Times" (Twain), 148
East Alabamian (LaFayette), 251, 252
"Easter" (Hayne), 244
Eaton, Clement, 282
Eaves, T. C. Duncan, 408
Eble, Kenneth, 140
Eddings, Dennis W., 383
Eddis, William, 4
Edgar Allan Poe: Selected Prose and Poetry,
  378
Edgehill School, 21
Edwards, Harry Stillwell, 111
Eggleston, George Cary, 175–76, 180
Ekstrom, Kjell, 82
"Eldorado" (Poe), 370
"Electioneering on Big Injun Mounting"
  (Murfree), 343
"Elegy on the Death of the Honorable Nicho-
  las Lowe, An" (E. Cook), 167
"Eleonora" (Poe), 368, 376
Eliot, George, 242, 339
Eliot, T. S., 247, 378
Ellie (J. E. Cooke), 175
Elliott, Charles Loving, 452, 457
Elliott, William, *205–11*; bibliography, 210–
  11; biography, 205–8; criticism of, 209–10;
  major themes, 208–9. Works: *Address to the
  People of St. Helena Parish*, 206, 208; *Car-
  olina Sports by Land and Water*, 207–9;
  Fiesco: A Tragedy, 207; "The Fire
  Hunter," 209; *The Letters of Agricola*, 207
Ellison, Curtis W., 52
Ellison, Ralph, 237
Ellison, Rhoda Coleman, 292
ELOGY (E. Cook), 166

"Emancipation: A Life Fable" (Chopin), 135
Emanuel, James A., 520
Emerson, Everett, 12, 156, 432
Emerson, Ralph Waldo, 120, 350, 373, 382, 531
Emory College, 314
Engel, Leonard, 383
English, Thomas Dunn, 369, 392, 436
English Classics, The . . . (Johnston), 278
"Entomologist, The" (Cable), 82
Eonchs of Ruby (Chivers), 119, 122, 124–25, 129
"Epimanes" (Poe), 367
"Equitable Set-Off, An" (Baldwin), 33
Erskine, John, 407
Erskine Honeymoon, The (Murfree), 340
Escape, The . . . (Brown), 48, 50
Essay on Cause and Effect (G. Tucker), 477
Essays, Moral and Metaphysical (G. Tucker), 477
Essays on the Ten Plagues . . . (Whitman), 515, 516
Essays on Various Subjects . . . (G. Tucker), 475
Essay Toward Facilitating Instruction, An . . . (Jefferson), 271
Estes, David C., 448
Estill, John Holbrook, 443
"Ethnogenesis" (Timrod), 13, 465, 469
Eureka (Poe), 369, 371, 374–75, 377, 378, 381–82
Eutaw (Simms), 8, 400
Evans, Virginia Young, 20
Evening Mirror, 368
"Evening Star" (Poe), 371
Evening Tales, 1893 (J. C. Harris), 230
"Evergreens" (Pinkney), 361
"Examining a Candidate for License" (Baldwin), 33
"Excerpts from the Portfolio of an Old Novelist" (Caruthers), 88
Experience . . . (Brown), 52
Extract from Captain Stormfield's Visit to Heaven (Twain), 149

"Fable, A" (St. G. Tucker), 496
"Face to Face" (Hayne), 244–45
"Facts Concerning the Carnival of Crime in Connecticut, The" (Twain), 155
"Facts in the Case of Monsieur Valdemar" (Poe), 376
Fairfax (J. E. Cooke), 181
Fair Mississippian, The (Murfree), 340

"Fairy Hill . . . " (St. G. Tucker), 497
"Fall of the House of Usher, The" (Poe), 9, 367, 375, 382, 383
Family Companion and Ladies' Mirror, 41, 449
"Family Sketch, A" (Twain), 157
"Farewell to America" (Wilde), 526
"Farewell to Frances" (Horton), 261
Farley, Mary Byrd, 474
Farm and the Fireside, The (C. H. Smith), 420
Farrell, Hubert, 170
Farris, Eliza, 132
Farrison, William Edward, 52, 266
Fatout, Paul, 158
Faulkner, William, xi, 9, 11, 13, 115, 220, 224, 237, 290, 312, 356
Fawcett, Edgar, 243
Fay, Fanny, 379
Federalist, The, 4
Felton, Cornelius, 406
"Female Creed, The" (Byrd), 63, 70
Ferguson, De Lancey, 155
Fetterley, Judith, 158
Fidler, William Perry, 539
Field, Eugene, 230
Field, Florence Lathrop, 351
Field, Henry, 353, 356
Field, Marshall, 351
Fiesco: A Tragedy (Elliott), 207
Figh, Margaret Gillis, 424
"Fight, The" (Longstreet), 10, 314, 317
Finch, Anne, 63
"Fire-Hunt, The" (W. T. Thompson), 445
"Fire Hunter, The" (Elliott), 209
Fischer, Victor, 159
Fisher, Benjamin Franklin IV, 383
"Fishing in the Appomattox" (Bagby), 21
Fishwick, Marshall, 181
Fitzgerald, Oscar P., 319
Fitzwilliam, Richard, 62
"Five Chapters to a History" (Johnston), 278
Flag of Our Union, 370
Flag of the Union, The, 292
Flanders, Bertram H., 449
Fletcher, Richard M., 381
Flint, Timothy, 458
"Flirts and Their Ways" (Murfree), 338
"Florence Vane" (P. P. Cooke), 184
Flower of the Chapdelaines, The (Cable), 78
Flush Times of Alabama and Mississippi (Baldwin), 11, 29–32, 34, 35

"Folio Club, The" (Poe), 376
"Folklore of the Southern Negroes" (J. C. Harris), 229
Following the Equator (Twain), 147, 157
Fontaine, John, 41
"For Annie" (Poe), 370, 376
Forayers . . . , The (Simms), 8, 400
Forclaz, Roger, 379, 381
Ford, Thomas W., 319
"Forest Maiden, The" (Simms), 403
"Forget Me Not" (Wilde), 526
Forman, Henry Chandlee, 293
Forrest, Mary, 538
Forrest, Nathan Bedford, 75
Forrest, William Mentzel, 380
Fortune, T. Thomas, 505, 507
Fosdick, Jane, 457
Foster, Francis Smith, 199
Foster, Stephen, 122, 127
"Fox Hunt, The" (Longstreet), 314
Franklin, Benjamin, 165, 199, 269, 505
Franklin, H. Bruce, 200
Frederick Douglass (Washington), 505, 509
"Freedman's Case in Equity, The" (Cable), 77
"Freedman's Triumphant Song, The" (Whitman), 516, 518
Freedom's Journal, 259
"Free Joe" (J. C. Harris), 233
Free Joe and Other Georgian Sketches (J. C. Harris), 6, 230, 234
Freeman, Mary Wilkins, 336–37
French and Indian Wars, 403
French realists, 297
French symbolists, 9
Friedman, Laurence J., 510
Froissart, Jean, 187
Froissart Ballads, and Other Poems (P. P. Cooke), 185, 187
From Clue to Climax (Harben), 214
"From the Woods" (Hayne), 244
Frontiersman, The (Murfree), 340
Fruit of Desire, The (Harben), 215
Fugitive Slave Act, 47
Fuller, Margaret, 378
Fuller, Thomas, 431
Future of the American Negro, The (Washington), 504, 507

Gabin, Jane S., 14, 309
Gabriel Tolliver (J. C. Harris), 231, 234
Gadsden, Christopher, 4
Gaines, Ernest, 237

Gaines, Francis Pendleton, 181, 293
Gale, Robert L., 159
Gales, Joseph, 259
Gales, Weston Raleigh, 259
"Gander Pulling, The" (Longstreet), 314, 318
Gargano, James, 382–83
Garmon, Gerald M., 439
Garrison, William Lloyd, 46, 194, 260
Gates, Henry Louis, Jr., 199
Gates, Jane Miller Singleton, 395–96
Gayarre, Charles, 243, 247
Generall Historie of Virginia . . . , The (J. Smith), 2, 429, 430
"Genius and Character of Edgar Allan Poe, The" (J. R. Thompson), 436
Gentlemen's Magazine, 185, 367
"Geoffrey Tetenoire" (P. P. Cooke), 187
George Balcombe (N. B. Tucker), 485–87
Georgia, University of, 278, 417
Georgians, The (Harben), 215
Georgia Scenes (Longstreet), 5, 10, 312–17, 319, 441, 447
Georgia Sketches (Johnston), 17, 278
"Georgia Theatrics" (Longstreet), 10, 314, 316–17
"Gertrude" (N. B. Tucker), 485
"Getting Married" (Bagby), 24
Gibson, Louise Catherine, 86
Gibson, William M., 156, 157
Gideon's Band (Cable), 78, 80
Gilbert Neal (Harben), 215
Gilded Age, The (Twain), 145–46, 151
Gilder, Richard Watson, 15, 76, 296, 390
Giles, Anna Malcolm, 396
Gilmer, Gertrude, 449
Girardin, Louis, 499
Gist, Mordecai, 325
Glasgow, Ellen, 8, 19, 115, 353
Glasscock, Christopher, 55–56
Gloster, Hugh, 265
Godey's Lady's Book, 367, 455
Gohdes, Clarence, 319
"Gold Bug, The" (Poe), 368, 376
Golden Age of Virginia, 177
Golden Christmas (Simms), 400, 404
Goldsmith, Oliver, 442, 495, 519
Goldstein, Michael, 510–11
Gompers, Samuel, 353
Gone with the Wind, 16
Gonzales, Ambrose Elliott, 207
"Good Eating" (Bagby), 21, 24
Goodman, Jennifer Robin, 432,

Goodwin, Katie, 466
Goodwin, Norma Lee, 490
"Goophered Grapevine, The" (Chesnutt), 18, 108, 110
Gordon, A. C., 350
Gordon Keith (Page), 352, 354–56
Gosnold, Bartholomew, 428
Gosse, Edmund, 350, 378
"Goth, A" (Page), 353
Gould, James, 313
Grady, Henry, 212, 230, 419, 422
Graham, George, 367, 368
Graham, Philip, 309
Graham, William, 289
Graham's, 185, 240, 368
Grandissimes, The (Cable), 17, 76, 80, 83, 115
Grant, Ulysses S., 146
"Grave, The" (Pinckney), 361
Graves, C. M., 438
Gray, Annie Elizabeth, 48, 287
Gray, Thomas, 495
"Grayling" (Simms), 403
Grayson, Louis, 476
"Gray Wolf's Ha'nt, The" (Chesnutt), 111
"Great South, The" (Cable), 76
"Great Strike, The" (Whitman), 518
Greeley, Horace, 260
Greene, Nathaniel, 8, 403
Greenough, Horatio, 525
Greenwood, F.W.P., 362
Gregories of Hackwood, The (P. P. Cooke), 186–87
Gregory, Eileen, 104
Gresham, John, 167
Gribben, Alan, 158, 320
Griffin, Benjamin F., 441
Griffin, Sarah, 91
Grigsby, Hugh Blair, 91
Griska, Joseph, 237
Griswold, Rufus W., 185, 331, 368, 378, 406, 436, 527
Gronberg, Douglas C., 528
Gross, Theodore L., 356, 520
Guilds, John C., 409–10
Gummere, Richard M., 70
Guy Rivers (Simms), 8, 397–98, 403

Habegger, Alfred, 539
Hahn, Michael, 457
Hakluyt, Richard, 430
Hall, James C., 27
Hall, Wade, 27, 282, 424

Halliburton, David, 382
Hamerick, Asger, 305
Hamilton, Alexander, 6, 35
Hammer and Rapier (J. E. Cooke), 176
Hammond, Alexander, 380
Hammond, James Henry, 398, 485
Harben, Will N., *212–19*; bibliography, 218–19; biography, 212–16; criticism of, 217–18; major themes, 216–17. Works: *Almost Persuaded*, 213, 215, 216; *Ann Boyd*, 215; *The Caruthers Affair*, 214; *The Cottage of Delight*, 216, 217; *The Desired Woman*, 215; *The Divine Event*, 216; *Dixie Hart*, 215; *From Clue to Climax*, 214; *The Fruit of Desire*, 215; *The Georgians*, 215; *Gilbert Neal*, 215; *The Hills of Refuge*, 216; *The Inner Law*, 215; *Jane Dawson*, 215, 217; *Kenneth Galt*, 215; *The Land of the Changing Sun*, 213, 217; *Mam' Linda*, 215, 217; *A Mute Confessor*, 213; *The New Clarion*, 215; *The North Walk Mystery*, 214; *Northern Georgia Sketches*, 214; "Old Buckskin . . . ," 212; *Paul Rundel*, 215; *Pole Baker*, 215; *The Redemption of Kenneth Galt*, 215; *Second Choice*, 215; *The Substitute*, 215; *The Triumph*, 215–17; *Westerfelt*, 214; "White Jane," 213; *White Marie*, 213; *The Woman Who Trusted*, 214
Hardendorff, Victor H., 247
Hariot, Thomas, 2, 168
Harkey, Joseph H., 319
Harian, Louis, 504, 510
Harlem Renaissance, 265
"Harnt' That Walks Chilhowee, The" (Murfree), 7, 337, 339, 342
Harper, Frances E. Watkins, 514
Harper's Magazine, 22, 407, 456
Harrell, Laura D. S., 393
Harris, George Washington, *220–26*, 13, 312, 336–39; bibliography, 225–26; biography, 220–21; criticism of, 224–25; major themes, 221–24. Works: "High Times and Hard Times," 223; *High Times and Hard Times*, 224; "The Knob Dance—A Tennessee Frolic," 222; *Sut Lovingood . . .* , 10, 13, 26, 223; "Sut Lovingood's Daddy, Acting Horse," 222; *Sut Lovingood's Yarns*, 224–25
Harris, Joel Chandler, *227–39*, 11, 14, 16, 27, 79, 111, 209, 212, 214, 336, 339, 389, 391, 392, 423, 448; bibliography, 237–393; biography, 227–32; criticism of, 235–37;

major themes, 232–235. Works: *Balaam and His Master*, 230, 233; *The Bishop and the Boogerman*, 231, 234; "Blue Dave," 233; *The Chronicles of Aunt Minery Ann*, 230; "Daddy Jake the Runaway," 233; *Daddy Jake the Runaway*, 230; *Evening Tales, 1893*, 230; "Folklore of the Southern Negroes," 229; "Free Joe," 233; *Free Joe and Other Georgian Sketches*, 16, 230, 234; *Gabriel Tolliver*, 231, 234; "Jeems Robinson," 229; "The Kidnapping of President Lincoln," 230; "Literature of the South," 230; *A Little Union Scout*, 231; "Mingo," 234; *Mingo and Other Sketches*, 230, 234; "Mom Bi," 233; *Nights with Uncle Remus*, 230; *On the Plantation*, 230, 236; *On the Wing of Occasions*, 230, 234; *Qua: A Romance of the Revolution*, 230; *The Romance of Rockville*, 229; *The Shadow Between His Shoulder Blades*, 231, 234; *Sister Jane*, 230, 236; *Stories of Georgia*, 230; "The Story of Mr. Rabbit and Mr. Fox," 229; *Tales of the Home Folks in Peace and War*, 230; *The Tar Baby and Other Rhymes*, 231; *Told by Uncle Remus*, 231; *Uncle Remus and His Friends*, 230–31; "Uncle Remus as a Rebel," 229; *Uncle Remus: His Songs and His Sayings*, 16, 229, 232, 235; *Uncle Remus's Magazine*, 231
Harris, Julia Collier, 236
Harris, Benjamin, 40
Harrison, James A., 128, 379
Harte, Bret, 336
Hartwell, Henry, 40
Harvard College, 2
Harvard University, 289
"Harvest Time" (Hayne), 245
Harwell, Richard Barksdale, 181
Hatch, Alden, 69
Hauck, Richard Boyd, 461
Hawkins, Hugh, 510
Hawkins, Mary, 359, 361
Hawthorne, Nathaniel, 9, 91, 242, 291, 297, 368, 377, 382, 438
Haycraft, Howard, 408
Hayhoe, George, 105
Hayne, Barrie, 461
Hayne, Emily McElhenney, 240
Hayne, Mary Middleton Michel, 244
Hayne, Paul Hamilton, *240–49*, xii, 13, 24, 398, 406–7, 465; bibliography, 248–49; biography, 240–43; criticism of, 246–48; ma-

jor themes, 243–46. Works: "An Anniversary," 244; "Ante-Bellum Charleston," 407; "Arolio," 244; *Arolio: A Legend of the Island of Cos*, 241; "The Ashley at the Battery," 243; "Aspects of the Pines," 244; "Beyond the Potomac," 245; "The Bonny Brown Hand," 244; "By the Grave of Henry Timrod," 244; "Cambyses and the Macrobian Bow," 245; "Charleston," 243, 245; "Closing In," 244; "Easter," 244; "Face to Face," 244, 245; "From the Woods," 244; "Harvest Time," 245; "Hints of Spring," 245; "In Harbor," 245; "In the Wheat Field,"245; *Legends and Lyrics*, 13, 242, 244; "Lines in the Death of Colonel Pierce M. Butler," 243; "A Little While I Fain Would Linger Yet," 244; "Love's Autumn," 244; "Midsummer (On the Farm)," 245; "Monody, 244; *The Mountain of the Lovers*, 13, 242, 244; "My Father," 144; "My Mother-Land," 243; "Nature the Consoler, An Ode," 244, 245; "On a Jar of Honey," 245; "The Pine's Mystery," 245; *Poems*, 13, 242, 244; *Poems (1855)*, 241; "The Return of Peace," 245; "Sesqui-Centennial Ode," 243; "The Snow Messenger," 245; *Sonnets and Other Poems*, 241, 244; "The Spirea," 245; "The Temptation of Venus," 241, 244; "To a Bee," 245; "The True Heaven," 245; "Under the Pine," 244; "Unveiled," 245; "The Voice of the Pines," 244; "The Wife of Brittany," 241, 244; "The Woodland," 244
Hayne, Robert Young, 240
Hayward, Edward F., 407
"Health, A" (Pinkney), 360, 362–63
"Heavenly Love" (Horton), 263
Heermance, J. Noel, 52, 116
Heir of Gaymount, The (J. E. Cooke), 7, 176
Helen Halsey (Simms), 399, 404
Hemings, Sally, 273
Hemingway, Ernest, 13
Henderson, James, 259
Henry, Patrick, 4, 6, 324
Henry St. John, Gentleman (J. E. Cooke), 7, 175
Hentz, Caroline Lee, 259, 260
Hentz, Nicholas, 259
Herbert, Henry William 457
Her Majesty the Queen (J. E. Cooke), 176
"Hermit of the Mountain" (St. G. Tucker), 500

Hermit of the Mountain (St. G. Tucker), 499

"Heroic Slave, The" (Douglass), 194, 196, 198, 201

Herrick, Sophia Bledsoe, 282

Herring, Henry, 370

Herron, Ima Honaker, 280, 282

"Her Virginia Mammy" (Chesnutt), 111

Hesperia (Wilde), 525, 526, 528

Hetherington, Hugh, 410

Higginson, Thomas Wentworth, 355, 369

"High Times and Hard Times" (G. W. Harris), 223

High Times and Hard Times (G. W. Harris), 224

Hill, Hamlin, 58, 155, 158, 224, 424, 461, 462

Hills of Refuge, The (Harben), 216

Hinckley, Anne Maria, 453

"Hints of Spring" (Hayne), 245

Hirsch, David, 383

Hirst, Robert, 156

History and Present State of Virginia, The (Beverley), 3, 38–40

"History of Nathaniel Bacon's Rebellion in Virginia" (E. Cook), 167, 168, 170, 171

History of South Carolina (Simms), 399, 403

History of the Dividing Line, The (Byrd), 3, 60–63, 66, 69–71

History of the United States (G. Tucker), 477

"History uv the Waw, by Mozis Addums" (Bagby), 27

His Vanished Star (Murfree), 343

Hitchcock, Bert, 280, 281, 283

Hive of "The Bee-Hunter," The (Thorpe), 456, 460

Hobson, Elisabeth, 21

Hoffman, Charles F., 406

Hoffman, Daniel, 381

Holliday, Carl, 247, 282, 319, 528

Holman, C. Hugh, 7, 319, 363, 392, 408, 410

Holman, Harriet R., 16, 356

Holmes, Oliver Wendell, 244, 246

Holmes, Sherlock, 214

Holmgren, Virginia C., 210

Home Culture Clubs, 78, 81

Hood, John Bell, 100

Hoole, W. Stanley, 254

Hooper, Archibald, 250

Hooper, Johnson Jones, *250–56*, 10, 33, 36, 312, 458; bibliography, 254–56; biography, 250–52; criticism of, 253–54; major themes, 252–53. Works: *Dog and Gun . . .* , 251;

Read and Circulate . . . , 252; *A Ride with Old Kit Knucker . . .* , 251; *Some Adventures of Captain Simon Suggs*, 11, 251–53; "Taking the Census in Alabama . . . ,'' 251; "Thirteen Sages of Antiquity Caricatured," 252; *The Widow Rugby's Husband . . .* , 251, 253

Hoover, Herbert, 273

Hope of Liberty, The (Horton), 9, 259–61, 263, 265

"Hop Frog" (Poe), 370

Horace, 170

"Horrible Scrape, A" (Bagby), 24

Horse-Shoe Robinson (Kennedy), 7, 286, 289–91

"Horse-Swap, The" (Longstreet), 314, 317

Horton, George Moses, *257–67*, xi, 9; bibliography, 266–67; biography, 257–63; criticism of, 265–66; major themes, 263–65. Works: *The Black Poet*, 262, 266; "Division of an Estate," 9, 261, 265; "Farewell to Frances," 261; "Heavenly Love," 263; *The Hope of Liberty*, 7, 259–61, 263, 265; *Naked Genius*, 206, 262–63; "Rachael or Virtue," 264; "Rosabella—Purity of Heart," 264

Horton, Hall, 261

Horton, James, 259–60

Horton, William, 257–58

Hotchkiss, William A., 442

"Hot-Foot Hannibal" (Chesnutt), 111

House Behind the Cedars, The (Chesnutt), 18, 108, 113, 115

Howe, Julia Ward, 297

Howell, Elmo, 224

Howells, William Dean, 77, 109, 146, 152, 214, 217, 242, 243, 246, 297, 352, 407

"How Sharp Snaffles Got His Capital and Wife" (Simms), 402

"How the Times Served the Virginians" (Baldwin), 33

"How to Kill Two Birds with One Stone" (W. T. Thompson), 446

"How to Write a Blackwood Article" (Poe), 376

Hubbell, Jay B., 20, 27, 67, 172, 180, 205, 209, 247, 282, 293, 301, 319, 331–32, 380, 392, 408, 449, 471, 500, 528, 538

Hubbs, G. Ward, 253

"Huck Finn and Tom Sawyer Among the Indians" (Twain), 150

Huckleberry Finn (Twain), 12, 146, 148, 149, 151–52, 157–58, 222

Hudson, Arthur Palmer, 315
Hugo, Victor, 47
Humor of the Old Southwest, 458, 461
"Humorous in American and British Litera-
    ture, The" (Simms), 404
Humphries, Jefferson, 384
Hunt, Harriet, 119
Hunt, Holman, 437
Hutchins, Mary O., 417
Hutchins, Nathan Lewis, 417
Huxley, Aldous, 378
Hyde, E. H., 314
Hyde, George M., 319

"If It Might Be" (Chopin), 134
I'll Take My Stand, 90
Imperial Agricultural Society of France, 207
"Imp of the Perverse, The" (Poe), 374
Impressionism, 383
"Inamorato L'Oiseaux" (Byrd), 59, 65, 71
"Indian Village, The" (Simms), 404
Inez: A Tale of the Alamo (Wilson), 14, 531
Inge, M. Thomas, 10, 202, 224, 319, 320
Inge, Tonette Bond, 141
Ingelow, Jean, 243
Ingram, John H., 379
"In Harbor" (Hayne), 245
"In Memory . . . " (E. Cook), 166
Inner Law, The (Harben), 215
Innocents Abroad, The (Twain), 145, 150–51
In Ole Virginia . . . (Page), 16
Intelligencer (Concordia, La.), 454
"Interesting Interview, An" (Longstreet), 314,
    318
In the Clouds (Murfree), 340, 342–44
In the "Stranger People's" Country (Mur-
    free), 340, 342–43
In the Tennessee Mountains (Murfree), 17,
    336–37, 339, 342–43, 346
"In the Wheat Field" (Hayne), 245
Iredell, James, 4, 327
Irving, Washington, 21, 35, 175, 291, 292,
    368, 382, 398, 452
Isaac, Rhys, 333
"Isadore" (Chivers), 129
"Island of the Fay, The" (Poe), 368, 376
"Israfel" (Poe), 9, 366, 371
Italian Lyric Poets, The (Wilde), 525, 527
"Italy" (Pinkney), 362
Ives, Sumner, 236

Jackson, Andrew, 6, 176, 252, 291, 360, 395,
    484

Jackson, Blyden, 521
Jackson, David K., 188
Jackson, Stonewall, 7, 518
Jacobs, Robert D., 188, 381, 383
James, Henry, 77, 82, 297
James, Jacqueline, 510
James, John J., 247
James, William, 154
Jane Dawson (Harben), 215, 217
Jane Eyre, 534
Jay, John, 474
"Jean-ah Poquelin" (Cable), 17, 79
"Jeems Robinson" (J. C. Harris), 229
Jefferson, Peter, 268
Jefferson, Thomas, *268–76*, xi, 4, 5, 9, 25–
    26, 35, 47, 50, 55, 67, 69, 90, 331, 475;
    bibliography, 273–76; biography, 268–70;
    criticism of, 273; major themes, 270–73.
    Works: *Autobiography*, 272; *An Essay To-
    ward Facilitating Instruction* . . . , 271;
    "My Head and My Heart," 269; *Notes on
    the State of Virginia*, 5, 67, 268–70
Jenner, Samuel, 60
Jeune, Francis, 350
Jewett, Sarah Orne, 336
"Jim Smiley and His Jumping Frog" (Twain),
    145
John Brown and Wm. Mahone . . . (Bagby), 25
John Carper, the Hunter of Lost River (P. P.
    Cooke), 187
John March, Southerner (Cable), 17, 77–78,
    81
John Marvel, Assistant (Page), 353–54, 356
"John M. Daniel's Latch-Key" (Bagby), 24,
    26
John's Alive; or the Bride of a Ghost (W. T.
    Thompson), 441, 444
Johns Hopkins University, 306
Johnson, Barbara, 383
Johnson, Nathan, 193
Johnson, Paul D., 200
Johnson, Robert Underwood, 15, 76, 355, 390
Johnson, Rose B., 217
Johnson, Samuel, 35
Johnston, Mrs. Joseph E., 99
Johnston, Richard Malcolm, *277–85*, 16, 17,
    227, 312, 448; bibliography, 283–85; biog-
    raphy, 277–79; criticism of, 281–83; major
    themes, 279–81. Works: *Dukesborough
    Tales*, 17, 277–80, 282; "Early Educational
    Life in Middle Georgia," 279; *The English
    Classics*, 278; "Five Chapters to a His-

tory,'' 278; *Georgia Sketches*, 17, 278; *Life of Alexander H. Stephens*, 278; *Little Ike Templin and Other Stories*, 278, 280; *Mr. Absalom Billingslea and Other Georgia Folk*, 278; *Mr. Billy Downs and His Likes*, 278, 280; *Mr. Fortner's Marital Claims and Other Stories*, 278, 280; ''Mr. Neelus Peeler's Conditions,'' 278; *Old Mark Langston: A Tale of Duke's Creek*, 279, 281; *Ogeechee Cross-Firings*, 279, 281; *Old Times in Middle Georgia*, 278–79, 280; *Other Georgia Folk*, 280; *Pearce Amerson's Will*, 279, 281; *The Primes and Their Neighbors*, 278, 280; *Two Gray Tourists*, 278; *Widow Guthrie*, 279, 281

Jones, Hugh, 167
Jones, John W., 531, 538
Jones, Joseph, 309
Jones, Lewis Pickney, 209
''Jones, Major'' (W. T. Thompson), 26
Joscelyn (Simms), 401, 403, 410
Journal of Julius Rodman, The (Poe), 367
Journey to the Land of Eden, A (Byrd), 3, 60, 64
''Judge with a Sore Rump, The'' (St. G. Tucker), 497
Juggler, The (Murfree), 340, 343
Jugurtha, Lillie Butler, 200
Julian, Count of Spain, 404
Jung, Carl, 383
Jurgen, 19
Justin, Henri, 384

Kafka, Franz, 51
Kammen, Michael, 330
Kaplin, Justin, 156
Kate Chopin Miscellany, A, 141
Kate Chopin Newsletter, The, 141
Katharine Walton (Simms), 400
Keats, John 242
Keller, Frances Richardson, 116
Kendall, John S., 393
Kennedy, J. Gerald, 383, 392
Kennedy, John Pendleton, *286–95*, xii, 7, 86, 89, 175, 179, 184, 185, 367, 368, 485, 486; bibliography, 293–95; biography, 286–90; criticism of, 291–93; major themes, 290–91. Works: ''The Border States,'' 289; ''Confessions of an Officeholder,'' 287; *Defense of the Whigs*, 289; *Horse-Shoe Robinson*, 7, 286, 289–91; *Memoirs of the Life of William Wirt*, 289; ''Mildred Lindsay'' (*Horse-Shoe Robinson*), 288; *Mr. Ambrose's*

Letters on the Rebellion, 289; *The Portico*, 287; *Quodlibet*, 288–93; *Red Book*, 287; *A Review of Mr. Cambreleng's Report*, 287; *Rob of the Bowl*, 7, 286, 288–92; *Swallow Barn*, 7, 286, 287, 289–93; ''The Swiss Traveler,'' 287

Kenneth Galt (Harben), 215
Kennon, Richard, 325
Kentuckian in New-York, The (Caruthers), 87, 89–90, 92
Kerney, Catherine, 440
Kesterson, David B., 381
Ketterer, David, 382
Kibler, James E., Jr., 410–11
''Kidnapping of President Lincoln'' (J. C. Harris), 230
Kilmer, Joyce, 217
Kimball, Marie, 273
Kincaid's Battery (Cable), 78
King, Edward, 15, 76
King, Grace, *296–302*, xi, 16–18; bibliography, 302; biography, 296–97; criticism of, 300–302; major themes, 297–300. Works: *Balcony Stories*, 18, 301; *Memories of a Southern Woman of Letters*, 18, 300; ''Monsieur Motte,'' 17, 296–98, 301; *Monsieur Motte*, 298; *The Pleasant Ways of St. Medard*, 299, 300; ''A Quarrel with God,'' 298; *Tales of a Time and Place*, 18, 301
King, Joseph L., 27
King, Kimball, 315, 320, 356
King, Sarah Ann Miller, 296
King, William Woodson, 296
King Leopold's Soliloquoy (Twain), 148
Kinsmen, The (Simms), 399
Kipling, Rudyard, 230, 350
Kirby, David, 301
Kirkland, Caroline, 458
Knickerbocker Magazine, 87, 88, 185, 398, 406, 437, 453, 456, 527
Knights and the Friars, The (St. G. Tucker), 494, 497
Knights of the Golden Horse-Shoe (Caruthers), 7, 88–89, 92–93
''Knob Dance—A Tennessee Frolic, The'' (G. W. Harris), 222
Knoxville, 221
Kolbenheyer, Frederick, 134
Kopley, Richard, 383
Krutch, Joseph Wood, 379
Ku Klux Klan, 49, 419
Kunitz, Stanley J., 408

La Guardia, Fiorello, 354
Lahontian, Baron de, 40
Laing, S., 509
Lamb, Charles, 21, 35
"Lament of the Captive, The" (Wilde), 525–26, 528
"Lament on the Death of My Mother" (Chivers), 129
Land of the Changing Sun (Harben), 213, 217
Land of the Spirit (Page), 355
"Landor's Cottage" (Poe), 370
"Landscape Garden" (Poe), 368–69
Lane, Ralph, 2
Langdon, Olivia (Clemens), 146
Lanier, Clifford, 392
Lanier, Henry, 508
Lanier, Mary Day, 306, 309
Lanier, Sidney, *303–11*, xii, 13, 242–44, 246–47, 289, 297, 339, 392, 466; bibliography, 309–11; biography, 304–6; criticism of, 308–9; major themes, 306–8. Works: *Centennial Edition of the Works of Sidney Lanier*, 309; *Centennial Meditation of Columbia*, 306; "Corn," 13, 305; "Little Ella," 305; "The Marshes of Glynn," 13, 307; *Poems*, 13; *The Science of English Verse*, 13, 306, 308; "Sunrise," 306–7; "The Symphony," 13, 307; *Tiger-Lilies*, 304, 308
La Rose, Esther, 228
"Last Indian, The" (P. P Cooke), 187
Latham, G. Woodville, 21
Lathrop, Barbour, 353
Lathrop, Bryan, 353
Latrobe, John H. B., 291
Lawrence, D. H., 373, 378, 380
Laws of Wages . . . , The (G. Tucker), 477
Lawson, John, 60
Leading American Writers, 407
Leary, Lewis, 225, 309, 490
Leather Stocking and Silk (J. E. Cooke), 7, 175, 181
Lecky, William E. H., 152
Lectures on Literature . . . (Johnston), 279
Lee, Arthur, 4
Lee, Richard Henry, 4, 324
Lee, Robert E., 7, 25–26, 349, 353
Lee, Mrs. Robert E., 99
Lee, Ulysses, 520
Leelah Misled (Whitman), 515, 517, 519
"Lee to the Rear" (J. R. Thompson), 438
Legends and Lyrics (Hayne), 13, 242, 244

Lemay, J. A. Leo, 3, 172, 333, 462
"Lenore" (Poe), 368
Lenz, William E., 320
Les Natchez (Chivers), 119
Letter . . . on . . . the Late Conspiracy of the Slaves (G. Tucker), 474
Letters (Byrd), 60, 63–66
"Letters from the Earth" (Twain), 149
Letters from the Earth (Twain), 153
"Letters from the Far West" (Thorpe), 454
Letters of Agricola, The (Elliott), 207
Letters of Mozis Addums to Billy Ivvins (Bagby), 11, 22
Letters of the British Spy, The (Wirt), 6, 486, 543, 544, 550, 552–54
Letters on the Epistle of Paul . . . (Longstreet), 314
Letter, to a Member of the General Assembly . . . , A (G. Tucker), 475
Levin, Harry, 380
Levine, Stuart G., 381
Lewis, Richard, 167, 200
Lewis, William H., 509
Lexington Union (Virginia), 30
Liberator, 194
Liberty, A Poem on the Independence of America (St. G. Tucker), 6, 494, 496
Library of Southern Literature, The, 27
Life and Times of Dante . . . , The (Wilde), 525
Life and Times of Frederick Douglass, 190
Life of Alexander H. Stephens (Johnston), 278
Life of Stonewall Jackson (J. E. Cooke), 176
Life of Thomas Jefferson, The (G. Tucker), 477
Life on the Mississippi (Twain), 12, 145–46, 151, 157
"Ligeia" (Poe), 367, 375, 382
Lilly, Paul R., Jr., 448
Lily and the Totem, The (Simms), 403
Lincoln, Abraham, 29, 175
Lindsay, Vachel, 353
"Lines from the Portfolio of H—" (Pinkney), 361
"Lines on the Death of Colonel Pierce M. Butler" (Hayne), 243
Link, Samuel A., 247, 319, 407
"Lionizing" (Poe), 367
Lippincott's, 24, 27, 214, 229, 230, 305, 338, 345
Lipscomb, Andrew Adgate, 243
"Literary Life of Thingum Bob, The" (Poe), 368

"Literati of New York City, The" (Poe), 369
"Literature in the Southern States" (Cable), 81
"Literature of the South, The" (Timrod), 465
"Literature of the South, 1879" (J. C. Harris), 230
"Little Ella" (Lanier), 305
Little Ike Templin and Other Stories (Johnston), 278, 280
Littleton, Mark, 287
Little Union Scout, A (J. C. Harris), 231
"Little While I Fain Would Linger Yet, A" (Hayne), 244
Live Indian, The (drama) (W. T. Thompson), 442
Ljungquist, Kent, 383
Local color writing, 16–17, 75, 134, 235, 277, 279, 300–301, 316, 336
Localism, 230
"Local Takes a Turn on the Ice, The" (Bagby), 21–22
Loggins, Vernon, 201, 265, 521
Lokke, Virgil L., 383
Lombard, Charles, 128
London Diary, The (Byrd), 59, 64, 65
London *Index*, 437
London *Standard*, 437
Long, E. Hudson, 159
Long, Frances Taylor, 281
Longfellow, Henry Wadsworth, 120, 222, 242–46, 369, 436, 520, 527
Longstreet, Augustus Baldwin, *312–22*, 10, 20, 36, 227, 278, 405, 441, 442, 447–48; bibliography, 320–22; biography, 312–15; criticism of, 319–20; major themes, 315–19. Works: "The Ball," 314; "The Character of a Native Georgian," 314, 318; "The Charming Creature as a Wife," 314, 316; "The Dance," 314; "The Debating Society," 314, 316; "Dropping to Sleep," 314; "The Fight," 10, 314, 317; "The Fox Hunt," 314; "The Gander Pulling," 314, 318; *Georgia Scenes*, 5, 10, 312, 313–17, 319, 441, 447; "Georgia Theatrics," 10, 314, 316, 317; "The Horse Swap," 314, 317; "An Interesting Interview," 314, 318; *Letters on the Epistle of Paul* . . . , *314*; *Master William Mitten*, 314, 319; "The Militia Company Drill," 314, 316; "The Mother and Her Child," 314, 316; "A Sage Conversation," 314, 318; *Shall South Carolina Begin the War?*, 314; "The Shooting-

Match," 314, 318; "The Song," 314, 316; *Stories with a Moral*, 314; "The Turf," 314; "The Turn Out," 314, 318; *A Voice from the South* . . . , 314, 442; "The Wax-Works," 314, 318
Longstreet, Fitz R., 314
Lorch, Fred. W., 158
"Lord Uther's Lament for Ella" (Chivers), 123
The Lost Pleiad (Chivers), 121, 122, 125, 128
Louisville *Journal*, 437
Lovejoy, Elijah P., 45
Loveman, Robert, 213, 214
Lovers of Louisiana (Cable), 78
"Love's Autumn" (Hayne), 244
Lovingood Papers, The, 224
Lowe, Bennett, 167, 171
Lowe, Henry II, 167, 171
Lowe, Nicholas, 171
Lowell, James Russell, 368–69, 378
Lumpkin, Joseph H., 317
Lynch, Anne, 369
Lynchburg *Express*, 21
Lynchburg *Virginian*, 21
Lynn, Kenneth S., 36, 69, 224, 254, 319
Lyrical and Other Poems (Simms), 397

Mabbott, Thomas O., 363, 368, 370, 379
Macaria (Wilson), 14, 532–33, 535–36, 538–39
Macaulay, Thomas, 47, 273
Mac Brady, J. E., 504
McCarthy, Carlton, 355
McCausland, Georgia, 359–60
McClary, Ben Harris, 224
McClung, Henry, 90
McClure, S. S., 352, 508
McDavid, Raven I., Jr., 424
McDermott, John F., 461
McElderry, Bruce R., Jr., 319
McElrath, T. L., 456
McIntosh, William, 404
McKeithan, Daniel M., 157, 247, 448
MacKethan, Lucinda H., 52, 199
McKinlay, Whitfield, 509
McKinley, William, 504
McLean, Robert Colin, 480
Macnaughton, William G., 158
Madame Bovary, 138
Madame Delphine (Cable), 17, 76, 80
"Madeline" (Timrod), 468
Madison, James, 4, 287, 475
"Maelzel's Chess Player" (Poe), 376

Magill, Franklin N., 383

Magnolia, 8, 88, 314, 399, 410

Magnum Opos . . . , 252

Main Currents in American Thought, 407

"Major Jones in Europe" (W. T. Thompson), 443, 444, 446–48

Major Jones's Courtship (W. T. Thompson), 10, 440–45, 447–49

Major Jones's Courtship: or Adventures of a Christmas Eve (drama) (W. T. Thompson), 442, 444

Major Jones's Sketches of Travel . . . (W. T. Thompson), 442, 444, 446–48

Making of a Statesman, The, 231

Mallarme, Stephane, 378

Malone, Dumas, 273

Malthus, Thomas, 477, 479

Mam' Linda (Harben), 215, 217

Manassas (Chesnut), 15, 101

Man Farthest Down, The (Washington), 505, 509

Mankowitz, Wolf, 379

Mann, William H., 314

"Man of the Crowd, The" (Poe), 374

Mansfield, Mary Frances, 277

"Man's Place in the Animal World" (Twain), 154

"Man That Corrupted Hadleyburg, The" (Twain), 12, 154

"Man That Was Used Up, The" (Poe), 368

Map of Virginia, A (J. Smith), 2, 429–31

Marambaud, Pierre, 67, 69, 70

Marble, Charles C., 393

Marbois, François de, 5

"Marginalia" (Poe), 369, 377

"Marie Roget" (Poe), 368

Marion, Francis, 8, 399, 403

Mark Twain. *See* Samuel Langhorne Clemens

Mark Twain-Howells Letters, 157

Mark Twain Journal, The, 159

Mark Twain Project, 156

Mark Twain's Autobiography (Twain), 157

Marrow of Tradition, The (Chesnutt), 18, 109, 114–15

"Marse Chan" (Page), 16, 350, 354

Marshall, Carl, 522

"Marshes of Glynn, The" (Lanier), 13, 307

Marston, Philip Bourke, 243

Martin, Isabella, 102

Martin, Jay, 301

Martin, Waldo E., Jr., 201

Martin Faber (Simms), 397

Mary Chesnut's Civil War, 14, 96, 101–5

Marylander, The, 360

Maryland Gazette, 2, 167

Maryland Muse, The (E. Cook), 4, 167, 171

Mason, Samuel W., 443

"Masque of the Red Death, The" (Poe), 368, 373

Massachusetts Anti-Slavery Society, 194

"Master of Bolton, The" (P. P. Cooke), 187

Master's House: A Tale of Southern Life, The (Thorpe), 456, 459

Master William Mitten (Longstreet), 314, 319

Mather, Cotton, 199

Mathews, Basil, 510

Mathews, J. Chesley, 528

Matlack, James, 201

"Matter of Principle, A" (Chesnutt), 112

Matthiessen, F. O., 224

May, David, 333

Meats, Stephen E., 410

Mechanics Institute, 23

"Meddler's Club Papers, The," 4

Meek, A. B., 292

"Meekins's Twinses" (Bagby), 27

Meier, August, 510

Meine, Franklin J., 224, 315, 319, 461

Mellichampe (Simms), 398

Melton, Wrightman F., 362

Melville, Herman, 291, 382, 398

Memoir (Brown), 48

Memoir of the Life and Character of John P. Emmet . . . (G. Tucker), 477

Memoirs of the Life of William Wirt (Kennedy), 289

Memoralia (Chivers), 119, 124

Memories of a Southern Woman of Letters (Murfree), 18, 300

Memphis *Daily Appeal*, 437

Memphis *Eagle and Enquirer*, 22

Mencken, H. L., 19

Mercer University, 277

Meriwether, James B., 320, 410

"Mesmeric Revelation" (Poe), 374, 382

Metcalf, E. W., Jr., 52

"Metzengerstein" (Poe), 366, 376

Mexican War, 454

Michael Bonham (Simms), 401

Michel, Mary Middleton, 240

Micklus, Robert, 225

"Midsummer (On the Farm)" (Hayne), 245

"Mighty Dead, The" (Chivers), 123

"Militia Company Drill, The" (Longstreet), 314

Millais, John Everett, 437
Miller, Henry Prentice, 447–49
Miller, John Carl, 379
Miller, John Rodney, 438
Miller, Jon C., 331, 333
Miller, Mary Boykin, 96
Miller, Stephen Decatur, 97
Milton, John, 242, 397
Mims, Edwin, 356
"Mingo" (J. C. Harris), 234, 401
Mingo and Other Sketches (J. C. Harris), 394
Minor, B. B., 188, 435
Miscegenation, 115
Mississippi, University of, 314
Missouri Compromise fo 1820, 484
Mr. Absalom Billingslea and Other Georgia Folk (Johnston), 278, 280
Mr. Ambrose's Letters on the Rebellion (Kennedy), 289
Mr. Billy Downs and His Likes (Johnston), 278, 280
Mr. Fortner's Marital Claims and Other Stories (Johnston), 278, 280
"Mr. Neelus Peeler's Conditions" (Johnston), 278
Mitchell, Donald Grant (Ik Marvel), 436
Mitchell, Maragaret, 352
Mobile Register, 24
Mohun (J. E. Cooke), 7, 176, 179–80
"Mom Bi" (J. C. Harris), 233
"Monitor Essays, The," 4
"Monody" (Hayne), 244
Monody . . . (Simms), 397
"Monsieur Motte" (King), 17, 18, 296–98, 301
Monsieur Motte (King), 298
Montgomery Mail, 250, 252
Mooney, Stephen, 380, 382
Moore, J. Quitman, 406
Moore, John Robert, 292
Moore, Rayburn S., 27, 242, 247
"Morella" (Poe), 375
Morning News (Savannah), 443
Morris, G. P., 127
Moses, Montrose T., 247
Moss, Sidney P., 379
"Mother and Her Child, The" (Longstreet), 314, 316
Mother Goose (Simms), 401
"Mother's Wail, A" (Timrod), 466, 468, 471
Mott, Valentine, 369
Moultrie, William, 403

"Mountain of the Lovers, The" (Hayne), 244
Mountain of the Lovers, The (Hayne), 13, 242, 244
Mt. Zion Academy, 277
"Mozis Addums" (Bagby) , 26
Mozis Addums' New Letters (Bagby), 11
"MS. Found in a Bottle" (Poe), 367, 372, 376
Muhlenfeld, Elisabeth S., 15, 96, 105, 301
Munford, Robert, 323–35, xi, 5; bibliography, 334–35; biography, 323–26; criticism of, 330–34; major themes, 326–30. Works: "Answer to a Winter Piece," 333; The Candidates, 5, 325–33; A Collection of Plays and Poems, 330; The Patriots, 5, 324–29, 331–33; "A Revolutionary Song," 325
"Murder of Cornstalk, The" (P. P. Cooke), 187
"Murders in the Rue Morgue, The" (Poe), 368, 376
Murfree, Fanny, 340, 344
Murfree, Mary Noailles [Charles Egbert Craddock], 336–47, 16, 17; bibliography, 346–47; biography, 337–40; criticism of, 344–46; major themes, 340–44. Works: Allegheny Winds and Waters, 339; The Amulet, 340; The Bushwhackers, 340; The Champion, 340; "The Dancin' Party at Harrison's Cave," 337–38, 341–42, 344; The Despot of Broomsedge Cove, 344; Down the Ravine, 339; "Drifting Down Lost Creek," 338, 343; "Electioneering on Big Injun Mounting," 343; The Erskine Honeymoon, 340; The Fair Mississippian, 340; "Flirts and Their Ways," 338; The Frontiersman, 340; "The Harnt' That Walks Chilhowee," 337, 339, 342; His Vanished Star, 343; In the Clouds, 340, 342–44; In the "Strange People's" Country, 340, 342–43; In the Tennessee Mountains, 17, 336–37, 339, 342–43, 346; The Juggler, 340, 343; "My Daughter's Admirers," 338; The Mystery of Witch-Face Mountain, 343; "On a Higher Level," 338; The Ordeal, 340; "The Panther of Jolton's Ridge," 338; The Prophet of the Great Smoky Mountains, 17, 336, 339, 342–44; "The Romance of Sunrise Rock," 342–43; A Spectre of Power, 340; "The Star in the Valley," 342–43; The Story of Duciehurst, 340; The Story of Old Fort Loudon, 340; "Taking the Blue Ribbon

at the County Fair," 338; *Where the Battle Was Fought*, 337, 339; *The Windfall*, 340
Murphy, James K., 217
Murray, Anna, 193
Murray, Margaret, 504
Murrell, John, 404
"Muscadines" (Hayne), 245
"Music in Camp" (J. R. Thompson), 438
Mute Confessor, A (Harben), 213
My Bondage and My Freedom (Douglass), 190, 194–95, 197, 198, 200, 201
"My Daughter's Admirers" (Murfree), 338
"My Father" (Hayne), 244
"My Head and My Heart" (Jefferson), 269
My Larger Education (Washington), 506, 509
"My Life is Like the Summer Rose" (Wilde), 525
"My Mother-Land" (Hayne), 243
"My Politics" (Cable), 79, 80
My Southern Home (Brown), 48
Mysteries of the Backwoods . . . ,The (Thorpe), 10, 454, 455, 459
Mysterious Stranger, The (Twain), 153, 156
"Mystery of Marie Roget, The" (Poe), 376
Mystery of Witch-Face Mountain (Murfree), 343
"Mystery Revealed, The" (W. T. Thompson), 445
"My Uncle Flatback's Plantation" (Bagby), 21

Nacoochee (Chivers), 119, 120, 124, 128
Naked Genius (Horton), 206, 262–63
Napier, J. E., 509
Narrative of Arthur Gordon Pym, The (Poe), 367, 377–78, 382–83
Narrative of the Life of Frederick Douglass . . . (Douglass), 9, 190, 194–200
Narrative of William W. Brown, A Fugitive Slave . . . , The (Brown), 9, 46, 50, 52
Nation, The, 406
National Association for the Advancement of Colored People, 109
National Gazette, 494
National Intelligencer, 289
Native Virginian (Orange County), 24
"Nature the Consoler, An Ode" (Hayne), 244, 245
Neal, John, 359, 366, 378
Negro in Business, The (Washington), 505, 508
Negro in the American Rebellion . . . ,The (Brown), 48

Negro in the South, The (Washington), 505, 508
Negro Question, The (Cable), 17, 79–81
Negro: The Southerner's Problem, The (Page), 16, 352, 355
Neider, Charles, 157
Nelson, Robert, 349
Nelson, William, 349
Neu-gefundenes Eden (Byrd?), 60
New American Cyclopaedia, 175
New Clarion, The (Harben), 365
New England Trials (J. Smith), 429–31
New Orleans *Crescent Monthly*, 22, 24, 437
New Orleans *Picayune*, 437
New Orleans *Sunday Delta*, 22
New Orleans *Times*, 390
Newport, Christopher, 1
New Princeton Review, 18, 297
New Voyage to Carolina, 60
New Yorker, 83
New York *Evening Post*, 24, 437
New York *Metropolitan Record*, 419
New York Review, 291
Nichols, William W., 200
Nicholson, Francis, 39
Niemtzow, Annette, 199
Night in Acadie, A (Chopin), 134, 137–38
Nights with Uncle Remus (J. C. Harris), 230
Noble, Donald R., Jr., 480
"No More" (Chivers), 129
Norman Maurice (Simms), 401
Norris, Frank, 231
North American Review, 360, 362, 406
Northern Georgia Sketches (Harben), 214
North Star (Frederick Douglass' Paper), 194
North Walk Mystery, The (Harben), 214
Not a Man Yet a Man (Whitman), 14, 515–17, 519, 522
"Notes of a Small Tourist" (Simms), 404
Notes on the State of Virginia (Jefferson), 5, 67, 268–70
Nugae (St. G. Tucker), 500
Nullification, 97, 206, 208, 240, 244, 401
"Number Eight" (Hooper's pseudonym), 25
"No. 44, The Mysterious Stranger" (Twain), 148, 154
"Numps and Robin" (St. G. Tucker), 497

"Ocean Fight, The" (Wilde), 524–25
O'Connor, Flannery, 11, 220, 312
O'Connors, T. P., 360
"Octoroon, The" (Whitman), 517–19
Odell, Alfred Taylor, 408

O'Flaherty, Katherine, 132
O'Flaherty, Thomas, 132
Ogeechee Cross-Firings (Johnston), 279, 281
Oglethorpe University, 304
"Old Bachelor, The" (St. G. Tucker), 499
Old Bachelor, The (Wirt), 546
"Old Buckskin . . . " (Harben), 212
Old Creole Days (Cable), 17, 76, 79
Old Dominion . . . , The (Page), 353
Old Gentlemen of the Black Stock (Page), 355
Old Mark Langston: A Tale of Duke's Creek
    (Johnston), 279, 281
Oldmixon, John, 39, 57
Old Times in Middle Georgia (Johnston), 278–
    80
"Old Times on the Mississippi" (Twain), 12,
    144, 146, 149
"Old Virginia Gentleman, The" (Bagby), 21,
    24, 26
Oliphant, Mary C. Simms, 408, 410
Olney, James, 198, 199
O'Meally, Robert G., 200
"On a Higher Level" (Murfree), 339
"On a Jar of Honey" (Hayne), 245
"On Leaving Florence" (Wilde), 526
On Newfound River (Page), 351
"On Parting" (Pinkney), 361
"On the Condition of Women" (Wirt), 544
On the Plantation (J. C. Harris), 230, 236
On the Wing of Occasions (J. C. Harris), 230,
    234
Orange Expositor, 24
Ordeal, The (Murfree), 340
*Original Letters of Mozis Addums to Billy
    Ivvins* (Bagby), 22
Orwell, George, 51
Osborne, William S., 292
Osgood, Frances, 369, 379
Osgood, James R., 157
Osthaus, Carl R., 449
Other Georgia Folk (Johnston), 280
Our Army at Monterey (Thorpe), 455
Our Army on the Rio Grande (Thorpe), 455
"Our Willie" (Timrod), 466–68
Outlook, 18, 505, 508
"Oval Portrait" (Poe), 368
Owens, Jimmy, 253
Owens, William, 229

Paddy McGann (Simms), 401, 410
Page, Elizabeth, 273
Page, Florence, 354
Page, Margaret Louther, 494

Page, Mary Frances, 176
Page, Thomas Nelson, *348–58*, 14, 15, 16,
    89, 111, 176, 230, 231, 234, 235, 293,
    389, 392; bibliography, 357–58; biography,
    348–54; criticism of, 355–56; major themes,
    354–55. Works: "Burial of the Guns," 356;
    Dante and His Influence, 354; *Gordon
    Keith*, 352, 354, 355–56; "A Goth," 353;
    *In Ole Virginia: Marse Chan and Other Sto-
    ries*, 16; *John Marvel, Assistant*, 353–56;
    Land of the Spirit, 355; "Marse Chan," 16,
    350, 354; *Marse Chan: A Tale of Old Vir-
    ginia*, 16; *The Negro: The Southerner's
    Problem*, 16, 352, 355; *The Old Dominion
    . . .* , 353; *The Old Gentlemen of the Black
    Stock*, 355; *On Newfound River*, 351; *Pas-
    time Stories*, 355; *The Peace Cross Book*,
    352; *The Red Riders*, 354–55; *Red Rock: A
    Chronicle of Reconstruction*, 16, 176, 351,
    355–56; *Robert E. Lee, Man and Soldier*,
    353; *Robert E. Lee, the Southerner*, 353;
    "Run to Seed," 355; *Two Little Confeder-
    ates*, 349; *Washington and Its Romance*,
    354
Page, Walter, 508
Paine, Albert Bigelow, 148, 153, 155, 157
Paine, Thomas, 328
Painter, F.V.N., 247
Paleologue, Theodore, 428
"Panther of Jolton's Ridge, The" (Murfree),
    338
Park, Robert E., 509
Parke, Daniel, 57
Parke, Frances Eliza, 313
Parke, Lucy, 24, 57, 58
Parker, Hershel, 157
Parker, Richard, 39, 499
Parks, Edd Winfield, 70, 188, 242, 247, 281–
    82, 309, 345, 409, 471, 526
Parks, Robert, 506
Parks, William, 2, 4, 167
Parrington, Vernon, 90, 92, 291, 319, 407,
    490
Partisan, The (Simms), 398, 403, 406
Partisan Leader . . . , The (N. B. Tucker), 7,
    485, 487–90
Party Leaders . . . (Baldwin), 30–32, 35
Pastime Stories (Page), 355
Path of Sorrow (Chivers), 119–20, 125–26
"Patriot Cool'd, The" (St. G. Tucker), 498
"Patriot Rous'd, The" (St. G. Tucker), 498,
    500

Patriots, The (Munford), 5, 324–29, 331–33

Pattee, Fred Lewis, 247, 301

Paulding, James Kirke, 87, 89–91, 398, 527

Paul Rundel (Harben), 215

Peabody, George, 289

Peabody Institute, 289

Peace Cross Book, The (Page), 352

Pearce Amerson's Will (Johnston), 279, 281

Pease, Donald, 383

Peden, William, 5

Pelayo, 404

Pelayo: A Story of the Goth (Simms), 398

Pendleton, Edmund, 286, 324

Pendleton, Maria, 174, 184

Pendleton, William Nelson, 349

Penn Magazine, The, 367, 368

Pennington, James W. C., 200

Pennsylvania, University of, 21, 86

Perceval, John, 56, 66

Perch, Philemon (Richard Malcolm Johnston), 17, 278

Percy, George, 2

Perry, Susan, 107

Personal Recollections of Joan of Arc (Twain), 147

Peterson, Merrill D., 5

Peterson, T. B., 443

Petigru, James Louis, 240

Pettit, Arthur G., 158

Phantasy Pieces (Poe), 368

Philbrick, Norman, 333

Philip, King, 403–4

"Philip Pendleton Cooke" (J. R. Thompson), 438

Phillips, David Graham, 353

Phillips, Mary E., 379

Phillips, Robert L., Jr., 282, 448

Philosophical Transactions, 56

"Philosophy of Composition, The" (Poe), 369, 377

"Piano in Arkansas, A" (Thorpe), 454

Picayune (New Orleans), 76, 437

Picken, Francis, 241

"Picture Song, A" (Pinkney), 361

Picturesque America, 457

Pike, Albert, 458

Pike, Wayne, 424

Pinkney, William, 287

"Pine's Mystery, The" (Hayne), 245

Pinkney, Edward Coote, *359–64*, 6; bibliography, 363–64; biography, 359–60; criticism of, 362–63; major themes, 360–62. Works:

"Evergreens," 361; "The Grave," 361; "A Health," 360; "Italy," 362; "Line: From the Port-Folio of H—," 361; "On Parting," 361; *Poems*, 360; "Prologue," 362; "Rodolph: A Fragment," 362; *Rodolph: A Fragment*, 359; "Serenade," 361, 363; "Song" ("Day departs this upper air"), 363; "Song" ("We break the Glass"), 363; "The Voyager's Song," 361, 363

Pioneer, The, 368

Pioneers of Southern Literature, 407

Piper, Henry Dan, 201

Pipes, Martha H., 345

"Pit and the Pendulum, The" (Poe), 368, 372

Pitcher, Edward, 383

Pitts, Helen, 195

"Plank, The" (Simms), 404

"Plantation novel," 7

Plater, Ormonde, 225

Pleadwell, Frank Lester, 363

Pleasant Ways of St. Medard, The (King), 299, 300

Pocahontas, 2, 403, 404, 428

Poe, David, Jr., 365

Poe, Edgar Allan, *365–88*, xi, 4, 6, 8, 118–19, 121–22, 128–29, 185, 188, 242, 316, 317, 319, 362–63, 392, 398, 406, 436, 438, 485; bibliography, 384–88; biography, 365–70; criticism of, 378–84; major themes, 370–78. Works: "Alone," 371; "Annabel Lee," 436; "The Assignation," 376; "Balloon Hoax," 368, 376; "The Bells," 370; "Berenice," 375; "The Black Cat," 374; "The Cask of Amontillado," 369, 373; "The City in the Sea," 9, 366, 372; "The Coliseum," 367; "The Colloquy of Monos and Una," 373, 377; *The Complete Works of Edgar Allan Poe*, 379; *The Conchologist's First Book*, 367; "The Conqueror Worm," 368, 373; "A Descent into the Maelstrom," 368, 372; *Doings of Gotham*, 368; "The Domain of Arnheim," 376; "A Dream," 371; "Dreams," 371; "A Dream Within a Dream," 371; *Edgar Allan Poe: Selected Prose and Poetry*, 378; "Eldorado," 370; "Eleonora," 368, 376; "Epimanes," 367; *Eureka*, 369, 371, 374–75, 377–78, 381–82; "Evening Star," 371; "The Facts in the Case of Monsieur Valdemar," 376; "The Fall of the House of Usher," 9, 367, 375, 383; "The Folio Club," 376; "For Annie," 370, 376; "The

Gold Bug," 368, 376; "Hop Frog," 370; "How to Write a Blackwood Article," 376; "The Imp of the Perverse," 374; "The Island of the Fay," 368, 376; "Israfel," 9, 366, 371; *The Journal of Julius Rodman*, 367; "Landor's Cottage," 370; "Landscape Garden," 368–69; "Lenore," 368; "Ligeia," 367, 375, 382; "Lionizing," 367; "The Literary Life of Thingum Bob," 368; "The Literati of New York City," 369; "Maelzel's Chess Player," 376; "The Man of the Crowd," 374; "The Man That Was Used Up," 368; "Marginalia," 369, 377; "Marie Roget," 368; "The Masque of the Red Death," 368, 373; "Mesmeric Revelation," 374, 382; "Metzengerstein," 366, 376; "Morella," 375; "MS. Found in a Bottle," 367, 372, 376; "The Murders in the Rue Morgue," 368, 376; "The Mystery of Marie Roget," 376; *The Narrative of Arthur Gordon Pym*, 367, 377–78, 382–83; "Oval Portrait," 368; *Phantasy Pieces*, 368; "The Philosophy of Composition," 369, 377; "The Pit and the Pendulum," 368, 372; *Poems*, 366; "The Poetic Principle," 360, 370, 374, 382; "A Predicament," 376; "The Premature Burial," 373; "The Purloined Letter," 376, 383; "Rationale of Verse," 368; "The Raven," 9, 122, 128–29, 368, 375; *The Raven and Other Poems*, 369; "The Scythe of Time," 376; "Shadow—A Parable," 376; "Silence—A Fable," 372, 376; "Sonnet—Silence," 372; *The Stylus*, 368–69; "Tales of the Folio Club," 366; *Tales of the Grotesque and Arabesque*, 367, 373, 376; "Tamerlane," 371; *Tamerlane and Other Poems*, 366; "The Tell Tale Heart," 368, 374; "To Helen," 9, 366, 370–71; "To My Mother," 370; "Ulalume," 128, 369, 376; "The Unparalled Adventure of One Hans Pfaall," 376; "Usher," 382; "The Valley of Unrest," 372; "The Visionary" ("The Assignation"), 367; "Von Kempelen and His Discovery," 370; "William Wilson," 367, 373
Poe, Elizabeth Arnold, 365
Poe, Virginia, 368–69
Poems (Lanier), 13
Poems (Pinkney), 360
Poems (Poe), 366
Poems (Russell), 392
Poems (1855) (Hayne), 13, 241, 242, 244

Poems Descriptive, Dramatic, Legendary and Contemplative (Simms), 401
Poems, Fugitive and Occasional (Wilde), 525–26
Poems of Sidney Lanier, 13
Poems on Several Occasions (Dawson), 4
"Poem Upon Some Ladies At Tunbridge 1700, A" (Byrd), 57
"Poet, The" (Chivers), 124
Poetic Works of George M. Horton, The, 261
"Poetic Principle, The" (Poe), 360, 370, 374, 382
"Point at Issue, A" (Chopin), 134
Pole Baker (Harben), 215
Polhemus, George W., 36
Political Economy for the People (G. Tucker), 477
"Politician, The" (Bagby), 24
Polk, James, 252, 258, 263
Polk, Noel, 225
Pollin, Burton R., 381
Ponce de Leon, Juan, 403–4
Pond, J. B., 82
Pope, Alexander, 186, 222, 397
Porter, William T., 10, 250, 251, 253, 278, 453, 456, 458, 461
Portico, The (Kennedy), 287
"Posson Jone" (Calbe), 17
Pound, Ezra, 247
Powers, Hiram, 525
Powhatan, 428
"Predicament, A" (Poe), 376
Prejudices, 19
"Premature Burial, The" (Poe), 373
Prentiss, S. S., 32
Present State of Virginia and the College, The, 40
Preston, Margaret Junkin, 242–44
Preston, Mary, 99
Preston, Sarah, 99
Pretty Mrs. Gaston (J. E. Cooke), 176
Price, Enoch, 45
Prima Donna, The (Simms), 399
Primes and Their Neighbors, The (Johnston), 278, 280
Prince, William S., 500
Prince and the Pauper, The (Twain), 146, 150–52, 154
Princeton College, 184
Private Mary Chesnut, The: The Unpublished Civil War Diaries (Chesnut), 15, 96
Probationary Odes of Jonathan Pindar, Esq. (St. G. Tucker), 6, 496, 497

Profits and Rent Investigated (G. Tucker), 477
"Profligate, The" (St. G. Tucker), 497
Progress of the United States . . . (G. Tucker), 477
Progress to the Mines, A (Byrd), 3, 60
"Prologue" (Pinkney), 362
Prophet of the Great Smoky Mountains, The (Murfree), 17, 336, 339, 342, 343, 344
Prose Romances of Edgar A. Poe, The, 368
Pro-Slavery Argument, The (Simms), 401
Public Discourse on the Dangers . . . (G. Tucker), 477
Public Discourse on the Literature of the United States (G. Tucker), 477
Puck, 390, 392
Puckman, Sarah, 435
Pudaloff, Ross, 71
Pudd'nhead Wilson (Twain), 1, 12, 115, 152, 154, 157
Pugh, Griffith Thompson, 82
Purchas, Samuel, 429–30
"Purloined Letter, The" (Poe), 376, 383
Putnam, George P., 289

Qua: A Romance of the Revolution (J. C. Harris), 230
"Quarrel with God, A" (King), 298
Quidor, John, 452
Quinn, Arthur Hobson, 181, 331, 356, 379, 380, 408
Quinn, Patrick, 380, 382, 383
Quodlibet (Kennedy), 288–91, 293

Rabelais, François, 222
Rabkin, Eric S., 383
"Rachael or Virtue" (Horton), 264
"Railroad Song" (Chivers), 126
Rainbow, The (Wirt), 553, 554
Raleigh, Sir Walter, 2
Raleigh *Register*, 259
Ramsay, David, 4, 292
Rancy Cottem's Courtship (W. T. Thompson), 443
Randall, Henry S., 273
Randolph, 359
Randolph, Frances Bland, 493
Randolph, Innes, 11, 12
Randolph, Jane, 268
Randolph, John, 35, 325, 485
Randolph, Peyton, 324
Randolph, Sarah N., 273
Rankin, Daniel S., 140

Rans, Geoffrey, 380
Ransom, John Crowe, 309
Rape of Florida, The (Twasinta's Seminoles) (Whitman), 516, 518–19, 522
"Rationale of Verse" (Poe), 368
"Raven, The" (Poe), 9, 122, 128–29, 368, 375
Raven and Other Poems, The (Poe), 369
Read and Circulate . . . (Hooper), 252
Reade, Charles, 242–43
"Rebel, The" (Randolph), 11, 12
"Recollections of the Florida Campaign of 1836" (W. T. Thompson), 441
Reconstruction, xi, 11, 101, 248, 416, 419, 422
Red Book (Kennedy), 287
Redding, Saunders, 201, 265, 520
Redemption of Kenneth Galt, The (Harben), 215
Redfield, Justus Starr, 400
Red Riders, The (Page), 354–55
Red Rock: A Chronicle of Reconstruction (Page), 16, 176, 351, 355–56
Reeve, Tapping, 313
"Reflections on Religion" (Twain), 153
Regan, Robert, 381
Rehan, Ada, 353
Reilly, John E., 383
Reminiscences of Charles L. Elliott, Artist (Thorpe), 457
Renan, Ernest, 297
Render, Sylvia Lyons, 116
Renza, Louis A., 384
"Reply to 'Pardon Jones,' of the N. O. 'Pic'" (W. T. Thompson), 449
Requa, Kenneth A., 71
"Resignation" (St. G. Tucker), 496
"Respectable Woman, A" (Chopin), 137
"Retirement" (Timrod), 469
"Retrospect, The" (Chivers), 126
"Return of Peace, The" (Hayne), 245
Review of Mr. Cambreleng's Report, A (Kennedy), 287
Revolutionary Committees, 327
"Revolutionary Song, A" (Munford), 325
Revolutionary War, xi, 174, 178, 396, 398–99, 400–401, 403, 409
Rhett, Edmund, 208
Rhett, Robert Barnwell, 207
Richard, Claude, 381
Richard Hurdis (Simms), 8, 398
Richardson, Thomas J., 83

Richmond, Annie, 379
Richmond, Merle A., 263, 266
Richmond *Daily Whig*, 22
Richmond *Dispatch*, 23–24
Richmond *Enquirer*, 24
Richmond *Evening News*, 24
Richmond *Examiner*, 24
Richmond Library Association, 23
Richmond *Whig*, 91
Rickels, Milton, 224, 225, 460, 461
Ride with Old Kit Knucker . . . , A (Hooper), 251
Ridgley, J. V., 292, 409–10
"Ripley" (Timrod), 470
Ripley, Robert L., 93
Rising Son, The (Brown), 48
Ritchie, Thomas, 499
Roach, Chevillette Eliza, 398
Roberson, William H., 83
Robert E. Lee, Man and Soldier (Page), 353
Robert E. Lee, the Southerner (Page), 353
Robinson, Douglas, 383
Robinson, William H., Jr., 521
Rob of the Bowl (Kennedy), 7, 286 , 288–92
Roch, John H., 67
Roderick the Goth, 404
"Rodolph: A Fragment" (Pinkney), 362
Rodolph: A Fragment (Pinkney), 359
Roemer, Kenneth M., 217
Rogers, Henry H., 147
Rogers, William W., 510
Romance of Rockville, The (J. C. Harris), 229
"Romance of Sunrise Rock, The (Murfree), 342–43
Rome *Commercial*, 419
Rome *Courier*, 419
Roosevelt, Franklin D., 273
Roosevelt, Theodore, 215, 231, 354
"Rosabella—Purity of Heart" (Horton), 264
Ross, Charles Hunter, 362
Ross, Stephen M., 225
Rossetti, Dante Gabriel, 121
Roughing It (Twain), 145, 150
Rourke, Constance, 224, 378, 461
Royal Society, 56
Rubin, Louis D., Jr., 82, 172, 209, 309, 363, 392, 410–11, 462, 521
Rudwick, Elliott M., 511
Ruffin, Edmund, 67, 485
Ruffner, Lewis, 502
Ruggles, David, 193
"Run to Seed" (Page), 355

Russell, Elizabeth Allen, 389
Russell, Irwin, *389–94*, 14; bibliography, 393–94; biography, 389–91; criticism of, 392–93; major themes, 391–92. Works: "Christmas-Night in the Quarters," 14, 392; *Poems*, 392
Russell, William McNab, 390
Russell's Magazine, 207, 241, 406, 465
Ryan, Father Abram Joseph, 12

Sabine, Lorenzo, 406
Sack and Destruction of the City of Columbia, S.C. (Simms), 401
"Sacred Furniture Warehouse, The" (Bagby), 21
"Sage Conversation, A" (Longstreet), 314, 318
"Sahara of the Bozart, The," 19
St. Armand, Barton Levi, 383
St. Domingo: Its Revolutions and Its Patriots (Brown), 48
St. Elmo (Wilson), 14, 533, 537–39
Saint Louis *Times*, 45
St. Nicholas Magazine, 157, 392
Saintsbury, George, 378
Saliba, David, 383
Salley, H. S., 409
Salomon, Roger B., 158
Saltonstall, Samuel, 429
Saltos, Francis, 243
Sampson, Ann Maria, 107
"Samuel Hele, Esq. . . . " (Baldwin), 33
Sandburg, Carl, 353
Sanford, Charles, 380
Saturday Courier, 366
Saturday Evening Post, 102, 231
Saturday Review, 339
Saturday Visiter, 367
Sayer, E. Sanford, 251
Scafidel, Beverly, 209
Schachner, Nathan, 273
Schmitz, Neil, 462
Scholes, Robert, 383
School History of Georgia, A (C. H. Smith), 421
Schooner, Elizabeth, 46
Science of English Verse, The (Lanier), 13, 306, 308
Scott, Emmett, J, 506
Scott, Jesse, 90
Scott, Sir Walter, 35, 186, 193, 242, 293, 360, 397, 408, 486, 520
Scout, The (Simms), 399

Scribner, Robert, 325

Scribner's Monthly, 76, 278, 350, 390, 392

Scriven, J. P., 250

"Scythe of Time, The" (Poe), 376

Sea Grammer, A (J. Smith), 429–30

Search After Truth (Chivers), 119–20

Second Choice (Harben), 365

Secret Diary, The (Byrd), 57, 59

Secret History of the Line, The (Byrd), 3, 60, 61, 63–67, 69, 71

Seddon, James A., 435

Seelye, John, 69, 158

Seilhamer, George O., 331

Sekora, John, 198, 199, 202

"Seminole Dance, The" (W. T. Thompson), 441

Sendall, Thomas, 427

Sentinel (Longstreet), 314

"Serenade" (Pinkney), 361, 363

"Sesqui-Centennial Ode" (Hayne), 243

Severn, John K., 516

Seward, William H., 23

Seyersted, Per, 18, 141

"Shadow—A Parable" (Poe), 376

Shadow Between His Shoulder Blades, The (J. C. Harris), 231, 234

Shadwell, Thomas, 40

Shakespeare, William, 35, 222, 242

Shall South Carolina Begin the War? (Longstreet), 314

"Sharp Snaffles" (Simms), 404

Shaw, Francis, 510

Shaw, George Bernard, 378

Sheffield, John, 40

Shelley, Percy Bysshe, 123, 464

Shelton, Elmira Royster, 370

Shenstone, William, 495

"Sheriff's Children, The" (Chesnutt), 113

Sherman, Joan R., 521

Sherman, William Tecumseh, 181, 442

Shew, Marie Louise, 369

Shillingsburg, Miriam, 410, 411

Shippey, Herbert, 448

"Shooting-Match, The" (Longstreet), 314, 318

Shreeven, William Van, 325

Siebert, Donald T., Jr., 71

" 'Sieur George" (Cable), 17

"Silence—A Fable" (Poe), 372, 376

Silent South, The (Cable), 17, 77

Silverman, Kenneth, 319, 333

Simmons, J. P., 363

Simms, Chevillette, 401, 405

Simms, L. Moody, Jr., 392

Simms, William Gilmore, *395–415*, xi, 7, 8, 24, 63, 86, 89, 121, 181, 240–44, 291, 292, 369, 392, 436, 465, 485–86, 527; bibliography, 411–15; biography, 395–402; criticism of, 406–11; major themes, 402–6. Works: "Apostrophe to Ocean," 404; *Areytos*, 399, *As Good as a Comedy*, 400, 410; *Atalantis. A Story of the Sea*, 397, 404; "Bald-Head Billy Bauldy," 402; *Beauchampe*, 399, 404; *Book of My Lady*, 397, 403; *Border Beagles*, 399; *The Cassique of Accabee*, 399; *The Cassique of Kiawah*, 397, 400, 403, 405; *Castle Dismal*, 399; *Charlemont*, 404; *Confession*, 399, 404; "Cortes and the Conquest of Mexico," 403; "The Cub of the Panther," 402; *The Damsel of Darien*, 7, 398, 403; *Donna Florida*, 399, 403; *Early Lays*, 397; *Eutaw*, 8, 400; *The Forayers . . .* , 8, 400; "The Forest Maiden," 403; *The Golden Christmas*, 400, 404; "Grayling," 403; *Guy Rivers*, 8, 397–98, 403; *Helen Halsey*, 399, 404; *History of South Carolina*, 399; "How Sharp Snaffles Got His Capital and Wife," 402; "The Humorous in American and British Literature," 404; "The Indian Village," 404; *Joscelyn*, 401, 403, 410; *Katharine Walton*, 400; *The Kinsmen*, 399; *The Lily and the Totem*, 403; *Lyrical and Other Poems*, 397; *Martin Faber*, 397; *Mellichampe*, 398; *Michael Bonham*, 401; *Monody . . .* , 397; *Mother Goose*, 401; *Norman Maurice*, 401; "Notes of a Small Tourist," 404; *Paddy McGann*, 401, 410; *The Partisan*, 398, 403, 406; *Pelayo: A Story of the Goth*, 398; "The Plank," 404; *Poems Descriptive, Dramatic, Legendary and Contemplative*, 401; *The Prima Donna*, 399; *The Pro-Slavery Argument*, 401; *Richard Hurdis, 8, 398; Sack and Destruction of the City of Columbia, S.C.*, 401; *The Scout*, 399; "Sharp Snaffles," 404; *The Social Principle*, 399; *South Carolina in the Revolutionary War*, 401; *Southern Passages and Pictures*, 398; *Southward Ho!*, 401; *The Sword and the Distaff*, 400; *The Tri-Color*, 397; *Vasconselos*, 7, 401, 403; "Vasco Nunez," 403; *Views and Reviews in American Literature, History and Fiction*, 399, 403–5, 410; *The Vision of Cortes, Cain, and Other Poems*,

7, 397, 403; *Voltmeier*, 397, 402, 410; *War Poetry of the South*, 403, 405; "Wisdom, Love, and Folly," 405; *Woodcraft*, 400, 410–11; *The Yemassee*, 8, 397–98, 403, 408, 410

Simons, Harris, 467

"Simon Suggs, Jr., Esq. . . . " (Baldwin), 33

Simpson, Joshua McCarter, 518

Simpson, Lewis P., 5, 69

Simpson, Stephen, 360

Sinclair, William, 288

"Singular Episode, A" (Twain), 157

"Sis's Becky's Pickaninny" (Chesnutt), 111

Sister Jane (J. C. Harris), 230, 236

Skaggs, Merrill Maguire, 16, 319

Skardon, B. N., 209

Skelton, Martha Wayles, 268

Sketches of the Life and Character of Patrick Henry (Wirt), 6, 546–49, 551

Skinner, John, 207

Slade, M.D.J., 251

Slavery, xi, 8, 52, 61, 103, 115, 119, 194–97, 208, 228, 281

Sloane, Hans, 65

Slosser, George E., 383

Smith, Ann Hutchinson, 206

Smith, Asahel Reed, 416

Smith, Bradford, 431–32

Smith, Caroline Maguire, 416

Smith, Charles Henry ["Bill Arp"], *416–26*, 10, 20, 227; bibliography, 424–26; biography, 416–21; criticism of, 424; major themes, 421–24. Works: *Bill Arp: From the Uncivil War to Date*, 420; *Bill Arp, So Called*, 11, 419–20, 422; *Bill Arp's Peace Papers*, 420, 423; *Bill Arp's Scrap Book*, 420; "A Cousin in Berlin," 420; *The Farm and the Fireside*, 420; *A School History of Georgia*, 421

Smith, Daniel C., 506

Smith, F. Hopkinson, 111

Smith, George, 427

Smith, Gerald J., 319

Smith, Henry Nash, 156–58

Smith, Howard Winston, 254

Smith, John, *427–34*, xi, 2, 7, 8, 40, 399, 403; bibliography, 432–34; biography, 427–30; criticism of, 431–32; major themes, 430–31. Works: *An Accidence*, 429–30; *Advertisements*, 2, 429–31; *A Description of New England*, 429–31; *The Generall Historie of Virginia . . .* , 2, 429, 430; *A Map of Virginia*, 2, 429–31; *New England Trials*, 429–31; *A Sea Grammer*, 429–30; *A True Relation*, 2, 428, 430; *The True Travels*, 429–30

Smith, Lucy Ann, 484

Smith, Marian, 421

Smith, Mary, 63

Smith, Roswell, 76

Smith, Seba, 444

Snavely, Tipton R., 480

"Snow Messengers, The" (Hayne), 245

"Soaring Swan, The" (Chivers), 121

Social Principle, The (Simms), 399

"Solomon and the Genie" (Wilde), 526

Some Adventures of Captain Simon Suggs (Hooper), 11, 251–53

"Song" ("Day departs this upper air") (Pinkney), 363

"Song" ("We break the Glass") (Pinkney), 363

"Song, A" (Byrd), 63

"Song, The" (Longstreet), 314, 316

"Song of the Sioux Lovers, The" (P. P. Cooke), 187

"Sonnet on the Death of Zachary Taylor" (J. R. Thompson), 438

Sonnets and Other Poems (Hayne), 241, 244

"Sonnet—Silence" (Poe), 372

"Sonnet to Lord Byron" (Wilde), 528

Sot-Weed Factor, The (E. Cook), 3, 4, 165–72

Sotweed Redivivus (E. Cook), 167–69

South Carolina College, 315

South-Carolina Gazette, 2, 4

South Carolina in the Revolutionary War (Simms), 401

Southern Agriculturalist, 206

Southern and Western (Simms), 8, 399

Southern cavalier, 174

Southern Field and Fireside, 314, 437

Southern Literary Gazette, 240, 397, 409

Southern Literary Journal, 207

Southern Literary Messenger, 6, 8, 10, 21–26, 30, 128–29, 174, 185, 188, 240, 316, 319, 367, 406, 436, 438, 485, 527

Southern Miscellany (Madison, Ga.), 442, 446

Southern Passages and Pictures (Simms), 398

Southern Quarterly Review, 6, 8, 83, 399–400, 410

Southern realism, 115

Southern Recorder, 314

Southern Renascence, xi

Southern Standard, 207

Southey, Robert, 360
"Southland's Charms . . . ,The" (Whitman), 518
Southward Ho! (Simms), 401
Southwell, Robert, 56
Southwest Humorists, xi, 310, 438
Southworth, E.D.E.N., 14
Sparks, W. H., 313
Sparta Academy, 277
Spaulding, James Reed, 532
Speckled Bird, A (Wilson), 534, 537
Spectre of Power, A (Murfree), 340
Spenser, Edmund, 242
Sperry, Watson R., 437
Spiller, Robert E., 301
"Spirea, The" (Hayne), 245
Spirit of the Times, 10, 30, 222, 224, 250–52, 453, 458
Spotswood, Alexander, 7, 41, 58, 60, 92
"Spring" (Timrod), 470
Springer, Marlene, 141
"Squire A. and the Fritters" (Baldwin), 33
Stamp Tax, 4
Stanard, Mrs. Jane, 371
Standard, 437
Standring, George, 152
"Star in the Valley, The" (Murfree), 342–43
Starke, Aubrey Harrison, 309
Starling, Marion Wilson, 201
States Rights Sentinel, 314, 441
Statute Law Controversy, 166, 167
Stauffer, Donald, 383
Staunton Academy, 29
Stedman, E. C., 175, 176, 242, 243, 246, 279, 281–82, 438, 529
Stein, Judith, 510
Stephens, Alexander, 277, 283, 417
Stephens, Linton, 277
Stepto, Robert B., 52, 199, 200–201
Sterne, Laurence, 35
Stevenson, Eva C., 78
Stevenson, Robert Louis, 154
Stockton, Frank, 278
Stoddard, Richard Henry, 438
Stone, Albert, 198, 199
Stone, Edward, 356
Stone, Herbert S., 135
Stories of Georgia, 1896 (J. C. Harris), 230
Stories with a Moral (Longstreet), 314
"Storm, The" (Chopin), 18, 140
"Story of an Hour, The" (Chopin), 18, 137
"Story of Bras-Coupé, The" (Cable), 17, 80

Story of Duciehurst, The (Murfree), 340
"Story of Mr. Rabbit and Mr. Fox, The" (J. C. Harris), 229
Story of My Life and Works, The (Washington), 505, 507
Story of Old Fort Loudon, The (Murfree), 340
Story of the Negro, The (Washington), 506, 509
Stovall, Floyd, 379–82
Stowe, Harriet Beecher, 14, 50, 127, 200, 230, 456, 459, 532
Strange True Stories of Louisiana (Cable), 77
Strickland, Betty Jo, 410
Striker, Laura Polanyi, 431
Strindburg, Johann August, 378, 381
Strong Hearts (Cable), 78, 82
Strother, David H., 184, 289
Strother, Francis, 32
Stuart, J.E.B., 7, 103, 175, 437
Stylus, The (Poe), 368, 369
Substitute, The (Harben), 215
Suggs, Simon, 26
Sumner, Charles, 525
Sumter, Thomas, 403
"Sunrise" (Lanier), 306, 307
Surry of Eagle's Nest (J. E. Cooke), 7, 176, 179, 181
Survey of London, 430
Sutherland, Judith, 383
Sut Lovingood . . . (G. W. Harris), 10, 13, 26, 223
"Sut Lovingood's Daddy, Acting Horse" (G. W. Harris), 222
Sut Lovingood's Yarns (G. W. Harris), 224–25
Swain, David, 260
Swallow Barn (Kennedy), 7, 286, 287, 289–93
Swedenborg, Emanuel, 119, 120, 122, 124
Swift, Jonathan, 40, 222, 474, 495
Swinburne, Algernon Charles, 243
"Swiss Traveler, The" (Kennedy), 287
Sword and the Distaff, The (Simms), 400
Sydnor, Charles, 332
Symons, Julian, 379
"Symphony, The" (Lanier), 13, 307

Takaki, Ronald T., 201
"Taking the Blue Ribbon at the County Fair" (Murfree), 338
"Taking the Census in Alabama . . . " (Hooper), 251
Tales (Poe), 369
Tales of a Time and Place (King), 18, 301
"Tales of the Folio Club" (Poe), 366

Tales of the Grotesque and Arabseque (Poe), 367, 373, 376

Tales of the Home Folks in Peace and War (J. C. Harris), 230

Talley, Susan Archer, 370

Talvande, Ann Marson, 97

"Tamerlane" (Poe), 371

Tamerlane and Other Poems (Poe), 366

Tandy, Jennette, 35, 319

Tar Baby and Other Rhymes, The (J. C. Harris), 231

Tarbell, Ida, 353

Tarleton, Banastre, 404

Tasistro, Louis, 378

Tate, Allen, 373–74, 378, 380, 382

Taylor, Bayard, 243, 438

Taylor, John, 6, 429

Taylor, Maria, 59

Taylor, William R., 409

Taylor, Zachary, 459

Taylor Anecdote Book, The (Thorpe), 455

"Tell Tale Heart, The" (Poe), 368, 374

Temperance Society, 87

Temple, Sir William, 71

"Temptation of Venus, The" (Hayne), 241, 244

Tenant, Mary, 287

Tenney, Thomas, 156, 159

Tennyson, Alfred, Lord, 47, 242, 247, 437, 464, 466, 470

Territorial Enterprise (Virginia City, Nev.), 144

Thackeray, Anne, 437

Thackeray, William Makepeace, 102, 242, 400, 437

"Theory of Poetry, A" (Timrod), 465

"Thirteen Sages of Antiquity Caricatured" (Hooper), 252

Thomas, Dwight R., 379

Thomas, J. Wesley, 409

Thompson, Daniel P., 91

Thompson, Edgar E., 254

Thompson, G. R., 379, 381, 383

Thompson, H. T., 466

Thompson, John Reuben, *435–39*, 185, 188, 242, 243, 398; bibliography, 439; biography, 435–37; criticism of, 438–39; major themes, 437–38. Works: "Ashby," 438; "The Burial of Latane," 438; "The Genius and Character of Edgar Allan Poe," 436; "Lee to the Rear," 438; "Music in Camp," 438; "Philip Pendleton Cooke," 438; "Sonnet on the Death of Zachary Taylor," 438

Thompson, Louisa A., 476

Thompson, Maurice, 243, 246

Thompson, William Tappan, *440–51*, 10, 227, 252, 278, 312, 448; bibliography, 450–51; biography, 440–44; criticism of, 447–50; major themes, 444–47. Works: "Boss Ankles . . . ," 445; "The Burglars of Iola," 446; *Chronicles of Pineville*, 442, 445, 447; "The Duel," 445; "The Fire-Hunt," 445; "How to Kill Two Birds with One Stone," 446; *John's Alive; or, The Bride of a Ghost*, 441, 444; *The Live Indian* (drama), 442; *Major Jones's Courtship*, 10, 440–45, 447–49; *Major Jones's Courtship; or Adventures of a Christmas Eve* (drama), 442, 444; "Major Jones in Europe," 443, 444, 446–48; *Major Jones's Sketches of Travel . . .* , 442, 444, 446–48; "The Mystery Revealed," 445; *Rancy Cottem's Courtship*, 443; "Recollections of the Florida Campaign of 1836," 441; "Reply to 'Pardon Jones,' of the N. O. 'Pic,' " 449; "The Seminole Dance," 441; *Truth at the Botton of a Well . . .* , 443; *The Vicar of Wakefield* (dramatic adaptation), 442; *A Voice from the South . . .* , 314, 442

Thomson, James, 530

Thoreau, Henry David, 200, 382

Thornbrough, Emma Lou, 510

Thorp, Willard, 254

Thorpe, Thomas Bangs, *452–63*, 10, 34, 36, 312; bibliography, 462–63; biography, 452–58; criticism of, 460–62; major themes, 458–60. Works: "American Pictures," 458; "Art and Drama," 457; "The Big Bear of Arkansas," 10, 452–54, 456, 460–62; *The Big Bear of Arkansas . . .* , 454, 458; "The Devil's Summer Retreat," 454; "The Disgraced Scalp-Lock," 454; *The Hive of "The Bee-Hunter"*, 456, 460; "Incidents in the Life of Audubon," 455; "Letters from the Far West," 454; *The Master's House . . .* , 456, 459; *The Mysteries of the Backwoods . . .* , 10, 454, 455, 459; *Our Army at Monterey*, 455; *Our Army on the Rio Grande*, 455; "A Piano in Arkansas," 454; *Reminiscences of Charles L. Elliott, Artist*, 457; "A Search for the Picturesque," 457; "Sugar and Sugar Regions of Louisiana," 456; *The Taylor Anecdote Book*, 455; "Tom Owen, the Bee-Hunter," 453, 454, 461

Thorpe, Willard, 301

"Those Extraordinary Twins" (Twain), 154
Three Years in Europe (Brown), 47
Tiger-Lilles (Lanier), 304, 308
Tillotson, John, 65
Timrod, Henry, *464–72*, xii, 6, 13, 24, 240–
    42, 244, 247, 398, 417; bibliography, 471–
    72; biography, 464–66; criticism of, 471;
    major themes, 467–71. Works: "The Arctic
    Voyager,"465; "Carmen Triumphale," 470;
    "Carolina," 470; "Charleston," 13, 470;
    "The Cotton Boll," 13, 465, 469; "A Cry
    to Arms," 13, 470; "Ethnogenesis," 13,
    465, 469; "The Literature of the South,"
    465; "Madeline," 468; "A Mother's
    Wail," 466, 468, 471; "Our Willie," 466–
    68; "Retirement," 469; "Ripley," 470; "A
    Theory of Poetry," 465; "The Unknown
    Dead," 467, 470; "A Vision of Poesy,"
    468
Tinling, Marion, 67
"To a Bee" (Hayne), 245
"To Allegra Florence in Heaven" (Chivers),
    129
"To Col. Lovelace of the British Guards" (St.
    G. Tucker), 497
"To Helen" (Poe), 9, 366
Told by Uncle Remus (J. C. Harris), 231
Tomlinson, David O., 293
"Tom Owen, the Bee-Hunter" (Thorpe), 453,
    454, 461
Tom Sawyer (Twain), 12, 145, 149, 151, 158
Tom Sawyer Abroad (Twain), 147, 150, 157
"Tom Sawyer's Conspiracy" (Twain), 148,
    150
"To My Mother" (Poe), 370
Toombs, Robert, 252, 417
Toth, Emily, 141
"To the Mockingbird" (Wilde), 528
"To the Person Sitting in Darkness" (Twain),
    148
Tradescant, John, 429
Tragedy of Pudd'nhead Wilson, The (Twain),
    147
Traits of American Humor, 456
Tramp Abroad, A (Twain), 146–47, 152
Transcript (Boston), 369
Transylvania University, 119
Trent, William P., 392, 402, 407
Tribune (Chamberc County, Ala.), 251
Tri-Color, The (Simms), 397
Triumph, The (Harben), 215–16, 217
Trotter, William Monroe, 505

"True Heaven,The" (Hayne), 245
True Relation, A (J. Smith), 2, 428, 430
"True Story, A" (Twain), 12
True Travels, The (J. Smith), 429–30
Truth at the Botton of a Well (W. T. Thomp-
    son), 443
Tucker, Beverley D., 490, 500
Tucker, Edward L., 188, 528
Tucker, George, *473–82*, 7, 89, 486; bibliog-
    raphy, 480–82; biography, 473–78; criticism
    of, 480; major themes, 478–80. Works: *A
    Century Hence*, 477, 479; *Essay on Cause
    and Effect*, 477; *Essays, Moral and Meta-
    physical*, 477; *Essays on Various Subjects of
    Taste . . .* , 475; *History of the United
    States*, 477; *The Laws of Wages . . .* , 477;
    *Letter . . . on . . . the Late Conspiracy of the
    Slaves*, 474, 477; *A Letter, to a Member of
    the General Assembly*, 475; *The Life of
    Thomas Jefferson*, 477; *Memoir of the Life
    and Character of John P. Emmet . . .* , 477;
    Political Economy for the People, 477; *Prof-
    its and Rent Investigated . . .* , 477; *Progress
    of the United States . . .* ," 477; *Public Dis-
    course on the Dangers . . .* , 477; *Public
    Discourse on the Literature of the United
    States*, 477; *The Valley of the Shenandoah*,
    7, 476, 478–79, 486; *A Voyage to the
    Moon*, 476
Tucker, Nathaniel Beverley, *483–91*, 7, 330,
    398, 500; bibliography, 490–91; biography,
    483–86; criticism of, 489–90; major themes,
    486–89. Works: *George Balcombe*, 485–88;
    "Gertrude," 485, 488; *The Partisan
    Leader*, 7, 485, 487–90
Tucker, St. George, *492–501*, xi, 5, 91; bibli-
    ography, 501; biography, 492–95; criticism
    of, 500; major themes, 495–500. Works:
    "The Belles of Williamsburg," 494; *Black-
    stone's Commentaries*, 494; "Carmen Secu-
    lare . . .* ," 495; *A Dissertation on Slavery*,
    6, 479; "A Dream," 498; "The Dreamer,"
    499; "A Fable," 496; "Fairy Hill . . .* ,"
    497; *Hermit of the Mountain*, 499, 500;
    "The Judge with a Sore Rump," 497; *The
    Knights and the Friars*, 494, 497; *Liberty, A
    Poem on the Independence of America*, 6,
    494, 496; *Nugae*, 500; "Numps and Ro-
    bin," 497; "Ode to Peace," 497; "The Old
    Bachelor," 499; "The Patriot Cool'd," 498;
    "The Patriot Rous'd," 498, 500; *Probation-
    ary Odes . . .* , 496–97; "The Profligate,"

497; "Resignation," 495–96; "To Col. Lovelace of the British Guards," 497; "To Sleep," 497; "Up and Ride," 497; "The Wheel of Fortune," 497
Tucker, Thomas Tudor, 473
Tuckerman, Henry T., 290
Tuckey, John S., 156
Tunbrigalia . . . (Byrd), 59
Tupper, Martin, 378
"Turf, The" (Longstreet), 314
Turner, Arlin, 82, 461
Turner, Darwin T., 202
"Turn Out, The" (Longstreet), 314, 318
Turrentine, Percy Winfield, 490
Tuskegge Institute, 18
Twain, Mark. *See* Clemens, Samuel Langhorne
Twasinta's Seminoles . . . (Whitman), 14, 520
Two Country Houses, The (P. P. Cooke), 186
Two Gray Tourists (Johnston), 278
Two Little Confederates (Page), 349
Two Years; or the Way We Lived Then (Chesnut), 15, 101

"Ulalume" (Poe), 128, 369, 376
Ulrich, Henry Albert, 506
Uncle Remus and His Friends (J. C. Harris), 230–31
"Uncle Remus as a Rebel" (J. C. Harris), 229
Uncle Remus: His Songs and His Sayings (J. C. Harris), 16, 229, 232, 235
Uncle Remus's Magazine (J. C. Harris), 231
Uncle Tom's Cabin, 14, 50, 200, 438, 456, 532
"Uncle Wellington's Wives" (Chesnutt), 112
Underground Railroad, 46
"Under the Pine" (Hayne), 244
Underwood, J.W.H., 417
"Unknown Dead, The"(Timrod), 467, 470
"Unparalled Adventure of One Hans Pfaall, The" (Poe), 376
"Unrenowned Warrior . . . , An" (Bagby), 23
"Unveiled" (Hayne), 245
"Up and Ride" (St. G. Tucker), 497
Up From Slavery (Washington), 18, 502, 503, 505–6, 508
"Upon a Fart" (Byrd), 63
"Upon a Sigh," 63
Upshur, Abel P., 485, 488
"Uv Wimmin" (Bagby), 27

Valery, Paul, 378
Valley of the Shenandoah, The (St. G. Tucker), 7, 476, 478–79, 486

"Valley of Unrest, The" (Poe), 372
Van Borcke, Heros, 437
Van Buren, Martin, 252, 291
Van Deburg, William L., 201
Van Doren, Carl, 181, 407–8
Vanity Fair, 102
Vasconselos (Simms), 7, 401, 403
"Vasco Nunez" (Simms), 403
Vashti . . . (Wilson), 14, 533
Veler, Richard P., 380–81
"Veteran, The" (Whitman), 516, 518
Vethake, Henry, 87
The Vicar of Wakefield (drama adaptation) (W. T. Thompson), 442
Vidal, Gore, 273
Views and Reviews in American Literature, History and Fiction (Simms), 399, 403–5, 410
"Virgil of Aiden, The" (Chivers), 122
Virginalia (Chivers), 119, 124, 125
Virginia, University of, 5, 174, 366, 435
Virginia: A History of the People (J. E. Cooke), 176–77
Virginia Cavaliers, The (Caruthers), 7
Virginia Comedians, The (J. E. Cooke), 7, 175–76, 178–79
"Virginia Editor, The" (Bagby), 22
Virginia Gazette, 2, 4, 324
Virginia Historical Society, 23
Virginia Literary Museum, The, 477
Virginian Argus, 6
"Virginia Negro, The" (Bagby), 24
"Visionary, The" ("The Assignation") (Poe), 367
Vision of Cortes, Cain, and Other Poems (Simms), 7, 397, 403
"Vision of Poesy, A" (Timrod), 468
Voice from the South . . . , A (Longstreet and W. T. Thompson), 314, 442
Voice of the People, The, 19
"Voice of the Pines, The" (Hayne), 244
Voice to America, A, 456–57
Voltmeier (Simms), 397, 402, 410
"Von Kempelen and His Discovery" (Poe), 370
"Voyager's Song, The" (Pinkney), 361, 363
Voyages, 430
"Voyage to Maryland, A" (*The Sot-Weed Factor*) (E. Cook), 168
Voyage to the Moon, A (G. Tucker), 476
Voyles, Jimmy Ponder, 281–82

Wade, John Donald, 319, 449
Wade, Mary Augusta, 444

Wagenknecht, Edward, 156, 379
Wager, Willis, 157
Waight, Phebe, 205
Wakelyn, Jon L., 410
Walker, David, 259–60
Walker, James, 45
Walker, Marym 390
Walker, Peter F., 201
Walser, Richard, 266
Walsh, John E., 379
Ward, John Shirley, 538
Warden, Blanche, 290, 293
Warner, Charles Dudley, 145, 278, 297, 338
War of 1812, 48
War Poetry of the South (Simms), 401
"War Prayer, The" (Twain), 148
Warren, Robert Penn, 11, 220, 273, 309
Wahington, Booker T., *502–13*, 18, 109, 113,
    522; bibliography, 511–13; biography, 502–
    7; criticism of, 510–11; major themes, 507–
    10. Works: *Black Belt Diamonds*, 504, 507;
    Frederick Douglass, 505, 509; *The Man
    Farthest Down*, 505, 509; *My Larger Edu-
    cation*, 506, 509; *The Negro in Business*,
    505, 508; *The Negro in the South*, 505, 508;
    The Story of My Life and Works, 505, 507;
    The Story of the Negro, 506, 509; *Up From
    Slavery*, 18, 502–3, 505–6, 508; *Working
    with the Hands*, 508
Washington, George, 6, 26, 175, 268–69, 474
Washington, Madison, 196, 201
Washington and Its Romance (Page), 354
Watkins, Floyd C., 363, 392
Watson, Charles S., 410–11
Watson, David, 499
Watson, Ritchie D., Jr., 182
Watts, Charles Henry, 128
"Wax-Works, The" (Longstreet), 314, 318
Wearing of the Gray (J. E. Cooke), 176
Weathers, Willie T., 70
Webb, Charles Henry, 533
Webb, William A., 282
Webber, Edgard, 507
"Web of Circumstance, The" (Chesnutt), 113
Webster, Charles L., 157
Webster, Daniel, 244
Wector, Dixon, 155
Weekly Anglo-African (New York), 48
Weekly Constitution (Atlanta), 229
Weeks, Stephen B., 282
Weems, Mason Locke, 6

Welland, Dennis, 158
Westerfelt (Harben), 214
Western Continent (Baltimore), 442
"Western Emigrants, The" (Simms), 404
Westward Ho! (Caruthers), 84
Wharton, Henry, 431
"What I Did with My Fifty Millions"
    (Bagby), 27
"What is Man?" (Twain), 148, 153–54
Wheatley, Phillis, 263
"Wheel of Fortune, The" (St. G. Tucker),
    497
Where the Battle Was Fought (Murfree), 337,
    339
"Which Was It?" (Twain), 148
Whig (Wetumpka, Ala.), 251
Whipple, E. P., 242–43, 246
Whipple, Leonidas Rutledge, 140
White, John, 2, 40, 168
White, Thomas W., 185, 367, 485
"White Jane" (Harben), 213
White Marie (Harben), 213
Whitman, Albery Allson, *514–23*, 14; bibliog-
    raphy, 522–23; biography, 514–16; criticism
    of, 520–22; major themes, 516–20. Works:
    Drifted Leaves, 516; *Essays on the Ten Pla-
    gues . . .*, 515, 516; "The Freedman's
    Triumphant Song," 516, 518; "The Great
    Strike," 518; *An Idyl of the South . . .*, 516;
    Leelah Misled, 515–17; 519; *Not a Man Yet
    a Man*, 14, 515–17, 519, 522; "The Octo-
    roon," 517–19; *The Rape of Florida (Twa-
    sinta's Seminoles)*, 14, 516, 518–20, 522;
    "The Southland's Charms . . .," 518; "The
    Veteran," 516, 518; *The World's Fair
    Poem*, 516; "Ye Bards of England," 518
Whitman, Sarah Helen, 370, 379, 383, 436
Whitman, Walt, 14, 242, 247, 369, 382
Whitmarsh, Thomas, 2
Whittier, John Greenleaf, 146, 243–46
Widow Guthrie (Johnston), 279, 281
Widow Rugby's Husband . . . , The (Hooper),
    251, 253
"Wife of Brittany, The" (Hayne), 241, 244
"Wife of His Youth, The" (Chesnutt), 108,
    111, 112
Wife of His Youth and Other Stories . . . ,
    (Chesnutt), 108
Wiggins, Robert Lemuel, 236
Wigwam and the Cabin, The (Simms), 403,
    405
Wilbur, Richard, 375, 380, 382–83

Wilde, Richard Henry, *524–29*, 6, 398; bibliography, 528–29; biography, 524–26; criticism of, 527–28; major themes, 526–27. Works: "At Night," 526; *Conjectures and Researches . . .*, 525; "Farewell to America," 526; "Forget Me Not," 526; *Hesperia*, 525–26, 528; *The Italian Lyric Poets*, 525, 527; "The Lament of the Captive," 525–26, 528; *The Life and Times of Dante*, 525; "My Life is Like the Summer Rose," 525; "The Ocean Fight," 524–25; "On Leaving Florence," 526; *Poems, Fugitive and Occasional*, 525–26; "Solomon and the Genie," 526; "Sonnet to Lord Byron," 528; "To the Mockingbird," 528

Wiley, Bell Irvin, 104

William and Mary Quarterly, 331

William Gilmore Simms (Trent), 407

Williams, Cratis D., 344

Williams, Fannie Barrier, 504, 509

Williams, Kenney J., 521

Williams, William Carlos, 378, 380

"William Wilson" (Poe), 367, 373

Willis, N. P., 368, 378

Willoughby, Lord de Eresby, 427

Wilmer, Lambert A., 367

Wilmot, John, Earl of Rochester, 40

Wilson, Augusta Jane Evans, *530–40*, xi, 14; bibliography, 539–40; biography, 530–34; criticism of, 538–39; major themes, 534–37. Works: *At the Mercy of Tiberius*, 534–35; *Beulah*, 14, 531–33, 539; *Devota*, 534; *Inez: A Tale of the Alamo*, 14, 531; *Macaria*, 14, 532–33, 535–36, 538–39; *A Speckled Bird*, 534, 537; *St. Elmo*, 14, 533, 537–39; *Vashti . . .*, 14, 533

Wilson, Edmund, 83, 104, 181, 224, 301, 378, 380

Wilson, James Southall, 379

Wilson, Lorenzo Madison, 533

Wilson, Woodrow, 273, 354

Wimsatt, Mary Ann, 7, 410–11

Windfall, The (Murfree), 340

Winters, Yvor, 378

Winwar, Frances, 379

Wirt, William, *541–56*, 6, 287, 289, 486, 495, 499; bibliography, 554–56; biography, 541–48; criticism of, 553–54; major themes, 548–53. Works: *The Letters of the British Spy*, 6, 486, 543, 544, 550, 552–54; "On the Condition of Women," 544; *The Old*

Bachelor, 546; *The Rainbow*, 550, 553, 554; *Sketches of the Life and Character of Patrick Henry*, 6, 546–49, 551

"Wisdom, Love and Folly" (Simms), 405

"Wiser Than a God" (Chopin), 134, 136

Wolcot, John, 496

Wolfe, Charles, 467

Woman Who Trusted, The (Harben), 214

Women's suffrage, 194

Wood, Clara Ruth Coleman, 283

Wood, Gordon S., 326–27

Wood, N. B., 504

Woodberry, George Edward, 379

Woodcraft (Simms), 400, 410–11

Woodfin, Maude H., 67

"Woodland, The" (Hayne), 244

Woodward, C. Vann, 15, 96, 105

Woodward, Thomas S., 252

Woolson, Constance Fenimore, 243

Wordsworth, William, 88, 242, 371, 397, 464

Working with the Hands (Washington), 508

World's Fair Poem, The (Whitman), 516

Wormeley, Ralph, 40

Wright, Louis B., 40, 67, 69

Wright, Nathalia, 346

Wroth, Lawrence C., 171

Wynes, Charles E., 522

Wynne, T. H., 67

Wythe, George, 268, 494

Yancey, William L., 251

Yanella, Donald, 67

Yankee (Boston), 366

Yats, Norris W., 224, 254, 461

Yeates, William Butler, 378

"Ye Bards of England" (Whitman), 518

Yellin, Jean Fagan, 52

Yemassee, The (Simms), 8, 397–98, 403, 408, 410

"Yorktown and Appomattox" (Bagby), 25

Young, Alfred, 510

Young, Bird H., 254

Young, John, 44

Young, Stark, 115, 220, 392

Young, Thomas Daniel, 363, 392

Young America, 405

"Young Doctor Gosse" (Chopin), 135

Youth's Companion, 213, 338, 340

Zeitz, Lisa Margaret, 200

Ziff, Larzer, 140

Contributors

RICHARD E. AMACHER, Hargis Professor Emeritus of American Literature at Auburn University, also taught at Yale, Rutgers, Carnegie Tech, Rensselaer Polytech, and Henderson State in Arkansas. He lectured in Germany as a Fulbrighter during 1961–62 (Wurzburg) and 1969–70 (Konstanz) in seminars headed by Professor Wolfgang Iser at these two universities. His publications in Southern literature include articles on William Wirt and Robert Penn Warren and a monograph on Joseph Glover Baldwin; in early American literature, two books on Benjamin Franklin and encyclopedia articles on Franklin, Samuel Sewall, Matthew Carey, and William Duane as well as a book on *American Political Writers, 1588–1800*; and in literary criticism, an anthology of literary criticism, edited with Victor Lange (*New Perspectives in German Literary Criticism*—1979).

WILLIAM L. ANDREWS is Professor of English at the University of Wisconsin–Madison. He has coedited *Southern Literary Culture: 1969–1975* and is the author of *The Literary Career of Charles W. Chesnutt* (1981). His interest in antebellum black Southern writing is reflected in his most recent book, *To Tell a Free Story: The First Century of Afro-American Autobiography, 1760–1865* (1986).

ROBERT D. ARNER, Professor of English at the University of Cincinnati and an authority on the literature of the eighteenth-century Colonial South, wrote the chapter on that subject for *The History of Southern Literature*. He has written numerous articles on Colonial American and Southern American writers; his articles have appeared in such journals as *Early American Literature, Mississippi Quarterly*, and the *Southern Literary Journal*.

JAMES C. AUSTIN is Professor Emeritus, Southern Illinois University at Edwardsville. He is author of *Fields of the Atlantic Monthly* (1953) and *American Humor in France* (1978), and three titles in Twayne's United States Authors Series: *Artemus Ward* (1964), *Petroleum V. Nasby* (1965), and *Bill Arp* (1970); besides articles in American and foreign scholarly journals on American literature, humor, popular literature, and literary dialect. He also dabbles in jazz, cartooning, poetry, and comic opera.

ROBERT BAIN, Professor of English and Bowman and Gordon Gray Professor of Undergraduate Teaching at the University of North Carolina at Chapel Hill, is the author of *H. L. Davis* and coeditor of *Colonial and Federalist American Writing* and *Southern Writers: A Biographical Dictionary*. He was a contributor to *A Bibliographical Guide to the Study of Southern Literature* and to *Southern Writers* and *The History of Southern Literature*.

ERIC W. CARLSON, Emeritus Professor of English, University of Connecticut, was a founding member and first president of the Poe Studies Association, 1973–78, and has been editor of its *Newsletter* since 1973. Since 1967 he has been on the Board of Editors of *Poe Studies*. His publications include *The Recognition of Edgar Allan Poe: Selected Criticism since 1829* (1966); *Introduction to Poe: A Thematic Reader* (1967); *Poe: "The Fall of the House of Usher"* (casebook, 1971); *Poe on the Soul of Man* (1973); *Emerson's Literary Criticism* (1979); *Selections from the Critical Writings of Edgar Allan Poe*, with J. Lasley Dameron (a reissue with new preface and introduction, 1981); *Critical Essays on Edgar Allan Poe* (1986).

WILLIAM CARROLL is Associate Professor of English at Norfolk State University. He holds degrees from Norfolk State University, Temple University, and the University of North Carolina at Chapel Hill. He is coauthor of *Rhetoric and Readings for Writing*, and his articles on Horton have appeared in various publications including *The Dictionary of Literary Biography*.

EUGENE CURRENT-GARCIA is Hargis Professor Emeritus of American Literature at Auburn University, where he taught nineteenth-century American and Southern literature from 1947 until his retirement in 1978. He helped to found the *Southern Humanities Review* in 1967 and served as editor and coeditor until 1979. Since the 1940s, his articles and reviews have appeared in such journals as *American Literature, American Quarterly, Studies in Short Fiction*, the *Southern Review*, and *Mississippi Quarterly* among others; and his book publications include *What Is the Short Story?, O. Henry, Realism and Romanticism in Fiction, Short Stories of the Western World, American Short Stories* (now in its fourth edition), and *The American Short Story Before 1850*.

ANNE MARGARET DANIEL, a native of Richmond, Virginia, was graduated from Harvard University in 1985 with an A.B. in English and American

Literature and Language and American History. Her honors thesis is entitled "Robert Beverley's *History and Present State of Virginia*: Tradition Before Transition."

CURTIS CARROLL DAVIS, of Baltimore, Maryland, is a writer in the field of American historical biography, with special attention to its belletristic aspects. His interests have led to article and book-length treatments of factual or literary topics in both the Carolinas and the Virginias, and his *Revolution's Godchild* ... (1976) is the authorized account of the North Carolina Society of the Cincinnati. Formerly an officer with the Central Intelligence Agency, Dr. Davis also reviews widely in the fields of espionage, military intelligence, and related subjects.

MARY KEMP DAVIS received her B.A. from Florida A & M University, her M.A. from Atlanta University, and her Ph.D. from the University of North Carolina at Chapel Hill. After teaching a year at the University of Houston-Downtown, she returned to Chapel Hill as a postdoctoral fellow. She is now on the faculty there, and is currently at work on a study of fictional treatments of the Nat Turner Revolt.

JACK DE BELLIS is Professor of English at Lehigh University. He has written widely on the literature of the South. Among his works are *Sidney Lanier* (1972) and *Sidney Lanier, Henry Timrod and Paul Hamilton Hayne: A Reference Guide* (1978).

CARL R. DOLMETSCH is Professor Emeritus of American literature at the College of William and Mary. He is the author of *The Smart Set: A History & Anthology* and coeditor of *The Poems of Charles Hansford*. Among his publications on Southern writers are studies of H. L. Mencken, William Byrd II, and St. George Tucker, whose unpublished essays and plays he is preparing for a collected edition. He is now at work on a book about Mark Twain's sojourn in Vienna, 1897–99.

ELIZABETH DUNN teaches American literature at the University of Texas at Tyler. She has written articles and delivered papers on the works of Ralph Waldo Emerson and others. A student of the Age of Emerson, Professor Dunn received her doctorate from the University of North Carolina at Chapel Hill in 1985.

EVERETT EMERSON, Professor of English and American Studies at the University of North Carolina at Chapel Hill, is the author of *The Authentic Mark Twain: A Literary Biography of Samuel L. Clemens* (1984). Since 1969 he has been editor of the journal *Early American Literature*. His "Southern experience" includes living in Louisiana, Virginia, North Carolina (from the mountains to the sea), and Florida.

ALLISON R. ENSOR is Professor of English at the University of Tennessee, Knoxville. She is the author of *Mark Twain and the Bible*, editor of the Norton Critical Edition of *A Connecticut Yankee in King Arthur's Court*, and chairman of the editorial board of *Tennessee Studies in Literature*. Most of her scholarly articles have concerned nineteenth-century American literature, especially Mark Twain.

JOSEPH M. FLORA is Professor of English and chairman of the Department at the University of North Carolina at Chapel Hill. He edited James Branch Cabell's *The Cream of the Jest* (1975) and is editor of *The English Short Story 1880–1945* (1985) and coeditor of *Southern Writers: A Biographical Dictionary* (1979). He is the author of *Vardis Fisher* (1965), *William Ernest Henley* (1970), *Frederick Manfred* (1974), and *Hemingway's Nick Adams* (1982).

JANE S. GABIN received her Ph.D. in English from the University of North Carolina at Chapel Hill in 1977. She has taught at Queens College of the City University of New York, UNC-Chapel Hill, UNC-Greensboro, Chapel Hill Senior High School, and the Duke Institute for Learning in Retirement. Currently a business owner and independent scholar in Chapel Hill, she is the author of *A Living Minstrelsy: The Poetry and Music of Sidney Lanier* (1985).

GERALD M. GARMON, Professor of English at West Georgia College, has attended the University of Richmond, Auburn University, and the University of Virginia. A member of MLA, CEA, and SAMLA, he has given papers and chaired seminars in these and other scholarly organizations and published on Joseph Conrad, D. H. Lawrence, Tolkien, Poe, Faulkner and others. His book on John Reuben Thompson (1979) is in the Twayne series.

JENNIFER R. GOODMAN teaches at Texas A & M University. Her Harvard Bowdoin Prize essay on Captain John Smith appeared in *Virginia Magazine of History and Biography*. She has also published on Chaucer, Malory, William Caxton, and stage history.

HARRIET R. HOLMAN, Professor Emerita of English Literature of Clemson University, retired to Anderson, South Carolina, where she grew up. She earned degrees from Winthrop College, the University of Michigan, and Duke University. She served as a reference librarian and reader's adviser at Winthrop and Duke and taught English at Winthrop College, Erskine College, and Clemson University. She found the intricacies of scholarly research, most of it on nineteenth-century writers, fascinating, and classroom teaching fun.

M. THOMAS INGE is Blackwell Professor of Humanities at Randolph-Macon College in Ashland, Virginia. He has written critical essays on Faulkner and other Southern writers, collected in two volumes the writings of humorist George Washington Harris, and edited the three-volume *Handbook of American Popular Culture*. He is writing a study of Melville in popular culture.

BLYDEN JACKSON is Professor of English, Emeritus, University of North Carolina at Chapel Hill and former teacher of junior high school English in Louisville, Kentucky; assistant and associate professor of English at Fisk University; professor of English, Chairman of Department and, eventually, Graduate Dean at Southern University. He is author (with Louis Rubin) of *Black Poetry in America* and author of *The Waiting Years*. He was a senior editor of *The History of Southern Literature*.

DAVID KIRBY, a Johns Hopkins Ph.D., is currently Professor of English at Florida State University in Tallahassee. Among his nine books is the Twayne United States Authors Series book on Grace King. Also a poet, he recently received a fellowship from the National Endowment for the Arts.

JON KUKLA, a native of Wisconsin, took the Ph.D. in History at the University of Toronto and has directed the publications program of the Virginia State Library since 1976. His published works include "Order and Chaos in Early America: Political and Social Stability in Pre-Restoration Virginia" in the *American Historical Review* (April 1985) and *Speakers and Clerks of the Virginia House of Burgesses, 1743–1776* (1981). He is working on an edition of the poems of Sir Francis Wyatt and a book entitled *Virginia and the Origins of American Statecraft*.

WILLIAM E. LENZ is Assistant Professor of English and Director of the Writing Program at Chatham College. He has written on Mark Twain, George Washington Harris, Bill Arp, Augustus Baldwin Longstreet, William Dean Howells, Hugh Henry Brackenridge, and American Humor; his book *Fast Talk and Flush Times: The Confidence Man As a Literary Convention*, has recently been published by the University of Missouri Press (1985). Current research projects include a study of the Antarctic in nineteenth-century American fiction and the function of women in Southwestern Humor.

CHARLES M. LOMBARD received his Ph.D. in French literature at the University of Wisconsin and was Professor Emeritus of French at the University of Illinois, Chicago. His work on Southern writers includes *Thomas Holley Chivers* (1946) and *Chivers' Complete Works*, reprints published by Scholars Facsimiles. He also published on Poe and French Romanticism. Professor Lombard died on 5 October 1985.

LUCINDA H. MACKETHAN is a Professor of English at North Carolina State University where she teaches Southern literature and directed the Freshman Composition Program. Her publications include *The Dream of Arcady: Place and Time in Southern Literature* (1980) and articles on Joel Chandler Harris, Flannery O'Connor, and Afro-American literature. She is completing a study of American slave narratives begun during her year as a fellow at the National Humanities Center in 1984–85.

JON C. MILLER earned his Ph.D. at the University of North Carolina at Chapel Hill. For his dissertation, he edited and wrote an introduction to the poems and plays of Robert Munford. He teaches at the North Carolina School of Science and Mathematics and continues to pursue his interests in seventeenth- and eighteenth-century literature.

RAYBURN S. MOORE, Professor of English at the University of Georgia, is author of *Constance Fenimore Woolson* (1963) and *Paul Hamilton Hayne* (1972); editor of collections of Constance Woolson's short fiction (1967) and Hayne's letters (1982); and a senior editor of *The History of Southern Literature* (1985). He is a past president of the Society for the Study of Southern Literature.

MERRITT W. MOSELEY, JR., received his Ph.D. from the University of North Carolina at Chapel Hill. His scholarly interests range from the Victorian novel to contemporary American humorous writing, and he has published criticism on Ring Lardner, Artemus Ward, and H. L. Mencken. He is an Associate Professor of Literature at the University of North Carolina at Asheville.

ELISABETH S. MUHLENFELD is Associate Professor of English at Florida State University, where she teaches graduate and undergraduate courses in Southern American literature. Since 1984, she has been Dean of Undergraduate Studies at Florida State. In addition to her work on Chesnut, Muhlenfeld has written extensively on nineteenth- and twentieth-century Southern writers, especially on William Faulkner.

JAMES K. MURPHY, Associate Professor of English at West Georgia College, Carrollton, Georgia, received his B.A., M.A., and Ph.D. from the University of Chattanooga, the University of Kentucky, and George Peabody College for Teachers respectively. He is the author of *Will N. Harben* in the Twayne series on American writers and has published several articles on Harben for national periodicals. He is a member of various professional organizations, including the National Council of Teachers of English, the Conference on College Composition and Communication, the South Atlantic Modern Language Association, the Georgia–South Carolina College English Association, and the Society for the Study of Southern Literature.

DONALD R. NOBLE teaches American literature and American Studies at the University of Alabama. He is the editor of George Tucker's *A Century Hence* and the coeditor, with Joab L. Thomas, of *The Rising South*, as well as the author of numerous articles and reviews in such journals as the *Southern Literary Journal*, the *Mississippi Quarterly*, and the *Southern Quarterly*. He was recently Senior Fulbright Lecturer in American Literature, University of Osijek, Yugoslavia.

SONDRA O'NEALE teaches at Emory University in Atlanta, Georgia. Specializing in nineteenth-century American literature, Afro-American literature, and the Bible as literature, she has published in *Obsidian, Melus*, and in the *Dictionary of Literary Biography*, and she has written books on Phillis Wheatley and Jupiter Hammon.

WILLIAM PEDEN is Professor of English, Emeritus, University of Missouri–Columbia, and fiction editor, *Missouri Review*. His work on Jefferson includes a University of Virginia doctoral dissertation, *Thomas Jefferson: Book Collector, Bibliophile, & Critic*; an edition of *Notes on the State of Virginia* (University of North Carolina Press, 1954; reissued, *Norton Books That Live*). He is coeditor, 1972 (with Adrienne Koch), of *Life & Selected Writings of Thomas Jefferson*, Random House/Modern Library, 1944; reissued, the Franklin Library, 1982. He is the author of many articles.

ROBERT L. PHILLIPS teaches Southern and American literature at Mississippi State University. He has published widely on Southern writers and was Managing Editor of *The History of Southern Literature*. In addition, he edits the *Newsletter* for the Society for the Study of Southern Literature.

J. V. RIDGELY is Professor of English at Columbia University. Among his works on Southern literature are *William Gilmore Simms* (1962); *John Pendleton Kennedy* (1966); and *Nineteenth-Century Southern Literature* (1980).

ANNE E. ROWE received her M.A. and Ph.D. from the University of North Carolina at Chapel Hill. She is Professor of English at Florida State University where she teaches American literature, including courses on Southern literature. She is the author of *The Enchanted Country: Northern Writers in the South, 1865–1910* (LSU Press) as well as *The Idea of Florida in the American Literary Imagination* (1986).

REED SANDERLIN, professor of English at the University of Tennessee at Chattanooga, also serves as Executive Director of the Southern Humanities Conference. He coedited *Politics, Society, and the Humanities* and has published a volume of poems.

JOHN SEKORA teaches Southern and American literature at North Carolina Central University in Durham. He has published widely on black American writers. With Darwin T. Turner, he edited *The Art of Slave Narrative* (1982).

LYNNE P. SHACKELFORD teaches at Furman University. She has published essays on James Branch Cabell, Nathaniel Hawthorne, and Henry James.

HERBERT SHIPPEY teaches English at Andrew College in Cuthbert, Georgia. He has published brief articles on William Tappan Thompson for the *Dictionary of Literary Biography* and the *Dictionary of Georgia Biography*. Presently, he is gathering and editing Thompson's uncollected fictional writings.

C. MICHAEL SMITH has taught at UCLA and Winthrop College, where he has been chair of the English department and is currently Dean of the Faculty and Academic Vice President. He has published articles in *Modern Fiction Studies* and elsewhere.

L. MOODY SIMMS, JR., is Professor of History and former chairman of the department at Illinois State University. He has published widely on the social, cultural, and intellectual history of the South. His work on Southern literature has appeared in such journals as *Mississippi Quarterly, Southern Studies, Resources for American Literary Study, American Literary Realism 1870–1910*, and *Mid-South Folklore*.

ROBERT O. STEPHENS is Professor of English and chairman at the University of North Carolina, Greensboro. Besides several essays on Cable, he has written *Hemingway's NonFiction: The Public Voice* (1968) and edited *Ernest Hemingway: The Critical Reception* (1977), and published articles on Hemingway, colonial American writing, and Texas oil folklore.

DAVID O. TOMLINSON is Professor of English and former chairman of the Department at the United States Naval Academy. He has published on William Cullen Bryant and William Gilmore Simms as well as on John Pendleton Kennedy. His bibliography of work by and about Kennedy appeared in 1979 in *Resources in American Literature*; and an article on Kennedy's literary apprenticeship that published manuscript letters for the first time. With librarian Lyn Hart, he organized the sesquicentennial exhibition of manuscripts of *Swallow Barn* and the celebration for the occasion at the Peabody Library in Baltimore.

EDWARD L. TUCKER, Professor of English at Virginia Polytechnic Institute and State University, is the author of two books: *Richard Henry Wilde: His Life and Selected Poems* and *The Shaping of Longfellow's "John Endicott."* He has published articles on several antebellum Southern magazines, and on Thomas Holley Chivers; John Fox, Jr.; Jesse Stuart; and William Faulkner.

RITCHIE D. WATSON, JR., is Professor of English at Randolph-Macon College. He has published a number of articles and essays dealing with his area of specialization, Virginia fiction. The LSU Press has recently published his book *The Cavalier in Virginia Fiction*, which examines the ways Virginia's writers have developed the aristocratic character type in their fiction.

MARY ANN WIMSATT teaches Southern and American literature at Southwest Texas State University in San Marcos. She has published numerous articles on William Gilmore Simms and was Associate Editor of *The History of Southern Literature*. A past president of the Society for the Study of Southern Literature, she is completing a book on Simms.

HAROLD WOODELL is an Associate Professor of English at Clemson University, where he teaches Southern literature. He received his B.A. and M.A. from Wake Forest University and his Ph.D. from the University of North Carolina at Chapel Hill. He has published articles and reviews on Southern literature in the *South Carolina Review*, the *South Atlantic Bulletin*, *Pembroke Magazine*, the *CLA Journal*, and the *Southern Literary Journal*.

MARLENE YOUMANS teaches American literature and creative writing at the State University of New York at Potsdam. In addition to her scholarship in American literature, she has published her poetry in such journals as *Southern Poetry Review*, the *South Carolina Review*, *Ploughshares*, the *Laurel Review*, and the *Carolina Quarterly*.